EMOTIONS IN
SOCIAL PSYCHOLOGY

2005

2

10

Key Readings in Social Psychology

General Editor: ARIE W. KRUGLANSKI, University of Maryland at College Park

The aim of this series is to make available to senior undergraduate and graduate students key articles in each area of social psychology in an attractive, user-friendly format. Many professors want to encourage their students to engage directly with research in their fields, yet this can often be daunting for students coming to detailed study of a topic for the first time. Moreover, declining library budgets mean that articles are not always readily available, and course packs can be expensive and time-consuming to produce. **Key Readings in Social Psychology** aims to address this need by providing comprehensive volumes, each one of which will be edited by a senior and active researcher in the field. Articles will be carefully chosen to illustrate the way the field has developed historically as well as current issues and research directions. Each volume will have a similar structure, which will include:

- an overview chapter, as well as introductions to sections and articles,
- Questions for class discussion,
- Annotated bibliographies,
- Full author and subject indexes.

Published Titles

The Self in Social Psychology	Roy F. Baumeister
Stereotypes and Prejudice	Charles Stangor
Motivational Science	E. Tory Higgins and Arie W. Kruglanski

Titles in Preparation

Social Psychology	Arie W. Kruglanski and E. Tory Higgins
Social Cognition	David Hamilton
Close Relationships	Harry Reis and Caryl Rusbult
Group Processes	John Levine and Richard Moreland
Intergroup Relations	Michael Hogg and Dominic Abrams
Language and Communication	Gün R. Semin
Attitudes and Persuasion	Richard E. Petty, Shelly Chaiken, and Russell Fazio
Social Psychology of Culture	Hazel Markus and Shinobu Kitayama
Social Psychology of Health	Peter Salovey and Alexander J. Rothman
Human Sexuality	Roy F. Baumeister

EMOTIONS IN SOCIAL PSYCHOLOGY
Essential Readings

Edited by

W. Gerrod Parrott
Georgetown University

USA	Publishing Office:	PSYCHOLOGY PRESS
		A member of the Taylor & Francis Group
		325 Chestnut Street
		Philadelphia, PA 19106
		Tel: (215) 625-8900
		Fax: (215) 625-2940
	Distribution Center:	PSYCHOLOGY PRESS
		A member of the Taylor & Francis Group
		7625 Empire Drive
		Florence, KY 41042
		Tel: 1-800-634-7064
		Fax: 1-800-248-4724
UK		PSYCHOLOGY PRESS
		A member of the Taylor & Francis Group
		27 Church Road
		Hove
		E. Sussex, BN3 2FA
		Tel: +44 (0)1273 207411
		Fax: +44 (0)1273 205612

EMOTIONS IN SOCIAL PSYCHOLOGY: Essential Readings

1 2 3 4 5 6 7 8 9 0

Printed by Edwards Brothers, Ann Arbor, MI, 2001.
Cover design by Ellen Seguin.
Edited by Hilary Ward and Joe Madia.
Cover art, The Feast of St. Nicholas by Jan Havicksz Steen, supplied by the Rijksmuseum, Amsterdam.

A CIP catalog record for this book is available from the British Library.
∞ The paper in this publication meets the requirements of the ANSI Standard Z39.48-1984 (Permanence of Paper).

Library of Congress Cataloging-in-Publication Data
Emotions in social psychology : essential readings edited by W. Gerrod Parrott.
p. cm.
Includes bibliographical references and index.
ISBN 0-86377-682-5 (hbk. : alk. paper) — ISBN 0-86377-683-3 (pbk. : alk. paper)
1. Emotions—Social aspects. I. Parrott, W. Gerrod.

BF531 .E523 2000
152.4—dc21
00-042544

ISBN: 0-86377-682-5 (case)
ISBN: 0-86377-683-3 (paper)

Dedication

To Nick, Andy, and Henry

Contents

About the Editor

W. Gerrod Parrott is a Professor of Psychology at Georgetown University. He received his Ph.D. in 1985 from the University of Pennsylvania, and was a postdoctoral fellow at the University of Illinois at Urbana-Champaign. He was Editor of the journal *Cognition and Emotion* from 1995-1999 and, with Rom Harré, was co-editor of the book *The Emotions: Social, Cultural and Biological Dimensions* (Sage, 1996). W. Gerrod Parrott is the author of over 50 scholarly chapters and articles. His research spans a variety of topics in the psychology of emotion, including the nature of human emotion; emotions' social and cultural foundations, functions, and dysfunctions; social emotions such as envy, jealousy, shame, embarrassment, and guilt; and the influence of emotion and emotional self-regulation on thinking.

Acknowledgements

The Authors and Publishers are grateful to the following for permission to reproduce the articles in this book:

Reading 1: P. Shaver, J. Schwartz, D. Kirson, & C. O'Conner, Emotion knowledge: Further exploration of a prototype approach. Journal of Personality and Social Psychology, 52, 1061–1086. Copyright ©1987 by the American Psychological Association. Reprinted with permission.

Reading 2: N. H. Frijda, The laws of emotion. American Psychologist, 43, 349–358. Copyright © 1988 by the American Psychological Association. Reprinted with permission.

Reading 3: S. Schachter, & J. E. Singer, Cognitive, social, and physiological determinants of emotional state. Psychological Review, 69, 379-399. Copyright ©1962 by the American Psychological Association. Reprinted with permission.

Reading 4: C. A. Smith, & R. S. Lazarus, Appraisal components, core relational themes, and the emotions. Cognition and Emotion, 7, 295–323. Copyright © 1993 by Taylor and Francis, Inc. Reprinted with permission.

Reading 5: H. R. Markus, & S. Kitayama, The cultural construction of self and emotion: Implications for social behavior. In S. Kitayama & H. R. Markus (Eds.), Emotion and culture: Empirical studies of mutual influence (pp. 89–130). Washington, DC: American Psychological Association. Copyright ©1994 by the American Psychological Association. Reprinted with permission.

Reading 6: D. M. Buss, R. J. Larsen, D. Westen, & J. Semmelroth, Sex differences in jealousy: Evolution, physiology, and psychology. Psychological Science, 3, 251–255. Copyright © 1992 by Blackwell Publishers. Reprinted with permission.

Reading 7: D. A. DeSteno, & P. Salovey, Evolutionary origins of sex differences in jealousy: Questioning the "fitness" of the model. Psychological Science, 7, 367–372. Copyright © 1996 by Blackwell Publishers. Reprinted with permission.

Reading 8: M. D. Robinson, J. T. Johnson, & S. A. Shields, The gender heuristic and the database: Factors affecting the perception of gender-related differences in the experience and display of emotions. Basic and Applied Social Psychology, 20, 206–219. Copyright © 1998 by Lawrence Erlbaum Associates. Reprinted with permission.

Reading 9: D. Keltner, & J. Haidt, Social functions of emotions at four levels of analysis. Cognition and Emotion, 13, 505–521. Copyright © 1999 by Taylor and Francis, Inc. Reprinted with permission.

Reading 10: P. Salovey, C. K. Hsee, & J. D. Mayer, Emotional intelligence and the self-regulation of affect. In D. M. Wegner & J. W. Pennebaker (Eds.), Handbook of Mental Control (pp. 258–277). Englewood Cliffs, NJ: Prentice-Hall. Copyright © 1993 by Prentice-Hall. Reprinted with permission.

Reading 11: J. P. Forgas & G. H. Bower, Mood effects on person-perception judgments. Journal of Personality and Social Psychology, 53, 53–60.

Emotions in Social Psychology: Volume Overview

W. Gerrod Parrott

Emotions are at the heart of social psychology and are part of what makes social psychology so interesting. Over the past several decades, emotion has become an important topic for research in social psychology. Some of this research concerns the nature of emotion itself: the types of emotions, their causes, and their properties. Other research concerns how emotions influence social phenomena: their effects on thought and behavior, their social functions. Altogether, emotion has emerged both as a special topic of study and as an important aspect of all of social psychology. Students beginning to learn about social psychology will want to have some introduction to emotion and its social effects, and those already with a background in social psychology will want to learn in depth about emotions. The readings in this volume include both classic studies and cutting-edge research, selected to provide the reader with a good background in all these aspects of emotion.

The purpose of this overview chapter is to provide some background for the study of emotion and its importance in social psychology. It explains why emotion is intrinsically part of social psychology. It presents some of the basic issues and definitions that underlie research on emotion, and it summarizes the theories, research, and controversies that have shaped the field.

Social Emotions, and Emotions in Social Phenomena

Emotion and social psychology are deeply intertwined, with interconnections running in both directions. Emotions are themselves social, and the phenomena of social psychology are themselves often emotional. Understanding the relations between emotion and the social world is essential for understanding why research on emotion must include the social psychological approach and why research on social psychology must so often include the study of emotions.

Consider first the idea that emotions are social. One justification for this assertion is that the social world is what most emotions are *about*. We are jealous of our relationships with others. We feel loneliness or belonging depending on our sense of being connected to others. We experience anger about others' blameworthy actions, appreciation for others' help, admiration for their virtues, and contempt for their vices. We compare ourselves to others and feel superior or inferior, pity or envy. Our social identities are contradicted during an interaction and we become embarrassed. Our flaws are publicly exposed and we feel shame. We cause others hurt or trouble and feel guilt. Toward other people we feel love or hate—or both. Certainly not all emotions are necessarily social—there need be nothing particularly social about our fear of heights or our happiness at reaching a goal. Yet, it is remarkable how many of our fears are of social confrontations or public speaking, and how often the cause of our happiness is helping others or gaining a friend. Thus, many emotions seem intrinsically social, and the rest are frequently social because of the social nature of most of our goals, concerns, and self-conceptions.

Apart from their being about the social world, there are other reasons for regarding emotions as social (Parkinson, 1996). The roles people play and the identities they assume in social interactions specify which emotions are to be displayed and which moods are to permeate an occasion (Goffman, 1959; Hochschild, 1979). Culture influences the meanings that are given to events—whether the funeral tends to produce sadness or happiness, or whether the athletic victory is felt to elevate one's solitary self or one's club and coach, depends on interpretations derived from a cultural system of meaning (Markus & Kitayama, 1991; Shott, 1979). The rewards of positive emotions and the aversiveness of negative emotions make them a powerful means of social control (Harré & Parrott, 1996; Shott, 1979). Emotions communicate one's perceptions and intentions to others, and they can be contagious, spreading from one person to another (Fridlund, 1994; Hatfield, Cacioppo, & Rapson, 1994). In the deepest sense, emotions are social by being shaped by culture. Cultures promote different attitudes, values, reactions, and self-conceptions. *Social constructionism* (alternatively *constructivism*) is the name for one approach to emotion that depicts emotions as born from the matrix of meanings, identities, and relationships supplied by a culture (Averill, 1980; Harré, 1986). On this account, emotions are as much the product of socialization as of biology. Because emotions are social in all these ways, they cannot be studied without keeping in mind their social and cultural aspects, and, not surprisingly, social psychologists have been deeply involved in this research.

Consider now the idea that the phenomena of social psychology are emotional. In fact, emotions are involved in most of the topics studied by social psychologists. There is not a chapter in a social psychology text that does not involve emotions in some form. Many of the connections are obvious: aggression is clearly linked with anger and hostility, close relationships with attraction and love, prejudice with fear and hostility, "groupthink" with threat and the desire to belong, and persuasion with moods and fear-inducing messages. Other connections emerge clearly only with some analysis and research. Conformity has been linked to social anxiety about appearing foolish, just as obedience to malevolent authority has been linked to embarrassment and aversion to face-to-face confrontation (Sabini & Silver, 1982). The most famous contemporary research on altruism concerns careful distinctions among distress, empathy, sympathy, and relief from guilt (Batson, 1998). The pluralistic ignorance that gives rise to unhelpful bystanders has its roots in fear of embarrassment (Miller & McFarland, 1987), and the arousal that produces social facilitation often originates in anxiety about evaluation (Cottrell, 1968). Moods can bias person perception, social judgments, stereotyping, and other forms of social cognition (Kunda, 1999). Cognitive dissonance involves a variety of emotions, including discomfort, self-anger, and guilt (Harmon-Jones & Mills, 1999). Thus, to study social psychology is necessarily to study emotions and their effects.

To understand social psychology, one must understand emotions—what they are, how they work, how they influence social interactions. The reverse is also true: to understand emotions fully, one must also understand social psychology. It's no surprise, then, that social psychologists have conducted much of the basic research on the nature of emotion, as well as studying emotions' role in social processes.

Basic Terms and Concepts

What is emotion? A widely-accepted definition has proved elusive. As a pair of psychologists famously remarked, "Everyone knows what an emotion is, until asked to give a definition. Then, it seems, no one knows" (Fehr & Russell, 1984). This elusiveness is probably not a failure, but rather a useful clue about the concept of emotion, which psychologists have inherited from ordinary language. The everyday concept of "emotion" in fact has no precise definition. Data gathered by Fehr and Russell (1984) suggest that the everyday conception of emotion is more like a prototype than a definition. It is represented by some clear examples, such as happiness, anger, and sadness. Membership in the category is determined more by similarity to these prototypes than by any fixed rule. Thus, the boundaries of the category are ill-defined or "fuzzy."

Social psychologists use the word "emotion" somewhat more precisely than do everyday speakers, if only because social psychologists have focused on a subset of the meanings that the everyday term can have. When psychologists speak of emotions, they refer to ongoing states of mind that are marked by mental, bodily, or behavioral symptoms. Thus, although everyday language allows one to speak of loving someone for 30 years, the psychologists' meaning of emotion would not extend to this use of an emotion word. Psychologists would refer instead to a person as having a "disposition" to experience love during these three decades, or speak of the person as having an "attitude" of love during this period, and would reserve the term "emotion" for those times the person was consciously aware of loving, was physically agitated by love, or acted in a loving manner.

Likewise, a person's general tendency to experience emotion is distinguished from that person's actual experiences of emotion. This is referred to as the "state/trait distinction." For example, a person who is easily or frequently angered may be referred to as an "angry person" in everyday language, but the meaning of this expression ascribes the trait of anger, not the state of anger, to that person. Angry people (in the trait sense) are not always angry (in the state sense). It is the state sense that is usually meant by the psychologist's term "emotion." Social psychologists do study emotional traits as well as states, however.

Finally, psychologists use the term "emotion" more in the sense of the English language expression "having an emotion" than in the sense of the expression "being emotional." In everyday speech, at least in the United States, "being emotional" has decidedly negative connotations, including excessive emotion, lack of control, bias, confusion, unpleasantness, maladaptiveness, weeping, and irrationality (Parrott, 1995b). These connotations may not exist in other languages or cultures. Some of these connotations are also expressed by the now somewhat old-fashioned-sounding term, "passion." To the extent that social psychologists study the phenomena of "passion" and "being emotional," it tends to be under the rubric of "motivated social cognition" rather than under that of "emotion."

An important and often confusing distinction concerns the difference between an emotion and a mood. There is some disagreement about what underlies this distinction, but the approach that seems most successful and widely accepted is based on the concept of having an object—what philosophers have called *intensionality* (Kenny, 1963) or *object directedness* (Nissenbaum, 1985). That is, emotions are about, or directed toward, something in the world. In the English language, they are *about* something, *at* something, *of* something, or *that* something. A person is angry about the mess a roommate did not clean, or afraid of an upcoming examination, or happy at receiving an unexpected present, or sad that a pet dog has died. In contrast, moods lack this quality of object directedness; a person in an irritable mood is not necessarily angry about anything in particular—he or she is just generally grumpy. Moods either have no object, or else have a very general object, such as one's entire life situation or the world at large (Lazarus, 1991). Moods therefore have a global, free-floating quality that tends to color reactions to events and situations encountered while in the mood.

In reality, moods and emotions may alternate, or even co-occur. A mood makes it more likely that one will experience the corresponding emotion about something in particular. Likewise, an emotion sometimes induces the corresponding mood and thus spreads beyond the object on which it was initially focused. It is helpful to keep in mind the conceptual distinction based on object directedness, lest these alternations lead to confusion.

The fluctuation that moods and emotions undergo brings up an important point about the nature of emotions: They are not static phenomena, but rather develop over time (Parkinson, Totterdell, Briner, & Reynolds, 1996). Certain everyday emotion concepts seem to have the idea of dynamic change built into them. "Grief" and "jealousy," for example, often suggest a sequence of reactions that coheres by forming a narrative about a response to an initial cause. Psychologists sometimes distinguish these complex, emotional chain reactions from simpler, single-reaction emotions, by referring to the former as "emotional episodes" and the latter as "emotions" (Frijda, Mesquita, Sonnemans, & Van Goozen, 1991; Parrott, 1991).

Social psychologists are interested in all of these emotional phenomena—moods, emotions, and emotional episodes—and all are represented in the readings in this volume. Usually the focus is on one or another, as appropriate for the topic under study, but sometimes psychologists wish to consider all emotional feelings more broadly, and for this purpose they often use the terms *affect* or *affective states*. "Affect" refers to any psychological state that is felt and in some way is evaluative or valenced (positive or negative). Indeed, the range of phenomena encompassed by the term "affect" includes not only moods, emotions, and emotional episodes, but also pleasures, pains, likes, and dislikes.

It is possible to distinguish a large number of emotional states. One imperfect index of the number of states distinguished by a culture is the number of words in that culture's language devoted to emotions. In English, researchers agree that there are over 500 words having emotional connotations (Ortony, Clore, & Foss, 1987), with at least 200 of these naming affective states (Fehr & Russell, 1984; Shaver, Schwartz, Kirson, & O'Connor, 1987). Clearly, however, people are capable of distinguishing more states than they have words. For example, English speakers sometimes feel pleasure or satisfaction at the misfortune of another person, but their language does not supply a word for this emotion. When English speakers learn that the German language has a word for this emotion—*schadenfreude*—they recognize that they have had an emotion for which they lacked a word, and may subsequently borrow *schadenfreude* from German because it is useful to have such a word. This example demonstrates that the number of emotional states cannot be equated with a language's lexicon for emotions, and demonstrates more generally the importance of distinguishing emotion words from emotional states themselves.

A Brief History of the Psychology of Emotion

Early Approaches

The earliest psychological approaches to emotion did not emphasize its social aspects. Rather, the emphasis of William James (1884), Charles Darwin (1872), and Walter Cannon (1927) was on the body, biology, and the nervous system. The reasons for this emphasis are partly historical. There is a long tradition of emphasizing the biological aspects of emotion that traces its modern origins to Descartes and extends back to the Ancient Greeks (Averill, 1974). Yet, history alone cannot explain this modern emphasis, because there are also long traditions of emphasizing the cognitive and social aspects of emotion, including Spinoza and extending back to the Ancient Stoics and Aristotle (Nussbaum, 1994). The nineteenth-century emphasis on biology in emotion may stem from the tendency prevalent at that time to contrast emotion with reason. Emotion was characterized as impulsive, irrational, and primitive, and considered as something brutish that humans share with animals. This emphasis naturally led to linking emotions to bodily physiology and to sub-cortical regions of the brain. These regions show similarity to structures in mammalian and reptilian brains and are distinct from the neocortical regions associated with human language and reason (Averill, 1974).

William James' influential theory depicted emotional feelings as arising from the sensation of bodily changes. This view suggested that differences between emotional feelings resulted from corresponding differences in bodily activity. The activity initially considered most promising was that produced by arousal of the sympathetic nervous system (SNS), but subsequent research found little difference in the way that the SNS was activated for different emotions. In 1927 Walter Cannon published an influential paper attacking James' theory on these grounds. Although subsequent research has led to some qualifications to Cannon's critique, James' theory is no longer considered plausible, largely because the required correspondence between distinct emotions and bodily changes was never established. Bodily changes are not consistently associated with specific emotions, nor does the loss of ability to feel changes in the body result in the loss of emotional feelings (Chwalisz, Diener, & Gallagher, 1988; Ginsburg & Harrington, 1996).

Certain of James' ideas continue to influence the social psychology of emotion, however. Bodily changes, although not the sole or even the primary source of emotional feelings, have been found to contribute to emotional experience (Laird & Bresler, 1992; Stepper & Strack, 1993). The tendency of people to mimic the bodily postures and movements of those they are interacting with may contribute to emotions' spread from one person to another (Hatfield, Cacioppo, & Rapson 1994). The occurrence of bodily changes during some emotions can be exploited as a measure of emotion by social psychologists wishing an alternative to relying on people's own reports (Cacioppo, Klein, Berntson, & Hatfield, 1993).

Cannon's (1927) alternative to James' approach was to understand emotions as the result of activity in certain regions of the brain. Cannon's work began a tradition of brain research that continues to the present day. A number of emotional behaviors are now known to rely on information processing and motor control occurring in subcortical structures of the brain, such as the amygdala (LeDoux, 1995).

Of the early scientific approaches to emotion, Darwin's was perhaps the most social in its emphasis, focusing on expressions and communication of emotion. Darwin's (1872) book on expressions of emotion retained the emphasis on the primitive, however, stressing the similarities between humans and animals. Furthermore, unlike modern evolutionary approaches, this book did not characterize emotion as functioning in adaptive ways. Rather, it was Darwin's work on general evolutionary theory, later reapplied to emotion by others in the twentieth century, that led to appreciation of how emotions might have evolved through natural selection (Fridlund, 1994).

Two-factor Theory

The first major contribution of modern social psychology to the theory of emotion was the famous paper written by Stanley Schachter and Jerome Singer in 1962. These theorists accepted Cannon's claim that SNS activation was essentially identical for most emotions, yet they retained James' intuition that SNS activity contributed importantly to the experience of emotion. They therefore proposed that SNS activity was necessary but not sufficient for the experience of emotion. They theorized that SNS activity provided the feeling and intensity of emotion, but that it was ambiguous, possibly indicating an emotion but possibly being the result of exercise, fever, or some other nonemotional cause. Schachter and Singer asserted that SNS arousal had to be "labeled" as emotional, a cognitive process that interacted with arousal to produce an emotional state. Cognitive labeling was never fully explained by Schachter and Singer, but it clearly added not only a cognitive element to emotion, but social elements as well. First, the theory suggested that cognitive labeling was based not only on a person's knowledge but also on his or her social situation: examples of situations included parties, arguments, and being near beautiful people. The second social element came from the cognition itself, which eventually came to be understood as an attribution for the cause of the SNS arousal, thereby placing emotion in the province of social cognition rather than in that of nonsocial cognitive psychology.

It is difficult to understate the influence of two-factor theory during the next 20 years. It was the subject of literally hundreds of experiments; it was applied to many different emotions; it was revised and extended to address a wide variety of phenomena. These phenomena included not only emotional ones, such as aggression (Zillman, Johnson, & Day, 1974), sexual attraction (Dutton & Aron, 1974), and guilt (Dienstbier & Munter, 1971), but also such disparate phenomena as cognitive dissonance (Zanna & Cooper, 1974), obesity (Rodin, 1981), and insomnia (Storms & Nisbett, 1970). Its influence was felt as much outside psychology as within. Two-factor theory was welcomed by many cultural relativists and social constructionists because its emphasis on labeling appeared to provide a way in which society and culture might shape emotion (Greenwood, 1994). Philosophers saw the theory as contributing insights about sources of feelings that had been neglected by philosophy's cognitive and linguistic emphasis (Lyons, 1980).

This influence was achieved despite several major shortcomings. The initial experiment produced strikingly weak effects, some not even statistically significant, and all of them difficult to replicate (Mezzacappa, Katkin, & Palmer, 1999). The initial theory suffered from a number of ambiguities (Gordon, 1978). The building block of its most important predictions—unexplained SNS arousal—was unlikely to be a factor in more than a subset of emotions, thus making the theory ill suited as a general theory of emotion. So, why did two-factor theory achieve such prominence in the first place? Four reasons may be suggested. First, two-factor theory seemed to capture, however inadequately, the everyday intuition that emotion involves both mind and body. Second, Stanley Schachter was one of the cleverest experimentalists the field of social psychology has ever known, and the sheer ingenuity of Schachter and Singer's experiment (reprinted in this volume as Reading 3) made the theory compelling despite the shortcomings of the theory and results. Third, the proposal of two-factor theory coincided with the rise of interest in attribution theory, with which it was highly compatible and in terms of which it was soon reinterpreted. Finally, although many of the theory's predictions have not been borne out, one prediction did receive considerable experimental support: Emotional states can indeed be intensified when arousal from an irrelevant source is misattributed to them (Reisenzein, 1983). Some of the most famous findings in the two-factor tradition were of this type.

By 1980, the two-factor theory was losing its popularity. Its most promising applications had been explored, and its assumptions appeared increasingly open to question. Evidence suggested that autonomic arousal was unnecessary for emotional experience (Chwalisz, Diener, & Gallagher, 1988), that autonomic arousal was not identical for all emotional states (Ekman, Levenson, & Friesen, 1983), and that cognition was of importance in producing arousal in the first place, not merely in labeling the arousal after it occurred. Misattribution, of arousal as well as of other feelings states, remains an important emotional phenomenon (Schwarz & Clore, 1983), but the two-factor theory is no longer considered adequate as a general account of emotion.

Contemporary Approaches

No single theory can be said to have taken the place of two-factor theory in the psychology of emotion, but subsequent theories do tend to share several themes that contrast with two-factor theory. The first of these themes is to view emotions as more complex than two-factor theory depicted. Recent theories tend to depict emotions as involving multiple components that tend to be correlated, albeit imperfectly. Emotions are understood as involving evaluative perceptions about events ("appraisals"); preparations for action; expressive movements, vocalizations, and faces; physiological changes; and conscious experiences (Frijda, 1986; Scherer, 1984). These components are interrelated, and each can influence the others, but they are not enmeshed in unified "affect systems" as some theorists once predicted (e.g., Tomkins, 1962). Each is also influenced by factors unrelated to emotion, and it is not uncommon to detect evidence of emotion in one component but not in another (Cacioppo et al., 1993). Related to this theme is the idea that emotions can be studied at various levels of analysis. Although some researchers focus on biology, others on cognition, and still others on social and cultural aspects of emotion, theorists generally recognize that these approaches are interrelated and that complete understanding of emotions requires knowledge of all the levels of analysis.

A second theme of contemporary theories is a greater tendency to acknowledge the unique properties of specific emotions. Anger, shame, happiness, and the rest are considered to have their unique characteristics not just cognitively (as in two-factor theory) but physiologically, behaviorally, and socially as well. This is not to say that emotion theorists have abandoned the general category of emotion, but only that the generalizations of current theorizing tend to be more abstract, with a noticeable appreciation that particular emotions have unique morphology and functions. Many current theories depict the various types of emotion as discrete categories, each possessing its own constellation of features.

The final theme has to do with understanding the functions of emotions. This theme is perhaps the most characteristic feature of contemporary approaches to emotion. Two-factor theory focused researchers' attention the malleability of attributions for feelings of emotional arousal, and it was not particularly concerned with what purpose emotions served. In contrast, the function of emotion is the dominant theme of emotion research over the past 20 years (Oatley & Jenkins, 1992). Theorists taking a biological approach now argue that emotions would not have evolved unless they served adaptive functions, at least in the environments inhabited by proto-human ancestors (Plutchik, 1980). The evolutionary functions that have been postulated include escape from harm, communication, facilitation and regulation of social interaction, energizing and directing physical reactions, alertness to danger, preservation of sexual fidelity, maintenance of romantic relationships, and protection of offspring. Theorists focusing on a cognitive level of analysis have stressed how moods and emotions provide information about one's judgments and coping resources (Morris, 1992; Schwarz, 1990). Emotions' cognitive functions include reallocating mental resources according to new priorities, altering specific cognitive processes such as attention and memory, and adjusting cognitive processing style in ways that are likely to be beneficial under the circumstances that give rise to the emotion (Frijda, 1986; Oatley, 1992). Theorists focusing on social and cultural levels of analysis posit that not only do the previously mentioned evolutionary and cognitive functions have profound social consequences, but emotions also sustain social values and norms, and reinforce social roles and hierarchies (Armon-Jones, 1986; Hochschild, 1979; Shott, 1979).

These themes are evident in a variety of theories. Izard's (1991) differential emotions theory and Ekman's (1972) neurocultural theory are well-known examples that have emphasized facial expressions of emotion. Both theories maintain that a small number of basic emotions are innate and universal in humans. These theories maintain that each of these emotions is elicited under certain circumstances; each involves characteristic expressions, physiological reactions, and behaviors; and each evolved to serve adaptive functions. Culture-specific rules and customs are said to modify these behaviors.

The cognitive labeling of two-factor theory has been replaced by appraisal theories, which aim to specify the cognitive aspects of emotion. An appraisal is a perception-like evaluation of the meaning of a situation in terms of a person's own cares, concerns, goals, and well-being. An appraisal is a type of cognition, but it is distinguished from general beliefs or knowledge because it relates a situation to a person's own concerns and because it has a direct, perceptual quality (Arnold, 1960). This view of cognition is quite different from that of two-factor theory, which construed cognition as unemotional without SNS arousal. In contrast, appraisal is an intrinsically emotional awareness of a situation (Frijda, 1986). The foundations of appraisal theories were set out by Magda Arnold (1960), who first defined the concept. Subsequently, research on stress and coping by Richard Lazarus (1966) demonstrated that altering a person's way of thinking about an event could also alter that person's emotional response. Lazarus's research led to a distinction between "primary appraisal," which concerns the meaning of the situation in relation to a person's concerns, and "secondary appraisal," which concerns that person's options for coping with the situation. Appraisal theories vary with respect to details about the nature and sequence of cognitions and their role in producing emotions. Research on specific emotions, such as anger or guilt, often concerns the nature of the appraisals associated with each emotion. Examples of appraisal theories, and criticism of them, will be found later in this volume.

Contemporary psychological theories of emotion are being influenced by approaches outside of psychology. Two examples may serve to illustrate this trend. The idea that human emotions have been shaped by evolution has led some theorists to draw on theories and methods from evolutionary biology, sociobiology, and ethology. The evolutionary psychology of Buss (2000) and the ethological approach to facial expressions of Fridlund (1994) are good examples of this trend. Second, the idea that human emotions are shaped by culture has led other theorists to draw on concepts and methods from anthropology and sociology. Markus and Kitayama's (1991) theory of how the concept of self influences the experience of emotions across cultures would exemplify this approach, as would social constructionism, the theory of how emotions are formed by social customs and practices (Averill, 1980; Harré, 1986).

Finally, much contemporary research on emotions is concerned not so much with the nature of emotion itself but with how emotions affect thinking, behavior, and social interaction. For example, social psychologists have been interested in how emotion affects social cognition, decision making, and communication. Research on emotion's effects shows it can function both adaptively and maladaptively, which in turn has encouraged research on how emotion is regulated and controlled.

Current Controversies in the Psychology of Emotion

The themes that were highlighted in the previous section emphasize the points of relative agreement among contemporary emotion researchers. They provide some idea of the history of psychological research on emotion and of the directions it is now taking. No overview of the contemporary research scene would be complete without some discussion of disagreements—the field has plenty of those as well! This section will present a brief synopsis of some of the major controversies that have arisen in recent years. These disagreements often center on fundamental questions that highlight not only where we need better answers, but also where we need better questions.

The Structure of Emotions

The sheer number of emotions can be overwhelming, and can obscure similarities and regularities that exist. For this reason psychologists have searched for valid ways of simplifying matters by organizing or structuring the emotions. A number of methods have been proposed, each of which has its strengths and weaknesses.

One approach is to seek a small number of dimensions that capture the most important similarities and differences among emotions. These dimensions may be found by asking people to describe each emotion using rating scales, or to rate how similar each emotion is to every other emotion being studied. These ratings are then subjected to a statistical analysis designed to construct a small number of measures from a larger number that are correlated (e.g., factor analysis) or to plot emotions in a small number of dimensions while preserving information about their similarities and differences (e.g., multidimensional scaling). These methods often suggest that just two factors or dimensions are adequate to account for much of the difference between emotions. One of the dimensions involves the pleasantness or unpleasantness of the emotion. The other dimension involves the degree of activation, arousal, or intensity. Such findings certainly suggest that if one were seeking the two most generally useful ways of capturing the overall similarity of emotions, pleasantness and intensity would be the two. Beyond that, researchers disagree.

Some researchers have proposed that when emotions are plotted in the two-dimensional space defined by pleasantness (the x-axis) and activation (the y-axis), the points corresponding to the various emotions will form a circle (Russell, 1980). That is, fairly intense positive emotions such as happiness and euphoria will tend to be found in the pleasant and active quadrant of the graph (near one and two on the face of a clock), whereas positive emotions of fairly low activation such as satisfaction and serenity will be found in the pleasant and unactive quadrant (near four and five o'clock). Fairly intense negative emotions such as fear and anger will be found in the unpleasant and active quadrant (near ten and eleven o'clock), whereas negative emotions of low activation such as sadness and boredom will be found in the remaining quadrant (near seven and eight o'clock). The resulting circle of points is known as a *circumplex*, and Russell (1980) has proposed that it reflects both the everyday conception of affect as well as the actual structure of affect. Not all researchers agree, however. One objection to this conclusion is that, in fact, there are not many emotion words in the parts of the circle corresponding to the neutral middle region of the pleasantness-unpleasantness dimension (six or twelve o'clock). Most graphs of the circumplex therefore tend to look not so much like a circle as like a pair of parentheses.

One way to avoid this problem is to reorient the two axes defining the two-dimensional space. Watson and Tellegen (1985) have proposed just this, suggesting that it is more useful to think of the two-dimensional space as being defined not by pleasantness and activation, but rather by two independent types of affect, called *positive affect* and *negative affect*. Positive affect, in their scheme, ranges from its extreme of elated euphoria (which was 1:30 on the original clock) to its minimum of sluggishness (the former 7:30). Negative affect ranges from an extreme of nervous hostility (the former 10:30) to a minimum of relaxation (the former 4:30). One advantage of these dimensions is that they correlate with well-known measures of personality. Measures of persons' positive affect correlate with measures of their extraversion, whereas measures of negative affect correlate with their neuroticism (Meyer & Shack, 1989). Yet, this interpretation has not been without its difficulties, either. For example, positive affect and negative affect are supposed to be uncorrelated with each other, but in fact this correlation varies with the intensity of the affect, the time period over which it is measured, and with how people interpret the task of rating their affect (Parkinson et al., 1996).

In summary, viewing the multitude of moods and emotions as variations in just two dimensions can be useful for understanding the most general qualities of emotion. It is also useful for creating measures of affect that are applicable under a wide variety of circumstances. Nevertheless, it is a mistake to consider emotions as holding a fixed location in two-dimensional space independent of context. Furthermore, two-dimensional schemes omit much of the rich variety of affective states. Anger and fear are close neighbors on the circumplex, reflecting their strong negativity and high activity (or their high negative affect and low positive affect), yet they certainly seem very different in other ways. Capturing these differences requires a different approach.

Several alternatives to dimensional representations of emotions have been developed. Some researchers have analyzed ratings of similarity using a technique called cluster analysis, which yield a hierarchical structure rather than a two-dimensional space (see Reading 1, by Shaver, et al., 1987). This approach suggests that emotions can be grouped in clusters, the number of clusters varying with the level of specificity one desires. One could select just two clusters (positive and negative emotions) or a much larger number. Shaver and colleagues suggested that a useful level of specificity for many purposes was the one with five clusters, which consisted of affection, happiness, sadness, anger, and fear.

Other researchers have abandoned the entire approach of grouping emotions based on ratings of global similarity. The problem with such ratings is that they force raters to settle on a single rating, whereas in fact the similarity of two emotions may vary depending on what aspect of the emotion is being considered. Anger and fear are very similar when their pleasantness and activity are focused on, but they are rather dissimilar with respect to their tendencies to motivate approach or withdrawal. These researchers have preferred to group emotions based on other criteria, such as the components of their appraisals (e.g., Scherer, 1984) or the aspects of events that give rise to an emotion (Ortony, Clore, & Collins, 1988). The structure of these groupings varies, but is typically a hierarchy or a grid. A reasonable compromise might be to allow that there is no single structure for emotions, but that different structures are optimal for different purposes.

The Role of Cognition

In most cases there is a good deal of agreement between a person's way of thinking and the emotions that person feels. People who believe they have achieved a major goal usually feel happy; those who believe they have suffered the irrevocable loss of something they cherished usually feel sad, and so on. But sometimes people's emotions do not seem to fit with their beliefs—they can seem irrational even to the person having the emotion! There is controversy about how to resolve this paradox.

As we have seen, appraisal theorists resolve the paradox by distinguishing appraisal from other types of cognition. Appraisals can be automatic and unconscious, and, if they differ from consciously held beliefs, will produce emotions that conflict with those beliefs (Frijda, 1986). According to appraisal theorists, feeling jealousy while consciously reassuring oneself that one's partner is faithful merely indicates a habitual appraisal of insecurity, not an emotion that occurs without any cognition at all.

This solution to the paradox of irrational emotions is not universally endorsed, however. The best-known dissenter from this approach is Robert Zajonc, who proposes that cognition and emotion should be conceived as two independent systems, often working together, but capable of being at odds. In a series of famous papers, Zajonc (1980, 1984) argued for the independence of emotion from cognition, brandishing such slogans as "preferences need no inferences" and "affect is primary." A prominent appraisal theorist, Richard Lazarus (1984), joined in debate with Zajonc, dissenting instead that "cognition is primary." This debate continued for several years, and its early contributions are among the most highly cited papers on the topic of emotion.

Close analysis of Zajonc's arguments suggests that the thesis "affect is primary" actually consisted of at least five separate claims: (1) that affect becomes conscious before cognition does, (2) that affect accounts for more behavior than cognition does, (3) that affect is effortless and uncontrollable, (4) that affect is irrevocable by subsequent cognition, and (5) that affect can occur in response to a stimulus without intervening cognition (Parrott & Sabini, 1989). Many of these claims were attacking a straw person, however. Some of the claims assume that "cognition" is conscious, verbal, and controllable, but, as we have seen, appraisal was never thought necessarily to have any of these qualities. Other claims are actually compatible with appraisal theory. Actually, the most significant part of Zajonc's critique was the fifth point, that cognition does not always precede emotion, and that will be discussed below. Lazarus's rejoinder that "cognition is primary" attempted to clarify some of these issues, but the rhetoric about primacy tended to obscure the issues that actually were at stake. These papers by Zajonc and Lazarus surely would have been included in this book were it not for the large number of misunderstandings that characterized this debate. Although there indeed are deep issues concerning the relation between cognition and emotion (Calhoun, 1984; Dalgleish & Power, 1999), this debate did not do them justice, as even one of its participants acknowledges (see Lazarus, 1999). In the present volume the pair of readings on anger—Reading 20 by Leonard Berkowitz and Reading 21 by James Averill—represent the perspectives and approaches that defined the Zajonc-Lazarus debate.

The debate did yield some useful outcomes. Critics of cognitive approaches became more aware that the cognition being proposed by appraisal theorists was not the conscious, deliberate, verbal cogitation that some had assumed. Advocates of a cognitive approach, on the other hand, greatly refined their theories. Modern appraisal theories have become much more explicit about the types of cognition being included. Some, called "multi-level theories," explicitly recognize qualitatively distinct types of information, such as sensory, perceptual, and symbolic representations, that contribute to emotional appraisals (Teasdale, 1999).

More recent criticisms of research on appraisal have focused on whether appraisals are necessary causes of emotion. Critics contend that appraisals are but one of many causes of emotions, some of which are best understood at the social or physiological levels of analysis (Parkinson & Manstead, 1993). These criticisms are leading to improvements in research methods. They are also leading to refinements in our understanding of appraisal. For example, rather than understanding appraisals as necessarily *causing* emotion, it may be more reasonable to conceive of appraisals as a *part* of emotions. That is, although it may be usual for an appraisal of loss to cause sadness, it may be possible for other things to cause sadness too. In this latter case, the most the cognitive approach may be able to assert is that an appraisal of loss is part of the nature of sadness, regardless of its cause.

Causal and Normative Explanations

The preceding discussion of cognition concluded by alluding to an issue of which it is good to be aware: the nature of scientific explanation. In all areas of social psychology, one can find two quite different models of science being used. One model is derived from the physical sciences and is based on the idea of causality. The aim of science, according to this model, is to specify what causes the phenomenon one is studying. This approach to social psychology tends to treat social and mental phenomena in a mechanistic manner, attempting to discover laws that allow one to predict later events from knowledge of prior circumstances. In the case of emotion, this approach leads to specifying the circumstances that produce emotions, and the effects that emotions have on subsequent thinking and behavior. This mode of science seems natural for anyone familiar with physics or chemistry. The question whether it is appropriate for understanding social psychology.

Some social psychologists believe it is not. These critics argue that many social events transpire as they do not because of causes impinging on people but because people interpret situations, have goals, understand social norms and roles, and decide to act accordingly. This approach to social psychology treats people as agents who have choice and who can be held responsible for their actions. It understands these actions as being based on reasons rather than on causes. These critics point out how odd it would seem to say that a person driving a car was *caused* to stop the car by a light that turned red. There's nothing about the red light that physically causes the person to stop the car. The red light has its force not from anything it causes but from the *meaning* it has to drivers of cars (Harré, Clarke, & De Carlo, 1985).

For our purposes it is not important to try to resolve this issue, but only to realize that it exists and to be alert for it when reading research on emotion. These two approaches to science are raised explicitly only in Part 10 of this book, but there are many examples of each approach to science in the nine preceding parts. Critical readers will be alert to which approach is being employed in any given reading and will consider in each case whether it is appropriate and why. Each approach has its place, because some aspects of social psychology operate in a rather mechanistic manner and other aspects operate only as part of a system of meaning and free choice.

Basic Emotions and Neglected Emotions

Some researchers have proposed that there exists a small set of "basic emotions" that are innate and universal. They are built into the brain, although they may not develop for months or years after birth. They are identified on the basis of brain structures, patterns of physiological activity, facial expressions, and patterns of appraisal and action readiness. Non-basic emotions are considered to be variations, elaborations, or blends of the basic emotions. Well-known proponents of basic emotions include Tomkins (1962), Ekman (1992), Izard (1991), and Oatley (1992).

The idea that there exist basic emotions can be criticized in several ways (Ortony & Turner, 1990). One problem is that the various criteria for basic emotions do not reliably co-occur. Another problem is that basic emotion concepts include the cultural assumptions of the English language (Wierzbicka, 1999). A third problem is that the various proposals for basic emotions disagree about how many basic emotions there are and which emotions are considered basic. It may be that different emotions seem basic depending on one's criteria and purposes. Critics of basic emotions tend to view emotions as built from components that are not themselves emotional. They argue either that there are no basic emotions, or that there are only two general ones, such as positive and negative affect.

Related to the question of whether there are basic emotions is the question of what is included among the emotions. For a variety of reasons the list of emotions most studied by psychologists is not quite the same as the list of emotions deemed most prototypical in everyday language. Ranking high on prototypicality are such emotions as love, hate, compassion, sympathy, and lust, which are not studied in academic psychology as much as their prototypicality might suggest. Psychologists sometimes argue that a neglected emotion plays an important role in social life and deserves more recognition and study. An example would be the recent proposal by Baumeister and Leary (1995) suggesting that *belonging* is such an emotion. Similarly, psychologists sometimes argue that states widely regarded as emotional are not. An example would be the argument by Ortony, Clore, and

Collins (1988) that surprise is quite unusual for an emotion in that it can be positive, negative, or neutral and for that reason may best be considered not to be one.

Nature and Nurture

The extent to which emotions are malleable by culture has not been determined, and psychologists have hypothesized a variety of solutions to the nature-nurture problem. These solutions range from proposing a fairly high degree of genetic and biological determinism that limits the possibility of cultural variation to proposing a fairly high degree of malleability that permits or even requires cultural and social processes to supply many of the components of emotions. An example of the former extreme would be evolutionary psychology; an example of the latter would be social constructionism. Many psychologists appreciate points made by both extremes, which leads them to suspect either that some intermediate position is warranted or that the extreme positions are not addressing themselves to quite the same phenomena.

It is important to realize that each of these extremes includes a place for both biology and culture. Even the most biologically oriented theorists believe that culture determines the significance of many events and the appropriateness of various emotional behaviors and expressions. What these theorists want to assert is that there is a core emotional response nestled between appraisal and self-regulation that is universal across cultures. These theorists tend to believe that emotions are part of a basic human nature that is present in people in all cultures and walks of life. Likewise, even the most culturally relativist theorists must assign a crucial role to genetics and biology. Unless humans evolved a brain that was capable of learning a variety of roles and responses, there is no way that people growing up in different cultures could learn different emotions. Without this biological plasticity, human emotions would be as tied to instinct as are their analogues in other species. Thus, in their way, social constructionist theories posit a crucial role for evolution and biology in emotions.

This controversy seems to rest partly on matters of fact and partly on matters of emphasis and definition. There are factual questions about the degree to which emotions differ cross-culturally that cannot yet be resolved simply because the right data have not yet been collected—much cross-cultural data is anecdotal, or concerns conceptions of emotion or the language of emotion rather than emotional states. But there are also differences in approach and emphasis that must be acknowledged. Those emphasizing biology tend to regard the essence of emotion as something that is unchangingly present despite changes in context, cognitive elaboration, cultural valuation, and other transformations that are not considered to have altered the emotion's unchanging essence. Those emphasizing social construction tend to be more attuned to nuance and more cognizant of the role of cognition and cultural meaning in influencing conscious experience.

Feelings

Preconceptions about the role of feelings in emotions may underlie other controversies in the field. One reason to think that emotion and cognition must be distinct is to assume that cognition does not involve feeling whereas emotion does. One reason to think that emotions must involve arousal of the SNS is to assume that cognition alone cannot produce feelings whereas arousal can. One reason to think that there are basic emotions, or to think that emotions cannot be modified by culture to any significant extent, is to assume that feelings must be the result of innate brain structures and hormone systems.

Are these assumptions valid? One reason to question them is that there is much more to emotions than feelings. The entire emphasis on feelings in both everyday and academic approaches to emotion may be exaggerated—not all cultures or periods of history empha-size feelings. Not only is the current Western preoccupation with internal experiences some-what exceptional, there are compelling philosophical arguments to suggest that the mean-ing of emotion concepts could never be based purely on private experiences (Wittgenstein, 1953).

But suppose we accept that feelings are part of the current Western conception of emo-tion. Where do emotional feelings come from? There are many answers to this question. Some answers single out one facet of emotion as the source of feelings: physiological activity, emotional behavior, and cognition have all been proposed. Other answers involve combinations of several facets. There are really two matters at issue: first, what are the sources of feelings, and, second, how do feelings arise from their sources? Let us consider each of these matters in turn.

First, numerous sources of feelings have been proposed. Some of these sources are bodily. For example, some theorists propose that activity of certain regions of the brain directly give rise to emotional feelings (e.g., Buck, 1988). And, as we have seen, James (1884) and Schachter and Singer (1962) suggested arousal of the SNS as a source of emotional feel-ings. James (1884) also proposed that sensory feedback from bodily actions contributed to emotional feelings, and modern experiments have suggested that expressive actions such as facial expressions, posture, and gaze patterns can contribute to the quality and intensity of emotional experience (Laird & Bresler, 1992; Stepper & Strack, 1993). Emotions in-volve not only actions, but preparations for action, and awareness of these may also con-tribute to emotional experience (Frijda, 1986).

Cognition has been proposed to contribute to emotional experience in a variety of ways. Awareness of one's patterns of cognitive activity appears to give rise to distinctive phe-nomenological states, such as when contradiction of one's framework for understanding events leads to a feeling of confusion, or when one is biased toward optimistic interpreta-tions or vigilant for possible threats (Parrott, 1988). Awareness of appraisals and their implications may also influence conscious experience because of the personal importance of what they signify, because they refer to future pleasures or pains, or because they sug-gest that certain actions ought to be attempted (Frijda, 1986). Because of the ways that social and cultural factors can shape cognition, any cognitive source of feeling must be considered a potential social and cultural source as well.

The second issue concerns the ways in which these sources come to be experienced as emotional. Three approaches to this issue can be distinguished. Some theorists have pro-posed that physiological and bodily activities lead directly to feelings without the need for intervening cognition (Buck, 1988; Stepper & Strack, 1993). Other theorists have pro-posed that some conscious, cognitive interpretation such as labeling is required for feel-ings to be emotional (Schachter & Singer, 1962). The third approach argues that cognition is necessary for emotional feelings to occur, but that this cognition is implicit and percep-tual. Like the perception of size, which is based on cognitions about depth and visual angle that are not consciously experienced, emotional feelings may be the end-product of a pro-cess that involves considerable unconscious cognition. One example of this approach is the self-preception theory of Laird and Bresler (1992), which depicts emotional experience as a form of self-knowledge based on observation and interpretation of one's emotional be-haviors. Another example would be the phenomenological theory of Frijda (1986), which depicts emotional experience as perception-like awareness that the world has properties relating to oneself and to one's goals and values.

The large number of hypotheses just reviewed may suggest more controversy than in fact exists. The many possible sources of feelings may be somewhat redundant, given that some of them influence others. Furthermore, the hypotheses about sources need not be mutually exclusive—it may be that all of them can contribute to emotional feelings, al-though not all of them may be necessary for these feelings to occur (Parrott, 1995a). The more controversial issue is over how these sources become feelings and whether cognition is required to do so. What evidence is available at present suggests that conscious cognition is not required but that perception-like cognition may indeed be necessary. Research showing that attributions modify emotional experience suggests that identical sensations can produce different emotional experiences depending on the inferences that are made of those sensations (Schwarz, 1990). Many sources of emotional feelings appear to be learned, not innate (Laird & Bressler, 1992).

The Social Nature of Emotions

Interestingly, the very premise of the present volume is somewhat controversial. This chapter began with the argument that emotions are social, yet this emphasis is missing from much research that treats emotion as a purely intrapsychic phenomenon. The assumption of such research is that emotion happens within a person; that it results from the activity of one person's brain; that it involves one person's perceptions, concerns, and reactions; that it is a private conscious experience.

These assumptions may seem natural for members of Western cultures, but it is worth noting that in many languages the words corresponding most closely to Western emotion words do not have these connotations. Rather, they often refer to publicly observable aspects of a person's behavior, to types of social situations, or to alterations in interpersonal relationships (Russell, 1991). These differences may reflect differences in the cultures themselves. Western cultures, valuing the independence of individuals, may tend to emphasize the individual's perspective and subjective experience. Other cultures may place more value on relationships and the community, and may therefore have folk psychologies that emphasize those aspects of emotions (Markus & Kitayama, 1991).

Thus, within the Western tradition, the social nature of emotions can come across as something of a discovery. A number of theorists have argued that emotions are social, including de Rivera (1984), Markus and Kitayama (1991), Averill (1980), Parkinson (1996), and Baumeister, Stillwell, and Heatherton (1994). The social aspects of emotion are arguably of more interest and importance to social psychology than to any other discipline, so they are a major theme of this book. Nevertheless, the social nature of emotion is not universally accepted, and the extent to which emotions should be considered an internal feeling state or a social transaction is presently an open question. Controversy is evident in two pairs of articles in this volume, one dealing with guilt (Readings 17 and 18), the other with anger (Readings 20 and 21). In each pair, one article takes a more intrapsychic approach and the other a more social approach.

About this Volume

The articles that are reprinted in this volume have been carefully selected to represent the topics in which emotion figures importantly in social psychology. The general organization of the book is that the first half focuses on the nature of emotion, and the second half on the ways in which emotions affect social events and processes. In the first half of the book are articles on the aspects of emotion most important in social psychology: the concept of emotion, the various types of emotion, and schemes for structuring or grouping emotions; the basic ways in which emotion involves thought, preparation for action, expression, and behavior; the roles of cognition, culture, and evolution. In the second half of the book are articles on how emotions affect social phenomena such as social cognition, social contagion, and facial expressions. The second half of the book is also where specific emotions are considered: shame, guilt, envy, jealousy, and anger are featured. In the middle of the book is the pivotal topic of function. As I have argued in this overview, function is the central theme of contemporary emotion research, and it is what connects the first part of this book to the second. How emotions function and are regulated is intrinsic to our understanding of what emotions are, and is also the basis of how emotions affect social life. The topics of function and regulation therefore complete the first part of the book while setting the stage for the second.

The primary challenge of editing a volume such as this one is to represent the field's rich variety of topics and approaches within a very limited space. The solution involved several strategies. One was to address the volume specifically to the field of social psychology. Emotion is by its nature multidisciplinary; it has physiological, cognitive, and sociological aspects as well as social psychological ones, but articles outside of social psychology were not included. Several of the included articles, however, are superb examples of the ways in which good social psychology draws on insights and methods from other disciplines. Effort has been made to discuss topics from outside social psychology in this overview chapter where they are important for the study of emotions.

Another strategy was to select articles that address more than one topic. Note that this strategy was pursued without relying on review articles; most of the articles in this collection report empirical data. Many articles address two or more subjects that easily could have warranted separate articles. Just as examples, the first reading in the book includes discussions and data pertaining to the circumplex model of emotions, hierarchical representations of emotions, as well as the prototypical nature of conceptions of emotions. The last reading in the book reports data on anger while also discussing the theory of social constructionism and the rational and causal modes of explanation. The important topic of how altruism is influenced by moods is addressed at the end of the article on emotional intelligence and self-regulation. The editor's nomination for the most under-appreciated social emotion, embarrassment, did not receive its own chapter but is discussed at the end of the article on the social functions of emotions. Thus, there is much more in this book than may first meet the eye!

Nevertheless, achieving balanced coverage with just 21 articles required selectivity, and each part of this book presents only a sample of the rich area it represents. These articles were therefore chosen carefully. Many are classics that continue to be widely referenced. Many have notable breadth. Because a major use of this volume will be for teaching, clear and accessible prose was favored, and articles were grouped to facilitate discussion and contrast. In addition, each of the ten sections of this volume begins with an introduction that provides background, highlights important aspects of each study, and links each to subsequent work. Each section concludes with an annotated list of suggestions for further reading, which provides a guide to other important studies and approaches for the reader wishing to learn more about a topic.

It was necessary to edit some of the selections to reduce their length. Fewer than half of the articles have been edited, and cuts were always made carefully and with the aim of preserving the article's structure and aims. Extra details and peripheral points were the main targets. In a few cases only one of two experiments has been included where the experiments made essentially the same point.

This book is the result. May it be useful to both students and experts with an interest in understanding the emotional heart of social psychology!

Acknowledgments

The editor's task in preparing this volume was aided by thoughtful suggestions from a panel of expert reviewers. Roy Baumeister, Tony Manstead, Peter Salovey, Norbert Schwarz, and June Tangney, as well as two anonymous reviewers, all commented on an already-too-long list of proposed readings, and their suggestions were very helpful in refining this list as well as in choosing the topics to cover in this overview and in the introductions. Two other colleagues, Agneta Fischer and Richard Smith, also provided helpful suggestions. All their contributions are gratefully acknowledged. That some of their suggestions are not reflected in this volume is almost always due to their suggestions being of the form "add this" whereas the necessity facing the editor was more often of the form "delete that." This volume is certainly the better for having had the benefit of their suggestions.

REFERENCES

Armon-Jones, C. (1986). The social functions of emotion. In R. Harré (Ed.), *The social construction of emotions* (pp. 57–82). Oxford, England: Basil Blackwell.

Arnold, M. B. (1960). *Emotion and personality: Vol. 1. Psychological aspects.* New York: Columbia University Press.

Averill, J. R. (1974). An analysis of psychophysiological symbolism and its influence on theories of emotion. *Journal for the Theory of Social Behaviour, 4,* 147–190.

Averill, J. R. (1980). A constructivist view of emotion. In R. Plutchik & H. Kellerman (Eds.), *Emotion: Theory, research and experience: Vol. 1. Theories of emotion* (pp. 305–339). New York: Academic Press.

Batson, C. D. (1998). Altruism and prosocial behavior. In D. T. Gilbert, S. T. Fiske, & G. Lindzey (Eds.), *The handbook of social psychology* (4th ed., Vol. 2, pp. 282–316). New York: McGraw-Hill.

Baumeister, R. F., & Leary, M. R. (1995). The need to belong: Desire for interpersonal attachments as a fundamental human motivation. *Psychological Bulletin, 117,* 497–529.

Baumeister, R. F., Stillwell, A. M., & Heatherton, T. F. (1994). Guilt: An interpersonal approach. *Psychological Bulletin, 115,* 243–267.

Buck, R. (1988). *Human motivation and emotion* (2nd ed.). New York: Wiley.

Buss, D. M. (2000). *The dangerous passion: Why jealousy is as necessary as love and sex.* New York: Free Press.

Cacioppo, J. T., Klein, D. J., Berntson, G. G., & Hatfield, E. (1993). The psychophysiology of emotions. In M. Lewis & J. M. Haviland (Eds.), *Handbook of emotions* (pp. 119–142). New York: Guilford.

Calhoun, C. (1984). Cognitive emotions? In C. Calhoun & R. C. Solomon (Eds.), *What is an emotion: Classic readings in philosophical psychology* (pp. 327–342). New York: Oxford University Press.

Cannon, W. B. (1927). The James-Lange theory of emotions: A critical examination and an alternative theory. *American Journal of Psychology, 39,* 106–124.

Chwalisz, K., Diener, E., & Gallagher, D. (1988). Autonomic arousal feedback and emotional experience: Evidence from the spinal cord injured. *Journal of Personality and Social Psychology, 54,* 820–828.

Cottrell, N. B. (1968). Performance in the presence of other human beings: Mere presence, audience, and affiliation effects. In E. C. Simmel, R. A. Hoppe, & G. A. Milton (Ed.), *Social facilitation and imitative behavior* (pp. 91–110). Bonson: Allyn & Bacon.

Dalgleish, T., & Power, M. (Eds.). (1999). *Handbook of cognition and emotion.* Chichester, England: Wiley.

Darwin, C. (1872). *The expression of the emotions in man and animals.* London: John Murray.

De Rivera, J. (1984). The structure of emotional relationships. In P. Shaver (Ed.), *Review of personality and social psychology, Vol. 5: Emotions, relationships, and health* (pp. 116–145). Beverly Hills, CA: Sage.

Dienstbier, R. A., & Munter, P. O. (1971). Cheating as a function of the labeling of natural arousal. *Journal of Personality and Social Psychology, 17,* 208–213.

Dutton, D. G., & Aron, A. P. (1974). Some evidence for heightened sexual attraction under conditions of high anxiety. *Journal of Personality and Social Psychology, 34,* 774–781.

Ekman, P. (1972). Universals and cultural differences in facial expressions of emotion. In J. K. Cole (Ed.), *Nebraska symposium on motivation* (Vol. 19, pp. 207–283). Lincoln, NE: University of Nebraska Press.

Ekman, P. (1992). An argument for basic emotions. *Cognition and Emotion, 6,* 169–200.

Ekman, P., Levenson, R. W., & Friesen, W. V. (1983). Autonomic nervous system activity distinguishes among emotions. *Science, 221,* 1208–1210.

Fehr, B., & Russell, J. A. (1984). Concept of emotion viewed from a prototype perspective. *Journal of Experimental Psychology: General, 113,* 464–486.

Fridlund, A. J. (1994). *Human facial expression: An evolutionary view.* San Diego, CA: Academic Press.

Frijda, N. H. (1986). *The emotions.* Cambridge, England: Cambridge University Press.

Frijda, N. H., Mesquita, B., Sonnemans, J., & Van Goozen, S. (1991). The duration of affective phenomena, or emotions, sentiments and passions. In K. Strongman (Ed.), *International review of studies on emotion* (Vol. 1, pp. 198–225). Chichester, England: Wiley.

Ginsburg, G. P., & Harrington, M. E. (1996). Bodily states and context in situated lines of action. In R. Harré & W. G. Parrott (Eds.), *The emotions: Social, cultural and biological dimensions* (pp. 229–258). London: Sage.

Goffman, E. (1959). *The presentation of self in everyday life.* Garden City, NY: Doubleday.

Gordon, R. M. (1978). Emotion, labelling and cognition. *Journal for the Theory of Social Behaviour, 8,* 125–135.

Greenwood, J. D. (1994). *Realism, identity and emotion.* London: Sage Publications.

Harmon-Jones, E., & Mills, J. (Eds.). (1999). *Cognitive dissonance: Progress on a pivotal theory in social psychology.* Washington, DC: American Psychological Association.

Harré, R. (Ed.). (1986). *The social construction of emotions.* Oxford, England: Basil Blackwell.

Harré, R., Clarke, D., & De Carlo, N. (1985). *Motives and mechanisms: An introduction to the psychology of action.* London: Methuen.

Harré, R., & Parrott, W. G. (Eds.). (1996). *The emotions: Social, cultural, and biological dimensions.* London: Sage.

Hatfield, E., Cacioppo, J. T., & Rapson, R. L. (1994). *Emotional contagion.* Cambridge, England: Cambridge University Press.

Hochschild, A. R. (1979). Emotion work, feeling rules, and social structure. *American Journal of Sociology, 85,* 551–575.

Izard, C. E. (1991). *The psychology of emotions.* New York: Plenum.

James, W. (1884). What is an emotion? *Mind, 19,* 188–205.

Kenny, A. (1963). *Action, emotion and will.* London: Routledge & Kegan Paul.

Kunda, Z. (1999). *Social cognition: Making sense of people.* Cambridge, MA: MIT Press.

Laird, J. D., & Bresler, C. (1992). The process of emotional experience: A self-perception theory. In M. S. Clark (Ed.), *Review of personality and social psychology: Vol. 13. Emotion* (pp. 213–234). Newbury Park, CA: Sage.

Larsen, R. J., & Diener, E. (1992). Promises and problems with the circumplex model of emotion. In M. S. Clark (Ed.), *Review of personality and social psychology: Vol. 13. Emotion* (pp. 25–59). Newbury Park, CA: Sage.

Lazarus, R. S. (1966). *Psychological stress and the coping process.* New York: McGraw-Hill.

Lazarus, R. S. (1984). On the primacy of cognition. *American Psychologist, 39,* 124–129.

Lazarus, R. S. (1991). *Emotion and adaptation.* New York: Oxford University Press.

Lazarus, R. S. (1999). The cognition-emotion debate: A bit of history. In T. Dalgleish, & M. Power (Eds.), *Handbook of cognition and emotion* (pp. 3–19). Chichester, England: Wiley.

LeDoux, J. E. (1995). In search of an emotional system in the brain: Leaping from fear to emotion and consciousness. In M. S. Gazzaniga (Ed.), *The cognitive neurosciences* (pp. 1049–1061). Cambridge, MA: MIT Press.

Lyons, W. (1980). *Emotion.* Cambridge, England: Cambridge University Press.

Markus, H. R., & Kitayama, S. (1991). Culture and the self: Implications for cognition, emotion, and motivation. *Psychological Review, 98,* 224–253.

Meyer, G. J., & Shack, J. R. (1989). The structural convergence of mood and personality: Evidence for old and new 'directions'. *Journal of Personality and Social Psychology, 57,* 691–706.

Mezzacappa, E. S., Katkin, E. S., & Palmer, S., N. (1999). Epinephrine, arousal, and emotion: A new look at two-factor theory. *Cognition and Emotion, 13,* 181–199.

Miller, D. T., & McFarland, C. (1987). Pluralistic ignorance: When similarity is interpreted as dissimilarity. *Journal of Personality and Social Psychology, 53,* 298–305.

Morris, W. N. (1992). A functional analysis of the role of mood in affective systems. *Review of personality and social psychology: Vol. 13. Emotion* (pp. 256–293). Newbury Park, CA: Sage.

Nissenbaum, H. F. (1985). *Emotion and focus.* Stanford, CA: Center for the Study of Language and Information.

Nussbaum, M. C. (1994). *The therapy of desire: Theory and practice in Hellenistic ethics.* Princeton, NJ: Princeton University Press.

Oatley, K. (1992). *Best laid schemes: The psychology of emotions.* New York: Cambridge University Press.

Oatley, K., & Jenkins, J. M. (1992). Human emotions: Function and dysfunction. *Annual Review of Psychology, 43,* 55–85.

Ortony, A., Clore, G. L., & Collins, A. (1988). *The cognitive structure of emotions.* Cambridge, England: Cambridge University Press.

Ortony, A., Clore, G. L., & Foss, M. A. (1987). The referential structure of the affective lexicon. *Cognitive Science, 11,* 341–364.

Ortony, A., & Turner, M. J. (1990). What's basic about basic emotions? *Psychological Review, 74,* 431–461.

Parkinson, B. (1996). Emotions are social. *British Journal of Psychology, 87,* 663–683.

Parkinson, B., & Manstead, A. S. R. (1993). Making sense of emotions in stories and social life. *Cognition and Emotion, 7,* 295–323.

Parkinson, B., Totterdell, P., Briner, R. B., & Reynolds, S. (1996). *Changing moods: The psychology of mood and mood regulation.* London: Longman.

Parrott, W. G. (1988). The role of cognition in emotional experience. In W. J. Baker, L. P. Mos, H. V. Rappard, & H. J. Stam (Eds.), *Recent trends in theoretical psychology* (pp. 327–337). New York: Springer-Verlag.

Parrott, W. G. (1991). The emotional experiences of envy and jealousy. In P. Salovey (Ed.), *The psychology of jealousy and envy* (pp. 3–30). New York: Guilford.

Parrott, W. G. (1995a). Emotional experience. In A. S. R. Manstead & M. Hewstone (Eds.), *The Blackwell encyclopedia of social psychology* (pp. 198–203). Oxford, England: Basil Blackwell.

Parrott, W. G. (1995b). The heart and the head: Everyday conceptions of being emotional. In J. A. Russell, J.- M. Fernández-Dols, A. S. R. Manstead, & J. C. Wellenkamp (Eds.), *Everyday conceptions of emotions: An introduction to the psychology, anthropology and linguistics of emotion* (pp. 73–84). Dordrecht: Kluwer.

Parrott, W. G., & Sabini, J. (1989). On the "emotional" qualities of certain types of cognition: A reply to arguments for the independence of cognition and affect. *Cognitive Therapy and Research, 13,* 49–65.

Plutchik, R. (1980). *Emotion: A psychoevolutionary synthesis.* New York: Harper & Row.

Reisenzein, R. (1983). The Schachter theory of emotion: Two decades later. *Psychological Bulletin, 94,* 239–264.

Rodin, J. (1981). Current status of the internal-external hypothesis for obesity: What went wrong? *American Psychologist, 36,* 361–372.

Russell, J. A. (1980). A circumplex model of affect. *Journal of Personality and Social Psychology, 39,* 1161–1178.

Russell, J. A. (1991). Culture and the categorization of emotions. *Psychological Bulletin, 110,* 426–450.

Sabini, J., & Silver, M. (1982). *Moralities of everyday life.* Oxford, England: Oxford University Press.

Schachter, S., & Singer, J. (1962). Cognitive, social, and physiological determinants of emotional state. *Psychological Review, 69,* 379–399.

Scherer, K. R. (1984). On the nature and function of emotions: A component process approach. In K. R. Scherer, & P. Ekman (Eds.), *Approaches to emotion* (pp. 293-317). Hillsdale, NJ: Erlbaum.

Schwarz, N. (1990). Feelings as information: Informational and motivational functions of affective states. In E. T. Higgins & R. M. Sorrentino (Eds.), *Handbook of motivation and cognition* (Vol. 2, pp. 527–561). New York: Guilford Press.

Schwarz, N., & Clore, G. L. (1983). Mood, misattribution, and judgments of well-being: Informative and directive functions of affective states. *Journal of Personality and Social Psychology, 45,* 513–523.

Shaver, P., Schwartz, J., Kirson, D., & O'Connor, C. (1987). Emotion knowledge: Further exploration of a prototype approach. *Journal of Personality and Social Psychology, 52*, 1061–1086.

Shott, S. (1979). Emotion and social life: A symbolic interactionist analysis. *American Journal of Sociology, 84*, 1317–1334.

Storms, M. D., & Nisbett, R. E. (1970). Insomnia and the attribution process. *Journal of Personality and Social Psychology, 16,* 319–328.

Stepper, S., & Strack, F. (1993). Proprioceptive determinants of emotional and nonemotional feelings. *Journal of Personality and Social Psychology, 64*, 211–220.

Teasdale, J. D. (1999). Multi-level theories of cognition-emotion relations. In T. Dalgleish & M. Power (Eds.), *Handbook of cognition and emotion* (pp. 665–681). Chichester, England: Wiley.

Tomkins, S. S. (1962). *Affect, imagery, consciousness: Vol. 1. The positive affects.* New York: Springer.

Watson, D., & Tellegen, A. (1985). Toward a consensual structure of mood. *Psychological Bulletin, 98*, 219–235.

Wierzbicka, A. (1999). *Emotions across languages and cultures: Diversity and universals.* Paris: Cambridge University Press.

Wittgenstein, L. (1953). *Philosophical investigations.* Oxford, England: Blackwell.

Zajonc, R. B. (1980). Feeling and thinking: Preferences need no inferences. *American Psychologist, 35,* 151–175.

Zajonc, R. B. (1984). On the primacy of affect. *American Psychologist, 39*, 117–123.

Zanna, M. P., & Cooper, J. (1974). Dissonance and the pill: An attribution approach to studying the arousal properties of dissonance. *Journal of Personality and Social Psychology, 29,* 703–709.

Zillman, D., Johnson, R. C., & Day, K. D. (1974). Attribution of apparent arousal and proficiency of recovery from sympathetic activation affecting excitation transfer to aggressive behavior. *Journal of Experimental Social Psychology, 10,* 503–515.

The Nature of Emotion

What *are* emotions? To answer this question, it is necessary to address two subtly interrelated issues: what do people *mean* by the word "emotion," and what does research tell us about these states to which the word "emotion" refers? Each of the articles in this section focuses on one of these issues.

To understand why the concept of emotion requires research, it is necessary to realize that this concept did not originate as a scientific term with a precise definition. Rather, the general category of "emotion," as well as specific emotion words such as "anger" or "embarrassment," has its origins in everyday language and folk psychology. Research on emotion concepts informs us about what people mean when they speak or think of emotions.

There is a subtle interrelation between conceptions of emotion and emotions themselves. Although it is certainly possible that people might be wrong to some extent about the nature of their emotions, they cannot be completely wrong. If scientists were to study some phenomenon that differed too much from our everyday conception of what an emotion is, we would say that the scientist was not studying emotion at all, and, if research revealed no mental phenomena that closely resembled the folk conception of emotion, we would say that emotions do not exist, not that the folk conception of emotion was wildly incorrect. Understanding the everyday conception of emotion therefore serves at least two important purposes: it makes explicit what people believe about everyday emotion concepts, and it provides the starting point and general limits for scientific research on emotion.

Two more purposes become clear if we consider how emotions might be influenced by culture. The word "emotion" is English, but, even though most Western languages have some word that is roughly equivalent, some languages lack such a term and some folk psychologies lack such a category (Russell, 1991). The English language itself has not always contained the word "emotion." Research on conceptions of emotion therefore allows comparison of contemporary English conceptions of emotion with those of other languages and cultures. Finally, consider that our conceptions of emotion may play a role in the ways that emotion affects social interaction, in the ways in which emotion is regulated by social customs, and in our experience of emotion (Armon-Jones, 1986; Hochschild, 1990). Studying emotion concepts therefore may contribute to our understanding of emotion's effect on social behavior and of the nature of emotional experience itself.

The paper on emotion knowledge by Shaver, Schwartz, Kirson, and O'Connor (1987) provides a good introduction to these issues, and aptly summarizes a number of classic studies and builds upon them. Of particular importance is an earlier paper by Fehr and Russell (1984), which presented evidence that the everyday concept of emotion may not have a single, clear definition. Fehr and Russell showed that some emotions (such as happiness, anger, and sadness) are better representatives of emotion than are other emotions (such as respect, boredom, and calmness). Their findings also suggested that there is no set of properties that is necessary and sufficient for determining that a psychological state belonged to the category of "emotion." Shaver and colleagues built upon these findings. They too found that a large list of possible emotion names will include some words that nearly everyone agrees are "definitely" an emotion, other words that nearly everyone agrees are "definitely not" an emotion, and the remaining words spread in between. Their list of English emotion names, sorted in order of

rated prototypicality, is itself useful as a demonstration of the variety and typicality of various English emotion names. Their findings, like those of Fehr and Russell, suggest that "emotion" is a category with fuzzy boundaries, and that family resemblance, not a precise definition, determines membership in the category, at least in everyday speech and thought.

Shaver and colleagues then address the problem of how best to represent the relations among all these emotions. They asked people to rate how similar each emotion is to every other emotion on their list, and then explored three ways of summarizing these data. Two involve a mathematical method known as *multidimensional scaling*, which preserves as much of the similarity information as possibly while displaying the emotions on a two- or three-dimensional graph. The third method employs the statistical technique of *cluster analysis* to generate a multilevel hierarchical structure from the similarity data. The result from cluster analysis is strikingly different from that of multidimensional scaling, and in many ways more satisfactory. The hierarchical chart suggests that one can make distinctions between emotional states at various levels of abstraction. The most general simply distinguishes positive and negative emotions, the most specific consists of the 135 emotion words, and there are several levels intermediate. One of these is deemed the "basic level" by the authors, and consists of five clusters: affection, happiness, sadness, anger, and fear. This is a useful way of categorizing emotions, although it is interesting to note what is gained and lost at higher and lower levels of abstraction. This aspect of our knowledge of emotions is lost when multidimensional scaling is used.

In a second study, Shaver and colleagues investigated the five basic level emotions in more detail. They collected accounts of actual emotional experiences, as well as descriptions of what would be typical experiences, and summarized the prototypical features for each emotion in figures that depict each prototype as having a script-like structure. The scripts have three parts, corresponding to the conditions that elicit the emotion, the nature of the emotional response, and ways of controlling or resolving the emotion. Note that the similarity data that generated these prototypes came from the authors, not from the participants.

This paper has been influential by increasing appreciation of emotion categories as prototypes and as structured knowledge. Some of the methods used by these researchers were quite innovative, and have since been extended to other emotions, such as embarrassment, and to other issues, such as the accuracy of emotion stereotypes (Parrott & Smith, 1991). These methods have proved very useful for comparing emotion categories from different cultures. Shaver and colleagues, for example, compared the emotion hierarchy they found in the United States with hierarchies in Italy and China, finding some similarities but some interesting differences as well (Shaver, Wu, & Schwartz, 1992). Likewise, Church, Katigbak, Reyes, and Jensen (1998) used these methods to analyze Filipino emotion words and to compare them to words from other languages.

In the second selection, we turn our attention from the concept of emotion to emotional states themselves. Nico Frijda (1988) provides a succinct and insightful summary of what psychologists have learned about the nature of emotion by proposing a dozen "laws of emotion." These

"laws," which Frijda readily concedes are really just statements of empirical regularities, aptly summarize much recent research on emotion and provide a coherent overview of what has been learned. Although not all psychologists agree with Frijda's perspective, the 12 laws he proposes introduce some of the most important themes, concepts, and phenomena to emerge from research on the nature of emotion.

Noteworthy is Frijda's explicit acknowledgement that research on emotion must grow in "bootstrapping" fashion out of our everyday conceptions of emotion, refining and expanding what we know from everyday experience. The laws summarize emotion's profound effects on perspective, preparation for action, goals, behavior, attention, and thought. They demonstrate that certain types of cognition are part of emotion, even though nonemotional cognition is distinct and sometimes at odds. In emphasizing the lawlike nature of these phenomena, Frijda draws attention to why emotions require self-control, the means of which range from coping and self-regulation to motivated cognition and self-deception.

One limitation of Frijda's article is its focus on the individual and on processes occurring within the individual—one might wish to propose some amendments to these laws to more fully address the more social aspects of emotion. As later selections will make clear, emotion's effects on others, its regulation by social roles and rules, and its modification by culture provide a social dimension that is especially important in social psychology.

REFERENCES

Armon-Jones, C. (1986). The thesis of constructionism. In R. Harré (Ed.), *The social construction of emotions* (pp. 32–56). Oxford, England: Basil Blackwell.

Church, A. T., Katigbak, M. S., Reyes, J. A. S., & Jensen, S. M. (1998). Language and organization of Filipino emotion concepts: Comparing emotion concepts and dimensions across cultures. *Cognition and Emotion, 12,* 63–92.

Fehr, B., & Russell, J. A. (1984). Concept of emotion viewed from a prototype perspective. *Journal of Experimental Psychology: General, 113,* 464–486.

Frijda, N. H. (1988). The laws of emotion. *American Psychologist, 43,* 349–358.

Hochschild, A. R. (1990). Ideology and emotion management: A perspective and path for future research. In T. D. Kemper

(Ed.), *Research agendas in the sociology of emotions* (pp. 117–142). Albany, NY: State University of New York Press.

Parrott, W. G., & Smith, S. F. (1991). Embarrassment: Actual vs. typical cases, classical vs. prototypical representations. *Cognition and Emotion, 5,* 467–488.

Russell, J. A. (1991). Culture and the categorization of emotions. *Psychological Bulletin, 110,* 426–450.

Shaver, P., Schwartz, J., Kirson, D., & O'Connor, C. (1987).

Emotion knowledge: Further exploration of a prototype approach. *Journal of Personality and Social Psychology, 52,* 1061–1086.

Shaver, P. R., Wu, S., & Schwartz, J. C. (1992). Cross-cultural similarities and differences in emotion and its representation. In M. S. Clark (Ed.), *Review of personality and social psychology: Vol. 13. Emotion* (pp. 175-212). Newbury Park, CA: Sage.

Discussion Questions

1. In one minute, list as many emotions as you can. Compare the emotions on your list. What, if anything, do they have in common? Do some seem to be "better" examples of emotion than do others?
2. Consider the following as "feelings": hunger, confidence, sexual arousal, insecurity, superiority, confusion, intelligence. Should any of these feelings be considered to be emotions? Why or why not? For each of these feelings, what aspects seem emotional and what aspects do not?
3. Should social psychologists accept the everyday definitions of emotion concepts such as "love," "jealousy," and "emotion," or should they develop more precise, technical definitions of their own? Discuss the strengths and weaknesses of each alternative.
4. The emotions "fear" and "anger" are located very close to each other in a two-dimensional circumplex, but fall into different basic emotion clusters in a multilevel hierarchical structure. What similarities are being captured by the circumplex, and what differences are being captured by the hierarchy?
5. Think about a typical episode of pride or shame. Did you think of information representing all three parts of an emotion script: the eliciting conditions, the emotional symptoms, and the means of regulation or resolution? What does this suggest to you about our beliefs about emotions?
6. Some of Frijda's laws of emotion depict emotions as proceeding in mechanical fashion, outside of an individual's control, whereas other laws depict ways in which emotions are controlled and regulated. Do these laws contradict each other? Why or why not?

Suggested Readings

Clore, G. L., Ortony, A., & Foss, M. A. (1987). The psychological foundations of the affective lexicon. *Journal of Personality and Social Psychology, 53,* 751–766. This article tests the validity of a scheme for distinguishing emotion words from the perplexing variety of related words. The resulting delineation of words into groups emphasizing emotion, cognitive aspects of emotion, and behavioral aspects of emotion, among others, is very helpful in making sense of the relation between emotions words and their closest lexical neighbors.

Cornelius, R. R. (1996). *The science of emotion: Research and tradition in the psychology of emotion.* Upper Saddle River, NJ: Prentice Hall. Students wishing for a succinct and readable introduction to the psychology of emotion will find this to be just the book.

Cornelius' clearly presents each of four major theoretical traditions that form the psychology of emotion: the evolutionary, the physiological, the cognitive, and the social constructivist.

Russell, J. A. (1991). In defense of a prototype approach to emotion concepts. *Journal of Personality and Social Psychology, 60,* 37–47. ALSO Clore, G. L., & Ortony, A. (1991). What more is there to emotion concepts than prototypes? *Journal of Personality and Social Psychology, 60,* 48-50. This pair of articles nicely presents the arguments both for considering emotion concepts to be prototypes and for considering them to entail other types of representation as well.

Russell, J. A., Fernández-Dols, J.-M., Manstead, A. S. R., & Wellenkamp, J. C. (Eds.). (1995). *Everyday conceptions of emotion: An introduction to the psychology, anthropology and linguistics of emotion.* Dordrecht: Kluwer Academic Publishers. This book contains papers presented at a conference devoted to the topic of the ordinary person's conceptualization of emotion. It presents a variety of viewpoints: the authors include not only psychologists from a variety of subdisciplines, but also anthropologists and linguists.

Wierzbicka, A. (1999). *Emotions across languages and cultures: Diversity and universals.* Paris: Cambridge University Press. The author of this book is a linguist, and in this book she summarizes several decades of research on semantic primitives and lexical universals. She argues that English emotion words are laden with European cultural constructs, and therefore are misleading if used to label emotional states of people not belonging to such a culture.

Emotion Knowledge: Further Exploration of a Prototype Approach

Phillip Shaver, Judith Schwartz, Donald Kirson, and Cary O'Connor
• University of Denver

Recent work on natural categories suggests a framework for conceptualizing people's knowledge about emotions. Categories of natural objects or events, including emotions, are formed as a result of repeated experiences and become organized around prototypes (Rosch, 1978); the interrelated set of emotion categories becomes organized within an abstract-to-concrete hierarchy. At the basic level of the emotion hierarchy one finds the handful of concepts (love, joy, anger, sadness, fear, and perhaps, surprise) most useful for making everyday distinctions among emotions, and these overlap substantially with the examples mentioned most readily when people are asked to name emotions (Fehr & Russell, 1984), with the emotions children learn to name first (Bretherton & Beeghly, 1982), and with what theorists have called basic or primary emotions. This article reports two studies, one exploring the hierarchical organization of emotion concepts and one specifying the prototypes, or scripts, of five basic emotions, and it shows how the prototype approach might be used in the future to investigate the processing of information about emotional events, cross-cultural differences in emotion concepts, and the development of emotion knowledge.

Ordinary people know a great deal about emotion. When given posed or natural photographs of common emotional expressions, people around the world can reliably name the emotion being expressed (Ekman, Friesen, & Ellsworth, 1982a, 1982b). People from a variety of cultures agree on which emotion generally follows a particular set of abstract antecedents, such as insult, loss, and danger (Boucher & Brandt, 1981; Brandt & Boucher, 1984; Ekman, 1984; Roseman, 1984; Sullivan & Boucher, 1984). Both children and adults can report and agree on typical antecedents of several common emotions (Harris, 1985; Masters & Carlson, 1984; C. Smith & Ellsworth, 1985). They can also talk about methods for controlling the expression of negative emotions (Hochschild, 1983; Johnson, 1983; Masters & Carlson, 1984; Saarni, 1979, 1984). Children as well as adults agree about the similarity or distinctiveness of a diverse array of emotions, and their similarity ratings, when multidimensionally scaled or factor analyzed, reliably form a two- or three-dimensional structure, with positive-negative valence, activity or arousal, and potency or dominance being the most frequently obtained dimensions (e.g., Averill, 1975; Osgood, Suci, & Tannenbaum, 1957; Russell, 1978, 1979, 1980; Russell & Ridgeway, 1983; Schlosberg, 1952, 1954). Because emotions play a central role in individual experience and interpersonal relations, it is no wonder that people are highly knowledgeable about them.

With few exceptions (e.g., Averill, 1982; de Rivera, 1981a; Scherer, 1984), emotion knowledge has been studied piecemeal, some studies focusing on antecedents, some on emotional expressions and responses, others on self-control of these responses, and still others on the dimensions underlying the large emotion lexicon. But an extensive body of research and theory in cognitive and cognitive-social psychology suggests that the various components of emotion knowledge are likely to be parts of an organized whole. Numerous studies have shown that repeated experiences with similar objects or events lead to the construction of generic mental representations of the important elements, and the relations among elements, of these objects or events (e.g., Bobrow & Norman, 1975; Posner & Keele, 1968; Rumelhart & Ortony, 1977). Although generic representations go by a variety of different names in the scientific literature-schemas (Bartlett, 1932; Mandler, 1984), scripts (Schank & Abelson, 1977), prototypes (Rosch, 1978), and stereotypes (Hamilton, 1981)—all have in common the notion that features shared by many or most members of a category occupy central places in an organized mental representation.

Emotion knowledge, organized into generic representations, almost certainly plays an important part in social interaction. A substantial part of interaction involves interpreting one's own and other people's emotional reactions, predicting reactions from antecedent events, controlling emotional expressions, attempting to influence others' emotions, and sharing and talking about emotional reactions to past and present events (Goffman, 1959; Jones & Pittman, 1982; Kelley, 1984). Moreover, an important part of reading and writing fiction and of watching films and stage productions is anticipating characters' emotional reactions and making attributions about likely causes of such reactions when they occur (Schwartz & Shaver, 1987).

For our long-term purposes, which include mapping both the overall structure of the domain of emotion knowledge and the content and structure of typical emotion episodes, prototype theory and research are especially useful. Rosch (1973, 1978; Rosch, Mervis, Gray, Johnson, & Boyes-Braem, 1976), the originator of prototype analysis, has

proposed that category systems or taxonomies can be viewed as having both a vertical and a horizontal dimension. The vertical dimension concerns the hierarchical relations among categories in treelike taxonomies. Often the vertical dimension can be analyzed in terms of three major levels of inclusiveness: the *superordinate* (furniture, for example), the *basic* (chair), and the *subordinate* (kitchen chair).

Rosch calls the middle level "basic" because research has revealed that it is special in several respects. Basic-level categories are learned first during language acquisition; are accessed most quickly when a relevant stimulus is encountered; are likely to have short, single-word names; and are the most abstract categories that can be represented by a single visual image (Mervis & Crisafi, 1982; Rosch, Mervis, Gray, Johnson, & Boyes-Braem, 1976). Basic-level concepts accomplish two important functions of categorization: They convey more, and more specific, information about category members than superordinate categories do, and at the same time, they are superior to subordinate-level concepts in identifying major distinctions between categories. Because the basic level offers the best compromise between informativeness and cognitive economy, people seem naturally to prefer basic-level categorization for much of their everyday conversation and thought.

Category systems also have a horizontal dimension that, according to Rosch (1978), "concerns the segmentation of categories at the same level of inclusiveness" (p. 30)—categories such as chair, table, and sofa. Prototype researchers argue that many such categories used in everyday cognition are best conceptualized as "fuzzy sets" separated by vague rather than sharp boundaries. (Objects such as loveseats and chaises lounges, literally "long chairs," illustrate the vagueness of the boundaries between *chair*, *sofa*, and *bed*.) Each of these fuzzy categories is defined, not by a conclusive set of necessary and sufficient features (such as might define the category of even numbers), but rather by a *prototype*—an abstract image or set of features representing the best, most representative, most typical example of the category (e.g., the "prototypical" chair). Categorization decisions are made by comparing instances with this prototype. Individual objects vary in their degree of similarity or "family resemblance" to the prototype—the degree to which they are good examples of the category.

Empirical studies have demonstrated that people can make reliable judgments of object prototypicality (e.g., Rosch, 1973, 1975; Rosch & Mervis, 1975; E. E. Smith, Shoben, & Rips, 1974), that prototypical objects are more quickly and more frequently identified as category members than are less prototypical objects (e.g., McCloskey & Glucksberg, 1978; Rosch, Simpson, & Miller, 1976), and that people often fill gaps in information about an object by inserting features that are consistent with the category prototype (e.g., Cantor & Mischel, 1977; Franks & Bransford, 1971; Posner & Keele, 1970; Reitman & Bower, 1973; Schank & Abelson, 1977). Thus, the view of categories as fuzzy sets organized around abstract prototypes—categories whose members bear a family resemblance to one another—seems to fit people's representation of common categories.

In the years since Rosch and her colleagues introduced the prototype approach to the categorization of colors and physical objects, other researchers have applied it to a wide variety of domains, including grammatical categories (Maratsos & Chalkley, 1980), person categories (Cantor & Mischel, 1979a; Chaplin, John, & Goldberg, 1986; Hampson, John, & Goldberg, 1986), psychiatric categories (Cantor, Smith, French, & Mezzich, 1980; Horowitz, French, & Anderson, 1982; Horowitz, Wright, Lowenstein, & Farad, 1981), and categories of social situations (Cantor, Mischel, & Schwartz, 1982) and environmental scenes (B. Tversky & Hemenway, 1983). In each of these areas, prototype researchers have learned a great deal about categorization and representation processes and about the actual structure of the domains being categorized or represented. In fact, it is common for prototype researchers, following Rosch (1978), to argue that the structure of representation necessarily reflects the gross structure of reality, or at least the distinct features of reality that are most important for human transactions with the world. This suggests that a prototype analysis of the emotion domain might produce useful information not only about the cognitive representation of emotion episodes but also about the actual nature of human emotion.

Viewing emotion knowledge from a prototype perspective suggests why it has been difficult for psychologists to agree on a number of fundamental issues concerning emotion. For example, there is no agreement on a formal definition of the construct; as Fehr and Russell (1984) have observed, "Everyone knows what an emotion is, until asked to give a definition" (p. 464). If the category *emotion* is itself "fuzzy" defined mainly by prototypical members or features, there may be no classical definition associated with it. Moreover, most emotion theorists have claimed that there is a set of basic emotions, the term basic supposedly pointing to underlying biological substrates. But there has been considerable variability in published lists of basic emotions (e.g., Ekman et al., 1982a, 1982b, Epstein, 1984; Izard, 1977; Roseman, 1984; Tomkins, 1984). Prototype theory suggests that the most salient and frequently used categories, at least as used by ordinary people, are basic in Rosch's sense; that is, they occupy the basic level of categorization. The reason for making everyday distinctions at this level remains to be discovered, biological "basicness" being just one of several possibilities. It has also proved difficult to say why, if there is a mere handful of basic emotions, the emotion lexicon in most modern languages contains hundreds of emotion names (Averill, 1975). What exactly is the need for so many nonbasic terms? Prototype theory suggests that they are used to make subordinate-level distinctions—fine distinctions that are not needed for most everyday purposes. Finally, what are the most appropriate statistical techniques for detecting and representing cognitive relations among emotions (or emotion names)? Emotion researchers have tended to use dimensional techniques such as factor analysis or multidimensional scaling. The prototype approach suggests the use of hierarchical cluster analysis, which, although occasionally used in the past (e.g., Fillenbaum & Rapaport, 1971; Scherer, 1984), has rarely been used within a theoretical context.

Although studies of ordinary people's cognitive representations of emotion episodes, and of the emotion domain as a whole, cannot resolve scientific debates about the nature of emotion, they may be able to reveal the origins of emotion theorists' intuitions (e.g., the intuition that there are such things as basic emotions) and, at the same time, by providing details of such intuitions that have been neglected in the past, may suggest deficiencies in current emotion theories. Aside from these outcomes, studies of emotion knowledge should open up new avenues for research on social perception and memory for social events.

Emotion Categories as Fuzzy Sets

In recent years, several authors have suggested that the term emotion and specific emotion terms such as anger, fear, and sadness designate fuzzy sets, indicating that the emotion domain might fruitfully be analyzed from a prototype perspective. For example, Russell (1980), at the time writing within the psychometric tradition, asserted that "each emotion word can . . . be considered a label for a fuzzy set, defined as a class without sharp boundaries, in which there is a gradual but specifiable transition from membership to nonmembership" (p. 1165). In a 1981 footnote, de Rivera, writing within the phenomenological tradition, said, "It is conceivable that . . . all the different instances of anger . . . simply bear . . . a 'family resemblance' to each other . . . To the extent this were true, one might want to use the tactic that Rosch (1973) has described" (1981b, p. 78). Averill, the leading proponent of the social-constructionist approach to emotion, stated in his 1982 book on anger, "Emotional categories . . . form taxonomies, with categories like anger, fear, and hope representing the basic level" (p. 330). Working from a psycholinguistic perspective, Lakoff and Kovecses (1983) concluded that "the metaphors and metonymies . . . we have investigated so far converge on a certain prototypical cognitive model of anger" (p. 20). Writing about emotions within the context of close relationships, Kelley (1983) observed,

> The varieties of love and commitment are reflected in the fact that, in natural language, each concept refers to a "fuzzy category." Like other such categories . . . , love and commitment include a number of different phenomena that are distinguishable as to their prototypicality. (pp. 313–314)

Writing about the emotion-elicitation process, Ekman (1984) said, "In automatic appraisal an event is instantly matched with one of the prototypic situations, thereby setting off emotion-specific changes in expression and physiology" (p. 338). Finally, Kagan (1984) suggested

> that variations in bodily change, incentive, and evaluation lead to a family of feeling states, each of which has a prototypic core. These prototypes include the emotions we call fear, worry, anger, sadness, joy, guilt, shame, empathy, contentment, and interest. I am not certain how many prototypes are needed to account for all of the basic human feelings. (p. 169)

Despite the promise evident in these converging insights, there has been little empirical research to follow them up. In 1984, however, Fehr and Russell reported a seminal series of studies, based on Rosch's ideas, that supported the hypothesis that emotion itself is a fuzzy category. Although no compelling classical definition of emotion exists, Fehr and Russell found that people are quite able to say which emotions are better and which are worse examples of the category.

> An emotion's goodness of example (prototypicality) . . . was found to predict how readily it comes to mind when one is asked to list emotions, how likely it is to be labeled as an emotion when asked what sort of thing it is, how readily it can be substituted for the word emotion in sentences without their sounding unnatural, and the degree to which it resembles other emotion categories in terms of shared features. (Fehr & Russell, 1984, p. 464; see also Fehr, Russell, & Ward, 1982)

A similar approach to the concept of emotion has been taken in recent papers by Conway and Bekerian (1985) and Tiller and Harris (1984).

Although Fehr and Russell (1984) hypothesized in their Discussion section that "what we are calling the middle level of emotion categories is the basic level" (p. 481) and that "middle level emotion categories possess an internal structure and fuzzy boundaries" (p. 482), these hypotheses remained untested. Fehr and Russell indicated the probable scriptlike nature of basic-level emotion knowledge, using fear as an example, in the following passage:

> Although we often speak of fear as a thing, a more apt description may be a sequence of events. . . . [To] know the meaning of the word fear is to know some such sequence. It is to know a *script* . . . [that includes] prototypical causes, beliefs, physiological reactions, feelings, facial expressions, actions, and consequences. The notion of script can thus be seen to extend to episodes the notion of prototype. (1984, p. 482)

Overview of the Present Studies

In the remainder of this article we will explore further the notion that emotion knowledge may be represented hierarchically, with one level corresponding to what both emotion theorists and prototype researchers, for seemingly different reasons, have wanted to call "basic." Fehr and Russell

(1984) speculated about the contents of this level, basing their ideas on evidence concerning which emotions are brought to mind most readily as examples of "emotion": "We have short names for many of the concepts at the middle level: fear, anger, love, hate, and so forth" (p. 482). They did not examine the treelike structure of the domain of emotion concepts, however, to see where their candidates for basicness actually fall. Besides pursuing that matter here, we have attempted to learn more about people's emotion prototypes, or scripts, on the assumption that descriptively rich prototypes will prove useful in future research on emotion knowledge, including research on the role such knowledge plays in everyday social interaction (Schwartz & Shaver, 1987). At the end of this article we will consider potential applications and extensions of the prototype approach to emotion knowledge.

Study 1: Hierarchical Structure of the Emotion Domain

As explained earlier, a prototype analysis of people's knowledge of a particular domain consists of two parts: (a) description of the hierarchical structure of the domain's categories and (b) specification of category prototypes. In Study 1, we explore the hierarchical organization of the emotion domain and compare it with multidimensional structures identified repeatedly by factor-analytic and multidimensional-scaling techniques. Our goal is not to argue that a hierarchical representation is superior to these other structures for all purposes, but to show that it is intuitively reasonable, hence plausibly related to everyday emotion categorization, compatible with prototype theory, and informative in distinctive ways.

English and many other languages contain hundreds of terms that seem to refer to emotions. It is obvious that some of the emotional states referred to are closely related (e.g., anger, annoyance, hatred, and rage), whereas others (e.g., contentment and despair) are quite distinct. If emotion knowledge has the kind of hierarchical structure that Rosch and others have shown to exist in domains as different as furniture, food items, physical and social environments, and personality types, it should be reflected in subjects' similarity sorts of emotion names. Moreover, if data from similarity

sorts are submitted to hierarchical cluster analysis, they should reveal a multitiered hierarchy in which one level can reasonably be called more basic than others. By "reasonably," we mean that (a) the basic-level concepts will correspond roughly to the ones Fehr and Russell (1984) found to be elicited most frequently in response to the instruction "Please list [in 1 min] as many items of the category 'EMOTION' as come readily to mind" (p. 468). The emotions listed by more than 40% of 200 subjects were happiness, anger, sadness, love, fear, hate, and joy. (b) The basic-level concepts will correspond roughly to emotion theorists' lists of basic or primary emotions. There are many such lists. Izard's (1977), one of the longest, includes interest, joy, surprise, distress, anger, fear, shame, disgust, contempt, and guilt. Ekman and his colleagues (summarized in Ekman, 1984) focused their research on fear, anger, surprise, disgust, sadness, and happiness. Epstein's list (1984) includes "fear, anger, sadness, joy, and possibly love and affection" (p. 68). (c) The basic-level concepts will correspond roughly to the ones that children name first in spontaneous speech. Bretherton and Beeghly (1982) reported that the emotion names used most frequently by 28-month-olds are love, like, mad, scared, happy, and sad.

Because the same similarity-sorting data can be submitted to multidimensional scaling analysis, the resulting structures can be compared to determine what each reveals about the organization of emotion knowledge. Providing such a comparison is an additional goal of Study 1.

Choosing Exemplars of the Emotion Category

How should emotion terms be chosen for a similarity-sorting study? In reviewing previous attempts to characterize the structure of emotion knowledge, we found that some investigators (e.g., Fillenbaum & Rapaport, 1971) had used too few terms to reveal much in the way of hierarchical structure, especially because most of their terms were taken from what we will call the basic level. Other investigators used so many terms (e.g., 235 in Scherer's, 1984, study) that no available computer program could analyze the resulting similarity matrix; besides, many of the terms were debatable as names of emotions and appeared in different parts of speech—some as adjectives, some as nouns, some as adverbs, and so forth—which may have confused subjects. Finally, some researchers, especially those who favor a circumplex (two-dimensional circle) model of emotion (e.g., Russell, 1980), added such terms as *sleepy* to their lists to fill out the low-arousal portion of the circumplex, even though almost no one believes that sleepiness is an emotion (see the tests for "emotionness" developed by Ortony & Clore, 1981, and the prototypicality data reported by Fehr & Russell, 1984).

The prototype approach suggests solutions to these problems. Even if the concept of emotion is fuzzy, subjects ought to be able to report reliably whether a particular mental or physical state word—for instance, anger, happiness, sleepiness, or hunger—denotes a relatively good or a relatively poor example of the concept. In fact, recent studies conducted by unrelated research teams in England (Conway & Bekerian, 1985; Tiller & Harris, 1984), British Columbia (Fehr & Russell, 1984), and the United States (Averill, 1975; the present authors, see next section) demonstrate that subjects can easily make such judgments and that the results correlate highly across studies, despite somewhat different emotionness measures and different subject populations. Tiller and Harris (1984) reported correlations above .80 between ratings they obtained in England and ratings obtained by Fehr and Russell (1984) in British Columbia. We computed correlations between our ratings, gathered in Colorado, and Fehr and Russell's two sets of ratings of 20 emotion names, gathered 5 months apart. The resulting correlations, .94 and .96, were almost perfect. Correlations between our ratings or Fehr and Russell's ratings and ratings obtained by Averill (1975) in Massachusetts and California were all around .80. (The drop from .95 to .80 may be due to Averill's use of adjective forms of the nouns that we and Fehr and Russell used.)

In other words, although English speakers around the world have difficulty giving an explicit rulelike definition of emotion, they have little trouble agreeing that a particular psychological-state name designates a relatively good or a relatively poor example of the emotion category. We decided, therefore, to include in Study 1 a sizable number of emotion names that subjects could agree were representative of the category *emotion*.

Method

SELECTION OF EMOTION TERMS: PROTOTYPICALITY RATINGS

Subjects. One hundred twelve students in introductory psychology courses participated in the prototypicality-rating phase of the study. They completed the rating task during regular class sessions.

Procedure. A list of 213 emotion names, to be rated for prototypicality or emotionness, was compiled in the following way. We began with Averill's (1975) Semantic Atlas of Emotional Concepts, which contains 558 words "with emotional connotations" (p. 1), and supplemented these with the few nonoverlapping terms in Davitz's (1969) and de Rivera's (1977) lists of emotion words. To eliminate redundancy, we then removed all but one of each set of words formed from the same root (e.g., fury and furious) and converted all of the remaining words to their noun forms (e.g., *pitying* in Averill's list became *pity* in ours). Any words that did not have familiar noun forms (e.g., *blasé*) were eliminated. Noun forms were chosen so that the emotions would be cognitively parallel to the "objects" studied in most prototype research. We also eliminated words that seemed to name traits (e.g., brave, patriotic, religious) rather than emotions and metaphorical emotion terms that include the word *heart* (heartrending). This left 213 words, shown in Table 1.1, that could reasonably be considered emotion names.

Subjects rated the states named by each of these 213 terms, in alphabetical order, on a 4-point scale ranging from *I definitely* would not *call this an emotion* (1) to *I definitely* would *call this an emotion* (4). (They were also given the option of saying that they were not sure what the word meant. As a result, 4 words, identified in Table 1.1, were eliminated for being relatively unfamiliar to more than a quarter of the subjects, even though they satisfied our other criteria.) Mean prototypicality ratings were computed and used to select 135 "good" examples of the emotion domain. This number was chosen to sample the domain extensively without burdening subjects with an unmanageable number of terms to sort. The final 135 words, along with their mean prototypicality scores, are marked with superscripts in Table 1.1. They are the ones subjects rated highest on the 4-point emotionness scale, with one exception: *Sur-*

prise was included because emotion theorists have so often designated it a basic emotion, even though, with a mean of 2.69, it did not quite reach the cutoff for the other 134 terms (above 2.75). The proportion of subjects who indicated that "I'm not sure what this word means" is also shown for each word in Table 1.1.

SIMILARITY SORTING

Subjects. One hundred students in introductory psychology courses (50 men and 50 women) participated in the similarity-sorting phase of the study. They were tested individually and received course credit for participating. None of them had participated in the prototypicality-rating task.

Procedure. Each of the 135 terms was printed on a small white card, and the cards were presented to subjects with the following oral instructions:

> This study has to do with human emotions. Specifically, we want to find out which emotions people think are similar to each other (which "go together"), and which emotions seem different and therefore belong in different categories. We've prepared 135 cards, each containing the name of an emotion. We'd like you to sort these cards into categories representing your best judgments about which emotions are similar to each other and which are different from each other. There is no one correct way to sort the cards—make as few or as many categories as you wish and put as few or as many cards in each group as you see fit. Spread the cards out on the table and keep moving them around until the groupings make sense to you. This requires careful thought; before you stop, be sure you are satisfied that each word fits best in the category where you have placed it.

After receiving these instructions, each subject performed the sorting task, finishing in an hour or less. Because no limit was placed on either the number of categories or the number of terms within each category, these parameters varied widely across subjects. One person put all 135 terms into two categories (positive and negative), and one put them into 64 categories. Category size ranged from 1 to 90 terms.

Results and Discussion

For each subject, a 135 × 135 co-occurrence matrix was constructed, with 1 indicating that two terms were placed in the same category and 0 in-

dicating that they were not. These matrices were added across the 100 subjects to form a single 135 × 135 matrix in which cell entries could range from 0 to 100, representing the number of subjects who placed a particular pair of words in the same category. This matrix was analyzed using the BMDP 1M Cluster Analysis Program's average distance method (Everitt, 1980; Hartigan, 1981). The results are shown in Figure 1.1.

What we will consider subordinate clusters of words are listed along the bottom of the figure, each one having a cluster strength greater than 50. This means that across all pairs of words in that subgroup, the average frequency of co-occurrence (number of subjects placing the two pair members in one category) was greater than 50. For example, in the bottom-left corner of the figure, there are three such clusters: (a) adoration, affection, and so forth; (b) arousal, desire, lust, and so forth; and (c) longing. Each of the first two groups has a cluster strength greater than 50; *longing* forms a category by itself; and the three small clusters combine to form a larger cluster labeled *love*, which has a strength of approximately 27.5 (indicated by the scale on the left). All cluster strengths below 50 can be determined in the same way by referring to the 0-to-50 scale. For the sake of simplicity and figure size, we have placed single-word subcategories (contempt, dismay, distress, dread, hysteria, mortification, and sentimentality) into the nearest larger subcategory, with the exception of longing, relief, and torment, each of which co-occurred with the nearest subcluster at a level less than 30, suggesting substantial distinctiveness.

Inspection of the figure suggests that there are five or six separate clusters that might reasonably be considered basic. (Later, we will suggest that one of the six, surprise, may not qualify for basic-level status.) The names of these large groups, appearing about halfway up the figure, were determined as follows. For each of the 135 emotion words, two scores were calculated: (a) the average number of co-occurrences with all other words in the same large cluster and (b) the average number of co-occurrences with all words outside that cluster. For each word, the second number was subtracted from the first, and the difference was interpreted as a measure of within-category centrality or prototypicality. (This definition of centrality is similar to Rosch, Mervis, Gray, Johnson, and Boyes-Braem's, 1976, notion of "cue valid-

Table 1.1. Mean Prototypicality Ratings and Unfamiliarity Proportions (UP) for 213 Emotion Words

Emotion word	M	UP	Emotion word	M	UP	Emotion word	M	UP	Emotion word	M	UP
love[a]	3.94	.00	agitation[a]	3.29	.01	triumph[a]	2.95	.00	calmness	2.63	.00
anger[a]	3.90	.00	outrage[a]	3.28	.00	joviality[a]	2.94	.05	respect	2.62	.00
hate[a]	3.84	.00	resentment[a]	3.28	.00	wrath[a]	2.93	.07	somberness	2.62	.02
depression[a]	3.83	.00	dislike[a]	3.27	.00	arousal[a]	2.92	.03	vehemence	2.62	.34
fear[a]	3.83	.00	glee[a]	3.24	.02	attraction[a]	2.92	.00	sulkiness	2.59	.03
jealousy[a]	3.81	.00	alienation[a]	3.23	.01	contentment[a]	2.92	.04	encouragement	2.58	.01
happiness[a]	3.77	.00	distress[a]	3.23	.01	grumpiness[a]	2.92	.00	frenzy	2.58	.01
passion[a]	3.75	.00	enjoyment[a]	3.23	.00	irritation[a]	2.92	.00	obsession	2.58	.00
affection[a]	3.72	.01	relief[a]	3.23	.00	malevolence	2.92	.32	success	2.56	.00
sadness[a]	3.68	.00	gloom[a]	3.21	.00	ferocity[a]	2.91	.00	forgiveness	2.55	.00
grief[a]	3.65	.01	misery[a]	3.20	.02	enthrallment[a]	2.90	.13	indignation	2.55	.17
rage[a]	3.64	.00	euphoria[a]	3.19	.16	revulsion[a]	2.88	.10	discomfort	2.54	.00
aggravation[a]	3.63	.03	bliss[a]	3.18	.07	alarm[a]	2.87	.00	vindictiveness	2.54	.13
ecstasy[a]	3.63	.00	gladness[a]	3.17	.00	eagerness[a]	2.87	.00	aversion	2.52	.25
sorrow[a]	3.62	.00	regret[a]	3.16	.00	hysteria[a]	2.87	.00	power	2.52	.00
joy[a]	3.61	.00	rejection[a]	3.16	.00	liking[a]	2.87	.00	vibrance	2.52	.13
compassion[a]	3.62	.00	pride[a]	3.14	.01	neglect[a]	2.87	.00	sheepishness	2.50	.14
envy[a]	3.58	.00	gaiety[a]	3.13	.04	insult[a]	2.86	.00	jitteriness	2.49	.01
fright[a]	3.58	.00	homesickness[a]	3.13	.00	mortification[a]	2.85	.04	virtue	2.48	.01
terror[a]	3.57	.00	jolliness[a]	3.12	.00	tenseness[a]	2.85	.00	mirth	2.47	.36
elation[a]	3.55	.10	nervousness[a]	3.12	.00	contempt[a]	2.84	.03	demoralization	2.46	.05
guilt[a]	3.53	.00	woe[a]	3.12	.05	amazement[a]	2.83	.00	fierceness	2.46	.01
excitement[a]	3.51	.00	longing[a]	3.11	.00	amusement[a]	2.83	.00	effervescence	2.44	.43
anguish[a]	3.49	.01	loathing[a]	3.10	.05	zeal[a]	2.83	.00	fervor	2.44	.23
embarrassment[a]	3.49	.00	satisfaction[a]	3.10	.01	scorn[a]	2.82	.02	complacency	2.42	.27
worry[a]	3.49	.00	hope[a]	3.08	.00	zest[a]	2.82	.03	nostalgia	2.42	.03
panic[a]	3.48	.00	abhorrence	3.06	.30	astonishment[a]	2.80	.00	modesty	2.40	.00
unhappiness[a]	3.48	.00	insecurity[a]	3.06	.00	titillation	2.80	.27	disgruntlement	2.37	.20
anxiety[a]	3.46	.00	defeat[a]	3.05	.01	torment[a]	2.80	.02	inconsolableness	2.37	.34
desire[a]	3.45	.00	dread[a]	3.05	.00	optimism[a]	2.78	.01	belligerence	2.33	.20
horror[a]	3.45	.00	fondness[a]	3.05	.00	vengefulness[a]	2.78	.03	disconsolateness	2.33	.41
sympathy[a]	3.45	.00	enthusiasm[a]	3.05	.00	impatience	2.75	.00	determination	2.30	.00
shame[a]	3.44	.00	sentimentality[a]	3.05	.00	persecution	2.75	.01	doubt	2.30	.00
lust[a]	3.43	.00	hopelessness[a]	3.04	.01	viciousness	2.75	.01	superiority	2.29	.00
disgust[a]	3.42	.00	annoyance[a]	3.03	.00	edginess	2.74	.05	vanity	2.28	.05
hostility[a]	3.41	.00	cheerfulness[a]	3.03	.00	awe	2.73	.03	acceptance	2.26	.00
jubilation[a]	3.41	.01	displeasure[a]	3.03	.00	despondency	2.73	.30	abandonment	2.23	.01
loneliness[a]	3.41	.01	melancholy[a]	3.02	.02	gratitude	2.73	.00	carefreeness	2.22	.00
delight[a]	3.40	.00	glumness[a]	3.01	.02	mellowness	2.71	.00	exhaustion	2.19	.00
pleasure[a]	3.40	.00	shock[a]	3.01	.00	vexation	2.71	.32	craving	2.16	.00
tenderness[a]	3.40	.00	spite[a]	3.01	.01	enchantment	2.70	.01	inclination	2.16	.00
pity[a]	3.39	.00	suffering[a]	3.01	.00	exultation	2.70	.15	approval	2.14	.00
bitterness[a]	3.38	.00	dismay[a]	3.00	.01	sullenness	2.69	.06	distraction	2.14	.01
disappointment[a]	3.38	.00	exasperation[a]	3.00	.02	surprise[a]	2.69	.00	freedom	2.13	.00
humiliation[a]	3.38	.00	infatuation[a]	3.00	.04	discontentment	2.67	.00	startle	2.11	.01
dejection[a]	3.37	.04	apprehension[a]	2.99	.03	discouragement	2.66	.00	indecision	2.02	.01
despair[a]	3.37	.01	caring[a]	2.98	.01	boredom	2.65	.01	interest	1.96	.00
frustration[a]	3.37	.00	isolation[a]	2.98	.00	exuberance	2.65	.05	self-control	1.95	.00
hurt[a]	3.37	.00	exhilaration[a]	2.96	.00	forlornness	2.65	.25	alertness	1.94	.00
adoration[a]	3.36	.07	rapture[a]	2.96	.11	lividness	2.65	.20	carefulness	1.84	.00
agony[a]	3.36	.01	uneasiness[a]	2.96	.00	moroseness	2.65	.25	practicality	1.75	.00
thrill[a]	3.34	.00	grouchiness[a]	2.95	.00	dolefulness	2.64	.40	deliberateness	1.73	.05
fury[a]	3.33	.01	ire	2.95	.57	wonderment	2.64	.01	intelligence	1.57	.00
remorse[a]	3.30	.03									

Note. Ratings were made by 112 subjects on a 4-point scale ranging from 1 (I definitely would not call this an emotion) to 4 (I definitely would call this an emotion). The words abhorrence, ire, malevolence, and titillation were excluded from the sorting study because many subjects were unfamiliar with them.

[a]Words used in the emotion-sorting study.

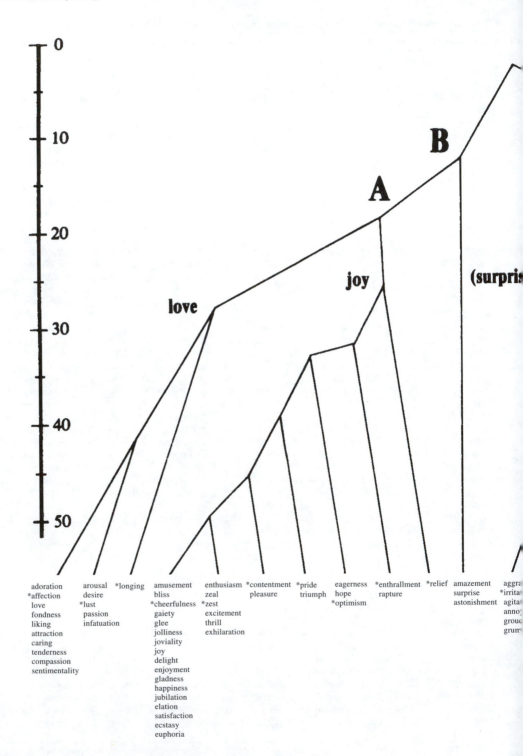

FIGURE 1.1 ■ Results of a hierarchical cluster analysis of 135 emotion names. (Cluster strength can be determined by referring

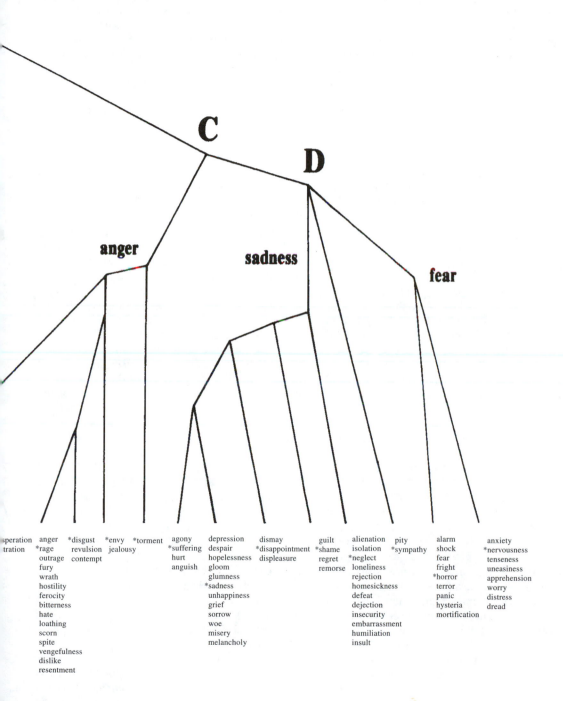

esperation tration	anger *rage outrage fury wrath hostility ferocity bitterness hate loathing scorn spite vengefulness dislike resentment	*disgust revulsion contempt	*envy jealousy	*torment	agony *suffering hurt anguish	depression despair hopelessness gloom glumness *sadness unhappiness grief sorrow woe misery melancholy	dismay *disappointment displeasure	guilt *shame regret remorse	alienation isolation *neglect loneliness rejection homesickness defeat dejection insecurity embarrassment humiliation insult	pity *sympathy	alarm shock fear fright *horror terror panic hysteria mortification	anxiety *nervousness tenseness uneasiness apprehension worry distress dread

to numerical scale at left. Asterisks indicate empirically selected subcluster names.)

ity" and to A. Tversky and Kahneman's, 1982, notion of "representativeness.") Among the few highest scoring words in each of the six major clusters, an emotion could always be found that at least some theorists have included in their lists of basic emotions. We decided to retain those names—love, joy, surprise, anger, sadness, and fear—even though in four cases a synonym received a slightly higher score: *affection* rather than *love*, *happiness* rather than *joy*, *amazement* rather than *surprise*, and *depression* rather than *sadness*.

In some respects, *affection* may actually be a better name than *love* for the leftmost basic category, which includes *fondness* and *liking*. Similarly, *happiness* may be a better general name than *joy*, which intuitively seems briefer and more intense than happiness. On the other hand, *sadness* seems more general than *depression* and, hence, deserves to be the category label, even though our college-student subjects apparently use the more specific clinical term to such an extent that to them it seems slightly more prototypical than *sadness* (see ratings in Table 1.1). Notice that in each of the three cases, the term often favored by emotion theorists and the term generated by analysis of co-occurrence data fell within the same subordinate category. For purposes of this article, we will use the labels *love, joy, surprise, anger, sadness,* and *fear*. Future work may persuade us and other researchers to replace some of these with more general synonyms.

When the same kind of analysis was performed on all categories in the hierarchy above what we are calling the basic level (see the nodes labeled A, B, C, and D in Figure 1.1), Node A was labeled *joy*, B was labeled *cheerfulness*, C was labeled *sadness*, and D was also labeled *sadness*. These results seem to indicate that above the basic level, the only meaningful distinction is the one between positive and negative emotions. Because no general term such as *negative emotion* was included in the sorting study, the analysis was forced to select names that seem inappropriate labels for their subordinates—sadness, for example, is an odd superordinate label for categories such as rage and panic. When the analysis was performed on each of the subordinate categories (those below the basic level) containing more than one term, the labels shown with asterisks in Figure 1.1 were chosen: *affection, lust,* and *longing* (for the love category); *cheerfulness, zest, contentment, pride, optimism, enthrallment,* and *relief* (for the joy cat-

egory); *irritation, exasperation, rage, disgust, envy,* and *torment* (for the anger category); *suffering, sadness, disappointment, shame, neglect,* and *sympathy* (for the sadness category); *horror* and *nervousness* (for the fear category). (There were no subcategories within the small surprise group.)

The cluster-analytic results therefore provide three sets of candidates for basicness: a 2-term list at a high level of abstraction (essentially, positive vs. negative emotions), a 5- or 6-term list, and a 25-term list. Given these alternatives, we have tentatively decided to accept the 5- or 6-term list, which conforms most closely to the three basicness criteria listed earlier: (a) correspondence with Fehr and Russell's (1984) exemplar-listing data, (b) correspondence with several emotion theorists' lists of basic or primary emotions, and (c) correspondence with data on language learning in early childhood.

Recall that Fehr and Russell's emotion-naming procedure produced a list topped by happiness, anger, sadness, love, fear, hate, and joy. If happiness and joy are accepted as synonyms, only hate in Fehr and Russell's list and surprise in ours fail to correspond. In comparison with the lists proposed by various emotion theorists, ours matches Epstein's (1984) except for *surprise* in our list; it matches the list of emotions studied extensively by Ekman (1984) except for *disgust* in his list and *love* in ours; finally, five of our six basic emotions are included in Izard's (1977) list (all but *love*), in addition to which he included interest, distress, shame, disgust, contempt, and guilt. In comparison with Bretherton and Beeghly's (1982) list of emotion terms learned early by American children, ours contains *surprise* but is otherwise the same—assuming that *love* and *like* in the children's list are closely related. In all respects, then, it seems reasonable to adopt as a working hypothesis that the labeled level of the hierarchy in Figure 1.1 is the basic level of emotion knowledge, at least for our subjects. Only Izard's(1977) list of basic emotions, which we chose for comparison because of its unusual length, is very different from ours, and even in that case, five of our six categories appear on his list.

We have reservations concerning the *surprise* cluster, which is obviously much smaller and less differentiated than the others. In Fehr and Russell's (1984) exemplar-listing study, only 8.5% of the subjects listed surprise within a minute, whereas between 41% and 76% listed each of the other five basic-level terms. In Bretherton and Beeghly's (1982) study, well over half (57% to 87%) of 28-month-olds used the words *sad, happy, scared, mad,* and *love,* whereas only 13% used *surprise.* We have therefore chosen in this article to examine prototypes of only five basic-level categories—fear, sadness, anger, joy, and love-although we retain surprise in our examination of results from multidimensional scaling analyses. Future research will be needed to clarify the unique status of surprise.

If we accept as a working hypothesis that there are five basic-emotion categories, what kinds of distinctions seem to be added to the differences among these five when one moves to the subordinate level? First, notice that each basic category includes one large subcluster containing the basic-level term. These subclusters seem to designate a generic, core, or nonspecialized form of the emotion in question. For example, within the love category, the affection subcategory seems to designate the generic form of love, which Sternberg and Grajek (1984) found applies to friendship, family relationships, marital relationships, and so forth, whereas the lust (or passion) subcategory refers only to romantic or sexualized love. Similarly, in the joy category, the cheerfulness subcategory contains fairly general names for joyful or happy feelings, whereas the other subcategories (zest, contentment, pride, etc.) have more specialized meanings.

To test the hypothesis that what we are calling core or generic subordinate categories are more central or representative members of their basic-level categories, we performed a new analysis. This involved computing mean within-category (within the basic category, in this case) centrality or prototypicality scores (the ones used to select category names) for terms in the core subclusters and separately for terms in the noncore (more specialized) subclusters. A *t* test was used to compare the two means ($M = 41.02$ for the core subclusters and 28.09 for the noncore subclusters), and the difference was found to be highly significant, $t(130) = 8.31, p < .001$. When five separate such comparisons were made, one for each basic-level category, four of the five were highly significant (all but the analysis for the fear category). Thus, the core subcategories are more representative of their basic-level clusters, on the average, than are the noncore subcategories. Theoretically, this representativeness should be reflected in judgments of the de-

gree to which various terms are judged prototypical of the category *emotion* because the basic-level emotions themselves are highly prototypical (Fehr & Russell, 1984). This implication was tested by comparing the prototypicality (or emotionness) ratings of two groups of words: those contained in core subclusters ($M = 3.29$) and those contained in noncore subclusters ($M = 3.17$). The difference was significant, $t(130) = 2.29, p < .03$.

One might expect the naming analysis described earlier to have selected the basic-level term within each core subcluster as that subcluster's name. Except in the case of sadness, however, that did not happen. Recall that the selection of names was based on the difference between a term's average co-occurrence with other terms within its subcluster and its average co-occurrence with all terms outside its subcluster. Although the basic-level names co-occurred frequently with terms that fell within their core or generic subclusters, they also co-occurred frequently with words appearing in other subclusters of the same basic-level category. Instead of the basic-level term, then, the analysis selected the term that tended most strongly to co-occur with terms in the core or generic subcluster and *not* with other terms in the same basic-level category.

Core or generic love (*affection*) is similar to what social psychologists have called *companionate* love (e.g., Walster & Walster, 1978). It is usually contrasted with *passionate* love, which corresponds to the second large subcluster (*lust*) within the love category in Figure 1.1. Interestingly, several recent studies have shown that descriptions of different kinds of close relationships (e.g., friendships, sibling relationships, parent-child relationships) have a core construct of love in common, whereas romantic love seems to be conceptualized as this core kind of love plus passion, sexual attraction, and so forth (e.g., Davis & Todd, 1982; Sternberg, 1986; Sternberg & Grajek, 1984).

The joy category contains a core or generic subcategory (*cheerfulness*) containing the words *joy* and *happiness,* plus subcategories that our statistical procedures labeled excitement, zest, contentment, pride, optimism, enthrallment, and relief. Each of these subordinate-level clusters makes sense as a distinct category, and together they suggest that the major reasons for the evolution of a large and differentiated emotion lexicon are twofold: The lexicon marks differences in intensity within each of the basic emotion categories (e.g., contentment vs. ecstasy) and communicates some-thing about the conditions or context in which the basic emotion under consideration arises (e.g., *pride* indicates that the self is the agent of a joy-producing outcome; *optimism*, that one expects a joy-producing outcome in the future).

The anger category contains a core or generic subcategory (*rage*), which includes the word *anger*, plus five additional subcategories: irritation, exasperation, disgust, envy, and torment (which subjects may have misunderstood). *Hate*, which Fehr and Russell (1984) found to be among the most psychologically accessible emotion names, appears within the core anger subcluster, indicating that subjects closely associated it with anger. Disgust, which many emotion theorists have treated as a basic emotion in its own right (because of its distinct facial expression and supposed links to innate reactions to bad tastes and smells), is clearly part of the basic-level anger category in the present study. (This fits with such everyday remarks as "I was disgusted when I heard that he got promoted" or "Did you hear Reagan's commercial about how much he has helped poor people?—Disgusting!") Thus, although disgust may be a separate, identifiable physical reaction across the life span, in the adult emotion lexicon it becomes metaphorically transformed into a type of anger akin to contempt. This transformation is neither arbitrary nor limited to our culture. Cross-cultural studies of emotional expressions (e.g., Ekman, Sorensen, & Friesen, 1969) and emotion antecedents (e.g., Boucher & Brandt, 1981) reveal frequent worldwide confusion between anger and disgust expressions and elicitors. A study of Pacific islanders' emotion classification yielded results similar to ours, with disgust being seen as a type of anger (Lutz, 1982).

Sadness includes, besides a core or generic subcluster (*sadness*), suffering, disappointment, shame, neglect, and sympathy. The substructure containing pity and sympathy is fairly distinct from the others because several subjects placed these in a category with love words, from the other side of the positive–negative divide. (*Longing* is a relatively detached member of the love cluster for a similar reason; many subjects classified it as a form of sadness.) Fear comes in two major forms: core, or generic, fear (*horror*) and anxiety—a distinction that corresponds well to the clinical-psychological distinction between fear and anxiety. Within the sadness and fear categories, we see again that

subordinate-level distinctions have mainly to do with intensity differences and with the antecedents or context in which the emotion in question arises.

HIERARCHY, CIRCUMPLEX, OR THREE-DIMENSIONAL SPACE?

Next, we consider how the hierarchical representation of the emotion domain compares with the more common circumplex and multidimensional portraits. To make comparisons most directly, using our own data, we subjected the 135 × 135 co-occurrence matrix to a classical nonmetric multidimensional scaling analysis (using the ALSCAL-4 program; Young & Lewyckyj, 1979; see also Kruskal, 1964). An elbow test, which involves plotting Kruskal stress coefficients as a function of solution dimensionality, indicated that the three-dimensional solution provided a good fit to the data. The stress coefficient was .20 for the one-dimensional solution, .15 for the two-dimensional solution, and .10 for the three-dimensional solution; little reduction in stress resulted from adding further dimensions. Because several contemporary emotion researchers (e.g., Plutchik, 1980; Russell, 1980, 1983) have favored a two-dimensional circumplex representation of the emotion domain, we will discuss both the two- and three-dimensional solutions.

A computer-generated summary of the two-dimensional solution is shown in Figure 1.2. Members of different basic-level emotion clusters in Figure 1.1, including surprise, are represented in Figure 1.2 by different symbols (*hearts* for love words, *circles* for joy words, *clubs* for surprise words, *squares* for anger words, *diamonds* for sadness words, and *crosses* for fear words). The large symbols designate the words naming the basic-emotion categories: love, joy, surprise, anger, sadness, and fear. Four features of the results merit discussion: (a) Even though the 135 terms were not preselected to fit a circumplex pattern, or any other theoretically significant configuration, they fall roughly around the perimeter of a circle defined by two orthogonal dimensions, which can be interpreted as evaluation (positive vs. negative hedonic tone) and intensity or arousal. (b) Despite the large number of terms included, many parts of the circle are unoccupied, suggesting (in line with Scherer, 1984) that more perfect-looking circumplex analyses, such as Russell's (1980, 1983), require the inclusion of words that most

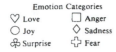

Emotion Categories
♡ Love   □ Anger
○ Joy   ◇ Sadness
♣ Surprise ♧ Fear

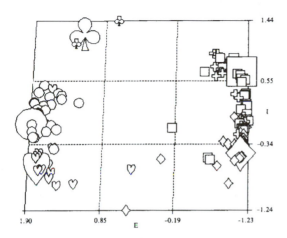

E: Evaluation (Positive to Negative)
I: Intensity (Low to High)

FIGURE 1.2 ■ Two-dimensional solution from a multidimensional scaling analysis of the emotion co-occurence matrix. (Each of the six kinds of symbols—hearts, circles, and so on—represents a different basic-level cluster in Figure 1. The large symbol of each type indicates the location of the word naming the basic-level cluster—love, joy, and so on.)

people would not call emotions (e.g., *sleepy, relaxed*). (c) Within each of the basic categories (according to Figure 1.1) one finds terms that differ with respect to intensity or arousal. These include *rage* vs. *grouchiness*, *terror* vs. *worry*, and *ecstasy* vs. *contentment*. Differences between these terms within basic categories are almost as responsible for the intensity dimension's appearance in the analysis as are intensity differences between basic emotion categories. (d) The clusters of terms labeled *fear* and *anger* in Figure 1.1, which most people see as quite distinct, are almost completely intermingled in Figure 1.2 (notice the intermingling of crosses and squares). In general, the two-dimensional solution provides no basis for separating terms that, according to both intuition and hierarchical cluster analysis (e.g., fear and anger), belong to qualitatively different emotion categories. (The large cross representing the word *fear* is nearly obscured by the large square designating the word *anger*; only two of its arms protrude at the top and left of the large square.)

A computer-generated summary of the three-

dimensional solution is shown in Figure 1.3. Just as the two-dimensional solution corresponds well with two-dimensional solutions reported by previous investigators, the three-dimensional solution corresponds well with three-dimensional solutions obtained earlier by, for example, Schlosberg (1954), Osgood et al. (1957), and Russell and Mehrabian (1977). The first, horizontal dimension corresponds with what Osgood et al. called "evaluation." The second and third, extending back and up, respectively, are formed by splitting Figure 1.2's intensity dimension into two separate vectors, which Osgood et al. called "potency" and "activity." The major contributions of moving from two to three dimensions are (a) to reveal that anger-related emotions (e.g., anger, rage, fury, and spite) tend to be high in potency, sadness-related emotions (e.g., loneliness, melancholy, and sadness) tend to be low in potency, and the other four emotion categories (including surprise) tend to be inteimediate in potency, although there is substantial variation within categories; and (b) to reveal that fear (e.g., alarm, shock, fear, and panic) and especially surprise are high in activity, love-related emotions are somewhat low in activity, and the other emotion categories are intermediate in activity. The three-dimensional solution helps to differentiate between what the cluster analysis suggests are separate basic-emotion categories, and it

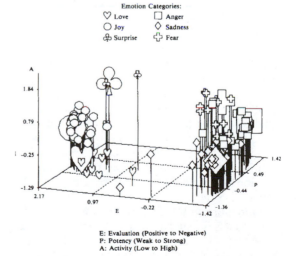

Emotion Categories:
♡ Love   □ Anger
○ Joy   ◇ Sadness
♣ Surprise ♧ Fear

E: Evaluation (Positive to Negative)
P: Potency (Weak to Strong)
A: Activity (Low to High)

FIGURE 1.3 ■ Three-dimensional solution from a multidimensional scaling analysis of the emotion co-occurrence matrix. (The meaning of the large and small symbols and of the six different types of symbols is the same as in Figure 2.)

is clearly more informative as a representation of emotion knowledge than the two-dimensional solution. Nevertheless, there is still some overlap between categories (reflecting their fuzziness) and no way within the multidimensional scaling analysis to tell that frustration, for example, is conceptually closer to anger than to fear or sadness—a fact revealed by cluster analysis. Moreover, the meaningful subordinate-level structure within each of the basic categories, so clear in the cluster analysis, is difficult to derive from the multidimensional scaling analysis (even when all of the names are included, which they cannot be in the small figure shown here).

SUMMARY OF STUDY 1

The prototype approach to emotion proved useful in guiding the selection of emotion terms to be included in the analysis (those that were judged relatively prototypical), in suggesting the use of nouns ("objects in natural categories"; Rosch, Mervis, Gray, Johnson, & Boyes-Braem, 1976) rather than other parts of speech, and in pointing to hierarchical cluster analysis as a technique that reveals features of categorical structure not revealed by the more usual multidimensional scaling techniques. It seems possible, given the results, that all of the terms in the emotion lexicon—at least the hundred or so that are most prototypical of the category *emotion*—refer in one way or another to a mere handful of basic-level emotions. Each term seems to specify either the intensity of the basic emotion in question (e.g., *jubilation* vs. *satisfaction*, *rage* vs. *grouchiness*, *terror* vs. *worry*) or the antecedent context in which the emotion arises (*disappointment* vs. *grief*; *pride* vs. *hope*). In other words, the emotion lexicon, containing hundreds of terms (only 135 of which were included here), may refer to the particular basic emotion in question and to its intensity, specific eliciting context, or both. If so, the structure of emotion knowledge is not as complex as one might initially expect.

A three-dimensional representation of co-occurrence data from Study 1 was also shown to be statistically justifiable and highly interpretable. Thus, the very same similarity or categorization judgments are meaningfully compatible with both hierarchical and dimensional representations, and the two forms of representation reveal different aspects of emotion knowledge.

Study 2: Contents of Basic Emotion Prototypes

The prototype approach to mental representation suggests that comparisons among named emotions involve comparisons of prototypes or prototypical features. Moreover, as discussed briefly by Fehr and Russell (1984, p. 482), the approach suggests that real emotional events, or exemplars of emotion, are perceived and understood with reference to emotion prototypes or scripts. Finally, it suggests that the initial encoding of an emotion episode is likely to occur at the basic level of the emotion hierarchy. For these reasons, it seemed important to delineate prototypes of the basic emotions, along the lines pioneered by Averill (1982) and de Rivera (1981b) in analyses of anger, and to examine their structures and contents. That was the purpose of Study 2.

Like other prototype researchers (e.g., Cantor & Mischel, 1979a; Horowitz et al., 1982) and cognitively oriented emotion researchers (e.g., Roseman, 1984; Smith & Ellsworth, 1985), we began with the assumption that people's descriptions of specific instances of a category reflect underlying category prototypes. The average young adult has witnessed thousands of emotion episodes and has experienced thousands more. If contemporary cognitive psychology is correct in claiming that repeated experiences with similar events lead to the construction of generic mental representations, then ordinary, untrained subjects should construct emotion prototypes and implicitly use them when witnessing and recounting emotion episodes. Just as story readers construct generic story schemas (Mandler, 1984) and regular restaurant patrons construct restaurant scripts (Schank & Abelson, 1977), observers and experiencers of emotion should, whether they are aware of it or not, construct basic emotion prototypes.

Method

SUBJECTS AND PROCEDURE

One hundred twenty students in introductory psychology courses wrote accounts of emotional experiences. The accounts were of two kinds, *self* and *typical*. Subjects in the self condition (30 men and 30 women) wrote descriptions of actual episodes in which they experienced fear, sadness, anger, joy, and love. For each emotion, they were free to choose any incident from their own experience. To elicit a complete account of the relevant episode, subjects were given a questionnaire (similar to ones used by Averill, 1982; Fehr & Russell, 1984; and Scherer, Summerfield, & Wallbott, 1983) containing the following instructions and questions, with blank spaces provided for their responses:

> Think of a real incident in which you were AFRAID [SAD, ANGRY, JOYFUL; in the love condition, "in which you felt particularly IN LOVE or LOVING"]. Take a few moments to recall as many details of the incident as you can.
> 1. Tell *in detail* what happened to cause you to feel afraid [sad, etc.]
> 2. Tell in as much detail as you can
>   —what you were feeling and thinking
>   —what you said, if anything, and how you said it
>   —what physical signs of fear [sadness, etc.] you showed, if any; and
>   —what you did, how you acted.
> 3. About how long did the feeling last? How was it resolved? What caused it to change or subside?
> 4. Can you add anything that would help to describe the emotion episode more fully?

Subjects in the *typical* condition (30 men and 30 women) described their impressions of typical emotion episodes—telling what generally happens when a person becomes afraid, sad, angry, joyful, or loving. The typical condition was included to allow comparisons between descriptions of personal emotional experiences, on the one hand, and beliefs about the emotional experiences of people in general, on the other. The typical version of the questionnaire directly paralleled the self version, but it asked subjects to "think about times when people are afraid," "tell *in detail* what typically causes a person to feel afraid," and so forth.

SAMPLE ACCOUNTS

Subjects responded easily to both versions of the questionnaire, producing rich and informative accounts of emotional episodes. An 18-year-old woman, for example, wrote the following description of an actual (self) anger experience:

> My boyfriend overheard a friend of his giving me some very nice compliments and being a little suggestive. Because I did not return soon, he assumed something was going on. When I did re-

turn, he told me to get out of his life and that "we were over." I didn't know the reason for his behavior, and I became very defensive and angry. He went to beat up his friend; I tried to stop him in the elevator by not allowing the doors to close. Then I let him go and went to my room, slamming every door in my path.

> I was confused because I didn't know why he was so mad and being so mean to me. I was angry with him for acting the way he was over what *I* felt was no big deal. (I didn't know his assumptions; I at first did not know he had even heard part of what his friend had said.) I was also sad and scared about our relationship ending, but anger overrode these feelings.

> I called him a jerk. I yelled at him. I said (excuse me, please) "fuck you" and called him a "shit head." I also tried to tell him he was wrong to act the way he was over no big deal. I hit and kicked and cursed him repeatedly.

> The anger lasted about 2 days. It subsided after he found out what really happened and apologized. He got my side of the story and talked with his friend (not a good talk), and our stories of course matched. He then felt really bad and silly about his actions.

An 18-year-old man wrote the following account of an actual joy experience:

> I had the opportunity to direct the first all-student musical ever done at my high school. I was producer-director, which put a lot of pressure and responsibility on me. But to see the final play and know that I contributed and brought it all together was great! The lady who usually directs the plays went up to the principal and asked him what they needed her for if the students could do it this well!

> I was so proud. I have never had as much fun or excitement as I did that closing night. Everyone was congratulating me, and it made me very naturally high. Everyone could tell I was excited and joyful. I just kept saying, "We did it, and we did it great!" I had the biggest smile on my face, and I was hugging all of the cast members. I was on Cloud 9 for a long time. I acted so proud, I guess like a new father or something.

> The feeling lasted for about 2 or 3 days. The thing that made it subside was when I realized that it was over, and all the fun and excitement ended.

Finally, a 19-year-old woman wrote this description of typical sadness experiences:

> Disappointments, and deaths of people that one really cares about. When the person has really put

everything he has into something (like a relation-ship, a business venture, an application for a com-petitive scholarship) and that something doesn't work out, it's a disappointment and the person is sad. Another, more severe sadness is grief over the death of somebody the person really cared about. Someone who has made a significant mark on a person's life, but now they are gone. This creates a feeling of loss or emptiness which is also a form of sadness.

A sad person typically feels empty; they have lost something of great value. They may also feel lost. They don't know what to do next or where to turn. A sad person typically feels unable to rem-edy the situation. There is no way to make things better or erase what has happened. For example, the dead loved one is dead, and there's nothing you can do about it. A job not gotten is a job not gotten.

A sad person speaks with both words and ac-tions. He might actually tell a close friend how he feels: "Something terrible has happened and I can't help it; I feel devastated, lost, and empty." But people on the street can tell it even if he doesn't say anything. He doesn't initiate conversation; he seems weary with everything. He is likely not to be at his physical best—perhaps his clothes are unironed, his hair uncombed; maybe he doesn't smile even at people he knows. The person might look physically exhausted and drooped over, like he hasn't slept in days. Circles under the eyes, et-cetera. Generally run down.

Sad people usually act as if nothing they are doing has much significance. As if at work, or at home or whatever, they are just going through the motions of living.

CODING THE ACCOUNTS

Six coders read a sample of the 120 accounts for a given emotion and generated, through group dis-cussion, a list of features (antecedents, expressions, feelings, physiological reactions, and behaviors) that they could agree appeared in at least a few of these accounts. This feature list served as the cod-ing system for the relevant emotion. Three of the six coders then independently evaluated each ac-count, judging each feature in the coding system to be either present or absent in that account. Interrater reliabilities (average proportion of agree-ment between pain of coders) ranged from .65 to 1.00. Of the 127 prototypical features, 125 were coded with reliability equal to or greater than .70.

The coders' judgments were used to produce a feature summary of each narrative account. A fea-ture was scored as present in a given account if at least two of three coders agreed that it was present. On the basis of these codings, we determined the prototypical features of the basic emotion catego-ries. Following the convention established by Horowitz et al. (1981) and Cantor and Mischel (1979a), a feature was retained in the prototype of a given emotion if it was present in at least 20% of either the self or typical accounts for that emo-tion. Although somewhat arbitrary, this cutoff re-sulted in the elimination of infrequent, idiosyn-cratic features.

These procedures produced a list of 23 to 29 prototypical features for each emotion category. Although informative in themselves, in simple list form the features failed to convey the temporally organized, scriptlike structure of subjects' ac-counts, which seemed potentially important for future research and theorizing (Schwartz & Shaver, 1987). To organize each emotion prototype into temporal and functional feature groupings, an ad-ditional step was taken. We arranged the features for each emotion in random order on a sheet of paper, and the six coders, all of whom had read scores of accounts of each emotion, independently rated all possible pairs of features on a 5-point functional similarity scale. (See Mandler, 1984, for a similar procedure.) If two features played very different functional roles in the emotion episodes (e.g., an intense expression, such as screaming and an attempt to control such expressions by "trying to keep it inside"), that pair was given a rating of 1. If two features performed very similar functions (e.g., two causal antecedents such as "getting what was not wanted" and "not getting what was wanted"), the pair was given a rating of 5. Corre-lations between all pairs of raters were computed for each emotion, and Cronbach's alpha was com-puted as an index of reliability from the resulting correlation matrix. All of the alphas were high: .90 for love, .94 for joy, .93 for anger, .94 for sad-ness, and .91 for fear.

For each prototype, the matrices of ratings pro-duced by the six coders were averaged and sub-mitted to hierarchical cluster analysis (again us-ing the BMDP 1M program's average distance method) to produce the prototype diagram for that emotion. (This is the procedure used by Horowitz et al., 1981.) Although not completely objective, because the six coders (including the authors) had held many discussions about emotions, emotion accounts, and so forth, the structures shown in Figures 1.4 through 1.8 are more systematic than intuitive author summaries. They stand as working hypotheses concerning the internal organization of basic-emotion scripts.

Results and Discussion

Figures 1.4 through 1.8 present the prototypes of fear, sadness, anger, joy, and love, respectively. A glance at the five figures reveals a consistent general structure, highlighted by heavy lines surrounding the large exterior boxes. All five prototypes contain a set of *antecedents* (listed in the uppermost of the heavily outlined boxes) and a diverse collection of experiential, physiological, cognitive, expressive, and behavioral *responses* (contained in the second and largest heavily outlined box). Each of the three negative emotions—fear, sadness, and anger—also includes a set of *self-control procedures*, appearing in the third and smallest heavily outlined box. The number in the upper right-hand corner of each box represents the average functional similarity rating (on a 5-point scale) of all pairs of features in that box. Higher numbers identify "tighter" clusters—those containing features judged to be highly similar to one another. All clusters with strengths of at least 2.75 are indicated by boxes in the diagrams. The number in brackets following each feature indicates the percentage of 120 subjects mentioning that feature. (Some of the percentages are less than 20 because the 20% cutoff applied to either the self or the typical subjects, whereas proportions from these two groups of subjects have been averaged in the figure.) Despite this common gross structure, each emotion prototype exhibits unique contents and fine structure. We turn now to a consideration of some of these details.

FEAR

The fear prototype is presented in Figure 1.4. Examination of the antecedents reveals that fear accounts begin with an interpretation of events as potentially dangerous or threatening to the self—most commonly, an anticipation of physical harm, loss, rejection, or failure. The fear antecedents also include a set of situational factors (unfamiliar situation, being in the dark, being alone) that probably increase the person's perceived vulnerability to such threats and impede his or her chances of

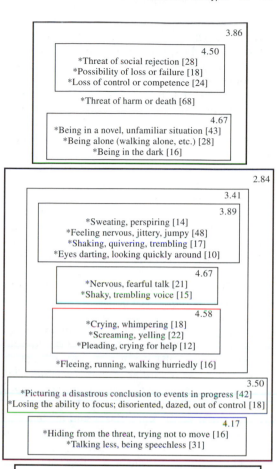

FIGURE 1.4 ■ The Prototype of Fear.

coping effectively. Thus, as various authors have pointed out (Osgood, May, & Miron, 1975; Roseman, 1984) the fearful person describes himself or herself as relatively weak or low in potency; some aspect of the self (e.g., physical well-being, social position, or sense of competence) is potentially under attack and the fearful person is relatively helpless to do anything about it other than flee or hide.

A central element of the person's response to this dangerous and weak position seems to be arousal of the autonomic nervous system in preparation for flight (as Cannon, 1927, and others have argued); the person feels jittery and jumpy, perspires, trembles, and looks quickly around. The person's voice shakes or trembles and he or she verbalizes nervousness or fear. Other commonly reported vocal expressions include screaming or yelling, crying, and pleading for help. This last response is presumably an attempt to avert the imagined disaster, as is flight (fleeing, running, walking hurriedly). These features may explain fear's relatively high standing on the activity dimension of the three-dimensional emotion space (see Figure 1.3). The remaining responses include an additional pair of coping attempts (hiding from the threat or freezing, and being quiet) and a pair of internal reactions (picturing disaster and becoming disoriented or cognitively impaired). Finally, the fear prototype includes self-control mechanisms. One of these, comforting oneself, is primarily internal and seems designed to reduce fear. Another, acting unafraid, is a form of self-presentation that in many accounts seems designed to reduce the likelihood of a threatening person's (or gang's) attack.

If one were to try to convey fear, say in a novel or a film, Figure 1.4 suggests that one would want to communicate the threat of harm or death, if possible in an unfamiliar or unpredictable environment and in a situation in which the protagonist is vulnerable or lacking in control; to portray the potential victim's jitteriness and tendency to imagine disaster (perhaps in "flash-forwards"); and to show the victim either screaming or utterly speechless. Taken together, these elements of fear, which of course are often used to depict this emotion, could not possibly be mistaken for any other basic emotion.

SADNESS

The prototype of sadness is presented in Figure 1.5. If fear accounts begin with a description of events as potentially dangerous or threatening to the self, sadness accounts begin with a situation in which the threat has already been realized. The sad person has experienced an undesirable outcome; often he or she has experienced one of the events that the fearful person dreads-death of a loved one, loss of a relationship, or social rejection. Like fear, sadness involves "discovering that one is powerless, helpless, or impotent" to change the unhappy circumstances (cf. Seligman, 1975). This may explain the especially low potency ratings given to sadness-related words in multidimensional-scaling studies of the emotion domain.

Because the sad person (or someone with whom

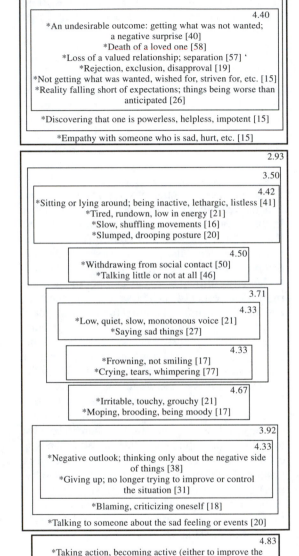

FIGURE 1.5 ■ The Prototype of Sadness.

he or she empathizes) has received the negative outcome that the fearful person only anticipates receiving his or her reported responses are quite different from those contained in the fear prototype. Attempts to flee or avoid harm would be useless because the harmful event has already occurred. Unlike the fearful person, who becomes aroused and vigilant, the sad person becomes inactive, lethargic, and listless—low, compared with the fearful person, in activity. He or she withdraws from social contact and talks little or not at all, frequently expressing sadness by crying or whimpering. Sadness channels the person's cognitions in a negative direction, leading him or her to think only about the unhappy aspects of events. This negative outlook, and the conviction that the situation is hopeless, are reflected in the sad person's tendency to give up—to withhold futile efforts to improve circumstances. Often, however, the sad person reportedly manages to put an end to this downward spiral by enacting some kind of self-control procedure, most frequently by deliberately trying to become more energetic and active.

ANGER

Figure 1.6 contains the prototype of anger. The cognitive antecedents that initiate the anger process, as inferred from subjects' accounts, can be summarized as follows: Something (usually another person, in these accounts) interferes with the person's execution of plans or attainment of goals (by reducing the person's power, violating expectations, frustrating or interrupting goal-directed activities). Alternatively, the person perceives another as harming him or her in some way (inflicting physical or psychological pain). Finally, as de Rivera (1981b) pointed out, the angry person makes the judgment that the frustration, interruption, power reversal, or harm is illegitimate—that the situation is contrary to what ought to be. This last element is the most frequent feature in the anger prototype, occurring in fully 95% of the self anger accounts.

Unlike the fearful person, who tends to flee from the source of danger, and the sad person, who becomes inactive and withdrawn, the angry person reports becoming stronger (higher in potency) and more energized in order to fight or rail against the cause of anger. His or her responses seem designed to rectify injustice—to reassert power or status, to frighten the offending person into compliance, to restore a desired state of affairs. Thus, the angry person reports attacking the cause of anger verbally, in a loud and ferocious voice, and also communicating anger nonverbally (e.g., by walking out and slamming doors). He or she frequently imagines attacking the target physically (e.g., "I thought about slugging him") and sometimes does. Displaced attacks against inanimate objects are also

2.97
*Predisposition to anger, either because of previous similar or related experiences or became of stress, overload, fatigue, etc. [18]

4.04

4.44
*Reversal or sudden loss of power, status, or respect; insult [43]
*Violation of an expectation; thing not working out as planned [54]
*Frustration or interruption of a goal-directed activity [33]
*Real or threatened physical or psychological pain [57]

*Judgment that the situation is illegitimate, wrong, unfair, contrary to what ought to be [78]

2.92

3.50

3.75

4.44
*Obscenities, cursing [30]
*Verbally attacking the cause of anger [69]
*Loud voice, yelling, screaming, shouting [59]
*Complaining, bitching, talking about how lousy thing are [18]

4.04

4.83
*Hands or fists clenched [22]
*Aggressive, threatening movements or gestures [21]

4.33
*Attacking something other than the cause of anger (e.g., pounding on something, throwing things) [35]
*Physically attacking the cause of anger [26]
*Incoherent, out-of-control, highly emotional behavior [18]
*Imagining attacking or hurting the cause of anger [31]

3.87

4.08
*Heavy walk, stomping [11]
*Tightness or rigidity in body; tight, rigid movements [17]
*Nonverbally communicating disapproval to the cause of anger (e.g., slamming doors, walking out) [25]

4.25
*Frowning, not smiling, mean or unpleasant expression [18]
*Gritting teeth, showing teeth, breathing through teeth [13]
*Red, flushed face [33]

3.50
*Crying [17]
*Feelings of nervous tension, anxiety, discomfort [17]

4.00
*Brooding; withdrawing from social contact [14]

4.50
*Narrowing of attention to exclude all but the anger situation; not being able to think of anything else [16]
*Thinking "I'm right, everyone else is wrong" [38]

4.00
*Suppressing the anger; trying not to show or express it [20]
*Redefining the situation or trying to view it in such a way that anger is no longer appropriate [11]

FIGURE 1.6 ■ The Prototype of Anger.

common (pounding on something, throwing things). Anger reports mention several physical signs, most of which seem designed to intimidate the target (frowning, showing teeth, clenching fists, etc.). The most commonly mentioned physical sign is a hushed, red face, probably associated with "blood flow ... to the head and chest to support threat displays and fighting responses" (Scherer, 1984, p. 47; see Ekman, Levenson, & Friesen, 1983, for evidence that the metaphorical "heat" of anger, sometimes associated with flushing and reddening, is literally measurable by skin-temperature sensors). Like the other emotions, anger has a channeling influence on perceptions and thoughts, often expressed in the angry person's conviction that he or she is right and the rest of the world is wrong. Finally, like those for fear and sadness, the anger prototype includes a self-control component, frequently exhibited in the tendency to suppress expressions of the emotion.

JOY

The joy prototype is presented in Figure 1.7. Theory, research, and common sense indicate that joy, or happiness, and sadness are opposite concepts (e.g., de Rivera, 1977; Plutchik, 1962; Russell, 1980), and comparison of the relevant prototypes confirms this. Whereas sadness accounts begin with undesirable outcomes (getting what is not wanted, suffering social rejection, losing a valued relationship), joy accounts begin with positive outcomes—getting something desired or desirable. In contrast to the losses and failures that trigger sadness, the desirable outcome that initiates happiness is frequently a gain or success in the achievement domain (task success, achievement) or in the social domain (receiving esteem or affection).

Reported joy responses contrast sharply with those of sadness. Whereas the sad person is withdrawn and uncommunicative, the happy person is socially outgoing; he or she seeks contact with others (acts friendly, hugs people, etc.) and tends to communicate and share his or her good feelings. Whereas sadness is associated with inactivity and lack of energy, joy is portrayed as energetic, active, and bouncy. Whereas sadness is expressed by crying, whimpering, and not talking, joy is expressed by laughing, smiling, and talking enthusiastically. Finally, whereas the sad person's thoughts are characterized by negativity,

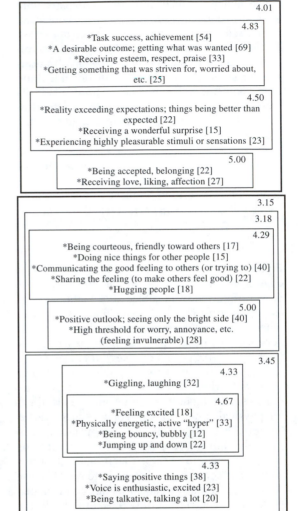

FIGURE 1.7 ■ The Prototype of Joy.

by seeing only the dark side of events, the happy person has a positive outlook, focuses on the bright side of things, and feels relatively invulnerable to trouble, worry, or annoyance.

LOVE

Figure 1.8 displays the love prototype. Two common antecedents of love illustrate its similarity to joy—the judgment that the loved one provides something the person wants, needs, or likes and the realization that the target person loves, needs, or appreciates the person writing the account.

These two antecedents are very much like the joy-eliciting judgments that one has gotten something wanted or desirable and that one is liked or loved. In the joy episodes, these antecedents promote a general sense of well-being; in the case of love, they promote a similar sense of well-being that is personalized (i.e., that is attributed to the presence or existence of the love object). Love is marked by several additional antecedents. According to our subjects, love can occur because one has shared time or special experiences with the other person, because one finds the other physically or psychologically attractive, because one enjoys exceptionally good communication with the other person, or because one feels open and trusting in the person's presence.

The responses that typify love include several prototypical joy responses—for example, smiling and feeling excited and energetic. In addition, the person who is experiencing love reports seeking social contact, but contact of a highly specific nature. Whereas the joyful person's gregariousness is fairly general, the loving person typically wants to see and be near the love object, to hug, kiss, and hold him or her and to communicate loving feelings. That love may be conceptualized as a personalized form of joy is suggested again by subjects' explicit mention of happiness and joy and by cognitive biases similar to those mentioned in joy episodes: In addition to being obsessed with thoughts of the love object, the loving person tends to see only the positive side of things and feels self-confident and invulnerable, just as the happy person does. Loving subjects also report feeling warm, trusting, and secure when in the presence of (or when thinking about) the loved person. This may explain why love is viewed as somewhat less active than joy, according to Figure 1.3—contentment and security being placid forms of pleasure.

OBSERVATIONS AND COMMENTS

The basic-emotion prototypes suggest some tentative generalizations about the cognitive representation of emotion episodes. Figure 1.9 presents, in diagram form, the model of emotion that seems to be implicit in subjects' accounts of self and typical emotion episodes. Examination of the antecedent clusters and subclusters of the prototype diagrams (Figures 1.4–1.8) reveals that emotions are conceptualized as beginning with appraisals of the way in which circumstances or events bear on a

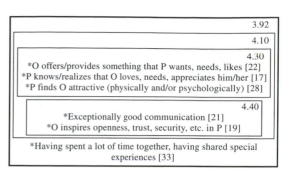

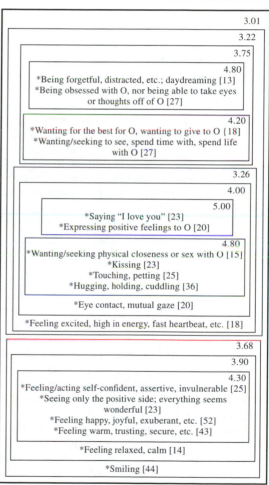

FIGURE 1.8 ■ The Prototype of Love.

person's motives, goals, values, or desires (Arnold, 1960). In other words, prototypical emotion episodes begin with an interpretation of events as good or bad, helpful or harmful, consistent or inconsistent with a person's motives (cf Roseman, 1984). We believe this is why emotions and emotion categories—around the world, evidently (e.g., Lutz,

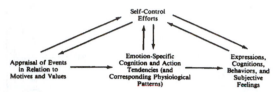

FIGURE 1.9 ■ A dynamic model of the emotion process implicit in subjects' accounts of emotion episodes.

1982; Osgood et al., 1975; Russell, 1983)—are arrayed into good and bad superordinate categories.

When a situation is judged to be motive-inconsistent, it also seems to be appraised with respect to the potential efficacy of active, forceful responses (Epstein, 1984). The combination of appraisals then determines which set of basic-emotion responses is elicited. (The manner in which the appraisals physically elicit emotional responses is not revealed by subjects' accounts and is one of the areas in which scientific emotion theory must go beyond "folk" conceptions of the emotion process.) Once one of the basic emotions is elicited, its characteristic action tendencies, cognitive biases, and physiological patterns seem to arise automatically unless they are countered by self-control efforts. This automaticity probably accounts for the common opinion (analyzed historically by Averill, 1982) that emotions "overtake," "grab," and "hit" us, even though they are consequences of our own appraisals of situations. Self-control efforts can be initiated at any stage of the emotion process and can be directed at any of the components of emotion. Appraisals can be reevaluated, action tendencies can be stifled or suppressed, and subjective feelings can be denied, distorted, or disattended. Often, however, an emotion unfolds before control can be successfully exerted.

An emotion episode, then, is more comprehensive, in perceivers' minds at least, than many contemporary theories of emotion suggest. For example, Schachter (1971) focused on physiological arousal and post hoc cognitive labels; Roseman (1984) and Smith and Ellsworth (1985) on cognitive antecedents; Ekman (1984) and Izard (1977) on facial expressions; and Bower (e.g., Bower & Cohen, 1982) and Isen (1984) on cognitive biases caused by emotional states. The basic-emotion prototypes suggest that all of these different facets of emotion are included in ordinary people's organized representations of emotion episodes.

Emotion theories will probably seem more lifelike when they, too, become comprehensive.

When people judge the similarity or distinctiveness of two emotions, say frustration and anger, it seems likely to us that they do so in terms of prototypical features rather than positions on abstract dimensions such as evaluation, potency, and activity, although this matter obviously requires study in its own right. For the moment, we suspect that the three abstract dimensions of emotion are emergent properties of emotion prototypes, not active elements in everyday processing of emotional information. When subjects in an emotion-sorting or similarity-rating study compare two emotions, or two mental representations of emotions, they may think about antecedents, responses, self-control efforts, or all three. It may be a mistake, therefore, to think of the abstract dimensions of emotion—evaluation, potency, and activity—as properties of appraisals or responses or subjective experiences, or of any other single aspect of emotion.

Certain basic emotions are closely connected in Figure 1.1 because some subjects placed terms from more than one category in a single pile when sorting them for similarity. It seems likely that the similarity of certain forms of sadness and fear is due primarily to their common antecedents: real or threatened harm, loss, rejection, and the inability to control or rectify these. In contrast, the response components of the two emotions are quite distinct because fear mobilizes a person to cope with or escape from a threatening situation, whereas sadness is immobilizing. Thus, fear and sadness are reactions to similar situations, but situations that differ enough to produce highly dissimilar responses. Love and joy are similar, as we mentioned, in many of their antecedents and responses. These examples point to the complexity of the similarity judgments made by subjects in Study 1 and give reason for wariness concerning emotion theories that try to explain the structure of emotion solely in terms of antecedents or expressions or subjective feelings.

SELF VERSUS TYPICAL PERSPECTIVES

Out of 127 feature-by-feature comparisons between self and typical accounts, 66 were significant at the .05 level or less. Of these, 20 had significance levels less than .01 but greater than .001, and 34 had significance levels less than .001. Given the large number of analyses performed, the weaker differences should be interpreted with caution.

A few interesting patterns can be noted in the results of these comparisons. First, cognitive biases and distortions (e.g., negative outlook and giving up in the sadness prototype, narrowing of attention and thinking "I'm right, everyone else is wrong" in the anger prototype, positive outlook and high threshhold for worry in the joy prototype, being forgetful and distracted in the love prototype) were mentioned more frequently in typical than in self accounts, suggesting that people are not very aware of their own narrow focus and cognitive biases when describing personal experiences of emotion. When someone else is angry, we easily notice his or her one-sidedness, proneness to distortion, and bullheadedness; when we are angry we tend to see only the virtues of our own position, and this difference shows up in people's emotion accounts. This is one of two major kinds of self-typical differences discovered in the data, both of which are related to the well-known actor-observer distinction (Jones & Nisbett, 1972; Storms, 1973).

Actors and observers have different perspectives on actors' experiences and behavior. Actors have access to privileged information concerning their own desires, perceptions, thoughts, and intentions (Andersen, 1984; Bem, 1972; Wilson & Stone, 1985), whereas observers have privileged access to certain features of the actors' appearance and behavior. In the case of emotion, subjects asked to write about personal examples more often mentioned their predispositions (e.g., predisposition to anger), interpretations of events (e.g., reversal or loss of power, violation of expectation, and judgment of illegitimacy in the anger prototype; task success, receiving esteem, and getting something striven for in the joy prototype) and self-control efforts (e.g., taking action, becoming active in the sadness prototype; redefining the situation in the anger prototype), all of which can be present without necessarily manifesting themselves in behavior. Subjects asked to write about typical emotion episodes more often mentioned expressions and reactions manifested in the person's physical appearance and overt behavior (e.g., eyes darting, fleeing, and hiding in the fear prototype; sitting or lying around, slow or shuffling movements, slumped posture, and saying sad things in the sadness prototype; yelling and screaming, aggressive gestures, and red, flushed face in the anger prototype; being bouncy, saying positive things, and smiling in the joy prototype). These generalizations regarding actor-observer effects do not describe every one of the 66 comparisons that reached the .05 significance level, but nearly all of the differences fit this pattern. Despite these differences, both groups of subjects frequently revealed the gap filling, schematic nature of emotion prototypes by saying such things as "probably my face was red," "I suppose I turned pale," or "Probably the person thinks, 'This isn't fair.'"

General Discussion

The results of Studies 1 and 2 indicate, in line with suggestions by several authors and research by Fehr and Russell (1984), that a prototype approach provides useful ways to probe and represent adults' emotion knowledge. Study 1 revealed that hierarchical cluster analysis, a method suggested by the prototype approach, yields a rather different picture of the domain of emotion knowledge than that provided by the more commonly used multidimensional scaling method. Cluster analysis of emotion-similarity sorts produced a multilevel hierarchy, the top level of which distinguished positive from negative emotions and the middle level of which distinguished among love, joy, surprise, anger, sadness, and fear. These emotion categories, which we hypothesize are the basic-level concepts in most people's emotion lexicons, correspond to the ones that Fehr and Russell's subjects named most readily as examples of the emotion category. They are similar to Bretherton and Beeghly's (1982) list of emotion terms learned first in early childhood, and they overlap extensively with various theorists' lists of basic or primary emotions. Surprise was considered questionable as a basic-level category because of its small size and poor showing in previous studies. Below what we interpreted as the basic level were 25 subordinate-level categories, with tentative names such as affection, lust, cheerfulness, pride, irritation, rage, disappointment, shame, horror, and nervousness. Within each basic-level category, one subcluster, containing the basic-level term, appeared to designate a generic or core form of the emotion in question, whereas the other subclusters seemed to designate more specialized forms. Words in the core subclusters were shown to be more representative of their basic-level categories and more prototypical examples of the category *emotion* than their noncore counterparts. We suggested that subordinate-level categories within each basic-level category are designed primarily to distinguish levels of intensity and details of eliciting context.

Multidimensional scaling analyses of the data used for the hierarchical cluster analysis indicated that a three-dimensional solution fit the similarity matrix well. The three dimensions were the ones that previous investigators have found by using similar methods: evaluation, potency, and activity. Within the three-dimensional space, the five basic-level emotion categories could be seen to differ from one another in systematic ways. Thus, both hierarchical and dimensional representations can be used to shed light on the structure of emotion concepts.

Study 2 was an initial attempt to derive prototypical features of basic-level emotion scripts from two kinds of protocols: subjects' descriptions of typical emotion episodes and of personal (self) examples of these same emotions. Results from the two different kinds of accounts were very similar, suggesting either that basic-level emotion prototypes are derived from personal experiences similar to the ones subjects reported, that prototypes guide memory and reporting of personal experiences, or both. Whichever the case, there seems to be a generic scriptlike representation of each of the basic-level emotions. The content of these prototypes helps to explain the similarity judgments made by subjects in Study 1; fear and sadness were seen as more similar than sadness and anger, for example, and this seems attributable to the substantial overlap between the antecedents of fear and sadness.

We believe that the prototypes are compatible with an implicit model of emotion processes, according to which emotions begin with appraisals of events in relation to motives or preferences. The various patterns of appraisal, then, elicit one or more sets of basic-level emotional responses, each including expressions, action tendencies, subjective feelings, and associated physiological states. An emotion may or may not be manifested directly in behavior, depending on the application of self-control efforts. Not surprisingly, this model, implicit in ordinary people's representation of emotion episodes, is paralleled by several contemporary scientific theories (e.g., Lazarus, 1985; Roseman, 1984; Scherer, 1984; Smith & Ellsworth, 1985; Weiner, 1985) and by much earlier philosophical theories of emotion (e.g., those of Aristotle and Spinoza).

Two limitations of the methods used in Study 2 deserve mention. First, the information about basic-emotion prototypes was elicited by a series of questionnaire prompts. We know from pilot studies in which subjects were simply asked, without specific prompting, to describe actual or typical emotion episodes that such accounts tend to be vague and sketchy. Only when specifically instructed, "Tell in detail what happened to cause you to feel . . . ," "Tell . . . what you said, if anything, and how you said it," and so forth, do most subjects provide the kind of detail needed to construct rich and reliable prototypes. Unfortunately, the prompts may have contributed to the narrative structure subsequently derived from subjects' accounts and summarized in Figure 1.9. Subjects seemed to find the narrative structure implicit in the questionnaire natural and comfortable, but that may be due as much to the generality of story grammars (Mandler, 1984) as to the particular organization of emotion knowledge. In other words, we cannot be sure that natural emotion accounts have a predictable antecedents/responses/self-control structure independent of our questioning procedure. This obviously deserves further study.

Second, we encountered some difficulty in determining the appropriate level of abstraction at which to code particular features of emotion accounts. We noticed, after gaining some experience with our methods, that we were coding antecedents at a fairly abstract level, whereas we were coding behavioral responses, facial expressions, and physiological reactions more concretely. Evidently, there are many more ways for an environmental event to bear on a person's motives than there are of expressing emotional reactions. If we were to code every specific source of joy, sadness, anger, fear, and love in its own terms, we would have a nearly infinite list of all of life's experiences. Because such a list would be impossible to compile, investigators are forced to impose abstract coding categories on the specific elements mentioned in subjects' accounts. Comparisons of results from different studies would be greatly facilitated if the studies were similar in the level of abstraction adopted when coding protocols. One goal of future research, then, should be to develop explicit guidelines regarding the most appropriate levels of abstraction to be used in coding various features.

Extensions and Applications

Future research on the prototype approach to emotion knowledge might proceed in several directions, four of which we will mention here.

The prototype approach suggests that prototypes of subordinate-level emotions are more similar to the basic-level prototype with which they are associated than to any of the other basic-level prototypes. This is a testable implication of the approach. We anticipate, however, that certain subordinate-level emotions—the ones that facial expression researchers have called *blends* (e.g., Ekman et al., 1982b)—will prove related to more than one basic-level prototype.

The emotion *hurt*, for example, although it appears within the sadness cluster in Figure 1.1, seems to be a blend of sadness and anger. (We say this on the basis of its appearance in descriptions of both sadness and anger in Study 2 and on the basis of a pilot study of hurt itself.) A person feels hurt, according to subjects' accounts, when he or she has been wronged in a way that warrants anger (i.e., in a way that is unfair, inappropriate given agreed-upon roles or rules) but believes that the offender does not care enough to rectify matters, even if a reasonable objection were to be raised (cf. de Rivera, 1977). Not surprisingly, hurt is an emotion mentioned more frequently by people who perceive themselves to be the weaker (less potent) party in a relationship.

Longing and sympathy, two more examples of blended emotion categories, seem to refer to mixtures of sadness and love—in one rase, a painful feeling related to separation from a loved one; in the other, a feeling of sadness for a person we care about. In other words, these emotion categories share antecedents—and perhaps responses as well—with both love and sadness.

Similar analyses could be made of states such as jealousy and envy, which appear in the anger cluster in Figure 1.1 but have been defined by researchers as mixed emotions that occur in certain kinds of relationship situations (e.g., Bringle &

Buunk, 1985). Prototype methods should prove useful in delineating the precise blended composition of mental representations of such states.

A prototype analysis of emotion knowledge may have implications for models of everyday processing of emotion-related information. Prototype researchers have already shown, in a variety of content domains, that both the vertical and the horizontal dimensions of category hierarchies have predictable effects on information processing.

Regarding the vertical dimension, the claim that the emotion hierarchy contains a basic level implies that perception, cognition, and communication tend to occur at this level, unless there are special reasons for being either more detailed or more general. It should be possible to show that the basic level of emotion knowledge is the level of choice for maximizing information about an emotional event while maintaining cognitive and communicational economy (Cantor & Mischel, 1979a; Rosch, Mervis, Gray, Johnson, & Boyes-Braem, 1976). Moreover, stimuli described in basic-level terms (e.g., "an angry person") should prove more cognitively vivid or imaginable than those described in superordinate terms (e.g., "a person who is experiencing negative emotion") (Rosch, 1978). Rosch, Mervis, Gray, Johnson, and Boyes-Braem (1976) found that basic-level, but not superordinate, categories are associated with scripted or programmed sequences of actions (motor programs). Thus, people can probably say how they typically feel and act in response to another's anger, fear, or happiness (e.g., by protecting the self, protecting or comforting the fearful person, or joining the fun, respectively), but they cannot do so for more abstract levels of the emotion hierarchy.

Rosch (1978) suggested that "objects may be first seen or recognized as members of their basic category, and . . . only with the aid of additional processing can they be identified as members of their superordinate or subordinate category" (p. 35). When people encounter an emotional person in real life, fiction, or film, they are likely to notice first that the person is angry, sad, or whatever, and then only with additional cognitive work realize that the person is actually annoyed, disappointed, and so forth. Regarding memory, a subject who hears or reads about someone's dejection, panic, or delight might be expected to recall later that the person was sad, afraid, or happy.

Regarding the horizontal dimension, prototypicality has been shown to affect "virtually all of the major dependent variables used as measures in psychological research" (Rosch, 1978, p. 38). Items are judged to be category members faster, more frequently, and with greater certainty the more prototypical they are (e.g., McCloskey & Glucksberg, 1978; Rosch, Simpson, & Miller, 1976). In the emotion domain, therefore, subjects should be quicker and more confident in judging that the emotion experienced by a fictional character is sadness, for example, if the story contains features that are highly prototypical of the sadness category than if the elements of the story are less prototypical. Moreover, when a perceiver has incomplete information about a person or event that has been identified as a category member, he or she often fills gaps in the available information by inserting features contained in the category prototype (e.g., Bartlett, 1932; Cantor & Mischel, 1977, 1979b; Schank & Abelson, 1977). In the emotion domain we would expect unpresented but prototypical features of a particular emotion category to intrude into subjects' recall or recognition memory for information about an episode in which that emotion was experienced.

CROSS-CULTURAL COMPARISONS OF EVERYDAY CONCEPTIONS OF EMOTION

Psychologists have documented the cross-cultural universality of facial expressions associated with certain emotions, including fear, sadness, anger, surprise, and happiness (e.g., Ekman et al., 1982), and the pervasiveness, if not universality, of the two- or three-dimensional structure that seems to underlie or characterize similarity ratings of various emotions. Despite these hints that fundamental characteristics of emotion knowledge, and of emotions themselves, are quite similar across cultures, some social scientists have argued that emotions are "socially constructed" (Averill, 1982) or, at least, that conceptions of emotion differ substantially across cultures (Lutz, 1982). Kagan (1984), for example, reasoned that

> Because each emotional name is a classification category, the extraordinary diversity among cultures in presuppositions and values should be accompanied by differences in how feeling states are categorized. . . . The influence of culture on the choice of emotional terms is nicely illustrated in C. Lutz's (1982) study of the emotion words used by the approximately five hundred people living on the small island atoll of Ifaluk, located in the Western Caroline Islands of Micronesia. (p. 166)

Careful study of Lutz's data indicates, however, that her results, based on similarity sorts of 31 words by only 15 natives of Ifaluk, are remarkably similar to those summarized in Figure 1.1. Hierarchical cluster analysis of her data yielded five basic-level categories (although she did not use that term), four of which clearly parallel ours. Her first cluster, *emotions of good fortune*, is very similar to a combination of our love and joy clusters; she translated words in this category as pride/love, playful happiness, happiness/excitement, and liking, for example. Lutz's second cluster, *emotions of danger*, clearly corresponds to our fear cluster. The third, *emotions of connection and loss*, corresponds to many of the terms in our sadness cluster. Her fourth cluster contains words translated as hate, irritation, short-temper, justified anger, frustration/grief, and jealousy/competitiveness, among others; clearly, this corresponds to our anger cluster. Only Lutz's fifth cluster, which she called *emotions of inability*, fails to correspond to one of ours, but it is also, by her account, the least "unified" and so may prove unreliable.

Lutz's mistake was to compare a cluster analysis of her Ifaluk data with conclusions drawn from multidimensional scaling studies done in Western societies. As we have shown in relation to Study 1, these two methods produce different-looking results even when the same data are used. If cross-cultural studies were done with sufficiently large samples of emotion terms and subjects, and if the data were analyzed by both hierarchical cluster analysis and multidimensional scaling, it would be more feasible to draw valid conclusions about cross-cultural similarities and differences. We expect that the basic level of the emotion hierarchy will look more or less the same across cultures, whereas the subordinate level will look rather different. To the extent that basic-level emotions are biologically based, they should be the same everywhere (although self-control rules may vary); subordinate-level emotion concepts, in contrast, because they seem designed to designate intensity levels and fairly specific situational antecedents, could differ substantially across cultures. (For relevant data, see Scherer et al., 1983.)

DEVELOPMENT OF EMOTION KNOWLEDGE

Knowledge about emotions develops dramatically between birth and adulthood. By early childhood, children establish a rudimentary emotion vocabulary (Bretherton & Beeghly, 1982), can recognize and label emotions based on photographed facial expressions (Reichenbach & Masters, 1983), and know something about both the situational antecedents of some of the basic emotions (Harter, personal communication, 1985; Masters & Carlson, 1984) and about methods for controlling the: expression of negative emotions (Masters & Carlson, 1984; Saarni, 1979, 1984). They also know, as early as 8 years of age, how to sort emotion words in ways that produce the ubiquitous evaluation and intensity dimensions (Russell & Ridgeway, 1983). With age, these areas of knowledge expand, and older children become capable of inferring the interpretations that a person must have made of a situation in order to have reacted emotionally in a particular way (Masters & Carlson, 1984).

Developmental research (e.g., Anglin, 1977; Blewitt & Durkin, 1982; Mervis & Crisafi, 1982; Rosch, Mervis, Gray, Johnson, & Boyes-Braem, 1976) indicates that the usual sequence of acquiring knowledge about categorization hierarchies is basic level first, superordinate and subordinate levels later. As mentioned earlier, there is evidence in a recent article by Bretherton and Beeghly (1982) that what we have identified as basic-level emotion terms are acquired first. We expect, therefore, that a more complete developmental study would reveal that the emotion lexicon grows with age as children (and possibly adults) learn to use more, and more subtly nuanced, subordinate-level terms and more abstract superordinate terms (e.g., feeling good) but that the underlying basic-level structure remains the same.

Harter and her colleagues (personal communication, 1985) have interviewed children between the ages of 4 and 12, asking them which emotions they can name and what causes these emotions. The 4-year-olds spontaneously mentioned only happy, sad, mad, and scared, but could talk about love if asked to, although they did not usually mention it themselves. What is most striking about the children's descriptions of emotion antecedents is how conceptually similar they are across the age range studied by the Harter group, and between their subjects and our own. Specifics change with age: Broken toys, monsters, and being tickled or bitten give way to social and achievement failures and successes and to perceived injustices of various kinds. Viewed in terms of abstractly conceptualized antecedents, however, continuity is more evident than change.

Other research indicates that young children first learn to identify others' emotional states from facial expressions and only gradually learn to infer them from knowledge of antecedents (Reichenbach & Masters, 1983). Moreover, very young children seem to have little explicit knowledge of procedures for controlling emotional responses, but by early elementary school age they can talk about controlling feelings by taking direct action (e.g., "wipe the tears off," "just hold the mad feelings in," "cuddle against my dolly"), and by age 10 or 12 by altering their own appraisals (e.g., "think to myself that [the situation] is not that bad," "think about what you're doing—why you're sad and how not to be that way"; Johnson, 1983). It seems likely, therefore, that children must in some sense know about particular emotion components—first expressions and, later, interpretive antecedents—before being able to exercise self-control over them (Saarni, 1984).

Conclusion

The prototype approach to emotion knowledge promises to contribute in several ways to the understanding of emotion representation in everyday life. Results of the two studies reported here are highly compatible with the approach; the emotion lexicon can be reasonably portrayed as a hierarchy with a basic level, and both typical and actual emotion episodes can be meaningfully characterized in terms of basic-emotion prototypes. The many subordinate-level emotion terms seem to specify the eliciting context and intensity level of one of the five or six basic-level emotions or to indicate blends of basic-level emotions. The prototype approach should be useful in determining how emotion-related information is processed in a variety of real-life situations, including social interactions. It should also clarify and provide a means of integrating findings concerning cross-age and cross-cultural similarities and differences in emotion concepts. As further research is conducted on ordinary people's implicit models of emotion processes, these models may provide new and valuable clues about the nature of emotion itself.

REFERENCES

Andersen, S. M. (1984). Self-knowledge and social inference: II. The diagnosticity of cognitive/affective and behavioral data. *Journal of Personality and Social Psychology, 46,* 294–307.

Anglin, J. M. (1977). *Word, object, and conceptual development.* New York: Norton.

Arnold, M. B. (1960). *Emotion and personality.* New York: Columbia University Press.

Averill, J. R. (1975). A semantic atlas of emotional concepts. *JSAS: Catalog of Selected Documents in Psychology, 5,* 330. (Ms. No. 421)

Averill, J. R. (1982). *Anger and aggression: An essay on emotion.* New York: Springer-Verlag.

Bartlett, F. C. (1932). *Remembering.* Cambridge: Cambridge University Press.

Bem, D. J. (1972). Self-perception theory. In L. Berkowitz (Ed.), *Advances in experimental social psychology* (Vol. 6, pp. 1–62). New York: Academic Press.

Blewitt, P, & Durkin, M. (1982). Age, typicality, and task effects on categorization of objects. *Perceptual and Motor Skills, 55,* 435–445.

Bobrow, D. G., & Norman, D. A. (1975). Some principles of memory schemata. In A. Collins & D. G. Bobrow (Eds.), *Representation and understanding: Studies in cognitive science* (pp. 131–149). New York: Academic Press.

Boucher, J. D., & Brandt, M. E. (1981). Judgment of emotion: American and Malay antecedents. *Journal of Cross-Cultural Psychology, 12,* 272–283.

Bower, G. H., & Cohen, P. R. (1982). Emotional influences in memory and thinking: Data and theory. In M. S. Clark & S. T. Fiske (Eds.), *Affect and cognition: The Seventeenth Annual Carnegie Symposium on Cognition* (pp. 291–331). Hillsdale, NJ: Erlbaum.

Brandt, M. E., & Boucher, J. D. (1984, August). *Judgments of emotions from antecedent situations in three cultures.* Paper presented at the meeting of the International Congress of Cross-Cultural Psychology, Acapulco, Mexico.

Bretherton, I., & Beeghly, M. (1982). Talking about internal states: The acquisition of an explicit theory of mind. *Developmental Psychology, 18,* 906–912.

Bringle, R. G., & Buunk, B. (1985). Jealousy and social behavior: A review of person, relationship, and situational determinants. In P Shaver (Ed.), *Review of personality and social psychology* (Vol. 6, pp. 241–264). Beverly Hills, CA: Sage.

Cannon, W. B. (1927). The James–Lange theory of emotions: A critical examination and an alternative theory. *American Journal of Psychology, 3,* 106–124.

Cantor, N., & Mischel, W. (1977). Traits as prototypes: Effects on recognition memory. *Journal of Personality and Social Psychology, 35,* 38–48.

Cantor, N., & Mischel, W. (1979a). Prototypes in person perception. In L. Berkowitz (Ed.), *Advances in experimental social psychology* (Vol. 12, pp. 3–52). New York: Academic Press.

Cantor, N., & Mischel, W. (1979b). Prototypicality and personality: Effects on free recall and personality impressions. *Journal of Research in Personality, 13,* 187–205.

Cantor, N., Mischel, W., & Schwartz, J. (1982). A prototype analysis of psychological situations. *Cognitive Psychology, 14,* 45–77.

Cantor, N., Smith, E., French, R. de S., & Mezzich, J. (1980). Psychiatric diagnosis as prototype categorization. *Journal of Abnormal Psychology, 89,* 181–193.

Chaplin, W. F, John, O. P., & Goldberg, L. R. (1986). *On the distinction between states and traits: An empirically based prototype model.* Eugene, OR: Oregon Research Institute.

Conway, M. A., & Bekerian, D. A. (1985). *Organization of emotional knowledge.* Unpublished manuscript, MRC Applied Psychology Unit, Cambridge, England.

Davis, K. E., & Todd, M. J. (1982). Friendship and love relationships. In K. E. Davis (Ed.), *Advances in descriptive psychology* (Vol. 2, pp. 79–122). Greenwich, CT: JAI Press.

Davitz, J. (1969). *The language of emotion.* New York: Academic Press.

de Rivera, J. (1977). A structural theory of the emotions. *Psychological Issues, 10*(4, Monograph No. 40).

de Rivera, J. (Ed.). (1981a). *Conceptual encounter: A method for the exploration of human experience.* Washington, DC: University Press of America.

de Rivera, J. (1981b). The structure of anger. In J. de Rivera (Ed.), *Conceptual encounter: A method for the exploration of human experience* (pp. 35–81). Washington, DC: University Press of America.

Ekman, P. (1984). Expression and the nature of emotion. In K. S. Scherer & P. Ekman (Eds.), *Approaches to emotion* (pp. 319–343). Hillsdale, NJ: Erlbaum.

Ekman, P., Friesen, W. V., & Ellsworth, P. C. (1982a). What are the similarities and differences in facial behavior across cultures? In P. Ekman (Ed.), *Emotion in the human face* (2nd ed., pp. 128–143). Cambridge: Cambridge University Press.

Ekman, P., Friesen, W. V., & Ellsworth, P. C. (1982b). What emotion categories or dimensions can observers judge from facial behavior? In P. Ekman (Ed.), *Emotion in the human face* (2nd ed., pp. 39–55). Cambridge: Cambridge University Press.

Ekman, P., Levenson, R. W, & Friesen, W. V. (1983). Autonomic nervous system activity distinguishes between emotions. *Science, 221,* 1208–1210.

Ekman, P., Sorensen, E. R., & Friesen, W. V. (1969). Pancultural elements in facial displays of emotion. *Science, 164,* 86–88.

Epstein, S. (1984). Controversial issues in emotion theory. In P. Shaver (Ed.), *Review of personality and social psychology* (Vol. 5, pp. 64–88). Beverly Hills, CA: Sage.

Everitt, B. (1980). *Cluster analysis* (2nd ed.). New York: Halstead Press.

Fehr, B., & Russell, J. A. (1984). Concept of emotion viewed from a prototype perspective. *Journal of Experimental Psychology: General, 113,* 464–486.

Fehr, B., Russell, J. A., & Ward, L. M. (1982). Prototypicality of emotions: A reaction time study. *Bulletin of the Psychonomic Society, 20,* 253–254.

Fillenbaum, S., & Rapaport, A. (1971). *Structures in the subjective lexicon.* New York: Academic Press.

Franks, J. J., & Bransford, J. D. (1971). Abstraction of visual patterns. *Journal of Experimental Psychology, 90,* 65–74.

Goffman, E. (1959). *The presentation of self in everyday life.* Garden City, NY: Doubleday/Anchor.

Hamilton, D. L. (1981). *Cognitive processes in stereotyping and intergroup behavior.* Hillsdale, NJ: Erlbaum.

Hampson, S. E., John, O. P., & Goldberg, L. R. (1986). Category breadth and hierarchical structure in personality: Studies of asymmetries in judgments of trait implications. *Journal of Personality and Social Psychology, 51,* 37–54.

Harris, P. (1985). What children know about the situations that provoke emotion. In M. Lewis & C. Saarni (Eds.), *The socialization of affect* (pp. 161–185). New York: Plenum Press.

Hartigan, J. A. (1981). Cluster analysis. In W. J. Dixon (Ed.), *BMDP statistical software 1981* (pp. 447–463). Berkeley: University of California Press.

Hochschild, A. (1983). *The managed heart: The commercialization of human feeling.* Berkeley: University of California Press.

Horowitz, L. M., French, R. de S., & Anderson, C. A. (1982). The prototype of a lonely person. In L. A. Peplau & D. Perlman (Eds.), *Loneliness: A sourcebook of current theory, research and therapy* (pp. 183–205). New York: Wiley-Interscience.

Horowitz, L. M., Wright, J. C., Lowenstein, E., & Farad, H. W. (1981). The prototype as a construct in abnormal psychology: 1. A method for deriving prototypes. *Journal of Abnormal Psychology, 90,* 568–574.

Isen, A. M. (1984). Toward understanding the role of affect in cognition. In R. S. Wyer, Jr. & T. K. Srull (Eds.), *Handbook of social cognition* (Vol. 3, pp. 179–236). Hillsdale, NJ: Erlbaum.

Izard, C. E. (1977). *Human emotions.* New York: Plenum Press.

Johnson, D. L. (1983). *The development of children's theories of emotional control.* Unpublished master's thesis, University of Denver, CO.

Jones, E. E., & Nisbett, R. E. (1972). The actor and the observer: Divergent perceptions of the causes of behavior. In E. E. Jones, D. E. Kanouse, H. H. Kelley, R. E. Nisbett, S. Valins, & B. Weiner (Eds.), *Attribution: Perceiving the causes of behavior* (pp. 79–94). Morristown, NJ: General Learning Press.

Jones, E. E., & Pittman, T. S. (1982). Toward a general theory of strategic self-presentation. In J. Suls (Ed.), *Psychological perspectives on the self* (pp. 231–262). Hillsdale, NJ: Erlbaum.

Kagan, J. (1984). *The nature of the child.* New York: Basic Books.

Kelley, H. H. (1983). Love and commitment. In H. H. Kelley, E. Berscheid, A. Christensen, J. H. Harvey, T. L. Huston, G. Levinger, E. McClintock, L. A. Peplau, & D. R. Peterson (Eds.), *Close relationships* (pp. 265–314). New York: W. H. Freeman.

Kelley, H. H. (1984). Affect in interpersonal relations. In P. Shaver (Ed.), *Review of personality and social psychology* (Vol. 5, pp. 89–115). Beverly Hills, CA: Sage.

Kruskal, J. B. (1964). Nonmetric multidimensional scaling. *Psychometrika, 29,* 1–27, 115–129.

Lakoff, G., & Kovecses, Z. (1983). *The cognitive model danger inherent in American English* (Report No. 10). Berkeley, CA: Berkeley Cognitive Science Program.

Lazarus, R. S. (1985). *Classic issues about emotion from the perspective of a relational and cognitive theory.* Paper presented at the meeting of the Summer Institute on Cognition-Emotion Relations, Winter Park, CO.

Lutz, C. (1982). The domain of emotion words on Ifaluk. *American Ethnologist, 9,* 113–128.

Mandler, J. M. (1984). *Stories, scripts, and scenes: Aspects of schema theory.* Hillsdale, NJ: Erlbaum.

Maratsos, M., & Chalkley, M. A. (1980). The internal language of children's syntax: The ontogenesis and representation of syntactic categories. In K. Nelson (Ed.), *Children's language* (Vol. 2, pp. 127–214). New York: Gardner.

Masters, J., & Carlson, C. R. (1984). Children's and adults' understanding of the causes and consequences of emotional states. In C. E. Izard, J. Kagan, & R. B. Zajonc (Eds.), Emotions, cognition, and behavior (pp. 438–463). Cambridge: Cambridge University Press.

McCloskey, M. E., & Glucksberg, S. (1978). Natural categories: Well defined or fuzzy sets? *Memory and Cognition, 6,* 462–472.

Mervis, C. B., & Crisafi, M. A. (1982). Order of acquisition of subordinate-, basic-, and superordinate-level categories. *Child Development, 53,* 258–266.

Ortony, A., & Clore, G. L. (1981). Disentangling the affective lexicon. *Proceedings of the Third Annual Conference of the Cognitive Science Society* (pp. 90–95). Berkeley, CA: Cognitive Science Society.

Osgood, C. E., May, W. H., & Miron, M. S. (1975). *Cross-cultural universals of affective meaning.* Urbana: University of Illinois Press.

Osgood, C. E., Suci, G. J., & Tannenbaum, P. H. (1957). *The measurement of meaning.* Urbana: University of Illinois Press.

Plutchik, R. (1962). *The emotions: Facts, theories, and a new model.* New York: Random House.

Plutchik, R. (1980). *Emotion: A psychoevolutionary synthesis.* New York: Harper & Row.

Posner, M. I., & Keele, S. W (1968). On the genesis of abstract ideas. *Journal of Experimental Psychology, 77,* 353–363.

Posner, M. L., & Keele, S. W. (1970). Retention of abstract ideas. *Journal of Experimental Psychology, 83,* 304–308.

Reichenbach, L., & Masters, J. C. (1983). Children's use of expressive and contextual cues in judgments of emotion. *Child Development, 54,* 993–1004.

Reitman, J. S., & Bower, G. H. (1973). Storage and later recognition of exemplars of concepts. *Cognitive Psychology, 4,* 328–350.

Rosch, E. (1973). On the internal structure of perceptual and semantic categories. In T. E. Moore (Ed.), *Cognitive development and the acquisition of language* (pp. 111–144). New York: Academic Press.

Rosch, E. (1975). Cognitive representations of semantic categories. *Journal of Experimental Psychology: General, 104,* 192–233.

Rosch, E. (1978). Principles of categorization. In E. Rosch & B. B. Lloyd (Eds.), *Cognition and categorization* (pp. 27–48). Hillsdale, NJ: Erlbaum.

Rosch, E., & Mervis, C. B. (1975). Family resemblances: Studies in the internal structure of categories. *Cognitive Psychology, 7,* 573–605.

Rosch, E., Mervis, C. B., Gray, W D., Johnson, D. M., & Boyes-Braem, P. (1976). Basic objects in natural categories. *Cognitive Psychology, 8,* 382–439.

Rosch, E., Simpson, C., & Miller, R. S. (1976). Structural

bases of typicality effects. *Journal of Experimental Psychology: Human Perception and Performance, 2,* 491–502.

Roseman, I. J. (1984). Cognitive determinants of emotion: A structural theory. In P. Shaver (Ed.), *Review of personality and social psychology* (Vol. 5, pp. 11–36). Beverly Hills, CA: Sage.

Rumelhart, D. E., & Ortony, A. (1977). The representation of knowledge in memory. In R. C. Anderson, R. J. Spiro, & W. E. Montague (Eds.), *Schooling and the acquisition of knowledge* (pp. 99–135). Hillsdale, NJ: Erlbaum.

Russell, J. A. (1978). Evidence of convergent validity on the dimensions of affect. *Journal of Personality and Social Psychology, 36,* 1152–1168.

Russell, J. A. (1979). Affective space is bipolar. *Journal of Personality and Social Psychology, 37,* 345–356.

Russell, J. A. (1980). A circumplex model of affect. *Journal of Personality and Social Psychology, 39,* 1161-1178.

Russell, J. A. (1983). Pancultural aspects of the human conceptual organization of emotions. *Journal of Personality and Social Psychology, 45,* 1281–1288.

Russell, J. A., & Mehrabian, A. (1977). Evidence for a three-factor theory of emotions. *Journal of Research in Personality, 11,* 273–294.

Russell, J. A., & Ridgeway, D. (1983). Dimensions underlying children's emotion concepts. *Developmental Psychology, 19,* 795–804.

Saarni, C. (1979). Children's understanding of display rules for expressive behavior. *Developmental Psychology, 15,* 424–429.

Saarni, C. (1984). An observational study of children's attempts to monitor their expressive behavior. *Child Development, 55,* 1504–1513.

Schachter, S. (1971). *Emotion, obesity, and crime.* New York: Academic Press.

Schank, R., & Abelson, R. (1977). *Scripts, plans, goals, and understanding.* Hillsdale, NJ: Erlbaum.

Scherer, K. R. (1984). Emotion as a multicomponent process: A model and some cross-cultural data. In P. Shaver (Ed.), *Review of personality and social psychology* (Vol. 5, pp. 37–63). Beverly Hills, CA: Sage.

Scherer, K. R., Summerfield, A. B., & Wallbott, H. G. (1983). Cross-national research on antecedents and components of emotion: A progress report. *Social Science Information, 22,* 355–385.

Schlosberg, H. (1952). The description of facial expressions in terms of two dimensions. *Journal of Experimental Psychology, 44,* 229–235.

Schlosberg, H. (1954). Three dimensions of emotion. *Psychological Review, 61,* 81–88.

Schwartz, J. C., & Shaver, P. (1987). Emotions and emotion knowledge in inter personal relations. In W. Jones & D. Perlman (Eds.), *Advances in personal relationships* (Vol. 1, pp. 197–241). Greenwich, JAI Press.

Seligman, M. E. P. (1975). *Helplessness: On depression, development, and death.* San Francisco: Freeman.

Smith, C., & Ellsworth, P. (1985). Patterns of cognitive appraisal in emotion. *Journal of Personality and Social Psychology, 48,* 813–838.

Smith, E. E., Shoben, E. J., & Rips, L. J. (1974). Structure and process in semantic memory: A featural model for semantic decisions. *Psychological Review, 81,* 214–241.

Sternberg, R. J. (1986). A triangular theory of love. *Psychological Review, 93,* 119–135.

Sternberg, R. J., & Grajek, S. (1984). The nature of love. *Journal of Personality and Social Psychology, 47,* 233–464.

Storms, M. D. (1973). Videotape and the attribution process: Reversing actors' and observers' points of view. *Journal of Personality and Social Psychology, 27,* 165–175.

Sullivan, B. N., & Boucher J. D. (1984, August). *Commonalities of meaning in antecedents to emotions across four cultures.* Paper presented at the meeting of the International Congress of Cross-Cultural Psychology, Acapulco, Mexico.

Tiller, D. K., & Harris, P. L. (1984). *Prototypicality of emotion concepts: A discussion of normative data.* Unpublished manuscript, Oxford University, Oxford, England.

Tomkins, S. S. (1984). Affect theory. In K. S. Scherer & P. Ekman (Eds.), *Approaches to emotion* (pp. 163–195). Hillsdale, NJ: Erlbaum.

Tversky, B., & Hemenway, K. (1983). Categories of environmental scenes. *Cognitive Psychology, 15,* 121–149.

Tversky, A., & Kahneman, D. (1982). Judgments of and by representativeness. In D. Kahneman, P. Slovic, & A. Tversky (Eds.), *Judgment under uncertainty: Heuristics and biases* (pp. 84–98). New York Cambridge University Press.

Walster, E., & Walster, G. W. (1978). *A new look at love.* Reading, MA: Addison-Wesley.

Weiner, B. (1985). An attributional theory of achievement motivation and emotion. *Psychological Review, 92,* 548–573.

Wilson, T. D., & Stone, J. I. (1985). Limitations of self-knowledge: More on telling more than we can know. In P. Shaver (Ed.), *Review of personality and social psychology* (Vol. 6, pp. 167–183). Beverly Hills, CA: Sage.

Young, F. W., & Lewyckyj, R. (1979). *ALSCAL 4 user's guide* (2nd ed.). Chapel Hill, NC: Data Analysis and Theory Associates.

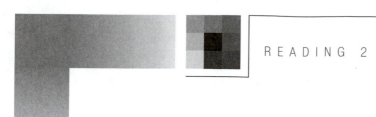

READING 2

The Laws of Emotion

Nico H. Frijda • University of Amsterdam, The Netherlands

It is argued that emotions are lawful phenomena and thus can be described in terms of a set of laws of emotion. These laws result from the operation of emotion mechanisms that are accessible to intentional control to only a limited extent. The law of situational meaning, the law of concern, the law of reality, the laws of change, habituation and comparative feeling, and the law of hedonic asymmetry are proposed to describe emotion elicitation; the law of conservation of emotional momentum formulates emotion persistence; the law of closure expresses the modularity of emotion; and the laws of care for consequence, of lightest load, and of greatest gain pertain to emotion regulation.

For a long time, emotion was an underprivileged area in psychology. It was not regarded as a major area of scientific psychological endeavor that seemed to deserve concerted research efforts or receive them.

Things have changed over the last 10 or so years. Emotion has become an important domain with a coherent body of theory and data. It has developed to such an extent that its phenomena can be described in terms of a set of laws, the laws of emotion, that I venture to describe here.

Formulating a set of laws of emotion implies not only that the study of emotion has developed sufficiently to do so but also that emotional phenomena are indeed lawful. It implies that emotions emerge, wax, and wane according to rules in strictly determined fashion. To argue this is a secondary objective of this article. Emotions are lawful. When experiencing emotions, people are subject to laws. When filled by emotions, they are manifesting the workings of laws.

There is a place for obvious a priori reservations here. Emotions and feelings are often considered the most idiosyncratic of psychological phenomena, and they suggest human freedom at its clearest. The mysticism of ineffability and freedom that surrounds emotions may be one reason why the psychology of emotion and feeling has advanced so slowly over the last 100 years. This mysticism is largely unfounded, and the freedom of feeling is an illusion. For one thing the notion of freedom of feeling runs counter to the traditional wisdom that human beings are enslaved by their passions. For another, the laws of emotion may help us to discern that simple, universal, moving forces operate behind the complex, idiosyncratic movements of feeling, in the same way that the erratic path of an ant, to borrow Simon's (1973) well-known parable, manifests the simple structure of a simple animal's mind.

The word *law* may give rise to misunderstanding. When formulating "laws" in this article, I am discussing what are primarily empirical regularities. These regularities—or putative regularities—are, however, assumed to rest on underlying causal mechanisms that generate them. I am suggesting that the laws of emotion are grounded in mechanisms that are not of a voluntary nature and that are only partially under voluntary control. Not only emotions obey the laws; we obey them. We are subject to our emotions, and we cannot engender emotions at will.

The laws of emotion that I will discuss are not all equally well established. Not all of them originate in solid evidence, nor are all equally supported by it. To a large extent, in fact, to list the laws of emotion is to list a program of research. However, the laws provide a coherent picture of emotional responding, which suggests that such a research program might be worthwhile.

The Law of Situational Meaning

What I mean by laws of emotion is best illustrated by the "Constitution" of emotion, the *law of situational meaning: Emotions arise in response to the meaning structures of given situations; different emotions arise in response to different meaning structures*. Emotions are dictated by the meaning structure of events in a precisely determined fashion.

On a global plane, this law refers to fairly obvious and almost trivial regularities. Emotions tend to be elicited by particular types of event. Grief is elicited by personal loss, anger by insults or frustrations, and so forth. This obviousness should not obscure the fact that regularity and mechanism are involved. Emotions, quite generally, arise in response to events that are important to the individual, and which importance he or she appraises in some way. Events that satisfy the individual's goals, or promise to do so, yield positive emotions; events that harm or threaten the individual's concerns lead to negative emotions; and emotions are elicited by novel or unexpected events.

Input some event with its particular kind of meaning; out comes an emotion of a particular kind. That is the law of situational meaning. In goes loss, and out comes grief. In goes a frustration or an offense, and out comes anger. Of course, the law does not apply in this crude manner. It is meanings and the subject's appraisals that count—that is, the relationship between events and the subject's concerns, and not events as such. Thus, in goes a personal loss that is felt as irremediable, and out comes grief, with a high degree of probability. In goes a frustration or an offense for which someone else is to blame and could have avoided, and out comes anger—almost certainly. The outputs are highly probable, but are not absolutely certain because the inputs can still be perceived in different fashions. One can view serious, irremediable personal loss as unavoidable, as in the na-

ture of things; there will be resignation then instead of grief. Frustration or offense can be seen as caused by someone powerful who may have further offenses in store, and fear then is likely to supplant anger as the emotional response. These subtleties, rather than undermining the law of situational meaning, underscore it. Emotions change when meanings change. Emotions are changed when events are viewed differently. Input is changed, and output changes accordingly.

The substance of this law was advanced by Arnold (1960) and Lazarus (1966). Evidence is accumulating that it is valid and that a number of subsidiary laws—for the elicitation of fear, of anxiety, of joy, and so forth—can be subsumed under it. The evidence is indirect because it consists mainly of correlations between subjects' reports of their emotional states and their conscious appraisals of events, which are not faithful reflections of the cognitive antecedents. Still, the correlations are strong (see, e.g., Frijda, 1987; Smith & Ellsworth, 1987) and suggest mechanisms. In fact, a computer program has been written that takes descriptions of event appraisals as its input and that outputs plausible guesses of the emotion's names. It shows the beginnings of success. When given the descriptions by 30 subjects of affective states corresponding to 32 emotion labels, the computer achieved a hit rate of 31% for the first choice and of 71% for the first five choices (with chance percentages of 3% and 17%, respectively; Frijda & Swagerman, 1987).

The law of situational meaning provides the overarching framework to organize findings on the cognitive variables that account for the various emotions and their intensity (see also Ortony, Clore, & Collins, 1988). These cognitive variables pertain not merely to how the individual thinks the events might affect him or her but also to how he or she might handle these events. They include secondary as well as primary appraisals, in Lazarus's (1966) terms. Fear involves uncertainty about one's ability to withstand or handle a given threat; grief involves certainty about the impossibility of reversing what happened. Analyses of self-reports and of the semantics of emotion terms offer converging conclusions on the major variables involved (see Scherer, 1988, for a review). Experimental studies corroborate the importance of many of them. Outcome uncertainty affects fear intensity (e.g., Epstein, 1973). Causal attributions have been shown to influence emotions of anger, pride, shame, and gratitude (Weiner, 1985). Unpredictability and uncontrollability contribute to the shaping of emotional response (Mineka & Hendersen, 1985). They may lead to depressive mood (Abramson, Seligman, & Teasdale, 1978) or reactance (Wortman & Brehm, 1975), depending on one's cognitive set. Erratic behavior in one's friends enrages when one is used to control and saddens when one is used to being controlled.

The workings of the law of situational meaning are not always transparent because they can be overridden by conscious control or by less conscious counterforces that I will discuss later. The law is most evident when resources for control and counterforces fail, such as in illness or exhaustion. Posttraumatic syndromes show that, under these conditions, almost every obstruction is a stimulus for angry irritation, every loss or failure one for sorrow, every uncertainty one for insecurity or anxiety, and almost every kindness one for tears.

Under more normal circumstances, too, the automatic workings of the law of situational meaning are evident. I mention two examples. One is "sentimentality," the almost compulsive emergence of tearful emotions when attachment themes are touched on in films or stories about miracle workers (Efran & Spangler, 1979), brides marrying in white, or little children who, after years of hardship, find a home or are lovingly accepted by their grandfathers. Tears are drawn, it seems, by a precise kind of sequence: Latent attachment concerns are awakened; expectations regarding their nonfulfillment are carefully evoked but held in abeyance; and then one is brusquely confronted with their fulfillment. The sequence is more potent than the observer's intellectual or emotional sophistication, a fact to which probably every reader can testify.

The other example concerns falling in love. Data from questionnaire studies (Rombouts, 1987) suggest that it is also triggered by a specific sequence of events, in which the qualities of the love-object are of minor importance. A person is ready to fall in love because of one of a number of reasons—loneliness, sexual need, dissatisfaction, or need of variety. An object then incites interest, again for one of a number of reasons, such as novelty, attractiveness, or mere proximity. Then give the person a moment of promise, a brief response from the object that suggests interest. It may be a confidence; it may be a single glance, such as a young girl may think she received from a pop star. Then give the person a brief lapse of time—anywhere between half an hour or half a day, the self-reports suggest—during which fantasies can develop. After that sequence, no more than a single confirmation, real or imagined, is needed to precipitate falling in love.

In the emergence of emotions people need not be explicitly aware of these meaning structures. They do their work, whether one knows it or not. One does not have to know that something is familiar in order to like it for that reason (Zajonc, 1980). Distinct awareness comes after the fact, if it comes at all.

Emotions

In the preceding section, I have not specified what I mean by "emotions" nor what it is that the laws of emotion involve. There is no consensus about the definition of emotion; one may quarrel endlessly about the word. The issue can be approached somewhat empirically, however, in bootstrapping fashion, by first assuming that what we loosely call "emotions" are responses to events that are important to the individual, and then by asking of what the responses to such events consist. Those responses are what the laws are about.

First of all, those responses—"emotions"—are subjective experiences. Their core is the experience of pleasure or pain. That core is embedded in the outcome of appraisal, the awareness of situational meaning structure. Emotional experience contains more, however, that emotion psychology seems to have almost forgotten.

Introspections produce a wealth of statements that refer to what I call "awareness of state of action readiness." Subjects report impulses to approach or avoid, desires to shout and sing or move, and the urge to retaliate; or, on occasion, they report an absence of desire to do anything, or a lack of interest, or feelings of loss of control (Davitz, 1969; Frijda, 1986, 1987).

What is interesting about these felt states of action readiness is that the kinds of states reported correspond to the kinds of state of action readiness that are manifest in overt behavior, as for instance, facial expression and organized action. Awareness of state of action readiness is a rough reflection of state of action readiness itself.

State of action readiness is a central notion in emotion. All emotions—all states, that is, that one would want to call "emotions"—involve some change in action readiness: (a) in readiness to go at it or away from it or to shift attention; (b) in sheer excitement, which can be understood as being ready for action but not knowing what action; or (c) in being stopped in one's tracks or in loss of interest. Several emotions can be unambiguously defined in terms of a particular form of action readiness; they can be defined in terms of some form of action tendency or some form of activation or lack thereof. This is the case with the emotions usually considered as primary or basic (Izard, 1977; Plutchik, 1980). Joy, for instance, is a sense of pleasure plus the urge toward exuberance and contact-seeking. Anger is a sense of displeasure plus the urge to do some of the things that remove or harm its agent. Shame is a sense of displeasure plus the compelling desire to disappear from view. Sadness is a sense of displeasure plus the ebbing away of any urge except for the desire for the lost object or opportunity, which is known to be unfulfillable. The identifications of particular emotions with particular forms of action readiness originate in the functional analysis of expressive behavior. Sadness, for example, characteristically is manifest in listlessness and the averted glance, or in the helplessness pattern of weeping. Fear is manifest in mixtures of avoidant, self-protective, and attentive facial patterns. The identifications correspond to self-reports of emotional awareness. For the more "basic" emotions, correspondence between reported states of action readiness and emotion labels is quite specific (Dijker, 1987; Frijda, 1987); discriminant analysis yielded 46.3% correct predictions in a study with 32 emotion labels (Kuipers, 1987).

Emotions other than the "basic" ones are not characterized by a particular form of action readiness; jealousy and guilt feelings are examples. Still, some change in action readiness is involved whenever a response is called an "emotion." Admiration makes one want to emulate, or follow, or sit motionless, or cry, if it is worth its salt as an emotion; the changes are called forth by the object's enthralling or overpowering aspects. The emotion evoked by the feeling of guilt makes one restlessly want to undo the deed or tends to paralyze one's actions and lets one impotently suffer; which form of action readiness ensues follows from what stares one in the face—the deed or one's worthlessness.

The law of situational meaning can now be phrased more precisely. Meaning structures are lawfully connected to forms of action readiness. Events appraised in terms of their meanings are the emotional piano player's finger strokes; available modes of action readiness are the keys that are tapped; changes in action readiness are the tones brought forth.

The keys, the available modes of action readiness, correspond to the behavior systems and general response modes with which humans are endowed. These include the programs for innate behavioral patterns, of which elementary defensive and aggressive behaviors, laughter and crying, and the universal facial expressions (Ekman, 1982) are elements. They further include the general activation or deactivation patterns of exuberance, undirected excitement, and apathetic response, and the pattern of freezing or inhibition. They also include the various autonomic and hormonal response patterns—those of orienting, of active or passive coping, and the like, described by the Laceys (Lacey & Lacey, 1970), Obrist (1981), and Mason (1975), among others. These physiological patterns form, so to speak, the logistic support of the action readiness changes involved. And last, the response modes include the action control changes that are manifest in behavioral interference and that we experience as preoccupation and urgency; sometimes, these are the only aspect of our change in action readiness that we feel or show.

The Law of Concern

The law of situational meaning has a necessary complement in the *law of concern: Emotions arise in response to events that are important to the individual's goals, motives, or concerns.* Every emotion hides a concern, that is, a more or less enduring disposition to prefer particular states of the world. A concern is what gives a particular event its emotional meaning. We suffer when ill befalls someone because, and as long as, we love that someone. We glow with pride upon success and are dejected upon failure when and because we strive for achievement, in general or in that particular trade. Emotions point to the presence of some concern. The concern may be different from one occurrence of an emotion to another. We fear the things we fear for many different reasons. Note that the law of concern joins different and even opposite emotions. One suffers when a cherished person is gravely ill; one feels joy at his or her fortune or recovery; one is angry at those who harm him or her. Emotions arise from the interaction of situational meanings and concerns.

One may question whether a concern can be found behind every single instance of emotion. It would not be meaningful to posit a "concern for the unexpected" behind startle (but, also, it may not be meaningful to regard startle as an emotion; cf. Ekman, Friesen, & Simons, 1985). But by and large, the law of concern holds and is of considerable value in understanding emotions. Why does someone get upset at the news of another person's illness? Because he or she seems to love that person. Why does someone feel such terrible jealousy? Because, perhaps, he or she yearns for continuous possession and symbiotic proximity. Emotions form the prime material in the exploration of an individual's concerns.

The Law of Apparent Reality

According to the law of situational meaning, emotions are dictated by the way a person perceives the situation. One aspect of this perception is particularly important for the elicitation of emotion. I will call it the situation's "apparent reality." Emotions are subject to the *law of apparent reality: Emotions are elicited by events appraised as real, and their intensity corresponds to the degree to which this is the case.*

What is taken to be real elicits emotions. What does not impress one as true and unavoidable elicits no emotion or a weaker one. The law applies to events taken to be real when in fact they are not. It also applies to events that are real but that are not taken seriously. Whatever is present counts; whatever lies merely in the future can be taken lightly or disregarded, however grim the prospects. Mere warnings usually are not heeded. Examples are found in the responses to nuclear energy dangers that tend to evoke emotions only when consequences are felt. Unrest arose when restrictions on milk consumption were imposed after Chernobyl. Symbolic information generally has weak impact, as compared to the impact of pictures and of events actually seen—the "vividness effect" discussed in social psychology (Fiske & Taylor, 1984). A photograph of one distressed child in Vietnam had more effect than reports about thousands killed. Although people have full knowledge

of the threat of nuclear war, they tend to remain cool under that threat, except for the emotions rising during a few weeks after the showing of a film such as *The Day After* (Fiske, 1987).

Examples abound from less dramatic contexts. Telling a phobic that spiders are harmless is useless when the phobic sees the crawling animal. Knowing means less than seeing. When someone tells us in a friendly fashion that she or he does not appreciate our attentions, we tend not to heed her or him. Words mean less than tone of voice. When someone steps on our toes, we get angry even when we know that he or she is not to blame. Feeling means more than knowing.

I call this the law of apparent reality and use the word *reality* to characterize the stimulus properties at hand; Ortony, Clore, and Collins (1988) extensively discuss the issue under the same heading. The preceding anecdotal examples are paralleled by experimental results. Bridger and Mandel (1964) showed that a conditioned fear response, established by the warning that shock would follow a signal light, extinguished at once when shock electrodes were removed. It did not, however, when a single strong shock reinforcement had actually been delivered. Conditioned electrodermal response persisted indefinitely after shock, in the same way that a smell of burning evokes a sense of panic in anyone who has ever been in a conflagration. The powerlessness of verbal reassurance to diminish phobic anxiety contrasts with the abatement of phobia sometimes obtained by "live modeling plus participation," that is, by making the subject actually touch the snake or spider after seeing a model do it (Bandura, 1977). Smaller effects, but still effects, are obtained by having the subject imagine touching the snake or spider, provided that true, vivid imagery is achieved (Lang, 1977).

The law of apparent reality applies to numerous instances of strong emotion in everyday life and explains important phenomena, such as the absence of strong emotions where one might have expected them. Grief dawns only gradually and slowly after personal loss. Emotions often do not arise when being told of loss, and the loss is merely known. They break through when the lost person is truly missed, when the arm reaches out in vain or the desire to communicate finds its target to be absent (Parkes, 1972). The law also accounts for the weakness of reason as opposed to the strength of passion. "Reason" refers to the consideration of satisfactions and pains that are far away and only symbolically mediated. "Passion" refers to the effects of the present, of what is actually here to entice or repel.

What is the source of the law of apparent reality? What do actual stimuli such as shock, fires, live encounters, truly missing someone, and actions such as touching a snake have in common? It is, I think, their "reality." Stimuli appraised as "real" include (a) unconditioned affective stimuli such as pain, startle stimuli, and perceived expressive behaviors (Lanzetta & Orr, 1986; Ohman & Dimberg, 1978); (b) sensory stimuli strongly associated to such stimuli; and (c) events involving the actual ineffectuality of actions, such as not receiving an answer to one's calls. Several guesses can be made as to why these are the emotionally effective stimuli; a plausible one is that the modes of action readiness are biological dispositions that need sensory stimuli as their unconditioned releasers. It is sensory stimulations that have the proper input format for the emotion process. Notice that vivid imagination, too, has the properties of "reality." It is capable of eliciting or abating strong emotions. Imagination, conceivably, serves to transform symbolic knowledge into emotionally effective stimulation. The effects of imaginal stimuli—fantasies, films, songs, pictures, stories— underline the major problem behind the law of apparent reality: to explain why one kind of cognition is not equivalent to another.

The Laws of Change, Habituation, and Comparative Feeling

The nature of events that elicit emotions must be still further specified because emotions obey the *law of change: Emotions are elicited not so much by the presence of favorable or unfavorable conditions, but by actual or expected changes in favorable or unfavorable conditions.* It is change that does it—change with respect to current adaptation level. Everyday examples of the importance of change abound. Subjective satisfactions, these days, are not superior to those in, say, 1937, when economic conditions were incomparably inferior. They probably are not superior to subjective satisfactions in any developing country that suffers no outright famine or oppression. Or, take the common observation that spouses who were taken for granted and were even felt to be sources of irrita-

tion are gravely missed after they die or leave. "One never stops to wonder, until a person's gone," as Dory Previn (1970) put it, "one never stops to wonder, 'til he's left and carried on."

The greater the change, the stronger the subsequent emotion. Having overcome uncertainty results in a pleasure of considerably larger magnitude than that produced by the same event without prior challenge or suspense. Basketball fans enjoy the victory of their team most when both teams' chances of winning are even (Ortony & Clore, 1988). Laughter generally follows what has been called the "suspense-mastery" or "arousal-safety" sequence (Rothbart, 1973): During infants' rough-and-tumble play, for instance, laughter is evoked only at the stage of development in which the event is just on the verge between being under control and being beyond control (Sroufe & Waters, 1976). A similar sequence accounts for the enjoyment of suspense in crime and adventure tales and perhaps even for that of mountain climbing and stunt riding where, on occasion, it results in peak experience (Piët, 1987).

The law of change can take treacherous forms, because adaptation level is not its only frame of reference. Hopes and perspectives on the future contribute. Goal-gradient phenomena seem to find their root herein. War pilots went on their missions with bravura, which tended to shift to anxiety and depression when possible survival once again became a real option toward the end of their tour of duty (Janis, 1951).

The law of change, to a large extent, is based on the *law of habituation: Continued pleasures wear off; continued hardships lose their poignancy.* Habituation is known experimentally mainly from the orienting response. There is more evidence, however, from repeated exposures to phobic objects or electric shocks (e.g., Epstein, 1973). Daily life offers ample illustrations again, partly consoling ones, partly saddening ones. The pains of loss of love abate with time, but love itself gradually loses its magic. Continued exposure to inhumanities blunts both suffering and moral discernment.

The law of change has many variants. One is the law of affective contrast. Loss of satisfaction does not yield a neutral condition, but positive misery. Loss of misery does not yield a sense of normality, but positive happiness. The law of affective contrast was formulated by Beebe-Center (1932) as resulting from adaptation level shifts and by Solomon (1980) as due to "opponent processes." Whatever its source, it is a law of considerable practical consequence. It is the basis of the play of take-and-give that proves so effective in, for instance, brainwashing. One takes privileges away and subsequently gives them back in part, and the emotions of gratitude and attachment result.

The law of change itself expresses a more encompassing generality that we can name the *law of comparative feeling: The intensity of emotion depends on the relationship between an event and some frame of reference against which the event is evaluated.* The frame of reference is often the prevailing state of affairs, but it can also be an expectation, as it is in the conditions for relief, disappointment, or the enhancement of joy by previous suspense. Or it can be provided by the fate and condition of other people. Ratings of subjective well-being have been shown to vary with prior exposure to descriptions of the past as times of poverty or as times of personal closeness. One tends to feel less well off when others fare better. Envy and *Schadenfreude* are names for emotions rooted in comparisons of this kind.

Generally speaking, the frame of reference that determines what counts as an emotional event consists of that which is deemed possible. This holds with considerable generality. Those who wring their hands in despair still entertain hopes; they have not really abandoned desiring. Those who grieve and mourn have not really taken their leave from the departed person; they still expect him or her at the other end of their arms, bed, or table. Those who feel that they should be able to cope suffer when they cannot cope. The point needs to be stressed and elaborated because internal locus of control, achievement motivation, and being in control are generally held to be factors that contribute to coping with stress. They are and do as long as there exist ways to cope. They bring extra burdens when there are no such ways. Anecdotal evidence from concentration camps and trauma research, as well as experimental studies with animals and humans (Rothbaum, Weisz, & Snyder, 1982; Weiss, 1971; Wortman & Brehm, 1975), support this conclusion.

The Law of Hedonic Asymmetry

The laws of habituation and comparative feeling operate only within certain limits. There exists, it

would seem, misery that one does not get used to; there is deprivation to which one does not adapt. This fact has, it appears, no counterpart for positive emotions. Joy, bliss, and fascination invariably tend to fade toward neutrality or some pale contentment. One must, I think, posit a law *of hedonic asymmetry*, the law of asymmetrical adaptation to pleasure or pain: *Pleasure is always contingent upon change and disappears with continuous satisfaction. Pain may persist under persisting adverse conditions.* One gets used to the events that, earlier, delighted and caused joy; one does not get used to continuous harassment or humiliation. Fear can go on forever; hopes have limited duration. The law predicts a negative balance for the: quality of life, unless self-deceit and self-defense intervene, which of course they do. It may not be as bad as that when life is not filled with adverse conditions, but for many people life is filled in that manner. Remember that the joys of freedom, for those who suffered oppression, do not last as long as tile sorrows of oppression did. True enough, the situations underlying these examples are not altogether transparent. It is difficult to disentangle the effects of repetition, accumulation, and sheer persistence of a given state of affairs. Oppression makes itself known each day; liberty, as an event, occurs only at the day of liberation. Be that as it may, at a gross level the law appears to hold and to manifest itself in many ways, dramatic as well as commonplace. The grief upon one's partner's being gone is much, much more poignant and enduring than the joy caused by his or her presence a month before or the joy after his or her return one month later.

The law of hedonic asymmetry is a stern and bitter law. It seems almost a necessary one, considering its roots, which, theoretically, are so obvious. Emotions exist for the sake of signaling states of the world that have to be responded to or that no longer need response and action. Once the "no more action needed" signal has sounded, the signaling system can be switched off, there is no further need for it. That the net quality of life, by consequence, tends to be negative is an unfortunate result. It shows the human mind to have been made not for happiness, but for instantiating the blind biological laws of survival.

On the other hand, the law's outcomes are not unavoidable. Adaptation to satisfaction can be counteracted by constantly being aware of how fortunate one's condition is and of how it could have been otherwise, or actually was otherwise before—by rekindling impact through recollection and imagination. Enduring happiness seems possible, and it can be understood theoretically. However, note that it does not come naturally, by itself. It takes effort.

The Law of Conservation of Emotional Momentum

The law of change, or at least the law of habituation, shows a further restriction. One of its, consequences seems to be that emotions diminish with time. This supposition, or one of its forms, is expressed in the common adage that time heals all wounds. That adage, however, is untrue. Time heals no wounds. On the contrary, what accounts for habituation is repeated exposure to the emotional event within the bounds of asymmetry of adaptation. It is repetition that does it, when it does, not time. Time does not really soften emotions. We may phrase the *law of conservation of emotional momentum* thus: *Emotional events retain their power to elicit emotions indefinitely, unless counteracted by repetitive exposures that permit extinction or habituation, to the extent that these are possible.*

The law will be difficult to prove because it asserts resistance against change when nothing happens. Yet, it is of value to propose it, and there is evidence to support it. As regards its value, behavior therapy and trauma theory both appear to hold the silent supposition that enduring trauma effects need explanation in terms of avoidance, denial, secondary gain, or whatever. Yet, traditional extinction theory as well as the interference theory of forgetting make it more reasonable to assume that the emotional impact of traumatic events never really wanes; it can only be overwritten. As regards the evidence, it is ample, although only clinical or anecdotal. Loss of a child never appears to become a neutral event (Lehman, Wortman, & Williams, 1987). The persistence or recurrence of other trauma effects is of course well-known. Emotions surge up when stimuli resembling the original stimuli are encountered or when aroused by "unbidden" images (the term is Horowitz's, 1976) in nightmares or even while awake. The sudden fear—shivering, palpitations, a sense of panic—upon the smell of burning in former fire victims is a more common occurrence. Equally common is the unexpected outburst of tears when, many years later, a letter, a toy, or a piece of clothing belonging to a child who died is stumbled upon, or the blood that rushes to one's face when recalling an embarrassing act committed years ago. The emotional experiences tend to be fresh, as poignant and as articulable as they were at the original occasion, or perhaps even more so. Certain old pains just do not grow old; they only refer to old events.

The Law of Closure

In the preceding sections, I have discussed the lawful determination of emotional reactions, mentioning the determinants of situational meaning, concerns, apparent reality, change, and momentum. Emotional response itself, too, has its lawful properties, which can be subsumed under the *law of closure: Emotions tend to be closed to judgments of relativity of impact and to the requirements of goals other than their own.* They tend to be absolute with regard to such judgments and to have control over the action system.

It may be, according to the law of change, that the causes of emotion are relative ones, relative, that is, to one's frame of reference—emotional response does not know this relativity and does not recognize it. For someone who is truly angry, the thing that happened is felt to be absolutely bad. It is disgraceful. It is not merely a disgraceful act but one that flows from the actor's very nature and disposition. Somebody who has acted so disgracefully is disgraceful and thus will always be. The offense and the misery it causes have a character of perpetuity. In strong grief the person feels that life is devoid of meaning, that life cannot go on without the one lost. Each time one falls in love, one feels one never felt like that before. One dies a thousand deaths without the other. Every feature or action of the love object has an untarnishable gloss for as long as the infatuation lasts. In the presence or strong desires—think of trying to lose weight, stop smoking, or get off drugs—one feels as if one will die when they are not satisfied and that the pain is insupportable, even while one knows that the pang of desire will be over in a minute or two. Verbal expressions of emotions tend to reflect this absoluteness in quality and time: "I could kill him" or "I cannot live without her."

The closure of emotion is manifest not only in the absoluteness of feeling but also in the fact that emotions know no probabilities. They do not weigh likelihoods. What they know, they know for sure. Could it be that your friend is meeting someone else? Your jealousy is certain. Could it be that your partner is an inattentive person? Your anger is certain. Does she love me? Love now is certain that she does, and then is certain that she does not. When jealous, thoughts of scenes of unfaithfulness crop up, and one suffers from images self-created. It is the same for the delights and the anxieties of love. Love is consummated 10 times before it actually is, and, when one is uncertain whether the loved one will be at the rendezvous, one prepares the reproachful speech over the telephone in advance.

The absoluteness of feelings and thinking is mirrored by what people do. They tend to act upon this absoluteness. The primary phenomenon of emotion, one may argue, is what can be called the "control precedence" of action readiness (Frijda, 1986). The action readiness of emotion tends to occupy center stage. It tends to override other concerns, other goals, and other actions. It tends to override considerations of appropriateness or long-term consequence. Control precedence applies to action as well as to nonaction, to fear's impulse to flee as well as to grief or despair's lethargy. It applies to single actions, such as shouting or crying, as well as to the execution of long-term plans, such as when passionate love makes a person neglect his or her obligations. It applies to attentional control (Mandler, 1984). It also applies to the information processing involved in action preparation and execution, where it shows in the effects of emotion on performance—activating under some conditions and interfering under others.

Closure, or control precedence, may well be considered the essential feature of emotion, its distinguishing mark, much more so than autonomic arousal or the occurrence of innate responses such as crying or facial expressions. The notion of control precedence captures in some sense the involuntary nature of emotional impulse or apathy, its characteristic of being an "urge," both in experience and in behavior.

The law of closure expresses what I think is the major, basic, theoretical fact about emotion: its modularity (Fodor, 1981). Emotion can be considered the outflow of a module serving the regulation of activity for safeguarding the satisfaction of the individual's major goals or concerns. Modularity is the conception that best accounts for the central properties of emotional response hinted at in this section (see Frijda & Swagerman, 1987).

The Law of Care for Consequence

Emotion is not always as absolute as just sketched. Emotions do manifest deliberation, calculation, or consideration. Infatuation can be stingy, and anger can be prudent. However, I argue, closure and absoluteness reflect the basic modular shape of emotion. The manifestations of that basic shape may run into opposite tendencies, though, that stem from the *law of care for consequence: Every emotional impulse elicits a seondary impulse that tends to modify it in view of its possible consequences.* The major effect is response moderation. Its major mechanism is response inhibition.

Presence of a tendency toward moderation or inhibition of response—that is, presence of emotion control—must be considered a ubiquitous fact of emotion. Its ubiquity, and thus the validity of the law, paradoxically is evident in those rare instances when control power fails, as happens in blind panic or anger, with neurological interferences such as temporal epilepsy (Mark & Ervin, 1970) or experimental decortication (Bard, 1934), and under toxic influences like those of alcohol. Normal fury or passion, however violent, is nonetheless controlled. In anger, one rarely smashes one's truly precious objects. When madly in love, one still waits to get home before consummating. Something snaps when going from there to frenzy, to blind impulse.

The law of care for consequence, too, is a law of emotion. Control, in large measure, is an emotional response. Anxiety—rigid anxiety, freezing—in fact is its most complete expression; the drying up of emotional freedom before critical onlookers is a more moderate version. Like other emotional responses, control is elicited or maintained by stimuli. The stimuli for control are the signals for possible adverse consequences of uninhibited response such as retaliation, reprobation, or miscarriage of plans. The notion that inhibition is triggered by anticipation of adverse response consequences, of course, comes from Gray (1982).

The fact that involuntary emotion control itself is an emotional response implies that the other laws of emotions apply to it, notably the law of apparent reality. One cannot at will shed restraint, as little as one can at will shed anxiety or timidity.

Emotional spontaneity is a function of how the environment is perceived to respond. Environmentally induced inhibition is illustrated by audience effects like the one just mentioned, familiar from examinations or auditions and from social facilitation research. Opposite, disinhibitory effects are found in the surprising emotional responsiveness, the increase in susceptibility to weeping and sexual excitement, in groups that are sympathetic toward such impulses. Therapy groups, sensitivity training groups, and meetings in sects like those led by Baghwan Rajneesh illustrate what is meant. The point is of much more relevant consequence because it provides a basis for explaining certain aspects of mass behavior. According to deindividuation theory (e.g., Zimbardo, 1970), mass enthusiasm, mass ecstasy, and mass violence are consequences of decreases in self-monitoring and of focusing attention on a leader and a common objective. These mass phenomena, in other words, result from a decrease in control due to the absence of stimuli that signal adverse response consequences and to the presence of stimuli that signal approbation of unhampered impulse expression.

The Laws of the Lightest Load and the Greatest Gain

Emotion control is not dictated entirely by external cues, or, more precisely, to the extent that it is dominated by external cues, those cues themselves are, within limits, at the subject's discretion. One can focus now upon this, then upon that, aspect of reality. One can complement reality with imagination or detract from it by not thinking of particular implications. The construction of situational meaning structures, in other words, offers leeway for emotional control that has its origins within the object himself or herself. Situational meaning structures can be chosen in ways that decrease emotional intensity, prevent occurrence of emotion, or make events appear more tolerable or more pleasing. The situational meaning structure that dictates emotion, in accordance with our first law, is in part shaped and transformed by its own expected outcomes and consequences. Transformation follows various principles. One of these can be phrased as the *law of the lightest load: Whenever a situation can be viewed in alternative ways, a tendency exists to view it in a way that mini-*

mizes negative emotional load. "Negative emotional load" refers to the degree to which a situation is painful and hard to endure.

Defensive denial is commonplace and has been widely described (see Lazarus & Folkman, 1984). The many ways to minimize emotional load, however, merit emphasis; mechanisms exist to ensure it at different levels of the process by which meaning structures are constructed. Denial, avoidant thinking, and entertaining of illusionary hopes operate at almost the conscious, voluntary level (see Weisman's, 1972, concept of "middle knowledge"). People often claim that they had always known that their illness would be fatal, that the loss they suffered would be permanent, or that the malfunctioning in the nuclear plant was dangerous, their earlier denials notwithstanding. Note that such knowledge does not prevent the denials from being resistant to correction, presumably because the load reduction they effect is so considerable.

Other mechanisms of load lightening operate at a much more elementary level. This applies particularly to the mechanisms that transform one's sense of reality and block the occurrence of hedonic appreciations. What I am referring to are the mechanisms of depersonalization, the occurrence of the sense of unreality, the veil over emotional feeling. Depersonalization occurs under all conditions of shock, severe trauma, severe threat, and severe pain. It has been described contingent upon accidents, serious loss or failure, torture, and sexual abuse (e.g., Cappon & Banks, 1961).

Denial and depersonalization are by no means the only ways in which load minimizing operates. The interplay of emotion and cognition can take many shapes that often are, for the subject, as difficult to recognize as they are difficult to bear. Examples are provided by the occurrence of painful emotions that, there are reasons to suppose, replace still more devastating ones. Sometimes, for instance, people entertain a "worst case hypothesis," preferring the apparent certainty of a disastrous prospect over the uncertainty of a future unknown. They convince themselves, for instance, that they are suffering from fatal illness in order to shield themselves from the possible shock of being told unpreparedly. An even more complex interplay is found in the cognitive strategy that leads people to view themselves as responsible when in fact they have been victims of arbitrary maltreatment. The guilt feelings that, paradoxically, are so common in victims of sexual or other child abuse appear to serve to retain the view that adults are dependable and right in what they do. These guilt feelings are the lesser price to pay compared to the utter despair and disorientation that would otherwise follow. They permit the victim to see sense in a fate that contains none (Kroon, 1986).

The law of the lightest load blends into the *law of the greatest gain: Whenever a situation can be viewed in alternative ways, a tendency exists to view it in a way that maximizes emotional gain.* Emotions produce gains that differ from one emotion to another. Anger intimidates and instills docility. Fear saves the efforts of trying to overcome risks. Guilt feelings for misdeeds done confer high moral standing. Grief provides excuses, confers the right to be treated with consideration, and gives off calls for help. Often, when crying in distress or anger, one casts half an eye for signs of sympathy or mollification. Anticipation of such consequences, it can be argued, belongs to the factors that generate one particular situational meaning structure rather than another, and thus brings one particular emotion rather than another into existence. The mechanism involved is transparent. One focuses, for instance, on the idea that another is to blame in order to permit emergence of an anger that makes the other refrain from what he or she is doing. The mechanism operates in jealousy, and the coercive effects perpetuate much marital quarreling. Even if the pains of jealousy may not originate in the wish to prevent the partner from being unfaithful, that wish strongly sustains jealousy; it does so particularly when the partner yields and gives up part of his or her freedom of action. Who would wish to make one suffer so? Here, too, certain painful emotions appear to result from something resembling choice—choice of a painful emotion over a still more painful one. That process in fact is rather general. Grief upon loss, for instance, tends to be willfully prolonged, not only because it provides excuses but also because it keeps the lost person nearby, so to speak. When grief is over, true loneliness sets in.

Concluding Remarks

The purpose of this article was to show that the study of emotion has advanced to a point that a coherent account of emotion can be given. The account is one that fits reasonably well into the framework developed for other domains, such as those of cognitive processes and motivation. A further purpose was to show that emotions are governed by laws. Emotions emerge and manifest themselves the way they do because lawfully operating mechanisms dictate response. We are subjected to these mechanisms and obey the laws.

Clearly, humans are not entirely and blindly subjected to these mechanisms. Not even all of human emotion is dictated by the emotion laws. One can seek occasions for certain emotions and avoid other ones. One can willfully supplant the situational meaning structure of a given event with prospects of the future and with those considerations of long-term gain or loss that represent the voice of reason. One can exert voluntary emotion control and substitute deliberate action for impulsive emotional response. It is not clear, though, how the relationship and difference between the two modes of action control—control by situational meaning structure and impulse, and by deliberate intent—are to be viewed. There is a current distinction between automatic and controlled processing. It is not evident, however, that this distinction illuminates the present context more than did the old distinction between Emotions and the Will (Bain, 1859) because the major problem is their opposition and, on occasion, persisting conflict, as manifest in emotion's control precedence. Perhaps the concept of an emotion module ready to intrude on top-level control, as suggested earlier, comes closer to how the relationship should be conceptualized.

Even if not subjected blindly to the laws of emotion, still we are subjected to them. When falling in love, when suffering grief for a lost dear one, when tortured by jealousy, when blaming others or fate for our misfortunes, when saying "never" when we mean "now," when unable to refrain from making that one remark that will spoil an evening together, one is propelled by the big hand of emotion mechanism. I would like, in conclusion, to return to the issue touched on in the beginning of this article: the opposition one may feel between the lawfulness of emotions and the sense of personal freedom.

Note, first, that there is comfort in the notion of the lawfulness of emotion and in one's participation in the laws of nature that that notion implies. It is the comfort that resides in the recognition of necessity generally I mentioned previously the law of comparative feeling—emotions are proportional to the difference between what is and what is deemed possible. Recognizing necessity where there is necessity, where nature limits one's control, can considerably decrease emotional load. More important, there is, I think, no true opposition between lawfulness and freedom. Personal freedom, wrote Spinoza (1677/1955) consists in acting according to one's own laws rather than to those imposed by someone else.

Second, as I hinted at earlier in this article, neither is there a fundamental opposition between Emotion and Reason. It may be argued that reason consists of basing choices on the perspectives of emotions at some later time. Reason dictates not giving in to one's impulses because doing so may cause greater suffering later. Reason dictates nuclear disarmament because we expect more sorrow than pleasure from nuclear war, if not for ourselves then for our children, whose fate fills us with emotion. The only true opposition is that between the dictates of the law of apparent reality, which tend to attach to the here and now, and the anticipations of later emotions, which tend not to be so dictated and thereby lack emotional force.

It is here that the laws of emotion and reason may meet and where both emotion and reason can be extended so as to make them coincide more fully with one's own laws. Following reason does not necessarily imply exertion of the voluntary capacities to suppress emotion. It does not necessarily involve depriving certain aspects of reality of their emotive powers. On the contrary, our voluntary capacities allow us to draw more of reality into the sphere of emotion and its laws. They allow us to turn the law of apparent reality into a law of reality, that is, to let reality—full reality, including long-term consequences—be what determines emotion. They allow one's emotions to be elicited not merely by the proximal, or the perceptual, or that which directly interferes with one's actions, but by that which in fact touches on one's concerns, whether proximal or distal, whether occurring now or in the future, whether interfering with one's own life or that of others. This is accomplished with the help of imagination and deeper processing. These procedures, as I have suggested, can confer emotive power on stimuli that do not by their nature have it. They can extend the driving forces of emotion to the spheres of moral responsibility, for instance. The laws of emotion can extend to the calls of reason as much as to those of immediate interests.

REFERENCES

Abramson, L., Seligman, M., & Teasdale, J. (1978). Learned helplessness in humans: Critique and reformulation. *Journal of Abnormal Psychology, 87,* 49–74.

Arnold, M. B. (1960). *Emotion and personality* (Vols. 1, 2). New York: Columbia University Press.

Bain, A. (1859). *The emotions and the will.* London: Longmans.

Bandura, A. (1977). *Social learning theory.* Englewood Cliffs, NJ: Prentice Hall.

Bard, P. (1934). On emotional expression after decortication with some remarks on certain theoretical views. *Psychological Review, 38,* 309–329; 424-449.

Beebe-Center, J. G. (1932). *The psychology of pleasantness and unpleasantness.* New York: Van Nostrand.

Bridger, W. H., & Mandel, J. J. (1964). A comparison of GSR fear responses produced by threat and electrical shock. *Journal of Psychiatric Research, 2,* 31–40.

Cappon, D., & Banks, R. (1961). Orientation perception: A review and preliminary study of distortion in orientation perception. *Archives of General Psychiatry, 5,* 380–392.

Davitz, J. R. (1969). *The language of emotion.* New York: Academic Press.

Dijker, A. J. M. (1987). Emotional reactions to ethnic minorities. *European Journal of Social Psychology, 17,* 305–325.

Efran, J. S., & Spangler, T. J. (1979). Why grown-ups cry: A two-factor theory and evidence from *The Miracle Worker. Motivation and Emotion, 3,* 63–72.

Ekman, P. (Ed.). (1982). *Emotion in the human face* (2nd ed.). New York: Cambridge University Press.

Ekman, P. E., Friesen, W. V., & Simons, R. C. (1985). Is the startle reaction an emotion? *Journal of Personality and Social Behavior, 49,* 1416–1426.

Epstein, S. (1973). Expectancy and magnitude of reaction to a noxious UCS. *Psychophysiology, 10,* 100–107.

Fiske, S. T. (1987). People's reactions to nuclear war: Implications for psychologists. *American Psychologist, 42,* 207–217.

Fiske, S. T., & Taylor S. E. (1984). *Social cognition.* New York: Random House.

Fodor, J. (1981). *The modularity of mind.* Cambridge, MA: MIT Press.

Frijda, N. H. (1986). *The emotions.* London: Cambridge University Press.

Frijda, N. H. (1987). Emotions, cognitive structure and action tendency. *Cognition and Emotion, 1,* 115–144.

Frijda, N. H., & Swagerman, J. (1987). Can computers feel? *Cognition and Emotion, 1,* 235–258.

Gray, J. (1982). *The neuopsychology of anxiety: Inquiry into the septohippocampal system.* Oxford, England: Clarendon Press.

Horowitz, M. J. (1976). *Stress response syndrome.* New York: Jason Aronson.

Izard, C. E. (1977). *Human emotions.* New York: Plenum Press.

Janis, I. L. (1951). *Air war and emotional stress.* New York: McGraw-Hill.

Kroon, R. M. C. (1986). *De wereld op zijn kop: Een literatuurstudie naar parentificatie en incest* [The world upside down: A literature survey on parentification and incest]. Unpublished master's thesis, Amsterdam University.

Kuipers, P. (1987). *Appraisal and action readiness in emotions.* Unpublished doctoral dissertation, Amsterdam University.

Lacey, J. I., & Lacey, B. C. (1970). Some autonomic-nervous system relationships. In P. Black (Ed.), *Physiological correlates of emotion* (pp. 205–227). New York: Academic Press.

Lang, P. (1977). Imagery and therapy: An information processing analysis of fear. *Behavior Therapy, 8,* 862–886.

Lanzetta, J. T, & Orr, S. P. (1986). Excitatory strength of expressive faces: Effects of happy and fear expressions and context on the extinction of a conditioned fear response. *Journal of Personality and Social Behavior, 50,* 190–194.

Lazarus, R. S. (1966). *Psychological stress and the coping process.* New York: McGraw-Hill.

Lazarus, R. S., & Folkman, S. (1984). *Stress, appraisal and coping.* New York: Springer.

Lehman, D. R., Wortman, C. B., & Williams, A. F. (1987). Long-term effects of losing a spouse or child in a motor vehicle crash. *Journal of Personality and Social Behavior, 52,* 218–231.

Mandler, G. (1984). *Mind and body: The psychology of emotion and stress.* New York: Norton.

Mark, V. H., & Ervin, F. R. (1970). *Violence and the brain.* New York: Harper & Row.

Mason, J. W. (1975). Emotion as reflected in patterns of endocrine integration. In L. Levi (Ed.), *Emotions: Their parameters and measurement* (pp. 143–181). New York: Raven Press.

Mineka, S., & Hendersen, R. W. (1985). Controllability and predictability in acquired motivation. *Annual Review of Psychology, 36,* 495–529.

Obrist, P. A. (1981). *Cardiovascular psychophysiology: A perspective.* New York: Plenum Press.

Öhman, A., & Dimberg, U. (1978). Facial expressions as conditioned stimuli for electrodermal responses: A case of "preparedness"? *Journal of Personality and Social Psychology, 36,* 1251–1258.

Ortony, A., & Clore, G. L. (1988). *Report on emotions in basketball fans.* Manuscript in preparation.

Ortony, A., Clore, G. L., & Collins, A. (1988). *The cognitive structure of emotions.* London: Cambridge University Press.

Parkes, C. M. (1972). *Bereavement: A study of grief in adult life.* New York: International Universities Press.

Piët, S. (1987). What motivates stuntmen? *Motivation and Emotion, 11,* 195–213.

Plutchik, R. (1980). *Emotion: A psychoevolutionary synthesis.* New York: Harper & Row.

Previn, D. (1970). Soared to be alone (Song). In D. Previn, *On my way to where* (Album, UAG 29176). United Artists.

Rombouts, H. (1987). *The emotion of being in love.* Manuscript submitted for publication.

Rothbart, M. K. (1973). Laughter in young children. *Psychological Bulletin, 80,* 247–256.

Rothbaum, F. Weisz, J. R.. & Snyder, S. S. (1982). Changing the world and changing the self: A two-process model of perceived control. *Journal of Personality and Social Psychology, 42,* 5–37.

Scherer, K. R. (1988). Cognitive antecedents of emotions. In V. Hamilton, G. H. Bower, & N. H. Frijda (Eds.), *Cognition, motivation and affect* (pp. 89–126). Dordrecht, The Netherlands: Nijhoff.

Simon, H. A. (1973). *The sciences of the artificial.* Cambridge, MA: MIT Press.

Smith, C. A., & Ellsworth, P. C. (1987). Patterns of appraisal and emotion related to taking an exam. *Journal of Personality and Social Psychology, 52,* 475–488.

Solomon, R. L. (1980). The opponent-process theory of acquired motivation. *American Psychologist, 5,* 691–712.

Spinoza, B. (1955). *Ethics* (R. H. M. Elwes, Trans.). New York: Dover Books. (Original work published 1677)

Sroufe, L. A., & Waters, E. (1976). The ontogenesis of smiling and laughter: A perspective on the organization of development in infancy. *Psychological Review, 83,* 173–189.

Weiner, B. (1985). An attributional theory of achievement motivation and emotion. *Psychological Review, 92,* 548–573.

Weisman, A. D. (1972). *On dying and denying.* New York: Behavior Publications.

Weiss, J. M. (1971). Effects of punishing a coping response (conflict) on stress pathology in rats. *Journal of Comparative and Physiological Psychology, 77,* 14–21.

Wortman, C. B., & Brehm, J. W. (1975). Responses to uncontrollable outcomes: An integration of reactance theory and the learned helplessness model. In L. Berkowitz (Ed.), *Advances in experimental social psychology* (Vol. 8, pp. 277–336). New York: Academic Press.

Zajonc, R. B. (1980). Thinking and feeling: Preferences need no inferences. *American Psychologist, 35,* 151–175.

Zimbardo, P. G. (1970). The human choice: Individuation, reason and order versus deindividuation, impulse and chaos. In W. J. Arnold & D. Levine (Eds.), *1969 Nebraska Symposium on Motivation* (Vol. 16). Lincoln: University of Nebraska Press.

INTRODUCTION TO PART 2

The Role of Cognition

One of the ways in which emotions are social is that the social world is what they are usually *about*. Our social triumphs and trials, our interpersonal connections and conundrums, are what typically lead to our emotions. Emotions thus would seem to require some evaluation of our social circumstances. We must monitor social interactions and norms to become embarrassed, evaluate responsibility and blame to feel anger or guilt, have a sense of self to feel pride or shame, and monitor our relationships with others to experience belonging or jealousy. Emotions, therefore, seem to involve some type of cognitive activity, and social psychologists have concerned themselves with understanding the role of cognition in emotion.

Reprinted in this part of the book are two articles that represent the primary approaches social psychologists have taken to understanding the cognition that leads to emotion. Few studies of emotion have attained the fame and influence of the first of these articles, by Schachter and Singer (1962). This classic article proposed the "two-factor" theory of emotion and reported its first and most famous experimental test. Two-factor theory proposed that emotion requires both bodily arousal and cognition: arousal of the sympathetic nervous system, such as that caused by epinephrine (adrenalin), as well as cognition that links this arousal to an emotional source. According to two-factor theory, cognition without arousal will not result in an emotional state, nor will arousal that is understood as being caused by something other than emotional circumstances.

It is difficult not to love the experiment that Schachter and Singer report: the zany stooge, the fictitious vitamin "Suproxin," the insulting questionnaire, the hula-hoop! For many emotion theorists, however, it is also difficult not to hate it. As explained in the Overview chapter, the results of this experiment were quite weak

71

when they were statistically significant at all, and they have proved quite difficult to replicate (Reisenzein, 1983). Furthermore, two-factor theory dominated the social psychology of emotion for the next 20 years, even though the theory in several respects was ill-suited to serve as a general theory of emotion. By the 1980s, the two-factor theory was losing its popularity. Its most promising applications had been explored, and its assumptions appeared increasingly open to question (see the Overview chapter for details, and also see Reading 15 by Ekman, Friesen, & Ancoli, 1980).

Appraisal theories have replaced two-factor theory as explanations of the role of cognition in producing emotion. Appraisal theories postulate that certain types of thinking are necessary for emotions to occur, and that different emotions are associated with different patterns of thinking. The basic premise of appraisal theories is simple enough: Everyday emotions appear, by and large, to be related to the interpretations that people place on events. Specific appraisal theories differ in their details, but all assert that appraisals are a type of cognition; all assert that appraisals differ from other types of cognition in that they relate events or circumstances to one's own cares, concerns, goals, or well-being; all assert that appraisals need not be conscious, controllable, or verbal. There are numerous variations on this idea. Most, but not all, appraisal theories see appraisals as being a *cause* of emotions. Most, but not all, assert that appraisals are *necessary* for emotions to occur. Much of the debate among appraisal theorists concerns how best to represent appraisals. Some theorists consider each emotion to have its own, unique appraisal, whereas others think that all possible appraisals draw on the same fixed set of evaluative dimensions, and still others postulate a hierarchy of appraisals (some of which apply to many

emotions, others only to a few). Some theorists think that appraisal components are considered one at a time, in sequence from basic to refined, whereas others propose that all aspects of appraisal are considered in parallel.

The article that represents appraisal theory in this book describes one of the most influential theories. One of its authors, Richard Lazarus, is a founder of appraisal theory, and the other, Craig Smith, is a leading proponent. In this paper, Smith and Lazarus (1993) describe their theory and report an empirical test. Their theory makes a distinction between primary and secondary appraisal that has proved useful for understanding stress and coping as well as emotion. Their distinction between appraisal components and core relational themes is a recent theoretical innovation that links two ways of representing appraisals that previously had been opposed. Appraisal components are found on a more microscopic level of analysis; they are the details that must be evaluated, such as whether a situation is relevant to one's concerns and who is responsible for the situation. Core relational themes, on the other hand, summarize the overall import of the particular constellation of appraisal components that correspond to each emotion. For example, the appraisal components of guilt—relevance to one's concerns, incongruence with one's desires, and self-accountability for the situation—are aptly summarized in guilt's core relational theme of self-blame.

Although Smith and Lazarus's (1990) general theory addresses a large number of emotions, the experiment that they report examined only four, all of them negative: anger, guilt, fear/anxiety, and sadness. Appraisals were manipulated by composing scenarios, which participants read and imagined vividly. The scenarios were varied so that they depicted either the other-blame that is part of the appraisal for anger, the self-blame that is part of the appraisal for guilt, the threat of fear/anxiety, or the loss and helplessness of sadness. Participants reported their imagined appraisals and emotions on a questionnaire. The statistical analyses of appraisal research tend to get rather complex, but Smith and Lazarus lay out their results clearly. By and large, the manipulation of the scenarios produced the expected effects both on appraisals and on core relational themes, which in turn had the expected effects on emotions (although the associations were weak for sadness).

These authors have demonstrated in other papers that an appraisal is different from other types of cognition, such as general knowledge or attributions. That is, it is not one's beliefs about the "facts" of the situation that determine one's emotions, but rather one's construal of how these facts concern one's own concerns and well-being (Lazarus & Smith, 1988; Smith, Haynes, Lazarus, & Pope, 1993).

As discussed in the Overview chapter, appraisal theories and research have been criticized in a number of ways. Some critics, such as Zajonc (1980), reject entirely the idea that cognition plays any necessary role in emotion. These critics often seem to use the term "cognition" more narrowly than do appraisal theorists, and they also seem to use the term "emotion" more broadly, yet they have pointed out some of the limits of appraisal theory as well as prompted some clarifications. Other critics (e.g., Parkinson & Manstead, 1993) have focused on the limitations of the research methods that have been used. They argue that imagined scenarios may produce less self-involvement than do real emotions, and may prepackage events in verbal form more than does real life. These critics question whether hypothetical laboratory tasks can yield insight into how emotions are generated in everyday life. At present, appraisal theorists are trying to meet these challenges by exploring a variety of new methods that avoid such limitations. For example, some research has studied appraisals that occur in real-life emotions (e.g., Levine, 1996), and other research has attempted to manipulate appraisals in real time and to use physiological measures as well as conscious self-report (Kappas & Pecchinenda, 1999).

REFERENCES

Ekman, P., Friesen, W. V., & Ancoli, S. (1980). Facial signs of emotional experience. *Journal of Personality and Social Psychology, 39,* 1125–1134.

Kappas, A., & Pecchinenda, A. (1999). Don't wait for the monsters to get you: A video game task to manipulate appraisals in real time. *Cognition and Emotion, 13,* 119–124.

Lazarus, R. S., & Smith, C. A. (1988). Knowledge and appraisal in the cognition-emotion relationship. *Cognition and Emotion, 2,* 281–300.

Levine, L. J. (1996). The anatomy of disappointment: A naturalistic test of appraisal models of sadness, anger, and hope. *Cognition and Emotion, 10,* 337–359.

Parkinson, B., & Manstead, A. S. R. (1993). Making sense of emotions in stories and social life. *Cognition and Emotion, 7,* 295–323.

Reisenzein, R. (1982). The Schachter theory of emotion: Two decades later. *Psychological Bulletin, 94,* 239–264.

Schachter, S., & Singer, J. (1962). Cognitive, social, and physiological determinants of emotional state. *Psychological Review, 69,* 379–399.

Smith, C. A., Haynes, K. N., Lazarus, R. S., & Pope, L. K. (1993). In search of the "hot" cognitions: Attributions, appraisals, and their relation to emotion. *Journal of Personality and Social Psychology, 65,* 916–929.

Smith, C. A., & Lazarus, R. S. (1990). Emotion and adaptation. In L. A. Pervin (Ed.), *Handbook of personality: Theory and research* (pp. 609–637). New York: Guilford.

Smith, C. A., & Lazarus, R. S. (1993). Appraisal components, core relational themes, and the emotions. *Cognition and Emotion, 7,* 295–323.

Zajonc, R. B. (1980). Feeling and thinking: Preferences need no inferences. *American Psychologist, 35,* 151–175.

Discussion Questions

1. Can you think of times when you have reacted more intensely than usual because you have recently exercised or have just been startled? Apply the two-factor theory to such an example. It is convincing as an explanation?
2. What do Schachter and Singer mean by "labeling" a state of physiological arousal? Specify what steps are involved. Some theorists believe that "labeling" actually involves more than one cognitive step—what do you think?
3. Can you think of emotions that do not seem to be characterized by the presence of elevated epinepherine levels?
4. What is a primary appraisal, and what is a secondary appraisal?
5. Think of a time when you knew that a friend was angry but your friend denied it at first (admitting it later). What are the implications of denied anger for theories of appraisal? What do they tell us about the nature of appraisal (or, about the existence of appraisal)?

Suggested Readings

Reisenzein, R. (1982). The Schachter theory of emotion: Two decades later. *Psychological Bulletin, 94,* 239–264. This highly cited article provides an excellent review of the first 20 years of the two-factor theory. Both theoretical and empirical issues are reviewed and critically evaluated.

Dienstbier, R. A. (1979). Emotion-attribution theory: Establishing roots and exploring future perspectives. In H. E. Howe, Jr. (Series Ed.) & R. A. Dienstbier (Vol. Ed.), *Nebraska Symposium on Motivation: 1978. Human emotion* (pp. 237–306). Lincoln, NE: University of Nebraska Press. This chapter synthesizes research on two-factor theory and shows how it influenced social psychology.

Frijda, N. H. (Ed.) (1993). Appraisal and beyond: The issue of cognitive determinants of emotion [Special issue]. *Cognition and Emotion, 7*(3&4). The article by Smith and Lazarus that is reprinted in this volume was first published in a Special Issue of the journal *Cognition and Emotion.* The rest of that issue contains valuable contributions by other appraisal theorists (Frijda, Reisenzein, and Scherer), as well as by critics (Parkinson and Manstead).

Parkinson, B. (1997). Untangling the appraisal-emotion connection. *Personality and Social Psychology Review, 1,* 62–79. This article clearly explores the variety of ways in which appraisal might be related to emotion, and provides a critical review of the evidence to date. The author argues that the evidence obtained so far is consistent with a variety of interpretations.

Ortony, A., Clore, G. L., & Collins, A. (1988). *The cognitive structure of emotions.* Cambridge: Cambridge University Press. This book nicely articulates the cognitive richness implicit in many emotions. The authors develop a helpful hierarchical structure for grouping emotions based on their eliciting conditions.

Zajonc, R. B. (1980) Feeling and thinking: Preferences need no inferences. *American Psychologist, 35,* 151–175. ALSO Lazarus, R. S. (1982). Thoughts on the relations between emotion and cognition. *American Psychologist, 37,* 1019–1024. ALSO Leventhal, H., & Scherer, K. (1987). The relationship of emotion to cognition: A functional approach to a semantic controversy. *Cognition and Emotion, 1,* 3–28. The article published by Robert

Zajonc in 1980 set off a furious round of debate about the nature of emotion and the role of cognition. The article by Richard Lazarus is one well-known example of the many responses to Zajonc. The debate was mostly exhausted within seven years, and the article by Leventhal and Scherer is representative of the outcome. That article reviews the debate between Robert Zajonc and Richard Lazarus and attempts to resolve it by arguing that their disagreements were largely matters of definition. It also sets out a scheme that is typical of contemporary cognitive approaches, delineating the variety of mental processes that are included within the general term "cognition."

Cognitive, Social, and Physiological Determinants of Emotional State

Stanley Schachter • Columbia University
Jerome E. Singer • Pennsylvania State University

The problem of which cues, internal or external, permit a person to label and identify his own emotional state has been with us since the days that James (1890) first tendered his doctrine that "the bodily changes follow directly the perception of the exciting fact, and that our feeling of the same changes as they occur *is* the emotion" (p. 449). Since we are aware of a variety of feeling and emotion states, it should follow from James' proposition that the various emotions will be accompanied by a variety of differentiable bodily states. Following James' pronouncement, a formidable number of studies were undertaken in search of the physiological differentiators of the emotions. The results, in these early days, were almost uniformly negative. All of the emotion states experimentally manipulated were characterized by a general pattern of excitation of the sympathetic nervous system but there appeared to be no clearcut physiological discriminators of the various emotions. This pattern of results was so consistent that Cannon (1929) offered, as one of the crucial criticisms of the James-Lange theory, the fact that "the same visceral changes occur in very different emotional states and in non-emotional states" (p. 351).

More recent work, however, has given some indications that there may be differentiators. Ax (1953) and J. Schachter (1957) studied fear and anger. On a large number of indices both of these states were characterized by a similarly high level of autonomic activation but on several indices they did differ in the degree of activation. Wolf and Wolff (1947) studied a subject with a gastric fistula and were able to distinguish two patterns in the physiological responses of the stomach wall. It should be noted, though, that for many months they studied their subject during and following a great variety of moods and emotions and were able to distinguish only two patterns.

Whether or not there are physiological distinctions among the various emotional states must be considered an open question. Recent work might be taken to indicate that such differences are at best rather subtle and that the variety of emotion, mood, and feeling states are by no means matched by an equal variety of visceral patterns.

This rather ambiguous situation has led Ruckmick (1936), Hunt, Cole, and Reis (1958), S. Schachter (1959) and others to suggest that cognitive factors may be major determinants of emotional states. Granted a general pattern of sympathetic excitation as characteristic of emotional states, granted that there may be some differences in pattern from state to state, it is suggested that one labels, interprets, and identifies this stirred-up state in terms of the characteristics of the precipitating situation and one's apperceptive mass. This suggests, then, that an emotional state may be considered a function of a state of physiological arousal[1] and of a cognition appropriate to this state of arousal. The cognition, in a sense, exerts a steering function. Cognitions arising from the immediate situation as interpreted by past experience provide the framework within which one understands and labels his feelings. It is the cognition which determines whether the state of physiological arousal will be labeled as "anger," "joy," "fear," or whatever.

In order to examine the implications of this formulation let us consider the fashion in which these two elements, a state of physiological arousal and cognitive factors, would interact in a variety of situations. In most emotion inducing situations, of course, the two factors are completely interrelated. Imagine a man walking alone down a dark alley, a figure with a gun suddenly appears. The perception-cognition "figure with a gun" in some fashion initiates a state of physiological arousal; this state of arousal is interpreted in terms of knowledge about dark alleys and guns and the state of arousal is labeled "fear." Similarly a student who unexpectedly learns that he has made Phi Beta Kappa may experience a state of arousal which he will label "joy."

Let us now consider circumstances in which these two elements, the physiological and the cognitive, are, to some extent, independent. First, is the state of physiological arousal alone sufficient to induce an emotion? Best evidence indicates that it is not. Marañon[2] (1924), in a fascinating study, (which was replicated by Cantril & Hunt, 1932, and Landis & Hunt, 1932) injected 210 of his patients with the sympathomimetic agent adrenalin and then simply asked them to introspect. Seventy-one percent of his subjects simply reported their physical symptoms with no emotional overtones; 29% of the subjects responded in an apparently emotional fashion. Of these the great majority described their feelings in a fashion that Marañon labeled "cold" or "as if" emotions, that is, they made statements such as "I feel *as if* I were afraid" or "*as if* I were awaiting a great happiness." This is a sort of emotional "déjà vu" experience; these subjects are neither happy nor afraid, they feel "as if" they were. Finally a very few cases apparently reported a genuine emotional experience. However, in order to produce this reaction in most of these few cases, Marañon (1924) points out:

One must suggest a memory with strong affective force but not so strong as to produce an emotion in the normal state. For example, in several cases we spoke to our patients before the injection of

their sick children or dead parents and they responded calmly to this topic. The same topic presented later, during the adrenal commotion, was sufficient to trigger emotion. This adrenal commotion places the subject in a situation of "affective imminence" (pp. 307–308).

Apparently, then, to produce a genuinely emotional reaction to adrenalin, Marañon was forced to provide such subjects with an appropriate cognition.

Though Marañon (1924) is not explicit on his procedure, it is clear that his subjects knew that they were receiving an injection and in all likelihood knew that they were receiving adrenalin and probably had some order of familiarity with its effects. In short, though they underwent the pattern of sympathetic discharge common to strong emotional states, at the same time they had a completely appropriate cognition or explanation as to why they felt this way. This, we would suggest, is the reason so few of Marañon's subjects reported any emotional experience.

Consider now a person in a state of physiological arousal for which no immediately explanatory or appropriate cognitions are available. Such a state could result were one covertly to inject a subject with adrenalin or, unknown to him, feed the subject a sympathomimetic drug such as ephedrine. Under such conditions a subject would be aware of palpitations, tremor, face flushing, and most of the battery of symptoms associated with a discharge of the sympathetic nervous system. In contrast to Marañon's (1924) subjects he would, at the same time, be utterly unaware of why he felt this way. What would be the consequence of such a state?

S. Schachter (1959) has suggested that precisely such a state would lead to the arousal of "evaluative needs" (Festinger, 1954), that is, pressures would act on an individual in such a state to understand and label his bodily feelings. His bodily state grossly resembles the condition in which it has been at times of emotional excitement. How would he label his present feelings? It is suggested,

---

[1]Though our experiments are concerned exclusively with the physiological changes produced by the injection of adrenalin, which appear to be primarily the result of sympathetic excitation, the term physiological arousal is used in preference to the more specific "excitation of the sympathetic nervous system" because there are indications, to be discussed later, that this formulation is applicable to a variety of bodily states.

[2]Translated copies of Marañon's (1924) paper may be obtained by writing to the senior author.

of course, that he will label his feelings terms of his knowledge of the immediate situation.[3] Should he at the time be with a beautiful woman he might decide that he was wildly in love or sexually excited. Should he be at a gay party, he might, by comparing himself to others, decide that he was extremely happy and euphoric. Should he be arguing with his wife, he might explode in fury and hatred. Or, should the situation be completely inappropriate he could decide that he was excited about something that had recently happened to him or, simply, that he was sick. In any case, it is our basic assumption that emotional states are a function of the interaction of such cognitive factors with a state of physiological arousal.

This line of thought, then, leads to the following propositions

1. Given a state of physiological arousal for which an individual has no immediate explanation, he will "label" this state and describe his feelings in terms of the cognitions available to him. To the extent that cognitive factors are potent determiners of emotional states, it could be anticipated that precisely the same state of physiological arousal could be labeled "joy" or "fury" or "jealousy" or any of a great diversity of emotional labels depending on the cognitive aspects of the situation.

2. Given a state of physiological arousal for which an individual has a completely appropriate explanation (e.g., "I feel this way because I have just received an injection of adrenalin") no evaluative needs will arise and the individual is unlikely to label his feelings in terms of the alternative cognitions available.

Finally, consider a condition in which emotion inducing cognitions are present but there is no state of physiological arousal. For example, an individual might be completely aware that he is in great danger but for some reason (drug or surgical) remain in a state of physiological quiescence. Does he experience the emotion "fear"? Our formulation of emotion as a joint function of a state of physiological arousal and an appropriate cognition, would, of course, suggest that he does not, which leads to our final proposition.

3. Given the same cognitive circumstances, the individual will react emotionally or describe his feelings as emotions only to the extent that he experiences a state of physiological arousal.[4]

Procedure

The experimental test of these propositions requires (a) the experimental manipulation of a state of physiological arousal, (b) the manipulation of the extent to which the subject has an appropriate or proper explanation of his bodily state, and (c) the creation of situations from which explanatory cognitions may be derived.

In order to satisfy the first two experimental requirements, the experiment was cast in the framework of a study of the effects of vitamin supplements on vision. As soon as a subject arrived, he was taken to a private room and told by the experimenter:

> In this experiment we would like to make various tests of your vision. We are particularly interested in how certain vitamin compounds and vitamin supplements affect the visual skills. In particular, we want to find out how the vitamin compound called 'Suproxin' affects your vision.
>
> What we would like to do, then, if we can get your permission, is to give you a small injection of Suproxin. The injection itself is mild and harmless; however, since some people do object to being injected we don't want to talk you into anything. Would you mind receiving a Suproxin injection?

If the subject agrees to the injection (and all but 1 of 185 subjects did) the experimenter continues with instructions we shall describe shortly, then leaves the room. In a few minutes a physician enters the room, briefly repeats the experimenter's instructions, takes the subject's pulse and then injects him with Suproxin.

Depending upon condition, the subject receives one of two forms of Suproxin—epinephrine or a placebo.

---

[3]This suggestion is not new for several psychologists have suggested that situational factors should be considered the chief differentiators of the emotions. Hunt, Cole, and Reis (1958) probably make this point most explicitly in their study distinguishing among fear, anger, and sorrow in terms of situational characteristics.

[4]In his critique of the James-Lange theory of emotion, Cannon (1929) also makes the point that sympathectomized animals and patients do seem to manifest emotional behavior. This criticism is, of course, as applicable to the above proposition as it was to the James-Lange formulation. We shall discuss the issues involved in later papers.

Epinephrine or adrenalin is a sympathomimetic drug whose effects, with minor exceptions, are almost a perfect mimicry of a discharge of the sympathetic nervous system. Shortly after injection systolic blood pressure increases markedly, heart rate increases somewhat, cutaneous blood flow decreases, while muscle and cerebral blood flow increase, blood sugar and lactic acid concentration increase, and respiration rate increases slightly. As far as the subject is concerned the major subjective symptoms are palpitation, tremor, and sometimes a feeling of flushing and accelerated breathing. With a subcutaneous injection (in the dosage administered to our subjects), such effects usually begin within 3–5 minutes of injection and last anywhere from 10 minutes to an hour. For most subjects these effects are dissipated within 15–20 minutes after injection.

Subjects receiving epinephrine received a subcutaneous injection of ½ cubic centimeter of a 1:1000 solution of Winthrop Laboratory's Suprarenin, a saline solution of epinephrine bitartrate.

Subjects in the placebo condition received a subcutaneous injection of ½ cubic centimeter of saline solution. This is, of course, completely neutral material with no side effects at all.

MANIPULATING AN APPROPRIATE EXPLANATION

By "appropriate" we refer to the extent to which the subject has an authoritative, unequivocal explanation of his bodily condition. Thus, a subject who had been informed by the physician that as a direct consequence of the injection he would feel palpitations, tremor, etc. would be considered to have a completely appropriate explanation. A subject who had been informed only that the injection would have no side effects would have no appropriate explanation of his state. This dimension of appropriateness was manipulated in three experimental conditions which shall be called: Epinephrine Informed (Epi Inf), Epinephrine Ignorant (Epi Ign), and Epinephrine Misinformed (Epi Mis).

Immediately after the subject had agreed to the injection and before the physician entered the room, the experimenter's spiel in each of these conditions went as follows:

Epinephrine Informed. I should also tell you that some of our subjects have experienced side effects from the Suproxin. These side effects are transitory, that is, they will only last for about 15 or 20 minutes. What will probably happen is that your hand will start to shake, your heart will start to pound, and your face may get warm and flushed. Again these are side effects lasting about 15 or 20 minutes.

While the physician was giving the injection, she told the subject that the injection was mild and harmless and repeated this description of the symptoms that the subject could expect as a consequence of the shot. In this condition, then subjects have a completely appropriate explanation of their bodily state. They know precisely what they will feel and why.

Epinephrine Ignorant. In this condition, when the subject agreed to the injection, the experimenter said nothing more relevant to side effects and simply left the room. While the physician was giving the injection, she told the subject that the injection was mild and harmless and would have no side effects. In this condition, then, the subject has no experimentally provided explanation for his bodily state.

Epinephrine Misinformed. I should also tell you that some of our subjects have experienced side effects from the Suproxin. These side effects are transitory, that is, they will only last for about 15 or 20 minutes. What will probably happen is that your feet will feel numb, you will have an itching sensation over parts of your body, and you may get a slight headache. Again these are side effects lasting 15 or 20 minutes.

And again, the physician repeated these symptoms while injecting the subject.

None of these symptoms, of course, are consequences of an injection of epinephrine, and, in effect, these instructions provide the subject with a completely inappropriate explanation of his bodily feelings. This condition was introduced as a control condition of sorts. It seemed possible that the description of side effects on the Epi Inf condition might turn the subject introspective, self-examining, possibly slightly troubled. Differences on the dependent variable between the Epi Inf and Epi Ign conditions might, then, be due to such factors rather than to differences in appropriateness. The false symptoms in the Epi Mis condition should similarly turn the subject introspective, etc., but the instructions in this condition do not provide an appropriate explanation of the subject's state.

Subjects in all of the above conditions were injected with epinephrine. Finally, there was a placebo condition in which subjects, who were injected with saline solutions, were given precisely the same treatment as subjects in the Epi Ign condition.

PRODUCING AN EMOTION INDUCING COGNITION

Our initial hypothesis has suggested that given a state of physiological arousal for which the individual has no adequate explanation, cognitive factors can lead the individual to describe his feelings with any of a diversity of emotional labels. In order to test this hypothesis, it was decided to manipulate emotional states which can be considered quite different—euphoria and anger.

There are, of course, many ways to induce such states. In our own program of research, we have concentrated on social determinants of emotional states and have been able to demonstrate in other studies that people do evaluate their own feelings by comparing themselves with others around them (S. Schachter, 1959; Wrightsman, 1960). In this experiment we have attempted again to manipulate emotional state by social means. In one set of conditions, the subject is placed together with a stooge who has been trained to act euphorically. In a second set of conditions the subject is with a stooge trained to act in an angry fashion.

EUPHORIA

Immediately[5] after the subject had been injected, the physician left the room and the experimenter returned with a stooge whom he introduced as another subject, then said:

> Both of you have had the Suproxin shot and you'll both be taking the same tests of vision. What I ask you to do now is just wait for 20 minutes. The reason for this is simply that we have to allow 20 minutes for the Suproxin to get from the injection site into the bloodstream. At the end of 20 minutes when we are certain that most of the Suproxin has been absorbed into the bloodstream we'll begin the tests of vision.

The room in which this was said had been deliberately put into a state of mild disarray. As he was leaving, the experimenter apologetically added:

> The only other thing I should do is to apologize for the condition of the room. I just didn't have time to clean it up. So, if you need any scratch paper or rubber bands or pencils, help yourself. I'll be back in 20 minutes to begin the vision tests.

As soon as the experimenter had left, the stooge introduced himself again, made a series of standard icebreaker comments, and then launched his routine. For observation purposes, the stooge's act was broken into a series of standard units, demarcated by a change in activity or a standard comment. In sequence, the units of the stooge's routine were the following:

1. Stooge reaches for a piece of paper and starts doodling saying, "They said we could use this for scratch, didn't they?" He doodles a fish for some 30 seconds, then says:
2. "This scrap paper isn't even much good for doodling" and crumples paper and attempts to throw it into wastebasket in far corner of the room. He misses but this leads him into a "basketball game." He crumples up other sheets of paper, shoots a few baskets, says "Two points" occasionally. He gets up and does a jump shot saying, "The old jump shot is really on today."
3. If the subject has not joined in, the stooge throws a paper basketball to the subject saying, "Here, you try it."
4. Stooge continues his game saying, "The trouble with paper basketballs is that you don't really have any control."
5. Stooge continues basketball, then gives it up saying, "This is one of my good days. I feel like a kid again. I think I'll make a plane." He makes a paper airplane saying, "I guess I'll make one of the longer ones."
6. Stooge flies plane. Gets up and retrieves plane. Flies again, etc.
7. Stooge throws plane at subject.

---

[5]It was, of course, imperative that the sequence with the stooge begin before the subject felt his first symptoms for otherwise the subject would be virtually forced to interpret his feelings in terms of events preceding the stooge's entrance. Pretests had indicated that, for most subjects, epinephrine-caused symptoms began within 3–5 minutes after injection. A deliberate attempt was made then to bring in the stooge within 1 minute after the subject's injection.

8. Stooge, flying plane, says, "Even when I was a kid, I was never much good at this."

9. Stooge tears off part of plane saying, "Maybe this plane can't fly but at least it's good for something." He wads up paper and making a slingshot of a rubber band begins to shoot the paper.

10. Shooting, the stooge says, "They [paper ammunition] really go better if you make them long. They don't work right if you wad them up."

11. While shooting, stooge notices a sloppy pile of manila folders on a table. He builds a tower of these folders, then goes to the opposite end of the room to shoot at the tower.

12. He misses several times, then hits and cheers as the tower falls. He goes over to pick up the folders.

13. While picking up, he notices, behind a portable blackboard, a pair of hula hoops which have been covered with black tape with a few wires sticking out of the tap. He reaches for these, taking one for himself and putting the other aside but within reaching distance of the subject. The stooge tries the hula hoop, saying, "This isn't as easy as it looks."

14. Stooge twirls hoop wildly on arm, saying, "Hey, look at this—this is great."

15. Stooge replaces the hula hoop and sits down with his feet on the table. Shortly thereafter the experimenter returns to the room.

This routine was completely standard, although its pace, of course, varied depending upon the subject's reaction, the extent to which he entered into this bedlam and the extent to which he initiated activities of his own. The only variations from this standard routine were those forced by the subject. Should the subject originate some nonsense of his own and request the stooge to join in, he would do so. And, he would, of course, respond to any comments initiated by the subject.

Subjects in each of the three "appropriateness" conditions and in the placebo condition were submitted to this setup. The stooge, of course, never knew in which condition any particular subject fell.

ANGER

Immediately after the injection, the experimenter brought a stooge into the subject's room, introduced the two and after explaining the necessity for a 20 minute delay for "the Suproxin to get from the injection site into the bloodstream" he continued, "We would like you to use these 20 minutes to answer these questionnaires." Then handing out the questionnaires, he concludes with, "I'll be back in 20 minutes to pick up the questionnaires and begin the tests of vision."

Before looking at the questionnaire, the stooge says to the subject,

> I really wanted to come for an experiment today, but I think it's unfair for them to give you shots. At least, they should have told us about the shots when they called us; you hate to refuse, once you're here already.

The questionnaires, five pages long, start off innocently requesting face sheet information and then grow increasingly personal and insulting. The stooge, sitting directly opposite the subject, paces his own answers so that at all times subject and stooge are working on the same question. At regular points in the questionnaire, the stooge makes a series of standardized comments about the questions. His comments start off innocently enough, grow increasingly querulous, and finally he ends up in a rage. In sequence, he makes the following comments.

1. Before answering any items, he leafs quickly through the questionnaire saying, "Boy, this is a long one."

2. Question 7 on the questionnaire requests, "List the foods that you would eat on a typical day." The stooge comments, "Oh, for Pete's sake, what did I have for breakfast this morning?"

3. Question 9 asks, "Do you ever hear bells?_____. How often?_____The stooge remarks, "Look at Question 9. How ridiculous can you get? I hear bells every time I change classes."

4. Question 13 requests, "List the childhood disease you have had and the age at which you had them" to which the stooge remarks, " I get annoyed at this childhood disease question. I can't remember what childhood diseases I had, and especially at what age. Can you?

5. Question 17 asks "What is your father's average annual income?" and the stooge says, "This really irritates me. It's none of their business what my father makes. I'm leaving that blank."

6. Question 25 presents a long series of items such

as "Does not bathe or wash regularly," "Seems to need psychiatric care," etc. and requests the respondent to write down for which member of his immediate family each item seems most applicable. The question specifically prohibits the answer "None" and each item must be answered. The stooge says, "I'll be damned if I'll fill out Number 25. 'Does not bathe or wash regularly'—that's a real insult." He then angrily crosses out the entire item.

7. Question 28 reads:

"How many times each week do you have sexual intercourse." 0–1____ 2–3____ 4–6____ 7 and over ____. The stooge bites out, "The hell with it! I don't have to tell them all this."

8. The stooge sits sullenly for a few moments then he rips up his questionnaire, crumples the pieces and hurls them to the floor, saying, "I'm not wasting any more time. I'm getting my books and leaving" and he stamps out of the room.

9. The questionnaire continues for eight more questions ending with: "With how many men (other than your father) has your mother had extramarital relationships?"

4 and under ____ : 5–9 ____ : 10 and over ____.

Subjects in the Epi Ign, Epi Inf and Placebo conditions were run through this "anger" inducing sequence. The stooge, again, did not know to which condition the subject had been assigned.

In summary, this is a seven condition experiment which, for two different emotional states, allows us (a) to evaluate the effects of "appropriateness" on emotional inducibility and (b) to begin to evaluate the effects of sympathetic activation on emotional inducibility. In schematic form the conditions are the following.

EUPHORIA	ANGER
Epi Inf	Epi Inf
Epi Ign	Epi Ign
Epi Mis	Placebo
Placebo	

The Epi Mis condition was not run in the Anger sequence. This was originally conceived as a control condition and it was felt that its inclusion in the Euphoria conditions alone would suffice as a means of evaluating the possible artifactual effect of the Epi Inf instructions.

MEASUREMENT

Two types of measures of emotional state were obtained. Standardized observation through a one-way mirror was the technique used to assess the subject's behavior. To what extent did he act euphoric or angry? Such behavior can be considered in a way as a "semiprivate" index of mood for as far as the subject was concerned, his emotional behavior could be known only to the other person in the room—presumably another student. The second type of measure was self-report in which, on a variety of scales, the subject indicated his mood of the moment. Such measures can he considered "public" indices of mood for they would, of course, be available to the experimenter and his associates.

OBSERVATION

Euphoria. For each of the first 14 units of the stooge's standardized routine an observer kept a running chronicle of what the subject did and said. For each unit the observer coded the subject's behavior in one or more of the following categories:

Category 1: Joins in activity. If the subject entered into the stooge's activities, e.g., if he made or flew airplanes, threw paper basketballs, hula hooped, etc., his behavior was coded in this category.

Category 2: Initiates new activity, A subject was so coded if he gave indications of creative euphoria, that is, if, on his own, he initiates behavior outside of the stooge's routine. Instances of such behavior would be the subject who threw open the window and, laughing, hurled paper basketballs at passersby; or, the subject who jumped on a table and spun one hula hoop on his leg and the other on his neck.

Categories 3 and 4: Ignores or watches stooge. Subjects who paid flatly no attention to the stooge or who, with or without comment, simply watched the stooge without joining in his activity were coded in these categories.

For any particular unit of behavior, the subject's behavior was coded in one or more of these categories. To test reliability of coding two observers independently coded two experimental sessions. The observers agreed completely on the coding of 88% of the units.

Anger. For each of the units of stooge behavior,

an observer recorded the subject's responses and coded them according to the following category scheme:

Category 1: Agrees. In response to the stooge the subject makes a comment indicating that he agrees with the stooge's standardized comment or that he, too, is irked by a particular item on the questionnaire. For example, a subject who responded to the stooge's comment on the "father's income" question by saying, "I don't like that kind of personal question either" would be so coded (scored +2).

Category 2: Disagrees. In response to the stooge's comment, the subject makes a comment which indicates that he disagrees with the stooge's meaning or mood; e.g., in response to the stooge's comment on the "father's income" question, such a subject might say, "Take it easy, they probably have a good reason for wanting the information" (scored –2).

Category 3: Neutral. A noncommittal or irrelevant response to the stooge's remark (scored 0).

Category 4: Initiates agreement or disagreement. With no instigation by the stooge, a subject, so coded, would have volunteered a remark indicating that he felt the same way or, alternatively, quite differently than the stooge. Examples would he "Boy I hate this kind of thing" or "I'm enjoying this" (scored +2 or –2).

Category 5: Watches. The subject makes no verbal response to the stooge's comment but simply looks directly at him (scored 0).

Category 6: Ignores. The subject makes no verbal response to the stooge's comment nor does he look at him; the subject, paying no attention at all to the stooge, simply works at his own questionnaire (scored –1).

A subject was scored in one or more of these categories for each unit of stooge behavior. To test reliability, two observers independently coded three experimental sessions. In order to get a behavioral index of anger, observation protocol was scored according to the values presented in parentheses after each of the above definitions of categories. In a unit-by-unit comparison, the two observers agreed completely on the scoring of 71% of the units jointly observed. The scores of the two observers differed by a value of 1 or less for 88% of the units coded and in not a single case did the two observers differ in the direction of their scoring of a unit.

SELF REPORT OF MOOD AND PHYSICAL CONDITION

When the subject's session with the stooge was completed, the experimenter returned to the room, took pulses and said:

> Before we proceed with the vision tests, there is one other kind of information which we must have. We have found, as you can probably imagine, that there are many things beside Suproxin that affect how well you see in our tests. How hungry you are, how tired you are, and even the mood you're in at the time—whether you feeel happy or irritated at the time of the time of testing will affect how well you see. To understand the data we collect on you, then, we must be able to figure out which effects are due to causes such as these and which are caused by Suproxin.

The only way we can get such information about your physical and emotional state is to have you tell us. I'll hand out these questionnaires and ask you to answer them as accurately as possible. Obviously, our data on the vision tests will only be as accurate as your description of your mental and physical state.

In keeping with this spiel, the questionnaire that the experimenter passed out contained a number of mock questions about hunger, fatigue, etc., as well as questions of more immediate relevance to the experiment. To measure mood or emotional state the following two were the crucial questions:

1. How irritated, angry or annoyed would you say you feel at present?

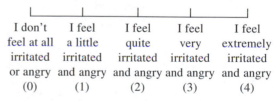

I don't feel at all irritated or angry (0)	I feel a little irritated and angry (1)	I feel quite irritated and angry (2)	I feel very irritated and angry (3)	I feel extremely irritated and angry (4)

2. How good or happy would you say you feel at present?

I don't feel at all happy or good (0)	I feel a little happy and good (1)	I feel quite happy and good (2)	I feel very happy and good (3)	I feel extremely happy and good (4)

To measure the physical effects of epinephrine and determine whether or not the injection had been successful in producing the necessary bodily state, the following questions were asked:

1. Have you experienced any palpitation (consciousness of your own heart beat)?

Not at all	A slight amount	A moderate amount	An intense amount
(0)	(1)	(2)	(3)

2. Did you feel any tremor (involuntary shaking of the hands, arms or legs)?

Not at all	A slight amount	A moderate amount	An intense amount
(0)	(1)	(2)	(3)

To measure possible effects of the instructions in the Epi Mis condition, the following questions were asked:

1. Did you feel numbness in your feet?
2. Did you feel any itching sensation?
3. Did you experience any feeling of headache?

To all three of these questions was attached a four-point scale running from "Not at all" to "An intense amount."

In addition to these scales, the subjects were asked to answer two open-end questions on other physical or emotional sensations they may have experienced during the experimental session. A final measure of bodily states was pulse rate which was taken by the physician or the experimenter at two times—immediately before the injection and immediately after the session with the stooge.

When the subjects has completed these questionnaires, the experimenter announced that the experiment was over, explained the deception and its necessity in detail, answered any questions, and swore the subjects to secrecy. Finally, the subjects answered a brief questionnaire about their experiences, if any, with adrenalin and their previous knowledge or suspicion of the experimental setup. There was no indication that any of the subjects had known about the experiment before-hand but 11 subjects were so extremely suspicious of some crucial feature of the experiment that their data were automatically discarded.

SUBJECTS

The subjects were all male, college students taking classes in introductory psychology at the Uni-

versity of Minnesota. Some 90% of the students in these classes volunteer for a subject pool for which they receive two extra points on their final exam for every hour that they serve as experimental subjects. For this study the records of all potential subjects were cleared with the Student Health Service in order to insure that no harmful effects would result from the injections.

EVALUATION OF THE EXPERIMENTAL DESIGN

The ideal test of our propositions would require circumstances which our experiment is far from realizing. First, the proposition that: "A state of physiological arousal for which an individual has no immediate explanation will lead him to label this state in terms of the cognitions available to him" obviously requires conditions under which the subject does not and cannot have a proper explanation of his bodily state. Though we toyed with such fantasies as ventilating the experimental room with vaporized adrenalin, reality forced us to rely on the disguised injection of Suproxin—a technique which was far from ideal for no matter what the experimenter told them, some subjects would inevitably attribute their feelings to the injection. To the extent that subjects did so, differences between the several appropriateness conditions should be attenuated.

Second, the proposition that: "Given the same cognitive circumstances the individual will react emotionally only to the extent that he experience, a state of physiological arousal" requires for its ideal test the manipulation of states of physiological arousal and of physiological quiescence. Though there is no question that epinephrine effectively produces a state of arousal, there is also no question that a placebo does not prevent physiological arousal. To the extent that the experimental situation effectively produces sympathetic stimulation in placebo subjects, the proposition is difficult to test, for such a factor would attenuate differences between epinephrine and placebo subjects.

Both of these factors, then, can be expected to interfere with the test of our several propositions. In presenting the results of this study, we shall first present condition by condition results and then evaluate the effort of these two factors on experimental differences.

Results

EFFECTS OF THE INJECTIONS ON BODILY STATE

Let us examine first the success of the injections at producing the bodily state required to examine the propositions at test. Does the injection of epinephrine produce symptoms of sympathetic discharge as compared with the placebo injection? Relevant data are presented in Table 3.1 where it can be immediately seen that on all items subjects who were in epinephrine conditions show considerably more evidence of sympathetic activation than do subjects in placebo conditions. In all epinephrine conditions pulse rate increases significantly when compared with the decrease characteristic of the placebo conditions. On the scales it is clear that epinephrine subjects experience considerably more palpitation and tremor than do placebo subjects. In an possible comparisons on these symptoms, the mean scores of subjects in any of the epinephrine conditions are greater than the corresponding scores in the placebo conditions at better than the .001 level of significance. Examination of the absolute values of these scores makes it quite clear that subjects in epinephrine conditions were, indeed, in a state of physiological arousal, while most subjects in placebo conditions were in a relative state of physiological quiescence.

The epinephrine injection, of course, did not work with equal effectiveness for all subjects; indeed for a few subjects it did not work at all. Such subjects reported almost no palpitation or tremor, showed no increase in pulse and described no other relevant physical symptoms. Since for such subjects the necessary experimental conditions were not established, they were automatically excluded from the data and all further tabular presentations

will not include such subjects. Table 3.1, however, does include the data of these subjects. There were four such subjects in euphoria conditions and one of them in anger conditions.

In order to evaluate further data on Epi Mis subjects it is necessary to note the results of the "numbness," "itching," and "headache" scales also presented in Table 3.1. Clearly the subjects in the Epi Mis condition do not differ on these scales from subjects in any of the other experimental conditions.

EFFECTS OF THE MANIPULATIONS ON EMOTIONAL STATE

Euphoria: Self-report. The effects of the several manipulations on emotional state in the euphoria conditions are presented in Table 3.2. The scores recorded in this table are derived, for each subject, by subtracting the value of the point he checks on the irritation scale from the value of the point he checks on the happiness scale. Thus, if a subject were to check the point "I feel a little irritated and angry" on the irritation scale and the point "I feel very happy and good" on the happiness scale, his score would be +2. The higher the positive value, the happier and better the subject reports himself as feeling. Though we employ an index for expositional simplicity, it should be noted that the two components of the index each yield results completely consistent with those obtained by use of this index.

Let us examine first the efforts of the appropriateness instructions. Comparison of the scores for the Epi Mis and Epi Inf conditions makes it immediately clear that the experimental differences are not due to artifacts resulting from the informed instructions. In both conditions the subject was

TABLE 3.1. The Effects of the Injections on Bodily State

Condition	N	Pulse		Self-rating of				
		Pre	Post	Palpitation	Tremor	Numbness	Itching	Headache
Euphoria								
Epi Inf	27	85.7	88.6	1.20	1.43	0	0.16	0.32
Epi Ign	26	84.6	85.6	1.83	1.76	0.15	0	0.55
Epi Mis	26	82.9	86.0	1.27	2.00	0.06	0.08	0.23
Placebo	26	80.4	77.1	0.29	0.21	0.09	0	0.27
Anger								
Epi Inf	23	85.9	92.4	1.26	1.41	0.17	0	0.11
Epi Ign	23	85.0	96.8	1.44	1.78	0	0.06	0.21
Placebo	23	84.5	79.6	0.59	0.24	0.14	0.06	0.06

TABLE 3.2. Self-Report of Emotional State in the Euphoria Conditions

Condition	N	Self-Report scales	Comparison	p^a
Epi Inf	25	0.98	Epi inf vs. Epi Mis	<.01
Epi Ign	25	1.78	Epi Inf vs. Epi Ign	.02
Epi Mis	25	1.90	Placebo vs. Epi Mis,	ns
Placebo	26	1.61	Ign, or Inf	

All p values reported throughout paper are two-tailed.

warned to expect a variety of symptoms as a consequence of the injection. In the Epi Mis condition, where the symptoms were inappropriate to the subject's bodily state the self-report score is almost twice that in the Epi Inf condition where the symptoms were completely appropriate to the subject's bodily state. It is reasonable, then, to attribute differences between informed subjects and those in other conditions to differences between informed subjects and those in other conditions to differences in manipulated appropriateness rather than to artifacts such as introspectiveness or self-examination.

It is clear that, consistent with expectations, subjects were most susceptible to the stooge's mood and consequently more euphoric when they had no explanation of their own bodily states than when they did. The means of both the Epi Ign and Epi Mis conditions are considerably greater than the mean of the Epi Inf condition.

It is of interest to note that Epi Mis subjects are somewhat more euphoric than are Epi Ign subjects. This pattern repeats itself in other data shortly to be presented. We would attribute this difference to differences in the appropriateness dimension. Although, as in the Epi Ign condition, a subject is not provided with an explanation of his bodily state, it is, of course, possible that he will provide one for himself which is not derived from his interaction with the stooge. Most reasonably he could decide for himself that he feels this way because of the injection. To the extent that he does so he should be less susceptible to the stooge. It seems probable that he would be less likely to hit on such an explanation in the Epi Mis condition than in the Epi Ign condition for in the Epi Mis condition both the experimenter and the doctor have told him that the effects of the injection would be quite different from what he actually feels. The effect of such instructions is probably to make it more dif-

ficult for the subject himself to hit on the alternative explanation described above. There is some evidence to support this analysis. In open-ended questions in which subjects described their own mood state, 28% of the subjects in the Epi Ign condition made some connection between the injection and their bodily state compared with the 16% of subjects in the Epi Mis condition who did so. It could be considered, then, that these three conditions fall along a dimension of appropriateness, with the Epi Inf condition at one extreme and the Epi Mis condition at the other.

Comparing the placebo to the epinephrine conditions, we note a pattern which will repeat itself throughout the data. Placebo subjects are less euphoric than either Epi Mis or Epi Ign subjects but somewhat more euphoric than Epi Inf subjects. These differences are not, however, statistically significant. We shall consider the epinephrine-placebo comparisons in detail in a later section of this paper following the presentation of additional relevant data. For the moment, it is clear that, by manipulating appropriateness has had a very strong effect on euphoria.

Behavior. Let us next examine the extent to which the subject's behavior was affected by the experimental manipulations. To the extent that his mood has been affected, one should expect that the subject will join in the stooge's whirl of manic activity and initiate similar activities of his own. The relevant data are presented in Table 3.3. The column labeled "Activity index" presents summary figures on the extent to which the subject joined in the stooge's activity. This is a weighted index which reflects both the nature of the activities in which the subject engaged and the amount of time he was active. The index was devised by assigning the following weights to the subject's activities: 5—hula hooping; 4—shooting with slingshot; 3—paper airplanes; 2—paper basketballs; 1—doodling; 0—does nothing. Pretest scaling on 15 college students ordered these activities with respect to the degree of euphoria they represented. Arbitrary weights were assigned so that the wilder the activity, the heavier the weight. These weights are multiplied by an estimate of the amount of time the subject spent in each activity and the summed products make up the activity index for each subject. This index may be considered a measure of behavioral euphoria. It should be noted that the same between-condition relationships hold for the two components of this index as for the index itself.

TABLE 3.3. Behavioral Indications of Emotional State in the Euphoria Conditions

Condition	N	Activity index	Mean number of acts initiated
Epi Inf	25	12.72	.20
Epi Ign	25	18.28	.56
Epi Mis	25	22.56	.84
Placebo	26	16.00	.54

	p value	
Comparison	Activity index	Initiates
Epi Inf vs. Epi Mis	.05	.03
Epi Inf vs. Epi Ign	ns	.08
or Inf	ns	ns

Tested by χ comparison of the proportion of subjects in each condition initiating new acts.

The column labeled "Mean number of acts initiated" presents the data on the extent to which the subject deviates from the stooge's routine and initiates euphoric activities of his own.

On both behavioral indices, we find precisely the same pattern of relationships as those obtained with self-reports. Epi Mis subjects behave somewhat more euphorically than do Epi Ign subjects who in turn behave more euphorically than do Epi Inf subjects. On all measures, then, there is consistent evidence that a subject will take over the stooge's euphoric mood to the extent that he has no other explanation of his bodily state.

Again it should be noted that on these behavioral indices, Epi Ign and Epi Mis subjects are somewhat more euphoric than placebo subjects but not significantly so.

Anger: Self-report. Before presenting data for the anger conditions, one point must be made about the anger manipulation. In the situation devised, anger, if manifested, is most likely to be directed at the experimenter and his annoyingly personal questionnaire. As we subsequently discovered, this was rather unfortunate, for the subjects, who had volunteered for the experiment for extra points on their final exam, simply refused to endanger these points by publicly blowing up, admitting their irritation to the experimenter's face or spoiling the questionnaire. Though as the reader will see, the subjects were quite willing to manifest anger when they were alone with the stooge, they hesitated to do so on material (self-ratings of mood and questionnaire) that the experimenter might see and only after the purposes of the experiment had been re-

vealed were many of these subjects willing to admit to the experimenter that they had been irked or irritated.

This experimentally unfortunate situation pretty much forces us to rely on the behavioral indices derived from observation of the subject's presumably private interaction with the stooge. We do, however, present data on the self-report scales in Table 3.4. These figures are derived in the same way as the figures presented in Table 3.2 for the euphoria conditions, that is, the value checked on the irritation scale is subtracted from the value checked on the happiness scale. Though, for the reasons stated above, the absolute magnitude of these figures (all positive) is relatively meaningless, we can, of course, compare condition means within the set of anger conditions. With the happiness-irritation index employed, we should, of course, anticipate precisely the reverse results from those obtained in the euphoria conditions; that is, the Epi Inf subjects in the anger conditions should again be less susceptible to the stooge's mood and should, therefore, describe themselves as in a somewhat happier frame of mind than subjects in the Epi Ign condition. This is the case; the Epi Inf subjects average 1.91 on the self-report scales while the Epi Ign subjects average 1.39.

Evaluating the effects of the injections, we note again that, as anticipated, Epi Ign subjects are somewhat less happy than placebo subjects but, once more, this is not a significant difference.

Behavior. The subject's responses to the stooge, during the period when both were filling out their questionnaires, were systematically coded to provide a behavioral index of anger. The coding scheme and the numerical values attached to each of the categories have been described in the methodology section. To arrive at an "Anger index" the numerical value assigned to a subject's responses to the stooge is summed together for the several units of stooge behavior. In the coding scheme

TABLE 3.4. Self-Report of Emotional State in the Anger Conditions

Condition	N	Self-Report scales	Comparison	p
Epi Inf	22	1.91	Epi Inf vs. Epi Ign	.08
Epi Ign	23	1.39	Placebo vs. Epi Ign or Inf	ns
Placebo	23	1.63		

used, a positive value to this index indicates that the subject agrees with the stooge's comment and is growing angry. A negative value indicates that the subject either disagrees with the stooge or ignores him.

The relevant data are presented in Table 3.5. For this analysis, the stooge's routine has been divided into two phases—the first two units of his behavior (the "long" questionnaire and "What did I have for breakfast?") are considered essentially neutral revealing nothing of the stooge's mood; all of the following units are considered "angry" units for they begin with an irritated remark about the "bells" question and end with the stooge's fury as he rips up his questionnaire and stomps out of the room. For the neutral units, agreement or disagreement with the stooge's remarks is, of course, meaningless as an index of mood and we should anticipate no difference between conditions. As can be seen in Table 3.5, this is the case.

For the angry units, we must, of course, anticipate that subjects in the Epi Ign condition will be angrier than subjects in the Epi Inf condition. This is indeed the case. The Anger index for the Epi Ign condition is positive and large, indicating that these subjects have become angry, while in the Epi Inf condition the Anger index is slightly negative in value indicating that these subjects have failed to catch the stooge's mood at all. It seems clear that providing the subject with an appropriate explanation of his bodily state greatly reduces his tendency to interpret his state in terms of the cognitions provided by the stooge's angry behavior.

Finally, on this behavioral index, it can be seen that subjects in the Epi Ign condition are significantly angrier than subjects in the Placebo condition. Behaviorally, at least, the injection of epi-

TABLE 3.5. Behavioral Indications of Emotional State in the Anger Conditions

Condtion	N	Neutral units	Anger units
Epi Inf	22	+0.07	−0.18
Epi Ign	23	+0.30	+2.28
Placebo	22*	−0.09	+0.79

Comparison for anger units	p
Epi Inf vs. Epi Ign	<.01
Epi Ign vs. Placebo	<.05
Placebo vs. Epi Inf	ns

*For one subject in this condition the sound system went dead and the observer could not, of course, code his reactions.

nephrine appears to have led subjects to an angrier state than comparable subjects who received placebo shots.

CONFORMATION OF DATA TO THEORETICAL EXPECTATIONS

Now that the basic data of this study have been presented, let us examine closely the extent to which they conform to theoretical expectations. If our hypotheses are correct and if this experimental design provided a perfect test for these hypotheses, it should be anticipated that in the euphoria conditions the degree of experimentally produced euphoria should vary in the following fashion:

$$\text{Epi Mis} \geq \text{Epi Ign} > \text{Epi Inf} = \text{Placebo}$$

And in the anger conditions, anger should conform to the following pattern

$$\text{Epi Ign} > \text{Epi Inf} = \text{Placebo}$$

In both sets of conditions, it is the case that emotional level in the Epi Mis and Epi Ign conditions is considerably greater than that achieved in the corresponding Epi Inf conditions. The results for the Placebo condition, however, are ambiguous for consistently the Placebo subjects fall between the Epi Ign and the Epi Inf subjects. This is a particularly troubling pattern for it makes it impossible to evaluate unequivocally the effects of the state of physiological arousal and indeed raises serious questions about our entire theoretical structure. Though the emotional level is consistently greater in the Epi Mis and Epi Ign conditions than in the Placebo condition, this difference is significant at acceptable probability levels only in the anger conditions.

In order to explore the problem further, let us examine the experimental factors identified earlier, which might have acted to restrain the emotional level in the Epi Ign and Epi Mis conditions. As was pointed out earlier, the ideal test of our first two hypotheses requires an experimental setup in which the subject has flatly no way of evaluating his state of physiological arousal other than by means of the experimentally provided cognitions. Had it been possible to physiologically produce a state of sympathetic activation by means other than injection, one could have approached this experimental ideal more closely than in the present setup. As it stands, however, there is always a reasonable alternative cognition available

TABLE 3.6. The Effects of Attributing Bodily State to the Injection on Anger in the Anger Epi Ign Condition

Condition	N	Anger index	p
Self-informed subjects	3	−1.67	ns
Others	20	+2.88	ns
Self-informed vs. Others			.05

to the aroused subject—he feels the way he does because of the injection. To the extent that the subject seizes on such an explanation of his bodily state, we should expect that he will be uninfluenced by the stooge. Evidence presented in Table 3.6 for the anger condition and in Table 3.7 for the euphoria conditions indicates that this is, indeed, the case.

As mentioned earlier, some of the Epi Ign and Epi Mis subjects in their answers to the open-end questions clearly attributed their physical state to the injection, e.g., "the shot gave me the shivers." In Tables 3.6 and 3.7 such subjects are labeled "Self-informed." In Table 3.6 it can be seen that the self-informed subjects are considerably less angry than are the remaining subjects; indeed, they are not angry at all. With these self-informed subjects eliminated the difference between Epi Ign and the Placebo conditions is significant at the .01 level of significance.

Precisely the same pattern is evident in Table 3.7 for the euphoria conditions. In both the Epi Mis and the Epi Ign conditions, the self-informed subjects have considerably lower activity indices than do the remaining subjects. Eliminating self-

TABLE 3.7. The Effects of Attributing Bodily State to the Injection on Euphoria in the Euphoria Epi Ign and Epi Mis Conditions

Epi Ign			
	N	Activity Index	p
Self-informed subjects	8	11.63	ns
Others	17	21.14	ns
Self-informed vs. Others			.05

Epi Mis			
	N	Activity Index	p
Self-informed subjects	5	12.40	ns
Others	20	25.10	ns
Self-informed vs. Others			.10

informed subjects, comparison of both of these conditions with the Placebo condition yields a difference significant at the .03 level of significance. It should be noted, too, that the self-informed subjects have the same score on the activity index as do the experimental Epi Inf subjects (Table 3.3).

It would appear, then, that the experimental procedure of injecting the subjects, by providing an alternative cognition, has, to some extent, obscured the effects of epinephrine. When account is taken of this artifact, the evidence is good that the state of physiological arousal is a necessary component of an emotional experience for when self-informed subjects are removed, epinephrine subjects give consistent indications of greater emotionality than do placebo subjects.

Let us examine next the fact that consistently the emotional level, both reported and behavioral, in Placebo conditions is greater than that in the Epi Inf conditions. Theoretically, of course, it should be expected that the two conditions will be equally low, for by assuming that emotional state is a joint function of a state of physiological arousal and of the appropriateness of a cognition we are, in effect, assuming a multiplicative function, so that if either component is at zero, emotional level is at zero. As noted earlier this expectation should hold if we can be sure that there is no sympathetic activation in the Placebo conditions. This assumption, of course, is completely unrealistic for the injection of placebo does not prevent sympathetic activation. The experimental situations were fairly dramatic and certainly some of the placebo subjects gave indications of physiological arousal. If our general line of reasoning is correct, it should be anticipated that the emotional level of subjects who give indications of sympathetic activity will be greater than that of subjects who do not. The relevant evidence is presented in Tables 3.8 and 3.9.

As an index of sympathetic activation we shall use the most direct and unequivocal measure available—change in pulse rate. It can be seen in Table 3.1 that the predominate pattern in the Placebo condition us a decreased in pulse rate. We shall assume, therefore, that those subjects whose pulse increases or remains the same give indications of sympathetic activity while those subjects whose pulse decreases do not. In Table 3.8, for the euphoria condition, it is immediately clear that subjects who give indications of sympathetic activity are considerably more euphoric than are subjects who show no sympathetic activity. This relation-

TABLE 3.8. Sympathetic Activation and Euphoria in the Euphoria Placebo Condition

Subjects whose:	N	Activity index	p
Pulse decreased	14	10.67	ns
Pulse increased or remained same	12	23.17	ns
Pulse decrease vs. pulse increase or same			.02

ship is, of course, confounded by the fact that euphoric subjects are considerably more active than noneuphoric subjects—a factor which independent of mood could elevate pulse rate. However, no such factor operates in the anger condition where angry subjects are neither more active nor talkative than calm subjects. It can be seen in Table 3.9 that Placebo subjects who show signs of sympathetic activation give indications of considerably more anger than do subjects who show no such signs. Conforming to expectations, sympathetic activation accompanies an increase in emotional level.

It should he noted, too, that the emotional levels of subjects showing no signs of sympathetic activity are quite comparable to the emotional level of subjects in the parallel Epi Inf conditions (see Tables 3.3 and 3.5). The similarity of these sets of scores and their uniformly low level of indicated emotionality would certainly make it appear that both factors are essential to an emotional state. When either the level of sympathetic arousal is low or a completely appropriate cognition is available, the level of emotionality is low.

Discussion

Let us summarize the major findings of this experiment and examine the extent to which they

TABLE 3.9. Sympathetic Activation and Anger in Anger Placebo Condition

Subjects whose:	N[a]	Activity index	p
Pulse decreased	13	+0.15	ns
Pulse increased or remained same	8	+1.69	ns
Pulse decrease vs. pulse increase or same			.01

[a]N reduced by two cases owing to failure of sound system in one case and experimenter's failure to take pulse in another.

support the propositions offered in the introduction of this paper. It has been suggested, first, that given a state of psyiological arousal for which an individual has no explanation, he will label this state in terms of the cognitions available to him. This implies, of course, that by manipulating the cognitions of an individual in such a state we can manipulate his feelings in diverse directions. Experimental results support this proposition for following the injection of epinephrine, those subjects who has no explanation for the bodily state thus produced, gave behavioral and self-report indications that they had been readily manipulable into the disparate feeling states of euphoria and anger.

From this first proposition, it must follow that given a state of physiological arousal for which the individual has a completely satisfactory explanation, he will not label this state in terms of the alternative cognitions available. Experimental evidence strongly supports this expectation. In those conditions in which subjects were injected with epinephrine and told precisely that they would feel and why, they proved relatively immune to any effects of the manipulated cognitions. In the anger condition, such subjects did not report or show anger; in the euphoria condition, such subjects reported themselves as far less happy than subjects with an identical bodily state but no adequate knowledge of why they felt the way they did.

Finally, it has been suggested that given constant cognitive circumstances, an individual will react emotionally only to the extent that he experiences a state of physiological arousal. Without taking account of experimental artifacts, the evidence in support of this proposition is consistent but tentative. When the effects of "self-informing" tendencies in epinephrine subjects and of "self-arousing" tendencies in placebo subjects are partialed out, the evidence strongly supports the proposition.

The pattern of data, then, falls neatly in line with theoretical expectations. However, the fact that we were forced, to some extent, to rely on internal analyses in order to partial out the effects of experimental artifacts inevitably makes our conclusions somewhat tentative. In order to further test these propositions on the interaction of cognitive and physiological determinants of emotional state, a series of additional experiments, published elsewhere, was designed to rule out or overcome the operation of these artifacts. In the first of these, S. Schachter and Wheeler (1962) extended the range of manipulated sympathetic activation by employing three experimental groups—epinephrine, placebo, and a group injected with the sympatholytic agent, chlorpromazine. Laughter at a slapstick movie was the dependent variable and the evidence is good that amusement is a direct function of manipulated sympathetic activation.

In order to make the epinephrine-placebo comparison under conditions which would rule out the operation of any self-informing tendency, two experiments were conducted on rats. In one of these Singer (1961) demonstrated that under fear inducing conditions, manipulated by the simultaneous presentation of a loud bell, a buzzer, and a bright flashing light, rats injected with epinephrine were considerably more frightened than rats injected with a placebo. Epinephrine-injected rats defecated, urinated, and trembled more than did placebo-injected rats. In nonfear control conditions, there were no differences between epinephrine and placebo groups, neither group giving any indication of fear. In another study, Latané and S. Schachter (1962) demonstrated that rats injected with epinephrine were notably more capable of avoidance learning than were rats injected with a placebo. Using a modified Miller-Mowrer shuttlebox, these investigators found that during an experimental period involving 200 massed trials, 15 rats injected with epinephrine avoided shock an average of 101.2 trials while 15 placebo-injected rats averaged only 37.3 avoidances.

Taken together, this body of studies does give strong support to the propositions which generated these experimental tests. Given a state of sympathetic activation, for which no immediately appropriate explanation is available, human subjects can be readily manipulated into states of euphoria, anger, and amusement. Varying the intensity of sympathetic activation serves to vary the intensity of a variety of emotional states in both rats and human subjects.

Let us examine the implications of these findings and of this line of thought for problems in the general area of the physiology of the emotions. We have noted in the introduction that the numerous studies on physiological differentiators of emotional states have, viewed en masse, yielded quite inconclusive results. Most, though not all, of these studies have indicated no differences among the various emotional states. Since as human beings, rather than as scientists, we have no difficulty identifying, labeling, and distinguishing

among our feelings, the results of these studies have long seemed rather puzzling and paradoxical. Perhaps because of this, there has been a persistent tendency to discount such results as due to ignorance or methodological inadequacy and to pay far more attention to the very few studies which demonstrate *some* sort of physiological differences among emotional states than to the very many studies which indicate no differences at all. It is conceivable, however, that these results should be taken at face value and that emotional states may, indeed, be generally characterized by a high level of sympathetic activation with few if any physiological distinguishers among the many emotional states. If this is correct, the findings of the present study may help to resolve the problem. Obviously this study does *not* rule out the possibility of physiological differences among the emotional states. It is the case, however, that given precisely the same state of epinephrine-induced sympathetic activation, we have, by means of cognitive manipulations, been able to produce in our subjects the very disparate states of euphoria and anger. It may indeed be the case that cognitive factors are major determines of the emotional labels we apply to a cognitive state of sympathetic arousal.

Let us ask next whether our results are specific to the state of sympathetic activation or if they are generalizable to other states of physiological arousal. It is clear that from our experiments proper, it is impossible to answer the question for our studies have been concerned largely with the effects of an epinephrine created state of sympathetic arousal. We would suggest, however, that our conclusions are generalizable to almost any pronounced internal state for which no appropriate explanation is available. This suggestion receives some support from the experiences of Nowlis and Nowlis (1956) in their program of research on the effects of drugs on mood. In their work the Nowlises typically administer a drug to groups of four subjects who are physically in one another's presence and free to interact. The Nowlises describe some of their results with these groups as follows:

At first we used the same drug for all 4 men. In those sessions seconal, when compared with a Placebo, increased the checking of such words as expansive, forceful, courageous, daring, elated, and impulsive. In our statistical analysis we were confronted with the stubborn fact that when the same drug is given to all 4 men in a group, the N that has to be entered into the analysis is 1, not 4. This increases the cost of an already expensive experiment by a considerable factor, but it cannot be denied that the effects of these drugs may be and often are quite contagious. Our first attempted solution was to run tests on groups in which each man had a different drug during the same session, such as 1 on seconal, 1 on benzedrine, 1 on dramamine, and 1 on placebo. What does seconal do? Cooped up with, say the egotistical benzedrine partner, the withdrawn, indifferent dramimine partner, and the slightly bored lactose man, the seconal subject reports that he is distractible, dizzy, drifting, glum, defiant, languid, sluggish, discouraged, dull, gloomy, lazy, and slow! This is not the report of mood that we got when all 4 men were on seconal. It thus appears that the moods of the partners do definitely influence the effect of seconal (p. 350).

It is not completely clear from this description whether this "contagion" of mood is more marked in drug than in placebo groups, but should this be the case, these results would certainly support the suggestion that our findings are generalizable to internal states other than that produced by an injection of epinephrine.

Finally, let us consider the implications of our formulation and data for alternative conceptualizations of emotion. Perhaps the most popular current conception of emotion is in terms of "activation theory" in the sense employed by Lindsley (1951) and Woodworth and Schlosberg (1958). As we understand this theory, it suggests that emotional states should be considered as at one end of a continuum of activation which is defined in terms of degree of autonomic arousal and of electroencephalographic measures of activation. The results of the experiment described in this paper do, of course, suggest that such a formulation is not completely adequate. It is possible to have very high degrees of activation without a subject either appearing to be or describing himself as "emotional." Cognitive factors appear to be indispensable elements in any formulation of emotion.

Summary

It is suggested that emotional states may be considered a function of a state of physiological arousal and of a cognition appropriate to this state of arousal. From this follows these propositions:

1. Given a state of physiological arousal for which an individual has no immediate explanation, he will label this state and describe his feelings in terms of the cognitions available to him. To the extent that cognitive factors are potent determiners of emotional states, it should he anticipated that precisely the same state of physiological arousal "joy" or "fury" or "jealousy" or any of a great diversity of emotional labels, depending on the cognitive aspects of the situation.
2. Given a state of physiological arousal for which an individual has a completely appropriate explanation, no evaluative needs will arise and the individual is unlikely to label his feelings in terms of the alternative cognitions available.
3. Given the same cognitive circumstances, the individual will react emotionally or describe his feelings as emotions only to the extent that he experiences a state of physiological arousal.

An experiment is described which, together with the results of other studies, supports these propositions.

REFERENCES

Ax, A. F. (1953). Physiological differentiation of emotional states. *Psychosomatic Medicine, 15,* 433–442.
Cannon, W. B. (1929). *Bodily changes in pain, hunger, fear, and rage* (2nd ed.) New York: Appleton.
Cantril, H., & Hunt, W. A. (1932). Emotional effects produced by the injection of adrenalin. *American Journal of Psychology, 44,* 300–307.
Festinger, L. (1954). A theory of social comparison processes. *Human Relations, 7,* 114–140.
Hunt, J. McV., Cole, M. W., & Reis, E. E. (1958). Situational cues distinguishing anger, fear, and sorrow. *American Journal of Psychology, 71,* 136–151.
James, W. (1890). *The principles of psychology.* New York: Holt.
Landis, C., & Hunt, W. A. (1932). Adrenalin and emotion. *Psychological Review, 39,* 467–485.
Latané, B., & Schachter, S. (1962). Adrenalin and avoidance learning. *J. Comp. Physiol. Psychol., 65,* 369–372.
Lindsley, D. B. (1951). Emotion. In S. S. Stevens (Ed.), *Handbook of experimental psychology* (pp. 473–516). New York: Wiley.
Marañon, G. (1924). Contribution à l'étude de l'action émotive de l'adrénaline. *Revue Française d' Endocrinologie, 2,* 301–325.
Nowlis, V., & Nowlis, H. H. (1956). The description and analysis of mood. *Annals of the Academy of Sciences, 65,* 345–355.
Ruckmick, C. A. (1936). *The psychology of feeling and emotion.* New York: McGraw-Hill.
Schachter, J. (1957). Pain, fear, and anger in hypertensives and normotensives: A psychophysiologic study. *Psychosomatic Medicine, 19,* 17–29.

Schachter, S. (1959). *The psychology of affiliation*. Stanford, CA: Stanford University Press.

Schachter, S., & Wheeler, L. (1962). Epinephrine, chlorpromazine, and amusement. *Journal of Abnormal Psychology, 65,* 121–128.

Singer, J. E. (1961). *The effects of epinephrine, chlorpromazine and dibenzyline upon the fright responses of rats under stress and non-stress conditions.* Unpublished doctoral dissertation, University of Minnesota.

Wolf, S., & Wolff, H. G. (1947). *Human gastric function.* New York: Oxford University Press.

Woodworth, R. S., & Schlosberg, H. (1958). *Experimental psychology.* New York: Holt..

Wrightsman, L. S. (1960). Effects of waiting with others on changes in level of felt anxiety. *Journal of Abnormal Psychology, 61,* 216–222.

Appraisal Components, Core Relational Themes, and the Emotions

Craig A. Smith • Vanderbilt University
Richard S. Lazarus • University of California, Berkeley

This study experimentally tests the contributions of specific appraisals, considered at both molecular (appraisal components) and molar (core relational themes) levels of analysis, to the experience of four emotions (anger, guilt, fear/anxiety, and sadness) using a two-stage directed imagery task. In Stage 1, subjects imagined themselves in scenarios designed to evoke appraisals hypothesised to produce either anger or sadness. In Stage 2, the scenarios unfolded in time to produce a second manipulation designed to systematically evoke the appraisals hypothesised to produce each of the four emotions under study. The results provided substantial support for the theoretically specified appraisal-emotion relationships for anger, guilt, and fear/anxiety. However, support for the predictions for sadness was weaker, partially due to ineffective manipulation of the relevant appraisals. Implications for the further development and testing of emotion theory are discussed.

Recent evidence is consistent with a key premise of all cognitive theories of emotion (e.g., Frijda, 1986; Lazarus & Folkman, 1984; Leventhal, 1984; Roseman, 1984; Scherer, 1984), namely, that certain relational meanings concerning the implications of one's circumstances for personal well-being, achieved via cognitive appraisal, are associated with specific emotions (e.g., Conway & Bekerian, 1987; Frijda, Kuipers, & ter Schure, 1989; Roseman, Spindel, & Jose, 1990; Shaver, Schwartz, Kirson, & O'Connor, 1987; Smith & Ellsworth, 1985).

Although this evidence contributes to a comprehensive theory of cognition and emotion, a number of problems limit the conclusions that can presently be drawn. One of the most important of these is the way appraisal is conceptualised (see Lazarus & Smith, 1988; Smith & Lazarus, 1990).

Appraisal is an evaluation of what one's relationship to the environment implies for personal well-being. Each positive emotion is said to be produced by a particular kind of appraised benefit, and each negative emotion by a particular kind of appraised harm. The emotional response is hypothesised to prepare and mobilise the person to cope with the particular appraised harm or benefit in an adaptive manner, that is, to avoid, minimise, or alleviate an appraised harm, or to seek, maximise, or maintain an appraised benefit. Whether a particular set of circumstances is appraised as harmful or beneficial depends, in part, on the person's specific configuration of goals and beliefs. Appraisal thus serves the important mediational role of linking emotional responses to environmental circumstances on the one hand, and personal goals and beliefs on the other.

We have proposed that two distinct but related types of cognition are involved in achieving this linkage, but that only one of these directly results in emotion (e.g., Lazarus, 1991a; Lazarus & Folkman, 1984; Lazarus & Smith, 1988; Smith & Lazarus, 1990; Smith, Haynes, Lazarus, & Pope, 1993). First, a well-developed construal of the factual nature of one's circumstances, reflecting one's *knowledge* or *beliefs* about what is happening, is necessary. However, we do not believe this construal by itself is sufficient to produce emotion. Instead, we propose that the "facts" as represented in this construal must be evaluated, or *appraised*, with respect to their significance for personal harm or benefit for emotion to result. The implications for personal well-being that emerge from this appraisal comprise the relational meaning that, we think, lies at the heart of emotion. In our usage, appraisal is meant to encompass the most proximal cognitive variables that directly result in emotion.[1] We consider appraisal to be a sufficient condition of emotion, as well as a necessary one, although this latter position is clearly controversial (see Lazarus, 1991b).

Previous examinations of cognition and emotion have tended to treat knowledge and appraisal as interchangeable. The resulting models intermix components of appraisal with components of knowledge and the subjective properties of the emotional response, producing considerable theoretical and empirical unclarity (cf. Lazarus & Smith, 1988; Scherer, 1988). Thus, the main goal of the present research was to isolate appraisal (as we have defined it) as best we could, and to examine the relationships between it and emotion. Further, in developing our specific appraisal model, we attempted to maximise the model's theoretical coherence by explicitly integrating it into the more general theory of stress and coping previously developed by Lazarus and his colleagues (e.g., Lazarus, 1966; Lazarus & Folkman, 1984).

The present research tests predictions of our model for four emotions—anger, guilt, sadness, and fear/anxiety—commonly thought to be responses to (appraised) actual or potential harm. Therefore, a brief summary of the model's predictions for these emotions follows. More complete treatment of the model and its theoretical underpinnings can be found elsewhere (Smith, 1991; Smith & Lazarus, 1990).

In describing the model, we should point out that it differs in several respects from the one currently advanced by Lazarus (1991a, 1991c). The discrepancies arise because in the time since the collaborative research reported here was performed, Lazarus has made changes in his analysis of the appraisal components and core relational themes postulated for several emotions. However, the present model is not obsolete. Smith continues to advance it, and it provides the foundation of his research programme (e.g., Smith, Ellsworth, & Pope, 1990; Smith & Pope, 1992. [. . .]

APPRAISAL COMPONENTS AND CORE RELATIONAL THEMES

We describe the relational meaning underlying each emotion at two levels of analysis, which represent complementary ways of conceptualising and assessing this meaning. The first level is molecular, and describes the specific judgements made by a person to evaluate particular relational harms and benefits. The adaptational issues at this level are single *components* of appraisal, which correspond closely to appraisal dimensions described in previous work (e.g., Frijda et al., 1989; Roseman, 1991; Scherer, 1984; Smith & Ellsworth, 1985). We have attempted to refine the components to reflect more clearly our conceptualisation of appraisal (cf. Lazarus & Smith, 1988).

To this we have added a second, more molar level of analysis that combines the individual appraisal components into summaries, or perhaps more accurately, gestalts of relational meaning, referred to as core relational themes.[2] A *core rela-*

---

[1] In the present discussion we focus on the *contents* of adult appraisal rather than the formal cognitive processes underlying these contents or the precursors of these contents in infants. In particular, we do not mean to imply that appraisals are necessarily conscious or deliberate. Instead, we have consistently maintained that appraisal may often be unconscious and automatic (e.g., Lazarus, 1966, 1991a; Smith & Lazarus, 1990). Nor do we mean to imply that the appraisals relevant to emotion are necessarily identical for adults and infants. Although beyond the scope of the present article, we consider both the development of appraisal-emotion relationships and the formal cognitive processes underlying appraisal to be important research topics.

[2] We are aware that Luborsky (1977, 1984) has used a similar term, "core conflictual relationship themes," with meanings that overlap but also differ from our core relational themes.

(continued)

tional theme is simply the central (therefore core) harm or benefit that underlies each of the negative and positive emotions. Whereas the individual appraisal components describe the specific questions evaluated in appraisal, the core relational themes efficiently capture the central relational meaning derived from the configuration of answers to these appraisal questions, which differs in each emotion.

For example, the core relational theme for sadness is proposed to be irrevocable loss. This relational meaning draws on more than a single appraisal component. There must be an appraised loss which, in turn, stems from evaluating (1) a goal commitment as being (2) threatened or harmed in a manner that (3) cannot be avoided or repaired. In our analysis, there are, in effect, three separate and distinct appraisal components, each of which makes an essential contribution to the complex relational meaning hypothesised to produce the emotion, but none of which individually constitutes the whole meaning.

Notably, the answers to the appraisal component questions are not conceptualised as causing the core relational themes in a mechanistic sense. Instead, the relationship between the appraisal components and core relational themes is one of logical or analytic causality: Each core relational theme is *defined* by a specific configuration of answers to several appraisal component questions. Thus, a specific configuration of appraisal components *implies* a particular relational meaning and vice versa—without any necessary causal ascription. In short, the appraisal components and core relational themes provide alternative ways of representing the *same* relational meanings associated with the various emotions. However, if one compares the appraisal components taken individually with the molar relational meanings as captured by the core relational themes, we would expect the

latter to be more efficient in predicting emotion because they capture the meaning of the full configuration of appraisal components in a way that transcends the components' individual meanings— much in the way a sentence captures a complex idea that goes beyond the meanings of its individual words. The two levels of analysis have different properties, which, as we discuss later, provide for different uses in the study of emotion.

SPECIFIC APPRAISALS IN ANGER, GUILT, FEAR/ANXIETY, AND SADNESS

Each appraisal component addresses one of the two general appraisal issues originally proposed by Lazarus and his colleagues as relevant to well-being under stress (e.g., Lazarus, 1966; Lazarus & Folkman, 1984): *primary appraisal* concerns whether and how the encounter is relevant to the person's well-being; and *secondary appraisal* concerns the person's resources and options for coping with the encounter.

The model utilises six appraisal components, two of primary appraisal, and four of secondary appraisal. The components of primary appraisal are motivational relevance and motivational congruence (or incongruence). *Motivational relevance* is an evaluation of the extent to which the encounter touches upon personal commitments (issues the person cares about), and thus the degree to which the encounter is personally relevant. *Motivational congruence* refers to the extent to which the encounter is consistent or inconsistent with the person's desires or goals.

The four components of secondary appraisal are accountability, problem-focused coping potential, emotion-focused coping potential, and future expectancy. *Accountability* determines who or what (oneself or someone/something else) is to receive the credit (if the encounter is motivationally congruent) or the blame (if it is motivationally incongruent) for the outcome of the encounter, and therefore who or what should be the target of any subsequent coping efforts. The two components of coping potential correspond to the two main means of reducing discrepencies between one's circumstances and one's desires and motivations (cf. Folkman & Lazarus, 1988; Kimble, 1990; Smith & Lazarus, 1990): *problem-focused coping potential* reflects evaluations of the person's ability to act directly upon the situation to bring or keep it in accord with the person's desires; and

His usage refers to the central and recurrent interpersonal scenarios of a troubled person. An example might be persons with a constant need to assert themselves with others, including loved ones, which, when enacted, leads to the vicious circle of rejection by the other, withdrawal by the needy person, and renewed but counterproductive efforts at assertion (see also Horowitz, 1988, on role relationship schemas). A major difference between Luborsky's usage and ours is the classic distinction between emotion traits and states. Because Luborsky is concerned with psychotherapy for dysfunctional people, his construct focuses on stable or recurrent themes, whereas ours focuses on the momentary themes of specific encounters.

emotion-focused coping potential refers to the perceived prospects of adjusting pyschologically to the encounter by altering one's interpretations, desires, and/or beliefs. *Future expectancy* refers to the possibilities, for any reason, of there being changes in the actual or psychological situation which could make the encounter seem more or less motivationally congruent.

Specific patterns of appraisals along the above components, we suggest, shape each of the four emotions under study. The postulated appraisal components and core relational themes for each emotion are listed in Table 4.1. The four emotions under study are *all* associated with various types of harm, and thus are characterised by motivational relevance and motivational incongruence. The components of secondary appraisal further define and differentiate the core relational themes that produce these emotions, and thus determine which specific emotion(s) will be experienced in the harmful or threatening encounter.

To illustrate, the core relational theme for anger is "other-blame," which is defined by combining primary appraisals of motivational relevance and motivational incongruence with a secondary appraisal of other accountability. Both the primary appraisals and other-accountability are necessary for an appraisal of other-blame, because accountability does not translate to blame in the absence of motivational incongruence. If one's circumstances are appraised as beneficial (i.e., motivationally relevant and motivationally congruent) an appraisal of other-accountability will contribute to a core relational theme of "other-credit" and a very different affective state, such as gratitude, will result (cf. Smith, 1991).

The core relational theme for guilt is "self-blame". This theme is also defined by combining primary appraisals of motivational relevance and motivational incongruence with accountability, but in this case the accountability is assigned to oneself. As with other-blame, both the primary appraisals and self-accountability are required to produce self-blame; under beneficial conditions the appraisal of self-accountability contributes to a core relational theme of "self-credit" and results in feelings of pride (Smith, 1991).

The core relational theme for fear/anxiety is "danger" or "threat"—the perception that one will not be able to psychologically adjust to a harm should it occur. In this theme, with its focus on the inability to adjust to potential harm, the primary appraisals of motivational relevance and motivational incongruence are combined with secondary appraisals of low emotion-focused coping potential. In contrast, for sadness the core relational theme is one of *irrevocable loss* or *helplessness about loss*, which emphasises the inability to restore the loss or eliminate the harm. This theme is defined by combining secondary appraisals of low problem-focused coping potential and negative future expectations with primary appraisals of motivational relevance and motivational incongruence.

TABLE 4.1. Appraisal Components and Core Relational Themes Associated with 4 Harm-related Emotions

Emotion	Core Relational Theme	Important Appraisal Components
Anger	Other-blame	1. Motivationally relevant 2. Motivationally incongruent 3. Other-accountability
Guilt	Self-blame	1. Motivationally relevant 2. Motivationally incongruent 3. Self-accountability
Fear/Anxiety	Danger/Threat	1. Motivationally relevant 2. Motivationally incongruent 3. Low/Uncertain (emotion-focused) coping potential
Sadness	Irrevocable loss Helplessness about harm or loss	1. Motivationally relevant 2. Motivationally incongruent 3. Low (problem-focused) coping potential 4. Low future-expectancy

Method

The present research was designed to provide an experimental test of the above appraisal model for anger, guilt, fear/anxiety, and sadness. We elected to examine four harm-related emotions because we believed manipulating appraisals associated with these emotions, which differ with regard to secondary appraisal components, would provide a more sensitive test of the discriminant validity of the model than could be obtained by contrasting one or two benefit-related emotions with one or two harm-related ones.

Our strategy was to manipulate the relevant appraisals twice. Once by systematically varying the conditions to which subjects were initially exposed, and a second time by systematically attempting to vary the subjects' appraisals during the experimental encounter. We think the second manipulation provides a more powerful test of the strength and specificity of the appraisal-emotion relationships than has been possible in most previous studies, which have relied more heavily on retrospective techniques. We reasoned that by dynamically manipulating specific appraisals during an encounter we would be able to rule out a host of third factor explanations for any observed appraisal-emotion relationships. A directed imagery task was employed because of the use of imagery appears to be a reliable technique for evoking emotion in the laboratory (e.g., Lang, 1979; Smith, 1989; Smith, McHugo, & Lanzetta, 1986), and it affords a high degree of experimental control.

OVERVIEW OF RESEARCH DESIGN

Four hypothetical scenarios, each involving multiple stages of an emotional encounter as it unfolded over time, were written to manipulate appraisal. These scenarios were administered in a between-subjects design. Two of the scenarios were designed to evoke initially appraisals of other-blame, theoretically associated with anger. One of these was learning that a friend had betrayed a confidence (the friend scenario); the other described being persecuted by a teaching assistant (the TA scenario). The remaining two scenarios were designed to evoke appraisals of irrevocable loss and helplessness, theoretically associated with sadness. One involved learning that a favourite relative had cancer (the cancer scenario); the other,

learning that one had performed poorly in an important course (the course scenario) .

The story of each scenario unfolded in two stages. The *first stage* established the motivational relevance for the central character (whose role the subject was instructed to assume), as well as both the motivational incongruence (or conflict) and the component(s) of secondary appraisal appropriate to the relational theme the scenario was intended to evoke. Thus the friend and TA scenarios emphasised other-accountability, whereas the cancer and course scenarios emphasised low coping potential and low future expectancy.

To allow a more explicit examination of the emotional effects of changes in appraisal over time, multiple versions of the *second stage* were written for each scenario, creating a second manipulation nested within the first. Whereas in Stage 1 each scenario was associated with a single appraisal condition, in Stage 2 different versions of each scenario were written to create four appraisal conditions: other-blame; self-blame; threat; and loss/ helplessness. To provide closure, there was also a *third stage* in which subjects were asked to resolve the scenario.

Subjects sequentially imagined themselves in the events of their assigned scenario, and at the end of Stages 1 and 2 they reported on their appraisals and emotions in that stage. This allowed systematic manipulations of appraisals as the scenario progressed and assessment of how these appraisals affected the emotions experienced. Table 4.2 summarises the overall experimental design.

SUBJECTS, EXPERIMENTAL DESIGN, AND SCENARIO CONTENTS

Subjects were 193 University of California at Berkeley undergraduates (89 males, 104 females) who participated as part of an introductory psychology course requirement. Subjects were tested individually, and each was randomly assigned to one of 16 experimental cells, resulting in between 11 and 13 subjects being assigned to each cell (see Table 4.2).

The experiment was organised as a 2 (Stage 1 manipulation) × 4 (Stage 2 manipulation) between-subjects design. There were two scenarios for each condition, serving as replications, to yield the 16 experimental cells. Subjects sequentially imagined themselves within each stage to simulate the experience of the encounter as it unfolded. By vary-

TABLE 4.2. Overview of the Experimental Design

Scenario Content	Appraisals Manipulated within Each Experimental Cell		
	Stage 1	Stage 2	Cell *N*
Friend	Other-blame	Other-blame	12
		Self-blame	13
		Threat	12
		Loss/Helplessness	12
TA	Other-blame	Other-blame	12
		Self-blame	12
		Threat	13
		Loss/Helplessness	12
Cancer	Loss/Helplessness	Other-blame	12
		Self-blame	11
		Threat	12
		Loss/Helplessness	12
Course	Loss/Helplessness	Other-blame	12
		Self-blame	12
		Threat	12
		Loss/Helplessness	12

ing the descriptions subjects received to guide their imagery, appraisal, at the level of both appraisal components and core relational themes, was manipulated in the first and second stages. All descriptions avoided any mention of emotional reactions to the depicted events to ensure that the subjects' reactions were guided by the provided contextual and cognitive cues.

For example, the first stage of the friend scenario established the subject's situation as important and motivationally incongruent, and suggested other-accountability:

You have a very close friend with whom you share much intimate detail about your life and emotions. This relationship is very important to you and the friend is your only confidant. You have revealed to him (her) that although you have an intimate, long-standing love relationship, you have also been seeing someone on the side. You impress upon your friend that it is very important to you that what you've revealed remains a strict secret, because you don't want your main lover to find out about the other relationship.

One day after class, you are talking to another student, who, in passing, indicates he (she) knows your secret.

Four distinct versions of the second stage for each scenario were used to create the Stage 2 manipulation. These versions correspond to the four appraisal conditions. Each version consisted of two parts. The first part was the same for each version, and simply added a factual development to the encounter. To illustrate, in the friend scenario:

You seek out your friend and confront him (her) with your suspicion that he (she) has revealed your secret. At first your friend denies being the source of the leak, but under intense questioning admits that he (she) told the other student and tries to make light of the whole incident.

The second part contained the appraisal manipulation and necessarily differed across appraisal conditions. In addition to motivational relevance and motivational incongruence, the four versions emphasised the secondary appraisal components defining the themes of other-blame, self-blame, threat, and loss/helplessness, respectively, as well as the themes themselves.

The other-blame version emphasised someone else's accountability. In the friend scenario:

You can't believe your friend betrayed your trust like this, especially since he (she) knew how important this secret was to you. You believe that for the first time you're seeing your friend for what he (she) really is, and that what he's (she's) done is totally inexcusable. You wonder why you ever liked him (her).

In contrast, the self-blame version emphasised the subjects' own accountability:

You realise that you've made a mess of things, and are largely to blame for what has happened. You now think that you were very wrong to cheat on your main lover in the first place, and you now see that the knowledge of your affair was simply too much of a burden to place upon your friend.

The threat version emphasised the subject's low emotion-focused coping potential by raising uncertainties about both the long-term implications of the encounter and the subject's ability to adapt to those implications:

You wonder how far your secret has spread, who knows about your affair, and how much social harm you will suffer now that they know. You realise there is serious danger that you won't be able to salvage things if your main lover learns of your secret.

Finally, the loss/helplessness version emphasised both the subject's inability to alter the undesirable situation (low problem-focused coping potential) and the absence of any expectation for improvement (low future expectancy):

You wish that you could change your friend so that he (she) wouldn't do things like this, but you know that there's nothing you can do. You realise that because of what's happened the close trust you once shared with this person is gone, and you're certain that you will never be able to feel the same way about this person again. The end of this trust and friendship is a great personal loss.

The complete text for the first two stages of the other three scenarios is presented in the Appendix. The third stage simply provided the subjects with an opportunity to resolve the episode.

PROCEDURE

Subjects participated in the experiment as part of a study of "emotion, stress, and coping." They were provided with three clearly labelled envelopes containing the three stages of their assigned scenario. They were told that for each stage they should:

Read through the description of the stage, and picture the situation that is described to you in your mind as best you can. Pretend that you are actually living through this experience ... Try to mentally create the thoughts and feelings you would have if you were actually in this situation. When you . . . are experiencing the feelings it [the situation] evokes, please answer the questions that follow . . . as you think you would if you were actually experiencing the situation.

For each stage, subjects first imagined themselves in the described situation, and then to ensure engagement in the imagery task, they wrote a few sentences describing their reactions. Next, they completed three questionnaires designed to measure their appraisals of the stage (in terms of both components and relational themes) and their emotional reactions to it. The order in which the questionnaires were presented was counterbalanced across subjects, with each subject receiving the same order for all stages. After completing the questionnaires for a stage, the subjects repeated the entire procedure for the next stage, until all three stages had been completed. At that time, the research purposes were explained and any questions were answered.

MEASURES

Appraisal Components. The subjects' appraisals for each stage were assessed with seven face-valid items designed to measure motivational relevance, motivational incongruence, accountability, problem-focused coping potential, emotion-focused coping potential, and future expectancy. A single item was used to measure each component, with the exception of two accountability items to measure self-accountability (i.e., "To what extent do you consider YOURSELF responsible for this situation?") and other-accountability (i.e., "To what extent do you consider SOMEONE ELSE responsible for this situation?"). Four items were rated on scales ranging from 1 (not at all) to 11 (extremely). The three scales measuring future expectancy and coping potential were bipolar and ranged from –5 (low coping potential, negative expectations) to +5 (high coping potential, positive expectations).

Core Relational Themes. A second questionnaire contained 42 face-valid items representing the core relational themes hypothesised to be associated with a variety of emotions. Each item reflected a core relational theme for a particular emotion (e.g., two items measuring irrevocable loss/ helplessness were: "I feel helpless"; and "Nothing can ever be done to fix this bad situation"). Subjects indicated on 9-point scales (1–9) the extent to which each statement characterised their thoughts during the stage they had just imagined. Four scales, measuring the core relational themes theoretically associated with anger, guilt, fear/anxiety, and sadness, were recovered for analysis. Scale scores were computed by taking the mean of the contributing items. Internal consistencies were estimated by computing the mean coefficient alpha for the first two scenario stages. The recovered scales and their estimated reliabilities were: other-blame (6 items: $\alpha = 0.89$); self-blame (3 items: $\alpha = 0.89$); threat (3 items: $\alpha = 0.69$); and loss/ helplessness (6 items: $\alpha = 0.89$).

Emotions. An emotion questionnaire (Ellsworth & Smith, 1988a) required subjects to rate on 9-point scales (1–9) the extent to which each of 33 emotional adjectives characterised their emotional state during the stage they had just imagined. Using the same procedures as for the core relational theme measures, scales were recovered to measure anger (6 items: $\alpha = 0.86$), guilt (3 items: $\alpha = 0.69$), fear/anxiety (3 items: $\alpha = 0.95$), and sadness (3 items: $\alpha = 0.73$).

ANALYTIC STRATEGY

Two sets of analyses within each stage were conducted for each of the four emotions to examine the effectiveness of the manipulations in eliciting the desired appraisals, and to assess the effects of the appraisals on emotion. Multiple regression equations using a priori contrasts examined the overall effects of the appraisal manipulations (Cohen & Cohen, 1983, pp. 204–217; Rosenthal & Rosnow, 1985). Then, path analyses evaluated the hypothesised causal sequence from scenario to appraisal to emotion, for each emotion separately. In addition, two sets of follow-up analyses were conducted to examine further the discriminant and predictive validity of the appraisal model.

Stage 1 Manipulation. The effects of the Stage 1 manipulation were measured by three orthogonal contrasts. Conceptually, this manipulation created two experimental conditions, other-blame and loss/helplessness, both with two replications involving different scenarios. The first contrast tested the main effects of the manipulation, and the second and third contrasts tested the replicability of any significant manipulation effects by testing for differences between the two scenarios within each condition.

Stage 2 Manipulation. The effects of the Stage 2 manipulation were measured with 12 additional contrasts that completed the partitioning of the full 16-cell between-subjects design. To adequately test for the predicted effects, the set of contrasts differed for each emotion.

The first three contrasts tested the main effects of the Stage 2 manipulation. The first is of greatest theoretical interest, and pitted the condition hypothesised to produce the appraisal of interest (i.e., the other-blame condition for anger, the self-blame condition for guilt, the threat condition for fear/anxiety, and the loss/helplessness condition for sadness) against the other three combined conditions. To determine the next two contrasts the two conditions involving blame were paired, as were the ones involving loss-helplessness and threat. The remaining member of the pair split by the first contrast was pitted against the other two conditions to form the second contrast. The third contrast pitted these latter two conditions against each other. For example, the first three contrasts of the anger analysis were: (1) other-blame vs. the other three conditions; (2) self-blame vs. combined loss/helplessness and threat; and (3) loss/ helplessness vs. threat.

The remaining nine contrasts always tested for interactions between the main effects of the Stage 2 manipulation (as coded by the first three contrasts of the set) and the effects of the Stage 1 manipulation (as reflected in the three Stage 1 contrasts).

For the analysis of each emotion (in both stages), the variables consisted of the emotion, its proposed core relational theme (other-blame for anger; self-blame for guilt; threat for fear/anxiety; and loss/ helplessness for sadness), and the appraisal components hypothesised to define that theme. Motivational relevance and motivational incongruence were always included, but the components of secondary appraisal were limited to those most theoretically relevant to the emotion (other-accountability for anger; self-accountability for guilt; emotion-focused coping potential for fear/anxiety; and both problem-focused coping potential and future expectancy for sadness).

In addition, to assess accurately the effectiveness of the Stage 2 manipulation in *changing* appraisal and emotion, all analyses in this stage statistically controlled for all relevant Stage 1 variables (i.e., the emotion, the theme, and the relevant appraisal components) by entering them into the analyses prior to the variables of interest.

In constructing the theoretically derived path analyses the contrasts coding the manipulation effects were always assumed to be first in the causal sequence and to be followed, in order, by the appraisal components, the core relational themes, and the emotions. No attempt was made to assign causal priority among the appraisal components.

The ordering of the appraisal components and core relational themes was not intended to reflect a true causal process, because, as discussed above, the components and themes reflect alternative descriptions of the *same* relational meanings. Instead, the ordering of the appraisal variables reflects the emergent status of the core relational themes. Treating the components as "causally prior" to the themes allowed us to examine the degree to which the individual appraisal components contributed to the *definition* of the core relational themes, as hypothesised.

The direct effects on each variable were estimated by regressing the variable simultaneously on all causally prior variables. Thus, in Stage 1 the independent variables included any prior appraisal variables and the three scenario contrasts. In Stage 2 they included any causally prior variables from the second stage, all 15 contrasts, and all relevant Stage 1 variables.

Due to the complexity of the experimental design the results to be presented were simplified as follows: first, in presenting the findings for Stage 2, the effects of variables from the first stage are not depicted because they reveal little beyond significant stability across stages for all variables. In addition, all significant effects (at $P < 0.05$, two-tailed) directly relevant to the experimental hypotheses (e.g., main effects of the appraisal manipulations) are presented, but additional effects (e.g., manipulation-by-scenario interactions) are discussed only if they in some way qualify the interpretation or generalisability of a theoretically relevant effect. Finally, in depicting the results of the second appraisal manipulation, simple change scores (from Stage 1 to Stage 2) are presented in lieu of the regression residuals upon which the statistical inferences are based, because the change scores preserve information about the absolute direction of change that is lost in the residuals, and the change scores were highly correlated with the residuals for each variable (average $r = 0.94$).

PREDICTIONS

Two sets of predictions corresponded to the two sets of appraisal manipulations. First, in Stage 1 the friend and TA scenarios were designed to evoke appraisals of other-blame, whereas the cancer and course scenarios were designed to evoke appraisals of loss/helplessness. Because both themes involve appraisals of high motivational relevance and high motivational incongruence, no systematic differences were anticipated for these appraisal components. However, the friend and TA scenarios, relative to the cancer and course ones, were expected to be high in both other-accountability and other-blame, whereas the cancer and course scenarios were expected to be relatively low in problem-focused coping potential and future expectancy and relatively high in loss/helplessness. These appraisal differences were expected to result in relatively high levels of anger in the friend and TA scenarios, and relatively high levels of sadness in the cancer and course scenarios. No systematic predictions were advanced for self-accountability, self-blame, and guilt, or for emotion-focused coping potential, threat, and fear-anxiety.

For the Stage 2 manipulation, motivational relevance and motivational incongruence were again not expected to vary across conditions. However, through appropriate changes in the relevant component(s) of secondary appraisal, each manipulation condition was expected to produce elevated levels of the targeted core relational theme, and it was expected that these themes would be associated with increases in the theoretically linked emotion. Thus, other-accountability, other-blame, and anger were expected to be elevated in the other-blame condition; self-accountability, self-blame, and guilt were expected to be elevated in the self-blame condition; emotion-focused coping potential was expected to be depressed, and both threat and fear/anxiety were expected to be elevated in the threat condition; and depressed levels of both problem-focused coping potential and future expectancy were expected to be accompanied by elevations in loss/helplessness and sadness in the loss/helplessness condition.

In all cases the path analyses were expected to provide support for the hypothesised sequence. The appraisal manipulation was expected to have direct effects on the relevant components of secondary appraisal, but, because these components help to define the core relational themes, the effects on the core relational themes were expected to be mediated through the appraisal components (as evidenced by direct effects of the components on the themes after controlling for the effects of the manipulation)

In addition, effects of the manipulation on emotion were expected to be mediated through the relational meanings (considered at both molecular and molar levels of analysis). However, because we consider the core relational themes to be more efficient summaries of the relational meanings than the individual appraisal components, we anticipated the themes would demonstrate direct effects on the emotions even after controlling for the contributions of the individual appraisal components. Conversely, to the extent that the core relational themes effectively captured the contributions of the individual appraisal components, the components of secondary appraisal (hypothesised to be responsible for differentiating one core relational theme from another) were not expected to exert direct effects on the emotions after controlling for the contributions of the themes.

Results and Discussion

The results for both sets of manipulations are presented for each of the four emotions in turn, and the follow-up analyses are presented last. Table 4.3 presents the means depicting the main effects

of the appraisal manipulations on all variables considered (i.e., appraisal components, core relational themes, and emotions).

ANGER

Stage 1 Manipulation. Examination of Table 4.3 indicates that, as assumed, appraisals of motivational relevance (overall $M = 10.03$) and motivational incongruence (overall $M = 9.52$) were generally rated high. However, both appraisal components were higher in the loss/helplessness condition than in the other-blame one, and although small in absolute magnitude, these differences were statistically significant (motivational relevance: $\beta = -0.24$, $t(189) = -3.40$, $P < 0.001$; motivational incongruence: $\beta = -0.18$, $t(189) = -2.52$, $P < 0.05$).

More importantly, however, the appraisal manipulation produced the anticipated differences in other-accountability and other-blame, and these differences were accompanied by the predicted differences in anger. Other-accountability, $\beta = 0.28$, $t(189) = 5.07$, $P < 0.001$, other-blame, $\beta = 0.66$,

TABLE 4.3. Means for Main Effects of both Appraisal Manipulations

Measure	Stage 1 Manipulation		Stage 2 Manipulation			
	Other-blame	Loss/Helplessness	Other-blame	Self-blame	Threat	Loss/Helplessness
Appraisal components						
Motivational relevance	9.72	10.34	−0.44	−0.25	0.10	−0.13
Motivational incongruence	9.18	9.87	−0.29	−0.48	0.22	0.08
Other-accountability	7.72	6.00	1.27	−2.42	−0.33	−0.02
Self-accountability	6.13	6.31	−1.38	1.88	−0.35	−0.81
Emot. foc. coping pot.	1.45	1.63	0.38	0.40	−0.51	−0.48
Prob. foc. coping pot.	0.22	−0.65	−0.19	0.38	−0.10	−0.27
Future expectancy	1.27	0.60	−0.65	−0.21	−0.96	−0.71
Core relational themes						
Other-blame	5.06	2.32	1.21	−1.05	0.53	−0.04
Self-blame	4.34	3.89	−0.97	1.60	0.10	−0.47
Threat	4.44	4.54	−0.47	−0.63	0.88	−0.08
Loss/Helplessness	3.96	4.63	0.37	−0.05	0.78	0.79
Emotions						
Anger	6.07	4.26	0.50	−0.93	0.11	−0.36
Guilt	4.29	5.11	−0.74	1.24	−0.05	−0.31
Fear/Anxiety	4.87	6.36	−0.92	−0.64	0.95	−0.30
Sadness	5.56	6.72	−0.40	−0.09	−0.07	0.22

Note. All means for Stage 1 reflect raw ratings for each scale. All means for Stage 2 reflect change scores from Stage 1 to Stage 2. Although change scores are reported here and in the text to preserve information about the absolute sign of change, all inferential statistics for Stage 2 data are based on residualised Stage 2 scores, obtained for each variable by partialling out the variance attributable to that variable in Stage 1.

$t(189) = 12.64$, $P < 0.001$, and anger, ß = 0.51, $t(189) = 8.69$, $P < 0.001$, were each significantly higher in other-blame condition than in the loss/helplessness one.

The path analysis provided clear support for the proposed model. As predicted, controlling for the effects of the manipulation, other-accountability contributed directly to the core relational theme of other-blame, ß = 0.38, $t(186) = 6.17$, $P < 0.001$, which in turn, had a strong direct effect on anger, even after controlling for the contributions of the individual appraisal components, ß = 0.51, $t(185) = 6.84$, $P < 0.001$. After controlling for other-blame, however, other-accountability did not contribute directly to anger, ß = − 0.01, $t(185) < 1$, ns.

Contrary to expectations, comparison to the two different scenarios of loss/helplessness revealed a dissociation between other-accountability and other-blame in the cancer scenario. Comparison of the cancer and course scenarios indicated that other-accountability was elevated in the cancer scenario (cancer $M = 8.35$, course $M = 3.65$), ß = 0.56, $t(189) = 9.96$, $P < 0.001$, but that this did not translate to either other-blame or anger. The cancer and course scenarios did not differ in the levels of other-blame they evoked (cancer $M = 2.33$, course $M = 2.32$), ß = 0.01, $t(189) < 1$, ns, and anger was actually significantly lower in the cancer scenario ($M = 3.54$) than in the course scenario ($M = 4.97$), ß = −0.28, $t(189) = −4.89$, $P < 0.001$.

Stage 2 Manipulation. The results of the Stage 2 manipulation offer strong support for the predictions for anger. As reflected in the means shown in Table 4.3, relative to the other three conditions, the other-blame condition resulted in elevated levels of other-accountability, ß = 0.28, $t(172) = 5.82$, $P < 0.001$, other-blame, ß = 0.26, $t(172) = 6.55$, $P < 0.001$, and anger, ß = 0.18, $t(172) = 3.60$, $P < 0.001$. Further, although not anticipated (but consistent with the model), relative to the combined threat and loss/helplessness conditions, the self-blame condition resulted in significantly reduced levels of other-accountability, ß = −0.22, $t(172) = −4.54$, $P < 0.001$, other-blame, ß = −0.23, $t(172) = −5.87$, $P < 0.001$, and anger, ß = −0.15, $t(172) = −3.05$, $P < 0.01$.

The effects on anger of the other-blame manipulation did not interact with the first appraisal manipulation. However, the effectiveness of the self-blame manipulation in reducing anger did. This manipulation reduced other-accountability ($M =$

−3.08), other-blame ($M = −1.91$), and anger ($M = −1.61$) more in the two scenarios in which they had previously been elevated (friend and TA), than in the scenarios originally associated with loss/helplessness (cancer and course; other-accountability: $M = −1.69$, ß = −0.18, $t(172) = −3.68$, $P < 0.001$; other-blame: $M = −0.17$, ß = −0.23, $t(172) = −5.96$, $P < 0.001$; anger: $M = −0.21$, ß = −0.18, $t(172) = −3.68$, $P < 0.001$).

The path analysis indicated that, in accord with predictions, changes in other-accountability directly contributed to changes in other-blame, ß = 0.43, $t(169) = 8.31$, $P < 0.001$, which, in turn, directly influenced the changes in anger, ß = 0.39, $t(168) = 3.80$, $P < 0.001$. As in the first stage, after controlling for the changes in other-blame, changes in other accountability did not contribute directly to the changes in anger, ß = 0.07, $t(168) < 1$, ns.

GUILT

Stage 1 Manipulation. The Stage 1 manipulation was not expected to influence appraisals of self-blame or feelings of guilt systematically, and consistent with this expectation, the first stage analyses of self-accountability, self-blame, and guilt primarily revealed effects specific to individual scenarios that will not be considered in detail. However, comparison of the cancer and course scenarios revealed a dissociation between emotion and appraisal in the cancer scenario somewhat analogous to the one observed for anger. Both self-accountability ($M = 4.13$) and self-blame ($M = 2.43$) were significantly lower in the cancer scenario than in the course scenario (self-accountability, $M = 8.50$, ß = −0.52, $t(189) = −9.80$, $P < 0.001$; self-blame: $M = 5.35$, ß = −0.45, $t(189) = −7.88$, $P < 0.001$). However, guilt was elevated equally in both scenarios (Cancer $M = 5.10$, Course $M = 5.11$), ß = 0.00, $t(189) < 1$, ns. The net effect of this dissociation was that although the combined loss/helplessness scenarios did not reliably differ from the combined other-blame ones in terms of either self-accountability, ß = −0.03, $t(189) < 1$, ns, or self-blame, ß = 0.10, $t(189) = 1.73$, $P = 0.09$, guilt was significantly higher in the loss/ helplessness scenarios ($M = 5.11$) than in the other-blame ones ($M = 4.29$), ß = −0.21, $t(189) = −3.74$, $P < 0.001$.

This one anomaly aside, the results of the path analysis for guilt were largely consistent with predictions. Appraisals of self-accountability contributed directly to self-blame, ß = 0.71, $t(186)$ = 12.91, $P < 0.001$, which, in turn, directly influenced guilt, ß = 0.38, $t(185)$ = 4.24, $P < 0.001$, but self-accountability did not contribute directly to guilt, ß = 0.15, $t(185)$ 1.59, $P = 0.11$.

Stage 2 Manipulation. The results of the Stage 2 manipulation were straightforward. As can be seen in Table 4.3, relative to the other three conditions, the self-blame condition resulted in elevated levels of self-accountability, ß = 0.39, $t(172)$ = 8.28, $P < 0.001$, self-blame, ß = 0.37, $t(172)$ = 7.90, $P < 0.001$, and guilt, ß = 0.35, $t(172)$ = 6.37, $P < 0.001$. Further, the path analysis indicated that changes in self-accountability contributed directly to changes in self-blame, ß = 0.55, $t(169)$ = 8.82, $P < 0.001$, and changes in self-blame contributed directly to changes in guilt, ß = 0.32, $t(168)$ = 3.24, $P < 0.005$. In addition, the changes in self-accountability contributed directly to the changes in guilt, ß = 0.27, $t(168)$ = 2.79, $P < 0.01$.

FEAR/ANXIETY

Stage 1 Manipulation. The Stage 1 manipulation did not directly vary appraisals relevant to fear/anxiety. Nonetheless, as indicated in Table 4.3, fear/anxiety was significantly higher in the loss/helplessness scenarios than in those involving other-blame, ß = –0.31, $t(189)$ = –4.68, $P < 0.001$, but the corresponding effects were not observed for either emotion-focused coping potential or threat, both $ts < 1$, ns. Rather, examination of the individual scenarios indicated that fear/anxiety and its theoretically relevant appraisals (low emotion-focused coping potential and high threat) were elicited in the two loss/helplessness scenarios (which did not significantly differ) and, to a lesser degree, in the friend scenario. Relative to the TA scenario, emotion-focused coping potential tended to be depressed in the friend scenario (Friend $M = 0.98$; TA $M = 1.92$), ß = –0.13, $t(189)$ = –1.87, $P = 0.06$, and both threat (Friend $M = 5.02$; TA $M = 3.86$), ß = 0.23, $t(189)$ = 3.23, $P < 0.01$, and fear (Friend $M = 5.84$; TA $M = 3.90$), ß = 0.29, $t(189)$ = 4.40, $P < 0.001$, were elevated.

The path analysis indicated that the observed variation in fear/anxiety was largely mediated through appraisal: Low emotion-focused coping potential contributed to the theme of threat, ß = – 0.53, $t(186)$ = –8.88, $P < 0.001$, which, in turn, had a positive direct effect on fear-anxiety, ß =

0.40, $t(185)$ = 5.70, $P < 0.001$. Emotion-focused coping potential did not directly affect fear/anxiety, however, ß = –0.02, $t(185) < 1$, ns.

Stage 2 Manipulation. The results of the Stage 2 manipulation provide further support for the predictions for fear/anxiety. As shown in Table 4.3, relative to the other three conditions, the threat condition resulted in reduced levels of emotion-focused coping potential, ß = –0.10, $t(172)$ = –2.10, $P < 0.05$, and elevated levels of both threat, ß = 0.15, $t(172)$ = 2.82, $P < 0.01$, and fear, ß = 0.18, $t(172)$ = 4.40, $P < 0.001$. Further, although not anticipated, relative to the combined self- and other-blame conditions, the loss/helplessness condition produced reduced levels of emotion-focused coping potential, ß = –0.13, $t(172)$ = –2.72, $P < 0.01$, and elevated levels of threat, ß = 0.25, $t(172)$ = 4.84. $P < 0.001$, and fear/ anxiety, ß = 0.23, $t(172)$ = 5.28, $P < 0.001$. The path analysis indicated that reductions in emotion-focused coping potential contributed directly to increases in threat, ß = – 0.44, $t(169)$ = –5.61, $P < 0.001$, which in turn directly influenced increases in fear/anxiety, ß = 0.31, $t(168)$ = 4.96, $P < 0.001$. In addition, reductions in emotion-focused coping potential contributed directly to increases in fear/anxiety, ß = –0.17, $t(168)$ = –2.44, $P < 0.05$.

SADNESS

Stage 1 Manipulation. As indicated in Table 4.3, the main effects of the Stage 1 manipulation for sadness were largely consistent with predictions. The loss/helplessness scenarios produced more pessimistic appraisals of problem-focused coping potential than did the other-blame ones, ß = 0.18, $t(189)$ = 2.60, $P < 0.05$, and tended to produce more pessimistic appraisals of future expectancy, ß = 0.12, $t(189)$ = 1.80, $P = 0.07$. These appraisals were accompanied by increased levels of loss/helplessness, ß = –0.19, $t(189)$ = 2.69, $P < 0.01$, and sadness, ß = –0.32, $t(189)$ = 2.60, $P < 0.05$.

However, inspection of the individual scenarios indicates that these anticipated differences primarily were due to the cancer scenario which, relative to the course scenario, produced particularly pessimistic appraisals of problem-focused coping potential (Cancer $M = -1.54$, Course $M = 0.25$), ß = –0.26, $t(189)$ = –3.76, $P < 0.001$, and future expectancy (Cancer $M = -0.52$, Course $M = 1.73$), ß = –0.30, $t(189)$ = –4.33, $P < 0.001$; and elevated levels of loss/helplessness (Cancer $M = 5.05$,

Course $M = 4.23$), $\beta = 0.16$, $t(189) = 2.21$, $P < 0.01$, and sadness (Cancer $M = 7.07$, Course $M = 6.37$), $\beta = 0.13$, $t(189) = 2.06$, $P < 0.05$. Further, although there were no differences on any relevant appraisal variables (i.e., problem-focused coping potential, future expectancy, or loss/helplessness), the friend scenario resulted in significantly more sadness than the TA scenario (Friend $M = 6.35$; TA $M = 4.77$), $\beta = 0.32$, $t(189) = 4.90$: $P < 0.001$.

Although unable to account for this latter effect, the path analysis nonetheless indicated that the Stage 1 variations in sadness were generally consistent with the theoretical model. Controlling for scenario content, appraisals of both problem-focused coping potential, $\beta = -0.47$, $t(185) = -6.62$, $P < 0.001$, and future expectancy, $\beta = -0.19$, $t(185) = -2.66$, $P < 0.01$, contributed negatively to the core relational theme of loss/ helplessness, which in turn directly influenced feelings of sadness, $\beta = 0.20$, $t(184) = 2.69$, $P < 0.01$. Neither future expectancy, $\beta = 0.01$, $t(184) < 1$, ns, nor problem-focused coping potential, $\beta = -0.12$, $t(184) = 1.50$, $P = 0.14$, contributed directly to sadness.

Stage 2 Manipulation. The results of this manipulation provide, at best, tentative support for the model for sadness. Examination of Table 4.3 indicates that the loss/helplessness manipulation was largely ineffective in eliciting the intended appraisals. Problem-focused coping potential was only marginally more pessimistic in the loss/helplessness condition than the other three, $\beta = -0.10$ $t(171) = -1.66$, $P = 0.10$, and future expectancy did not significantly differ in this condition relative to the other three, $\beta = -0.03$, $t(171) < 1$, ns.

Although the core relational theme of loss/helplessness increased from the first to second stages in the loss/helplessness condition as intended, this increase was not reliably different from the changes in the other three conditions, $\beta = 0.09$, $t(171) = 1.55$, $P = 0.12$, largely because loss/ helplessness also increased significantly in the threat condition relative to the combined self- and other-blame conditions, $\beta = 0.12$, $t(171) = 2.11$, $P < 0.05$. However, sadness was not significantly higher in the loss/helplessness condition relative to the other three, $\beta = 0.06$, $t(171) = 1.20$, ns, nor was it significantly elevated in the threat condition relative to the blame conditions, $\beta = 0.05$, $t(171) = 1.04$, ns. Thus sadness did not accompany these elevations in loss/helplessness.

Nonetheless, although not attributable to the appraisal manipulation, the path analysis indicated that the between-subject variation in sadness was consistent with the proposed model: Changes in both problem-focused coping potential, $\beta = -0.30$, $t(167) = -4.26$, $P < 0.001$, and future expectancy, $\beta = -0.26$, $t(167) -3.17$, $P < 0.005$, contributed directly to changes in loss/helplessness, which, in turn, contributed directly to changes in sadness, $\beta = 0.28$, $t(166) = 3.52$, $P < 0.001$. Neither problem-focused coping potential, $\beta = 0.00$, $t(166) < 1$, ns, nor future expectancy, $\beta = 0.15$, $t(166) = 1.66$, $P < 0.10$, contributed directly to changes in sadness.

FOLLOW-UP ANALYSES OF DISCRIMINANT AND PREDICTIVE VALIDITY

We believe the above analyses provide strong support for the predictions of the appraisal model for anger, guilt, and fear/anxiety, with the predictions for sadness receiving weaker support. By demonstrating that the various manipulations differentially produced the intended changes in appraisal components and core relational themes, and that these changes were associated with predicted changes in emotion, they suggest considerable discriminant validity for the model.

However, by considering each emotion separately, the above analyses do not preclude the possibility that, in addition to being associated with their theoretically relevant appraisals, the emotions are just as strongly associated with other appraisals theoretically associated with different emotions. For instance, it is possible that appraisals of threat are as closely associated with appraisals of future expectancy as they are with emotion-focused coping potential, or that fear/anxiety is as strongly associated with appraisals of loss/helplessness as with threat, and so on.

Further, the above analyses were designed to examine the relationships between appraisals and emotion considering both levels of relational meaning (i.e., appraisal components and core relational themes) simultaneously. However, the relative abilities of appraisal components and core relational themes to predict emotions are also of considerable interest.

In the path analyses the core relational themes consistently exerted strong direct effects on their associated emotions after controlling for the contributions of the appraisal components, but the secondary appraisal components did not consistently exert direct effects on the emotions after controlling for the contributions of the core relational themes. This lends support to our view of the themes as efficient molar summaries of the relational meanings associated with the various emotions.

Nevertheless, the presence of the themes in these analyses may have obscured the ability of the appraisal components to predict the emotions. One possibility is that the consistent effects of the themes were due to inadequate conceptualisation or measurement of the appraisal components. This possibility arises because our system of components is somewhat simpler than most previous dimensional systems (e.g., Ellsworth & Smith, 1988b; Frijda et al., 1989), and because the components were measured with single-item scales.

We performed two final sets of analyses to examine both of the above issues. The first set evaluated the discriminant and predictive validity of the overall appraisal model, and the second set directly compared the relative abilities of the appraisal components and core relational themes to predict their theoretically relevant emotions.

In the first set, the discriminant validity of the model was evaluated by examining the correlations between the components of secondary appraisal and the core relational themes, and between the core relational themes and the emotions, for both

Stages 1 and 2. To the extent that there is solid discriminant validity, each individual component of secondary appraisal should be most highly correlated with the core relational theme it was expected to help define, and each core relational theme should be most highly correlated with its theoretically associated emotion. The results of these analyses are presented in Table 4.4.

The results for both of the experimental stages are very similar, and their implications parallel those of the earlier emotion-specific analyses. The model received strong support for anger, guilt, and fear/anxiety, but the evidence in support of sadness was weaker. For the first three emotions the theoretically linked components of secondary appraisal and core relational themes were always significantly more highly correlated with each other than with any other theme or component, and the theoretically linked core relational themes and emotions always displayed similar relations.

For example, consistent with the hypothesised role of emotion-focused coping potential in distinguishing threat from other core relational themes, emotion-focused coping potential was more highly correlated with threat than with any other theme, and threat was more highly correlated with emotion-focused coping potential than with any other appraisal component. In addition, threat was more highly correlated with fear/anxi-

TABLE 4.4. Analyses of Discriminant Validity: Within-stage Correlations between Secondary Appraisal Components and Core Relational Themes, and between Core Relational Themes and Emotions

Secondary Appraisal Components	Stage 1 Core Relational Themes				Stage 2 Core Relational Themes			
	Other-blame	Self-blame	Threat	Loss/ Helplessness	Other-blame	Self-blame	Threat	Loss/ Helplessness
Other-accountability	0.44	−0.37	–	–	0.61	−0.34	–	–
Self-accountabilty	–	0.80	–	–	−0.28	0.79	–	–
Emot. foc. cop. pot.	–	–	−0.62	−0.39$_b$	–	–	0.59	−0.46$_b$
Prob. foc. cop. pot.	–	–	−0.25$_a$	−0.60	–	–	−0.28$_a$	−0.64$_c$
Future expectancy	–	–	−0.31$_a$	−0.46$_b$	–	–	−0.39$_a$	−0.58$_{b,c}$

Core Relational Themes	Emotions				Emotions			
	Anger	Guilt	Fear/ Anxiety	Sadness	Anger	Guilt	Fear/ Anxiety	Sadness
Other-blame	0.64	−0.26$_a$	−0.24$_a$	−0.26$_a$	0.65	−0.25	–	–
Self-blame	0.29$_b$	0.53	0.31$_b$	0.26$_b$	–	0.56	–	–
Threat	–	0.27$_b$	0.52	0.32$_b$	0.33$_a$	–	0.63	0.43$_a$
Loss/Helplessness	–	–	0.29$_b$	0.39$_b$	–	–	0.46$_a$	0.48$_a$

Note. For clarity of presentation only correlations significantly different from zero at $P < 0.001$ are presented. For each of the four analyses, all coefficients within each row or column not sharing a common subscript differ significantly at $P < 0.05$.

ety than with any other emotion; and fear/anxiety was more highly correlated with threat than with any other core relational theme.

Although analogous patterns were observed for the appraisals associated with anger and guilt, the differentiation was less evident for sadness. Some support was obtained for the hypothesised differentiation of loss/helplessness from threat; problem-focused coping potential was consistently more strongly correlated with loss/helplessness than it was with threat, and this correlation was significantly higher than the correlation between loss/helplessness and emotion-focused coping potential. However, the contribution of future-expectancy to the definition of loss-helplessness was less clear. Moreover, loss/helplessness did not show its predicted unique relationship with sadness. Despite being correlated with fear/anxiety significantly less than was threat, loss/helplessness was as highly correlated with fear/anxiety as it was with sadness, and in an analogous fashion, sadness was as highly correlated with threat as it was with loss/helplessness.

In the second set of analyses, the relative predictive abilities of the appraisal components and the core relational themes were examined by regressing each emotion first on just its hypothesised core relational theme, and second on just the set of three or four appraisal components hypothesised to define that theme (see Table 4.1). These regression analyses were repeated for both stages of the experimental task. Table 4.5 lists the proportion of emotion variance accounted for in each analysis (shrunken R^2, Cohen & Cohen, 1983, pp. 105–107).

As Table 4.5 indicates, with the exception of anger, for which the appraisal components were substantially less predictive than was the core relational theme, the appraisal components and core relational themes predicted the emotions to similar degrees. Moreover, these levels of prediction compare quite favourably to those obtained by Ellsworth and Smith (1988b). Using a somewhat more complicated dimensional model, these investigators were able to account for 25%, 23%, and 21% of the variance in guilt, fear/anxiety, and sadness, respectively.

The relative inability of the appraisal components to predict anger appears to be due to the already noted dissociation between other accountability and other-blame within the cancer scenario. When this scenario was removed from consideration, and the analyses were repeated on the 146 subjects who imagined themselves in one of the other three scenarios, the three anger-relevant appraisal components accounted for 28% and 38% of the variance in anger in the first and second stages, respectively (both $Ps < 0.001$). These levels compare favourably to the 31% and 43% of the variance in anger accounted for by other-blame in these same subjects, and to the 36% of the variance in anger accounted for by Ellsworth and Smith (1988b).

Thus, with the exception of anger within the cancer scenario, both the individual appraisal components and the core relational themes were found to be associated with their theoretically relevant emotions to similar degrees, and at levels comparable to previous findings. These results suggest that our conceptualisation and measurement of the appraisal components were adequate, and they support our view of the appraisal components and

TABLE 4.5. Relative Predictive Validity of Appraisal Components and Core Relational Themes for Each Emotion

Emotion	Proportion of Variance Accounted for By:			
	Appraisal Components		Core Relational Themes	
	Stage 1	Stage 2	Stage 1	Stage 2
Anger	0.03	0.16	0.40	0.42
Guilt	0.29	0.28	0.28	0.31
Fear/Anxiety	0.24	0.32	0.27	0.40
Sadness	0.22	0.28	0.15	0.23

Note. The coefficients in each column reflect the shrunken multiple squared correlations for each emotion within each stage obtained by regressing that emotion on either the three or four appraisal components or the single core relational theme hypothesised to be theoretically relevant to that emotion (See Table 1). With the exception of the coefficient obtained for anger in Stage 1 using the appraisal components, which is significantly different from 0 at $P < 0.05$, all listed coefficients are significantly different from 0 at $P < 0.001$.

core relational themes as alternative descriptions of the relational meaning that underlies each emotion.

General Discussion

The present data provide, we believe, strong experimental support for the predictive and discriminant validity of the specific appraisal model we proposed for anger, guilt, and fear/anxiety, but they provide weaker support for sadness. Not only were the first three emotions highly correlated with the theoretically appropriate appraisals, but they were more highly correlated with those appraisals than with any others.

That much of the emotion-related variation in appraisal was directly produced by the experimental manipulations provides particularly strong evidence for the strength and specificity of the observed relationships. Manipulation of the appraisals theoretically relevant to anger in Stage 1 produced predicted differences in reported anger. In Stage 2, the appraisals theoretically associated with anger, guilt, and fear/anxiety were successfully manipulated within each of the four scenarios, and these manipulations resulted in the predicted changes in reported emotion. This model, therefore, provides a firm theoretical foundation upon which to base the further development and testing of a comprehensive theory of emotion.

We believe that an important contribution of this model is that it describes relational meaning, which we view as the core of an emotion, at two distinct levels of analysis, molar and molecular. The molar analysis synthesises the essence of the relational meaning into a single complex concept, and the molecular analysis identifies the individual appraisal components that, together in a particular configuration, imply that meaning. The simultaneous consideration of appraisal at both levels provides a theoretical bridge for relating dimensional appraisal models (e.g., Frijda et al., 1989; Scherer, 1984; Smith & Ellsworth, 1985), which have conceptualised appraisal in a manner akin to our appraisal components, to models of discrete emotions (e.g., Plutchik, 1980), which have treated appraisal more categorically in a manner akin to our core relational themes.

Even more importantly, the two levels of analysis are complementary, and, we believe, their respective properties lend them to different uses in the study of emotion. For example, the individual appraisal components, which reflect the issues that must be evaluated in a particular way for an emotion to be generated, should be especially useful for investigating the environmental and dispositional antecedents of emotion, as well as for predicting how these characteristics combine to produce the relational meanings for each emotion (see Lazarus, 1991a; Smith & Lazarus, 1990; and Smith & Pope, 1992, for theory and research along these lines).

In addition, given a particular emotional reaction, knowledge of the specific appraisal components that led to that reaction represents an important inferential tool for diagnosing the basis of the emotional reaction—for instance, why this particular individual responded to this particular set of circumstances in this particular way. This knowledge, in turn, could be quite useful clinically in designing interventions to alleviate troubled person-environment relationships (cf. Lazarus, 1989; Smith, 1993; Smith & Lazarus, 1990).

The core relational themes, on the other hand, are more global, and reflect how the individual appraisal components combine into a central relational meaning for each emotion. These meanings are emergent in the sense that the relational harms and benefits they represent are holistic entities whose coherence is not easily captured by representing the relevant appraisals as a set of distinct judgements. We consider the core relational themes to be greater than the sum of the appraisal components that imply them, and to have properties and adaptational implications that cannot be easily derived from considering just the appraisal components taken individually.

Knowledge of the relevant core relational themes, because they efficiently represent the adaptational meanings around which emotions are organised (Smith & Lazarus, 1990), should be especially useful in investigating the effects of appraisal in shaping the physiological activities and the modes of action readiness associated with various emotions (e.g., Frijda, 1987; Frijda et al., 1989), as well as the influence of emotion on coping. The physiological activities and modes of action readiness are said to be organised around the adaptational requirements of the appraised encounter, and coping behaviours reflect the person's attempts to respond to those requirements. To us these adaptational requirements seem to be better expressed at the molar level than at the molecular level, and we would expect consideration of the core relational themes to be substantially more predictive of such things as action readiness and actual coping behaviour than consideration of the individual appraisal components.

In considering the utility of this model for future research, it is important to acknowledge that although most findings supported the model, there were unexpected results that raise important issues. Anger and guilt both demonstrated systematic dissociations from appraisal within the first stage of the cancer scenario, and the predictions for sadness generally received only weak support.

The failures of prediction for sadness can be partially attributed to ineffective manipulations or irrevocable loss/helplessness, the relational theme theoretically associated with that emotion. In the first manipulation, loss/helplessness was substantially elevated in only one of the two intended scenarios—the cancer scenario. It was no higher in the course scenario than in the two scenarios associated with other-blame (friend and TA). In the second manipulation, the loss/helplessness condition did not differentially produce increases in appraised loss/helplessness relative to the other conditions. Because the path-analyses for both Stages 1 and 2 indicated that the appraisal model nonetheless accounted for a significant amount of the variance in sadness, the predictions for sadness may gain more support with better manipulations of loss/helplessness.

However, we suspect the weak findings may also reflect more fundamental puzzles about the nature of sadness. The model we employed was unable to differentiate sadness from fear in either experimental stage. In contrast, fear/anxiety and guilt were successfully differentiated from the other emotions in both stages even though their relevant appraisals were not directly manipulated in the first stage. In addition, several previous studies have also failed to find strong, discriminable relationships between specific cognitions and sadness (e.g., Ellsworth & Smith, 1988b; Smith & Ellsworth, 1987), and the special anomalies of sadness have been noted by Lazarus (1991a, 1991c).

A major problem with sadness may be one of emotional *language*. Whereas the names of the other emotions examined—"anger," "fear/ anxiety," and "guilt"—appear to denote fairly specific and acute emotional states, the meaning of "sadness," at least in the vocabulary of our subject

population, appears to be considerably less specific. Perhaps many forms of sadness are really mood states rather than acute emotions. Also, as a counterpoint to "happy," which people use as a general-purpose adjective to describe a variety of emotional states associated with positive outcomes (cf. Ellsworth & Smith, 1988a; Weiner, 1985), we suspect, as Weiner (1985) has proposed, that people often use the term "sad" (and synonyms) nondifferentially to describe their emotional reactions to a variety of harmful circumstances. For example, the first stage of the friend scenario not only elicited fear/anxiety-relevant appraisals and fear-anxiety in a theory-consistent manner, but also elicited self-reported sadness in the relative absence of appraisals of loss/helplessness.

Nonetheless, our position differs from Weiner's (1985) in two important respects. First, the observed differentiation of sadness from both anger and guilt suggests that rather than a fully general-purpose adjective to describe responses to all kinds of harm, the term "sad" describes responses to harm in which the prospects of improvement are viewed as poor. Secondly, we do not consider the reactions subsumed by the term sadness to reflect a single undifferentiated state. Instead, we propose that the concept of sadness encompasses a number of distinct states, ranging from distress to resignation, that are associated with various stages of disengagement from a lost commitment (Lazarus, 1991a; Klinger, 1975; Smith & Lazarus, 1990). Each of these is hypothesised to be produced by distinct appraisals, and to have distinct motivational consequences.

We are also somewhat at a loss to explain the dissociations between appraisal and emotion within the cancer scenario, but we suspect they reflect subjects' attempts to cope with societal proscriptions against blaming helpless (and especially terminally ill and loved) victims. For instance, the dissociation of other-accountability and other-blame may have reflected subjects' attempts to deny being angry at their dying relative, even though they may have held that relative accountable for the disease, and perhaps the guilt they reported was in response to the very anger they were attempting to deny. Emotional states in these kinds of situations are likely to be complex and heavily laden with coping processes that address both the conditions producing these emotions and their social and intrapsychic implications.

Thus far, in conducting this study and in presenting and discussing the results, we have operated under the important, possibly controversial assumption that subjects were emotionally engaged while performing the imagery task. We assume that the subjects actively imagined themselves in the described scenarios, responded emotionally to the scenario contents, and then described their actual emotional reactions. Therefore, we would like to conclude by considering the implications of this assumption for interpreting our findings.

We made this assumption on the basis of previous imagery research which, using similar stimuli and instructions (e.g., Smith, 1989; Smith et al., 1986), has consistently demonstrated that subjects engaged in imagery produce (low-level) patterns of physiological activity consistent with the imagery-induced emotions they report experiencing. Although the physiological measures required to verify that our subjects were similarly engaged are not available in this study, we know of no compelling reason why subjects in the present study would have been systematically different from those in the previous ones.

Nonetheless, it is possible that our subjects might not have been emotionally engaged, but might have been performing a largely intellectual exercise in which they reported hypothetical emotions on the basis of their implicit emotional theories. If this were the case, we believe the conclusions to be drawn from the present experiment would change only a little. Instead of having directly demonstrated strong links between specific appraisals and actual emotional reactions, we would have demonstrated that these same strong appraisal-emotion linkages are present in our subjects' implicit theories of emotion.

In other words, at minimum we have demonstrated that our subjects' theories of emotion contain elaborate, specific, and shared hypotheses concerning the emotional consequences of specific appraisals. Because, as others have argued (e.g., Shaver et al., 1987), implicit theories are largely based on personal experience and tend to mirror that experience accurately, these hypotheses are likely to have considerable validity. In effect, we would then have indirectly demonstrated links between appraisal and emotion. Naturally, one would want to verify the validity of these links in subsequent research, but who would not want to do that in any event? Thus, whether one interprets our results as documenting the existence of actual appraisal-emotion relationships, or the presence of such relationships in our respondents' intuitive theories, we believe the present study provides a strong theoretical model upon which to base future research. [. . .]

REFERENCES

Cohen, J., & Cohen, P. (1983). *Applied multiple regression/ correlation analysis for the behavioral sciences* (2nd ed.). Hillsdale, NJ: Lawrence Erlbaum Associates.

Conway, M. A., & Bekerian, D. A. (1987). Situational knowledge and emotions. *Cognition and Emotion, 1,* 145–191.

Ellsworth, P. C., & Smith, C. A. (1988a). Shades of joy: Patterns of appraisal differentiating pleasant emotions. *Cognition and Emotion, 2,* 301–331.

Ellsworth, P. C., & Smith, C. A. (1988b). From appraisal to emotion: Differences among unpleasant feelings. *Motivation and Emotion, 12,* 271–302.

Folkman, S., & Lazarus, R. S. (1988). The relationship between coping and emotion: Implications for theory and research. *Social Science in Medicine, 26,* 309–317.

Frijda, N. H. (1986). *The emotions.* Cambridge University Press.

Frijda, N. H. (1987). Emotion, cognitive structure, and action tendency. *Cognition and Emotion, 1,* 115–143.

Frijda, N. H., Kuipers, P., & ter Schure, E. (1989). Relations among emotion, appraisal, and emotional action readiness. *Journal of Personality and Social Psychology, 57,* 212–228.

Horowitz, M. J. (1988). *Introduction to psychodynamics: A new synthesis.* New York: Basic Books.

Kimble, G. A. (1990). Mother nature's bag of tricks is small. *Psychological Science, 1,* 36–41.

Klinger, E. (1975). Consequences of commitment to and disengagement from incentives. *Psychological Review, 82,* 1–25.

Lang, P. J. (1979). A bio-informational theory of emotional imagery. *Psychophysiology, 16,* 495–512.

Lazarus, R. S. (1966). *Psychological stress and the coping process.* New York: McGraw-Hill.

Lazarus, R. S. (1989). Constructs of the mind in mental health and psychotherapy. In A. Freeman, K. M. Simon, L. E. Beutler, & H. Arkowitz (Eds.), *Comprehensive handbook of cognitive therapy* (pp. 99–121). New York: Plenum.

Lazarus, R. S. (1991a). *Emotion and adaptation.* Oxford University Press.

Lazarus, R. S. (199b). Cognition and motivation in emotion. *American Psychologist, 46,* 352–367.

Lazarus, R. S. (1991c). Progress on a cognitive-motivational-relational theory of emotion. *American Psychologist, 46,* 819–834.

Lazarus, R. S. & Folkman, S. (1984). *Stress, appraisal, and coping.* New York: Springer.

Lazarus, R. S. & Smith, C. A. (1988). Knowledge and appraisal in the cognition-emotion relationship. *Cognition and Emotion, 2,* 281–300.

Leventhal, H. (1984). A perceptual motor theory of emotion. In K. R. Scherer & P. Ekman (Eds.), *Approaches to emotion* (pp. 271–291). Hillsdale, NJ: Lawrence Erlbaum Associates.

Luborsky, L. (1977). Measuring pervasive psychic structures in psychotherapy: The core conflictual relationship. In N.

Freedman & S. Grand (Eds.), *Communicative structures and psychic structures: A psychoanalytic interpretation of communication*. New York: Plenum.

Luborsky, L. (1984). *Principles of psychoanalytic psychotherapy*. New York: Basic Books.

Plutchik, R. (1980). *Emotion: A psychoevolutionary synthesis*. New York: Harper & Row.

Roseman, I. J. (1984). Cognitive determinants of emotion: A structural theory. In P. Shaver (Ed.), *Review of personality and social psychology*, Vol. 5. *Emotions, relationships, and health* (pp. 11–36). Beverly Hills, CA: Sage .

Roseman, I. J. (1991). Appraisal determinants of discrete emotions. *Cognition and Emotion, 5,* 161–200.

Roseman, I. J., Spindel, M. S., & Jose, P. E. (1990). Appraisals of emotion-eliciting events: Testing a theory of discrete emotions. *Journal of Personality and Social Psychology, 59,* 895–915.

Rosenthal, R. & Rosnow, R. L. (1985). *Contrast analysis: Focused comparisons in the analysis of variance*. Cambridge University Press.

Scherer, K. R. (1984). On the nature and function of emotion: A component process approach. In K. R. Scherer & P. Ekman (Eds.), *Approaches to emotion* (pp. 293–317). Hillsdale, NJ: Lawrence Erlbaum Associates.

Scherer, K. R. (1988). Cognitive antecendents of emotion. In V. Hamilton, G. H. Bower, & N. H. Frijda (Eds.), *Cognitive perspectives on emotion and motivation* (pp. 89–126). Dordecht, The Netherlands: Kluwer.

Shaver, P., Schwartz, J., Kirson, D., & O'Connor, C. (1987). Emotion knowledge: Further exploration of a prototype approach. *Journal of Personality and Social Psychology, 52,* 1061–1086.

Smith, C. A. (1989). Dimensions of appraisal and physiological response in emotion. *Journal of Personality and Social Psychology, 56,* 335–353.

Smith, C. A. (1991). The self, appraisal, and coping. In C. R.

Snyder & D. R. Forsyth (Eds.), *Handbook of social and clinical psychology: The health perspective* (pp. 116–137). New York: Pergamon.

Smith, C. A. (1993). Evaluations of what's at stake and what I can do. In B. C. Long & S. E. Kahn (Eds.), *Women, work, and coping: A multidisciplinary approach to workplace stress*. Montreal: McGill-Queen's University Press.

Smith, C. A. & Ellsworth, P. C. (1985). Patterns of cognitive appraisal in emotion. *Journal of Personality and Social Psychology, 48,* 813–838.

Smith, C. A. & Ellsworth, P. C. (1987). Patterns of appraisal and emotion related to taking an exam. *Journal of Personality and Social Psychology, 52,* 475–488.

Smith, C. A., Ellsworth, P. C., & Pope, L. K. (1990, Abstract). Contributions of ability and task difficulty to appraisal, emotion, and autonomic activity. *Psychophysiology, 27,* S64.

Smith, C. A. & Lazarus, R. S. (1990). Emotion and adaptation. In L. A. Pervin (Ed.), *Handbook of personality: Theory and research* (pp. 609–637). New York: Guilford.

Smith, C. A., Haynes, K. N., Lazarus, R. S., & Pope, L. K. (1993). In search of the "hot" cognitions: Attributions, appraisals, and their relationship to emotion. *Journal of Personality and Social Psychology, 65,* 916–929.

Smith, C. A., McHugo, G. J., & Lanzetta, J. T. (1986). The facial muscle patterning of posed and imagery-induced expressions of emotion by expressive and nonexpressive posers. *Motivation and Emotion, 10,* 133–157.

Smith, C. A. & Pope, L. K. (1992). Appraisal and emotion: The interactional contributions of dispositional and situational factors. In M. S. Clark (Ed.), *Review of personality and social psychology*, Vol. 14. *Emotion and social behavior* (pp. 32–62). Newbury Park, CA: Sage.

Weiner, B. (1985). An attributional theory of achievement motivation and emotion. *Psychological Review, 92,* 548–573.

APPENDIX

COMPLETE TEXT OF THE TA, CANCER, AND COURSE SCENARIOS

TA

STAGE 1

You are enrolled in a course that is a prerequisite for your intended major. In general you are finding the course quite interesting and enjoyable, and you believe that you've chosen the right major. However, you don't get along with your TA. In your discussion section you often disagree with what he (she) says, and he (she) is highly critical of your comments. Recently you wrote a big paper for the class that your TA graded. You were really interested in the topic of the paper, and you wanted to show that you knew what you were talking about. So, you researched the topic very carefully, and put a lot of effort into writing what you believe is one of the best papers you'd ever written.

Today at the end of your discussion section the TA hands the papers back, and you see that you've been given a "C–."

STAGE 2

All Versions. After section the TA refused your request to regrade your paper, and said that you received the grade you did because the research was shoddy, and the paper was poorly written. In fact, he (she) said that the paper was one of the worst he (she) ever read, and that you should feel lucky to be getting a C–.

Other-blame. You can't believe that the TA is doing this to you. You know that the paper is nowhere near as bad as the TA says, and believe that he (she) had no right to persecute you like this.

Self-blame. Thinking back, you realise that you've been obnoxious and are at least partially to blame for this situation. You've given this person a very hard time. You've constantly argued with him (her), and because of you he's (she's) never been able to cover all the material he (she) planned to during section. Thinking about it, you realise that you've behaved badly, and really can't blame this person all that much for being hostile.

Threat. You don't know how you're going to get by in this course. The TA obviously can't stand you and isn't going to give you the benefit of the doubt, putting you in danger of serious academic trouble. You don't know whether there's anything you can do to straighten out things so that your work will be evaluated objectively and you'll receive the grade you deserve in this course.

Loss/Helplessness. You realise there's nothing you can do to please this person. You put out your very best effort and it was torn to shreds. This incident has ruined the whole course for you. Even though you had been enjoying the class, and had found the material and professor to be very interesting, you're certain that there's no way you'll be able to do well or enjoy the class as long as you have this TA. This is a great personal loss.

Cancer

STAGE 1

You have a relative (e.g., aunt, uncle, or grandparent) who was always your favourite when you were growing up. You love this relative dearly. He (she) always took you places and told you amusing stories. Even though he (she) is older, you've always been able to talk about your problems with him (her), and on several occasions he (she) has gotten you out of trouble with your parents. The only thing that bothers you about this relative is that he (she) is a heavy smoker. In the past you've tried to get him (her) to quit, but to no avail.

You've just been told that your relative is in the hospital with lung cancer, which you know is often fatal within a short time.

STAGE 2

All Versions. A couple of weeks have passed, and several days ago your relative had surgery. The news is bad. The cancer has spread so much that it's inoperable. Although the doctors will continue to do everything they can, they give your relative less than two months to live.

Other-blame. You can't understand why your relative let this happen to him(her)self. You don't understand why he (she) kept on smoking, even though he (she) knew it was dangerous, and even though you'd begged him (her) to quit. You also can't understand why he (she) waited so long before seeing a doctor. His (her) behaviour seems irresponsible and thoughtless of others.

Self-blame. You blame yourself for what has happened. You believe that you've let your relative down—that you weren't insistent enough in trying to get him (her) to stop smoking. If only you had made your relative realise how much you cared about him (her) and how important it was to you that he (she) quit smoking, then maybe this whole situation could have been avoided.

Threat. There is great danger he (she) will die, but no one can be sure. You don't know whether to believe the doctors or not. What if they're right and your relative dies? If that happens you don't know what you'll do without him (her) to turn to in times of trouble, or whether you'll ever again be able to enjoy the things you used to do together.

Loss/Helplessness. For the first time you're totally sure that your relative is going to die, and that there's nothing you or the doctors can do about it. You realise that you'll never again be able to go to this person with your problems, or share the enjoyable times you used to have with this relative. This is a great personal loss.

Course

STAGE 1

This semester you've been taking a course that is required for your intended major. You selected this major because you've always been interested in the field, and you believe that it's ideal preparation for your career aspirations, which you've held for a long time. You've found this course to be much more difficult than you expected, and you scored well below the median on the midterm. Realising that it was very important for you to do well on the final, you redoubled your efforts, studied as hard as you could, and Frequently sought out the TAs for help. You thought that the final was difficult, but left thinking that you had done fairly well.

The grades have just been posted, and you discover that you again scored well below the median, and have received a "C–" in the course.

STAGE 2

All Versions. When you talked to your professor about the grade, he (she) explained that your performance was really in the low "D" range, but because you were obviously trying so hard, he (she) already raised your grade to a "C–", and couldn't in good conscience raise it any further.

Other-blame. Thinking back over the semester, you realise that the TAs were not very helpful. They always seemed to be in a rush to get rid of you when you went to see them, and they didn't know how to explain things clearly so that you could understand them. You believe that if the TAs had been competent and had done their jobs properly, you would have done much better in the course.

Self-blame. Thinking back over the semester, you blame yourself for doing so poorly in the class. You realise that although you worked very hard you made a lot of mistakes. You almost always waited until the last minute before completing your assignments or going to the TAs for help. Because

of this the TAs were always very busy when you went to see them, and they couldn't devote much time to your problems. You believe that if only you had been more organised you would have done much better in the course.

Threat. You don't know what to do. You worked as hard as you could, and still you nearly flunked the course. You believe that if you stay with this major, no matter how hard you try you're in great danger of doing poorly in your classes and winding up with a rotten academic record. At the same time, however, because you've held your career aspirations for so long, and because they are so important to you, you really don't want to quit the major and abandon your dreams and plans.

Loss/Helplessness. You believe that you're not cut out for this major. You worked as hard as you could, and still you nearly flunked the course. You're certain that you should change your major and career plans. Right now, you're thinking about how long you've dreamed of achieving your career aspirations, how long you've been interested in this particular major, and how now you have to abandon these dreams and plans. This is a great personal loss.

Culture and Socialization

Social psychologists are increasingly appreciating the profound role of culture in emotion. Culture influences the meanings that events have for people, and thereby affects what emotions people will have. The cognitive perspective that was presented in the previous section therefore plays a role in explaining how culture influences emotion. Culture also influences norms of emotional expression, thereby affecting the self-regulation of emotion. Perhaps less obvious are ways in which culture can influence the nature of emotion itself. By influencing people's focus of attention—whether to their bodily states, to their personal goals, to their relation- ships, or to their reputations and obligations to others—culture alters the contents of consciousness and thereby, to an extent, alters the quality of emotional experience. To appreciate fully the pervasive influence of culture, it is necessary to learn how emotions are socialized. The practices that shape children's develop- ment vary across cultures, and it is via these that culture exerts its effects.

Theory and research on culture and emotion is undergoing rapid development at present. Social and developmental psychologists are comparing emotions and socialization practices across cultures and striving to understand how culture influences emotion. The most influential work to date in social psychology has been that of Hazel Rose Markus and Shinobu Kitayama, whose research has emphasized cross-cultural differences in the self (Markus & Kitayama, 1991). In the paper that is reprinted below, Markus and Kitayama (1994) apply their perspective to emotion and its socialization. In their theory they contrast European-American cultures with Asian cultures, drawing on evidence obtained mostly in the United States and Japan. Like much cross-cultural research, their contrast emphasizes the tendency of European (specifically, Northern European) and American cultures to place relatively more emphasis on the independence of individuals, whereas Asian cultures place relatively more emphasis on the interdependence of individuals.

Even the nature of emotion itself is influenced by culture. Markus and Kitayama speculate that the Western idea of emotions as involving private, subjective experiences may itself be the product of a culture that values independence. In interdependent cultures, emotion may be experienced more as a transformation in a social relationship than as an internal feeling state.

The first part of the paper aims to show that European-American and Asian cultures differ with respect both to the type of self that people develop and to the most common emotions they experience. European-Americans view themselves as differing from others in positive ways; they display the "false uniqueness effect" and typically report feeling good about themselves. Asians, in contrast, tend to display greater modesty and self-effacement and generally to devote less attention to their individual feelings than to harmonizing with others. The authors argue that emotions such as happiness, pride, anger, and frustration emphasize an individualist point of view and predominate in European-American cultures, whereas emotions such as friendliness, interpersonal harmony, indebtedness, and shame emphasize interdependence and interconnection and predominate in Asian cultures.

Markus and Kitayama next address how cultures socialize their members to have different concepts of self and different emotional repertoires. Evidence from a variety of sources is marshaled to argue that European-American cultures cultivate a positive sense of being distinct from others, whereas Asian cultures cultivate a positive sense of fitting in with others and of being respectable. Markus and Kitayama identify particular

socialization practices as bringing about this transformation. In the United States, for example, children tend to be generously praised regardless of their actual performance, in comparison with children in most other countries. This socialization practice contrasts with the well-documented Japanese tradition of *hansei*, the practice of deliberate self-criticism that is encouraged by parents and school teachers (White & LeVine, 1986), and with the Asian emphasis on encouraging children to fit in with their peers. In an interdependent culture, too many positive feelings about the individual self threaten one's fitting in with one's group; in such cultures, feeling too good (in the individualist sense) will in fact feel bad.

In a final section, Markus and Kitayama explore how differing emotions and senses of self may require modifying long-standing conclusions about such social processes as conformity to group pressure, stereotyping, and coping. In each case, the psychological literature reveals a European-American bias regarding what is desirable and what is undesirable.

Markus and Kitayama provide a compelling integration of four important topics in social psychology: the self, emotion, culture, and socialization, and their work has been extremely influential. Nevertheless, it has attracted some criticism, and recent research has begun to depart from their model in certain ways. Some researchers have argued that all cultures value both independence and interdependence, although in different ways (Raeff, 1997). Others have found broad dichotomies, such as that of independence versus interdependence, to be too broad to capture the unique character of a culture and have attempted more fine-grained distinctions. An interesting example would be research on conceptions of honor and how they affect emotions and other social psychological phenomena (Fischer, Manstead, & Rodriguez Mosquera, 1999; Nisbett & Cohen, 1996).

REFERENCES

Fischer, A. H., Manstead, A. S. R., & Rodriguez Mosquera, P. M. (1999). The role of honour-related vs. individualistic values in conceptualising pride, shame, and anger: Spanish and Dutch cultural prototypes. *Cognition and Emotion, 13,* 149–179.

Markus, H. R., & Kitayama, S. (1991). Culture and the self: Implications for cognition, emotion, and motivation. *Psychological Review, 98,* 224–253.

Markus, H. R., & Kitayama, S. (1994). The cultural construction of self and emotion: Implications for social behavior. In S. Kitayama & H. R. Markus (Eds.), *Emotion and culture: Empirical studies of mutual influence* (pp. 89–130). Washington, DC: American Psychological Association.

Nisbett, R. E., & Cohen, D. (1996). *Culture of honor: The psychology of violence in the South.* Boulder, CO: Westview.

Raeff, C. (1997). Individuals in relationships: Cultural values, children's social interactions, and the development of an American individualistic self. *Developmental Review, 17,* 205–238.

White, M. I., & LeVine, R. A. (1986). What is an *ii ko* (good child)? In Stevenson, H., Azuma, H., & Hakuta, K. (Eds.), *Child development and education in Japan* (pp. 55–62). New York: Freeman.

Discussion Questions

1. What does it mean to be a good person within a cultural framework of independence? Contrast this meaning with that which exists within a cultural framework of interdependence.

2. What does it mean to say that an emotion experienced by members of one culture corresponds approximately but not exactly to an emotion in another culture?

3. If European-American emotions differ from Asian emotions because a different type of self exists in these two types of cultures, which emotions would you expect to differ the most? Which would you expect to differ the least?

4. If you are familiar with a culture that is considered to promote independent selves by Markus and Kitayama, can you think of examples of independence in that culture? Can you also think of examples of interdependence? Does the "independent" label nevertheless seem apt, or does it seem to be something of a stereotype? If you are familiar with a culture that is considered to promote interdependent selves, perform this exercise for that culture, too.

Suggested Readings

Kitayama, S., & Markus, H. R. (1994). *Emotion and culture: Empirical studies of mutual influence.* Washington, DC: American Psychological Association. The article by Markus and Kitayama reprinted here first appeared in a book edited by the same authors, and the rest of the book makes good reading for those interested in learning more about emotion and culture. Eight of its chapters were written by other authors, and include psychologists, anthropologists, and linguists.

Harré, R. (Ed.). (1986). *The social construction of emotions.* Oxford: Basil Blackwell. Markus and Kitayama suggest that culture plays an important role in determining the nature of emotions. This thesis often goes under the rubric of "social constructionism." This volume, edited by Rom Harré, contains articles that advance a strong version the social constructionist thesis.

Lutz, C. A. (1988). *Unnatural emotions: Everyday sentiments on a Micronesian atoll & their challenge to Western theory.* Chicago: University of Chicago Press. In this book anthropologist Catherine Lutz reports on her fieldwork in Micronesia. Like Markus and

Kitayama, she also claims that differences in what cultures value will alter the nature of emotions within those cultures.

Russell, J. A. (1991). Culture and the categorization of emotions. *Psychological Bulletin, 110,* 426–450. This article reviews cross-cultural research and ethnographic studies to address the issue of whether humans in different cultures categorize emotions the same or differently. The author tentatively concludes that there is evidence that different cultures categorize emotions somewhat differently.

Saarni, C. (1993). Socialization of emotion. In M. Lewis & J. M. Haviland (Eds.), *Handbook of emotions* (pp. 435–446). This chapter provides a broad and systematic overview of what psychologists have learned about how emotions are socialized.

Fischer, A. H., Manstead, A. S. R., & Rodriguez Mosquera, P. M. (1999). The role of honour-related vs. individualistic values in conceptualising pride, shame, and anger: Spanish and Dutch cultural prototypes. *Cognition and Emotion, 13,* 149–179. Honor cultures, such as exist in Spain or in the American South, are a type of interdependent culture that is distinct from those of most Asian cultures. The authors of this paper investigate prototypes of three emotions in Spain and compare them with those in the Netherlands, where the culture places less value on honor and more on individualism. The results show that emotion concepts are influenced by these values.

The Cultural Construction of Self and Emotion: Implications for Social Behavior

Hazel Rose Markus and Shinobu Kitayama

In December 1992, the Japanese royal family announced that Crown Prince Naruhito had chosen Masako Owada, a bright, highly educated, fast-track member of the Foreign Ministry, to become the future Empress. Most Japanese were pleased at the prospect of having such a lively and accomplished Princess as part of their monarchy. But according to American press reports, many Americans, as well as many young Japanese women, could not begin to fathom how such a thoroughly modern, internationalized woman, even if she liked the Prince, could toss away a brilliant career to marry him and disappear into the conservative, humorless, controlling royal family where her life would never be her own again and her primary goal would be to produce a male heir to the throne.

As the June marriage approached, it seemed evident, according to analysts on both sides of the Pacific, that Masako Owada felt that it was her "duty" to marry the Prince. From an American perspective, the decision seemed to reflect forced compliance, self-denigration, and self-sacrifice. In giving up her hard-won career, she seemed, in the eyes of many, to be betraying the cause of individual determination, feminism in Japan, and ultimately, herself. The local controversy surrounding this particular social event is unlikely to be remembered for long, but it illustrates a classic problem in the analysis of social behavior and one that is at the heart of this chapter. From many European–American perspectives, the Princess's decision was "obviously" self-sacrificing and "natu-rally" accompanied by the emotion of unhappiness at not being able to realize some important defining attribute of the self. However, what is not evident in this analysis is the multileveled, dynamic interdependency among socially appropriate behavior, the self, and emotion.

The American understanding of this Japanese behavior is anchored in a particular individualist approach to the self. From a different orientation, one in which the individual is cast not as an independent entity but as one fundamentally interdependent with others, the decision to marry the Prince could be understood differently. It is possible from this other perspective that the Princess may not have felt sacrifice or injury to the self, but rather affirmation of a more connected, obligation-fulfilling, social self. She may indeed have felt content or "good" as a result of her decision to respond to the desires and expectations of others and many into the royal family. As is evident in this example and in studies from anthropology and cultural psychology (for recent reviews see Markus & Kitayama, 1991; Moghaddam, Taylor, & Wright, 1993; Shweder, 1991; Shweder & LeVine, 1984; Smith & Bond, 1993; Stigler, Shweder, & Herdt, 1990; Triandis, 1990), what is regarded as positive or negative normative social behavior can vary dramatically from one cultural group to another.

Emotions figure prominently in social behavior, although this is seldom explicitly acknowledged. Emotions are significant because they make possible the social regulation of behavior. Commonly observed social behavior, and its accounts, whether it is inclining naturally toward others and taking their expectancies into account when marrying in Japan, or distancing oneself just as naturally from the expectancies of others and relying on one's current, private, and personal feelings when marrying in the United States, is not merely the result of a blind adherence to powerful norms or of a principled holding fast to a system of values and beliefs. Normative behavior typically *feels* "good" or "right" (cf. D'Andrade, 1984; Spiro, 1961).

Good Feelings and Normative Behavior: The Role of the Self

We suggest that a cultural group's ways of feeling are shaped by the group's habitual and normative social behavior, and in turn, these ways of feeling influence the nature of this social behavior. Consequently, asking how the Princess might have made her decision and how she must have felt about it (whatever its merits or actual antecedents) and describing and analyzing any instance of a given social behavior—identity construction and maintenance, conformity to group pressure, stereotyping and intergroup behavior, or coping and adaptation—will be markedly enhanced by locating it within its dominant cultural frames. An analysis of the emotional responses that accompany various actions provides further access to the cultural and social meaning of these actions. At the same time, variation in normative social behavior provides a window on the interdependence between emotion and culture. Such variation implies that affective reactions, including what types of feeling states are commonly experienced and elaborated, as well as how, and under what conditions these states are experienced, may vary substantially.

Furthermore, we suggest that the nature of the "lock and key" arrangement between affective responses and the social order that has been of pervasive interest to psychologists, sociologists, and anthropologists alike (D'Andrade, 1984; Durkheim, 1953; James, 1890; Lutz, 1988; Radcliffe-Brown, 1952; Schieffelin, 1985; Shweder, 1993; Spiro, 1961) can be further understood with the idea of a self that provides a meeting point and a framework for the relation between the individual and the social world. Each person is embedded within a variety of sociocul-

tural contexts or cultures (e.g., country or region of origin, ethnicity, religion, gender, family, birth cohort, profession). Each of these cultural contexts makes some claim on the person and is associated with a set of ideas and practices (i.e., a cultural framework or schema) about how to be a "good" person. A sense of the "good" is an integral part of one's sense of the self, and one's sense of self shapes what is "good" (e.g., of value, concern, appropriate, etc.) and what is not (Markus & Kitayama, 1994; Oyserman & Markus, 1993).

The self, then, is an organized locus of the various, sometimes competing, understandings of how to be a person, and it functions as an individualized orienting, mediating, interpretive framework giving shape to what people notice and think about, to what they are motivated to do, and (the focus of this chapter) to how they feel and their ways of feeling. The self is not a special part of the person or of the brain, it is the entire person considered from particular points of view (Neisser, 1988), and it is the ways in which the person is made meaningful or given significance.

The concept of a self as the particularized locus of various sociocultural influences prevents an oversocialized conception of the person and helps to explain why two people, even those in similar sociocultural circumstances (e.g., twins in the same family) are unlikely to feel exactly the same way in a given set of circumstances. The self of any given individual is some organization of all the various influences of his or her individual social and developmental history. This organization, in which some sociocultural influences are elaborated and emphasized and others are resisted or ignored, affords the person considerable agency and idiosyncracy. The "I" who then feels an affective state or emotion has, as its referent, a particular configuration of self-representations and conceptions that reflect the individual's unique construction of experience. However, there are still ways of feeling that can be linked systematically to particular cultural frameworks, even though a given emotional state cannot be completely explained from these perspectives.[1]

In the marriage decision described here, the self that is being sacrificed or affirmed, depending on

---

[1] A specific focus on the nature of the self is an extension of the ideas of many emotion theorists. Frijda (1986) claimed that "emotions arise when events are relevant to the individual's concerns" (p. 359; see also Mowrer, 1960; Pribram, 1971). Lutz (1988) contended that emotions reflect

one's perspective, can assume a variety of forms and functions, depending on the cultural frameworks that have shaped it. The shape of the self (i.e., its various meanings and practices) will, in turn, determine the nature of "good" feelings and of the social behavior that will promote and foster these good feelings. This means that what is experienced as joyful or happy or as sad or angering depends on the mediating self. Aside from the good affective reactions that accompany sweet tastes or smells, or the bad affective reactions that result from extremely loud sounds, bright lights, or hissing snakes, most "good" or "bad" feelings depend on extensive emotional socialization. Through this process, people come to "have" feelings of the shape and variety that reflect the specific value commitments of their significant social groups. Basic to this argument is the idea that being moral (i.e., proper, right, or appropriate) according to one's group, feeling good, and being a person are all intimately connected. As the philosopher Taylor (1989) claimed, "to know who you [*are*] is to be oriented in moral space, a space in which questions arise about what is good or bad, what is worth doing and what is not, what has meaning and importance for you, and what is trivial and secondary" (p. 28).[2,3]

Linking Emotions to Culture-Specific Patterns of Behavior

Emotions as Meaningful Social Processes

From a theoretical point of view, emotions may be seen as some amalgam of component processes organized according to the nature of the functional relationship between the person and the environment, and more specifically, according to the relationship of the self, with relevant other people and groups of people (de Riviera, 1984). Emotions connect individuals to their social world and thus are the key to social integration and regulation because they are the basis of the reinforcement and reproduction of behavior (e.g., Zajonc, 1980). As such, they hold in place a group's dominant cultural tendencies, or coordinates, or emphases. For example, D'Andrade (1983) contended that "through the process of socialization individuals come to find achieving culturally prescribed goals and following cultural directives to be motivationally satisfying, and to find not achieving culturally prescribed goals and not following cultural directives to be anxiety producing" (p. 98). Similarly, with socialization, social behavior that is in line with a given cultural imperative or norm and is regarded as "positive" eventually comes to feel "good" and is relatively easily maintained and fostered. Social behavior that is in conflict with the dominant, cultural tendencies and is regarded as "negative" social behavior eventually comes to feel "bad" and is rejected and feared (see also Spiro, 1961).

In characterizing the pervasive nature of the cultural frame and its potential influence on emotion, we drew from a type of analysis set up by Bartlett (1932) where he characterized the precise role of the relationship between culture and memory. He wrote:

> Every social group is organized and held together by some specific psychological tendency . . . ,

---

commitment to seeing the world in particular ways and refer to "what is culturally defined and experienced as 'intensely meaningful'" (p. 8). These concerns and commitments converge in a view of self that structures ongoing experience and the very nature of emotional experience.

[2]The joint shaping of ways of being and ways or feeling can be differentiated from an emphasis on how certain patterns of appraisal, for example, is the event pleasurable, uncertain, or controllable (see Ellsworth, 1994, and Frijda & Mesquita, 1994), determine particular emotions. We are concerned here with questions such as what will feel "good," "proper," "pleasant," or "right," what will feel "bad," "unacceptable," or "unpleasant"; whether personal control and certainty will be experienced as part of feeling "good" or will, instead, be irrelevant to it; and why. The concern is with the mutual and reciprocal enculturation of self and emotions so that certain ways of being naturally feel good or positive, while others feel bad or negative.

[3]One might he tempted to conclude that if good feelings are those that promote or reinforce the self, and that bad feelings do the opposite, then the concept of the self is theoretically superfluous. Yet, the nature and course of social behavior (which includes the emotional experience and its instrumental consequences) will be pervasively influenced by whether good feelings are experienced, as in the example here, as realizing one's own attributes (e.g., ideas, motives, goals) or as fulfilling the expectations of significant others. The nature or the mediating self is thus significant. It is the self that is one of the personalized carriers of the social context. Many of the recent calls to "contextualize" psychological analyses (Gergen, 1992; Sampson, 1988) have gone largely unheeded because it is difficult to determine what is meant by the social context of a given behavior. However, the meanings and practices accorded to the self by a given cultural group are among the important features of the social context that can be localized, specified, and assessed.

which gives the group a bias in its dealings with external circumstances. The bias constructs the special persistent features of the group culture and this immediately settles what the individual will observe in his environment. It does this markedly in two ways. First, by providing that setting of interest, excitement, and emotion which favors the development of specific images, and secondly, by providing a persistent framework of institutions and customs which acts as a schematic basis for constructive memory. (p. 255)

Although Bartlett was not concerned with the source or the nature of a group's core psychological tendency, we suggest that this psychological tendency and the form of subjectivity that accompanies it derives from the cultural group's commitment to a particular meaning or approach to selfhood. We are interested here in charting the close relationship between this core tendency and emotional life. Taylor (1989) provided a useful starting point by sketching the nature of this interdependency:

My self-definition is understood as an answer to the question Who I am. And this question finds its original sense in the interchange of speakers. I define who I am by defining where I speak from, in the family tree, in social space, in the geography of social status and functions. . . . We first learn our languages of moral and spiritual discernment by being brought into an ongoing conversation by those who bring us up. The meanings that the key words first had for me are the meanings they have for us, that is, for me and my conversation partners together. . . . So I can only learn what anger, love, anxiety, the aspiration to wholeness, etc. are through my and others' experience for us, in some common space. (p. 35)

Cultural Frameworks

Our analysis suggests that one reason for which different types of events make different groups of people happy, sad, or joyful, and for which some groups experience feeling states that are relatively incomprehensible to others is because of formidable differences in the underlying cultural frames of these groups. A cultural frame refers to an interpretive grid, or meaning system, or schema (see Bruner, 1990; D'Andrade, 1987; Shweder, 1993; Wierzbicka, 1994). It consists of language and a set of tacit social understandings, which Quinn and Holland (1987) labeled "vital understandings" (p. 12), as well as of the social representations and practices that reflect and enact these understandings in daily life (Bourdieu, 1972; D'Andrade, 1984; Giddens, 1984; Quinn & Holland, 1987). Some of the elements of a shared cultural schema may be known and obvious to all (D'Andrade, 1987); other elements may be invisible, often taken for granted (Quinn & Holland, 1987), or may even be outside of conscious awareness (Moscovici, 1993).[4]

A CULTURAL FRAMEWORK OF INDEPENDENCE

In North America, a key element of the cultural framework is a set of beliefs about the self (Markus & Kitayama, 1991; Sampson, 1988; Shweder & LeVine, 1984; Triandis, 1990). These beliefs concern ways of being: what a self is and what to do with it. Such understandings as Taylor (1989) tried to draw out are not merely a metaphysical backdrop. Rather, they configure the nature of the fit between the individual and the cultural environment and structure the adaptive task and thus the nature of emotional reactions. Tied to an ideology of individualism, the self in North America and in much of Europe is defined as an independent, self-contained entity. Specifically, the model is that the self (a) comprises a unique configuration of internal attributes (e.g., traits, emotions, motives, values, and rights) and (b) behaves primarily as a consequence of these internal attributes (Markus & Kitayama, 1991). An explicit social goal from this perspective is to separate one's self from others and not to allow undue influence by others or connection to them.

[4]The term *cultural framework* is used because it seems to capture the central tendency of a large family of related terms. The dominant cultural framework includes the cultural group's ideas and ideals (e.g., its values, attitudes, beliefs, schemas, norms—its cultural software, and also its traditions, customs, and institutionalized social practices (e.g., its behavioral rituals, language, rules, legal practices—its cultural hardware) that codify and objectify these ideas and ideals and that make them relatively external, hard, obvious, and real (for a discussion of the importance of practices in cultural frames see Bourdieu, 1980; Gaskins, Miller, & Corsaro, 1992; and Miller, 1994). We intend for this term to cover and include other similar terms that we might also have used, such as cultural imperative, normal imperative, design for living, ethos, cultural schema, mode of operation, core psychological tendency, and cultural construal. A variety of important distinctions can and have been made among these terms, but in our use of the term here, we emphasize that a cultural frame is not just a set of ideas, beliefs, or cognitive representations stored in memory.

Most North Americans, as well as many Europeans, particularly those in northern and central Europe, live within societies that are structured according to this perspective of what it means to be a person. Such a perspective is multiply rooted in Western philosophical tradition and is linked to a Cartesian view in which the goal of existence is to objectify the self. According to Lebra (1992), the ontological goal of this perspective is to highlight the division between the experiencer and what is experienced or, in other terms, to separate the individual from the context. We have called the idea of a self as an entity containing significant dispositional attributes and detached from social context the *independent* view of self. It is an important part of the shared cultural frame of North America and Europe, and it is particularly characteristic of White, urban, male, middle-class, secularized, contemporary people.[5]

A CULTURAL FRAMEWORK OF INTERDEPENDENCE

Another model of the self that stands in significant contrast to the independent view is one that is characteristic of Japan, China, Korea, Southeast Asia, and much of South America and Africa. According to this perspective, the self is not and cannot be separate from others and the surrounding social context. The self is interdependent with the surrounding social context and it is the self-in-relation-to-other that is focal in individual experience (Markus & Kitayama, 1991). In fact, according to Kondo (1990), from the Japanese perspective, the self is fundamentally interrelated

with others and to understand the Japanese sense of self requires dissolving the self/other or self/society boundary that is such an obvious starting point in all Western formulations of the self. The cultural press in this alternate model of the self is not to become separate and autonomous from others but to fit-in with others, to fulfill and create obligation, and, in general, to become part of various interpersonal relationships. We have called this view the *interdependent* view of self.

According to Lebra (1992), this interdependent view of self can be traced to Buddhist and, especially in Japan, to Shintoist philosophical traditions within which the very goal of existence is different from that assumed in the West. From this view, the core notion is not to "objectify the self" but to submerge the self and "gain freedom from the self." The emphasis is on downplaying the division between the experiencer and the object of experience, and it is connection with, rather than separation from others and the surrounding context that is highlighted.[6]

Much more could and must be said about these apparently startling differences in ontological emphasis (see Lebra, 1992; and Markus & Kitayama, 1991, for extended discussions of these differences), and the variety of other ontologies that must also exist should be drawn out, but our purpose here is simply to underscore that these divergent views of what the self should be are critical underpinnings of emotional experience. These ways of being are significant elements of the cultural frame, and as sketched by Bartlett (1932), they form the framework for individual experience of emotions and social behavior. If the self func-

[5]There are, of course, other ideas about how to be a person, especially in a diverse society like the United Slates, some of which may even directly contradict the individualist or independent view, and many people may resist the dominant cultural frame in a variety of ways; but the general notion of the independence and autonomy of the individual from others is still influential in shaping social behavior because it is elaborated and given life in a broad net of social customs, practices, and institutions with a pervasive rang of influence. This view of a cultural frame allows us to explain how a set of ideas or values can remain influential even when some individuals do not actively endorse them or behave accordingly (Lave, Stepick,& Sailer, 1977). For example, many Americans would not claim that they are independent, autonomous entities, rather, they experience themselves as interdependent, highly social, and affiliative. Yet, they are constantly exposed to the individualist idea and its related practices because they live within a society created by and based on it.

[6]In earlier papers (Markus & Kitayama, 1991), we distinguished independence and interdependence as two broad sets of tasks that people need to perform in social life. Independence refers to a set of tasks for psychological tendencies to separate the self from the social context, encompassing goals of agency, autonomy, and disengagement from others. Interdependence, on the other hand, implies a set of tasks for psychological tendencies to connect the self with others, encompassing such goals as affiliation, communion, and engagement with others. We have suggested that these two tasks can be differently combined and incorporated into the definition and construction of the self, as well as into the pattern or cultural ideology, customs, and institutions. The two tasks—independence and interdependence—are assumed to be present in every culture, but cultures vary in the ways in which these tasks are weighted and organized in social life and manifest in individual thought and action.

tions as an interpretive, integrative, or orienting framework for individual behavior, then whether one has a self that is shaped by a European–American ontological tradition or by an Asian one has the potential to make an enormous difference in how life is lived—what kinds of experiences will feel "good" and what social behavior will be coded as "positive," and what kinds of experiences will produce "bad" feelings and will accompany "negative" social behavior.

In our work, we compare cultural groups from different regions of origin (European–Americans and Asians). Although many other cultural comparisons are possible and interesting, there is now sufficient empirical work on this particular cultural comparison to begin to evaluate hypotheses about the nature of the connections among emotions, self, and social behavior. For example, when comparing American university students with Japanese university students, we do not assume that all individuals in a given cultural group are alike. We suggest only that members of a given group are more likely to have been exposed to and have operated within a given cultural frame than members of the contrasting group, and thus members of the same cultural group may share some similar behavioral tendencies or patterns. Thus, the Japanese, the Chinese, and the Koreans share a powerful philosophical tradition that is strikingly different from that of the West. But these three groups, as well as the individuals within each group, are obviously different from each other in numerous other ways.

Emotion and the Cultural Framework

A cultural framework includes a group's sense of and attitudes toward emotions, that is, what emotions or feelings are, why they are experienced, and what their significance is in social life, as well as the implicit answers to questions like when does one feel, where does one feel, and how does one feel. The cultural framework also includes an understanding of what kinds of events emotions are, for example, are they considered to be individual products that are agentically produced and experienced privately and corporeally, or are they considered to be communicative processes or interpersonal moods that define the relationships among two or more people (Jenkins, 1991).

Miller (1994) suggested that cultures can diverge

even further in their understandings of emotions. Reviewing the anthropological evidence, she claimed that "many cultures do not share the concept of emotion assumed in psychological theory, with various cultures linking what might be considered to constitute emotional elicitors only to physical illness, making no distinction between thoughts and feelings or objectifying emotions" (p. 24; see also Gerber, 1975; Levy, 1973; Lutz, 1988; Lynch, 1990; Potter, 1988; Shweder, 1993). Lutz (1988) described an emotion concept as a confluence of cultural worldviews and scripts for social behavior. Specifically, she suggested that "to understand the meaning of an emotion is to be able to envisage (and perhaps to find oneself able to participate in) a complicated scene with actors, actions, interpersonal relationships in a particular state of repair, moral points of view, facial expressions, personal and social goals, and sequences of events" (p. 10).

Once it is acknowledged that emotions are more than just biologically prewired internal processes or bodily states (e.g., Kitayama & Markus, 1995; Lutz, 1988; Rosaldo, 1984; White 1994; Wierzbicka, 1994), it is evident that the very category of "emotion" can be constructed or assigned meaning in a variety of ways, and its very rank and standing among categories involved in the explanation of social behavior may vary dramatically.

Among those cultural groups that emphasize the importance of emotions in behavior, the answer given to the question "What is an emotion?" depends on how a group thinks about the nature of its functional relationship with the cultural environment. This understanding, in turn, will determine which aspect of the emotional experience or combination of aspects (e.g., the physiological, the subjective, the intersubjective, the instrumental action) will be emphasized and elaborated in experience as well as the role of these emotions in social behavior.

If an emotion is some amalgam of component processes that are organized by the nature of the functional relationship between the self and the cultural environment, then somewhat different sets of these components are highlighted and they are, in turn, combined in different ways depending on the pertinent cultural frame within which they are allowed to function. Specifically, given an independent frame for living and interacting with others, it may be the subjective part of one's emotional dynamics that is highlighted and elaborated; whereas given an alternative interdependent frame, it may be the interpersonal or intersubjective aspects of emotional experience that receive greater attention and elaboration. Furthermore, this divergent emphasis in emotional experience may in turn lead to correspondingly divergent definitions or emotion prototypes *feeling good*. This means that outer or external cultural frames are inscribed into the inner or internal emotional experience. In this way, emotion may serve as the most proximate or experience-near carrier of cultural imperatives or assumptions about what constitutes the self, others, and the relationship between the two.

Emotion as Subjective Versus Intersubjective

From an independent view of the self, the most important features of the self are the internal and private ones, and thus the corresponding individual, subjective experience will receive an elaborated and privileged place in the behavioral process (Levy, 1984). Key features of this subjectivity are a heightened awareness of one's inner attributes and the tendency to organize one's reactions and actions according to these attributes. The goal is to realize and express these internal attributes. Subjective experience is a result of these efforts that, in turn, fosters these efforts.

For example, in the United States, it is the emotional states that have the individual's internal attributes (his or her needs, goals, desires, or abilities) as the primary referent that are most commonly manifest. They typically result from the blocking (e.g., "I was treated unfairly") or the satisfaction or the confirmation (e.g., "I performed better than others") of one's internal attributes. The emotion of anger, even when caused by the actions of another person, focuses one on the individual goal that has been blocked or on the individual right that has been abridged. Consequently, apparently negative emotions like anger or frustration are not entirely undesirable (certainly not as undesirable as in Japan) because such emotions highlight individual, private, internal attributes and signal that the imperative of the cultural framework—in this case independence—is being served.

For example, many North American self-help groups now work with victims of rape or incest to turn what is regarded within the cultural frame as the passive and negative emotion of shame into the more productive and desirable emotion of anger (see Kitayama & Markus, in 1995). The tendency toward independence of the self from the other requires and fosters the emotions that promote the felt independence and disengagement of self from others. Pleasant feelings or emotional states (like happiness or pride) and unpleasant feelings (like anger and frustration) highlight the fundamental separation of self from others and will feel "natural," "right," or "good." From the perspective in which emotions are private and internal phenomena, some reasonable intensity and some variability in emotional state are positive and promote the felt independence of self.

By contrast, from an interdependent view of the self, the most important features of the self are external and public: status, roles, and relationships. In contrast to individual, subjective experience, it is the intersubjectivity that results from interdependence and connection that received a relatively elaborated and privileged place in the behavioral process. Key features of this intersubjectivity are a heightened sense of the other and of the nature of one's relation to the other and the expectation of some mutuality in this regard. The goal is not individual awareness, experience, and expression, but rather some attunement or alignment of one's reactions and actions with those of another, and intersubjective experience is a result of these efforts and, in turn, fosters these efforts.

Thus in Japan, it is the emotional states or feelings that accompany interdependence—friendly feelings, feelings of affiliation, calmness, smoothness, connectedness—that are regarded as positive or desirable. The emotional state of anger experienced in an in-group setting is very troubling anti regarded as extremely negative by the Japanese primarily because the manifestation of anger serves to break or disturb the relations producing interdependence.

The tendency toward interdependence of the self with others requires and fosters the relational, social emotions—sympathy, modesty (i.e., humility), agreeableness (i.e., harmony, balance, restraint). These emotions promote the felt interdependence of self with others and such engagement feels "right," and "good." The most common negative emotions are likely to be those that accompany a faltering of interdependence (anxiety, fear, shame) and a perceived disengagement of self from others. When these feelings are experienced, certain features of an interdependent relationship (e.g., harmony, tension, etc.) will be highlighted and the self will be perceived as being embedded and as-similated within the relationship. Thus, pleasant emotions (like feelings of closeness) highlight the unity and synchrony between the self and others in the relationship. Even unpleasant emotions in this category (feelings of indebtedness) focus at-tention not on the self, but on the relationship. These, then, are the emotions that have the most important social functions and the ones that will be promoted by "good" or "desirable" social be-havior. From this perspective, relatively low lev-els of intensity and a relative constancy in an emo-tional state will be experienced as positive.

This difference in the definition of what consti-tutes an emotional experience or in how an emo-tional state is defined can be illustrated with a con-crete recent empirical example. In a study comparing Americans with West Sumatrans (the Minangkabau), Levenson, Ekman, Heider, and Friesen (1992) found a remarkable cross-cultural divergence in the subjective experience of emo-tion along with an equally notable cross-cultural similarity in autonomic responses. Among Ameri-cans, they observed that posing the face to mimic positive and negative emotional expressions seems to cause systematic autonomic changes as well as the corresponding changes in subjective feelings. Thus, facial patterns that mimicked positive emo-tions resulted in positive subjective feelings, and those that mimicked negative emotions were linked with negative feelings. Among the Minangkabau respondents, the posed faces also caused similar autonomic changes, suggesting the presence of prewired and largely culture-free physiological and neurochemical networks connecting sensory sig-nals from facial musculature with the functioning of autonomic nervous systems. However, among the Minangkabau respondents the posed faces did not produce any corresponding change in subjec-tive feeling.

Later analysis of the cultural understandings of the Minangkabau by Levenson et al. (1992) re-vealed that these respondents may have had diffi-culty describing their emotional states because they were alone. Emotions for the Minangkabau, as with the Japanese, are typically experienced in the presence of others—relationally, interpersonally. By definition, an emotional event requires another person for its evocation, experience, and expres-sion. To extend their initial analysis, one could argue that the subjectivity of the Minangkabau was

keyed or tuned to the presence of others. So, in contract with the Americans, the activity of the autonomic nervous system stemming from the configuration of the facial musculature did not constitute an emotion. Such results are consistent with the suggestion that Americans and Minangkabaus define emotions differently, and that they have different expectations about when and why an emotion will be experienced. This is one of the important ways in which a group's way of being structures emotional experience.

If groups differ in what they regard as an emo-tion and in their views of what gives rise to par-ticular types of emotions, they are also likely to differ in what feelings they believe should prop-erly accompany these antecedent events, and in what to do about these feelings (i.e., what sorts of instrumental responses are appropriate or how to express or manage these feelings). It is likely, then, that there will be systematic variation in some as-pects of the emotional sequences or scripts that have been identified by emotion theorists (e.g., Frijda, 1986; Shweder, 1993).

In addition to determining what kind of an event an emotion is, cultural frames structure emotions in other, more specific ways. Specifically, many social events come "preappraised" in that there is no uncertainty or decision to be made about what kind or event has occurred nature of the event has been collectively determined at a time prior to the actual eliciting event. The individual does not have to participate actively in the appraisal process. The cultural frame determines which dimensions of appraisal are most relevant and often elaborates only one of the endpoints of these dimensions. Frijda and Mesquita (1994) call this preappraisal process *event-coding*. They contend that when cultures assign labels to events, such as terrorist attack, they also determine the appropriate affec-tive reaction. So for example, American are par-ticularly tuned to positive social events, and many events are already coded as positive and likely to be associated with good feelings. They are also tuned to "see" events in terms of their own efforts and to perceive them as personally controllable. Thus, a good grade on an exam for an American student is preappraised as a positive, controllable event—the good feeling is automatic.

In terms of Frijda and Mesquita's (1994) frame-work, cultural frames also shape emotion by in-scribing in the self habitual domains of concern and also patterns of action readiness and behavior that are tightly linked to particular appraisals. The understanding that the self is fundamentally interdependent with others highlights domains of concern and emphasizes particular patterns of appraisal and action readiness. By contrast, an understanding of the self as autonomous sets up distinctly different concerns and behavioral patterns. In this manner, ways of feeling are specifically and continually encultured in accordance with and commensurate with particular ways of being.

Divergent Ways of Being a Self and Feeling Good

In this section, we draw together studies conducted in different places for different purposes but that, together, begin to provide empirical support for the connections between self, emotion, and social behavior that have been hypothesized here. We illustrate the mutual and reciprocal relations between particular views of self, emotional experiences, and culture-specific patterns of thinking, acting, and interacting. The focus is on the simultaneous enculturation of independence and of pride and on individual happiness among North Americans and, similarly, on the simultaneous enculturation of interdependence and feelings of connection: and relatedness among Asians. We illustrate how ways of being and ways of feeling good are interrelated and, together, part and parcel of the ideas and practices of the dominant cultural frames. We can see here the outlines of a process whereby the stances and commitments of a given cultural frame are incorporated into each individual's subjectivity and intersubjectivity.

In North America and in large parts of Europe, identity formation is most typically tied to the need and the ability to distinguish one's self from others: to individuate the self progressively. European–American psychologists have repeatedly demonstrated what appears to be an extremely powerful and, presumably, universal motive to believe that one is somewhat better than one's peers (Harter, 1990). It is among the most robust and well-documented findings of psychology. American children as young as four believe themselves to be better than their peers. American adults typically consider themselves to be more intelligent, friendlier, and more attractive than the average adult. A recent finding is that, 70%, of people in a national sample thought that they were above av-

erage in leadership ability and that they were smarter, more considerate, and more in control than their peers (Myers, 1989). Furthermore, American adults have more positive expectations for themselves and their futures than they have for other people. They believe that they are more likely to own their own home and earn a large salary and are less likely to contract a deadly disease or get divorced than other people.

This well-known, well-documented tendency to underestimate the commonality of one's desirable behaviors has been called the *false uniqueness effect* (Mullen & Riordan, 1988; Myers, 1989). It is believed to be one clear method of enhancing self-esteem. The reason that being positively different from others produces a good feeling about the self is seldom broached (see Josephs, Markus, & Tarafodi, 1992, for a discussion (of this point). Typically, it is regarded as self-evident that being different in a positive sense produces a good feeling. One answer to such a question is that feeling positive about the self depends in part on realizing the approach to selfhood required by an independent culture. Realizing one's self as different in a positive sense validates, in Bartlett's (1932) terms, the group's core psychological tendency.

Yet, if a cultural group has a different core psychological tendency, as may be true of Asian cultural groups, then some very different social behavior may be associated with good feelings about the self. In this case, maintaining the self may assume a different form for more relational or interdependent selves. Positive feelings may not be linked with self-serving biases or with trying to see the self as positively unique. Good feelings may derive instead from realizing the approach to selfhood required by these independent cultures. Indeed, good feelings may be a function of good social relationships (i.e., fitting-in, belonging, maintaining harmony in one's relations, occupying one's proper place, engaging in appropriate action) while at the same time regulating one's inner personal thoughts and feelings so as to ensure interdependence. Such an interdependent perspective on the source and nature of good feelings may afford some understanding of why, on the occasion of her marriage to the Crown Prince of Japan, the Princess's mother could advise her daughter, "Be happy! Do the utmost to serve your country." From an independent perspective, happiness and serving one's country are not obvious partners.

In a study comparing a representative sample of Japanese college students in Japan and American college students in the United States, Markus and Kitayama (1991) found that it was the Americans who showed a distinct false uniqueness bias. When asked "What proportion of your peers is better than you are," in each of nine different domains, they believed that they were different from and better than others on all kinds abilities (mathematics, athletics, language, memory) with regard to their independence and autonomy and even with regard to their sympathy and warmheartedness. On average, American college students reported that only 30% of their peers were better than they. In a representative sample, if people answer questions in an unbiased way, the group estimate should hover at 50%, which would indicate no bias in estimation.

The Japanese college students did not reveal such a false uniqueness bias. For these respondents, their estimates did hover around 50%. The departure from this estimate that did occur was found to be for women who believed that most other Japanese people were somewhat better than they. Takata (1987) has suggested that these results reflect what could be called a self-harmonizing bias among the Japanese—a reflection of the core psychological tendency of the interdependent cultural frame—to see one's self as part of a whole with others and thus like others in important ways.

Stigler, Smith, and Mao (1985), in a study of elementary school children in the United States and China, found a similar persistent tendency for Chinese children not to distinguish themselves on ratings of self-worth and competence. The Chinese children rated themselves significantly lower than the American children on the cognitive, physical, and general subscales of Harter's Perceived Competence Scale for Children, which specifically requires children to compare themselves with other children. This study also found that, for American children, there was a strong correlation between general self-esteem and esteem for particular domains of self (i.e., cognitive, social, physical) (rs = .46–.53). These correlations were low for the Chinese children (rs = .23–.30). Stigler et al. (1985) suggested that the scale may have activated what they called "strong self-effacing tendencies" among the Chinese.

Both false uniqueness and false modesty or self-effacement may be viewed as social judgment tendencies or habits of cognitive behavior that support and reflect their underlying cultural frames. Many Americans find the Japanese behavior in these circumstances difficult to understand or believe. Could it really be the case that some Asians actually prefer to believe that, others are better than they are or, as has been shown in other studies, actually have more confidence in a test that showed them to be performing less well than their peers (Markus & Kitayama, 1991; Schwartz & Smith, 1976; Takata, 1987)? Could there actually be a concern that could rival good feelings about one's self and the continued pursuit of such positive self-feelings as a major life-organizing goal or motive (the Princess question again)?

Although there is probably little question that modesty is sometimes false, representing primarily an attempt at impression management, in many cases, self-effacement may follow naturally from a desire to maintain the self as an interdependent and respectable agent. Within an interdependent cultural frame, self-harmonizing can lead to a sense of fitting-in, the recognition of fully participating in a relationship, thereby meeting the criteria for positive social behavior and giving rise to a feeling of satisfaction that one is a worthy member of the community.

To answer questions regarding the authenticity of such social behavior requires understanding of the feeling states that accompany the self-serving, false uniqueness bias or the seemingly self-denying or self-harmonizing bias. In a recent study, Kitayama, Markus, and Kurokawa (1991) presented both Japanese college students in Japan and American college students in the United States with a number of labels for emotions, feelings, or sentiments—some indigenous to Americans and some indigenous to Japanese—and asked how frequently they experienced each of them in everyday life. The Americans reported an overwhelmingly greater frequency of experiencing positive than negative self-relevant feelings, but there was virtually no such effect among the Japanese.

Similarly, Akiyama (1992), in a national probability sample of 2,200 Japanese aged 60 years and older, found that the inverse correlation between negative affect and positive affect that characterized the American sample did not appear for the Japanese. There was virtually no correlation between negative and positive affect in the Japanese sample, and both positive and negative affect levels were considerably lower than those of

American respondents. Akiyama suggested that because Japanese are not socialized to monitor, elaborate, or express their own self-feelings, such feelings are less likely to be encoded and recalled. Consistent with this suggestion, Matsumoto (1992) found that Americans are more accurate than the Japanese at recognizing four of Ekman's six basic emotions. Perceiving or experiencing an emotion may require, as in the Levenson et al. (1992) study described earlier, the participation of others. Feelings about the self—the core of emotion for those with independent selves—may not be sufficient to experience an emotion.

In contrast, Americans tied to an independent cultural framework will highlight and emphasize their individual feeling states precisely be cause such feelings are self-definitional. Self-relevant feelings are necessary, important, and the more the better. This fits with the culturally shared imperative to create, or define, or objectify the self. As Wierzbicka (1994) pointed out, knowing that one feels, what one feels, and that one can instrumentally control one's emotions is extremely important in Anglo-American culture. Other observers have even claimed that Americans seem preoccupied with noting, registering, and in general, "working" on their emotions (e.g., Bellah, Madsen, Sullivan, Swidler, & Tipton, 1985). Positive self-feelings signal that a separate self or identity has been forged and will, in addition, function as an indicator of the adequacy and integrity of the self.

Positive *self* feelings are the basis of all good feeling. Self-esteem is typically operationalized as the total amount of good feelings directed toward the self (Epstein, 1973; Harter & Marold, 1991), and it is the basis of happiness American style, at least currently. Happiness indeed means "I feel good" and it plays a central role in American discourse and is the basis of psychological well-being (Wierzbicka, 1994). The American practice of smiling and being generally friendly is important because it is an indication that one has good self-feelings and such feelings reflect that one has the culturally required good inner self. That is, they indicate that the observed behavior is being directed by an autonomous self replete with positive attributes. Happiness and elation are apparently of a different nature in Japan and seem to require an awareness and assurance of connection and interdependence. [. . .]

Overall, among those assumed to have independent selves, the positive feelings produced by personal achievement and the attendant tendencies to self-enhance seem genuinely positive, capable of alleviating other negative feelings or sentiments, and associated with a general sense of happiness. In contrast, among those assumed to have selves with a more interdependent cast, general happiness or satisfaction, is related most closely to the confirmation of the self as part of the unitary, ongoing relationship, from this point of view, the self-harmonizing or self-effacement observed in the studies of false uniqueness can be conducive, much more than self-enhancement, to positive feelings or satisfaction.

Without some attention to what the cultural frame of interdependence requires for selfhood and good feeling, one could be led to believe, as some earlier investigators were, that the interdependent selves have difficulty constructing a positive identity and show excessive amounts of fatalism, dependence, and anxiety. For example, Hartnack (1987) has shown how British psychoanalysts identified these and other negative attributes as basic to the Indian personality and then used their findings to justify continued British rule. It is evident that a consideration of self and self-processes must reflect the cultural framework or what it means to be a self. The construct and maintenance of the self as well as all the hypothesized self-processes (self-evaluation, self-esteem, self-presentation, self-consciousness, self-effacement) are all conditioned by the meaning or significance that is attached to the self.

These studies begin to delineate the role of the self in shaping emotion and suggest how differences in the behaviors associated with self-construction and maintenance (e.g., self-aggrandizing or self-harmonizing) can be reconciled when these practices are located within their relevant cultural frame. Positive emotions serve many global and specific interpersonal functions. Initially, and very important, they signal the accomplishment of the important cultural task of being a person in the prescribed way. Thus, for those with interdependent selves, feeling good requires a connection to others, and a connection to others produces good feelings. Similarly, for those with independent selves, feeling good and positive emotions necessitate a separation from others, and beliefs and practices that emphasize this separation feel good and are the basis of self-esteem.

Shaping the Ways of Feeling Good

Given the demonstrated interdependence between models of the self and the meaning and nature of emotion, we can ask how this powerful interdependence is created. If, as these data suggest, American children experience happiness and an entire range of general good feelings when they have reason to believe that they have some qualities or attributes that distinguish them from others in a positive manner, we can ask why it is that "standing-out," at least to some extent, feels good. Similarly, we can ask why Japanese children feel good when they fit-in. One preliminary answer might come from a detailed analysis of emotional socialization practices. For example, many American children are constantly praised and rewarded for work that they have done and projects that they have created. These children are habitually encouraged to identify attributes of the self that are unique in a positive manner. Initially, the child's caretakers help with this (e.g., "Sarah, you did such a great job on that painting, I am proud of you") regardless of what Sarah has actually done. A recent study by Little, Oettingen, Stetsenko, and Baltes (1994), comparing Russian, German (East and West), and American elementary school children for the relationship between estimates of self-efficacy and actual performance, showed this correlation to be lower among American children than among other groups.

Young children in the United States receive a great deal of positive reinforcement that is not particularly contingent on actual performance. For example, in sharp contrast with schoolchildren in most other parts of the world, American children are rarely given information about their relative rank in the classroom. Increasingly, in elementary schools, students receive no grades, and activities that foster competition and thus provide information about one's standing relative to others (even sports activities) are discouraged. These educational practices set up a situation in which students' beliefs about themselves and their abilities are relatively unconstrained. In the early grades at least, situations are constructed so that children can hold a set of positive beliefs about themselves. Obviously, it does not work in all cases. Many American children still feel negatively about themselves; but, in general, such practices are likely to lead to beliefs in one's relative uniqueness.

Similarly, many current child-rearing practices are geared toward helping the child develop a distinct sense of self that he or she can feel good about. A recent study (Chao, 1993b) found that 64%, of European–American mothers in a California sample, as opposed to 8% of Chinese mothers in this sample, stressed building children's "sense of themselves" as an important goal of child rearing. Furthermore, criticism of children's actions was often explicitly avoided.

American children very quickly internalize the habit of identifying positive features in their own behavior, come to believe that they are better than others, and construct an identity that is built primarily around positive attributes. On average, the self-concepts of Americans contain about four to five times as many positive attributes as negative ones (Markus, Herzog, Holmberg, & Dielman, 1992). For North Americans, there is only one self, and it must be as positive as possible. In contrast, the Japanese self appears to be more fractionated, containing both a private self and a public self (Kuwayama, 1992; Rohlen, 1991). Given these two different aspects of self, there appears to be less concern among the Japanese in identifying and elaborating positive, personal attributes in the private self because it is the outside, public part of the self that makes contact with others and regulates social behavior. If one lives up to commitments, obligations, and responsibilities and their various roles, statuses and positions, it is decidedly less threatening to elaborate on shortcomings or negative aspects of the private self and to draw attention to them (Kim, 1994; Kim, Triandis, Kagitcibasi, Choi, Yoon, 1994; Rohlen, 1989, 1991). In fact, self-criticism is valued, desired, and promoted in Japan. Schoolchildren are often instructed to think about what they did wrong and how to improve their performance the next day. Adults also engage in self-criticism: Professional baseball players, for example, are required to find publicly the flaws in their own playing (Whiting, 1989).

On the basis of this collection of findings, we can hypothesize that those with independent selves will develop self-evaluative schemas that are especially sensitive or "tuned in" to positive information. These people will be motivated to feel unique in a positive manner and, when they are able to construct or locate such information, they will feel good. Discussing and expressing positive, internal attributes of the self is the "right" thing to do. By contrast, those with interdependent selves are habitually motivated to fit-in with or align themselves with the group. When children fit and find their proper place, they become part of the whole and are not distinctive. This does not automatically imply learning how to give up or sacrifice one's own interest and wishes for the good of the group (Choi & Choi, 1990; Kim, 1994; Kim et al., 1994). Rather, children learn that working together harmoniously is a way of creating and affirming the self. Kagitcibasi (1989) noted that whereas Canadian mothers are notable in efforts to "detach themselves" from their children, Japanese mothers do everything possible to convey a oneness between the mother and the child as the most desirable end state.

Peak (1991), in an examination of Japanese preschools, claimed that Japanese children are specifically taught about the "joy" of group life. In fact, Japanese mothers report that the primary reason for sending children to nursery school is to teach them how to fit in with their peers. It is the school's duty to teach group living (Peak, 1991; Rohlen, 1989). Recent studies reveal that Japanese teachers, in comparison with American teachers, direct their comments and questions to the group as a whole rather than to specific individuals (Hamilton, Blumenfeld, Akoh, & Miura, 1991). Similarly, Chinese children are encouraged to see the world as a network of relationships of which they are a part (Hsu, 1953). Chao (1993a) found that Chinese mothers explicitly stress fostering a happy, close, harmonious relationship with the child, as opposed to building self-esteem, as a goal of child rearing. When children learn to align their own goals with those of the group and find their proper place in a social network and "fit it," they are not distinctive.

The emphasis in interdependent child rearing is on attending to those circumstances in which the child is not aligned or does not fit-it. Deviations from the expectations of others need to be carefully monitored and, when detected, corrected. Here again, the caretaker plays a crucial role in helping the child find potential deficits or problems in his or her behavior. When a child is misbehaving, a caretaker might say "Kazuo, you are acting very strange; your friends may laugh at you if they see it." Attention is drawn to how the child is not behaving as expected, and the punishment involves being made to stand out, which poses a threat to the relationship between the child and the group. As a consequence, we can hypothesize

that the self-evaluative schemas of those from interdependent cultures will eventually become especially sensitive and tuned not to positive but to negative, self-relevant information. If children begin at an early age to embody the cultural imperative in this way, it is not surprising that, by college, these students will be much more sensitive and responsive to events that may cause them to feel bad about themselves.

A focus on emotional socialization can also provide insight into why the Japanese are motivated to believe that they fit with others and are not at all distinctive from others (i.e., why they show self-harmonizing or self-effacement rather than false uniqueness), and why it is that the most frequently experienced negative emotion among the Japanese is a fear of causing trouble or of burdening someone else (i.e., as observed in Kitayama et al., 1991). Children of interdependent cultures, then, may become relative experts with regard to the negative or bad aspects of their behavior and, in every case, bad feelings result from disturbances or difficulties with social relations (Rohlen, 1989). All good affective responses involve the realization or expression of close, secure, harmonious relations (Azuma, 1986). Although the practices involved are likely to be somewhat different, Kim (1994; Kim et al., 1994) reported that such socialization for interdependence has also been documented in Indian culture (Kakar, 1978; Sinha & Verma, 1987) and in Turkish culture (Kagitcibasi, 1989).

The data here are hardly sufficient or compelling, but they suggest the broad outlines of an enculturation process whereby the child comes to feel as his or her group does. The cultural framework is also created and reinforced through linguistic practices and through the artifacts, practices, and institutions of the society that reflect and promote this idea.[7] Although it may be difficult to fathom from an American viewpoint, within an interdependent cultural framework that what is labeled self-effacement can feel good, and an entire set of socialization practices works to ensure this link. Such apparently self-denying behavior is in the service of fitting in. These practices reinforce the sense of being fully participating in a relationship and the ultimate sense of satisfaction

---

[7]For a discussion of some of these other practices, see Markus and Kitayama (1994).

as a worthy member of the community. Living up to this idea of being a person is then related to good feelings and to contentment or satisfaction in one's own life. Labeling such behavior as *self-effacement* is misleading, because although one's personal attributes may not be the focus of attention—indeed they may be relatively ignored—the interdependent self (i.e., the self as a member of a community) is very much promoted and affirmed. Obviously, a great deal more needs to be done to specify fully the transformation of the cultural imperative into individual subjectivity; but even at this initial point, we can understand how it is that the Japanese future Empress may feel good about her decision to marry into the royal family, and we can draw out some implications for future study of social behavior in cross-cultural perspectives.

Implications for Social Behavior

If we assume that the emotional experiences that affirm the cultural frame are those that will be highlighted and emphasized, then certain social behavior that elicits, fosters, or reflects the focal emotions should be relatively common. The social behavior of various cultural groups can be analyzed productively for the emotions that accompany it. Accordingly, certain emotional states that are difficult to accept as positive or desirable from an American point of view (being modest, humble, or full of shame, and the accompanying social behavior of withdrawing, conforming, remaining silent) can, when located within the appropriate cultural frame, he more readily appreciated as positive and as desirable.

An appreciation of the emotional concomitants of various kinds of social behavior is one key to fathoming otherwise unfathomable behavior. This is the general notion behind the extensive study of values (Rokeach, 1973; Schwartz & Bilsky, 1990). Yet in most studies, values are regarded primarily as cognitive representations or beliefs that guide behavior. With a focus on feeling states, we seek to add to this analysis and delineate yet another powerful domain of contact between the social world and individual subjectivity and intersubjectivity. Certain social behavior is not only believed to be good or proper, it also feels natural or right and is experienced as desirable and necessary.

Several reviews of social psychology in a cross-cultural perspective (Moghaddam et al., 1993; Smith & Bond, 1993) suggest very little generalizability of the basic social psychological findings across various cultural groups, and the patterns of conflicting findings have not yet been reconciled. One route of understanding these differences and avoiding despair over the impossibility of making generalizations may be a consideration of the relation between the behavior being observed and the underlying cultural frame. When studies of social behavior are conducted within a single culture, the ways in which psychological functioning and theories about psychological functioning are culture specific and are conditioned by particular models of the self and the world is typically not obvious. For example, when a given social behavior has been induced or observed, social psychologists have rarely asked whether the behavior experienced is good and whether it reflects culture's notion of how to be a self or whether the behavior in question goes against the cultural grain.

Conformity to Group Pressure

In considering the phenomenon of conformity, Smith and Bond (1993) reported 24 published nonreplications of Asch's (1952) findings. Of the several studies done with Japanese respondents, the one using strangers as confederates found very low levels of conformity (Frager, 1970), and another found a high rate of errors when intact social groups were used (Williams & Sogon, 1984). Across all the reported studies on conformity, more errors in the direction of the confederate (i.e., conforming responses) were made by respondents in collectivist societies (Smith & Bond, 1993).

An analysis of differential conformity rates would be facilitated by an understanding of the affective responses that accompany being influenced by or responsive to others. From the perspective of a cultural frame that is rooted in the idea of a fundamental human relatedness, it is necessary, important, and feels good or right to be sensitive and responsive to the expectations of others, at least to those others within the in-group. Personal thoughts and opinions are often withheld for the purpose of promoting group harmony. From the perspective of an independent cultural frame, conformity takes a very different cast. Although conforming is viewed as a necessary integrative mechanism, it is viewed most often as "yielding" to the collective; it is something to fear. [. . .]

Stereotyping and Intergroup Behavior

Another important area of social behavior is stereotyping. The majority of research on stereotyping has been done with an independent cultural framework. From the point of view of the American melting pot ideology, all cultural differences should be submerged quickly (Moghaddam et al., 1993). Moreover, stereotyping is inherently negative from an independent perspective because it involves constructing people as group members and not as individuals. As Oakes and Turner (1990) noted, the idea that one is an exemplar of a social category or that individual freedom or agency is importantly configured by one's past or current group membership seems somehow undemocratic or un-American. Yet, from a framework in which people are taught from the earliest age about the joy of group life, a positive and distinctive group stereotype may well function for the group as a positive and unique self-concept does for the individual in North America.

When the group is the primary basis of self-definition, in-group membership takes on particular importance, the interdependent members of the group will evoke positive evaluations and the out-group members, negative evaluations (Jarymolvich, 1987; Reykowski, 1991). And if, as is often the case, among those in interdependent or collectivist cultural groups, self-interest is secondary and often subverted in the interest of the group (Triandis, 1994), then the desire to maintain a positive view of one's group may be extremely powerful. [. . .]

Coping and Adjustment

Another important area of social behavior concerns coping and adjustment. The burgeoning literature in health psychology has focused on trying to identify the features of good copers and bad copers. Good copers are those who maintain positive illusions about themselves, have high self-efficacy, focus on the problem rather than their own state, and have strong social support networks (Antonucci, 1990; Lazarus & Folkman, 1984; Taylor, 1989). People will be judged as good or as well-adjusted copers to the extent to which they can maintain this mode of operation after a crisis.

However, successful coping is tied to a cultural group's view of how to be a self. With a view of how to be a self that differs from the independent view, effective coping may take a different form.

In North America, prolonged grieving over the loss of a loved one and the failure to return to an autonomous lifestyle can be considered pathological, but this perspective is tied to a view of the self as a bounded, autonomous whole. As Stroebe, Gergen, Gergen, and Stroebe (1992) pointed out, from an interdependent perspective, the loss of another means a breaking of bonds and can destroy one's interdependent identity. Consequently, the bonds, even with the deceased, must be maintained or the self is threatened. Such a connection is maintained in some Japanese homes with a commemorative altar that allows for paying continued respect to one's ancestors.

Cross (1992) looked directly at the role of the self in coping. In a study with Asian international students, she found that those with interdependent selves suffered the most stress in American graduate schools, a place in which an independent cultural frame is clearly dominant. Those Asian students who coped best during graduate school were those who took on characteristics of an independent self.

Within different cultural frameworks, coping, mental health, and well-being can take different forms and are likely to be associated with different ways of feeling. For example, the avoidance of suffering may seem to be a universal goal, but as the work of Kleinman (1988) and Das (1992) in China and India documented, even this assumption may be questioned. According to some perspectives, suffering is a part of being human and can even be ennobling and associated with good feelings. If the pursuit of well-being is indeed a universal goal, research in this domain will be furthered by relating normative coping practices and desirable feeling states to the relevant cultural frame.

We have outlined here some of the ways in which culture, self, emotion, and social behavior constrain and afford each other. Initially, such a framing may seem to enlarge the scope of these phenomena to the point at which they are no longer tractable, but we believe that the type of framework offered here has the potential to generate specific, testable hypotheses. As social psychologists, we have focused in this last section on the implications of this interdependency for the analysis and explanation of social behavior. An understanding of the potential for systematic variation in emotional experience is one key to making sense of the conflicting set of results and failures to replicate that are increasingly reported in social psychology as considered in cross-cultural perspective. Specifically, we have argued that one of the specific and powerful ways in which cultural context influences individual behavior is through its influence on the meanings and practices of the self.

Each cultural context provides some message about, what it means to be a person. Through emotional socialization, ongoing social and linguistic processes, these cultural messages or imperatives are incorporated into the emotional system so that it feels "good" to behave in accordance with these imperative and it feels "bad" when one cannot or does not. In this way, the self shapes one's sense of the good by specifying one important set of criteria for what is "good" (and also how to feel good, when to feel good, why to feel good, etc.). As a consequence, the nature of the positive or good or the negative or bad emotions will depend on the supporting cultural frame. From a European–American cultural perspective, "good" emotions are experienced when one's own needs are met or one's own attributes are verified or expressed. From an Asian cultural perspective, "good" emotions entail fitting-in with others, seeking and fulfilling obligations, and becoming part of an ongoing relationship. This means that good feelings will be typically manifested as individual happiness from an independent perspective, but as sympathy or as feelings of similarity and connectedness from an interdependent perspective. These two different types of "good" feelings will be experienced differently—personally and subjectively in one case and interpersonally and intersubjectively in the other—and will be tied to different types of instrumental responses.

Out of this perspective comes a number of challenging ideas that are at odds with many current views on emotions and deserve further analysis (e.g., for some groups, sympathy is a basic emotion): that shame, or even humiliation, can be a desirable emotional experience for some groups (see Asad, 1987; Menon & Shweder, 1994), and that emotions are not experienced individually but relationally. This perspective also raises new questions about the functions of emotions, such as (a) do emotions serve the same cultural functions in all groups (Potter, 1988, argued that emotions are

essentially unimportant for the Chinese in the regulation of everyday action); (b) what makes an emotion basic; (c) what does it mean to experience emotions intersubjectively or relationally; (d) how does variation in the criteria for the generalized "good" or "bad" feelings influence the emotions of fear, anger, and surprise; (e) which aspects of the "good" feelings may be similar and which may be different from one another across cultural groups; and (f) how does a group's understanding and experience of emotion influence how the emotions should be observed, manipulated, or assessed (e.g., the questionnaires requiring reflections on one's own emotional state may be appropriate and adequate for groups with a private property view of emotion, but altogether inappropriate for groups who have a more interpersonal view of the nature and experience of emotion). Pursuing these questions may eventually allow an integration of two views of emotions that have remained separate and that have been pursued in distinct literature, that is, the view of emotions as discrete internal, personal products, and the view of emotions as moral, social, historical, political, and cultural products.

REFERENCES

Akiyama, H. (1992, June). *Measurement of depressive symptoms in cross-cultural research.* Paper presented at the International Conference on Emotion and Culture, University of Oregon, Eugene.

Antonucci, T. C. (1990). Social supports and social relationships. In R. H. Binstock & L. K. George (Eds.), *The handbook of aging and the social sciences* (3rd ed., pp. 205–226). San Diego, CA: Academic Press.

Asad, T. (1987). On ritual and discipline in medieval Christian monasticism. *Economy and Society, 16*(2), 159–203.

Asch, S. E. (1952). *Social psychology.* Englewood Cliffs, NJ: Prentice Hall.

Azuma, H. (1986). Why study child development in Japan? In H. Stevenson, H. Azuma, & K. Hakuta (Eds.), *Child development and education in Japan* (pp. 3–12). San Francisco: Freeman.

Bartlett, F. A. (1932). *Remembering: A study in experimental psychology.* Cambridge, England: Cambridge University Press.

Bellah, H. N., Madsen, R., Sullivan, W. M., Swidler, A., & Tipton, S. M. (1985). *Habits of the heart: Individualism and commitment in American life.* Berkeley: University of California Press.

Bourdieu, P. (1972). *Outline of a theory of practice.* Cambridge, England: Cambridge University Press.

Bourdieu, P. (1980). *The logic of practice.* Stanford, CA: Stanford University Press.

Bruner, J. (1990). *Acts of meaning.* Cambridge, MA: Harvard University Press.

Chao, R. K. (1993a, March). *Clarification of the authoritarian parenting style and parental control: Cultural concepts of Chinese child rearing*. Paper presented at the 60th Anniversary Meeting of the Society for Research in Child Development, New Orleans, LA.

Chao, R. K. (1993b). *East and West concepts of the self reflecting in mothers' reports of their child rearing*. Unpublished manuscript, University of California, Los Angeles.

Choi, S. C., & Choi, S. H. (1990, July). *We-ness: A Korean discourse of collectivism*. Paper presented at the First International Conference on Individualism and Collectivism: Psychocultural Perspectives for East and West, Seoul Korea.

Cross, S. E. (1992). *Cultural adaptation and the self: Self-construal, coping, and stress*. Unpublished doctoral dissertation, University of Michigan, Ann Arbor, MI.

D'Andrade, R. (1984). Cultural meaning systems. In R. A. Shweder & R. A. LeVine (Eds.), *Culture theory: Essays on mind, self and emotion* (pp. 88–119). Cambridge, England: Cambridge University Press.

D'Andrade, R. (1987). A folk model of the mind. In D. Holland & N. Quinn (Eds.), *Cultural models in language and thought*. Cambridge, England: Cambridge University Press.

Das, V. (1992). Moral orientations to suffering: Litigation, power and healing. In L. Chen, A. Kleinman, & N. Ware (Eds.), *Health and social change in international perspectives* (pp. 139–157). Boston: Harvard School of Public Health.

de Riviera, J. (1984). The structure of emotional relationships. In P. Shaver (Ed.), *Review of personality and social psychology: Vol. 5. Emotions, relationships, and health* (pp. 116–145). Beverly Hills, CA: Sage.

Durkheim, E. (1953). Individual representations and collective representations. In D. F. Pocock (Trans.), *Sociology and philosophy* (pp. 1–38). New York: Free Press. (Reprinted from *Revue de Métaphysique*, 1898, *6*, 274–302)

Ellsworth, P. C. (1994). Sense, culture, and sensibility. In S. Kitayama & H. R. Markus (Eds.), *Emotion and culture: Empirical studies of mutual influence* (pp. 23–50). Washington, DC: American Psychological Association.

Epstein, S. (1973). The self-concept revisited or a theory of a theory. *American Psychologist, 28*, 405´–416.

Frager, R. (1970). Conformity and anti-conformity in Japan. *Journal of Personality and Social Psychology, 15*, 203–210.

Frijda, N. (1986). *The emotions*. Cambridge, England: Cambridge University Press.

Frijda, N. H., & Mesquita, B. (1994). The social roles and functions of emotions. In S. Kitayama & H. R.. Markus (Eds.), *Emotion and culture: Empirical studies of mutual influence* (pp. 51–87). Washington, DC: American Psychological Association.

Gaskins, S., Miller, P. J., & Corsaro, W. A. (1992). Theoretical and methodological perspectives in the interpretive study of children. In W. A. Corsaro & P. J. Miller (Eds.), *Interpretive approaches in children's socialization* (pp. 5–23). San Francisco, CA: Jossey-Bass.

Gerber, E. (1975). *The cultural patterning of emotions in Samoa*. Unpublished doctoral dissertation, University of California, San Diego.

Gergen, K. J. (1992). Psychology in the postmodern era. *The General Psychologist, 28*, 10–15.

Giddens, A. (19984). *The constitution of society*. Oxford, England: Polity.

Hamilton, V. L., Blumenfeld, P. C., Akoh, H., & Miura, K. (1991). Group and gender in Japanese and American el-

ementary classrooms. *Journal of Cross-Cultural Psychology, 22*, 3.

Harter, S. (1990). Causes, correlates and the functional role of global self-worth: A life span perspective. In R. J. Sternberg & J. Kolligian, Jr. (Eds.), *Competence considered* (pp. 67–97). New Haven, CT: Yale University Press.

Harter, S., & Marold, D. B. (1991). A model of the determinants and mediational role of self-worth: Implications for adolescent depression and suicidal ideation. In G. R. Goethals & J. Strauss (Eds.), *Multidisciplinary perspectives on the self* (pp. 66–92). New York: Springer-Verlag.

Hartnack, D. (1987). British psychoanalysts in colonial India. In M. G. Ash & W. H. Woodward (Eds.), *Psychology in twentieth-century thought and society* (pp. 233–253). Cambridge, England: Cambridge University Press.

Hsu, F. L. K. (1953). *Americans and Chinese: Two ways of life*. New York: H. Schuman.

James, W. (1890). *Principles of psychology*. New York: Holt.

Jarymolvich, M. (1987). Perceiving one's own individuality. The estimation and attractiveness of self-distinctness from others. *Warsaw Psychological Monographs*. Warsaw, Poland: University of Warsaw Press.

Jenkins, J. H. (1991). Anthropology, expressed emotion, and schizophrenia. *Ethos, 19*, 4.

Josephs, R. A., Markus, H., & Tarafodi, R. W. (1992). Gender and self-esteem. *Journal of Personality and Social Psychology, 63*, 391–402.

Kagitcibasi, C. (1989). Family and socialization in cross-cultural perspective: A model of change. In K. A. Dienstbier & J. J. Berman (Eds.), *Nebraska Symposium on Motivation, 1989: Cross-cultural perspectives* (pp. 135–200). Lincoln: University of Nebraska Press.

Kakar, S. (1978). *The inner world: A psychoanalytic study of childhood and society in India*. London: Oxford University Press.

Kim, U. (1994). Introduction to individualism and collectivism: Conceptual clarification and elaboration. In U. Kim, H. C. Triandis, & C. Kagitcibasi (Eds.), *Individualism and collectivism: Theory, method, and applications*. Newbury Park, CA: Sage.

Kim, U., Triandis, H. C., Kagitcibasi, C., Choi, S. C., & Yoon, G. (1994). Introduction to individualism and collectivism: Social and applied issues. In U. Kim, H. C. Triandis, & C. Kagitcibasi (Eds.), *Individualism and collectivism: Theory, method, and applications*. Newbury Park, CA: Sage.

Kitayama, S., & Markus, H. R. (1995). Culture, self, and emotion: A cultural perspective to "self-conscious" emotions. In J. P. Tangney & K. W. Fisher (Eds.), *Shame, guilt, embarrassment, and pride: Empirical studies of self-conscious emotions*. New York: Guilford Press.

Kitayama, S., Markus, H. R., & Kurokawa, M. (1991, October). *Culture, self, and emotion: The structure and frequency of emotional experience*. Paper presented at the biannual meeting of the Society for Psychological Anthropology, Chicago.

Kleinman, A. (1988). *Rethinking psychiatry: From cultural category to personal experience*. New York: Free Press.

Kondo, D. (1990). *Crafting selves: Power, gender, and discourses of identity in a Japanese work place*. Chicago: University of Chicago Press.

Kuwayama, T. (1992). The reference other orientation. In N. W. Rosenberger (Ed.), *Japanese sense of self* (pp. 121–151). Cambridge, England: Cambridge University Press.

Lave, J., Stepick, A., & Sailer, L. (1977). Extending the scope of formal analysis. *American Ethnologist, 4,* 321–339.

Lazarus, R. S., & Folkman, S. (1991). *Stress, appraisal, and coping.* New York: Springer.

Lebra, T. S. (1992, June). *Culture, self and communication.* Paper presented at the University of Michigan, Ann Arbor, Michigan.

Levenson, K. W., Ekman, P., Heider, K., & Friesen, W. V. (1992). Emotion and autonomic nervous system activity in the Minangkabau of West Sumatra. *Journal of Personality and Social Psychology, 62,* 972–988.

Levy, R. I. (1973). *The Tahitians.* Chicago: University of Chicago Press.

Levy, R. I. (1981). Emotions in comparative perspective. In K. H. Scherer & P. Ekman (Eds.), *Approaches to emotion* (pp. 397–412). Hillsdale, NJ: Erlbaum.

Little, T. O., Oettingen, G., Stetsenko, A., & Baltes, P. B. (1994). *Children's school performance-related beliefs: How do American children compare to German and Russian children?* Berlin: Max Planck Institute for Human Development and Education.

Lutz, C. (1988) *Unnatural emotions: Everyday sentiments on a Micronesian atoll and their challenge to Western theory.* Chicago: University of Chicago Press.

Lynch, O. M. (1990). *Divine passions: The social construction of emotion in India.* Berkeley: University of California Press.

Markus, H. R., Herzog, A. H., Holmberg, D. E., & Dielman, L. (1992). *Constructing the self across the life span.* Unpublished manuscript, University of Michigan, Ann Arbor.

Markus, H., & Kitayama, S. (1991). Culture and the self: Implications for cognition, emotion, and motivation. *Psychological Bulletin, 98,* 221–253.

Markus, H. K., & Kitayama, S. (1994). A collective fear of the collective: Implications for selves and theories of selves. *Personality and Social Psychology Bulletin.*

Matsumoto, D. (1902). American-Japanese cultural differences in the recognition of universal facial expression. *Journal of Cross-Cultural Psychology, 23,* 1.

Menon, U., & Shweder, R. A. (1994). Kali's tongue: Cultural psychology and the power of shame in Orissa, India. In S. Kitayama & H. R. Markus (Eds.), *Emotion and culture: Empirical studies of mutual influence* (pp. 241–284). Washington, DC: American Psychological Association.

Miller, J. G. (1994). Cultural psychology: Bridging disciplinary boundaries in understanding the cultural grounding of self. In P. K. Pock (Ed.), *Handbook of psychological anthropology.* Westport, CT: Greenwood.

Moghaddam, F. M., Taylor, D. M., & Wright, S. C. (1993). *Social psychology in cross-cultural perspective.* San Francisco: Freeman.

Moscovici, S. (1993, Spring). The return of the unconscious. *Social Research, 60*(1).

Mowrer, O. H. (1960). *Learning theory and behavior.* New York: Wiley.

Mullen, B., & Riordan. C. A. (1988). Self-serving attributions in naturalistic settings: A meta-analytic review. *Journal of Applied Social Psychology, 18,* 3–22.

Myers, D. (1989). *Social psychology* (3rd ed.). New York: McGraw-Hill.

Neisser, U. (1988). Five kinds of self-knowledge. *Philosophical Psychology, 1,* 35–59.

Oakes, P. J., & Turner, J. C. (1990). Is limited information processing capacity the cause of social stereotyping? *European Review of Social Psychology, 1,* 111–135.

Oyserman, D., & Markus, H. R. (1993). The sociocultural self. In J. Suls (Ed.), *Psychological perspectives on the self* (Vol. 4, pp. 187–220). Hillsdale, NJ: Erlbaum.

Peak, L. (1991). *Learning to go to school in Japan: The transition from home to preschool life.* Berkeley: University of California Press.

Potter, S. H. (1988). The cultural construction of emotion in rural Chinese social life. *Ethos, 16,* 181–208.

Pribram, K. (1971). *Languages of the brain: Experimental paradoxes and principles of neuropsychology.* Englewood Cliffs, NJ: Prentice Hall.

Quinn, N., & Holland, D. (1987). Culture and cognition. In D. Holland & N. Quinn (Eds.), *Cultural models in language and thought* (pp. 3–40). Cambridge, England: Cambridge University Press.

Radcliffe-Brown, A. R. (1952). *Structure and function in primitive society.* New York: Free Press of Glencoe.

Reykowski, J. (1991). *The transition from collectivism: Introduction to a research project.* Unpublished manuscript, Polish Academy of Science, Warsaw.

Rohlen, T. P. (1989). Order in Japanese society: Attachment, authority, and routine. *Journal of Japanese Studies, 15,* 5–41.

Rohlen, T. P. (1991). *A developmental topography of self and society in Japan.* Paper presented at the Conference on Self and Society in India, China, and Japan, Honolulu, HI.

Rokeach, M. (1973). *The nature of human values.* New York: Free Press.

Rosaldo, M. Z. (1984). Toward an anthropology of self and feeling. In R. A. Shweder & R. A. LeVine (Eds.), *Culture therapy: Essays on mind, self, and emotion* (pp. 177–157). Cambridge, England: Cambridge University Press.

Sampson, E. E. (1988). The debate on individualism: Indigenous psychologies of the individual and their role in personal and societal functioning. *American Psychologist, 45,* 15–22.

Schieffelin, E. L. (1985). The cultural analysis of depressive affect: An example from New Guinea. In A. Kleinman & B. Good (Eds.), *Culture and depression: Studies in the anthropology and cross-cultural psychiatry of affect and disorder* (pp. 101–133). Berkeley: University of California Press.

Schwartz, S. H., & Bilsky, W. (1990). Toward a theory of the universal content and structure of values: Extensions between cross-cultural replications. *Journal of Personality and Social Psychology, 58,* 878–891.

Schwartz, J. M., & Smith, W. P. (1976). Social comparison and the inference of ability difference. *Journal of Personality and Social Psychology, 34,* 1268–1275.

Shweder, R. A. (1991). *Thinking through cultures: Expeditions in cultural psychology.* Cambridge, MA: Harvard University Press.

Shweder, R. A. (1993). The cultural psychology of the emotions. In M. Lewis & J. M. Haviland (Eds.), *Handbook of emotions* (pp. 417–431). New York: Guilford Press.

Shweder, R. A., & LeVine, R. A. (Eds.). (1984). *Cultural theory: Essays on mind, self, and emotion.* Cambridge, England: Cambridge University Press.

Sinha, J., & Verma, J. (1987). Structure of collectivism. In C. Kagitcibasi (Ed.), *Growth and progress in cross-cultural psychology* (pp. 201–203). New York: Swets North American.

Smith, P., & Bond, M. B. (1993). *Social psychology across cultures*. New York: Harvester Wheatsheaf.

Spiro, M. (1961). Social systems, personality, and functional analysis. In B. Kaplan (Ed.), *Studying personality cross-culturally* (pp. 93–127). New York: Harper & How.

Stigler, J. W., Shweder, H. A., & Herdt, G. (Eds.). (1990). *Cultural psychology: Essays on comparative human development.* Cambridge, England: Cambridge University Press.

Stigler, J., W., Smith, S., & Mao, L. (1985). The self-perception of competence by Chinese children. *Child Development, 56,* 1259–1270.

Stroebe, M., Gergen, M. M., Gergen, K. J., & Stroebe, W. (1992). Broken hearts or broken bonds: Love and death in historical perspective. *American Psychologist, 47,* 1205–1212.

Takata, T. (1987). Self-deprecative tendencies in self-evaluation through social comparison. *Japanese Journal of Experimental Social Psychology, 27,* 27–36.

Taylor, C. (1989). *Sources of the self: The making of modern identities.* Cambridge, MA: Harvard University Press.

Triandis, H. C. (1990). Cross-cultural studies of individualism and collectivism. In J. Berman (Ed.), *Nebraska Symposium on Motivation, 1989* (pp. 41–133). Lincoln: University of Nebraska Press.

Triandis, H. C. (1994). Major cultural syndromes and emotion. In S. Kitayama & H. R. Markus (Eds.), *Emotion and culture: Empirical studies of mutual influence* (pp. 285–306). Washington, DC: American Psychological Association.

White, G. M. (1994). Affecting culture: Emotion and morality in everyday life. In S. Kitayama & H. R. Markus (Eds.), *Emotion and culture: Empirical studies of mutual influence* (pp. 219–239). Washington, DC: American Psychological Association.

Whiting, R. (1989). *You gotta have wa.* New York: Macmillan.

Wierzbicka, A. (1994). Emotion, language, and cultural scripts. In S. Kitayama & H. R. Markus (Eds.), *Emotion and culture: Empirical studies of mutual influence* (pp. 133–196). Washington, DC: American Psychological Association.

Williams, T. P., & Sogon, S. (1984). Group composition and conforming behavior in Japanese students. *Japanese Psychological Research, 26,* 231–234.

Zajonc, R. B. (1980). Feeling and thinking: Preferences need no inferences. *American Psychologist, 35,* 151–175.

Gender Differences: Evolution, Socialization, and Stereotyping

This section of the book addresses a variety of topics that are grouped together because they are all associated with a common theme: the differences between men's and women's emotions. The first two articles debate the usefulness of evolutionary psychology in explaining sex differences in sexual jealousy. These articles introduce evolutionary psychology, an important approach in the social psychology of emotion, and they also introduce an important and very social emotion, jealousy. The third article addresses the conditions under which gender stereotypes are used to make judgments about people's emotions.

Evolutionary theory has been applied to a variety of topics in social psychology, including aggression, helping behavior, and mate selection, as well as emotion. These topics have a number of interesting common aspects. All of them are connected in some way to adaptive functioning, survival, or the procreation and rearing of offspring, and all of them have analogues in the social behavior of nonhuman species. One would expect emotions to be shaped by evolutionary forces not only because of their physiological underpinnings but because they motivate behavior that has implications for evolutionary fitness.

The two articles that debate the application of the evolutionary approach concern one particular emotion: sexual jealousy in heterosexual relationships. The first article advocates for the applicability of evolutionary psychology. Buss, Larsen, Westen, and Semmelroth (1992) present the evolutionary approach and demonstrate that it predicts a difference between males and females in many species. The difference is a subtle one in that it does not simply predict that one sex will experience more or less jealousy than the other. Rather, it predicts that the two sexes will tend to experience sexual jealousy for different reasons: males because of sexual infidelity per se, females because of a threat to their relationship with the male. Buss and colleagues report data from three studies that obtain the predicted sex differences. They conclude that their findings support the approach of evolutionary psychology, and outline ideas for future research, including the thesis that sex differences in jealousy are a human universal, applying across cultures.

This conclusion is challenged by DeSteno and Salovey (1996) in the following selection. These authors propose that these results are caused not by innate sex differences in the eliciting conditions of jealousy, but rather by learned gender differences in beliefs about whether one sort of infidelity implies that another sort of infidelity will occur. They report data supportive of this conclusion, and the first of their two studies is reprinted in this volume.

At the heart of this debate is an issue that neither team of researchers can directly assess, namely, whether an observed emotional phenomenon is best thought of as being the result of genetic causes or of socialization. Both articles discuss the conceptual and methodological issues that arise in trying to resolve this issue. The debate continues. Both teams have issued rebuttals, and other researchers have weighed in as well ("Sex differences in Jealousy," 1996). These skirmishes go on in the context of a more general debate about how to understand the role of genes and culture in explaining human social phenomena (e.g., Barkow, Cosmides, & Tooby, 1992).

As a final note, it is worth pointing out that not all jealousy is sexual jealousy. Jealousy exists not only with heterosexual couples, but also with homosexual couples, siblings, friends, teachers and students—virtually any human relationship. Evolutionary accounts of sex differences in sexual relationships are poorly suited to explain these other forms of jealousy. Furthermore, research on evolutionary predictions has not been particularly informative about the nature of jealous emotion itself—most of this research simply asks participants about "distress" or "upset." For more information about the nature of jealousy, the reader is referred to Reading 19 in this volume.

The final reading in this section addresses the common stereotype in Western cultures that "women are more emotional than men." The stereotype is actually more subtle: women are supposed to be more emotional when it comes to sadness, guilt, shame, empathy, and love, but men the more emotional when it comes to pride and anger. These differences stereotypically hold both for the intensity of subjective experience and for the display of public expressions—or so it is commonly believed. The question is whether the stereotype is accurate, and on that score the evidence is mixed. There is a pattern to the inconsistencies, however: when people report past emotions, or general tendencies toward emotions, then the data suggest the stereotype is accurate; however, when people report specific emotions that are ongoing or very recent, then stereotypic gender differences disappear (Fischer, 1993; LaFrance & Banaji, 1992; Shields, 1991). This pattern raises the possibility that the stereotype is false but that people use the stereotype when making estimates about emotions that are not vividly in mind. It is this possibility that the final paper in this section seeks to explore.

Robinson, Johnson, and Shields (1998) reported two particularly thorough experimental tests of this hypothesis, the first of which is reprinted in this volume. The results were entirely supportive of the hypothesis. No gender differences were found in participants who rated their emotions immediately after playing a game, but stereotypical gender differences appeared in ratings collected after a one-week delay. People who observed games likewise showed no gender differences in their ratings, either immediately or after a one-day delay, but people who were asked to imagine a game played against an average man or woman provided ratings that matched the gender stereotypes. These findings do not imply that there are no gender differences in emotion, of course, but only that, in one fairly normal setting, gender differences were not perceived unless the setting was imagined or recalled at a later time.

REFERENCES

Barkow, J. H., Cosmides, L., & Tooby, J. (Eds.). (1992). *The adapted mind: Evolutionary psychology and the generation of culture*. New York: Oxford University Press.

Buss, D. M., Larsen, R. J., Westen, D., & Semmelroth, J. (1992). Sex differences in jealousy: Evolution, physiology, and psychology. *Psychological Science, 3,* 251–255.

DeSteno, D. A., & Salovey, P. (1996). Evolutionary origins of sex differences in jealousy: Questioning the "fitness" of the model. *Psychological Science, 7,* 367–372.

Fischer, A. (1993). Sex differences in emotionality: Fact or stereotype? *Feminism and Psychology, 3,* 303–318.

LaFrance, M., & Banaji, M. (1992). Toward a reconsideration of the gender-emotion relationship. In M. S. Clark (Ed.), *Review of personality and social psychology: Vol.*

14. Emotion and social behavior (pp. 178–201). Newbury Park, CA: Sage.

Robinson, M. D., Johnson, J. T., & Shields, S. A. (1998). The gender heuristic and the database: Factors affecting the perception of gender-related differences in the experience and display of emotions. *Basic and Applied Social Psychology, 20,* 206–219.

Sex Differences in Jealousy [Special section]. (1996). *Psychological Science, 7*(6), 359–379.

Shields, S. A. (1991). Gender in the psychology of emotion: A selective research review. In K. T. Strongman (Ed.), *International review of studies on emotion* (Vol. 1, pp. 227–245). New York: Wiley.

Discussion Questions

1. The articles on sex differences in jealousy tend to focus on whether statistical tests reached significance, but it is also informative to consider the actual data. What percentage of men and women reported being more distressed by each type of infidelity? What do these numbers suggest about the predictions of evolutionary psychology?
2. Cultures differ with respect to many variables that may be relevant to sex differences in jealousy: rules for men and women about having multiple sexual partners, opportunities for men and women to obtain economic resources on their own, expectations about how much men and women will contribute to child rearing. How might such variables influence sex differences in jealousy?
3. What is the "double-shot hypothesis" of sex differences in sexual jealousy? If this hypothesis is correct, does it suggest that these sex differences are based on socialization, or could there be an evolutionary interpretation?
4. What gender stereotypes of emotion exist in your culture? Do you think these stereotypes are without basis, or that they are generally true under most circumstances, or only evident under certain circumstances?

Suggested Readings

Hinton, A. L. (Ed.). (1999). *Biocultural approaches to the emotions*. Cambridge, England: Cambridge University Press. The articles in this volume attempt to bridge the gap between evolutionary and cultural accounts of emotion. The authors are biological or cultural anthropologists, and for this volume the two camps tried to overcome their traditional divisions.

Sex Differences in Jealousy [Special section]. (1996). *Psychological Science, 7*(6), 359–379. The article by DeSteno and Salovey reprinted in this volume first appeared in an issue of the journal *Psychological Science* that contained five other articles on the same topic. These articles make interesting reading for those wishing to pursue this topic in greater depth. Two of these articles, like DeSteno and Salovey, reported research following up on the article by Buss and colleagues that is reprinted in this volume. The remaining three articles were commentaries on the three empirical reports. One of them, by Buss, Larsen, and Westen, defends the conclusions of the original article.

Buss, D. M. (2000). *The dangerous passion: Why jealousy is as necessary as love and sex.* New York: Free Press. This book presents a fuller account of the evolutionary approach to sexual jealousy. It is intended for the general reader and is written in an accessible style.

Fischer, A. H. (Ed.) (2000). *Gender and emotion: Social psychological perspectives*. Cambridge, England: Cambridge University Press. The 14 chapters in this volume represent the state of the art of research on emotion and gender. The literature on gender differences that is reviewed briefly in the article by Robinson, Johnson, and Shields can be explored in much more depth in several of these chapters. Other chapters address a variety of issues having to do with the general topic of the relation between gender and emotion.

Lutz, C. A. (1990). Engendered emotion: Gender, power, and the rhetoric of emotional control in American discourse. In C. A. Lutz & L. Abu-Lughod (Eds.), *Language and the politics of emotion* (pp. 69–91). Cambridge, England: Cambridge University Press. The author argues that gender differences in emotion stereotypes and emotion regulation relegate women to inferior status and thus have implications for social and political power.

Sex Differences in Jealousy: Evolution, Physiology, and Psychology

David M. Buss, Randy J. Larsen, Drew Westen and Jennifer Semmelroth
• University of Michigan

In species with internal female fertilization, males risk both lowered paternity probability and investment in rival gametes if their mates have sexual contact with other males. Females of such species do not risk lowered maternity probability through partner infidelity, but they do risk the diversion of their mates' commitment and resources to rival females. Three studies tested the hypothesis that sex differences in jealousy emerged in humans as solutions to the respective adaptive problems faced by each sex. In Study 1, men and women selected which event would upset them more—a partner's sexual infidelity or emotional infidelity. Study 2 recorded physiological responses (heart rate, electrodermal response, corrugator supercilii contraction) while subjects imagined separately the two types of partner infidelity. Study 3 tested the effect of being in a committed sexual relationship on the activation of jealousy. All studies showed large sex differences, confirming hypothesized sex linkages in jealousy activation.

In species with internal female fertilization and gestation, features of reproductive biology characteristic of all 4,000 species of mammals, including humans, males face an adaptive problem not confronted by females—uncertainty in their paternity of offspring. Maternity probability in mammals rarely or never deviates from 100%. Compromises in paternity probability come at substantial reproductive cost to the male—the loss of mating effort expended, including time, energy, risk, nuptial gifts, and mating opportunity costs. A cuckolded male also loses the female's parental effort, which becomes channeled to a competitor's gametes. The adaptive problem of paternity uncertainty is exacerbated in species in which males engage in some postzygotic parental investment (Trivers, 1972). Males risk investing resources in putative offspring that are genetically unrelated.

These multiple and severe reproductive costs should have imposed strong selection pressure on males to defend against cuckoldry. Indeed, the literature is replete with examples of evolved anticuckoldry mechanisms in lions (Bertram, 1975), bluebirds (Power, 1975), doves (Erickson & Zenone, 1976), numerous insect species (Thornhill & Alcock, 1983), and nonhuman primates (Hrdy, 1979). Since humans arguably show more paternal investment than any other of the 200 species of primates (Alexander & Noonan, 1979), this selection pressure should have operated especially intensely on human males. Symons (1979); Daly, Wilson, and Weghorst (1982); and Wilson and Daly (1992) have hypothesized that male sexual jealousy evolved as a solution to this adaptive problem (but see Hupka, 1991, for an alternative view). Men who were indifferent to sexual contact between their mates and other men presumably experienced lower paternity certainty, greater investment in competitors' gametes, and lower reproductive success than did men who were motivated to attend to cues of infidelity and to act on those cues to increase paternity probability.

Although females do not risk maternity uncertainty, in species with biparental care they do risk the potential loss of time, resources, and commitment from a male if he deserts or channels investment to alternative mates (Buss, 1988; Thornhill & Alcock, 1983; Trivers, 1972). The redirection of a mate's investment to another female and her offspring is reproductively costly for a female, especially in environments where offspring suffer in survival and reproductive currencies without investment from both parents.

In human evolutionary history, there were likely to have been at least two situations in which a woman risked losing a man's investment. First, in a monogamous marriage, a woman risked having her mate invest in an alternative woman with whom he was having an affair (partial loss of investment) or risked his departure for an alternative woman large or total loss of investment). Second, in polygynous marriages, a woman was at risk of having her mate invest to a larger degree in other wives and their offspring at the expense of his investment in her and her offspring. Following Buss (1988) and Mellon (1981), we hypothesize that cues to the development of a deep emotional attachment have been reliable leading indicators to women of potential reduction or loss of their mate's investment.

Jealousy is defined as an emotional "state that is aroused by a perceived threat to a valued relationship or position and motivates behavior aimed at countering the threat. Jealousy is 'sexual' if the valued relationship is sexual" (Daly et al., 1982, p. 11; see also Salovey, 1991; White & Mullen, 1989). It is reasonable to hypothesize that jealousy involves physiological reactions (autonomic arousal) to perceived threat and motivated action to reduce the threat, although this hypothesis has not been examined. Following Symons (1979) and Daly et al. (1982), our central hypothesis is that the events that activate jealousy physiologically and psychologically differ for men and women because of the different adaptive problems they have faced over human evolutionary history in mating contexts. Both sexes are hypothesized to be distressed over both sexual and emotional infidelity, and previous findings bear this out (Buss, 1989). However, these two kinds of infidelity

should be weighted differently by men and women. Despite the importance of these hypothesized sex differences, no systematic scientific work has been directed toward verifying or falsifying their existence (but for suggestive data, see Francis, 1977; Teismann & Mosher, 1978; White & Mullen, 1989).

Study 1: Subjective Distress Over Partner's External Involvement

This study was designed to test the hypothesis that men and women differ in which form of infidelity—sexual versus emotional—triggers more upset and subjective distress, following the adaptive logic just described.

Method

After reporting age and sex, subjects ($N = 202$ undergraduate students) were presented with the following dilemma:

> Please think of a serious committed romantic relationship that you have had in the past, that you currently have, or that you would like to have. Imagine that you discover that the person with whom you've been seriously involved became interested in someone else. What would distress or upset you more (*please circle only one*):
> (A) Imagining your partner forming a deep emotional attachment to that person.
> (B) Imagining your partner enjoying passionate sexual intercourse with that other person.

Subjects completed additional questions, and then encountered the next dilemma, with the same instructional set, but followed by a different, but parallel, choice:

> (A) Imagining your partner trying different sexual positions with that other person.
> (B) Imagining your partner falling in love with that other person.

Results

Shown in Figure 6.1 (upper panel) are the percentages of men and women reporting more distress in response to sexual infidelity than emotional infidelity. The first empirical probe, contrasting distress over a partner's sexual involvement with distress over a partner's deep emotional attachment, yielded a large and highly significant sex differ-

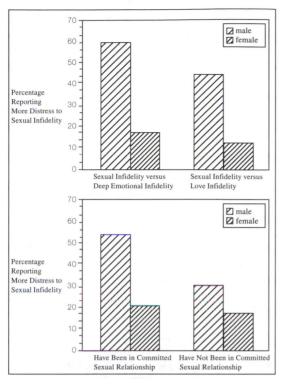

FIGURE 6.1 ■ Reported comparisons of distress in response to imagining a partner's sexual or emotional infidelity. The upper panel shows results of Study 1—the percentage of subjects reporting more distress to the sexual infidelity scenario than to the emotional infidelity (left) and the love infidelity (right) scenarios. The lower panel shows the results of Study 3—the percentage of subjects reporting more distress to the sexual infidelity scenario than to the emotional infidelity scenario, presented separately for those who have experienced a committed sexual relationship (left) and those who have not experienced a committed sexual realtionship (right).

ence ($\chi^2 = 47.56$, $df = 3$, $p < .001$). Fully 60% of the male sample reported greater distress over their partner's potential sexual infidelity; in contrast, only 17% of the female sample chose that option, with 83% reporting that they would experience greater distress over a partner's emotional attachment to a rival.

This pattern was replicated with the contrast between sex and love. The magnitude if the sex difference was large, with 32% more men than women reporting greater distress over a partner's sexual involvement with someone else, and the majority of women reporting greater distress over a partner's falling in love with a rival ($\chi2 = 59.20$, $df = 3$, $p < .001$).

Study 2: Physiological Responses to a Partner's External Involvement

Given the strong confirmation of jealousy sex linkage from Study 1, we sought next to test the hypotheses using physiological measures. Our central measures of autonomic arousal were electrodermal activity (EDA), assessed via skin conductance, and pulse rate (PR). Electrodermal activity and pulse rate are indicators of autonomic nervous system activation (Levenson, 1988). Because distress is an unpleasant subjective state, we also included a measure of muscle activity in the brow region of the face-electromyographic (EMG) activity of the *corrugator supercilii* muscle. This muscle is responsible for the furrowing of the brow often seen in facial displays of unpleasant emotion or affect (Fridlund, Ekman, & Oster, 1987). Subjects were asked to image two scenarios in which a partner became involved with someone else—one sexual intercourse scenario and one emotional attachment scenario. Physiological responses were recorded during the imagery trials.

Subjects

Subjects were 55 undergraduate students, 32 males and 23 females, each completing a 2-hr laboratory session.

Physiological Measures

Physiological activity was monitored on the running strip chart of a Grass Model 7D polygraph and digitized on a laboratory computer at a 10-Hz rate, following principles recommended in Cacioppo and Tassinary (1990).

ELECTRODERMAL ACTIVITY

Standard Beckman Ag/AgC1 surface electrodes, filled with a .05 molar NaCl solution in a Unibase paste, were placed over the middle segments of the first and third fingers of the right hand. A Wheatstone bridge applied a 0.5-V voltage to one electrode.

PULSE RATE

A photoplethysmograph was attached to the subject's right thumb to monitor the pulse wave. The signal from this pulse transducer was fed into a Grass Model 7P4 cardiotachometer to detect the rising slope of each pulse wave, with the internal circuitry of the Schmitt trigger individually adjusted for each subject to output PR in beats per minute.

ELECTROMYOGRAPHIC ACTIVITY

Bipolar EMG recordings were obtained over the *corrugator supercilii* muscle. The EMG signal was relayed to a wide-band AC-preamplifier (Grass Model 7P3), where it was band-pass filtered, full-wave rectified, and integrated with a time constant of 0.2 s.

Procedure

After electrode attachment, the subject was made comfortable in a reclining chair and asked to relax. After a 5-min waiting period, the experiment began. The subject was alone in the room during the imagery session, with an intercom on for verbal communication. The instructions for the imagery task were written on a form which the subject was requested to read and follow.

Each subject was instructed to engage in three separate images. The first image was designed to be emotionally neutral: "Imagine a time when you were walking to class, feeling neither good nor bad, just neutral." The subject was instructed to press a button when he or she had the image clearly in mind, and to sustain the image until the experimenter said to stop. The button triggered the computer to begin collecting physiological data for 20 s, after which the experimenter instructed the subject to "stop and relax." The next two images were infidelity images, one sexual and one emotional. The order of presentation of these two images was counterbalanced. The instructions for sexual jealousy imagery were as follows: "Please think of a serious romantic relationship that you have had in the past, that you currently have, or that you would like to have. Now imagine that the person with whom you're seriously involved becomes interested in someone else. *Imagine you find out that your partner is having sexual intercourse with this other person.* Try to feel the feelings you would have if this happened to you."

The instructions for emotional infidelity imagery were identical to the above, except the italicized sentence was replaced with "*Imagine that your partner is failing in love and forming an emotional attachment to that person.*" Physiological data were collected for 20 s following the subject's button press indicating that he or she had achieved the image. Subjects were told to "stop and relax" for 30 s between imagery trials.

Results

PHYSIOLOGICAL SCORES

The following scores were obtained: (a) the amplitude of the largest EDA response occurring during each 20-s trial; (b) PR in beats per minute averaged over each 20-s trial; and (c) amplitude of EMG activity over the corrugator supercilii averaged over each 20-s trial. Difference scores were computed between the neutral imagery trial and the jealousy induction trials. Within-sex t tests revealed no effects for order of presentation of the sexual jealousy image, so data were collapsed over this factor.

JEALOUSY INDUCTION EFFECTS

Table 6.1 shows the mean scores for the physiological measures for men and women in each of the two imagery conditions. Differences in physiological responses to the two jealousy images were examined using paired-comparison t tests for each sex separately for EDA, PR, and EMG. The men showed significant increases in EDA during the sexual imagery compared with the emotional imagery ($t = 2.00$, $df = 29$, $p < .05$). Women showed significantly greater EDA to the emotional infidelity image than to the sexual infidelity image ($t = 2.42$, $df = 19$, $p < .05$). A similar pattern was observed with PR. Men showed a substantial increase in PR to both images, but significantly more so in response to the sexual infidelity image ($t = 2.29$, $df = 31$, $p < .05$). Women showed elevated PR to both images, but not differentially so. The results of the *corrugator* EMG were similar, although less strong. Men showed greater brow contraction to the sexual infidelity image, and women showed the opposite pattern, although results with this nonautonomic measure did not reach significance ($t = 1.12$, $df = 30$, $p < .14$, for males; $t = -1.24$, $df = 22$, $p < .12$, for females). The elevated EMG contractions for both jealousy induction trials in both sexes support the hypothesis that the affect experienced is negative.

TABLE 6.1. Means and Standard Deviations on Physiological Measures During Two Imagery Conditions

Measure	Imagery type	Mean	SD
	Males		
EDA	Sexual	1.30	3.64
	Emotional	−0.11	0.76
Pulse rate	Sexual	4.76	7.80
	Emotional	3.00	5.24
Brow EMG	Sexual	6.75	32.96
	Emotional	1.16	6.60
	Females		
EDA	Sexual	−0.07	0.49
	Emotional	0.21	0.78
Pulse rate	Sexual	2.25	4.68
	Emotional	2.57	4.37
Brow EMG	Sexual	3.03	8.38
	Emotional	8.12	25.60

Note. Measures are expressed as changes from the neutral image condition. EDA is in microsiemen units, pulse rate is in beats per minute, and EMG is in microvolt units.

Study 3: Contexts that Activate the Jealousy Mechanism

The goal of Study 3 was to replicate and extend the results of Studies 1 and 2 using a larger sample. Specifically, we sought to examine the effects of having been in a committed sexual relationship versus not having been in such a relationship on the activation of jealousy. We hypothesized that men who had actually experienced a committed sexual relationship would report greater subjective distress in response to the sexual infidelity imagery than would men who had not experienced a high-investing sexual relationship, and that women who had experienced a committed sexual relationship would report greater distress to the emotional infidelity image than women who had not been in a committed sexual relationship. The rationale was that direct experience of the relevant context during development may be necessary for the activation of the sex-linked weighting of jealousy activation.

Subjects

Subjects for Study 3 were 309 undergraduate students, 133 men and 176 women.

Procedure

Subjects read the following instructions:

> Please think of a serious or committed romantic relationship that you have had in the past, that you currently have, or that you would like to have. Imagine that you discover that the person with whom you've been seriously involved became interested in someone else. What would distress or upset you more (*please circle only one*):
>
> (A) Imagining your partner falling in love and forming a deep emotional attachment to that person.
>
> (B) Imagining your partner having sexual intercourse with that other person.

Alternatives were presented in standard forced-choice format, with the order counterbalanced across subjects. Following their responses, subjects were asked: "Have you ever been in a serious or committed romantic relationship? (yes or no)" and "If yes, was this a sexual relationship? (yes or no)."

Results

The results for the total sample replicate closely the results of Study 1. A much larger proportion of men (49%) than women (19%) reported that they would be more distressed by their partner's sexual involvement with someone else than by their partner's emotional attachment to, or love for, someone else ($\chi^2 = 38.48$, $df = 3$, $p < .001$).

The two pairs of columns in the bottom panel of Figure 6.1 show the results separately for those subjects who had experienced a committed sexual relationship in the past and those who had not. For women, the difference is small and not significant: Women reported that they would experience more distress about a partner's emotional infidelity than a partner's sexual infidelity, regardless of whether or not they had experienced a committed sexual relationship ($\chi^2 = 0.80$, $df = 1$, ns).

For men, the difference between those who had been in a sexual relationship and those who had not is large and highly significant. Whereas 55% of the men who had experienced committed sexual relationships reported that they would be more distressed by a partner's sexual than emotional infidelity, this figure drops to 29% for men who had never experienced a committed sexual relationship ($\chi^2 = 12.29$, $df = 1$, $p < .001$). Sexual jealousy in men apparently becomes increasingly activated upon experience of the relevant relationship.

Discussion

The results of the three empirical studies support the hypothesized sex linkages in the activators of jealousy. Study 1 found large sex differences in reports of the subjective distress individuals would experience upon exposure to a partner's sexual infidelity versus emotional infidelity. Study 2 found a sex linkage in autonomic arousal to imagined sexual infidelity versus emotional infidelity; the results were particularly strong for the EDA and PR. Study 3 replicated the large sex differences in reported distress to sexual versus emotional infidelity, and found a strong effect for men of actually having experienced a committed sexual relationship.

These studies are limited in ways that call for additional research. First, they pertain to a single age group and culture. Future studies could explore the degree to which these sex differences transcend different cultures and age groups. Two clear evolutionary psychological predictions are (a) that male sexual jealousy and female commitment jealousy will be greater in cultures where males invest heavily in children, and (b) that male sexual jealousy will diminish as the age of the male's mate increases because her reproductive value decreases. Second, future studies could test the alternative hypotheses that the current findings reflect (a) domain-specific psychological adaptations to cuckoldry versus potential investment loss or (b) a more domain-general mechanism such that any thoughts of sex are more interesting, arousing, and perhaps disturbing to men whereas any thoughts of love are more interesting, arousing, and perhaps disturbing to women, and hence that such responses are not specific to jealousy or infidelity. Third, emotional and sexual infidelity are clearly correlated, albeit imperfectly, and a sizable percentage of men in Studies 1 and 3 reported greater distress to a partner's emotional infidelity. Emotional infidelity may signal sexual infidelity and vice versa, and hence both sexes should become distressed at both forms (see Buss, 1989). Future research could profitably explore in greater detail the correlation of these forms of infidelity as well as the sources of within-sex variation. Fi-

nally, the intriguing finding that men who have experienced a committed sexual relationship differ dramatically from those who have not, whereas for women such experiences appear to be irrelevant to their selection of emotional infidelity as the more distressing event, should be examined. Why do such ontogenetic experiences matter for men, and why do they appear to be irrelevant for women?

Within the constraints of the current studies, we can conclude that the sex differences found here generalize across both psychological and physiological methods-demonstrating an empirical robustness in the observed effect. The degree to which these sex-linked elicitors correspond to the hypothesized sex-linked adaptive problems lends support to the evolutionary psychological framework from which they were derived. Alternative theoretical frameworks, including those that invoke culture, social construction, deconstruction, arbitrary parental socialization, and structural powerlessness, undoubtedly could be molded post hoc to fit the findings—something perhaps true of any set of findings. None but the Symons (1979) and Daly et al. (1982) evolutionary psychological frameworks, however, generated the sex-differentiated predictions in advance and on the basis of sound evolutionary reasoning. The recent finding that male sexual jealousy is the leading cause of spouse battering and homicide across cultures worldwide (Daly & Wilson, 1988a, 1988b) offers suggestive evidence that these sex differences have large social import and may be species-wide.

REFERENCES

Alexander, R. D., & Noonan, K. M. (1979). Concealment of ovulation, parental care, and human social evolution. In N. Chagnon & W. Irons (Eds.), *Evolutionary biology and human social behavior* (pp. 436–453). North Scituate, MA: Duxbury.

Bertram, B. C. R. (1975). Social factors influencing reproduction in wild lions. *Journal of Zoology, 177,* 463–482.

Buss, D. M. (1988). From vigilance to violence: Tactics of mate retention. *Ethology and Sociobiology, 9,* 291–317.

Buss, D .M. (1989). Conflict between the sexes: Strategic interference and the evocation of anger and upset. *Journal of Personality and Social Psychology, 56,* 735–747.

Cacioppo, J. T., & Tassinary, L. G. (Eds.). (1990). *Principles of psychophysiology: Physical, social, and inferential elements.* Cambridge, England: Cambridge University Press.

Daly, M., & Wilson, M. (1988a). Evolutionary social psychology and family violence. *Science, 242,* 519–524.

Daly, M.. & Wilson, M. (1988b). *Homicide.* Hawthorne, NY: Aldine.

Daly, M., Wilson, M., & Weghorst, S. J. (1982). Male sexual jealousy. *Ethology and Sociobiology, 3,* 11–27.

Erickson, C. J., & Zenone, P. G. (1976). Courtship differences in male ring doves: Avoidance of cuckoldry? *Science, 192,* 1353–1354.

Francis, J. L. (1977). Toward the management of heterosexual jealousy. *Journal of Marriage and Family Counseling, 10,* 61–69.

Fridlund, A., Ekman, P., & Oster, J. (1987). Facial expressions of emotion. In A. Siegman & S. Feldstein (Eds.), *Nonverbal behavior and communication* (pp. 141–224). Hillsdale, NJ: Erlbaum.

Hrdy, S. B. G. (1979). Infanticide among animals: A review, classification, and examination of the implications for the reproductive strategies of females. *Ethology and Sociobiology, 1,* 14–40.

Hupka, R. B. (1991). The motive for the arousal of romantic jealousy: Its cultural origin. In P. Salovey (Ed.), *The psychology of jealousy and envy* (pp. 252–270). New York: Guilford Press.

Levenson, R. W. (1988). Emotion and the autonomic nervous system: A prospectus for research on autonomic specificity. In H. Wagner (Ed.), *Social psychophysiology: Theory and clinical applications* (pp. 17–42). London: Wiley.

Mellon, L. W. (1981). *The evolution of love.* San Francisco: W. H. Freeman.

Power, H. W. (1975). Mountain bluebirds: Experimental evidence against altruism. *Science, 189,* 142–143.

Salovey, P. (Ed.). (1991). *The psychology of jealousy and envy.* New York: Guilford Press.

Symons, D. (1979). *The evolution of human sexuality.* New York: Oxford University Press.

Teismann, M. W., & Mosher, D. L. (1978). Jealous conflict in dating couples. *Psychological Reports, 42,* 1211–1216.

Thornhill, R., & Alcock, J. (1983). *The evolution of insect mating systems.* Cambridge, MA: Harvard University Press.

Trivers, R. (1972). Parental investment and sexual selection. In B. Campbell (Ed.), *Sexual selection and the descent of man, 1871–1971* (pp. 136–179). Chicago: Aldine.

White, G. L., & Mullen, P. E. (1989). *Jealousy: Theory, research, and clinical strategies.* New York: Guilford Press.

Wilson, M., & Daly, M. (1992). The man who mistook his wife for a chattel. In J. Barkow, L. Cosmides, & J. Tooby (Eds.), *The adapted mind: Evolutionary psychology and the generation of culture.* New York: Oxford University Press.

Evolutionary Origins of Sex Differences in Jealousy?: Questioning the "Fitness" of the Model

David A. DeSteno and Peter Salovey • Yale University

Evolutionary psychology has become a popular framework for studying jealousy. Much of this popularity can be attributed to work by Buss and his colleagues showing an apparent relation between an individual's sex and jealousy for certain types of infidelity (i.e., sexual vs. emotional) that is consistent with evolutionary theory (Buss, Larsen, Westen, & Semmelroth, 1992). In two studies, we take issue with these findings and argue that the relation between sex and jealousy reported by Buss and his colleagues is more properly explained by considering individuals' beliefs concerning the covariation between sexual and emotional infidelity.

Evolutionary psychology has become a popular perspective from which to study jealousy. In accord with this perspective, the origins of jealousy are ascribed to the evolutionary history of humans (Buss, 1991, 1995), and the psychological mechanisms thought to be responsible for the evocation of jealousy are evaluated with respect to their present or past adaptive benefits (e.g., Wiederman & Allgeier, 1993). The popularity of the evolutionary perspective among investigators studying jealousy can be attributed in part to an influential article by Buss and his colleagues showing a sex difference in the intensity of jealousy in response to different types of infidelity (Buss, Larsen, Westen, & Semmelroth, 1992). Men reported more jealousy in situations involving sexual rather than emotional infidelity, but women reported more jealousy in situations involving emotional, as opposed to sexual, infidelity.

These sex differences in the elicitors of jealousy arise, according to the evolutionary model, as a consequence of their fitness-enhancing capabilities (Buss et al., 1992). Fitness refers to the ability to pass on genetic material by raising offspring to the age of sexual maturity (Daly & Wilson, 1983). Briefly stated, evolutionary theory predicts that males in species employing internal fertilization are vigilant of possible sexual contact by their mates with other males; this behavior is designed to prevent cuckoldry. Females of biparental species with internal fertilization have no doubt concerning their genetic link to offspring and are therefore predicted to be vigilant of threats concerning the absconding of the male, not of the sexual act itself; the male's continued presence aids in the successful rearing of the offspring (Buss et al., 1992; Daly & Wilson, 1983).

In order to evaluate these predictions for human jealousy, Buss et al. (1992) conducted three studies. In all the studies, the dependent variable of interest was which of two types of infidelity (sexual or emotional) would evoke more intense jealousy. As defined by Buss et al. (1992), sexual infidelity involves actual sexual contact between individuals; emotional infidelity involves the expression of a deep affection for and attachment to another individual. Participants in these studies were asked to imagine situations representing each type of infidelity. It was expected that men would be more distressed by sexual than by emotional infidelity and women would be more distressed by emotional than by sexual infidelity.

Two of the three studies presented subjects with a forced-choice question asking them simply to indicate which of the two types of infidelity would cause them more distress. In accordance with the evolutionary perspective, Buss and his colleagues found a significant sex difference in the choice of infidelity type; women were much more likely than men to indicate that the emotional infidelity event resulted in more distress. Also, physiological data were collected as a measure of emotional arousal in response to imagining each type of infidelity. Men showed significant elevations in electrodermal activity in response to imagining the sexual as compared with the emotional infidelity situation; the reverse pattern was found in women. Data from other physiological indices (pulse rate and electromyographic activity of the *corrugator supercilii*) were not as clear (Buss et al., 1992).

Based on these findings, Buss et al. (1992) concluded that their predictions were supported, and that only the "evolutionary psychological frameworks . . . generated the sex-differentiated predictions in advance and on the basis of sound evolutionary reasoning" (p. 255). We challenge this interpretation of these findings.

A major threat to the credibility of results based on a paradigm that does not use random assignment of participants to conditions is the influence of unmeasured variables (Abelson, 1995; Bollen, 1989). Such misspecification can lead to the acceptance of spurious results. When individuals are not assigned randomly to conditions, there is less assurance that the other dimensions upon which the individuals vary are balanced within the ensuing analyses. Consequently, causal claims with reference to the measured independent variable (or variables) may be compromised.

In the case at hand, individuals, of course, entered the study as men or women; sex cannot be assigned randomly. Therefore, the specter that

variables correlated with sex were not balanced in subsequent analyses must be a concern. This situation is not usually problematic when examining sex differences in a descriptive manner; if men behave a certain way because of a third variable that is correlated with sex, it may still make sense to speak in terms of a sex difference. However, when claims are attributed to sex based solely on genetically influenced predispositions, as opposed to other socially derived influences, lack of random assignment signals possible problems; there can be little confidence that observed sex differences are not due to other nongenetic variables correlated with sex. Extra care must be taken in such situations to examine the influence of alternative explanatory variables.

We suspect that the findings presented by Buss et al. (1992) can be explained by what we term the *double-shot hypothesis*. Simply stated, some individuals believe that emotional and sexual infidelity are not independent events. Consequently, they will select the type of infidelity that more implies the occurrence of the other when asked to indicate which one would make them more jealous. For instance, emotional infidelity, for certain individuals, may imply that sexual infidelity has occurred or soon will occur. These perceptions of nonindependence, moreover, may be correlated with sex in some samples, with women more likely than men to expect that emotional infidelity by their partners implies associated sexual infidelity. If the double-shot hypothesis is correct, it might explain the results obtained in the forced-choice paradigm used by Buss et al. (1992). According to this hypothesis, women select emotional infidelity as more distressing in the forced-choice paradigm because emotional infidelity really represents two types of infidelity as opposed to one. Certain types of infidelity bother individuals more than others because they represent a double shot of infidelity; the occurrence of both these types of infidelity is no doubt more troubling than either individually and also signals a greater threat to the relationship.

Such beliefs concerning the nonindependence of these two types of infidelity cannot be traced to genetic causes according to the usual evolutionary arguments in this domain; females should always be concerned with loss of attention and resources, whether or not males engage in extradyadic sexual activity. Instead, it seems more likely that perceptions of the nonindependence of these types of infidelity are derived through socialization; men and women, because of past experience, may hold differing beliefs concerning the implications of the each of the two types of infidelity. Moreover, perceptions of the nonindependence of sexual and emotional infidelity seem likely to vary not only across, but also within, sex. To the extent that this is the case, and to the extent that these perceptions account for variance in jealousy reported by individuals, perceptions of nonindependence would seem to create a more powerful and parsimonious account of jealousy than would an account based on evolution.

The following two studies were designed to evaluate this alternative explanation for the findings reported by Buss et al. (1992). In each case, we expected to show that the reported relation between biological sex and jealousy for certain types of infidelity was due to the association of sex with differing perceptions of the nonindependence of the two types of infidelity. We predicted that sex would provide no unique explanatory ability beyond that associated with these perceptions of nonindependence, and because sex is not the causal agent of such perceptions, but may simply covary with them, confirmation of these predictions would identify the relation between sex and infidelity choice as misspecified.

Study 1

We collected two measures from participants: a forced-choice measure identical to the one used by Buss et al. (1992), asking which type of infidelity they would find more distressing, and a measure estimating participants' beliefs concerning the independence of the two types of infidelity. In accordance with the double-shot hypothesis, we predicted that any association between sex and selection of infidelity type would be accounted for by perceptions of the nonindependence of the types of infidelity.

Method

PARTICIPANTS

The participants in this study were 114 undergraduate students (53 male and 61 female; mean

age = 19.8, SD = 1.40). They took part in the study voluntarily.

MATERIALS

As in the study by Buss et al. (1992), participants were asked to reflect on a present or past romantic relationship and then to indicate which of the following two events would distress them more: (a) their partner having passionate sexual intercourse with another person or (b) their partner forming a deep emotional attachment to another person.

So that we could measure the perceived nonindependence of the two types of infidelity, participants were told that the following two questions would ask them how likely typical members of the opposite sex were to behave in certain ways as a result of specific situations. They were also told to assume that the initials B.F. referred to a typical member of the opposite sex. Question 1 asked, "If B.F. develops a deep emotional attachment to someone of your gender, how likely is it that B.F. and this other individual are now, or soon will be, sleeping together?" Question 2 asked, "If B.F. has slept with someone of your gender, how likely is it that B.F. is forming, or will form, a deep emotional attachment to this individual?" Responses were recorded on 9-point scales ranging from "unlikely" to "very likely."

PROCEDURE

Participants completed these materials in groups. They completed the forced-choice measure first, followed by the measure of infidelity nonindependence.

Results and Discussion

EVOLUTIONARY PREDICTION

As Buss et al. (1992) found, women were more likely than men to indicate that emotional infidelity produced greater distress than did sexual infidelity, $\chi^2(1, N = 114) = 8.46, p = .004$. It is important to note, however, that only women showed a sizable difference in choosing between the two types of infidelity (46 women selected emotional infidelity as more distressing, 15 women selected sexual infidelity); the men were nearly evenly split (27 men selected sexual infidelity as more distressing, 26 men selected emotional infidelity), a pattern similar to that reported in Buss et al. (1992, Study 1). This pattern indicates that the predicted effect was driven primarily by women. There is little reason, according to the evolutionary perspective to expect that men should not show a differential preference for the infidelity types as well.

ALTERNATIVE EXPLANATION

According to the double-shot hypothesis, to the extent that individuals believe that emotional infidelity implies the occurrence of sexual infidelity, but not vice versa, they will report that emotional infidelity is the more distressing of the two. Moreover, to the extent that individuals perceive the two types of infidelity as equally likely to imply the occurrence of one another, their probability of selecting either should hover near .50. To index the differential likelihood of one type of infidelity implying the other, we subtracted participants' likelihood judgments of sexual infidelity implying emotional infidelity from their judgments of emotional infidelity implying sexual infidelity. This composite variable, hereafter referred to as the *differential infidelity implication* (DII), was positive if participants believed that emotional infidelity implied sexual infidelity more than the converse. A value of zero indicated that each type was as likely to follow the other, and a negative value of DII indicated that sexual infidelity implied emotional infidelity more than the converse. Thus, the more an individual's value of DII diverged from

zero, the less that individual believed that the two types of infidelity imply one another equally.

If the double-shot hypothesis is true, then based on the reported relation between sex and infidelity choice, we would expect to find that women have a positive mean value of DII, but the value for men is approximately zero; women showed a preference for selecting emotional infidelity, and men showed no differential preference in the forced-choice data. Indeed, women reported a greater DII value ($M = 2.62$, $SD = 3.10$) than did men ($M = 0.25$, $SD = 3.55$), $t(112) = 3.82$, $p < .001$.

TEST OF MISSPECIFICATION

To demonstrate that the relation between sex and infidelity choice reported by Buss et al. (1992) is due to a specification error, we conducted the series of logistic regression analyses reported in Table 7.1. In all models, the logits refer to the probability of selecting emotional infidelity as the more distressing type of infidelity. The first model outlined in Table 7.1 depicts the reported relation between sex and infidelity choice. The second model shows a strong relation between participants' DII values and their choice of infidelity type. Consonant with the double-shot hypothesis, increasingly positive values of DII corresponded to greater probabilities of selecting emotional infidelity as more distressing; to the extent that individuals believed emotional infidelity was more likely to

TABLE 7.1. Summary of Hierarchical Logistic Regression Analysis for Variables Predicting Choice of Infidelity Type as More Distressing in Study 1.

Variable	Parameter estimate	Standard error	Standardized parameter estimate	χ^2	p
Model 1:					
Sex	1.158	0.405	.320	8.19	.0042
Model 2:					
DII	0.265	0.067	.512	15.82	.0001
Model 3:					
Sex	0.722	0.443	.199	2.65	.1037
DII	0.233	0.068	.450	11.61	.0007

Note: For all models, −2 log likelihood probabilities are less than .05. Constant parameters for the models were −1.20, 0.21, and −0.83, respectively. In the coding of sex, male = 1 and female = 2. Logits (i.e., linear combinations of the parameter estimates) refer to the probability of selecting emotional infidelity as more distressing than sexual infidelity. Exact probabilities can be calculated as follows:

$$p = \frac{e^{x\beta}}{1 + e^{x\beta}},$$

where β represents the unstandardized parameter estimate(s). DII = differential infidelity implication (see the text).

imply sexual infidelity than the converse, they were more likely to select emotional infidelity as more distressing (see Figure 7.1a). Moreover, as predicted, a zero value of DII, indicating a belief that the two types of infidelity imply one another equally, was associated with a .55 probability of selecting emotional infidelity in this sample.

The third model regressed infidelity choice on both sex and DII. In this model, only participants' DII scores remained a reliable predictor of infidelity choice. Adding DII to Model I resulted in increased explanatory power ($\Delta\chi^2[1, N = 114] = 13.29$, $p < .001$), but adding sex to Model 2 did not ($\Delta\chi^2[1, N = 114] = 2.69$, $p = .10$); sex accounted for little unique variance in choice of the more distressing infidelity situation beyond the variance explained by DII. Thus, any significant association between sex and choice of the more distressing infidelity situation is explained by the differing expectations of men and women concerning the independence of the two types of infidelity.

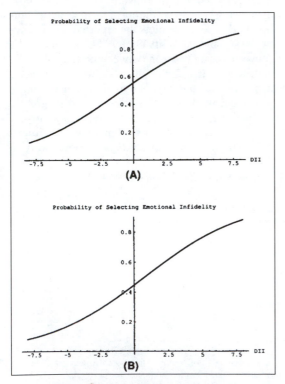

FIGURE 7.1 ■ Logistic regression curves representing estimates of the probability of selecting emotional infidelity as more distressing than sexual infidelity as a function of differential infidelity implication (DII) score for participants of Study 1 (a) and Study 2 (b).

Moreover, within-sex logistic regressions of infidelity choice on DII showed that most men and women selected the infidelity event that they believed more implied the subsequent occurrence of the other as well (DII parameters were 0.20, $p < .03$, and 0.28, $p < .01$, for men and women, respectively). These results further imply that perceptions of infidelity nonindependence constitute a more complete and parsimonious explanation of infidelity choice than does sex.

Study 2

Study 2 was designed as a replication of Study 1. The primary goal was again to show that the relation between sex and infidelity choice results from their correlation with a third variable, DII. Moreover, to increase the generalizability of these findings, we recruited a sample of nonstudent adults ranging in age from 17 to 70. [. . .]

General Discussion

The studies presented here show that the reported relation between sex and choice of the more jealousy-provoking infidelity type is rooted in a different sex difference: perceptions of the nonindependence of these two types of infidelity. Both men and women selected the infidelity event that they believed was more likely to signal the occurrence of the other type of infidelity as well, thereby supporting the double-shot hypothesis. Moreover, in both samples, the belief that emotional infidelity implies sexual infidelity was held to a greater degree by women than men. This reliable covariation between sex and beliefs about the nonindependence of the two types of infidelity accounts for the widely cited relation between biological sex and jealousy for the two types of infidelity.

In light of these findings, we assert that the choice between sexual infidelity and emotional infidelity is a false dichotomy for many individuals. Consequently, research that uses a forced choice between these two types of infidelity as the primary dependent variable without examining the influence of other variables is open to question. This argument extends to the use of physiological data as well. Although such procedures circumvent the error due to self-report, there remains no way to ensure that asking individuals to imagine an instance of emotional infidelity may not also trigger them to think about the possible sexual implications of such an event as well.

One further point is also worthy of note. Although the sex difference in infidelity choice reported by Buss et al. (1992) is readily replicable using the forced-choice paradigm, we have been unable to replicate it using continuous measures asking individuals to rate the amount of distress experienced in response to each type of infidelity.[1] Failures to find this effect using both manifest and latent multiple measures of jealousy led us to question the robustness of the originally reported sex difference outside of the forced-choice paradigm. It may be that the effect is dependent on choosing one type of infidelity over the other. In this case, if a person is forced to choose, we believe that he or she will choose the infidelity event that is more likely to result in a double shot.

The data presented here argue against an evolutionary interpretation of sex differences in jealousy (Buss et al., 1992; Daly & Wilson, 1983); there is no evidence that sex exerted any direct influence on the choice between sexual or emotional infidelity as more distressing. Rather, this relation appears to be due to a specification error; sex is correlated with perceptions of the nonindependence of these types of infidelity, and it is these perceptions, we argue, that influence choice of infidelity type. Evolutionary psychol-

ogy provides no basis for differential jealousy based on the nonindependence of types of infidelity; rather, each sex is theorized to focus on a specific type of fitness threat. The data presented here argue for an interpretation of infidelity choice based on expectations of subsequent behavior; infidelity events that imply the occurrence of other types of infidelity as well evoke more intense jealousy in both men and women specifically because of this augmentation.

In addition, unlike the psychological mechanism postulated in the evolutionary model, our findings show that the double-shot hypothesis not only explains differential choices of infidelity between men and women, but also explains variance in these choices among individuals of the same sex. The evolutionary model is incapable of explaining such within-sex differences. Consequently, we believe that our model provides a clear and parsimonious explanation of infidelity choice that is also more general than the one posed by Buss et al. (1992).

Jealousy, we believe, is a multifaceted phenomenon (DeSteno & Salovey, 1994, 1995; Salovey & Rothman, 1991). Evolutionary psychologists certainly share our view that socialization plays a role in shaping jealousy (Buss et al., 1992). In kind, we do not deny that jealousy may possess some adaptiveness with respect to fitness; nor are we arguing against the utility of the evolutionary perspective to study behavior in animals and humans. However, we do believe that, at present, conclusive empirical evidence has not been put forward to support the notion of evolutionary-based sex differences in the elicitation of jealousy.

[1]A study recently conducted in our laboratory illustrates the case. Sixty-five participants (34 men, 31 women) completed the standard forced-choice measure as well as a six-item jealousy measure (Cronbach's a = .90) for each of the two types of infidelity. Ratings were recorded on 9-point scales with the sum representing each participant's jealousy score. As expected, we replicated the usual relation between sex and choice of infidelity type for the forced-choice measure, $c^2(1, N = 65) = 10.20, p = .001$. The majority of women reported that emotional infidelity ($f = 27$) would cause more distress than sexual infidelity; only 4 women selected sexual infidelity as more distressing. Men, however, showed no such differential preference for sexual ($f = 17$) or emotional ($f = 17$) infidelity. Again, the lack of a differential preference in men is difficult to explain from the perspective of evolutionary psychology. More important, analyses of the continuous measures failed to show a relation between sex and the intensity of jealousy in response to the two types of infidelity. A 2 (sex) X 2 (infidelity type) mixed analysis of variance provided no evidence for the predicted interaction (for men, $M_{sexual\ infidelity} = 43.62, SD = 12.16$, and $M_{emotional\ infidelity} = 42.21$, $SD = 12.32$; for women, $M_{sexual\ infidelity} = 47.03, SD = 8.97$, and $M_{emotional\ infidelity} = 48.47, SD = 7.67$; $F[1, 62] = 1.78, p = .19$).

REFERENCES

Abelson, R. P. (1995). *Statistics as principled argument.* Hillsdale, NJ: Erlbaum.

Bollen, K. A. (1989). *Structural equations with latent variables.* New York: Wiley.

Buss, D. M. (1991). Evolutionary personality psychology. *Annual Review of Psychology, 42,* 459–491.

Buss, D. M. (1995). Evolutionary psychology: A new paradigm for psychological science. *Psychological Inquiry, 6,* 1–30.

Buss, D. M., Larsen, R. J., Westen, D., & Semmelroth, J. (1992). Sex differences in jealousy: Evolution, physiology, and psychology. *Psychological Science, 3,* 251–255.

Daly, M., & Wilson, M. (1983). *Sex, evolution, and behavior* (2nd ed.). Belmont, CA: Wadsworth.

DeSteno, D. A., & Salovey, P. (1994). Jealousy in close relationships: Multiple perspectives on the green-eyed monster. In A. L. Weber & J. H. Harvey (Eds.), Perspectives on close relationships (pp. 217–242). Needham Heights. MA: Allyn and Bacon.

DeSteno, D. A., & Salovey, P. (1995). Jealousy and envy. In A. S. R. Manstead & M. Hewstone (Eds.), *The Blackwell encyclopedia of social psychology* (pp. 342–343). Oxford, England: Basil Blackwell

Salovey, P., & Rothman, A. J. (1991). Envy and jealousy: Self and society. In P. Salovey (Ed.), *The psychology of jealousy and envy* (pp. 271–286). New York: Guilford Press.

Wiederman, M. W., & Allgeier, E. R. (1993). Gender differences in sexual jealousy: Adaptationist or social learning explanation? *Ethology and Sociobiology, 14,* 115–140.

The Gender Heuristic and the Database: Factors Affecting the Perception of Gender-Related Differences in the Experience and Display of Emotions

Michael D. Robinson • Department of Psychology, University of Illinois, Champaign
Joel T. Johnson • Department of Psychology, University of California, Davis
Stephanie A. Shields • Department of Psychology, Pennsylvania State University

We propose that gender stereotypes about emotion, an important influence on the self-concepts of men and women, are often used to "fill in" when concrete information about a situation is lacking (Shields, 1991). To examine these claims experimentally, we designed an emotion induction and varied the type and timing of emotion reporting. Participants either played or watched game conditions, or imagined themselves playing or watching the same game (hypothetical condition). Participants actually involved in the game made emotion judgments either immediately after the game (online condition) or after a time delay (delayed condition). Both in terms of self-reports of emotional experience and perceptions of the emotional displays of others, gender-related stereotypes had a significant influence on judgments of participants in the hypothetical condition but had no significant influence on online judgments. Furthermore, participants rating their own emotional experiences (after a 1-week delay) exhibited responses consistent with gender stereotypes, whereas participants rating the emotional displays of others (after a 1-day delay) did not show a gender-stereotypic response pattern. The results suggest that people tend to use an emotion-related gender heuristic when they lack a database of concrete situational experiences on which to base their judgments.

Based on the seminal efforts of key researchers (e.g., Allport, 1954; Hamilton, 1976; Tajfel, 1970), stereotypes are now seen as an inevitable consequence of the categorization process. However, considerable controversy has surrounded the issue of whether stereotypes influence social judgments when perceivers also have target-specific information. When we learn specific facts about a flesh-and-blood human being from a stereotyped social group, do stereotypes still exert an influence on our judgments of that person? Research on this question has sometimes yielded contradictory answers (Barn, Albright, & Malloy, 1995; Bodenhausen, 1988; Darley & Gross, 1983; Eagly & Steffan, 1984; Kunda & Sherman-Williams, 1993; Locksley, Borgida, Brekke, & Hepburn, 1980). [. . .]

Although informative and useful, they are limited in that they all utilize a common experimental paradigm. In all cases, the individuating information about the target was generated by the experimenters in the form of written descriptions, videotapes of the relevant behaviors, or programmed responses from an experimental confederate. None of these studies directly address the question of ultimate theoretical and practical interest: Do stereotypes still influence the inferences made by social perceivers when these perceivers are exposed to the actual behaviors of a real person from a stereotyped group? The research reported in this article confronts this question directly.

In addition, we examine the extent to which people generally apply gender stereotypes when they consider their own emotional experiences and displays as well as whether situational factors influence when these stereotypes are applied to the self. These issues have generally not been examined. The stereotype literature cited previously has not examined whether the application of gender-related schemas to the self may operate similarly to the application of gender stereotypes to judgments of others, in that the application of both types of stereotypes may be affected by the presence or absence of domain-specific individuating information.

Prior Research on Emotion-Related Gender Stereotypes

Many studies have established that people share gender stereotypes about emotion. Generally speaking, women are thought to display more emotion than men and to feel emotion more intensely (Grossman & Wood, 1993; Johnson & Shulman, 1988; Shields & Koster, 1989), and the term *emotional* is considered more typical of women than of men (Antill, 1987:. Shields, 1987; Spence et al., 1975). In terms of specific emotions, socially undesirable affect oriented toward the self (e.g., sadness and guilt), but socially desirable affect oriented toward others (e.g., love), is typically associated with women, whereas socially undesirable affect oriented toward others (e.g., anger) has been associated with men (Birnbaum, Nosanchuk, & Croll, 1980; Fabes & Martin, 1991; Grossman & Wood, 1993; Johnson & Boyd, 1995). Social observers, these studies suggest, may frequently use gender stereotypes to infer the emotions of specific women and men.

It is noteworthy that many of these gender stereotypes parallel self-reported gender differences, at least under certain conditions. Generally speaking, women report experiencing emotions more intensely (Diener, Sandvik, & Larsen, 1985; Fujita, Diener, & Sandvik, 1991) as well as displaying emotions more frequently and in a more extreme fashion (Grossman & Wood, 1993). In terms of specific emotional experiences, women report experiencing more socially undesirable self-oriented emotions such as shame and guilt (Stapley & Haviland, 1989; Tangney, 1990) as well as more depression (Nolen-Hoeksema, 1987). However, they also report experiencing more socially desirable other-oriented emotions like empathy (Eisenberg & Lennon, 1983). In terms of specific kinds of emotional expression, Balswick and Avertt (1977) found that women report displaying both more sadness (frequently a socially undesirable self-oriented feeling) and love (a socially desirable other-oriented feeling). Men, by contrast, report experiencing more socially desirable self-oriented emotions like pride (Tangney, 1990) as well as more socially undesirable other-oriented emotions like contempt (Stapley & Haviland, 1989).

In sum, gender differences in self-reports of emotion often correspond to emotion-specific gender stereotypes. Men are thought to experience and display more socially desirable self-oriented emotions (e.g., pride) and more socially undesirable other-oriented emotions (e.g., anger). Women are thought to experience and display more socially undesirable self-oriented emotions (e.g., guilt and sadness) and more socially desirable other-oriented emotions (e.g., love).

Recent literature reviews, however, suggest that self-reported gender differences in emotion are most likely to appear under certain conditions. LaFrance and Banaji (1992) noticed that gender differences in self-report are more likely to occur when self-reports are direct rather than inferred from other measures, when they concern emotional expression rather than emotional experience, when they are related to interpersonal rather than impersonal contexts, and when they involve global reports of emotionality rather than reports of specific feelings. In accord with the latter observations, Shields (1991, 1995) similarly concluded that gender differences in emotion self-reports are mote likely when they are global and retrospective rather than specific and concurrent with ongoing experience. For example, global retrospective reports about anger often yield a gender difference, with men reporting more frequent and intense occurrences than women. When Averill (1983) collected diary reports about recent experiences of anger, however, women and men reported feeling and expressing anger with equal frequency. Disparities between retrospective and concurrent reports of emotion have also been observed in studies of mood and the menstrual cycle. Slade (1984), for example, had women complete daily mood reports. Whereas retrospective studies often find that women report more negative affect premenstrually than at other times during the cycle, Slade's concurrent data showed no such pattern.

Why are self-reports that are removed from the occurrence of an emotion more likely to yield gender differences than to reflect gender stereotypes? We suggest that a gender stereotype is more likely to function as a heuristic device for estimating emotions, in self-reports and in impressions of others, when people lack a large and accessible database of relevant information on which to base their judgments. That is, gender stereotypes may be employed as a rule of thumb in judging the emotions of self and others when people lack easy access to target- and situation-specific information—a condition that characterizes many situations in which the individual is not concurrently experiencing the emotion or viewing the emotional display.

If so, two predictions follow. First, estimations of emotion in certain hypothetical situations should be more influenced by a gender heuristic than estimations of emotion in similar situations that are actually experienced. Second, retrospective ratings of emotion in these situations should be more influenced by a gender heuristic than concurrent or "online" ratings because retrospective ratings are removed from the experiences on which they are based.

We tested the first two predictions by systematically manipulating both the availability and the accessibility of the relevant database of emotional experience. Participants in the hypothetical condition estimated emotions in a hypothetical situation. In this condition, a directly relevant database was not available or accessible. By contrast, participants in the online condition estimated emotions immediately after experiencing the same situation, and participants in the retrospective condition made their estimations either 1 day or 1 week after their experience. In both the online and retrospective conditions, the relevant database would be available but in the retrospective condi-

tion, the data would be accessible.[1] We expected that responses in the hypothetical condition would be gender stereotypic owing to the lack of available episodic information, and that responses in the retrospective condtion would be gender stereotypic owing to the lack of accessible episodic information.

Method

OVERVIEW

To induce mild-to-moderate emotions in a nondeceptive manner, we used an involving word game. Participants were assigned to either player or observer conditions. Players competed in the word game and then rated their own emotional experiences, whereas observers monitored the game and then rated the players (not themselves) according to their emotional displays. Both players and observers were assigned one of three conditions: online, delayed, or hypothetical Players and observers in the online condition made their ratings immediately following the word game, whereas those in the delayed condition made their ratings at a later time. Finally, players and observers assigned to the hypothetical condition were not actually involved in the word game but were instead asked to imagine themselves (as either players or observers) in the same situation.

Players rated their own emotional experiences, whereas each observer rated the emotional displays of four players in the game. Accordingly, the responses of players and observers were not comparable, and the hypotheses of this study did not involve any comparison between them. Rather, we were interested in examining player and observer ratings separately to assess the effect of gender stereotypes on responses given in the online, delayed, and hypothetical conditions.

PARTICIPANTS AND DESIGN

Participants were 140 college students from the University of California at Davis (60 men and 80

---

[1] Social psychologists have made a distinction between the availability and accessibility of information retrieved from memory. Available information is information that exists in memory and thus could potentially be retrieved, whereas accessible information is information that is easy to retrieve. Given this distinction, information can be available without being accessible but could not be accessible without being available.

women) who chose to participate in the "Word Game Study" to earn extra credit for their psychology classes. Of these participants, 115 were designated players, and 30 were designated observers. Of the 115 players, 42 were assigned to the online condition (l9 men and 23 women), 41 to the delayed condition (19 men and 22 women), and 32 to the hypothetical condition (12 men and 20 women). Of the 30 observers (13 men and 17 women), 10 were assigned to the online condition, 11 to the delayed condition, and 9 to the hypothetical condition. Participants were randomly assigned to player or observer roles as well as randomly assigned to condition.

Target sex was a second variable of theoretical interest. For players, target sex was equivalent to participant sex, a between-subjects variable. For observers, target sex was a within-subject variable—that is, it was important to us that observers rated both male and female targets. Because participants were randomly assigned to player roles, this meant that observers who rated competitions involving only male or female players (five in total) were excluded from all analyses. Finally, all participants made ratings of both male- and female-stereotypic emotions. Thus, for both players and observers, the three- level variable of condition was crossed with the two-level variables of target sex and emotion stereotypicality (male-stereotypic emotions vs. female-stereotypic emotions). For both players and observers, condition was a between-subjects variable, and emotion stereotypicality was a within-subject variable. For players, target sex was a between-subjects variable, whereas for observers, target sex was a within-subject variable.

PROCEDURE

Participants randomly assigned to the hypothetical condition were taken by an experimenter to another room, where they completed questionnaires without actually playing in or observing the word game. Participants not assigned to the hypothetical condition remained in the first room. These participants were randomly assigned to competition groups and to roles within those groups. In each group, there was a red team, consisting of two players; a blue team, consisting of two players; and an observer. Within each of the teams (red and blue), one player was designated Player 1, and the other player was designated Player 2.

During the word game, Red Team Player 1 always competed against Blue Team Player 1, and Red Team Player 2 always competed against Blue Team Player 2. The red team wore red tags, the blue team wore blue tags, and the observer wore a white tag. The numbers of the players were prominently displayed on their tags, and the observer wore a tag with the word *observer*. After both oral and written instructions, players began the six rounds of the competition. During each round, players created words that had to include three particular target letters (e.g., *cap*) as well as preserve the order of those three letters within the words (e.g., *capture*, *catnip*, and *scrap* would be legal words, whereas *pack* would not). Each round lasted 1.25 min. The end of each round was prominently marked by a timer that made a loud popping sound when time had expired.

Players scored points for their team during an announcement period that followed each round. Competing players (e.g., Red Team Player 1 vs. Blue Team Player 1), who were always given the same three-letter combinations, took turns announcing their words. A player was given 0 points for announcing an illegal word, 1 point for announcing a legal word that his or her opponent did not have, and 2 points for a word that his or her opponent had but had not yet announced.

After both sets of opponents had finished announcing their words, individual totals for each round were calculated. The observer then added a player's points for that round to all the points that player had obtained in previous rounds and publicly announced the cumulative score of each competitor before proceeding to the next round. At the end of the competition, the observer announced final individual totals as well as final team totals. The team with the most points was publicly declared the winning team.

Prior to the first experimental session, online player questionnaires and delayed player information sheets were randomly intermixed, as were online observer questionnaires and delayed observer information sheets. After the competition, players and observers were randomly assigned to online and delayed conditions. For players in both of these conditions, dependent measures involved self-ratings of the intensity of certain feelings they experienced during the game. For observers in both conditions, dependent measures involved ratings of the extent to which each of the players had displayed certain feelings during the game.

Participants in the online condition completed their questionnaires immediately after the competition. Observers in the delayed condition returned 1 day later to complete their questionnaires, whereas players in the delayed condition completed them 1 week later. The difference in delay periods was based on our belief that, after a 1-week delay, players would still remember something about their own experiences but that observers would no longer remember the players in their competition groups (often complete strangers), much less the extent to which the players displayed various feelings. All delayed observers, and 41 of 42 delayed players, returned to complete the questionnaire.

INSTRUCTIONS

Hypothetical condition. Hypothetical players were told that we were interested in the ideas people have about what they might experience in certain highly specific situations. They were also told that we were interested in comparing their ideas of what they would experience in the word game to the perceptions of players who had actually played the game. Participants then read a one-page account describing the important features of the game: the task itself, the time limit, the number of rounds, and the announcement portion following each round. Hypothetical players were told that, if they actually competed in the game, they would have a teammate and an opponent. They were also told that an observer would watch them throughout the game, keep track of the individual point totals of all the players, and announce their scores after each of the six rounds. Finally, hypothetical players were told to imagine they were in the situation and rate how intensely they would feel a series of distinct feelings.

Hypothetical observers were given similar instructions. They were told that we would compare their ratings to the ratings of observers who actually watched players participating in the game. They then read an account similar to the one read by hypothetical players, except that hypothetical observers were told that their task was to watch the players. Finally, hypothetical observers were asked to rate the extent to which the average college-aged man and woman would be likely to display a number of distinct feelings (similar targets have been used by others, notably Martin, 1987, and Spence et al., 1975).

Actual experience conditions. Players and observers in actual competition groups were given both oral and written instructions describing the rules of the game. Observers, however, were also given additional written instructions describing how to set up each of the founds, how to total and announce individual and team point totals, and how to resolve disputes over the legality of particular words. Observers were also told to carefully watch the expressive reactions of each of the players.

DEPENDENT MEASURES

Player ratings. We employed two criteria when selecting the critical dependent measures for the study: (a) relevance to the game situation, and (b) evidence from prior research that the particular feelings might be considered gender stereotypic. All players were asked to judge how intensely they had felt each of 17 critical feelings during the game, specifically rating the "amount of the feeling, reaction sensation" that they experienced. All ratings were made on a 9-point scale, in which 1 was labeled *I felt none of this*, 3 was labeled *I felt a little of this*, 5 was labeled *I felt a moderate amount of this*, 7 was labeled *I felt quite a bit of this*, and 9 was labeled I felt an extreme amount of this.

The 17 feelings were grouped into four conceptual categories: (a) socially desirable emotions oriented toward the (self-satisfaction, pride, and satisfaction with the outcome (b) socially desirable emotions oriented toward others (sympathy toward opponent, friendliness toward opponent, friendliness toward partner, gratefulness to partner, and sympathy toward partner), (c) socially undesirable emotions oriented toward the self (disappointment with self, depression, criticism, guilt, and embarrassment), and (d) socially undesirable emotions oriented toward others (anger toward partner, hostility toward partner, anger toward opponent, and hostility toward opponent).

Based on the previous research summarized in the introduction, these emotion categories were combined a priori to form male- and female-stereotypic scales. The male-stereotypic scale included socially desirable emotions oriented toward the self and socially undesirable emotions toward others, whereas the female-stereotypic scale included socially desirable emotions oriented toward others and socially undesirable emotions oriented toward the self. (As we subsequently report, the a priori classification of the emotions as gender stereotypic received empirical validation in Study 2.)

Observer ratings. All observers were asked to judge the extent to which players displayed each of six critical feelings during the game, specifically rating "the amount of the feeling, reaction, or sensation that each player displayed." We included only six items (a subset of the 17 rated players) because online and delayed observers had to rate four targets, whereas players only had to rate themselves. Ratings were made on a 9-point scale, in which 1 was labeled *displayed none of this*, 3 was labeled *displayed a little of this*, 5 was labeled *displayed a moderate amount of this*, 7 was labeled *displayed quite a bit of this*, and 9 was labeled *displayed an extreme amount of this*.

Observers rated each of the players on disappointment with himself or herself, pride, friendliness toward his or her opponent, embarrassment, hostility toward his or her opponent and anger toward his or her partner. Adopting the definition used for player items, we classified the emotions into four emotion types that we predicted would be related to gender stereotypes: (a) socially undesirable emotions oriented toward the self (disappointment with himself or herself and embarrassment), (b) socially undesirable emotions oriented toward others (hostility toward his or her opponent and anger toward his or her partner), (c) socially desirable emotions oriented toward the self (pride), and (d) socially desirable emotions oriented toward others (friendliness toward his or her opponent). These emotion types were combined in the same manner as with the player categories, creating a male-stereotypic scale and a female-stereotypic scale.[2]

Reliability for the male- and female-stereotypic scales was assessed by Cronbach's alpha. For players in Study 1, alphas were .66 and .77, respectively. For observers in Study 1, alphas were .79 and .26, respectively, and similar values were ob-

tained in Study 2. Subsequent analyses revealed that the relatively low reliability obtained for the three-item female-stereotypic scale rated by observers was due to ratings of friendliness toward an opponent, which were not significantly correlated with either ratings of disappointment with self or ratings of embarrassment. In this connection, we note that friendliness toward an opponent, a socially desirable feeling directed toward others, belongs to a different conceptual category than the other two measures, which represent socially undesirable emotions directed toward the self. Further analyses, however, indicated that participants tended to rate both conceptual categories as stereotypic of women. It therefore appears that, although ratings of socially desirable emotion directed toward others tended to be orthogonal to ratings of socially undesirable emotion directed toward the self, both categories of emotion were nonetheless viewed as stereotypic of women.

Results

OVERVIEW OF STATISTICAL ANALYSES

Observers always rated at least one man and one woman, rendering target sex a within-subject variable for observers. Because target sex was instead a between-subjects variable for players, and because players and observers rated different sets of dependent measures, observer and player ratings were analyzed separately—that is, we never compare player ratings to observer ratings in any of the following analyses. For online and delayed observers, display means were calculated across all targets of the same sex. For instance, if a particular observer rated two men and two women, ratings given to each of the two men were averaged for each of the six feelings, as were ratings given to each of the two women. We report our analyses of observer data first.

ANALYSES OF OBSERVER DATA

In our initial and most inclusive analysis, rating condition was a three-level, between-subject variable (online vs. delayed vs. hypothetical), and target sex and emotion category (male-stereotypic vs. female-stereotypic emotions) were two-level, within-subjects variables. Results of the $3 \times 2 \times 2$ (Rating Condition × Target Sex × Emotion Category) univariate analysis of variance (ANOVA)

---

[2]In addition to the critical feelings, players rated an additional 15 filler items and observers rated a subset of 4 of these items. Filler items consisted largely of measures not considered emotions (e.g., interest, responsibility, difficulty in concentrating, and competitive spirit) and did not fit into any of the: four conceptual categories. Subsequent analyses revealed that, with the exception of ratings of competitive spirit, no filler items showed significant evidence of gender differences. A complete description of filler items is available from the authors.

indicated a main effect for emotion category, $F(1, 22) = 11.18$, $p < .003$, with higher estimations for female-than for male-stereotypic emotions as well as an omnibus main effect for rating condition, $F(2, 22) = 9.09$, $p < .001$, due to higher estimations in the hypothetical condition than in the other two conditions. There was no main effect for target sex, $F(1, 22) = 1.77$, $p > .15$, and no Target Sex × Rating Condition interaction ($F < 1$), indicating that observers in all three conditions saw no overall difference between men and women in the extent to which they displayed emotions in general.

The nature of the three remaining interactions, all of which reached conventional levels of significance, is graphically illustrated in Figure 8.1. As indicated by the figure, the Emotion Category × Rating Condition interaction, $F(2, 22) = 8.45$, $p < .002$, was due to the fact that hypothetical observers estimated that competitors would display more male-stereotypic than female-stereotypic emotions but that online and delayed observers believed that more female- than male-stereotypic emotions had been displayed. The Emotion Category × Target Sex interaction, $F(1, 22) = 12.06$, $p < .002$, indicated that men were rated higher than women on the display of male-stereotypic emotions, whereas women were rated higher than men on the display of female-stereotypic emotions.

More important, however, the Emotion Category × Target Sex × Rating Condition interaction, $F(2, 22) = 4.95$, $p < .02$, indicated that these gender-related differences varied significantly according to rating condition. Additional comparisons assessed whether the predicted Emotion Category × Target Sex interaction differed significantly between the hypothetical observer condition on the one hand and each of other two conditions on the other. Results of these comparisons indicated that the interaction was significantly stronger in the hypothetical condition than in both the online condition, $F(1, 22) = 4.60$, $p < .05$, and the delayed condition, $F(1, 22) = 9.54$, $p < .05$. Observers in the latter two conditions did not differ significantly from one another ($F < 1$). There were no significant four-way interactions involving the variable of observer sex, either with the omnibus test, $F(2, 19) = 1.36$, $p > .25$, or with any of the pairwise comparisons ($ps > .10$).

We also performed separate Target Sex × Emotion Category ANOVAs on the responses of participants in each of the three rating conditions, with data from all observers used to compute the error term. Results indicated that the Target Sex × Emotion Category interaction was highly significant among observers in the hypothetical condition, $F(1, 22) = 20.95$, $p < .001$, but did not approach

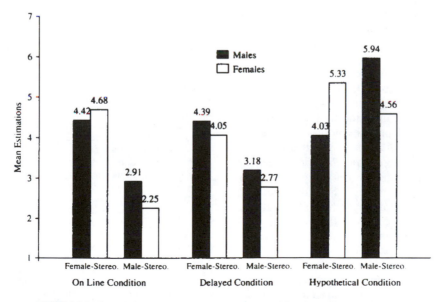

FIGURE 8.1 ■ Mean observer estimations of Emotional Display × Emotion Category.

significance among observers who had actually witnessed the game ($ps > .10$).[3]

In our initial and most inclusive analysis of player ratings, condition was a three-level, between-subject variable (online vs. delayed vs. hypothetical), participant sex was a two-level, between-subject variable, and emotion category (male vs. female stereotypic) was a two-level, within-subjects variable. This $3 \times 2 \times 2$ (Rating Condition × Emotion Category × Participant Sex) ANOVA revealed a significant main effect for rating condition, $F(2, 109) = 7.40$, $p < .005$, due to the fact that higher estimations were given in the hypothetical condition than in the other two conditions. In another parallel with observer data, there was a significant Emotion Category × Participant Sex interaction, $F(1, 109) = 9.95$, $p < .005$, indicating that men gave higher estimations of male-stereotypic emotions, whereas women gave higher estimations of female-stereotypic emotions. There was no significant main effect for participant sex ($F < 1$), indicating that female self-raters did not generally ascribe more intense emotions to themselves than male self-raters did, and there was no Participant Sex × Rating Condition interaction, $F(2, 109) = 2.11$, $p > .10$. There was also no effect for emotion category, $F(1, 109) = 1.88$, $p > .15$.

By contrast to the results for observers, the Emotion Category × Participant Sex × Rating Condition interaction was nonsignificant ($F < 1$). However, support for our predictions was obtained when we performed 2×2 (Emotion Category × Participant Sex) ANOVAs on ratings made in each of the three conditions, with data from all participants used to compute an error term. This interaction was nonsignificant in the online condition ($F < I$), and additional analyses indicated no significant gender-related differences on either male-stereotypic or female-stereotypic emotions alone. The Participant Sex × Emotion Category interaction, however, was significant in both the delayed, $F(1, 109) = 4.08$, $p < .05$, and hypothetical conditions, $F(1, 109) = 6.69$, $p < .025$. In the two conditions removed from the actual experience of the game, self-reports conformed to a gender-stereotypic pattern whereas they did not conform to this pattern in the on-line condition. Means of these three conditions are graphically displayed in Figure 8.2.[4]

Discussion

OBSERVER DISPLAY RATINGS

Our analyses of observer ratings of emotional display support our predictions. People who estimated emotional display in a hypothetical situation relied significantly more on the gender heuristic than people who had ready access to specific individuating information. Participants in the hypothetical condition, who did not witness the actual game competition, estimated significant gender-related differences in emotional display, believing that men would display more male-stereotypic emotions but that women would display more female-stereotypic emotions. However, neither observers who estimated emotional display immediately after the competition, nor observers who made their estimations 1 day later, showed evidence of a significant Target Sex × Emotion Category interaction. Gender stereotypes, it appears, dissipated in the two conditions in which people were able to

---

[3]Although all online and delayed observers viewed at least 1 man and 1 woman, groups differed somewhat in their gender composition. Recall that there were two one-on-one competitions within each of the groups, and that the gender of opponents was sometimes the same, but was sometimes different. A particular group might have two sets of same-sex opponents (man vs. man and woman vs. woman), two sets of opposite-sex opponents (two male vs. female competitions), or one set of each (e.g., man vs. woman and woman vs. woman). An ANOVA. however, revealed that this variable did not influence the extent to which the ratings of observers who witnessed the competition were consistent with gender stereotypes. That is, then was no three-way interaction involving this variable and the variables of target sex and emotion category ($F < 1$), and then was no four-way interaction involving these three variables and rating condition ($F < 1$).

[4]To determine whether self-reports of emotional experience by players in the competition were influenced by whether a participant's opponent was of the same or opposite gender, this variable was entered as a between-subjects factor in new analyses. Gender congruence of competitor (same gender vs. opposite gender) did not qualify the Target Sex × Emotion Category interaction ($F < I$), and there was no four-way interaction between the preceding three variables and rating condition ($F < 1$). An additional ANOVA that treated each specific four-person player group as a different level of a between-subjects variable indicated that player group did not modify the Target Sex × Emotion Category interaction ($p > .20$). The four-way interaction between these variables and rating condition was also nonsignificant ($F < 1$). These results suggest that, despite the potential for nonindependence among the responses of players in a particular group, it was nonetheless appropriate to treat individual player as the relevant unit of analysis in all relevant analyses.

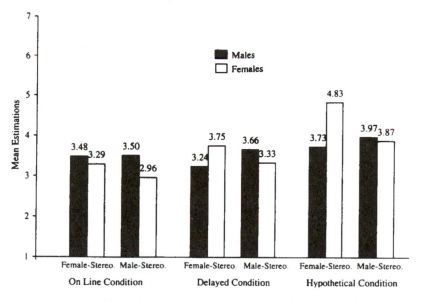

FIGURE 8.2 ■ Mean player estimations of Felt Emotional × Emotion Category.

access an available database of recent concrete experiences. Our results thus support the contention of Locksley and colleagues (Locksley, Borgida, Brekke & Hepburn, 1980; Locksley, Hepburn & Ortiz, 1982) that social perceivers disregard social stereotypes when they have access to target-specific information.

It is also noteworthy that none of the effects related to gender stereotypes were modified by the gender of the observers themselves. Male and female observers, in other words, appear to share the same gender-related stereotypes of emotional display and to utilize the gender heuristic in similar ways. These results generally complement those of other researchers (Birnbaum et al., 1980; Fabes & Martin, 1991; Johnson & Shulman, 1988), who found minimal evidence for Participant Sex × Target Sex interactions.

EXPERIENCE SELF-RATINGS

When asked to report on their subjective experiences immediately after playing the game, players, like observers, showed relatively little evidence of the use of a gender heuristic. Male and female players did not generally differ in their self-reports of their own emotional experiences, and player gender did not interact with whether the rated emotion was stereotypically male or stereo-

typically female. Consistent with the reasoning of Ellsworth (1991), these results suggest that, when men and women are placed in the same situation, they will often make similar appraisals and experience similar emotions.

The null result of the online condition can be contrasted with the gender-related differences in the hypothetical and delayed conditions. In the hypothetical condition, men tended to estimate that they would experience more intense male-stereotypic emotions, whereas women tended to estimate that they would experience more intense female-stereotypic emotions. Players reporting on their emotions 1 week later displayed a similar pattern of gender-related differences. These results are consistent with other research regarding self-reported gender differences in emotion. When not asked to report on recent, specific experiences, women report more socially undesirable emotions with self as the object (e.g., shame and guilt; Tangney, 1990) as well as more socially desirable emotions with another as the object (e.g., empathy; Eisenberg & Lennon, 1983). Under similar conditions, men report more socially undesirable emotions oriented toward others (e.g., contempt; Stapley & Haviland, 1989) as well as more socially desirable self-oriented emotions (e.g., pride; Tangney, 1990).

Our data are consistent with previous speculation that gender stereotypes of emotion are more likely to influence self-reports when men and women lack a database of recent, concrete experiences on which to base their inferences (Shields, 1991, 1995) as well as with findings indicating no significant gender differences when men and women are asked to report on recent specific experiences of anger (Averill, 1983). Our research also has some affinity with an earlier study by Frodi (1978), who intentionally provoked both male and female participants and then asked some of them to reflect on their experience. Results indicated some gender-related differences in self-reports of anger but only among those participants who engaged in retrospection (and perhaps used gender-related schemata to reconstruct their feelings). By contrast to these previous studies, however, our research examined gender-related differences in inferences of emotions in hypothetical versus actually experienced situations and also manipulated the temporal delay between the experimental situation and participants' evaluation of it. Even more strongly than these prior results, our data suggest that self-reported gender differences on a range of emotions may have more to do with use of a gender heuristic than with the nature of online emotional experience. [. . .]

General Discussion

In accord with our a priori classifications, significant Sex × Emotion Category interactions for both players and observers indicate that, when significant gender-related differences were found, participants indeed tended to rate men higher on emotions in the male-stereotypic category and to rate women higher on emotions in the female-stereotypic category. This tendency did not interact with the gender of the rater. More important, however, both studies indicate that estimates of gender-related differences in emotions may be influenced by the availability and accessibility of pertinent information.

Extensions of Stereotype Research

Shields (1991, 1995) suggested two important factors that may influence when these stereotypes will, and will not, be applied. First, she proposed that self-reported gender differences in emotion are more likely when participants make global,

retrospective judgments than when they make online reports about their emotions in specific situations. Second, she proposed that such differences are also more likely when one is evaluating hypothetical others than when one is evaluating oneself. One underlying explanation for the influence of both of these variables relates to the size and accessibility of the relevant database. People, that is, may be less likely to use gender as a heuristic for inferring emotional intensity when they have an available and readily accessible database of recent experiences on which to ground their judgments. [. . .]

In this study, we manipulated the presence versus absence of such a specific database and influenced its accessibility in memory by manipulating the temporal delay between the experience and its evaluation. Findings generally conformed to predictions. Among observers, only hypothetical ratings were gender-stereotypic. This suggests that, whereas gender stereotypes do not tend to impact the appraisal of online situational details, they are used to "fill in" reports when such situational details are lacking. In other words, gender stereotypes appear to be one source of generalized beliefs that serve as "default values" when the person lacks more specific information about the emotional situation.

The present results extend prior to stereotype research in several ways. First, the effects of specific information on the application of stereotypes to others (refs) may also pertain to the application of gender schemas to oneself. In either case, the presence of specific episodic information seems to eliminate the use of gender stereotypes. The present data further suggest that, although gender may be relatively central to the self-concept. [. . .]

Several theoretical ramifications of these findings merit further consideration. First, the findings of Study 1 extend stereotype research. Our results suggest that the effects of specific information on the application of stereotypes to others (Baron, Albright, & Malloy, 1995; Eagly & Steffen, 1984, 1986; Locksley et al., 1980; Locksley et al., 1982) may also pertain to the application of gender schemas to oneself. Responses of online players, who had a rich store of readily accessible information, showed no significant evidence of use of a gender heuristic, although the responses of hypothetical and delayed players did. These data further suggest that, although gender may be relatively central to the self-concept (Cross

& Markus, 1993; Spence, 1985), thus guiding hypothetical and delayed player ratings, it may be less important to the organization of ongoing experience. Second, results of both players and observers demonstrate that specific information may lessen the impact of gender stereotypes in a more naturalistic setting-one in which the information, instead of being generated by an experimenter, arises in the context of actual experience.

Issues Regarding Accuracy and Ecological Validity

It is important to note that neither of our studies resolve, or attempt to resolve, some significant issues regarding the relative accuracy of our participants' responses. Specifically one might argue that the responses of participants who are temporally remote from the game situation may, at least in some sense, actually be more valid than responses made online. Once the specific details of the experience had faded from their memory, participants in the delayed condition may have based their responses on their knowledge of their own previous behaviors in other, somewhat similar situations. This possibility suggests that, because they may be predicated on a wider database of personal experience, responses of participants in the delayed condition represent more valid generalizations of existing central tendencies than the responses of online participants do.

Although there is merit in this suggestion, we argue that it is highly likely that the responses of online participants are in fact more vertical indicators of the subjective intensity of emotions that were experienced online. The possibility that retrospective reports may reflect valid generalizations about prior feelings in other situations does not negate the fact that such reports may also entail distortions of the specific feelings that were experienced in the particular situation relevant to the self-report. Such distortions of accounts of specific experience by general knowledge structures are, of course, entirely consistent with our primary argument.

It is important to emphasize that we do not propose that gender differences in the online experience of emotions are invariably nonexistent. Grossman and Wood (1993), for example, reported some evidence of gender differences in self-reports of immediate reactions to emotion-inducing slides. Rather, we simply argue that temporal distance may facilitate a pattern of stereotype-consistent inferences, even when online reports indicate that gender-related differences were absent. When gender differences in online reports about subjective experience do not exist, that is, our findings suggest that retrospective reflection may create them. [. . .]

Another remaining issue concerns the ecological validity of our study. We might argue that the situation we chose was not representative of the variety of situations in which social observers judge men and women or that the emotions that participants assessed were not representative of the emotions experienced in everyday life. In this connection, it seems quite likely to us that gender differences in online self-reports of emotion may, in fact, occur in some daily situations (e.g., Grossman & Wood, 1993) and that the extent of such differences is likely related to the immediate salience of gender stereotypes and the intensity of the subjective experience. Situations that may entail salient gender stereotypes and elicit intense emotions may be somewhat more likely to produce gender differences in self-reports.

However, any situation or situations we chose would necessarily represent a very small subset of the wider range of situations to which people are exposed on a daily basis. By the same token, the emotions assessed were also necessarily limited to a subset of commonly experienced feelings. Nevertheless, our cooperative–competitive game context is similar to a wide variety of situations in which men and women cooperate, compete, or interact as relative strangers. In addition, the relatively moderate level of emotion that participants reported would seem quite typical of the level of affective intensity experienced by most people in most situations and is arguably more representative of daily life than the high level of emotion apparently elicited by slides used by Grossman and Wood (1993). In addition, the key emotions assessed (e.g., anger, sympathy, pride) are relatively common ones. Further research may be needed to identify the types of situations in which men and women differ, and do not differ, in the experience and display of emotions (for a further discussion of the context-specific nature of gender differences, see Deaux & Major, 1987). We would expect, however, that investigation of many other common affect-eliciting situations would reveal a similar pattern to our results—gender differences not reflected in online reports would nevertheless appear in prospective and retrospective accounts.

A final important objective for further research should be to investigate the mediation of our between-condition differences. Although our results suggest that immediate experience may defuse existing stereotypes, our research does not supply direct evidence on questions regarding the process that mediates this effect. For example, are gender stereotypes more influential in the delayed condition because details of the online experience are no longer accessible and because participants accordingly use existing general knowledge schemata as a basis for self-report? Alternatively, are memories of these details subjectively accessible but distorted or "confabulated" to fit existing stereotypes? By utilizing measures that assess the subjective accessibility and vividness of the relevant memories, and then by examining the role of accessibility and vividness as mediators, future research may furnish answers to these questions.

REFERENCES

Allen, B. P. (1995). Gender stereotypes are not accurate: A replication of Martin (1987) using diagnostic vs. self-report and behavioral criteria. *Sex Roles, 32,* 583–600.

Allport, G. W. (1954). *The nature of prejudice.* Reading, MA: Addison-Wesley.

Antill, J. K. (1987). Parents' beliefs and values about sex roles, sex differences, and sexuality: Their sources and implications. In P. Shaver & C. Hendrick (Eds.), *Review of personality and social psychology* (Vol. 7, pp. 294–328). Newbury Park. CA: Sage.

Averill, J. R. (1983). Studies on anger and aggression. Implications for theories of emotion. *American Psychologist, 38,* 1145–1160.

Balswick, J., & Avertt, C. P. (1977). Differences in expressiveness: Gender, interpersonal orientation, and perceived parental expressiveness as contributing factors. *Journal of Marriage and the Family, 39,* 121–127.

Baron, R. M., Albright, L., & Malloy, T. E. (1995). Effects of behavioral and social class information on social judgment. *Personality and Social Psychology Bulletin, 21,* 308–315.

Bem, S. L. (1981). Gender schema theory: A cognitive account of sex typing. *Psychological Review, 88,* 354–364.

Bem, S. L. (1982). Gender schema theory and self-schema theory compared: A comment on Markus, Crane, Bernstein, and Siladi's "Self-schemas and Gender." *Journal of Personality and Social Psychology, 13,* 1 92–1194.

Birnbaum, D. W., Nosanchuk, T. A., & Croll, W. L. (1980). Children's stereotypes about sex differences in emotionality. *Sex Poles, 6,* 435–443.

Crane, M., & Markus, H. (1982). Gender identity: The benefits of a self-schema approach. *Journal of Personality and Social Psychology, 43,* 1195–1197.

Cross, S. E., & Markus, H. R. (1993). Gender in thought, belief and action: A cognitive approach. In A. E. Beall & R. J. Sternberg (Eds.), *The psychology of gender* (pp. 55–98). New York: Guilford.

Deaux, K., & Major, B. (1987). Putting gender into context: An interactive model of gender-related behavior. *Psychological Bulletin, 94,* 369–389.

Diener, E., Sandvik. E., & Larsen, R. J. (1985). Age and sex effects for emotional intensity. *Developmental Psychology, 21,* 542–546.

Eagly, A. H., & Steffen, V. J. (1984). Gender stereotypes stem from the distribution of women and men into social roles. *Journal of Personality and Social Psychology, 46,* 735–754.

Eagly, A. H., & Steffen, V. J. (1986). Gender stereotypes, occupational roles, and beliefs about part-time employees. *Psychology of Women Quarterly, 10,* 252–262.

Eisenberg, N., & Lennon, R. (1983). Sex differences in empathy and related capacities. Psychological Bulletin, 94, 100–131.

Ellsworth, P. C. (1991). Some implications of cognitive appraisal theories of emotion. In K. T. Strongman (Ed.), International review of studies on emotion (Vol. 1, pp. 143–159). New York: Wiley.

Fabes, R. A., & Martin, C. L. (1991). Gender and age stereotypes of emotionality. *Personality and Social Psychology Bulletin, 17,* 532–540.

Frodi, A. (1978). Experimental and physiological responses associated with anger and aggression in women and men. Journal of Research in Personality, 12, 335–349.

Fujita, F., Diener, E., & Sandvik, E. (1991). Gender differences in negative affect and well-being: The case for emotional intensity. *Journal of Personality and Social Psychology, 61,* 427–434.

Grossman, M., & Wood, W. (1993), Sex differences in intensity of emotional expression: A social role interpretation. *Journal of Personality and Social Psychology, 65,* 1010–1022.

Hamilton, D. L. (1976). Cognitive biases in the perception of social groups. In J. S. Carroll & J. W. Payne (Eds.), *Cognition and social behavior* (pp. 81–93), Hillsdale. NJ: Lawrence Erlbaum Associates.

Johnson, J. T., & Boyd, K. R. (1995). Dispositional traits versus the content of experience: Actor/observer differences in judgments of the "authentic self." *Personality and Social Psychology Bulletin, 21,* 375–383.

Johnson, I. T., & Shulman, G. A. (1988). More alike than meets the eye. Perceived gender differences in subjective experience and its display. *Sex Roles, 19,* 67–79.

Kolar, D. W., Funder, D. C., & Colvin. C. R. (1996). Comparing the accuracy of personality judgments by the self and knowledgeable others. *Journal of Personality, 64,* 311–337.

LaFrance, M., & Banaji, M. (1992), Towards a reconsideration of the gender-emotion relationship. In M. S. Clark (Ed.), *Emotion and social behavior: Review of personality and social psychology* (Vol. 14. pp. 178–201). Newbury Park, CA: Sage.

Locksley, A., Borgida E., Brekke, N., & Hepburn, C. (1980). Sex stereotypes and social judgment. Journal of Personality and Social Psychology, 39, 821–831.

Locksley, A., Hepburn, C., & Ortiz. V. (1982). On the effects of social stereotypes on judgments of individuals: A comment on Grant and Holmes' "The integration of implicit personality theory schemas and stereotypic images." *Social Psychology Quarterly, 45,* 270–273.

Markus, H., Crane, M., Bernstein, S., & Siladi, M. (1982). Self-schemas and gender. *Journal of Personality and Social Psychology, 42,* 38–50.

Martin, C. L. (1987). A ratio measure of stereotyping. *Journal of Personality and Social Psychology, 52,* 489–499.

Nolen-Hoeksema, S. (1987). Sex differences in unipolar depression: Evidence and theory. *Psychological Bulletin, 101,* 259–282.

Shields, S. A. (1987). Women, men, and the dilemma of emotions. In P. Shaver & C. Hendrick (Eds.), *Sex and gender: Review of personality and social psychology* (Vol. 7, pp. 229–250). Newbury Park, CA: Sage.

Shields, S. A. (1991). Gender in the psychology of emotion: A selective research review. In K. T. Strongman (Ed.), *International review of studies on emotion* (Vol. 1, pp. 227–245). New York. Wiley.

Shields, S. A. (1995). The role of emotion beliefs and values in gender development. In N. Eisenberg (Ed.), *Review of personality and social psychology* (Vol. 15, pp. 212–232). Thousand Oaks. CA: Sage.

Shields, S. A., & Koster, B. A. (1989). Emotional stereotyping of parents in child rearing manuals, 1915–1980. *Social Psychology Quarterly, 52,* 44–55.

Slade, P. (1984), Premenstrual emotional changes in normal women: Fact or fiction? *Journal of Psychosomatic Research, 28,* 1–7.

Spence, J. T. (1985). Gender identity and its implications for concepts of masculinity and femininity. In T. B. Sonderegger (Ed.), *Nebraska symposium on motivation: Psychology of gender* (pp. 59–95). Lincoln: University of Nebraska Press.

Spence, J. T., Helmreich, R., & Stapp, J. (1975). Ratings of self and peers on sex role attributes and their relation to self-esteem and conceptions of masculinity and femininity. *Journal of Personality and Social Psychology, 32,* 29–39.

Stapley, J. C., & Haviland, J. M. (1989). Beyond depression: Gender differences in normal adolescents' emotional experiences. *Sex Roles, 20,* 295–308.

Tajfel, H. (1970). Experiments in intergroup discrimination. *Scientific American, 223,* 96–102.

Tangney, J. P. (1990). Assessing individual differences in proneness to shame and guilt: Development of the self-conscious affect and attribution inventory, *Journal of Personality and Social Psychology, 59,* 102–111.

The Social Functions of Emotions

Emotions clearly affect people, and many of these effects have profound social consequences. For example: emotions alter thinking and behavior; they direct attention and rearrange priorities; to others they communicate cares, intentions, and needs; they alter the feelings and behavior of other people; they are part of social roles, and mark social status; they influence the impression one person makes on another; they play a role in moral development, moral evaluation, and moral decision making. Many topics in social psychology, such as altruism and aggression, have emotions at their heart. Therefore, social psychologists' interest in emotions has not stopped at understanding the nature of emotion, but has extended to understanding how emotions influence social processes.

The social effects of emotions sometimes seem disruptive, but emotion theorists usually understand them as functioning in ways that have at least the potential for being useful and adaptive. The term "functionalism" has come to be applied to this approach to understanding emotion (Parrott & Schulkin, 1993). Functionalism has been applied to all aspects of emotion, including its biological, cognitive, and social effects, as well as its overall role in a society or culture. To understand how important emotion is to social psychology, it is necessary to see how emotion functions at all these levels of analysis; most articles, however, focus on only one. A strength of the next reading, by Keltner and Haidt (1999), is that it addresses four levels of analysis: the individual, the dyadic, the group, and the cultural. These levels span the range of ways in which emotions affect social psychology.

This reading serves as an introduction to the issue of social function, linking the aspects of emotion that were depicted in the preceding readings with the effects of emotion that will be described in subsequent readings. By describing the range of social functions attributed to emotions, Keltner and Haidt provide a framework for understanding how emotions influence virtually all social psychological phenomena. Another strength of this article is its application of the functionalist approach to one particular emotion, embarrassment, whose powerful influence in social interaction is often underappreciated. They demonstrate how embarrassment serves a variety of functions, which can be appreciated only by applying all four levels of analysis.

However, emotions are not always functional. In fact, when one considers the number of ways that emotions can cause dysfunction—leading to overreaction, loss of perspective, regrettable actions, mass hysteria, or clinical mood disorders—it can seem a miracle that they manage to function adaptively as much as they do. The key to emotions' adaptiveness, it seems, rests on their being deployed intelligently (Parrott & Schulkin, 1993).

Appraisals have to be accurate, feelings have to be interpreted correctly, and emotions must be acted on in a way well suited to the circumstances (Parrott, 1999). Two social psychologists who have considered these issues, Peter Salovey and John Mayer, have coined the term *emotional intelligence* to describe the cluster of abilities a person must have to take advantage of emotion's potential for contributing to adaptive functioning. In the chapter that has been reprinted in this book, Salovey, Hsee, and Mayer (1993) develop the concept of emotional intelligence. They describe its components, and they relate it to self-regulation. They conclude with an important example of emotion's involvement in social processes. Research on "prosocial behavior" (helping others) suggests that mood regulation may be a motive for choosing whether to come to another person's aid. The authors point out that many models of altruism, from the rather cynical Negative State Relief Model to more idealistic theories of pride and self-satisfaction, all point to emotions as underlying motivations to help or not to help.

REFERENCES

Keltner, D., & Haidt, J. (1999). Social functions of emotions at four levels of analysis. *Cognition and Emotion, 13,* 505–521.

Parrott, W. G. (1999). Multiple goals, self-regulation, and functionalism. In A. Fischer (Ed.), *Proceedings of the Xth Conference of the International Society for Research on Emotions* (pp. 37–40). Amsterdam: ISRE Publications.

Parrott, W. G., & Schulkin, J. (1993). Psychophysiology and the cognitive nature of the emotions. *Cognition & Emotion, 7,* 43–59.

Salovey, P., Hsee, C. K., & Mayer, J. D. (1993). Emotional intelligence and the self-regulation of affect. In D. M. Wegner & J. W. Pennebaker (Eds.), Handbook of mental control (pp. 258–277). Englewood Cliffs, NJ: Prentice-Hall.

Discussion Questions

1. Think of times when you have been embarrassed. In retrospect, can you think of ways in which you benefited from having been embarrassed? Try to think of benefits on each of the four levels of analysis proposed by Keltner and Haidt.

2. Think of times when you have become angry. Try to find one example of anger that served a productive purpose, and one example of anger that was mostly counterproduc-

tive. What determines whether your anger is functional or dysfunctional? What strategies could you follow in the future so that your regulation of anger exhibits more emotional intelligence?

3. What are some ways in which appraisals can affect whether emotions are functional or dysfunctional?

4. A cynic might assert that people are not truly altruistic when helping others, but rather are just trying to make themselves feel good and avoid feeling bad, which is really a sort of selfishness. Do you agree or not? How might studying the nature of emotions contribute to resolving this issue?

Suggested Readings

Frijda, N. H. (1986). *The emotions*. Cambridge, England: Cambridge University Press. This book is advanced, and it is not always easy reading, but it is undoubtedly a masterpiece, probably the most important book on the psychology of emotion in the past half century. It presents a theory of emotion that is noteworthy for its emphasis on the functions that emotions serve, and also for the extent to which self-regulation is conceived as being an integral part of emotions. It nicely extends the themes of the readings in this section for those who are ready for a more comprehensive treatment.

Armon-Jones, C. (1986). The social functions of emotion. In R. Harré (Ed.), *The social construction of emotions* (pp. 57–82). Oxford: Basil Blackwell. To the extent that cultures emphasize certain emotions and neglect others, it is often because of the functions emotions serve in a particular society. This chapter illustrates how emotional functions are understood from a social constructionist perspective.

Oatley, K. (1992). *Best laid schemes: The psychology of emotions*. New York: Cambridge University Press. Oatley's beautifully written book thoughtfully explores the idea that emotions usually function as prepackaged solutions to common problems, and that one way they function is by allocating priorities among the multiple goals that people pursue.

Frank, R. H. (1988). *Passions within reason*. New York: Norton. Economist Robert Frank ingeniously proposes ways in which certain intense, irrational, or otherwise seemingly dysfunctional states of mind could in fact serve adaptive functions. Frank's approach is helpful in developing an appreciation of the complex and sometimes unexpected ways that emotions can function in social life.

Parrott, W. G. (1993). Beyond hedonism: Motives for inhibiting good moods and for maintaining bad moods. In D. M. Wegner & J. W. Pennebaker (Eds.), *Handbook of mental control* (pp. 278–305). Englewood Cliffs, NJ: Prentice-Hall. The central argument of this chapter is that people have a variety of reasons to regulate their emotions, and that this variety is not always appreciated. Most research has assumed that people want to cheer themselves up, but almost no research has considered why people sometimes try to dampen their good moods or get themselves to feel bad moods, which people most certainly do. The reasons for inhibiting good moods and for maintaining bad moods mostly involve appreciating the adaptive functions of negative emotions and the undesirable effects of positive ones, thus demonstrating the link between functionalism and emotionally intelligent self-regulation.

Hochschild, A. R. (1979). Emotion work, feelings rules, and social structure. *American Journal of Sociology, 85,* 551–575. Hochschild's research on the sociology of emotion nicely demonstrates how that field often complements work in social psychology. Her research on societal "feeling rules" points out how emotions are often part of social roles, and she has coined the term "emotion work" to describe how people must manage their appearances and, indeed, their actual emotions, in order portray their roles effectively.

Batson, C. D., O'Quinn, K., Fultz, J., Vanderplas, M., & Isen, A. M. (1983). Influence of self-reported distress and empathy on egoistic versus altruistic motivation to help. *Journal of Personality and Social Psychology, 45,* 706–718. ALSO Cunningham, M. R. (1979). Weather, mood, and helping behavior: Quasi experiments with the sunshine Samaritan. *Journal of Personality and Social Psychology, 37,* 1947–1956. ALSO Cunningham, M. R., Steinberg, J., & Grev, R. (1980). Wanting to and having to help: Separate motivations for positive mood and guilt-induced helping. *Journal of Personality and Social Psychology, 38,* 181–192. These experiments investigate the influence of emotion on altruistic behavior. The first demonstrated that a person's emotional reaction to a person in need will influence the nature of that person's motivation to help and therefore the circumstances in which that person is likely to provide help. The second reported a series of naturalistic studies suggesting that sunshine and cloudiness, by affecting people's moods, can influence how helpful or generous they will tend to be. The third shows a distinction between helping that is motivated by good moods and helping that is motivated by feelings of guilt.

Baumeister, R. F., Heatherton, T. F., & Tice, D. M. (1994). *Losing control: How and why people fail at self-regulation.* San Diego, CA: Academic Press. This book provides a general reference on the topic of self-regulation. It addresses not only moods and emotions, but also thoughts, tasks, goals, and appetites. The book focuses on failures and how they arise.

Social Functions of Emotions at Four Levels of Analysis

Dacher Keltner • University of California, Berkeley

Jonathan Haidt • University of Virginia, Charlottesville, VA

In this paper we integrate claims and findings concerning the social functions of emotions at the individual, dyadic, group, and cultural levels of analysis. Across levels of analysis theorists assume that emotions solve problems important to social relationships in the context of ongoing interactions. Theorists diverge. however, in their assumptions about the origins, defining characteristics, and consequences of emotions, and in their preferred forms of data. We illustrate the differences and compatibilities among these levels of analysis for the specific case of embarrassment. We close by suggesting research strategies that incorporate a social-functional perspective.

The primary function is to mobilize the organism to deal quickly with important interpersonal encounters.

—Ekman, 1992, p. 171

Emotions are a primary idiom for defining and negotiating social relations of the self in a moral order.

—Lutz & White, 1986, p. 417

Early studies of emotion tended to focus on the "intrapersonal" aspects of emotion, mapping the determinants and characteristics of emotional response within the individual.[1] Many of the initial functional accounts of emotion similarly highlighted how emotions solve problems within the individual, for example as "interrupts" that prioritise multiple goals of the individual (e.g., Simon, 1967; Tomkins, 1962).

Several developments have led researchers to examine more closely the "interpersonal" functions of emotions. Researchers have begun to uncover how emotions structure relationships between parents and children (e.g., Bowlby, 1969), siblings (Dunn & Munn, 1985), and romantic partners (Levenson & Gottman, 1983). Emotions, such as anger and embarrassment, have been shown to have systematic effects on other individuals (e.g., Averill. 1980: Keltner & Buswell, 1997; Miller & Leary, 1992). Ethological studies suggest how emotions guide social interactions such as courtship and appeasement rituals (Eibl-Eibesfeldt, 1989). Finally, the growing contact between anthropologists (Abu-Lughod, 1986; Lutz & White, 1986) and psychologists (Haidt, Koller, & Dias, 1993; Markus & Kitayama, 1991; Mesquite & Frijda, 1992; Russell, 1991) in the new field of cultural psychology (Shweder, 1990) has led to greater awareness of the ways that emotions construct and are constructed by cultural practices and institutions.

---

[1] The obvious exception to this statement is the research on the interpersonal or inter-organismic functions or facial expressions, beginning with Darwin (1872/1965), and carried on since the 1960s by Ekman (1993), Izard (1977), and others.

These converging trends have inspired a wave of research and theory in a variety of disciplines on the connections between emotions and the social environment (Campos, Campos, & Barrett, 1989; Clark, 1990; Frijda, 1986; Kemper, 1993; Lutz & Abu-Lughod, 1990; de Rivera & Grinkis, 1956: Tooby & Cosmides, 1990). Frijda and Mesquita (1994) have written thoughtfully about the social functions of emotions, particularly anger, shame, and guilt. However, we think the time is right for a more general discussion of the assumptions, claims, and empirical findings that can be brought together into a social functional perspective on the emotions.

Our aims in this review are as follows. First, we discuss what it means to take a social functional approach in the study of emotion. Second, we review claims about the social functions of emotion in anthropology, ethology, history, psychology and sociology, highlighting illustrative empirical findings and conceptual issues. We then apply a social functional analysis to embarrassment, and conclude with a discussion of needed lines of empirical and theoretical inquiry.

We hope that this essay contributes some clarification to a growing field by distinguishing between social functions at four levels of analysis: (1) individual (intrapersonal); (2) dyadic (between two individuals); (3) group (a set of individuals that directly interact and has some temporal continuity); and (4) cultural (within a large group that shares beliefs, norms, and cultural models).[2] As we describe later, researchers working at each level differ in the systems they refer to, their preferred kinds of data, and the theoretical traditions within which they explain the origins and defining characteristics of emotions. Our aim will be to specify the differences and similarities in the accounts offered at each of the four levels, and to show how these levels can be put together to create a more complete understanding of the social functions of emotions.

Social-Functional Accounts of Emotion

Functional explanations, although a bit more recent to the field of emotion (Johnson-Laird & Oatley, 1992; Keltner & Gross, 1999), have long been used in biology and the social sciences. Functional explanations refer to the history of some object (e.g. behaviour or trait), as well as the regular consequences that benefit the system in which the object or trait is contained. As Merton (1968) stated, functional explanations hinge on "interpreting data by establishing their consequences for larger structures in which they are implicated".

Functional accounts vary according to the kind of system being analysed. For biological systems within an individual organism, a strong functionalism that specifies which features were shaped or selected for the consequences they bring about is usually appropriate. For example, the heart can only be understood as a pump working within a circulatory system "designed" by natural selection to fulfil a specific function—pumping blood at variable rates—within that larger system. At the cultural level of analysis, greater caution must be observed when making functional claims. Some institutions and cultural practices may have been designed to benefit the rich and powerful, as a Marxist might say, or to perpetuate themselves, as a meme theorist might say (Dawkins, 1976). But because there is no over-arching selection mechanism culling out inefficient or poorly adapted cultures, one cannot assume (as Malinowski did in his early pronouncements), that every practice and every artefact serves a "vital" function and "represents an indispensable part within a working whole" (Malinowski, 1926, quoted by Emmet, 1967). As a consequence, current cultural anthropologists generally employ a milder functionalism. They look at cultural facts and practices to see how they may play self-regulating or self-maintaining roles within larger systems, without assuming that every cultural practice has a conservative or stabilising effect. Because people have agency in a way that biological subsystems do not, it is now widely recognised that the best-laid plans of ruling elites are often contested and subverted by those they are meant to control.

Functional approaches to the emotions should therefore vary by level of analysis as well. Theorists working at the individual and dyadic levels of analysis, concerned with the effects of emotions within the individual or between interacting indi-

---

[2]Our framework was influenced by Averill's proposal (1992) that claims about emotions can be placed at the biological, psychological, or social levels of analysis. Although Averill's social level is clearly most relevant to the present paper, our review deals with studies that differ in their units of analysis, methods, and preferred forms of data, but would be classified at the social level. We therefore expanded Averill's social level into four different levels.

viduals (e.g., Bowlby, 1969; Ekman, 1992; Izard, l977; Nesse 1990; Ohman, 1986; Plutchik, 1980), espouse a functionalism that is consistent with adaptationist arguments found in evolutionary theory. These theorists argue that emotions were designed by natural selection, and that the core components of emotions are biologically based and genetically coded. Within an evolutionary framework it can be assumed that emotional expressions and action tendencies were selected because they produced consequences that improved the individual's inclusive fitness.[3]

Many theorists working at the group and cultural levels of analysis, in contrast, are engaged in what Geertz (1973) called an "interpretive science" in search of meaning, rather than an experimental science in search of laws and mechanisms. Emotions are seen as cultural products, constructed by individuals or groups in social contexts, and linked to constructs of the self, patterns of social hierarchy, language, or requirements of socioeconomic organisation (Lutz & Abu-Lughod, 1990). Social constructions often have consequences, but there is no equivalent to natural selection, selecting the emotional constructions with the best consequences. Rather, socially constructed emotions fit with social structures and other cultural facts in ways that make sense from an interpretive viewpoint, rather than an efficiency viewpoint.

Despite these differences, theorists at all levels of analysis address a few common questions, such as: Why do people have emotions? What are the consequences of having and expressing emotions, and how might those consequences reveal what emotions were designed or constructed to do? In answering these questions, theorists at all levels also share a few assumptions. First, social functional accounts of emotions assume that people are social by nature, and meet the problems of survival in relationships (e.g., Lutz & White, 1986). Second, social-functional accounts portray emotions as means of coordinating social interactions and relationships to address those problems (e.g., Averill, 1980; Eibl-Eibesfeldt, 1989; Ekman, 1992; Lutz & White, 1986; Tooby & Cosmides, 1990). Emotions are thought of as relatively automatic, involuntary, and rapid responses that help humans regulate, maintain, and use different social relationships, usually (though not always) for their own benefit (Bowlby, 1969; Frank, 1988; Hazan & Shaver, 1987; Lutz & White, 1986; Nesse, 1990; Johnson-Laird & Oatley, 1993). Third, emo-

tions are portrayed as dynamic processes that mediate the individual's relation to a continually changing social environment (Campos et al., 1989; Lazarus, 1991; Rosaldo, 1984), although the length of time that emotions are said to last varies from seconds or minutes (Ekman, 1992) to weeks or years (Frijda, Mesquita, Sonnemans, & Van Goozen, 1991).

Given these shared assumptions, there is every reason to believe that functional analyses of emotion will be "consilient" across levels (Wilson, 1998); that is, that emotion theorists can link and interrelate the four levels of analysis. We offer such a multilevel account of embarrassment near the end of this essay. But first, we summarise the claims and findings relevant to each of the four levels of analysis.

Social Functions of Emotions at the Individual Level of Analysis

At the individual level of analysis, researchers generally focus on the patterns of change of intraindividual components of emotion. The individual organism is the system with respect to which the functions of emotions are interpreted. Research investigates emotion-related changes in the endocrine, autonomic, and central nervous systems (Davidson, 1993; LeDoux, 1996; Levenson, 1992) and emotion-related appraisal, action tendency, memory, perception, and judgement (Clore, 1994; Frijda, 1986; Lazarus, 1991; Scherer, 1984; Schwarz, 1990; Smith & Ellsworth, 1985). The preferred forms of data include physiological measurement, self-reports of emotion phenomenology, and the effects of emotion on measures of judgement, memory, and social perception.

Although researchers interested in emotion-related physiology, experience, and cognition have tended to focus on patterns of intrapersonal change, some of these changes are understood as preparations for or reactions to specific problems that arise in social interaction. Specific brain structures and neurotransmitter systems underlie emotion-related play and dominant aggression (Panksepp, 1982). Some emotion-related action tendencies are motivated by social concerns, such as sharing or providing comfort (Frijda & Mesquita, 1994).

---

[3]Although any particular feature might have begun as an accidental "spandrel" (Gould, 1996) or as a "serviceable associated habit" (Darwin, 1872/1965), which was later shaped by selection pressures.

Theorists have proposed that emotional responses within the individual serve two broad social functions (Oatley & Jenkins, 1996). First, the conscious feeling of emotion produced by appraisal processes is believed to *inform the individual* about specific social events or conditions, typically needing to be acted upon and changed (Campos et al., 1989). Affect is a kind of information (Clore, 1994; Schwarz, 1990). As examples, theorists have proposed that the feeling of anger provides an assessment of the fairness of events (Solomon, 1990), love informs the individual of the level of commitment to another (Frank, 1988), happiness may signal the reproductive potential of certain social actions (Nesse, 1990), and shame informs the individual of his or her lower social status (Tangney, Miller, Flicker, & Barlow. 1996). As compelling as these claims seem, few empirical studies have directly examined whether specific emotions influence social judgements (for an exception, see Weiner, 1993, on the role of anger and sympathy in punitive judgements). Most studies of the effects of affect on cognition have examined more general positive and negative mood states (Schwarz, 1990).

Second, it has been claimed that certain emotion-related physiological (e.g., Levenson, 1992) and cognitive processes (Clore, 1994; Schwarz, 1990) *prepare the individual* to respond to problems or opportunities that arise in social interactions, even in the absence of any awareness of an eliciting event (Oatley & Jenkins, 1996). For example, empirical studies show that anger involves a shift of blood away from the internal organs towards the hands and arms (Levenson, Ekman, & Friesen, 1990), and heightened sensitivity to the injustices of other's actions (Keltner, Ellsworth, & Edwards, 1993), which presumably facilitates responses to threat or injustice. More generally, it follows that emotion-related physiology and cognition will be finely tuned to the specific nature of social events, as evident in brain-imaging studies showing that facial expressions of anger, disgust, fear, and sadness evoke activation in different brain regions in the perceiver (for a review, see Keltner & Ekman, 2000). It is also implied that emotional responses within the individual will change in response to changes in the emotion-eliciting event. A recent study reveals that the effects of anger on social cognition appear to diminish when the anger-producing injustice is redressed (Lerner, Goldberg, & Tetlock, 1998).

Social Functions of Emotions at the Dyadic Level of Analysis

At the dyadic level of analysis, researchers focus on how emotions organise the interactions of individuals in meaningful relationships. The interacting dyad is the system with respect to which the consequences of behaviours are interpreted. Researchers here focus on the communication of emotion in facial, vocal, and postural channels (e.g., DePaulo, 1992; Fernald, 1992; Fridlund. 1992: Klinnert, Campos, Sorce, Emde, & Svejda, 1983; Ohman, 1986: Scherer, 1986), properties of dyadic emotions, such as "contingency," "matching," "linkage," and "synchrony" (e.g., Field, Healy, Goldstein, & Uthertz, 1990; Levenson & Gottman, 1983; Tronick, 1989), and how emotions operate in other social interactions, such as greeting rituals (Eibl-Eibesfeldt, 1989), discourse (Bretherton, Fritz, Zahn-Waxler, & Ridgeway, 1986), and attachment and caregiving (Bowlby, 1969; Hazan & Shaver, 1957). The preferred forms of data are laboratory and naturalistic observations of interactions in humans and other species, and manipulations of emotional behaviour as social stimuli (e.g., Dimberg & Ohman, 1996).

Theorists working at the dyadic level of analysis have argued that emotional expressions *help individuals know others' emotions, beliefs, and intentions*, thus rapidly coordinating social interactions. Thus, relevant evidence indicates that the communication of emotion conveys information to receivers about senders': Current emotions (Ekman, 1993; Scherer. 1986), social intentions (Fridlund, 1992), and orientations towards the relationship, for example, as a dominant or submissive individual (Knutson, 1996). The communication of emotion also conveys information about objects in the environment: brief exposure to a model's fearful behaviour towards a phobic object (snake) leads observers to develop similar fearful responses to the phobic object (Mineka & Cook, 1993); and children rely on parents' facial emotion to assess whether ambiguous situations, stimuli, and people are safe or dangerous (Klinnert et al., 1983).

Second, emotional communication *evokes complementary and reciprocal emotions in others* that help individuals respond to significant social events. For example, research has documented that anger displays elicit fear-related responses, even when those displays are presented subliminally

(Dimberg & Ohman, 1996). Similarly, displays of distress elicit sympathy-related responses in observers (Eisenberg et al., 1989). In turn, emotions evoked in others are associated with behaviours, such as avoidance, helping, affiliation, and soothing, which help meet the goals of interacting individuals.

Third, emotions *serve as incentives or deterrents for other individuals' social behaviour* (Klinnert et al., 1983). Developmental research finds that emotional responses reward others' shifts in attention and goal-directed behaviour (Tronick, 1989), and thus play an important role in learning. In a similar vein, studies find that laughter occurs at the end of utterances (Provine, 1993), suggesting that laughter rewards desirable social behaviour.

Social Functions of Emotions at the Group Level of Analysis

At the group level of analysis, researchers focus on how emotions help collections of interacting individuals who share common identities and goals meet their shared goals, or the superordinate goals of the group. Groups, such as families, work groups, or social clubs, are the systems with respect to which the functions of emotion are interpreted. Researchers focus on phenomena such as: The differential distribution of emotion across group members (e.g., Collins, 1990; Kemper, 1993); collective emotion (Durkheim, 1915/1965; de Waal, 1996); emotion directed at other groups (e.g., Frijda & Mesquita, 1994); and role-related implications of emotional experience in group contexts (e.g., Clark, 1990). The preferred forms of data include the behaviour of group members in naturalistic and experimental concerts (e.g., Keltner, Young, Heerey, Oemig, & Monarch, 1998), ethnographies of small groups of people (Abu-Lughod, 1986; Briggs, 1970), and animal groups (e.g., de Waal, 1996), although such descriptions can sometimes be placed at the dyadic and cultural levels of analysis as well.

Although few empirical studies can be placed at the group level of analysis, theorists have made several provocative claims worthy of empirical study. First, emotions have been claimed to *help individuals define group boundaries and identify group members* (e.g., Durkheim, 1915/1965). Collective ecstasy and awe may give group members the sense of communal identity (Heise & O'Brien,

1993), whereas fear, hatred, and disgust towards nongroup members may sharpen group boundaries (Heise & O'Brien, 1993; Frijda & Mesquita, 1994). Consistent with these speculations, the experimental induction of fear of death has been shown to increase ingroup solidarity and outgroup derogation (Greenberg et al., 1990). Social anxiety additionally motivates individuals to avoid behaviours that would ostracise them from groups (Baumeister & Tice, 1990).

Within groups, the differential experience and display of emotion may *help individuals define and negotiate group-related roles and statuses* (e.g., Clark, 1990; Collins, 1990). Certain emotions are said to relate to, or constitute different roles and social statuses, for example, sympathy is part of playing a nurturant role, and displays of embarrassment mark lower status. Consistent with this view, empirical studies have documented association between an individual's status in a group and differences in joking and laughter (Coser, 1960), and embarrassment, anger, contempt, and fear (Keltner et al., 1998). Several cultures have a word that describes both a feeling, related to shame or embarrassment, and a deferential action directed at high-status individuals (*lajya* and *hasham*; see later). Additional research needs to establish whether the differential experience and display of emotion actually establishes an individual's role or status in a group, and whether these effects are independent of individual differences in the predisposition towards certain emotions.

Finally, recent animal evidence suggests that collective emotional behaviour may *help group members negotiate group-related problems.* In a suggestive study, chimpanzee groups were observed to engage in exuberant, celebratory affiliation just prior to the allocation of valuable resources (de Waal, 1996). This behaviour was believed to solidify social bonds that might be threatened by conflict related to distributing resources.

Social Functions of Emotions at the Cultural Level of Analysis

At the cultural level of analysis, researchers have focused on how emotions are shaped by historical and economic factors, on how emotions are embedded in cultural institutions and practices, and on the cultural norms and scripts for the proper expression and experience of emotions. The culture is the system with respect to which the functions of emotion are interpreted. Cultures are sometimes equated with nations or societies, but more often a culture is restricted to a community of shared meanings, as in D'Andrade's (1984, p. 116) treatment of culture as: "learned systems of meaning, communicated by means of natural language and other symbol systems, having representational, directive, and *affective functions*, and capable of creating cultural entities and particular senses of reality" (emphasis added). Culture not only creates the social world, it guides people in the affective reactions needed to function in that world. Some of the main areas of research include: How culture shapes emotion by shaping the self (Lutz, 1988; Markus & Kitayama, 1991); the social structures within which emotions are experienced (Abu-Lughod, 1986; Fiske, 1992); and culture-specific valuations of the experience and expression of emotion, for example in relation to gender, age, and social status (e.g., Lutz, 1990; Shweder & Haidt, 2000). The methodological emphasis is interpretive, and the preferred forms of data include ethnographies and "thick descriptions" (Geertz, 1973) of social practices; linguistic formations such as emotion lexicons (Russell, 1991), and metaphors (Lakoff; 1987); and historical documents and other meaning-laden cultural products, such as etiquette manuals (Elias, 1978) or cultural myths and legends (Miller, 1997).

Theorists working at the cultural level of analysis have attributed several social functions to emotion, some of which overlap with those at the group level of analysis. First, emotions are claimed to *play a critical role in the precesses by which individuals assume cultural identities*. Culture-specific concepts of emotional deviance are believed to motivate culturally appropriate behaviour (Thoits, 1985). Embarrassment (Goffman, 1967) motivates conformity and the proper playing of one's roles, whereas disgusts motivates the avoidance and shunning of people who violate key values within a culture (Rozin, Haidt, & McCauley, 2000).

Emotions are also embedded in socialisation practices that *help children learn norms and values of their culture*. For example, developmental (e.g., Bretherton, et al., 1986; Dunn & Munn, 1985) and cross-cultural studies (e.g., White, 1990) indicate that emotional conflicts engage individuals in conversations about cultural notions of right and wrong and redressing wrongdoing. Displays of disgust by parents, for example, are likely to be

important in toilet training and negative socialisation (Rozin et al., 2000). The emotional reactions of parents and other "local guardians of the moral order" (Shweder, Mahapatra, & Miller, 1987) may be the most important guides that children use in figuring out the contours of their moral world.

Finally, some theorists have asserted that cultural constructions of emotional experience *reify and perpetuate cultural ideologies and power structures* (e.g., Hochschild, 1990). Much as at the group level, the selective experience and expression of emotion for certain groups justifies their position with a culture. Thus, drawing on stereotypes of the emotions of subordinated groups, Lutz has argued that cultural discourses about female emotionality relegate women to positions of subordinate status (Lutz, 1990). It would be interesting to document how gender stereotypes of emotion are indeed used to justify subordinate positions for women, and whether these stereotypes actually create gender differences in emotional response.

Case Study: The Social Functions of Embarrassment

We have reviewed evidence and theory about the many social functions of emotion. Emotions inform people about social events and prepare their bodies and minds for action. Emotions co-ordinate social interactions. Emotions help individuals define their identities and play their roles within groups, and emotions mark or strengthen boundaries between groups. Finally, emotions simultaneously create and are shaped by cultural practices and symbol systems. All of these functions, interpreted with respect to four different kinds of systems, can occur simultaneously and in mutually interlocking ways. Although conflicts or incompatibilities across levels are possible in principle, in practice the social functions of emotion at one level are likely to work in tandem with the social functions of the adjoining levels. To illustrate the compatibility and consilience of these various functional perspectives, we will work through the case of embarrassment in detail.

Initially, most theorists ignored the social functions of embarrassment. Darwin's analysis of embarrassment focused on the blush, which he posited was simply a side-effect of social attention

(Darwin, 1872/1965). Although Goffman (1967) hinted at certain functions of embarrassment, he primarily concentrated upon its chaotic display and painful experience. Recent studies of the causes, characteristics, and social consequences of embarrassment, however, have led researchers to claim that embarrassment serves an appeasement function, reconciling social relations following transgressions of social norms (Keltner & Buswell, 1997; Miller & Leary, 1992). At each level of analysis, we see that embarrassment serves this appeasement function in a different way.

At the individual level of analysis, self-report narrative studies have revealed that prototypical forms of embarrassment typically follow some disruption in social interactions (Parrott & Smith, 1991; Silver, Sabini, & Parrott, 1987). Embarrassment is defined by the sense of personal failure and lowered status (e.g., Tangney et al., 1996), which may signal to the individual which social actions to avoid, thus motivating participants to stay within the bounds of appropriate behaviour. Consistent with this claim, evidence indicates that people will forego personal gain to avoid embarrassment, and once embarrassed, they engage in corrective behaviour that restores their social standing (see Keltner & Buswell, 1997).

Social transgressions require some form of appeasement or repair. Empirical studies at the dyadic level of analysis indicate that the display of embarrassment brings about reconciliation. Embarrassment is signalled by blushing, a controlled smile, face touching, downward movements of the head and eyes, and inhibited speech (Keltner & Buswell, 1997). These behaviours have been shown to signal the embarrassed person's commitment to social norms, and to prompt forgiveness in others (for a review, see Keltner, Young, & Buswell, 1997).

Theorists working at the group level of analysis have proposed, consistent with our general review, that embarrassment helps establish and maintain group hierarchies and norms (e.g., Clark, 1990). How might this work? One possibility is that embarrassment is embedded in group practices, which have specific consequences at the individual and dyadic levels of analysis. Group practices, such as teasing and shaming, produce different levels of embarrassment in group members (Keltner et al., 1998). For individuals, the differential experience of embarrassment in group contexts may signal their positions in the group hierarchy. Dyadic interactions in teasing and shaming may lead to reconciliation and enhanced group bonds.

Finally, recent ethnographies reveal how self-conscious emotions related to embarrassment are involved in the assumption of culturally appropriate identities and the perpetuation of cultural norms and values. Awlad-Ali Bedouins and Oriya Indians have long traditions of strong patriarchal authority in which open expressions of female sexuality bring dishonour and threaten to destabilise masculine authority. When in the presence of high-ranking men, it is considered a virtue for women to display *hasham* among the Awlad-Ali (Abu-Lughod, 1986) and to display *lajya* in Orissa, India (Menon & Shweder, 1994). Expressions of *hasham* and *lajya* honour patriarchal ideologies and hierarchies, and the possession of a well-cultivated liability to experience and express these emotions is a path to female honour and virtue in both cultures. Recent cross-cultural work demonstrates that if *lajya* must be equated with an English emotion word, that word is embarrassment (Haidt & Keltner, 1999). However, because North American middle class culture values hierarchy less and the expression of female sexuality more than do Oriyas, the experience of embarrassment cannot be equated with the experience of *lajya*. Embarrassment for Americans seems to lack the element of virtue and even pride that can be associated with the experiences of *lajya* and *hasham*.

Research Strategies for the Study of Social Functions of Emotions

We have attempted to place many lines of research on the social functions of. emotion into a taxonomy of four levels of analysis: Individual, dyadic, group, and cultural, all of which are complementary and interrelatable. In this final section, we look to the future and ask how a social-functional perspective, cognisant of different levels of analysis, can guide research. Most generally, we believe that integrative, cross-disciplinary work may be furthered by working at multiple levels of analysis, looking to adjoining levels for ideas and hypotheses. In terms of concrete research questions, we believe a social functional perspective points to two general issues that have recently begun to receive systematic attention.

First, social functional accounts assume that emotions solve social problems. Emotions arise in response to social problems (e.g., injustice, establishing attachments, negotiating status hierarchies), and presumably change as those problems (or opportunities) are met. The dynamic relations between elements of emotional response and changing social problems merit attention. At the individual level of analysis, emotions can be linked to specific kinds and features of changing social events (e.g., Kemper, 1993). At the dyadic level of analysis, research should continue to examine how specific emotions emerge in response to relational problems, as has been done in studies relating the emergence of adolescent social hierarchies and the development of embarrassment, shame, and social anxiety (Ohman, 1986). Finally, it should be possible to predict and measure changes in the emotional life of groups and cultures as new social problems arise. For example, as individualism, commercialism, and changing sex roles spread through the young generation of a traditional society, do elders try to elicit more shame, and engage in more teasing and shaming rituals? With so much of Asia rapidly adopting Western modes of commerce, dress, and even housing, it should be possible to document changes in the distribution and valuation of emotions (including patterns of use, and emotion concepts) over the course of a decade.

Second, social functional perspectives posit that inferences about social functions derive from analyses of the systematic consequences of emotions. Each emotion should have systematic effects on other individuals and features of the social environment that, for the most part, await discovery. Model research and relevant analytic procedures for ascertaining the social consequences of emotions have emerged in the study of more naturalistic emotional interactions between siblings (e.g., Dunn & Munn, 1985), romantic relationships (Levenson & Gottman, 1983), and parent-child interactions (e.g., Field et al., 1990). Experimental manipulations of emotional behaviour, as has been done in studies of the responses evoked by depressive maternal style (e.g., Cohn & Tronick, 1983) and posed facial expressions (Dimberg & Ohman, 1996), have the promise of making similar contributions to an understanding of the social functions of emotions.

In sum, the expansion of scholarship from intrapersonal to interpersonal functions of emotion points to several promising lines of enquiry that may integrate the insights and strengths of different disciplines. This conceptually and methodologically varied work can be understood and integrated by distinguishing among the individual, dyadic, group, and cultural levels of analysis. All four are necessary to understand the social functions of emotions.

REFERENCES

Abu-Lughod, L. (1986). *Veiled sentiments*. Berkeley. CA: University of California Press.

Averill, J. R. (1980). A constructivist view of emotion. In K. Plutchik & H. Kellerman (Eds.), *Emotions: Theory Research, and experience* (pp. 305–339). New York: Academic Press.

Averill, J. R. (1992). The structural bases of emotional behavior. In M. S. Clark (Ed.), *Emotion* (pp. 1–24). Newbury Park. CA: Sage.

Baumeister, R. F., & Tice, D. M. (1990). Anxiety and social exclusion. *Journal of Social and Clinical Psychology, 9,* 165–195.

Bowlby, J. (1969). *Attachment*. New York: Basic Books.

Bretherton, I., Fritz, J., Zahn-Waxler, C., & Ridgeway, D. (1986). Learning to talk about emotions: A functional perspective. *Child Development, 57,* 529–548.

Briggs, J. L. (1970). *Never in anger*. Cambridge. MA: Harvard University Press.

Campos, J. J., Campos, R. G., & Barrett, K. C. (1989). Emergent themes in the study of emotional development and emotion regulation. *Developmental Psychology , 25,* 394–402.

Clark, C. (1990). Emotions and the mircropolitics in everyday life: Some patterns and paradoxes of "Place.". In T. D. Kemper (Ed.), *Research agendas in the sociology of emotions* (pp. 305–334). Albany, NY: State University of New York Press.

Clore, G. (1994). Why emotions are felt. In P. Ekman & K. J. Davidson (Eds.), *The nature of emotion* (pp. 103–111). New York: Cambridge University Press.

Cohn, J. F., & Tronick, E. Z. (1983). Three month old infants' reactions to simulated maternal depression. *Child Development, 54,* 185–193.

Collins, R. C. (1990). Stratification, emotional energy, and the transient emotions. In T. D. Kemper (Ed.), *Research agendas in the sociology of emotions* (pp. 27–57). Albany, NY: State University of New York Press.

Coser, R. L. (1960). Laughter among colleagues. *Psychiatry, 2,* 81–95.

D'Andrade, R. G. (1984). Cultural meaning systems. In R. A. Shweder & R. A. LeVine (Eds.), *Culture theory*. Cambridge, UK: Cambridge University Press.

Darwin, C. (1965). *The expression of the emotions in man and animals*. Chicago, IL: University of Chicago Press. (Original work published 1872)

Davidson, R. J. (1997). Parsing affective space: Perspectives from neuropsychology and psychophysiology. *Neuropsychology, 7,* 464–475.

Dawkins, R. (1976). *The selfish gene*. London: Oxford University Press.

DePaulo, B. M. (1992). Nonverbal behavior and self-presentation. *Psychological Bulletin, 111,* 203–243.

de Rivera, J., & Grinkis, C. (1986). Emotions as social relationships. *Motivation and Emotion, 10.*

de Waal, F. B. M. (1996). *Good natured.* Cambridge, MA: Harvard University Press.

Dimberg, U., & Ohman, A. (1996). Behold the wrath: Psychophysiological responses to facial stimuli. *Motivation and Emotion, 20,* 149–182.

Dunn, J., & Munn, P. (1985). Becoming a family member: Family conflict and the development of social understanding in the second year. *Child development, 56,* 480–492.

Durkheim, E. (1965). *The elementary forms of the religious life* (J. W. Swain, Trans.). New York: The Free Press. (Original work published 1915)

Eibl-Eibesfeldt, I. (1989). *Human ethology.* New York: Aldine de Gruyter.

Eisenberg, N., Fabes, R. A., Miller, P. A., Fultz, J., Shell, R., Mathy, R. M., & Reno, R. R. (1989). Relation of sympathy and distress to prosocial behavior: A mulitmethod study. *Journal of Personality and Social Psychology, 57,* 55–66.

Ekman, P. (1992). An argument for basic emotions. *Cognition and Emotion, 6,* 169–200.

Ekman, P. (1993). Facial expression and emotion. *American Psychologist, 48,* 384–392.

Elias, N. (1978). *The history of manners. The civilizing process: Vol.* I (E. Jephcott, Trans.) New York: Pantheon. (Original work published 1939)

Emmet, D. M. (1967). Functionalism in sociology. *The encyclopedia of philosophy.* New York: Macmillan.

Fernald, A. (1992). Human maternal vocalizations to infants as biologically relevant signals: An evolutionary perspective. In J. H. Barkow, L. Cosmides, & J. Tooby (Eds.), *The adapted mind* (pp. 391–428). New York: Oxford University Press.

Field, T., Healy, B., Goldstein, S., & Guthertz, M. (1990). Behavior-state matching and synchrony in mother-infant interactions of depressed versus non-depressed dyads. *Developmental Psychology, 26,* 7–14.

Fiske, R. H. (1992). Four elementary forms of sociality: Framework for a unified theory of social relations. *Psychological Review, 99,* 689–723.

Frank, R. H. (1988). *Passions with reason.* New York: Norton.

Fridlund, A. J. (1992). The behavioral ecology and sociality of human faces. In M. S. Clark (Ed.), *Emotion.* Newbury Park, CA: Sage.

Frijda, N. (1986). *The emotions.* Cambridge. UK: Cambridge University Press.

Frijda, N. H., & Mesquita. B. (1994). The social roles and functions of emotions. In S. Kitayama & H. Marcus (Eds.), *Emotion and culture: Empirical studies of mutual influenced* (pp. 51–87). Washington, DC: American Psychological Association.

Frijda, N. N., Mesquita, B., Sonnemans, J., & Van Goozen. S. (1991). The duration of affective phenomena or emotions, sentiments, and passions. *International Review of Studies on Emotion, 1,* 187–225.

Geertz, C. (1973). Thick description: Toward an interpretive theory of culture. In C. Geertz (Ed.), *The interpretation of cultures.* New York: Basic Books.

Goffman, E. (1967). *Interaction ritual: Essays on face-to-face behavior.* Garden City, NY: Anchor.

Gould, S. J. (1996). *The mismeasure of man* (rev. ed.). New York: Norton.

Greenberg, J., Pyszczynski, T., Solomon, S., Rosenblatt, A.

V. M., Kirkland, S., & Lyon, D. (1990). Evidence for terror management theory: II. The effects of mortality salience on reactions to those who threaten or bolster the cultural worldview. *Journal of Personality and Social Psychology, 58,* 308–318.

Haidt, J., & Keltner, D. (1999). Culture and facial expression: Open-ended methods find more faces and a gradient of recognition. *Cognition and Emotion, 13,* 225–266.

Haidt, J., Koller, S., & Dias, M. (1993). Affect, culture, and morality, or is it wrong to eat your dog? *Journal of Personality and Social Psychology, 65,* 613–628.

Hazan, C., & Shaver, P (1987). Romantic love conceptualized as an attachment process. *Journal of Personality and Social Psychology, 52,* 511–524.

Heise, D. R., & O'Brien, J. (1993). Emotion expression in groups. In M. Lewis & J. M. Haviland (Eds.), *Handbook of emotions* (pp. 489–498). New York: Guilford Press.

Hochschild, A. R. (1990). Ideology and emotion management. In T. D. Kemper (Ed.), *Research agendas in the sociology of emotions* (pp. 117–142). Albany, NY: State University of New York Press.

Izard, C. E. (1977). *Human emotions.* New York: Plenum.

Johnson-Laird, P. N., & Oatley, K. (1992). Basic emotions, rationality, and folk theory. *Cognition and Emotion, 6,* 201–223.

Keltner, D., & Buswell, B. N. (1997). Embarrassment: Its distinct form and appeasement functions. *Psychological Bulletin, 122,* 250–270.

Keltner, D., & Ekman, P. (2000). Facial expressions of emotion. In J. Haviland & M. Lewis (Eds.), *Handbook of emotions (2nd ed.).* New York: Guilford Press.

Keltner, D., Ellsworth, P. C., & Edwards, K. (1993). Beyond simple pessimism: Effects of sadness and anger on social perception. *Journal of Personality and Social Psychology, 64,* 740–752.

Keltner, D., & Gross, J. (1999). Functional accounts of emotion. *Cognition and Emotion, 13,* 467–480.

Keltner, D., Young. R., & Buswell, B. N. (1997). Appeasement in human emotion, social practice, and personality. *Aggressive Behavior, 23,* 359–374.

Keltner, D., Young, R. C., Oemig, C., Heerey, E., & Monarch, N. D. (1998). Teasing in hierarchical and intimate relations. *Journal of Personality and Social Psychology, 75,* 1231–1247.

Kemper, T. D. (1993). Sociological models in the explanation of emotions. In M. Lewis & J. M. Haviland (Eds.), *Handbook of emotions* (pp. 41–51). New York: Guilford Press.

Klinnert, M., Campos, J., Sorce, J., Emde, R., & Svejda, M. (1983). Emotions as behavior regulators: Social referencing in infants. In R. Plutchik & H. Kellerman (Eds.), *Emotion theory, research, and experience: Vol. 2. Emotions in early development* (pp. 57–68). New York: Academic Press.

Knutson, B. (1996). Facial expressions of emotion influence interpersonal trait inferences. *Journal of Nonverbal Behavior 20,* 165–182.

Lakoff, G. (1987). *Women, fire and dangerous things.* Chicago: University of Chicago Press.

Lazarus, R. S. (1991). *Emotion and adaptation.* New York: Oxford University Press.

LeDoux, J. (1996). *The emotional brain.* New York: Simon & Schuster.

Lerner, J. S., Goldberg, J. H., & Tetlock, P. E. (1998). Sober second thought: The effects of accountability, anger, and authoritarianism on attributions of responsibility. *Personality and Social Psychology Bulletin, 24,* 563–574.

Levenson, R. W. (1992). Autonomic nervous system differences among emotions. *Psychological Science, 3,* 23–27.

Levenson, R. W., Ekman, P., & Friesen, W. V. (1990). Voluntary facial action generates emotion-specific autonomic nervous system activity. *Psycholphysiology, 27,* 363–384.

Levenson, R. W., & Gottman, J. M. (1983). Marital Interaction: Physiological linkage and affective exchange. *Journal of Personality and Social Psychology, 45,* 587–597.

Lutz, C. (1988). *Unnatural emotions.* Chicago: University of Chicago Press.

Lutz, C. (1990). Engendered emotion: Gender, power, and the rhetoric of emotional control in American discourse. In C. A . Lutz & L. Abu-Lughod (Eds.), *Language and the politics of emotion* (pp. 69–91). New York: Cambridge University Press.

Lutz, C. A., & Abu-Lughod, L. (1990). *Language and the politics of emotion.* New York: Cambridge University Press.

Lutz, C., & White, G. (1986). The anthropology of emotions. *Annual Review of Anthropology, 15,* 405–436.

Malinowski, B. (1926). Anthropology. *Encyclopedia Britannica* (13th ed.), supplement I.

Markus, H. R., & Kitayama. S. (1991). Culture and the self: Implications for cognition, emotion, and motivation. *Psychological Review, 98,* 224–253.

Menon, U., & Shweder, R. A. (1994). Kali's tongue: Cultural psychology, cultural consensus and the meaning of "shame" in Orissa, India. In H. Markus & S. Kitayama (Eds.), *Culture and the emotions* (pp. 241–284). Washington, DC: American Psychological Association.

Merton, R. K. (1968). *Social theory and social structure.* New York: Free Press.

Mesquita, B., & Frijda, N. (1992). Cultural variations in emotions: A review. *Psychological Bulletin, 112,* 179–204.

Miller, R. S., & Leary, M. R. (1992). Social sources and interactive functions of embarrassment. In M. Clark (Ed.), *Emotion and social behavior* (pp. 322–339). New York: Sage.

Miller, W. I. (1997). *The anatomy of disgust.* Cambridge, MA: Harvard University Press.

Mineka, S., & Cook, M. (1993). Mechanisms involved in the observational conditioning of fear. *Journal of Experimental Psychology : General, 122,* 23–38.

Nesse, R. (1990). Evolutionary explanations of emotions. *Human Nature, 1,* 261–289.

Oatley, K., & Jenkins, J. M. (1996). *Understanding emotions.* Oxford, UK: Blackwell.

Ohman, A. (1986). Face the beast and fear the face: Animal and social fears as prototypes for evolutionary analysis of emotion. *Psychophysiology, 23,* 123–145.

Panksepp, J. (1982). Toward a general psychobiological theory of emotions. With commentaries. *Brain and Behavioral Sciences, 5,* 407–467.

Parrott, W. G., & Smith, S. (1991). Embarrassment: Actual vs. typical cases, classical vs. prototypical representations. *Cognition and Emotion, 5,* 467–488.

Plutchik, R. (1980). *Emotion: A psychobioevolutionary synthesis.* New York: Harper & Row.

Provine, R. R. (1993). Laughter punctuates speech: Linguistic, social, and gender contexts of laughter. *Ethology, 95,* 291–298.

Rosaldo, M. (1984). Toward an anthropology of self and feeling. In R. Shweder & R. LeVine (Eds.), *Culture theory* (pp. 137–157). Cambridge, UK: Cambridge University Press.

Rozin, P., Haidt, J., & McCauley, C. (2000). Disgust. In M. Lewis & J. Haviland (Eds.), *Handbook of emotions (2nd ed.).* New York: Guilford Press.

Russell, J. A. (1991). Culture and the categorization of emotions. *Psychological Bulletin, 110,* 426–450.

Scherer, K. R. (1984). On the nature and function of emotion: A component process approach. In K. Scherer & P. Ekman (Eds.), *Approaches to emotion* (pp. 293–318). Hillsdale, NJ: Lawrence Erlbaum.

Scherer, K. R. (1986). Vocal affect expression: A review and a model for future research. *Psychological Bulletin, 99,* 143–165.

Schwarz, N. (1990). Feelings as information: Informational and motivational functions of affective states. In E. T. Higgins & R. M. Sorrentino (Eds.), *Handbook of motivation and cognition* (Vol. 2. pp. 527–561). New York: Guilford Press.

Shweder, R. (1990). Cultural psychology: What is it? In J. Stigler, R. Shweder, & G. Herdt (Eds.), *Cultural psychology: The Chicago symposium on culture and human development* (pp. 1–43). New York: Cambridge University Press.

Schweder, R. A., & Haidt, J. (2000). The cultural psychology of the emotions. In M. Lewis & J. M. Haviland (Eds.), *Handbook of emotions (2nd ed.).* New York: Guilford Press.

Shweder, R. A., Mahapatra, M., & Miller, J. (1987). Culture and moral development. In J. Kagan & S. Lamb (Eds.), *The emergence of morality in young children* (pp. 1–83). Chicago, IL: University of Chicago Press.

Silver, M., Sabini, J., & Parrott, W. G. (1987). Embarrassment: A dramaturgic account. *Journal of the Theory of Social Behaviour, 17,* 47–61.

Simon, H. A. (1967). Motivational and emotional controls of cognition. *Psychological Bulletin, 74,* 29–39.

Smith, C., & Ellsworth, P. (1985). Patterns of cognitive appraisal in emotion. *Journal of Personality and Social Psychology, 48,* 813–838.

Solomon, R. C. (1990). *A passion for justice.* Reading. MA: Addison-Wesley.

Tangney, J. P., Miller, R. S., Flicker, L., & Barlow, D. H. (1996). Are shame, guilt and embarrassment distinct emotions? *Journal of Personality and Social Psychology, 70,* 1256–1269.

Thoits, P. A. (1985). Self-labeling processes in mental illness and the role of emotional deviance. *American Journal of Sociology, 91,* 221–249.

Tomkins, S. (1962). *Affect, imagery, consciousness: Vol. I. The positive affects.* New York: Springer.

Tooby, J., & Cosmides, L. (1990). The past explains the present: Emotional adaptations and the structure of ancestral environments. *Ethology and Sociobiology, 11,* 375–424.

Tronick, E. Z. (1989). Emotions and emotional communication in infants. *American Psychologist, 44,* 112–119.

White, G. M. (1990). Moral discourse and the rhetoric of emotions. In C. A. Lutz & L. Abu-Lughod (Eds.), *Language and the politics of emotion* (pp 46–68). New York: Cambridge University Press.

Weiner, B. (1993). On sin versus sickness: A theory of perceived responsibility and social motivation. *American Psychologist, 48,* 957–965.

Wilson, E. O. (1998). *Consilience: The unity of knowledge.* New York: Knopf.

Emotional Intelligence and the Self-Regulation of Affect

Peter Salovey, Christopher K. Hsee and John D. Mayer

This chapter explores how individuals try to control their own feelings and the feelings of other people. In the service of this goal, we review, primarily, two lines of research. First we discuss a framework for understanding emotional regulation suggested by Salovey and Mayer (1990) called *emotional intelligence,* which is concerned with a set of skills expected to contribute to the accurate appraisal and expression of emotion in oneself and in others, the effective regulation of emotion in self and others, and the use of feelings to motivate, plan, and achieve in one's life. The emotional intelligence framework suggests that there may be individual differences in people's abilities to exert effective control over their emotional lives. Such individual differences will be the focus of the second section of this chapter. Finally, in the third section, we look at some behavioral strategies employed to self-regulate feelings. In this context, we present a theory of satisfaction proposed by Hsee (e.g., Hsee & Abelson, 1991; Hsee, Abelson, & Salovey, 1991), which claims that pleasure is determined not just by the value of outcomes that accrue to individuals but by their change from some baseline over time as well as the pattern of that change over time. We conclude by reviewing some research in the area of prosocial behavior suggesting that, at times, helping others may be usefully viewed as an affective self-regulatory strategy.

The Emotional Intelligence Framework

Emotional intelligence was proposed as a general framework that allows us to identify specific skills needed to understand and experience emotions most adaptively (Mayer & Salovey, 1993; Salovey & Mayer, 1990). More formally, we define emotional intelligence as "the ability to monitor one's own and others' feelings and emotions, to discriminate among them, and to use this information to guide one's thinking and actions" (Salovey & Mayer, 1990, p. 189).

Although, historically, scientists of human intelligence often contrasted rational thought with emotional experience (see summaries in Schaffer, Gilmer, & Schoen, 1940; Woodworth, 1940; Young, 1936), modern investigators recognize that emotions can serve as a source of information to individuals (cf. Schwarz, 1990), and individuals are more or less skilled at processing this information. For instance, Gardner (1983) described what he called personal intelligence in part as "access to one's own feeling life—one's range of affects or emotions: the capacity instantly to effect discriminations among these feelings and, eventually, to label them, to enmesh them in symbolic codes, to draw upon them as a means of understanding and guiding one's behavior" (p. 239).

The idea that there are different types of intelligences has a long history in psychology. In particular, intelligence theorists have struggled over how to define and measure the domain labeled *social intelligence* in which we would place emotional intelligence. We have reviewed the place of emotional intelligence in social intelligence frameworks elsewhere (Salovey & Mayer, 1990), and so we will not recapitulate that discussion here. However, it should be noted that whereas traditional conceptualizations of social intelligence largely ignored considerations of emotion, more modern work in this area has not (e.g., Cantor & Kihlstrom, 1987; Epstein & Meier, 1989; Sternberg & Smith, 1985). Briefly, emotional intelligence can be described in three primary domains, outlined in Figure 10.1: the accurate appraisal and expression of emotion (in self and in other people), the adaptive regulation of emotions (in self and in other people), and the utilization of emotions to plan, create, and motivate action.

Accurate Appraisal and Expression of Emotion

Perhaps most fundamental to the effective use of information provided by emotional experiences is the ability to recognize and identify accurately what one is feeling. Work with young children suggests that the ability to make faces that appropriately communicate an emotion to others as well as the ability to recognize these facial expressions in return increases linearly with age. Children as young as three years are able to pose voluntarily a facial expression suggested to them by an adult (Lewis, Sullivan, & Vasen, 1987). At about four years of age, children can identify correctly the emotion suggested by about half of the faces that they see. By six years of age, they are correct 75

percent of the time. For some emotions, such as happiness and disgust, correct identification on nearly every presentation is seen in children as young as four years (Profyt & Whissell, 1991).

Despite the skills demonstrated by young children, we all know adults who seem oblivious to their own feelings and insensitive to those of others (see Salovey & Mayer, 1991, for examples at annual psychology convention social hours). For instance, some individuals have great difficulty identifying the feelings communicated to them through the facial expressions of other people (Buck, 1984; Campbell, Kagan, & Krathwohl, 1971; Kagan, 1978; Rosenthal, Hall, DiMatteo, Rogers, & Archer, 1979). People also vary in their ability to use their own facial expressions (and other nonverbal behaviors) to communicate what they are feeling (Buck, 1979; Friedman, Prince, Riggio, & DiMatteo, 1980).

There are also vast differences in the ability to articulate feelings into words. Children begin to learn emotion words at quite a young age (Bretherton, Fritz, Zahn-Waxler, & Ridgeway, 1986). In one study, 74 five-, nine-, and thirteen-year-old boys and girls were able collectively to generate 1,169 synonyms for just seven "basic" emotions (Whissell & Nicholson, 1991). Despite such fluency with emotional language demonstrated by children, some adults grope wildly with the affective lexicon when trying to report on their feelings. Others, of course, are much more facile.

At the extreme, there seems to be a group of individuals who are simply unable to use words to describe feelings at all. Labeled *alexithymics* (literally, "no words for feelings"), these individuals are thought to be at risk for a variety of psychological disorders, especially psychosomatic illnesses, though the construct has been difficult to measure reliably (Apfel & Sifneos, 1979; Krystal, Giller, & Cicchetti, 1986; Sifneos, 1972, 1973; Taylor, 1984; Thayler-Singer, 1977).

In our recent work, we have been able to identify individuals who vary with respect to how much attention they pay to and the clarity with which they perceive their moods. (The instrument is called the Trait Meta-Mood Scale and will be described later; Salovey, Mayer, Goldman, Turvey, & Palfai, 1995.) Such perceptions may be related to the tendency to ruminate after distressing experiences and the frequency with which physical symptoms are reported in stressful situations (Goldman, Kraemer, Salovey, & Mayer, 1992). We

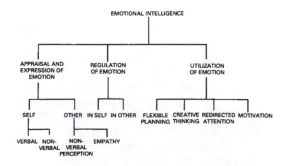

FIGURE 10.1 ■ Domains of Emotional Intelligence (Adapted from Salovey & Mayer, 1990).

will return to these studies later in the chapter when we discuss dispositional precursors to affective self-regulation.

Adaptive Regulation of Emotion

Historically, the ways in which people seek to understand and then take control over their emotional experiences has largely been ignored by researchers (but see Campos, Campos, & Barrett, 1989; Stein & Trabasso, 1989, for some recent exceptions). Perhaps this inattention was due to William James's (1890) belief that the influences of emotion terminate in the subject's own body and do not affect external events. Yet people engage in all kinds of activities to regulate their moods. They may try to control their thoughts, drink alcohol, seek the company of others, or jog (see Morris & Reilly, 1987, for a review, as well as Parrott, 1993).

The ability to regulate one's own feelings is recognized by children as young as four years old. For instance, Brown, Covell, and Abramovitch (1991) asked youngsters to listen to stories in which they might experience happy, sad, or angry emotions. They then indicated various cognitive (e.g., "try to think to yourself, 'it wasn't as bad as all that'") and behavioral (e.g., "go and do something that you would really like to do") strategies they would use in order to regulate that emotional experience. Four- to six-year-old children in this study were as likely to recognize effective emotion-control strategies as were teenagers. Later in this chapter we focus on two ways in which individuals attempt to regulate their emotions behaviorally—arranging the order of events and providing help to other people.

Emotional intelligence, however, includes more than just an ability to regulate feelings in oneself. It also pertains to the ability to regulate adaptively, the feelings of other people. We have all had the experience of being moved by a stirring orator, finding ourselves impressed by the professional demeanor of a job candidate, or becoming attracted to someone we hardly know. Some people seem to know how to create emotions in others that serve them in adaptive ways.

In the extreme, manipulating the feelings of another person for one's own gain may seem sociopathic or Machiavellian, but in less extreme situations we may simply label such individuals as "charismatic" or, merely, charming (Wasielewski, 1985). Moreover, some people simply feel good when they make others feel good, with no ulterior motive. The effective regulation of the feelings of other people has not been systematically investigated, although it does fall under the purview of impression management (Goffman, 1959). Often, a most advantageous strategy is to focus on the feelings of other people and inhibit a display of one's true emotional reactions to some situation. For example, Hochschild (1983) has studied the ways in which certain professionals, such as airline flight attendants, strongly regulate their displays of feelings and focus on and attempt to regulate the feelings of others. Such behavior is thought to extract a personal psychological toll and may even be a health hazard (Pennebaker, 1989; Pennebaker & Susman, 1988). Emotional regulation may be accentuated among helping professionals, which may account for their high incidence of burnout.

Utilization of Emotion-Based Knowledge

Individuals also differ in their ability to harness their own emotions to solve problems. Moods, generally, influence problem-solving outcomes. For instance, changes in feelings may facilitate the generation of multiple options (Mayer, 1986). And certain emotions may facilitate different kinds of problem-solving tasks. Creative and inductive reasoning, for example, may be improved by happy moods (Isen, Daubman, & Nowicki, 1987; Isen, Johnson, Mertz, & Robinson, 1985), and tasks requiring deductive reasoning and the careful consideration of multiple options may be facilitated by sad moods. In a recent set of studies, Palfai and Salovey (1993–1994) found that happy moods interfered with performance on a deductive reasoning task (such as those found on the LSAT exam), whereas sad moods led to slower performance on inductive reasoning problems, such as analogies.

It may be that happy and sad moods are associated with distinct information processing styles that can affect performance on different kinds of problem-solving tasks. Emotions that signal danger, such as sadness, fear, shame, and guilt, may switch individuals into a focused, sequential analytic mode of processing that leads to enhanced attention and reduced error on some kinds of problems (Kuhl, 1983). Anger and joy, on the other hand, may create a state of mind that allows for the diffuse, multiple processing characteristic of more intuitive and holistic tasks. An intuitive awareness of the kinds of cognitive tasks facilitated by different affective states may characterize the emotionally intelligent individual.

Mood also may facilitate problem solving by virtue of its impact on the organization and utilization of information in memory. Individuals find it easier to categorize aspects of problems as related or unrelated when happy (Isen & Daubman, 1984), which may facilitate creative thinking. It seems that when feeling good, individuals are better able to discover category organizing principles and then use these principles to integrate and remember new information (Isen, Daubman, & Gorgoglione, 1987).

Finally, the positive impact that pleasant moods have on creative problem-solving tasks may be mediated by changes in persistence. Happy individuals feel more confident about their abilities (Kavanagh & Bower, 1985; Salovey & Birnbaum, 1989) and so may be more likely to continue to work even in the face of unpleasant obstacles.

Summary

So far we have discussed *emotional intelligence* as an organizing framework for cataloguing abilities related to understanding, managing, and using feelings. Included in this array are abilities to recognize emotions in oneself and others and express emotion-laden concepts in words. Moreover, individuals functioning in an emotionally intelligent manner are able to regulate feelings in themselves and in other people and to utilize emotions to aid in problem solving and decision making. In the remainder of this chapter we discuss the aspect of emotional intelligence that is most relevant to mental control: emotional self-regulation—the strategies that people use to adjust their feelings. First, we discuss emotional self-regulation from an individual differences standpoint. We then turn to strategic behaviors that have affective consequences for their perpetrators.

Dispositional Precursors of the Self-Regulation of Affect

Several investigators have suggested that individuals differ in their ability to regulate their own feelings. Whether these efforts have produced ideas with discriminant (and construct!) validity remains

to be seen. Before describing our own foray into dispositional precursors of self-regulatory strategies, we shall mention briefly a few related efforts from other laboratories.

Levels of Emotional Awareness

Lane and colleagues have proposed that there are systematic individual differences in the maturity with which feelings are processed. Drawing on a Piagetian view of cognitive development as an analogy, they propose that individuals respond to emotionally evocative events in one of five different ways—with physiological sensations, body actions, undifferentiated feelings, differentiated emotions (blends of feelings), or multiple differentiated emotions (blends of blends of feelings), depending upon the level of emotional maturity that they have attained (Lane & Schwartz, 1987).

A Levels of Emotional Awareness Scale (LEAS) has been developed, although the predictive validity of emotional complexity measured in this way has not yet been explored (Lane, Quinlan, Schwartz, Walker, & Zeitlin, 1990). Individuals are presented with 20 scenes described in two to four sentences each. The scenes are organized around four emotions—anger, fear, happiness, and sadness. Subjects write about how they would feel and how others in the scenario would feel in response to the scene descriptions. Responses are then scored according to the level of emotional awareness represented (interrater reliability is reported to be reasonably high; Lane et al., 1990). So far, it seems, level of emotional awareness is associated with openness to experience, and maturity. The approach appears promising, although little research with this construct has been reported. Some recent findings argue that such discriminations in levels of emotional awareness can be made, at least psycholinguistically (Mayer, Salovey, Gomberg-Kaufman, & Blainey, 1991, Study 1).

Ambivalence about Emotional Expression

Even individuals with skills in the realm of emotional expression and appraisal may still feel ambivalent about such expression—either wishing they were more able to reveal their emotions to others, or desiring to hide them better (King & Emmons, 1990). King and Emmons (1990, 1991, Emmons, King, and Sheldon, 1993) have developed a scale that measures such ambivalences—the Ambivalence Over Emotional Expression Questionnaire (AEQ). The scale contains 28 items that are best characterized by a single, reliable ambivalence factor. Individuals who are less ambivalent about their emotional expressiveness seem to report greater happiness than those who express a variety of fears about emotional expression. Individuals who report wanting to express emotion and being unable to do so or expressing emotion but later regretting it are more likely to feel negative affect and a variety of psychiatric symptoms such as obsessive-compulsive tendencies, depression, and anxiety (King & Emmons, 1990, 1991).

Beliefs About Negative Mood Relief

In a similar line of work, Catanzaro and Mearns (1987, 1990) developed a 30-item measure concerning generalized expectancies for negative mood regulation: Do people believe that they can do something to alleviate their negative moods? In various studies, individuals who believe that negative moods can be relieved through their own actions are more likely to engage in problem-focused coping strategies and less likely to report depression and somatic complaints (Kirsch, Mearns, & Catanzaro, 1990).

These results have been replicated in subjects responding to a specific stresser, namely the breakup of a romantic relationship. Most interesting, individuals who believe that they can regulate their negative moods are less likely to become depressed in the face of romantic failure—and the predictive power of this variable in this context can be demonstrated prospectively, that is, prior to the breakup itself (Mearns, 1991). People with stronger expectancies concerning their ability to regulate negative moods seem to become less depressed following a distressing event than do individuals who lack these expectations. Individual differences in beliefs about the controllability of affect have also been measured and studied by Flett, Blanckstein, Bator, and Pliner (1989), Roger and Najarian (1989), and Riggio (1986), among others. The discriminant validity of this plethora of measures, however, still needs to be assessed.

Constructive Thinking

Constructive thinking, as described by Epstein (1990), refers to "a person's ability to think in a manner that solves everyday problems in living at a minimal cost in stress" (Katz & Epstein, 1991, p. 789). Particular attention is paid to how individuals manage their emotions, which is thought to be a major factor in determining how effectively intellectual abilities can be marshalled.

Constructive thinking is measured by the Constructive Thinking Inventory (CTI), which contains a global scale and six subscales (Epstein & Meier, 1989). Of particular relevance to the regulation of feelings are the 26-item global scale and the 9-item emotional coping subscale, which contains items such as "I tend to take things personally" and "I don't let little things bother me." Other subscales—naive optimism, negative thinking, and superstitiousness—also have implications for the management of feelings.

Constructive thinking is related to a variety of important life tasks including workplace achievement, romantic success, and emotional and physical well-being (Epstein & Meier, 1989). In a recent experiment (Katz & Epstein, 1991), good constructive thinkers were less likely to respond to laboratory stressors (e.g., mental arithmetic, mirror tracing) with negative affect, dysfunctional thoughts, and physiological arousal. The constructive thinking construct, at this point, seems well motivated theoretically, psychometrically sound, and has demonstrated validity as coping style in response to various stressors in different life domains (for a broader review, see Epstein, 1990).

The Meta-Mood Perspective

Moods are rarely experienced in a vacuum. Rather, pleasant and unpleasant experiences are nearly always accompanied by emotion-management related experiences (Mayer et al., 1991). Mayer and Gaschke (1988) distinguished between the direct experience of moods and a reflective experience that occurs simultaneously. The first is what we commonly consider a pleasant or unpleasant mood. The second, termed the *meta-mood experience,* arises in response to the direct perception of a mood and includes cognitions that monitor the mood (Scheier & Carver, 1982), and active attempts to alter the future course of the mood itself (Isen, 1984; Parrott, 1993). Extensive factor analytic research has revealed that the experience of mood is broader than its emotional content alone.

The mood experience encompasses emotion-management processes that modify perceptions of evocative situations that elicit an emotion. These *meta-mood experiences* typically involve broad attempts to regulate or change mood. The regulatory meta-experiences may in turn lead to direct-level thoughts concerning suppression and denial of the mood ("don't even think about it") and behavioral planning ("get help") that are also experienced as a part of mood (Mayer & Gaschke 1988; Mayer et al., 1991). When we asked subjects to imagine how they would feel across 32 different affectively charged situations, their responses factored into the usual pleasant–unpleasant and arousal–calm dimensions (Mayer & Volanth, 1985; see also Russell, 1979, and Green, Goldman, & Salovey, 1992). In addition, however, we also recovered management-related dimensions of denial and regulating thoughts. In a second study, three dimensions of emotion-management were recovered: suppression, denial, and thoughts of action (cf. Wegner, 1989).

We are interested in both transient thoughts about emotion-management (termed State Meta-Mood Experiences) and longer-standing dispositional orientations toward emotion management (Trait Meta-Mood Experiences). Mayer and Gaschke (1988) described a 60-item State Meta-Mood Scale (SMMS) that measures the kinds of thoughts an individual might have while experiencing moods, in particular whether they are under control, confusing or clear, acceptable, typical, and changeable. The State Meta-Mood dimensions differ depending on the mood experienced. For example, beliefs about the changeability of a mood are more likely to come to mind during unpleasant rather than pleasant experiences.

We recently completed work on a sister scale to the SMMS, the Trait Meta-Mood Scale (TMMS), containing 48 items that load on three factors— attention to feelings, clarity of moods and emotions, and beliefs about the desire to maintain or repair moods (Salovey et al., 1995). Scores on these scales are thought to represent stable, individual differences in the way in which people respond to their feeling states.

We have obtained some predictive validity for the constructs measured by the TMMS. In one experiment (Salovey et al., 1995), we asked subjects to view a distressing film concerning drunk driving and its victims. Then, in a purportedly unrelated experiment, subjects were asked to list at 30-second intervals any thoughts that came to mind. Subjects who experienced their emotions clearly had less distressing ruminations following the film than did those subjects who lacked this skill. They also recovered faster from the emotionally distressing event. Perhaps the clarity of their affective experience allowed these subjects to regulate their distress without engaging in aversive ruminative processes. Such individuals may know how they feel and may not need to engage in rumination in order to discern their feelings.

Behavioral Manifestations of the Self-Regulation of Affect

A Temporally Dynamic Perspective on Affect

In the previous sections we discussed how individuals differ in their reaction to and control of emotions. In this section we examine how people (in general) react to emotionally charged outcomes, particularly outcomes that unfold in time. In the section that follows we examine how people arrange the temporal order of such outcomes to maximize the pleasure experienced from them.

Historically, affect has largely been studied rather statically. Investigators have presented stimuli to subjects—shown them films, insulted them, threatened them with painful shocks—and then measured subjects' physiological, phenomenological, and behavioral reactions (for a review, see, for example, Leventhal & Tomarkin, 1986). But affectively charged stimuli impinging on the individual outside of the laboratory rarely involve the experience of such discrete, one-time events. Rather, we experience events that unfold in time. And our affective reactions may be determined as much by the pattern of these events over time as by any individual event itself. For instance, we may be aware of the absolute level of some outcome— is what I am experiencing now desirable? We may appreciate how this outcome has changed from some previous level—is this more desirable than what I experienced yesterday! And we may realize that this change from the previous level may be happening at some rate of speed—are things getting better at a faster or slower pace!

First of all, satisfaction with a desired outcome depends not only on the absolute value of the outcome, but also on the amount of change, or *displacement*, of the outcome from some baseline. Take a person who purchased a house as an investment as an example. Whether the person is happy with the investment depends not only on the current value of the house but also on the amount (and direction) the value has changed from some reference level, say, the value of the house when it was originally purchased—how much its value has increased (or decreased) over the years.

The idea that satisfaction with an outcome depends not just on the value of that outcome but also on its change from some baseline over time is not new in social psychological theory. For instance, studies of gain–loss phenomena suggest that individuals who first express negative attitudes toward us and later express positive attitudes are liked better than individuals who express positive attitudes all along (Aronson & Linder, 1965). Similarly, we experience as more devastating negative feedback received from someone who has always given us positive reinforcement than from someone whose negative feedback is typically expected. It should not be surprising, then, that we can only hurt the one we love.

Also relevant is the idea of hedonic relativity (Brickman & Campbell, 1971; cf. Kahneman & Tversky, 1979). People are more satisfied when an outcome first changes their lives as compared to later when they have gotten used to some standard of living. Studies of lottery winners, for instance, suggest that the greatest happiness is experienced immediately after winning the prize, but, over time, winners are no happier than losers (Brickman, Coates, & Janoff-Bulman, 1978). People seem ultimately to adapt to events, whether good or bad. Similar ideas can be found in Parducci's (1968, 1982) range-frequency theory, which suggests that one's past is used as the standard of comparison for evaluating present satisfaction (see Diener, 1984, for a more general review of the determinants of subjective well-being).

In addition to the fact that satisfaction depends on the change of an outcome, satisfaction also depends on the rate, or *velocity*, of the change (Hsee & Abelson, 1991). Take the person who invested in real estate described above. The feelings of this person depend not only on how much the value of the house has increased (or decreased), but also on how long the change takes place or how fast it is changing. Other things being equal, the person would be happier if the value of the house increased, say, $4,000 per year than, say, $4,000 in two years.

In a recent study (Hsee & Abelson, 1991) sub-jects rated their feelings about graphic displays on a computer screen that depicted the chances of winning a hypothetical game, the value of a stock, or their standing in a college class. In support of the velocity notion, subjects indicated greater satisfaction when these outcomes increased quickly than when they increased slowly, and greater dissatisfaction when they decreased quickly than when they decreased slowly, independent of the final outcome itself. It seems that individuals "do not just care how much an outcome has changed, but also how fast it changes" (Hsee & Abelson, 1991, p. 345). These data are consistent with Carver and Scheier's (1990) control-process view of affect, which holds that affect is determined by the rate at which goals are approached. [. . .]

So far we have discussed that pleasure is not just the result of how positive some outcome is, but also is a function of how fast that outcome is changing and how fast the rate of that change is itself changing. The idea that pleasure is multiply determined in this way poses a challenge to naive hedonism, the notion that the more we have of something we like, the happier we are (see Parrott's [1993] challenge to naive hedonism as well). In fact, happiness is not associated with wealth (e.g., Easterlin, 1973; Murray, 1988), and aversive experiences sometimes produce positive feelings (such as relief when they end), as predicted by opponent process theory (Solomon, 1980). What seems most important—and what emotions investigators have largely ignored—is the way in which affectively valent outcomes change over time (cf. Altman & Rogoff, 1987). This dynamic—indeed, *emodynamic*—view suggests that we are acutely sensitive to the pattern over which outcomes accrue in time, especially to their rate and shifts in that rate.

Arranging the Order of Events

In the previous section we examined how individuals react affectively to events that change over time. It appears that one's feelings depend not only on the final outcome of events, but also on the temporal pattern of these events. In this section we examine a related question: How do people strategically arrange the temporal pattern of events to optimize their feelings? In many situations, actions that we may take determine in part how we feel later. Thus, we can exert some control over future feelings. At dinner, should you eat the delicious prime rib steak before your least favorite vegetable, squash, or after it? At work, should you accept your boss's offer of a fixed annual salary for five years, or would you prefer a salary that starts lower than this amount and ends at a higher rate, even though the average is slightly less than the fixed option? And at the racetrack, would you feel better betting on a horse who always runs fairly well or taking a chance on a comer who used to be awful but has improved steadily race after race? We would like to argue that individuals prefer certain patterns of outcomes that they believe will maximize their pleasure. But even though we will state some general principles guiding these decisions, we also claim that there is considerable individual variability in people's knowledge of these principles and other factors that bear on how they will feel ultimately.

Suppose that you receive three boxes containing gifts on your birthday. You do not know what is inside each box, but you can guess their approximate value. In what order would you open these gifts? There are several competing predictions. If only the final outcome mattered, then you should have no systematic preference about the order with which you open the boxes. On the other hand, several factors suggest that people have a systematic preference. One is the *impatience* hypothesis. Economists have long believed that people prefer to consume or experience pleasant events as quickly as possible, presumably because the subjective value of a pleasant event will be less the longer the event is delayed (see Loewenstein, 1992, for a review). If this is the case, then people should open the gifts in the descending order, that is, the most-valued gift first and the least-valued gift last, because the most-valued gift carries the greatest weight and should be most susceptible to impatience.

A second factor is *savoring*. Sometimes people like to delay the consumption of a pleasant event so as to enjoy fully the pleasure derived from anticipation. For example, subjects in a questionnaire study indicated that they would rather kiss their favorite movie star in several days rather than right now (Loewenstein, 1987). Similarly, when subjects are provided an opportunity to choose the order in which they listen to musical pieces, they are more likely to listen to less pleasant pieces earlier and more pleasant pieces later (Breckler, Allen, & Konecni, 1985). Contrary to impatience, savoring would predict that you would open the gifts in the *ascending* order. Furthermore, when given a choice to open the gifts slowly or quickly, people should prefer to open the gifts slowly so as to enjoy fully the pleasure of anticipation .

A third factor that may influence one's preference of temporal pattern is the *velocity* effect. As discussed earlier, an increase in desired value will lead to greater satisfaction than a decrease, and a quick increase will lead to greater satisfaction than a sluggish increase. Like savoring, this velocity effect would lead us to expect people to open the gifts in the *ascending* order rather than in the descending order. But unlike savoring, the velocity notion would suggest that people prefer a *faster* ascending pattern rather than a slower ascending pattern. [. . .]

There is also a related literature on the way in which individuals attempt to cluster or separate experiences in the world systematically in order to self-regulate affect. In a fascinating paper, Linville and Fischer (1991) explored whether individuals prefer to separate or combine emotionally impactful events—whether they would prefer to experience two negative events in quick or distant succession; whether they would prefer two positive events to occur one right after the other or following a lengthier time lag. Across three different domains—academic, social, and financial—individuals separated large negative outcomes. They rarely preferred a "let's get it all over with at once" strategy, but rather preferred to deal with these losses one at a time. Similarly, for large positive events, individuals also preferred to experience them separately in time. It is as if they would rather savor each one on its own. Most interestingly, when subjects must experience mixed outcomes, such as a large gain and a small loss or a large loss and a small gain then they wanted to experience the two events in quick succession. It is as if they desire to buffer the negative outcome with the positive experience. These results suggest that people do not only passively experience emotions in response to external stimuli, they actively seek to organize external stimuli in a way that maximizes positive experiences. While doing so, they not only care about the total value of these experiences, but also about their temporal pattern.

Helping Others

In addition to arranging the order and patterning of outcomes to self-regulate feelings, individuals may also engage in specific interpersonal behaviors—affiliating with others, comparing with those less fortunate, basking in reflected glory—for their emotional consequences. One behavior that at times is used to manage feelings strategically is helping. There is a long history in social psychology of research concerning helping behaviors and how they may serve mood-regulatory strategies (see Salovey, Mayer, & Rosenhan, 1991; Schaller & Cialdini, 1990, for recent reviews). Positive feelings are thought to be maintained by helping others, and negative feelings relieved by such behaviors.

The positive mood maintenance hypothesis suggests that pleasant moods can be best maintained by engaging in altruistic and other helping behaviors because they foster further pleasant feelings (Clark & Isen, 1982; Isen & Simmonds, 1978). Many experiments have demonstrated that this indeed seems to be the case. When students are asked to help out an experimenter by volunteering to participate as subjects, they report feeling better (Yinon & Landau, 1987). Similar results have been obtained in other helping contexts as well (Harris, 1977; Williamson & Clark, 1989). Individuals seem to be aware of this positive consequence of helping others. When already happy, they avoid helping in situations that might threaten their positive moods (Forest, Clark, Mills, & Isen, 1979; Harada, 1983; Isen & Levin, 1972; Shaffer & Graziano, 1983).

Helping as a way of improving negative moods—the so-called Negative State Relief Model (Cialdini & Kenrick, 1976)—has received considerable support as well (Baumann, Cialdini, & Kenrick, 1981; Manucia, Baumann, & Cialdini, 1984). The classic test of the idea that individuals engage in helpful acts in order to make themselves feel more positively comes from experiments in which sadness is induced and avenues for improving mood are made available prior to a helping opportunity. For instance, if subjects are rewarded following negative mood induction but before they have an opportunity to help, they are no more likely to help than neutral mood control subjects (Cialdini, Darby, & Vincent, 1973; Cunningham, Steinberg, & Grev, 1980). Similarly, when subjects are led to believe that their moods cannot improve by helping—for instance, because they have been given a "drug" that locks their moods at current levels—they do not help following negative mood inductions (Manucia, Baumann, &

Cialdini, 1984, but see Schroeder, Dovidio, Sibicky, Mathews, & Allen, 1988, for a failure to replicate these kinds of effects).

Perhaps the most direct test of this idea is demonstrated in a study by Schaller and Cialdini (1988) who provided subjects with a variety of cheering-up strategies in addition to helping. When subjects had such alternatives available to them—for example, they could view humorous material—they were not as likely to help. It seems that individuals see helping in certain kinds of situations as one way in which to relieve a sad mood.

In other papers (e.g., Salovey, Mayer, & Rosenhan, 1991), we have suggested that people may help in order to self-regulate emotions over quite long periods of time by strategically delaying short-term pleasure for greater long-term rewards. We looked at literature concerning Christians who rescued Jews from the Nazis (e.g., London, 1970; Oliner & Oliner, 1988; Stein, 1988). It seems doubtful that such heroism was motivated by the kinds of short-term mood improvements typical of the laboratory experiments reviewed above. Rather, by providing haven for Jews, they "achieved" a longer-term goal of being able to look back on their actions and experience pride and great satisfaction (and, perhaps, reduced guilt). Living up to one's moral standards and engaging in altruistic behaviors and the like are social actions that may involve short-term costs but in the long term may be the most effective strategies for regulating emotions.

Conclusions

In this chapter we argued that there is a set of skills, organized around a framework we call emotional intelligence, concerned with the processing of emotion-relevant information. These skills can be grouped into three primary domains: the accurate appraisal and expression of emotion, the ability to utilize effectively emotion-based knowledge, and the adaptive regulation of emotion. This chapter was primarily concerned with this last domain.

Emotional self-regulation seems to require two precursors. The first is the predisposition to engage in such regulation. Although this issue has not been addressed directly, several constructs have appeared in recent years that may capture, in part, the desire to engage in emotional self-regulation—levels of emotional awareness, ambivalence about emotional expression, beliefs about negative state relief, constructive thinking, and meta-mood experiences. The second precursor to effective regulation of affect is an arsenal of behavioral strategies that affect one's feelings. We described two such strategies here: arranging the order of valenced events and helping other people.

The field of emotional self-regulation represents fertile, albeit largely unexplored, territory. Although developmental researchers have been concerned for quite some time with the ways in which children learn to regulate their emotional experiences—toddlers may stare at their mothers, for instance, while attempting a new, scary task—personality and social psychologists have become interested only recently in these issues. Much of emotional regulation is in some way a form of mental control. Our feelings are in part determined by how effectively we can control the contents of our minds (and the minds of other people as well). When the second volume of this handbook appears, perhaps research will have progressed to a stage where the links between mental control and emotional self-regulation have been demonstrated explicitly.

REFERENCES

Altman, I., & Rogoff, B. (1987). World views in psychology: Trait, interactional, organismic, and transactional perspectives. In D. Stokols & I. Altman (Eds.), Handbook of environmental psychology (pp. 7–39). New York: John Wiley.

Apfel, R. J., & Sifneos, P. E. (1979). Alexithymia: Concept and measurement. Psychotherapy and Psychosomatics, 32, 180–190.

Aronson, E., & Linder, D. (1965). Gain and loss of esteem as determinants of interpersonal attractiveness. Journal of Experimental Social Psychology, 1, 156–171.

Baumann, D. J., Cialdini, R. B., & Kenrick, D. T. (1981). Altruism as hedonism: Helping and self-gratification as equivalent responses. Journal of Personality and Social Psychology, 40, 1039–1046.

Breckler, S. J., Allen, R. B., & Konecni, V. J. (1985). Mood-optimization strategies in asthetic-choice behavior. Music Perception, 2, 459–470.

Bretherton, I., Fritz, J., Zahn-Waxler, G., & Ridgeway, D. (1986). Learning to talk about emotions: A functionalist perspective. Child Development, 57, 529–548.

Brickman, P., & Campbell, D. T. (1971). Hedonic relativism and planning the good society. In M. H. Appley (Ed.), Adaptation-level theory: A symposium (pp. 287–304). New York: Academic Press.

Brickman, P., Coates, D., & Janoff-Bulman, K. (1978). Lottery winners and accident victims: Is happiness relative? Journal of Personality and Social Psychology, 36, 917–927.

Brown, K., Covell, K., & Abramovitch, R. (1991). Time course and control of emotion: Age differences in understanding and recognition. Merrill-Palmer Quarterly, 37, 273–287.

Buck, R. (1979). Individual differences in nonverbal sending accuracy and electrodermal responding: The externalizing-internalizing dimension. In R. Rosenthal (Ed.), Skill in nonverbal communication: Individual differences. Cambridge, MA: Olegeshlager, Gunn, & Hain.

Buck, R. (1984). The communication of emotion. New York: Guilford Press.

Campbell, R. J., Kagan, N. I., & Krathwohl, D. R. (1971). The development and validation of a scale to measure affective sensitivity (empathy). Journal of Counseling Psychology, 18, 407–412.

Campos, J. J., Campos, R. G., & Barrett, K. C. (1989). Emergent themes in the study of emotional development and emotion regulation. Developmental Psychology, 25, 394–402.

Cantor, N., & Kihlstrom, J. F. (1987). Personality and social intelligence. Englewood Cliffs, NJ: Prentice Hall.

Carver, C. S., & Scheier, M. F. (1990). Origins and functions of positive and negative affect: A control-process view. Psychological Review, 97, 19–35.

Cantanzaro, S. J., & Mearns, J. (1987, August). Measuring generalized expectancies for negative mood regulation. Paper presented at the annual convention of the American Psychological Association, New York, N.Y.

Cantanzaro, S. J., & Mearns, J. (1990). Measuring generalized expectancies for negative mood regulation: Initial scale development and implications. Journal of Personality Assessment, 54, 546–563.

Cialdini, R. B., Darby, B. L., & Vincent, J. E. (1973). Transgression and altruism: A case for hedonism. Journal of Experimental Social Psychology, 9, 502–516.

Cialdini, R. B., & Kesrick, D. (1976). Altruism as hedonism: A social development perspective on the relationship of negative mood state and helping. Journal of Personality and Social Psychology, 34, 907–914.

Clark, M. S., & Isen, A. M. (1982). Toward understanding the relationship between feeling states and social behavior. In A. H. Hastorf & A. M. Isen (Eds.), Cognitive social psychology (pp. 73–108). New York: Elsevier North-Holland.

Cunningham, M. R., & Steinberg, J., & Grev, R. (1980). Wanting to and having to help: Separate motivations for positive mood and guilt-induced helping. Journal of Personality and Social Psychology, 38, 181–192.

Diener, E. (1984). Subjective well-being. Psychological Bulletin, 95, 542-575.

Easterlin, R. (1973). Does money buy happiness? The Public Interest, 30, 3–10.

Emmons, R. A., King, L. A., & Sheldon, K. (1993). Goal conflict and the self-regulation of action. In D. M. Wegner & J. W. Pennebaker (Eds.), Handbook of mental control (pp. 528–551). Englewood Cliffs, NJ: Prentice Hall.

Epstein, S. (1990). Cognitive-experiential self-theory. In L. Pervin (Ed.), Handbook of personality theory and research (pp. 165–191). New York: Guilford Press.

Epstein, S., & Meier, P. (1989). Constructive thinking: A broad coping variable with specific components. Journal of Personality and Social Psychology, 57, 332–350.

Flett, G. L., Blanckstein, K. R., Bator, C., & Pliner, P. (1989). Affect intensity and self-control of emotional behaviour. Personality and Individual Differences, 10, 1–5.

Forest, D., Clark, M. S., Mills, J., & Isen, A. M. (1979). Helping as a function of feeling state and nature of the helping behavior. Motivation and Emotion, 3, 701–711.

Friedman, H. S., Prince, L. M., Riggio, R. E., & DiMatteo,

M. R. (1980). Understanding and assessing nonverbal expressiveness: The Affective Communication Test. *Journal of Personality and Social Psychology, 39,* 333–351.

Gardner, H. (1983). *Frames of mind.* New York: Basic Books.

Goffman, E. (1959). *The presentation of self in everyday life.* Garden City, NY: Doubleday.

Goldman, S., Kraemer, R. D., Salovey, P., & Mayer, J. D. (1992). *Trait meta-mood as a moderator of the relation between negative emotional state, illness, and symptom reporting.* Manuscript submitted for publication.

Green, D. P., Goldman, S. L., & Salovey, P. (1992). *Measurement error masks bipolarity in affect ratings.* Manuscript submitted for publication.

Harada, J. (1983). The effects of positive and negative experiences on helping behavior. *Japanese Psychological Research, 25,* 47–51.

Harris, M. B. (1977). Effects of altruism on mood. *Journal of Social Psychology, 102,* 197–208.

Hochschild, A. R. (1983), *The managed heart: Commercialization of human feeling.* Berkeley: University of California Press.

Hsee, C. K., & Abelson, R. P. (1991). The velocity relation: Satisfaction as a function of the first derivative over time. *Journal of Personality and Social Psychology, 60,* 342–347.

Hsee, C. K., Abelson, R. P., & Salovey, P. (1991). The relative weighting of position and velocity in satisfaction. *Psychological Science, 2,* 263–266.

Isen, A. M. (1984). Toward understanding the role of affect in cognition. In R. S. Wyer & T. K. Srull (Eds.), *Handbook of social cognition* (Vol. 3, pp. 179–236). Hillsdale, NJ: Erlbaum.

Isen, A. M., & Daubman, K. A. (1984). The influence of affect on categorization. *Journal of Personality and Social Psychology, 47,* 1206–1217.

Isen, A. M., Daubman, K. A., & Gorgoglione, J. M. (1987). The influence of positive affect on cognitive organization: Implications for education. In R. Snow & M. Parr (Eds.), *Aptitude, learning, and instruction: Affective and cognitive factors.* Hillsdale, NJ: Erlbaum.

Isen, A. M., Daubman, K. A., & Nowicki, G. (1987). Positive affect facilitates creative problem solving. *Journal of Personality and Social Psychology, 52,* 1122–1131.

Isen, A. M., Johnson, M. S., Mertz, E., & Robinson, G. F. (1985). The effects of positive affect on the unusualness of word associations. *Journal of Personality and Social Psychology, 41,* 1413–1414.

Isen, A. M., & Levin, P. F. (1972). The effect of feeling good on helping: Cookies and kindness. *Journal of Personality and Social Psychology, 21,* 384–388.

Isen, A. M., & Simmonds, S. F. (1978). The effect of feeling good on a helping task that is incompatible with good mood. *Social Psychology, 41,* 345–349.

James, W. (1890). *The principles of psychology.* New York: Holt.

Kagan, N. (1978, September). *Affective sensitivity test: Validity and reliability.* Paper presented at the meeting of the American Psychological Association. San Francisco, CA.

Kahneman, D., & Tversky, A. (1979). Prospect theory: An analysis of decision under risk. *Econometrica, 47,* 263–291.

Katz, L., & Epstein, S. (1991). Constructive thinking and coping with laboratory-induced stress. *Journal of Personality and Social Psychology, 61,* 789–800.

Kavanagh, D. J., & Bower, G. H. (1985). Mood and self-efficacy: Impact of joy and sadness on perceived capabilities. *Cognitive Therapy and Research, 9,* 507–525.

King, L. A., & Emmons, R. A. (1990). Conflict over emotional expression: Psychological and physical correlates. *Journal of Personality and Social Psychology, 58,* 864–877.

King, L. A., & Emmons, R. A. (1991). Psychological, physical, and interpersonal correlates of emotional expressiveness, conflict, and control. *European Journal of Personality, 58,* 131–150.

Kirsch, I., Mearns, J., & Catanzaro, S. J. (1990). Mood regulation expectancies as determinants of depression in college students. *Journal of Counseling Psychology, 37,* 306–312

Krystal, J. H., Giller, E. L., & Cicchetti, D. V. (1986). Assessment of alexithymia in posttraumatic stress disorder and somatic illness: Introduction of a reliable measure. *Psychosomatic Medicine, 48,* 84–91.

Kuhl, J. (1983). Emotion, cognition, and motivation, II. *Sprache and Kognition, 4,* 228–253.

Lane, R. D., Quinlan, D. M., Schwartz, G. E., Walker, P. A., & Zeitlin, S. B. (1990). The levels of emotional awareness scale: A cognitive-developmental measure of emotion. *Journal of Personality Assessment, 55,* 124–134.

Lane, R. D., & Schwartz, G. E. (1987). Levels of emotional awareness: A cognitive-developmental theory and its application to psychopathology. *American Journal of Psychiatry, 144,* 133–143.

Leventhal, H., & Tomarkin, A. J. (1986). Emotion: Today's problems. *Annual Review of Psychology, 37,* 565–610.

Lewis, M., Sullivan, M. W., & Vasen, A. (1987). Making faces: Age and emotion differences in the posing of emotional expressions. *Developmental Psychology, 23,* 690–697.

Linville, P. W., & Fischer, G. W. (1991). Preferences for combining or separating events: A social application of prospect theory and mental accounting. *Journal of Personality and Social Psychology, 60,* 5–23.

Loewenstein, G. (1987). Anticipation and the valuation of delayed consumption. *Economic Journal, 97,* 666–684.

Loewenstein, G. (1992). The fall and rise of psychological explanations in the economics of intertemporal choice. In G. Loewenstein & J. Elster (Eds.), *Choice over time.* New York: Russell Sage.

London, P. (1970). The rescuers: Motivational hypotheses about Christians who saved Jews from the Nazis. In J. Macaulay & L. Berkowitz (Eds.), *Altruism and helping behavior* (pp. 241–250). New York: Academic Press.

Manucia, G. K., Baumann, D. J., & Cialdini, R. B. (1984). Mood influences on helping: Direct effects or side effects? *Journal of Personality and Social Psychology, 46,* 557–364.

Mayer, J. D. (1986). How mood influences cognition. In N. E. Sharkey (Ed.), *Advances in cognitive science* (Vol. 1, pp. 290–314). Chichester, UK: Ellis Horwood.

Mayer, J. D., & Gaschke, Y. N. (1988). The experience and meta-experience of mood. *Journal of Personality and Social Psychology, 55,* 102–111.

Mayer, J. D., & Salovey, P. (1993). The intelligence of emotional intelligence. *Intelligence, 17,* 433–442.

Mayer, J. D., Salovey, P., Gomberg-Kaufman, S., & Blainey, K. (1991). A broader conception of mood experience. *Journal of Personality and Social Psychology, 60,* 100–111.

Mayer, J. D., & Volanth, A. J. (1985). Cognitive involvement in the mood response system. *Motivation and Emotion, 9,* 261–275.

Mearns, J. (1991). Coping with a break-up: Negative mood regulation expectancies and depression following the end of a romantic relationship. *Journal of Personality and Social Psychology, 60,* 327–334.

Morris, W. N., & Reilly, N. P. (1987). Toward the self-regulation of mood: Theory and research. *Motivation and Emotion, 11,* 215–249.

Murray, C. (l988). *In pursuit of happiness and good government.* New York: Simon & Schuster.

Oliner, S. P., & Oliner, P. M. (1988). *The altruistic personality: Rescuers of Jews in Nazi Europe.* New York: Free Press.

Palfai, T. P., & Salovey, P. (1993–1994). The influence of depressed and elated moods on inductive and deductive reasoning. *Imagination, Cognition and Personality, 13,* 57–71.

Parducci, A. (1968). The relativism of absolute judgements. *Scientific American, 219,* 84–90.

Parducci, A. (1982, August). *Toward a relational theory of happiness.* Paper presented at the 90th annual convention of the American Psychological Association, Washington, DC.

Parrott, W. G. (1993). Beyond hedonism: Motives for inhibiting good moods and for maintaining bad moods. In D. M. Wegner & J. W. Pennebaker (Eds.), *Handbook of mental control* (pp. 278–305). Englewood Cliffs, NJ: Prentice-Hall.

Pennebaker, J. W. (1989). Confession, inhibition, and disease. In L. Berkowitz (Ed.), *Advances in experimental social psychology* (Vol. 22, pp. 211–244). San Diego: Academic Press.

Pennebaker, J. W., & Susman, J. R. (1988). Disclosure of traumas and psychosomatic processes. *Social Science and Medicine, 26,* 327–332.

Profyt, L., & Whissel, C. (1991). Children's understanding of facial expression of emotion: I. Voluntary creation of emotion-faces. *Perceptual and Motor Skills, 73,* 199–202.

Riggio, R. E. (1986). Assessment of basic social skills. *Journal of Personality and Social Psychology, 51,* 649–660.

Roger, D., & Najarian, B. (1989). The construction and validation of a new scale for measuring emotion control. *Personality and Individual Differences, 10,* 845–853.

Rosenthal, R., Hall, J. A., DiMatteo, M. R., Rogers, P. L., & Archer, D. (1979). *Sensitivity to nonverbal communication: The PONS Test.* Baltimore: Johns Hopkins University Press.

Russell, J. (1979). Affective space is bipolar. *Journal of Personality and Social Psychology, 37,* 1152–1168.

Salovey, P., & Birnbaum, D. (1989). Influence of mood on health-relevant cognitions. *Journal of Personality and Social Psychology, 57,* 539–551.

Salovey, P., & Mayer, D. (1990). Emotional intelligence. *Imagination, Cognition, and Personality, 9,* 185–211.

Salovey, P., & Mayer, J. D. (1991, Spring). On emotional intelligence. *Dialogue,* 9–10.

Salovey, P., Mayer, J. D., Goldman, S., Turvey, C., & Palfai, T. P. (1995). Emotional attention, clarity, repair: Exploring emotional intelligence using the Trait Meta-Mood Scale. In J. W. Pennebaker (Ed.), *Emotion, disclosure, and health* (pp. 125–154). Washington, DC: American Psychological Association.

Salovey, P., Mayer, J. D., & Rosenhan, D. L. (1991). Mood and helping: Mood as a motivator of helping and helping as a regulator of mood. In M. S. Clark (Ed.), *Prosocial behavior: Review of personality and social psychology* (Vol. 12, pp. 215–237). Newbury Park, CA: Sage Publications Inc.

Schaffer, L. F., Gilmer, B., & Schoen, M. (1940). *Psychology.* New York: Harper & Brothers.

Schaller, M., & Cialdini, R. B. (1988). The economics of empathic helping: Support for a mood management motive. *Journal of Experimental Social Psychology, 24,* 163–181.

Schaller, M., & Cialdini, R. B. (1990). Happiness, sadness, and helping: A motivational integration. In E. T. Higgins & R. M. Sorrentino (Eds.), *Handbook of motivation and cognition: Foundations of social behavior* (Vol. 2, pp. 265–296). New York: Guilford Press.

Scheier, M. F., & Carver, C. S. (1982). Cognition, affect, and self-regulation. In M. S. Clark & S. T. Fiske (Eds.), *Affect and cognition: The 17th annual Carnegie Symposium on Cognition* (pp. 157–183). Hillsdale, NJ: Erlbaum.

Schroeder, D. A., Dovidio, J. F., Sibicky, M. E., Mathews, L. L., & Allen, J. L. (1988). Empathic concern and helping behavior: Egoism or altruism? *Journal of Experimental Social Psychology, 24,* 333–353.

Schwarz, N. (1990). Feelings as information: Informational and motivational functions of affective states. In E. T. Higgins & R. M. Sorrentino (Eds.), *Handbook of motivation and cognition: Foundations of social behavior* (Vol. 2, pp. 527–561). New York: Guilford Press.

Shaffer, D. R., & Graziano, W. G. (1983). Effects of positive and negative moods on helping tasks having pleasant or unpleasant consequences. *Motivation and Emotion, 7,* 269–278.

Sifneos, P. E. (1972). *Short-term psychotherapy and emotional crisis.* Cambridge: Harvard University Press.

Sifneos, P. E. (1973). The presence of "alexithymic" characteristics in psychosomatic patients. *Psychotherapy and Psychosomatics, 22,* 225–262.

Solomon, R. L. (1980). The opponent process theory of acquired motivation: The costs of pleasure and the benefits of pain. *American Psychologist, 35,* 691–712.

Stein, A. (1988). *Quiet heroes: True stories of the rescue of Jews by Christians in Nazi-occupied Holland.* Toronto: Lester and Orpen Dennys.

Stein, N. L., & Trabasso, T. (1989). Children's understanding of changing emotional states. In C. Saarni & P. L. Harris (Eds.), *Children's understanding of emotion* (pp. 50–77). Cambridge, UK: Cambridge University Press.

Steinberg, R. J., & Smith, C. A. (1985). Social intelligence and decoding skills in nonverbal communication. *Social Cognition, 3,* 168–192.

Taylor, G. J. (1984). Alexithymia: Concept, measurement, and implications for treatment. *American Journal of Psychiatry, 141,* 725–732.

Thayler-Singer, M. (1977). Psychological dimensions in psychosomatic patients. *Psychotherapy and Psychosomatics, 28,* 13–27.

Wasielewski, P. L. (1985). The emotional basis of charisma. *Symbolic Interaction, 8,* 207–222.

Wegner, D. M. (1989). *White bears and other unwanted thoughts.* New York: Viking.

Whissell, C. M., & Nicholson, H. (1991). Children's freely produced synonyms for seven key emotions. *Perceptual and Motor Skills, 72,* 1107–1111.

Williamson, G. M., & Clark, M. S. (1989). Providing help

and desired relationship type as determinants of changes in moods and self-evaluations. *Journal of Personality and Social Psychology, 56,* 722–734.

Woodworth, R. S. (1940). *Psychology* (4th ed.). New York: Holt.

Yinon, Y., & Landau, M. O. (1987). On the reinforcing value of helping behavior in a positive mood. *Motivation and Emotion, 11,* 83–93.

Young, P. T. (1936). *Motivation of behavior.* New York: John Wiley.

Emotion and Social Cognition

In the preceding article, Salovey, Hsee, and Mayer proposed prosocial behavior as one example of how emotions influence social processes. In fact, emotion produces many effects at the level of the individual that figure in social psychological topics. Two further examples are presented in this section: person perception and persuasion.

In their research on person perception, Forgas and Bower (1987) build on previous research that suggests that moods and emotions automatically activate, or "prime," cognitive processes that are congruent with the emotional state. For example, a happy mood can direct a person's attention toward objects and ideas associated with happiness, leading to superior learning of that material. A happy mood can also prime memories that are associated with happiness, leading to enhanced recall of happy memories. These phenomena are called "mood-congruent learning" and "mood-congruent memory," respectively. They can be interpreted as being caused by automatic activation of mental representations that are linked to form a network of associations (Blaney, 1986; Bower, 1981).

In their research, Forgas and Bower investigated how cognitive changes brought about by changes in mood would manifest themselves in persons making judgments in a person-perception task. In order to create an experimental test, they needed to manipulate the moods of the participants. In this study they used the technique of providing participants with false information, telling them they did either very well or very poorly on a psychological test of personality. In order to emply this technique ethically, Forgas and Bower were careful to explain fully and convincingly the false nature of this information at the end of the study. After thus acquiring good or bad moods, participants were exposed to a series of sentences describing each of four characters. The participants' moods were found to have a number of effects on how they read the sentences, on the impressions that they formed of the characters, and on later memory for those characters. Of particular note is the finding that participants in good moods formed more favorable impressions of the targets than did participants in bad moods.

Subsequent research has found that the associative network model has serious limitations. One limitation is suggested by the results of this experiment. The effect of mood seemed more pronounced for good moods than for bad moods (although better evidence for this conclusion would be obtained if there were some sort of "neutral mood" control condition; see Parrott & Hertel, 1999). This asymmetry suggests that automatic cognitive priming cannot be the only mood-related effect that is occurring. If the participants in bad moods were trying to cheer themselves up, then their mood-regulation efforts may have attenuated the effects of automatic association in the bad mood condition relative to those in the good mood condition. An even stronger demonstration of such regulation has been found in research on how mood affects memory, where it sometimes happens that mood-*incongruent* memory is observed (Parrott & Sabini, 1990). Associative network theory cannot explain why people in a bad mood might remember events that are more positive than are the events remembered by people in a good mood, so the theory is either incomplete or wrong. One solution is to augment automatic priming theory with a supplemental theory that incorporates motivation; another is to abandon automatic priming theory altogether (Parrott & Spackman, 2000).

Another way in which moods affect social judgments is by serving as a source of information about the target. If you were asked how much you liked one of your neighbors, you might think about your neighbor and pay attention to how you were then feeling. In this case your feelings might serve as an index of your overall attitude toward your neighbor. However, if you did not believe that your feelings were caused by thinking about your neighbor—if you instead thought that they were caused by, say, gloomy weather—you might not use your mood to inform your judgment of your neighbor. The hypothesis that moods can serve as a source of information and that they can be discounted if they are attributed to a different cause was supported by a series of ingenious experiments by Schwarz and Clore (1983). In a manner somewhat reminiscent of the attributional version of Schachter's two-factor theory, they showed that attributions of mood states can determine whether moods will influence judgments. It is still unclear how to reconcile this approach with that of automatic priming.

With the second reading in this section we turn our attention away from the specific cognitive processes involved in learning and memory and toward what has been termed "cognitive processing style." Moods are thought to influence the general approach that people take to thinking and problem solving. Research suggests that people in good moods tend to adopt a quick, heuristic approach to solving problems. This style of thinking is open-minded and flexible, well suited for creative thinking, but not ideal for detailed analysis. In contrast, people in bad moods tend to adopt a more methodical, systematic, and analytical approach that tends to be accurate but rather careful and conventional (Fiedler, 2000; Isen, 1987; Schwarz & Bless, 1991).

The second reading in this section examines how mood-related changes in cognitive processing style affect one particular type of social influence: persuasion. Bless, Bohner, Schwarz, & Strack (1990) experimentally induced happy or sad moods by asking participants to recall a happy or sad experience. Participants were then presented with a persuasive message consisting either of strong or of weak arguments. The key overall finding in their two experiments was that participants in bad moods were more influenced by strong arguments than by weak arguments, but that participants in good moods were equally influenced by each.

These findings fit nicely with recent theorizing on the nature of persuasion. It has been proposed that people do not always process persuasive communications the same way. Sometimes people "elaborate" a message by attending carefully to the information and thinking critically about it (the "central route to persuasion"). Other times people do not elaborate the message, relying instead on heuristics and cues without scrutinizing the information contained in the message itself (the "peripheral route to persuasion") (Petty & Cacioppo, 1986; cf. Chaiken, Liberman, & Eagly, 1989). The results of the experiments performed by Bless and colleagues suggest that bad moods incline people to follow the central route whereas good moods incline them to follow the peripheral route.

Exactly why moods have this effect is a matter of some dispute that continues to occupy researchers. Some view these effects as automatic and possibly innate properties of moods (e.g., Ashby, Isen, & Turken, 1999), whereas others view them as potentially controllable and reversible (e.g., Clore, Schwarz, & Conway, 1994). Numerous specific hypotheses have been advanced, but none to date has achieved general support (Forgas, 2000).

There is little doubt that both general cognitive processing styles as well as specific cognitive processes are influenced by emotional states. The two articles in this section, plus the last article of the preceding section, have shown how these effects impact a variety of social phenomena: helping behavior, person perception, and persuasion. These are among the most important topics that have been studied, but it is important to realize that moods and emotions influence many other social phenomena as well. Intergroup relations, prejudice, and stereotyping are affected by moods and emotions, as are perceptions of attractiveness and mate selection. Social judgments, decision making, motivated reasoning, and the use of social scripts likewise are affected. In short, the topics in this section are but a sample of the myriad social phenomena that are influenced by moods and emotions.

REFERENCES

Ashby, F. G., Isen, A. M., & Turken, A. U. (1999). A neuro-psychological theory of positive affect and its influence on cognition. *Psychological Review, 106*, 529–550.

Blaney, P. H. (1986). Affect and memory: A review. *Psychological Bulletin, 99*, 229-246.

Bless, H., Bohner, G., Schwarz, N., & Strack, F. (1990). Mood and persuasion: A cognitive response analysis. *Personality and Social Psychology Bulletin, 16*, 331–345.

Bower, G. H. (1981). Mood and memory. *American Psychologist, 36*, 129–148.

Chaiken, S., Liberman, A., & Eagly, A. (1989). Heuristic and systematic information processing within and beyond the persuasion context. In J. Uleman & J. A. Bargh (Eds.), *Unintended thought* (pp. 212–252). New York: Guilford.

Clore, G. L., Schwarz, N., & Conway, M. (1994). Affective causes and consequences of social information processing. In R. S. Wyer & T. K. Srull (Eds.), *Handbook of social cognition* (2nd ed., Vol. 1, pp. 323–418). Hillsdale, NJ: Erlbaum.

Fiedler, K. (2000). Toward an integrative account of affect and cognition phenomena using the BIAS computer algorithm. In J. P. Forgas (Ed.), *Feeling and thinking: The role of affect in social cognition* (pp. 223–252). Cambridge, England: Cambridge University Press.

Forgas, J. P. (Ed.) (2000). *Feeling and thinking: The role of affect in social cognition*. Cambridge, England: Cambridge University Press.

Forgas, J. P., & Bower, G. H. (1987). Mood effects on person-perception judgments. *Journal of Personality and Social Psychology, 53*, 53–60.

Isen, A. (1987). Positive affect, cognitive processes and social behavior. In L. Berkowitz (Ed.), *Advances in experimental social psychology* (Vol. 20, pp. 203–253). New York: Academic Press.

Parrott, W. G., & Hertel, P. (1999). Research methods in cognition and emotion. In T. Dalgleish & M. Power (Eds.), *The handbook of cognition and emotion* (pp. 61–81). Chichester: John Wiley & Sons.

Parrott, W. G., & Sabini, J. (1990). Mood and memory under natural conditions: Evidence for mood incongruent recall. *Journal of Personality and Social Psychology, 59*, 321–336.

Parrott, W. G., & Spackman, M. (2000). Emotion and memory. In M. Lewis & J. Haviland-Jones (Eds.), *Handbook of emotions* (2nd ed.) (pp. 476–490). New York: Guilford.

Petty, R. E., & Cacioppo, J. T. (1986). *Communication and persuasion: Central and peripheral routes to attitude change*. New York: Springer-Verlag.

Schwarz, N., & Bless, H. (1991). Happy and mindless but sad and smart? The impact of affective states on analytic reasoning. In J. P. Forgas (Ed.), *Emotion and social judgments* (pp. 55–71). Oxford: Pergamon Press.

Schwarz, N., & Clore, G. L. (1983). Mood, misattribution, and judgements of well-being: Informative and directive functions of affective states. *Journal of Personality and Social Psychology, 45*, 513–523.

Discussion Questions

1. What do the terms "mood-congruent learning" and "mood-congruent recall" mean? Describe psychological processes that could produce each of these effects.
2. Mood-incongruent recall sometimes occurs, and so does mood-incongruent learning. What psychological processes could bring these about, and what does their existence imply about the mood-congruent effects that occur on other occasions?
3. Much social information is ambiguous. How might a person's emotional state influence his or her interpretation and response to a friend's ambiguous remark or gesture?
4. What are the "central" and the "peripheral" routes to persuasion?
5. Consider how moods might affect the use of stereotypes. In what ways might these effects be motivated, and in what ways might they be purely due to automatic changes in information processing?
6. Given the effects that emotions have on person perception, memory, and persuasion, under what conditions will good moods prove most useful? What about bad moods? What do your answers imply about mood regulation and emotional intelligence?

Suggested Readings

Forgas, J. P. (Ed.) (2000). *Feeling and thinking: The role of affect in social cognition*. Cambridge, England: Cambridge University Press. The chapters in this volume provide an up-to-date survey of research on how emotion affects social cognition.

Singer, J. A. & Salovey, P. (1993). *The remembered self: Emotion and memory in personality*. New York: Free Press. This book argues for a motivational approach to understanding how emotion affects memory. Motives such as self-regulation of mood and maintaining a self-concept are among those addressed in this highly readable book.

Parrott, W. G., & Spackman, M. (2000). Emotion and memory. In M. Lewis & J. Haviland-Jones (Eds.), *Handbook of emotions* (2nd ed.) (pp. 476–490). New York: Guilford. This chapter provides a clear overview of the principal ways in which emotion influences memory. It focuses on phenomena that are problematic for associative network theory, and reviews the motivational and constructionist theories that have been proposed as alternatives.

Forgas, J. P. (1995). Mood and judgment: The affect infusion model (AIM). *Psychological Bulletin, 117*, 39–66. The model described in this paper is the best known social psychological attempt to account for the multiple ways that mood can affect social judgment and to predict which will prevail under any given circumstances.

Clore, G. L., Schwarz, N., & Conway, M. (1994). Affective causes and consequences of social information processing. In R. S. Wyer & T. K. Srull (Eds.), *Handbook of social cognition* (2nd ed., Vol. 1, pp. 323–418). Hillsdale, NJ: Erlbaum. This chapter surveys theory and research on emotion and social cognition with particular reference to the theory that moods provide information.

Mood Effects on Person-Perception Judgments

Joseph P. Forgas • University of New South Wales, Australia
Gordon H. Bower • Stanford University

How does mood affect the way we learn about, judge, and remember characteristics of other people? This study looked at the effects of mood on impression formation and person memory. Realistic person descriptions containing positive and negative details were presented to subjects experiencing a manipulated happy or sad mood. Next, impression-formation judgments were obtained, and subjects' recall and recognition of details of the characters were assessed. Results showed that subjects spent longer learning about mood-consistent details but were faster in making mood-consistent judgments. Overall, happy subjects formed more favorable impressions and made more positive judgments than did sad subjects. Both cued recall and recognition memory were superior for mood-consistent characteristics. Positive mood had a more pronounced effect on judgments and memory than did negative mood. These findings are discussed in terms of recent theories of mood effects on cognition, and the likely implications of the results for everyday person-perception judgments are considered.

Does mood influence the time we spend examining positive or negative information about others? Does it influence the quality and latency of our person-perception judgments? Impression formation is a complex task largely based on inferences (Heider, 1958) that may be particularly sensitive to mood-induced biases (Forgas & Bower, 1988). Following recent theories of mood effects on cognition (cf. Bower, 1983; Clark & Isen, 1982), in this study we sought to show that people (a) will spend more time to learn about the mood-consistent characteristics of others, (b) will make more mood-consistent rather than inconsistent judgments, (c) will make mood-consistent judgments faster than inconsistent ones, and (d) will recall and recognize mood-consistent details about others better than inconsistent ones.[1] The demonstration of such mood-based distortions in person perception is of considerable practical im-portance and should provide direct evidence in the form of reaction time data for the kind of processing biases predicted by recent mood-cognition theories (Bower, 1981, 1983; Clark & Isen, 1982).

Researchers have recognized, at least since Asch's (1946) classic studies, that person perception is a constructive process in which expectations, predispositions, and implicit personality theories are sometimes more important than the actual characteristics of the people we judge (Schneider, 1973). In exploring this constructive

---

[1]The terms *mood consistent* and *mood congruent* are used throughout this article to refer to material whose evaluative valence matches the mood state of a subject. Thus any positive characteristic of a target person is mood consistent with a happy subject. This usage is based on Bower's (1981) semantic network model and represents an extension of earlier work in which mood consistency was primarily used to refer to words or events with an explicit affective loading.

aspect of person perception, many researchers have concentrated on the enduring cognitive expectations of the perceiver, often ignoring the short-term influence of fluctuating mood states. As Taylor (1981) noted, the perceiver is often thought of as a creature "out of a Camus novel: alone, bereft of language, without emotion, looking backwards" (p. 205). Yet much evidence suggests that the way the perceiver feels at the time is one of the most important influences on social judgments (Forgas & Moylan, 1987). Past studies have shown that people tend to find others more attractive when they feel good (Clark & Waddell, 1983; Gouaux, 1971; Gouaux & Summers, 1973; Griffitt, 1970), to judge others as more aggressive when they feel fearful (Feshbach & Singer, 1957), and to interpret facial expressions (Schiffenbauer, 1974), social events (Clore, 1985), or even interactive behaviors (Forgas, Bower, & Krantz, 1984) in accordance with their prevailing mood state.

Mood-based distortions in person perception have traditionally been interpreted either in terms of classical conditioning principles (Griffitt, 1970) or attributable to various dynamic or motivational factors, such as projection (Feshbach & Singer, 1957) or defensive biases (Freud, 1917/1952). In recent years, cognitively based models emphasizing the information-processing consequences of mood have gained ascendancy (Bower, 1981, 1983; Clark & Isen, 1982; Clore, 1985; Forgas & Bower, 1988). As Bruner (1957) stated some 30 years ago, perceiving an object or a person is essentially an act of categorization. Social judgments, in general, and person-perception judgments, in particular, involve the imposition of our internal cognitive constructs on the complex and often indeterminate characteristics of others (Heider, 1958; Kelly, 1955). Mood states may bias person perception by selectively influencing what people learn about others and by distorting the interpretations and associations they make (Bower, 1981; Clark & Isen, 1982). Indeed, at times it seems that "social behavior is almost a blank canvas onto which perceivers project a picture according to their moods" (Bower & Cohen, 1982, p. 307). Recent cognitive models imply specific mood-dependent biases in selective attention and judgment latencies that have not previously been demonstrated. To explicitly test these theories, we used a reaction-time paradigm to examine three different aspects of the way

mood states influence impression-formation judgments: learning and selective attention effects, judgmental biases, and memory biases.

In the first instance, we expected people to take longer to examine and encode mood-consistent information. There are three convergent reasons for these expected encoding biases. At the time of learning, "by spreading activation, a dominant emotion will enhance the availability of emotion-congruent interpretations and the salience of congruent stimulus materials for learning" (Bower, Gilligan, & Monteiro, 1981, p. 451). Because of the richer availability of mood-related categories and the larger number of potential associations and interpretations for such details, people should take longer to deal with and encode mood-consistent information into this enhanced associative base. Secondly, selective exposure effects may also contribute to the longer processing of mood-consistent information. The affective tone of observed characteristics enhances the intensity of congruent moods and reduces the intensity of incongruent feelings. Increased mood intensity may in turn motivate judges to give mood-consistent materials greater attention and to process them in greater detail and to a greater depth. Finally, mood-consistent materials are also more likely to selectively remind subjects of relevant episodes from their past, leading to the slower and deeper processing and superior recall of such details. Accordingly, we expected people to pay preferential attention to mood-consistent information and to take significantly longer to learn about and encode such characteristics about others.

Our predictions were quite different for actual judgments. We expected mood to bias the quality of subjects' impression-formation judgments (Forgas et al., 1984; Gouaux, 1971; Griffitt, 1970) and mood-consistent judgments to take less time to make than inconsistent judgments. As Craik and Tulving (1975) suggested, the richer the conceptual schema an event is related to at encoding, the more elaborate the memory trace and the faster the retrieval. At the time of judgment, we expected that mood-consistent information about the target person would be retrieved faster and in greater numbers than inconsistent information. Accordingly, happy subjects should make more positive judgments, sad judges should make more negative judgments, and such judgments should be made faster than mood-inconsistent judgments. Some evidence also suggests, however, that positive moods may be more effective than negative moods in influencing social judgments (Forgas & Bower, 1988; Forgas et al., 1984). Some models (cf. Clark & Isen, 1982) explicitly allow for the different influence of good as opposed to bad moods. In addition to the usual *automatic* processing strategy, *controlled* processing may be used to focus preferentially on positive materials to achieve a more positive mood state. This may limit the impact of negative mood effects on selective attention and memory. Our data will also be relevant to examining whether mood-induced biases in person perception are similar across good and bad moods.

Finally, the superior learning of mood-congruent materials should also influence our later memories about the people we encounter. Although mood may not have a robust effect on some retrieval processes (Blaney, 1986; Bower, 1985; Bower & Mayer, 1985), the richer associations and greater attention to mood-consistent characteristics at the time of encoding should result in better memory for such details (Craik & Tulving, 1975). There is some evidence that people tend to pay more attention to information consistent with their own mood and remember such details better (Blaney, 1986; Bower et al., 1981). In this study, we sought to expand these findings by directly measuring the time taken by happy or sad subjects to process each new item of positive or negative information about a person and to evaluate their later recall and recognition of such details.

Thus our first hypothesis is that judges should pay preferential attention to mood-consistent details of the targets. We expected happy people to take longer to deal with positive information and sad people to take longer to deal with negative information about others. Mood was also expected to influence both the quality and latency of impression-formation judgments. We expected happy subjects to make more positive and fewer negative judgments, and to make positive judgments faster. Exactly the opposite was expected for unhappy subjects. This pattern is consistent with the predicted better learning and greater availability of mood-consistent evidence and interpretational categories for use in judgments (cf. Bower, 1981, 1983; Clark & Isen, 1982; Forgas et al., 1984). Finally, we also expected recall and recognition

to be superior for the mood-congruent characteristics of the target persons.

Method

OVERVIEW

A positive or negative mood state was induced in subjects through manipulated feedback about their performance on a bogus test. Next, in an allegedly separate experiment, four realistic person descriptions were presented, each containing an equal number of positive and negative details. Impression-formation judgments of each character were also obtained. The exact time taken to read each descriptive sentence and to make each judgment was recorded. Finally, subjects' cued recall and recognition memory for details of the target persons were tested.

SUBJECTS

Fifty-two undergraduates (24 men and 28 women) participated in the study either for course credit or for money. Three additional subjects (2 women and 1 man) had to be eliminated from the analysis because of missing data owing to computer malfunction.

STIMULUS MATERIALS

We constructed four stimulus character descriptions, each consisting of 12 brief sentences. Each sentence communicated positive or negative information about the target character (e.g., "In grade school Bob was always very good at sports," "Cindy is short and very plain looking," "Steven is a generous and extraverted person"). The first and last sentences for each character were affectively neutral, describing common and banal features (e.g., catches the bus to work, lives in an apartment). The other 10 sentences were further subdivided, with 5 statements communicating information about the targets' socioemotional characteristics (e.g., friendliness, popularity) and 5 statements communicating information about his or her task competence (e.g., skill, intelligence). Thus each character description included relevant information about the two most common dimensions found in person perception research, namely, likability and competence (cf. Forgas, 1985).

Learning information about people depends not only on affective quality but also on many other characteristics, such as personal relevance, associations, information content, complexity, length, and so on. To control for such extraneous variables, we used two parallel stimulus lists within each mood condition, each incorporating lexically matched statements differing in affective quality only. This was achieved by switching only the evaluative descriptors between the two alternate sets. For example, if John was described in Set A as "always getting good marks at school," in Set B he was presented as "always getting bad marks school." Because the change of affective meaning was achieved by the substitution of single words (e.g., *good* for *bad*, *clever* for *stupid*), the two alternative versions of each character were as similar as possible in terms of length, semantic clarity, and syntactic complexity, and both occurred with the same frequency within each mood condition.

MOOD MANIPULATION TECHNIQUE

Mood was manipulated by giving subjects bogus feedback about their "good" or "bad" performance on a psychological test that allegedly measured social adjustment and personality. This technique, although it requires particularly careful debriefing (see Debriefing), had several advantages when compared with other mood manipulation procedures such as hypnosis (Bower, 1981), self-statements (Velten, 1968), or giving small presents (Clark & Isen, 1982). The false-feedback procedure can be used with any population, not just those who are highly hypnotizable. The resulting mood state is more personally relevant and enduring than commonly obtained by most nonhypnotic procedures. The procedure can induce both positive and negative moods, and the situational context is realistic and contains few demand characteristics.

A 50-item questionnaire assessing social adjustment and personality was used as the basis of the false-feedback manipulation. We selected items from published scales dealing with constructs such as social skills, loneliness, shyness, and self-monitoring. After completing the questionnaire, subjects were given detailed positive or negative feedback about their performance by trained confederates (see Procedure for details). Previous researchers have found this technique to result in a strong and enduring mood state that shows only a moderate decline even after 25 min of unrelated activity (cf. Forgas & Hepperlin, 1982). The present findings also confirm the technique's effectiveness (see Results).

PROCEDURE

Subjects were recruited to participate in two short, unrelated studies conducted by two different experimenters during a 1-hr session described as "a questionnaire study of personality and social adjustment" and an "experiment in person perception." On arrival, subjects were greeted by the first experimenter, a woman, who led them to a room equipped with chairs and tables and piles of blank or completed questionnaires. She reiterated that in order to save subjects' time, they would he asked to participate in two separate studies during the next hour. The first study involved the administration of a questionnaire that was described as measuring

> general social adjustment and personality in a student population that was found to be an extremely reliable and valid measure of these constructs in the past. Most people find it very useful in gaining a more objective and balanced view of themselves.

The questionnaire was then administered. Most subjects completed it in 8 to 10 min. The experimenter then informed subjects that she would score their answers immediately and give some feedback about their performance. She then proceeded to "score" the questionnaire using a prepared scoring template, jotting down several subscores and periodically consulting an impressive-looking bound "scoring manual." As the first scores became available, the experimenter would make increasingly strong signals indicating approval (head nods, smiles, mumbled comments such as "yes, yes," "good," "very good," "excellent") or disappointment (head shakes, frowns, mumbled comments such as "no," "bad," "pity," or "this is terrible"), depending on the mood condition to which the subject was assigned.

Once the scoring was completed, the experimenter would turn to the subject and say,

> This is very good (very bad). You have done much better (much worse) than the average score for students in your age group. You obviously have an excellent (problematic) personality, and you find most social situations very easy (quite diffi-

cult) to handle. If you have any more questions about this study, I will discuss it with you later but right now our time is up, and you will have to go to another room to participate in the second study you have to do today.

In addition to this verbal information, the interpersonal behavior of the experimenter was also carefully manipulated to communicate liking and admiration or dislike and condescension in the two mood conditions.

PROCEDURE IN THE PERSON-PERCEPTION EXPERIMENT

Following the mood manipulation, subjects were sent to an adjacent room where a second female experimenter introduced the person perception task. Subjects were told,

Information about different people will be presented sentence by sentence on a computer screen. Your task is to read each sentence carefully, trying to form as clear an impression about that person as possible. When you are finished with one sentence, press the space bar and the next sentence will appear. You will also be asked some questions about each of the characters, which you can also answer on the computer keyboard.

All necessary information, together with practice trials, was repeated on the computer screen. Subjects were left alone in an experimental cubicle until they had completed the task.

Subjects rated each character on eight 9-point rating scales. The scales were selected from the person-perception literature so as to tap the most common dimensions relevant to this task. These dimensions consisted of the following items: self-confident/shy, likable/dislikable, competent/incompetent, happy/unhappy, intelligent/unintelligent, good/hard to work with, likely/unlikely to have a good marriage, and likely/unlikely to do well in his or her job. In addition, to validate the effectiveness of the mood manipulation, at three different times during the procedure, covert questions (inserted among distracter items such as "Are you sitting comfortably?" Are you ready for the next sentence?) were used to ask subjects to rate their own mood state on 9-point happy–sad scales on the screen.

After reading about and making judgments of all four characters, a short (about 4 min) intervening period followed in which subjects were asked to perform some simple arithmetic calculations. At the end of this period, the experimenter, who was blind to the mood condition prior to this point, briefly inquired about the subject's performance on the personality questionnaire and indicated her belief in the reliability and validity of the instrument. This was done to reactivate the manipulated mood state. Next, subjects were given a cued recall test that asked them to "recall and write down everything you can remember about each of the characters you read about whose names appear on the top of each page."

Finally, a three-alternative forced-choice recognition test was administered. Each cluster consisted of one original and two distracter items. The first distracter was an evaluatively similar paraphrase of the original sentence. The second distracter was lexically identical to the original except for the evaluative term, which was replaced by its antonym.

DEBRIEFING

Because of the deceptive nature of the mood manipulation, an extensive and carefully designed debriefing session concluded the procedure. Care was taken to create a friendly and informal atmosphere in which the aims and rationale for the study were fully explained. The possible perseverance of the effects of the false feedback was described (cf. Ross, Lepper, & Hubbard, 1975), and subjects were invited to inspect all the materials used. All subjects understood and accepted the rationale of the procedure, and we found no evidence of any residual negative effects. The debriefing also revealed that the mood-manipulation procedure was accepted at face value by all subjects, and none of the subjects suspected a link between the mood manipulation and the person-perception task.

Results and Discussion

The results will be discussed in terms of the five main dependent variables we studied: (a) selective attention (reading times), (b) impression formation, (c) judgmental latencies, and (d) recall and (e) recognition memory for persons. As no significant differences owing to the subjects' sex or the two alternative lists of person descriptions were found, we will not consider these variables further.

EFFECTIVENESS OF THE MOOD MANIPULATION

To establish the effectiveness of our mood-manipulation procedure, we had subjects rate their own current mood state on 9-point happy–sad scales on three occasions during the procedure. An analysis of the average of these self-ratings showed a significant overall difference in mood between subjects in the happy and sad conditions, $F(1, 50) = 6.54$, $p < .025$, with only a moderate decline over time. We concluded that our mood manipulation procedure was effective in generating strong and enduring mood states. Our own observations, as well as comments by subjects during the debriefing, confirmed that all subjects took the false feedback they received seriously and reacted with the expected elated or depressed mood state.

READING TIMES: MOOD EFFECTS ON SELECTIVE ATTENTION

We next looked at the influence of mood on the way subjects attended to the various details of the target people. The time taken by subjects to read about the person stimuli was significantly affected by their mood state, $F(1, 50) = 8.21, p < .01$. Overall, subjects in a happy mood were almost 1 s faster in dealing with one unit of stimulus information than were subjects in a bad mood (6,074 ms vs. 7,056 ms). These results are consistent with the notion that a happy, elated mood is often associated with faster and more decisive information-processing strategies. Isen and Means (1983) also found that in dealing with complex and multidimensional information, "good-mood" subjects make faster decisions.

In accordance with our major hypothesis, we also found a significant interaction effect between the subjects' mood state and the evaluative valence of the material they read, $F(1, 50) = 12.30, p < .01$ (see Figure 11.1). Subjects in a good mood took longer to read positive than negative information (6,330 ms vs. 5,818 ms), $F(1, 50) = 6.01, p < .025$, and subjects who experienced a depressed mood spent longer reading about the negative than the positive characteristics of people (7,385 ms vs. 6,727 ms), $F(1, 50) = 5.58, p < .025$. This finding supported our expectation that mood-consistent information would receive more detailed attention and processing.

Mood activates richer and more elaborate background schemas relevant to the encoding of mood-congruent person descriptions, accounting for the longer processing of such details. Several models (Bower, 1983; Clark & Isen, 1982) specifically predict that mood increases the availability of mood-related thoughts or information. Because of the preactivation of an enriched associative base,

> pleasant events will receive more processing when people are in a pleasant mood, and unpleasant events will receive more processing when they are in an unpleasant mood. As a result, subjects should learn to a greater degree events that are congruent with their current emotion. (Bower et al., 1981, p. 453)

Selective attention to mood-consistent information can also be enhanced by motivational factors. Mood-consistent material may be focused on because it can serve to intensify existing feelings or to selectively remind us of relevant episodes from the past (Bower et al., 1981). The present results are the first empirically to demonstrate mood-based differences in selective attention and processing times in a realistic person-perception task, a finding of considerable theoretical and applied importance. The pattern of our results suggests that such attention and learning biases may occur both in good- and in bad-mood states (see Figure 11.1).

IMPRESSION FORMATION: MOOD AND THE QUALITY OF PERSON-PERCEPTION JUDGMENTS

We also predicted that overall, impression-formation judgments should be biased in the direction of the prevailing mood. An analysis of variance of mean impression-formation judgments (with low numbers corresponding to more positive impressions on a 9-point scale) indeed showed that happy subjects formed significantly more favorable impressions of the targets than did sad subjects (3.87 vs. 6.19), $F(1, 50) = 14.25, p < .01$.

Recent research has shown that many other everyday judgments (Forgas & Moylan, 1987), including interpretations of ongoing social behaviors (Forgas et al., 1984), can be influenced by transient mood. However, positive and negative mood had somewhat different effects on judgments in this as well as in several other studies (for a review, see Forgas & Bower, 1988). To gain further insight into such differences, we decided to analyze the actual number of positive and nega-

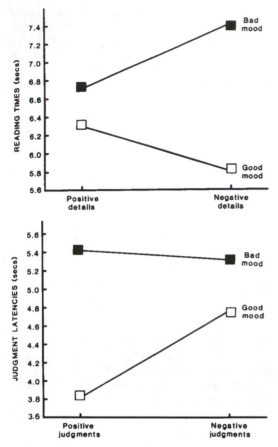

FIGURE 11.1 ▪ The effects of happy or sad mood on the time taken by subjects to learn about the positive or negative characteristics of people (top graph) and to make positive or negative impression-formation judgments (bottom graph).

impression-formation judgments (cf. Forgas et al., 1984; Gouaux, 1971; Gouaux & Summers, 1973), although this effect seems far more pronounced in positive than in negative moods in this as well as in other studies (cf. Forgas et al., 1984).

JUDGMENT LATENCIES

How did mood affect the time subjects took to make positive or negative person-perception judgments? For each judgmental dimension (e.g., happy–sad, likable–dislikable), we measured the average time taken by each subject in a happy or sad mood to make each judgment falling on the positive or the negative side of a scale. We found a mood main effect indicating that both kinds of judgments took longer to make in a bad mood than in a good mood (5,391 ms vs. 4,259 ms), $F(1, 50) = 13.97$, $p < .01$. A second main effect revealed that irrespective of mood, negative judgments took somewhat longer to make than did positive judgments (5,027 ms vs. 4,624 ms), $F(1, 50) = 4.99$, $p < .05$. This difference probably reflects the fact that the majority of our interpersonal judgments tend to be positive (Matlin & Stang, 1978) and to be made with a high degree of automaticity. Negative judgments, in contrast, are more uncommon and probably require more controlled and elaborate information processing than is the case with positive judgments.

In addition to these main effects, the expected significant Mood × Judgment Type interaction was also found, $F(1, 50) = 8. 13$, $p < .01$ (see Figure 11.1). When in a good mood, subjects made positive judgments considerably faster than they made negative judgments (3,8 13 ms vs. 4,706 ms), $F(1, 50) = 12.71$, $p < .01$. In a negative mood, negative judgments took marginally less time than did positive judgments (5,349 ms vs. 5,434 ms), although this difference was not significant. As hypothesized, these results show that mood-consistent judgments take less time to make than inconsistent judgments. These reaction-time differences may be partly related to the previous finding that mood-consistent judgments are also more frequently made, as quick response latency is often a characteristic of more frequent and dominant responses. The present study, however, is the first in which this frequency–latency relation has been demonstrated with respect to mood-primed materials.

The greater speed and frequency of mood-con-

tive judgments (defined as falling on either side of the neutral point on a scale) made by happy and sad subjects. The maximum number of person-perception judgments made by each subject was 32 (8 judgments of each of four stimulus persons). As expected, subjects in a good mood made considerably more favorable than unfavorable judgments (17.35 vs. 12.61). We found a similar but less pronounced pattern with subjects experiencing a bad mood (15.24 vs. 14.61). A statistical comparison of the judgmental patterns of good-mood as opposed to bad-mood subjects (based on the balance of positive over negative judgments for each group) again revealed a significant mood effect, $F(1, 50) = 7.69$, $p < .01$ (see Figure 11.2). This result confirms our hypothesis that temporary mood states indeed influence the quality of sistent judgments are theoretically consistent with the better learning and availability of mood-associated constructs (Bower, 1983; Clark & Isen, 1982). In the present case, the slower and more detailed encoding of mood-consistent details found earlier is likely to have resulted in the superior availability of evidence for mood-consistent judgments. In other words, selective attention and encoding biases probably account for a large part of the greater frequency and speed of mood-consistent impression-formation judgments found here. Interpretive biases may have played an additional, although smaller, role. As judgments of people are largely a matter of interpretation and inference (Forgas, 1983; Heider, 1958; Kelly, 1955), mood may function as "a 'cognitive set' to bias the way perceivers interpret social messages" (Bower et al., 1981, p. 453).

It is an interesting implication of cognitive-priming models that it is the slower and more thorough encoding of mood-consistent information that allows later mood-consistent judgments to be faster and more frequent. By directly demonstrating such a pattern in impression formation, our findings add significant new evidence to the growing number of studies that illustrate the importance of mood states in a variety of social judgments (Forgas & Bower, 1988). An interesting question is whether the same judgmental biases would also occur when encoding and judgmental moods are different, or when there is a greater temporal separation between the two events. We hope to explore this in the future.

It is noteworthy that mood-based distortions in judgmental latencies seem more pronounced in a good mood than in a bad mood. Although in the absence of a neutral condition we cannot be certain that this was caused by a genuine mood asymmetry, other evidence also suggests that the effects of negative mood states on social judgments are often subject to constraints. For example, bad mood is less likely to distort judgments of others than judgments of the self, both by depressed subjects (Hoehn-Hyde, Schlottmann, & Rush, 1982; Garber & Hollon, 1980) and by otherwise normal judges (Forgas et al., 1984; Pietromonaco & Markus, 1985). Several factors may contribute to the weakness or absence of negative mood biases when judging others. Perhaps as a result of internalized cultural norms, people learn to constrain the effects of their bad moods on social judgments. Ceiling effects may also have limited the impact of negative moods on judgmental latencies here, as judgments took far longer to make in a bad mood than in a good mood. Increasingly, evidence suggests that the basic and symmetrical mood effects predicted by cognitive theories such as the network model may be further modulated by a variety of social, cultural, and contextual factors that have received little attention to date (Forgas, 1981, 1983).

MOOD EFFECTS ON RECALL ABOUT PEOPLE

How did subjects' mood and the affective quality of the information influence memory for the stimulus characters? An analysis of the recall data indicated that good-mood subjects remembered slightly more of the 40 descriptive statements they read than did bad-mood subjects (16.75 vs. 15.31), but the difference was not significant, $F(1, 50) < 1.0$. The affective loading of the information had a significant influence on memory, $F(1, 50) = 4.33$, $p < .05$: Overall, more positive than negative details were remembered (8.80/20 vs. 7.23/20). The bias toward recalling more positive information exemplifies the positivity bias commonly found in many social judgments: All things being equal, people tend to see and remember others in a positive rather than a negative light, in accordance with the cultural expectations that regulate expected and desirable standards of conduct (Forgas, 1985).

Our major hypothesis predicted an interaction

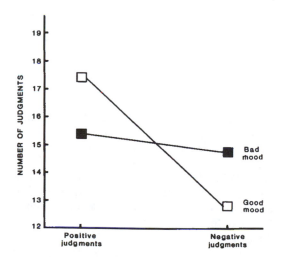

FIGURE 11.2 ■ The effects of happy or sad mood on the number of positive and negative person-perception judgments made by subjects.

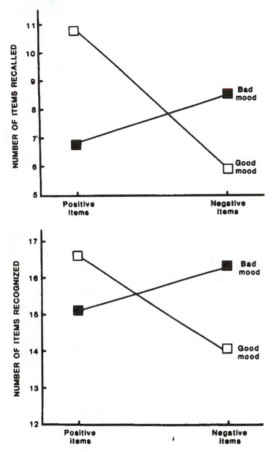

FIGURE 11.3 ■ The effects of happy or sad learning mood on subjects' ability to recall (top graph) and to recognize (bottom graph) the positive and negative details of the target characters.

between mood and the affective quality of the information leading to the superior learning and recall of mood-congruent items. Indeed, mood-congruent details were better remembered than mood-incongruent information, $F(1, 50) = 22.1$ 8, $p < .01$. Of a total of 20 positive and 20 negative characteristics shown to each subject, those in the good-mood condition remembered 10.83 positive and 5.92 negative items. $F(1, 50) = 9.09$, $p < .01$. In turn, subjects in a bad mood remembered somewhat more negative (8.54) than positive (6.77) details about the target persons, again a significant difference, $F(1, 50) = 4.27$, $p < .05$ (see Figure 11.3). Having already found a significantly longer processing time for mood-congruent descriptions of people, the superior recall of such information clearly reflects an encoding bias. This

finding extends the mood-congruity effect reported by Bower et al. (1981) and others to the domain of person-perception judgments. Interestingly, although retrieval mood effects on memory were not particularly robust (Blaney, 1986; Bower, 1985; Bower & Mayer, 1985), the present results suggest that encoding mood biases may play an important role in the kind of information that is later remembered about a person.

MOOD AND RECOGNITION MEMORY FOR PERSONS

In our recognition test, subjects were provided with three alternative choices for each of the person-description items they read: (a) the original statement, (b) an evaluatively similar distractor, and (c) a lexically similar distracter. The correct recognition data indicated similar but weaker mood effects than those found with the recall task. Neither the mood nor the evaluative valence of the information resulted in a significant main effect, $F(1, 50) < 1.0$. However, there was a small but significant Mood × Description Type interaction, $F(1, 50) = 9.09$, $p < .05$. This indicated that subjects in a good mood correctly recognized more positive than negative information about the targets (16.62 vs. 14.01), $F(1, 50) = 5.11$, $p < .01$, and subjects in a bad mood recognized somewhat more negative than positive details (16.27 vs. 15.13), $F(1, 50) < 1.0$ (see Figure 11.3). Such mood biases in recognition memory are of considerable interest because it is often assumed that the strong retrieval cues provided by recognition tasks generally mask the weaker mood effects (cf. Bower, 1981). Our findings suggest that recognition biases may in fact occur in person perception as a result of strong encoding (but probably not retrieval) of mood effects.

Of particular interest here is subjects' further analysis of incorrect recognition judgments ("false alarms"). We expected that evaluatively consistent distracters would be erroneously recognized as correct more frequently than would lexically consistent distracters (same words but different evaluative tone). We found some evidence to support this hypothesis. Overall, more mood-consistent distracters were recognized as correct than lexically consistent distractors (2.89 vs. 1.61), $F(1, 50) = 5.64$, $p < .025$. This tendency was equally characteristic of subjects irrespective of the happy or sad mood inductions they received. The most obvious explanation for such mood-consistent recognition errors is that subjects used their overall evaluative impressions about the target as a directive cue in identifying what they thought to be familiar information about others. What is remarkable is that evaluatively consistent but otherwise completely novel statements seemed to be more likely to trigger such false recognition judgments than statements that were lexically almost identical to the originals but different in evaluative tone.

Summary and Conclusions

We argued in this study that the congruence between the emotional state of a perceiver and the emotional character of information received about others may play a significant role in how person-perception judgments are commonly made. We found a wide range of evidence to support such a view. Subjects took longer to deal with mood-consistent information about others. Their later recall and recognition of such details was superior to their memory for incongruent characteristics. Their recognition errors also tended to be biased toward mood-consistent information. The quality and latency of person-perception judgments were also significantly influenced by mood. Mood-consistent judgments were made both more frequently and more quickly than mood-inconsistent judgments, probably as a result of the better encoding and availability of mood-consistent evidence. These findings are of considerable theoretical importance. They provide robust and unambiguous evidence for the kind of mood-contingent processing biases implied by the models put forward by Bower (1981, 1983), Clark and Isen (1982) and others. The different consequences of mood for encoding and judgmental latencies are consistent with these cognitive-priming theories.

Person perception is a highly complex process, involving a great deal of inference and reconstruction in the way observed details of a person are selectively encoded, stored, retrieved, and integrated (Asch, 1946; Heider, 1958; Kelly, 1955; Schneider, 1973). Apart from a few studies (cf. Feshbach & Singer, 1957; Forgas et al., 1984; Gouaux, 1971; Griffitt, 1970), the role of affect in this process has been relatively neglected (Forgas & Bower, 1988). Considering the widespread use of person-perception skills in the legal system, the helping professions, personnel selection, politics, and the like, evidence of affective biases in this process is clearly of considerable practical importance. Evaluating the conditions under which such mood-dependent biases can be controlled or eliminated is an obvious task for future research.

Theoretically, our findings are largely consistent with the semantic network–spreading activation model of Bower (1981, 1983) and similar formulations by Clark and Isen (1982) and others. When it comes to very complex kinds of social judgments, as in the present case, however, we are also likely to find various motivational, cultural, and normative influences superimposed on the purely cognitive processes assumed by such models. Cognitive-priming theories have difficulty accounting for the context sensitivity of mood effects found in several studies (Forgas et al., 1984). Clearly the incorporation of additional sociocultural variables in basic cognitive-priming models is an important theoretical task if the complex processes underlying everyday social judgments are to be fully understood (Clore, 1985; Forgas, 1981, 1983).

Other theoretical models are also relevant to certain aspects of our data. The long tradition of research in social psychology concerned with social comparison processes (Festinger, 1954; Wills, 1981) and the effects of self-esteem on person-perception judgments may account for some of the qualitative biases found here. Clore's (1985) interesting misattribution theory of mood effects on social judgments is also consistent with some of the impression-formation biases we demonstrated. Despite their obvious relevance, however, none of these models offers a parsimonious alternative explanation for all of our findings. In particular, predictions about reading and judgmental latencies and memory performance are not an integral part of these theories. Cognitive-priming models continue to offer the best overall explanation of our data at the present time (Bower, 1981, 1983; Clark & Isen, 1982).

Although a comparison of positive and negative mood effects is difficult without a neutral condition, it is interesting that positive mood effects appeared more robust than negative mood biases in our judgmental and memory (but not the reading times) data. Earlier research also showed that negative mood effects on social judgments are on the whole less pronounced and may depend on a variety of contextual factors (Forgas & Bower, 1988; Forgas et al., 1984). Clinical studies also suggest that mood-dependent biases in depression can be target and context specific (Garber & Hollon, 1980; Hoehn-Hyde et al., 1982; Pietromonaco & Markus, 1985). Clark and Isen's (1982) notion of controlled processing may indeed account for some of the less robust negative mood effects apparent here and elsewhere. A further exploration of the conditions under which controlled processing occurs may well indicate that cultural and normative factors play an important role in triggering such a processing strategy (Forgas, 1981, 1983). Given that person-perception judgments play a crucial role in many everyday decisions, and that such judgments in real life are probably even more fraught with emotional reactions than is the case in laboratory experiments, the investigation of mood-induced biases in impression formation in various social contexts should remain one of the major concerns of social cognition research.

REFERENCES

Asch, S. E. (1946). Forming impressions of personality. *Journal of Abnormal and Social Psychology, 41,* 258–290.

Blaney, P. H. (1986). Affect and memory: A review. *Psychological Bulletin, 99,* 229–246.

Bower, G. H. (1981). Mood and memory. *American Psychologist, 36,* 129–148.

Bower, G. H. (1983). Affect and cognition. *Philosophical Transactions of the Royal Society, 302*(B), 387–403.

Bower, G. H. (1985, May). *Review of research on mood and memory.* Paper presented at the meeting of the British Psychological Society, Oxford, England.

Bower, G. H., & Cohen, P. R. (1982). Emotional influences in memory and thinking: Data and theory. In M. S. Clark & S. T. Fiske (Eds.), *Affect and cognition* (pp. 291–331). Hillsdale, NJ: Erlbaum.

Bower, G. H., Gilligan, S. G., & Monteiro, K. P. (1981). Selectivity of learning caused by affective states. *Journal of Experimental Psychology: General, 110,* 451-473.

Bower, G. H., & Mayer, J. D. (1985). Failure to replicate mood-dependent retrieval. *Bulletin of the Psychonomic Society, 23,* 39–42.

Bruner, J. S. (1957). On perceptual readiness. *Psychological Review, 64,* 123–152.

Clark, M. S., & Isen, A. M. (1982). Towards understanding the relationship between feeling states and social behavior. In A. Hastorf & A. M. Isen (Eds.), *Cognitive social psychology* (pp. 73–108). New York: Elsevier.

Clark, M. S., & Waddell, B. A. (1983). Effects of moods on thoughts about helping, attraction and information acquisition. *Social Psychology Quarterly, 46,* 31–35.

Clore, G. L. (1985, September). *The cognitive consequences of emotion and feeling.* Paper presented at the annual convention of the American Psychological Association, Los Angeles.

Craik, F. I. M., & Tulving, E. (1975). Depth of processing and the retention of words in episodic memory. *Journal of Experimental Psychology: General, 104,* 268–294.

Feshbach, S., & Singer, R. D. (1957). The effects of fear arousal and suppression of fear upon social perception. *Journal of Abnormal and Social Psychology, 55,* 283–288.

Festinger, L. A. (1954). A theory of social comparison processes. *Human Relations, 7,* 117–140.

Forgas, J. P. (Ed.). (1981). *Social cognition: Perspectives on everyday understanding.* London: Academic Press.

Forgas, J. P. (1983). What is social about social cognition? *British Journal of Social Psychology, 22,* 129–144.

Forgas, J. P. (1985). *Interpersonal behavior: The psychology of social interaction.* Oxford: Pergamon Press.

Forgas, J. P., & Bower, G. H. (1988). Mood effects on social judgments. In K. Fiedler & J. P. Forgas (Eds.), *Affect, cognition and social behavior.* Toronto, Canada: Hogrefe.

Forgas, J. P., Bower, G. H., & Krantz, S. (1984). The influence of mood on perceptions of social interactions. *Journal of Experimental Social Psychology, 20,* 497–513.

Forgas, J. P., & Hepperlin, C. (1982). *The effects of mood on memory and social judgments.* Unpublished manuscript, University of New South Wales, Sydney, Australia.

Forgas, J. P., & Moylan, S. (1987). After the movies: The effects of mood on social judgments. *Personality and Social Psychology Bulletin, 13,* 467–477.

Freud, S. (1952). *A general introduction to psychoanalysis.* New York: Washington Square Press. (Original work published 1917)

Garber, J., & Hollon, S. D. (1980). Universal versus personal helplessness in depression: Belief in uncontrollability or incompetence? *Journal of Abnormal Psychology, 89,* 56–66.

Gouaux, C. (1971). Induced affective states and interpersonal attraction. *Journal of Personality and Social Psychology, 20,* 37–43.

Gouaux, C., & Summers, K. (1973). Interpersonal attraction as a function of affective state and affective change. *Journal of Research in Personality, 7,* 254–260.

Griffitt, W. (1970). Environmental effects on interpersonal behavior. Ambient effective temperature and attraction. *Journal of Personality and Social Psychology, 15,* 14–144.

Heider, E. (1958). *The psychology of interpersonal relations.* New York: Wiley.

Hoehn-Hyde, D., Schlottmann, R. S., & Rush, A. J. (1982). Perceptions of social interactions in depressed psychiatric patients. *Journal of Consulting and Clinical Psychology, 50,* 209–212.

Isen, A. M., & Means, B. (1983). The influence of positive affect on decision-making strategy. *Social Cognition, 2,* 18–31.

Kelly, G. A. (1955). *The psychology of personal constructs.* New York: Norton.

Matlin, M., & Stang, D. (1978). *The Pollyanna principle: Selectivity in language, memory and thought.* Cambridge, MA: Schenkman.

Pietromonaco, P. R., & Markus, H. (1985). The nature of negative thoughts in depression. *Journal of Personality and Social Psychology, 3,* 799–807.

Ross, L., Lepper, M., & Hubbard, M. (1975). Perseverance in self-perception and social perception: Biased attributional processes in the debriefing paradigm. *Journal of Personality and Social Psychology, 32,* 880–892.

Schiffenbauer, A. (1974). Effect of observer's emotional state on judgments of the emotional state of others. *Journal of Personality and Social Psychology, 30,* 31–35.

Schneider, D. J. (1973). Implicit personality theory: A review. *Psychological Bulletin, 79,* 294–309.

Taylor, S. E. (1981). On the interface of cognitive and social psychology. In J. Harvey (Ed.), *Cognition, social behavior and the environment* (pp. 241–276). Hillsdale, NJ: Erlbaum.

Velten, E. (1968). A laboratory task for induction of mood states. *Behavior Research and Therapy 6,* 473–482.

Wills, T. A. (1981). Downward comparison principles in social psychology. *Psychological Bulletin, 90,* 245–271.

Mood and Persuasion: A Cognitive Response Analysis

Herbert Bless and Gerd Bohner • Universität Heidelberg
Norbert Schwarz • Zentrum für Umfragen, Methoden und Analysen (ZUMA), Mannheim
Fritz Strack • Universität Mannheim

The impact of happy and sad moods on the processing of persuasive communications is explored. In Experiment 1, sad subjects were influenced by a counterattitudinal message only if the arguments presented were strong, not if they were weak. Happy subjects, however, were equally persuaded by strong and weak arguments unless explicitly instructed to pay attention to the content of the message. Subjects' cognitive responses revealed a parallel pattern suggesting that the findings reflect the impact of mood on cognitive elaboration of the message. In Experiment 2, working on a distractor task during message exposure eliminated the advantage of strong over weak arguments under bad-mood conditions. Good-mood subjects were not affected by a distracting task suggesting that they did not engage in message elaboration to begin with. It is concluded that subjects in a good mood are less likely to engage in message elaboration than subjects in a bad mood.

Attempts to persuade another person are often accompanied by efforts to change the other's mood state. In advertising, political campaigns, and informal social encounters, efforts to make the recipient feel good often precede the actual persuasion attempt. The frequent use of this persuasion strategy and the practitioners' faith in it suggest that it may actually be effective. However, the exact mechanisms by which recipients' affective states mediate persuasion processes are not yet understood.

The present article explores the impact of happy and sad moods on the processing of counterattitudinal communications in the context of a cognitive response approach to persuasion and attitude change. According to Petty and Cacioppo's (1986a, 1986b) elaboration likelihood model of persuasion, recipients of a persuasive communi-cation may either elaborate the content of the message ("central route to persuasion") or rely on simple cues that are unrelated to the message's content, such as the communicator's prestige or likableness ("peripheral route to persuasion"). These alternative routes constitute the extreme endpoints of an elaboration continuum. If the central route to persuasion is traveled, the resulting attitude change is a function of the recipients' cognitive responses to the message: The more thoughts that come to mind that support the position advocated in the message, the more pronounced the attitude change will be. Accordingly, messages that present strong arguments are more effective than messages that present weak or flawed arguments. The quality of the message affects attitude change less, however, if the peripheral route is traveled, because message elaboration is minimized.

Which "route to persuasion" is more likely to be used depends on recipients' motivation and ability. If the recipient is sufficiently motivated and able to process the content of the message, the "central route" is likely to predominate. The "peripheral route" is likely to be used if motivation and/or ability is low.

According to this general framework (cf. Chaiken, Liberman, & Eagly, 1989, for a related model), recipients' mood state may influence persuasion processes in several ways.[1] First, the recipient's mood itself may serve as a peripheral cue. As research on the informative functions of affective states has shown in other domains of judgment, individuals frequently simplify the judgmental task by asking themselves, "How do I feel about it?" In doing so, they use their affective reaction to the object of judgment as a basis for its evaluation (see Schwarz, 1990; Schwarz & Clore, 1988, for reviews). If individuals use their affective state as a peripheral cue, they should report more favorable attitudes toward the issue of the persuasive message under a good mood than under a bad mood. Second, the criteria used to evaluate the message may be influenced by the recipients' affective state, and recipients in a bad mood may use harsher criteria. Third, attitude judgments may be mediated by mood-congruent memory (see e.g., Bower, 1981), and recipients in a good mood may generate more positive associations than recipients who are in a bad mood. If so, recipients in a good mood should be more likely to be persuaded than recipients in a bad mood. In summary, all these hypotheses predict a main effect of mood such that individuals in a good mood are more likely to be persuaded than individuals in a bad mood.

Alternatively, however, it is conceivable that subjects' affective state influences the degree to which they elaborate the content of the message presented to them. For example, Isen and colleagues (for a review see Isen, 1987) suggested that individuals in a good mood may avoid cognitive effort that might interfere with their ability to maintain their pleasant affective state. If so, persons in a good mood may be unlikely to elaborate the message.

The effects of bad moods, however, are more difficult to predict. On the one hand, research on coping with bad moods (e.g., Rosenbaum, 1980) suggests that individuals in a bad mood may be motivated to distract themselves from unpleasant thoughts and may thus be particularly likely to engage in other activities that are irrelevant to the factors that produced their bad mood. Thus, they may concentrate on the message and elaborate its content. On the other hand, depressed moods have also been found to go along with decreased motivation (see e.g., Peterson & Seligman, 1984) and may thus decrease the likelihood of message elaboration.

Moreover, research on the effects of mood on problem solving suggests that good moods may facilitate the use of simple heuristics whereas bad moods may facilitate the use of detail-oriented, analytic processing strategies (see Fiedler, 1988, and Schwarz, 1990, for reviews). If individuals' affective state influences the degree to which they elaborate the content of the message, main effects of mood are unlikely to be obtained. Rather, the impact of recipients' mood should depend on the quality of the arguments presented to them. As a considerable body of research has shown, strong arguments are more persuasive the more the recipient engages in message elaboration. Conversely, weak arguments are less persuasive the more the recipient elaborates the content of the message, generating counterarguments. Accordingly, a comparison of the impact of affective states on the persuasiveness of strong and weak arguments allows an evaluation of the proposed hypotheses.

The currently available evidence bearing on these hypotheses is rather limited. The most germane study was reported by Worth and Mackie (1987). They found that subjects who were in an experimentally induced good mood were less influenced by the quality of message arguments than subjects whose mood was not manipulated. Their data suggest that this effect may be mediated by differences in the elaboration of the message, because similar patterns emerged for measures of attitude change and cognitive responses. Thus, being in a good mood may reduce the likelihood that a central route to persuasion is traveled, either because of a lack of motivation or because of a lack of ability. However, in their study, good mood was induced by an unexpected pleasant

---

[1]A more detailed presentation of these hypotheses and research is provided in an extended report of the present studies that may be requested by writing to the authors.

event—namely, finding a dollar bill that subjects ostensibly had won in a lottery. In contrast, neutral-mood subjects were not exposed to an unexpected event. Unexpected events, however, have been shown to instigate causal reasoning (e.g., Hastie, 1984; Weiner, 1985), and thinking about the pleasant surprise, rather than being in a good mood per se, may have interfered with the elaboration of the message. In addition, subjects in the Worth and Mackie (1987) study were instructed to imagine a delegate delivering a speech and to evaluate his performance. This instruction may focus subjects' attention on aspects other than the content of the message (e.g., how arguments are organized and presented) and may thus decrease elaboration likelihood to begin with. In contrast, if subjects' attention were focused on the message, mood effects might be limited or absent.

Experiment 1 was designed to explore the relative impact of good and bad moods on recipients' processing of persuasive communications that present strong or weak arguments under conditions that either do or do not focus their attention on the content of the message—that is, under conditions of either moderate or high elaboration likelihood. To induce a good or bad mood, subjects provided a vivid report of a pleasant or an unpleasant life event. As part of a purportedly independent second study, they were subsequently exposed to a tape-recorded communication that presented either strong or weak arguments in favor of an increase in student services fees. Half the subjects were asked to pay attention to the quality of the information provided. In contrast, the others were told that the study was concerned with language comprehension, focusing their attention on paraverbal aspects of the communication. Finally, subjects' attitudes toward an increase in student services fees, their cognitive responses to the message, their memory for the message's content, and their evaluation of the message were assessed.

Experiment 1

Method

SUBJECTS AND DESIGN

Eighty-seven nondepressive female students (Beck Depression Inventory scores less than 12, median = 4; assessed 1 week before Experiment 1) at the University of Heidelberg, West Germany, with a mean age of 22.3 years, were randomly assigned to the conditions of a 2 (positive vs. negative mood) × 2 (focus of attention on content vs. on language) × 2 (strong vs. weak arguments) factorial between-subjects design or to a nonfactorial control group. Number of subjects per cell ranged from 9 to 11. Subjects received DM 10 (approximately $5 at the exchange rate of the time) for their participation.

PROCEDURE

Overview. Subjects were run in groups of three to six and were seated at separate tables to minimize interaction. They were told in advance that they were to participate in two independent studies. The first was a study on personality, conducted by the experimenter as part of his thesis research, part of which would be the construction of a life-event inventory. This would be followed by another study, conducted by a research group at another university in the Heidelberg area, which the experimenter was ostensibly working for. This second study would involve listening to a tape recording and answering some questions. The "first study" contained the mood manipulation, and in the "second study" the persuasive message was presented and dependent variables were assessed.

Independent variables. Happy or sad moods were induced by asking subjects to provide a vivid and detailed written report of a happy or a sad life-event, purportedly to help with the construction of a "Heidelberg Life Event Inventory" that would make use of the reported events. This cover story has been found to successfully disguise the mood induction nature of the task (see Schwarz, 1987, for a discussion). Subjects were given 15 minutes to do so and were encouraged to relive the event in their mind's eye.

After completion of this task, subjects were thanked and were introduced to the "second study." They were first given a "Participants Questionnaire," printed on the letterhead of another university. Embedded in this questionnaire was a manipulation check that read, "How do you feel right now, at this very moment?" (1 = *very bad*; 9 = *very good*).

After completion of the Participants Questionnaire, the second study was introduced either as an experiment on the evaluation of arguments (*arguments focus condition*) or as an experiment on language comprehension (*language focus condition*). Subsequently, subjects listened to a tape-recorded communication that announced an increase in student services fees from DM 45 (approximately $22.50) to DM 65 (approximately $32.50) per semester, to take effect at the beginning of the following academic year at the subjects' university. This increase was justified either with 11 *strong arguments* or with 11 *weak arguments*. The two messages were of approximately equal length.

Pretest data based on 18 subjects indicated a reliable difference in the perceived quality of the arguments, $M = 6.6$ for the strong and 4.3 for the weak arguments on a 9-point scale (the scale ranged from 1, "not strong at all," to 9, "very strong"), $t(16) = 2.77$, $p < .02$. No differences in comprehensibility of the message or likability of the communicator emerged, all $ts < 1$.

Dependent variables. After exposure to the message, subjects reported their approval of an increase in student services fees along a rating scale from 1 (*strongly disapprove*) to 9 (*strongly approve*). Subsequently, they indicated the fee that they would consider appropriate.

Following the attitude measures, subjects rated the strength of the presented arguments (1 = *not strong at all* to 9 = *very strong*). Then they were instructed to list within 3 min "all thoughts that

had come to mind while listening to the tape recording, no matter if they seem important or unimportant to you." Subjects were provided a sheet with 10 boxes and were instructed to list only one thought per box. It was pointed out that they were not required to use all boxes.

After completion of this task, they marked each thought as "Favorable" (i.e., supporting the suggested increase), "unfavorable" (i.e., opposing an increase), or "neutral" (i.e., unrelated to the issue), following similar procedures used in other studies (e.g., Cacioppo, Harkins, & Petty, 1981).

Finally, subjects' memory for the arguments presented was assessed. They were given a surprise recall test and wrote down all arguments they could remember. Subsequently, they received a recognition test and indicated which of 30 arguments they had actually heard. The recognition list consisted of the 11 strong and 11 weak arguments plus 8 additional statements. Thus, there were 11 previously presented arguments and 19 foils for each subject. Subjects were given 3 min for each of these tasks.

Control group. Subjects in the nonfactorial control group were exposed to neither a mood manipulation nor a persuasive communication. They

TABLE 12.1. Attitude Change and Cognitive Responses as a Function of Mood, Message Quality, and Focus of Attention

	Focus of Attention			
	On Arguments		On Language	
	Mood		Mood	
	Good	Bad	Good	Bad
Attitude Change				
Approval				
Strong arguments	5.4*	7.3*	4.6*	5.4*
Weak arguments	3.0	3.0	4.7*	3.0
Recommended fee				
Strong arguments	53.98*	59.29*	51.11	54.00*
Weak arguments	47.78	45.63	56.43*	48.75
	Control group		Approval:	3.3
			Money:	48.44
Cognitive Responses				
Favorable thoughts				
Strong arguments	.19	.37	.14	.31
Weak arguments	.19	.15	.16	.06
Unfavorable thoughts				
Strong arguments	.48	.33	.55	.35
Weak arguments	.54	.49	.50	.59

Note: The recommended fee is given in deutsche marks. The possible range of values for approval is 1 (*strongly disapprove*) to 9 (*strongly approve*). The cognitive response data show the mean proportions of favorable and unfavorable thoughts.

*$p < .05$ for differences from the control group.

were only informed of the intended increase in student services fees and reported their attitudes toward this increase. No other dependent variables were assessed.

After completion of the procedures described above, all subjects were thoroughly debriefed and dismissed.

Results

Mood. As expected, subjects who had to describe a happy event reported being in a better mood ($M = 7.0$) than subjects who described a sad event ($M = 6.1$), $F(1, 70) = 5.01$, $p < .03$. This indicates that the mood manipulation was successful. No other significant effects emerged, all $Fs < 1$.

Attitude change. Both attitude questions were analyzed by a 2 (Mood) × 2 (Focus) × 2 (Quality of Arguments) MANOVA (all multivariate F ratios are based on Wilks's lambda). Because univariate analyses indicated the same results for each of the dependent variables, only the multivariate test are reported. The means of both variables are shown in the first part of Table 12.1 as a function of the experimental manipulations.

Subjects who were exposed to strong arguments reported more positive attitudes toward an increase in student services fees than subjects who were exposed to weak arguments, multivariate $F(2, 58) = 5.65$, $p < .01$.[2] This main effect was qualified by a significant interaction of argument quality and mood, multivariate $F(2, 58) = 5.26$, $p < .01$.

Subjects in a bad mood but not subjects in a good mood were differentially affected by strong and weak arguments. Specifically, subjects in a bad mood reported a higher approval of the intended increase, and suggested a higher fee as appropriate, when they were exposed to strong rather than weak arguments; multivariate $F(2, 62) = 8.58$, $p < .001$, for the simple main effect. Subjects in a good mood were equally affected by strong and weak arguments, multivariate $F < 1$.

In addition, a significant interaction of argument quality and focus of attention emerged, multivariate $F(2, 58) = 4.66$, $p < .02$, that was independent of the mood manipulation. Strong arguments were more influential than weak arguments when subjects were instructed to focus on the quality of the

information presented; multivariate $F(2, 62) = 8.17$, $p < .001$, for the simple main effect. When subjects were given a language comprehension set, however, argument quality did not exert a significant influence, multivariate $F < 1$.

Finally, the means of all experimental conditions were compared with the mean of the nonfactorial control group by planned comparison. The results of these tests, shown by asterisks in Table 12.1, indicate that strong but not weak arguments resulted in significant attitude change when subjects were in a bad mood, independent of the focus of attention manipulation. Subjects in a good mood, in contrast, were influenced by strong arguments but not by weak arguments when they were explicitly instructed to evaluate the quality of the arguments. Without this explicit instruction, good-mood subjects were equally influenced by strong and by weak arguments, although this pattern did not result in a significant triple interaction. Thus, being in a bad mood seemed functionally equivalent to being instructed to focus on the quality of the arguments presented, and either of these manipulations resulted in a differential impact of strong and weak arguments.

The results reported so far are incompatible with hypotheses that predict a main effect of mood, which was not obtained. Thus, it seems unlikely that subjects based their evaluation of the issue on their affective state at the time of judgment or that the impact of mood was mediated by more favorable associations under good than under bad mood. Rather, the findings suggest that subjects in a bad mood were more likely to elaborate the content of the message than subjects in a good mood, resulting in a greater impact of strong than of weak arguments under bad mood. Alternatively, subjects in a bad mood may have used harsher criteria to evaluate the quality of the message than subjects in a good mood, rendering the weak message less convincing. We will now turn to data that bear on these possibilities.

Perceived argument quality. As expected, subjects rated the strong arguments as stronger ($M = 6.0$) than the weak arguments ($M = 3.5$), $F(1, 70) = 27.48$, $p < .0005$. However, their evaluation of the arguments was not affected by their mood or by the induced focus of attention, all $Fs < 1$. Thus, the hypothesis that subjects in a good mood may have used more lenient criteria to evaluate the quality of the message received no support.

Cognitive responses. The average number of

---

[2]Eleven subjects did not indicate which fee they would consider appropriate. These refusals were independent of experimental conditions, $\chi^2(7) = 4.7$, n.s.

thoughts that subjects reported in the thought-listing task ($M = 5.6$, $s = 1.89$) was not significantly affected by the experimental manipulations, all $ps > .25$.

However, separate analyses of the proportions of favorable and unfavorable thoughts, shown in the lower part of Table 12.1, revealed systematic differences. Overall, subjects reported a higher proportion of favorable thoughts ($M = .25$) and a lower proportion of unfavorable thoughts ($M = .43$) in response to strong than in response to weak arguments ($Ms = .14$ and $.53$, respectively), $Fs(1, 70) = 7.50$ and 3.30, $ps < 01$ and $.08$, respectively. Again, this conclusion is qualified by significant interactions of argument quality and mood, $Fs (1, 70) = 8.65$ and 2.76, $ps < .005$ and $.11$, for proportions of favorable and unfavorable thoughts, respectively.

This effect of argument quality is due exclusively to the cognitive responses of subjects in a bad mood. These subjects generated a higher proportion of favorable and a lower proportion of unfavorable thoughts in response to the strong arguments than in response to the weak arguments, $ts(70) = 3.96$ and 2.43 $ps < .0005$ and $.003$, respectively, reflecting a high degree of systematic elaboration of the message. The cognitive responses generated by subjects in a good mood, in contrast, did not vary as a function of message quality, $ts < 1$, suggesting that the occurrence of favorable and unfavorable thoughts under a good mood was independent of the content of the message.

No other significant effects emerged either for the proportion of favorable or for the proportion of unfavorable thoughts, all $Fs < 1$; or did the proportion of neutral thoughts show any impact of the experimental manipulations.

In combination with the attitude data, these findings clearly support the hypothesis that the impact of mood on persuasion is mediated by its impact on the choice of processing strategies. Whereas subjects in a bad mood elaborated the content of the message according to a central route of persuasion, subjects in a good mood did not.

Recall and recognition data. Subjects' free recall data were categorized by two independent judges, who agreed on 97% of the listings, as either "correct" or "false." The mean number of recalled arguments was 6.7 (out of 11) and was not affected by the experimental manipulations, all $Fs < 1$.

To analyze subjects' recognition data, the difference between hits and false alarms was computed (Murdock, 1982). Overall, subjects showed a better recognition of weak than of strong arguments, $F(1, 70) = 5.83$, $p < .02$. No other effects emerged. Thus, there is no evidence that would suggest that subjects' mood or focus of attention affected their memory for the arguments.

Discussion

In combination, the findings of Experiment 1 suggest that recipients' moods affect their processing modes. Specifically, subjects in a good mood seem less likely to elaborate the arguments presented than subjects in a bad mood. Accordingly, subjects in a bad mood generated a higher proportion of favorable cognitive responses, and showed more attitude change, when exposed to a message that presented strong arguments than when exposed to a message that presented weak arguments. Subjects in a good mood, in contrast, were not differentially influenced by strong or weak arguments in either their cognitive responses or their attitude change, unless they were explicitly instructed to focus on the quality of the message. This pattern of findings suggests that subjects in a bad mood proceeded via a central processing route, which subjects in a good mood used only if they were explicitly instructed to do so.

We have to add, however, that subjects assigned to the bad-mood manipulation still reported a mood level above the midpoint of the mood scale, raising the possibility that they were in a "neutral" mood rather than in a pronounced bad mood. Note, however, that most people, most of the time, report being in a good mood (Bless & Schwarz, 1984; Matlin & Stang, 1978; Sommers, 1984). Accordingly, values in the middle range of a mood scale may already reflect the subjective experience of a negative deviation from one's usual mood. Moreover, additional comparisons with chronically depressed subjects (see note 1) indicated that their responses did not differ from those in the induced bad-mood conditions, supporting the assumption that the induction of a mildly depressed mood was successful.

Experiment 2

If the interaction of mood and message quality on attitude change obtained in Experiment 1 is mediated by the impact of moods on subjects' cognitive responses, this interaction should be affected by other variables that are known to influence message elaboration. Most important for our present purposes, distraction has been shown to interfere with the systematic processing of a message. As a consequence, distraction reduces the differential impact of strong and weak messages (see Petty & Brock, 1981).

Accordingly, one can test the hypothesis that the impact of mood on persuasion is mediated by its impact on subjects' cognitive responses by introducing a distraction manipulation. If subjects in a bad mood are likely to elaborate the message, while subjects in a good mood are less likely to do so, introducing a distraction manipulation should eliminate the mood effects obtained in Experiment 1. To test this hypothesis, subjects in a good or bad mood were exposed to strong or weak arguments and were or were not distracted during exposure. Because all subjects in Experiment 2 received the "language focus" instruction that had been used in Experiment 1, the two levels of the distraction factor constitute conditions of low versus moderate elaboration likelihood.

Method

SUBJECTS AND DESIGN

Seventy-five female students at the University of Heidelberg, with a mean age of 22.4 years, were randomly assigned to the conditions of a 2 (positive vs. negative mood) × 2 (strong vs. weak arguments) × 2 (no distraction vs. distraction) factorial design. Number of subjects per cell ranged from 8 to 11. Subjects received DM 8 (approximately $4) for their participation.

PROCEDURE

Except for the distraction conditions described below, the procedure and the independent and dependent variables were identical to those in language focus condition of Experiment 1. However, no free recall or recognition data were collected.

Distraction manipulation. Subjects assigned to the distraction conditions were shown 11 slides with simple computation tasks (e.g., $5 + 4 - 2 = ?$) during exposure to the tape. They had to solve these tasks and write down the answers on a solution

sheet. Following procedures used by Zimbardo, Snyder, Thomas, Gold, and Gurwitz (1970), subjects were told that their main task was to listen to the tape.

The pace of the slide presentation, 11.3 s per task, was pretested to ensure that the computation tasks would require a certain degree of cognitive capacity but that subjects would still be able to listen to the tape. Of the 38 subjects assigned to the distraction conditions, 36 solved all tasks correctly, and 2 subjects provided one incorrect solution.

Results

Mood. Subjects who had described a positive life event reported being in a better mood ($M = 6.3$) than subjects who had to describe a negative life event ($M = 5.4$), $F(1, 67) = 4.18$ $p < .04$; all other Fs < 1. Thus, the mood manipulation was successful.

Attitude change. As in Experiment 1, the influence of the persuasive communication was inferred from the recipients' approval of the suggested fee increase and the amount of increase they recommended, and multivariate analyses were computed. Both indexes are shown in Table 12.2 as a function of strength of arguments, subjects' induced mood, and distraction.

A specified triple interaction was predicted for this experiment, and this prediction was tested by a focused multivariate a priori contrast rather than an omnibus F test, following suggestions by Rosenthal and Rosnow (1985). The result of this analysis confirms the predicted triple interaction, $F(2, 61) = 3.02$, $p < .06$.[3] Diagnosis of this interaction indicates that the quality of the message affected *nondistracted* subjects when they were in a bad mood, $F(2, 61) = 4.21, p < .02$, but not when they were in a good mood, $F < 1$, resulting in a nonsignificant simple interaction of mood and argument quality, $F(2, 61) = 2.28, p < .12$. Additional univariate tests revealed a significant simple interaction for the "approval" measure, $F(1, 67) = 4.29$, $p < .05$, but not for the "amount of money" measure, $F(1, 62) = 2.14$, $p < .12$. Overall, this pattern of results replicates the findings of Experiment 1.

---

[3] Five subjects did not indicate which fee they would consider appropriate. These refusals were independent of experimental conditions, $\chi^2(7) = 8.5$, n.s.

Distracted subjects, in contrast, were not differentially affected by strong and weak arguments under either good or bad mood conditions, both *F*s < 1. Accordingly, no simple interaction of mood and argument quality emerged under distraction conditions, *F* < 1.

In summary, either being in a good mood or being distracted eliminated the advantage of strong over weak arguments. Moreover, no effect of mood on attitude change was obtained under distraction conditions, as suggested by the hypothesis that the impact of mood on attitude change is mediated by its impact on subjects' cognitive responses.

Perceived argument quality. As expected, subjects rated strong arguments as stronger (*M* = 5.58) than weak arguments (*M* = 3.86), *F*(1,67) = 11.75, *p* <.001. The evaluation of the arguments was affected neither by mood nor by the distraction tasks, all *ps* > .10. This indicates that all subjects, including the distracted ones, recognized the difference in argument quality. Thus, the pattern of the attitude results cannot be explained by differential evaluations of the quality of the arguments.

Cognitive responses. Overall, nondistracted subjects reported more thoughts in the thought-list-

ing task (*M* = 5.24) than distracted subjects (*M* = 4.83), *F*(1, 67) = 5.02, *p* < .03, indicating that the distraction manipulation was successful in reducing the total number of cognitive responses. No other significant effects on the total number of reported thoughts emerged.

Separate analyses of the proportion of favorable and unfavorable thoughts, presented in the lower part of Table 12.2, indicated that nondistracted subjects generated a smaller proportion of favorable thoughts (*M* = .17) and a higher proportion of unfavorable thoughts (*M* = .43) in response to the counterattitudinal message than distracted subjects (*Ms* = .23 and .31 respectively), *Fs*(1, 67) = 3.02 and 4.10, *ps* < .09 and .05, respectively. This finding further reflects the success of the distraction manipulation.

In addition, main effects of argument quality on both thought measures emerged. Subjects who were exposed to strong arguments reported a greater proportion of favorable thoughts (*M* = .25) and a smaller proportion of unfavorable thoughts (*M* = .29) than subjects who were exposed to weak arguments (*Ms* = .18 and .44, respectively), *Fs*(1, 67) = 2.06 and 6.37, *ps* < .16 and .02, respectively.

TABLE 12.2. Attitude Change and Cognitive Responses as a Function of Mood, Message, Quality, and Distraction

	Distraction Task			
	No		Yes	
	Mood		Mood	
	Good	Bad	Good	Bad
Contrast Weights				
Strong arguments	1	−3	1	1
Weak arguments	−1	3	−1	−1
Attitude Change				
Approval				
Strong arguments	4.3	5.3	4.7	4.0
Weak arguments	4.2	2.6	4.0	4.1
Recommended fee				
Strong arguments	51.00	52.55	53.75	53.10
Weak arguments	51.22	46.43	52.30	50.00
Cognitive Responses				
Favorable thoughts				
Strong arguments	.15	.35	.25	.27
Weak arguments	.14	.07	.29	.23
Unfavorable thoughts				
Strong arguments	.39	.29	.26	.23
Weak arguments	.41	.60	.31	.45

Note: The recommended fee is given in deutsche marks. The possible range of values for approval is 1 (*strongly disapprove*) to 9 (*strongly approve*). The cognitive response data show mean proportions of favorable and unfavorable thoughts.

As in Experiment 1, these main effects were qualified by interaction effects of mood and argument quality that parallel the attitude change data, $Fs(1, 67) = 3.15$ and 3.88, $ps < .08$ and $.06$, for the proportion of favorable and unfavorable thoughts, respectively.

Specifically, subjects in a bad mood reported a higher proportion of favorable thoughts ($M = .31$) and a smaller proportion of unfavorable thoughts ($M = .26$) after listening to strong arguments than after listening to weak arguments ($Ms = 26$ and 53); $Fs(1,67) = 5.45$ and 10.16, $ps < .05$ and $.01$, respectively, for the simple main effects. In contrast, subjects in a good mood were not affected by argument quality, either in the proportion of favorable thoughts ($M = .27$ and $.26$ for strong and weak arguments, respectively) or in the proportion of unfavorable thoughts ($M = .33$ and $.36$) that they reported $Fs(1, 67) < 1$ and 1.74, n.s., respectively, for the simple main effects.

Separate analyses under each distraction condition suggest that the interaction effects of mood and argument quality are due primarily to the behavior of nondistracted subjects. Specifically, nondistracted subjects in a bad mood reported a higher proportion of favorable thoughts ($M = .35$) and a smaller proportion of unfavorable thoughts ($M = .29$) in response to the strong rather than the weak arguments ($Ms = .07$ and $.60$, respectively), $ts(67) = 2.84$, and -2.62 $ps < .01$ and $.02$, respectively. This pattern was less pronounced when bad-mood subjects were distracted, $Ms = .27$ and $.23$, $t < 1$, for favorable thoughts in response to strong and weak arguments, and $Ms = .23$ and $.45$, $t(67) = -1.86$, $p < .07$, for unfavorable thoughts.

The cognitive responses reported by subjects in a good mood in contrast, were not affected by the distraction manipulation, all $ts < 1$, again paralleling the attitude change data. Finally, a contrast analysis was computed to test the significance of the predicted triple interaction, paralleling the analysis of the attitude change data. This analysis confirmed the statistical reliability of the described findings for the proportion of favorable thoughts, $t(67) = -2.41$, $p < .02$, but not for the proportion of unfavorable thoughts, $t(67) = 1.54$, $p < .10$.

In summary, either being distracted or being in a good mood interfered with subjects' elaboration of the message, as predicted by the hypothesis that the effects of mood on attitude change are mediated by subjects' cognitive responses.

General Discussion

In combination, the findings of the experiments reported indicate that mood affects recipients' processing modes. Specifically, subjects in a good mood seem less likely to elaborate the arguments presented than subjects in a bad mood. Accordingly, subjects in a bad mood generated a higher proportion of favorable cognitive responses and a smaller proportion of unfavorable cognitive responses and showed more attitude change when exposed to a message that presented strong arguments than when exposed to a message that presented weak arguments. Subjects in a good mood, however, were not differentially influenced by strong or weak arguments in either their cognitive responses or their attitude change.

Moreover, Experiment 2 provided direct evidence for the mediating role of recipients' cognitive responses: When subjects in a bad mood were distracted from processing the content of the message, their increased responsiveness to strong rather than weak arguments was eliminated, indicating that being in a bad mood is associated with systematic message elaboration. Subjects in a good mood, however, were not affected by a distracting task, suggesting that they did not engage in message elaboration to begin with. Thus, either being distracted or being in a good mood reduced recipients' elaboration of the message, suggesting that the two are functionally equivalent.

As a mirror image to this finding, Experiment 1 also demonstrated that subjects in a good mood did elaborate the message if explicitly instructed to do so. Subjects in a bad mood, in contrast, elaborated the message in the absence of explicit instructions. Thus, either being instructed to focus on the content of the message or being in a bad mood resulted in message elaboration, again suggesting that the two are functionally equivalent.

Note that this pattern of findings renders it unlikely that the impact of good mood on elaboration likelihood is due to limits on subjects' cognitive capacity: If good mood severely limited subjects' processing capacity, simply instructing them to pay attention to the message should not eliminate the mood effect. Rather, this finding suggests that the impact of mood is mediated by subjects' motivation to engage in effortful, detail-oriented processing of the content of the message. In this regard, the current results parallel findings in other domains that suggest that the likelihood of effortful, analytic processing of information decreases as mood states become more positive (see Fiedler, 1988; Schwarz, 1990, for reviews). As suggested elsewhere (Schwarz, 1990), being in a bad mood may inform the individual that his or her current situation is problematic and requires detailed attention. It may thus trigger the careful processing strategies that are adequate for handling problematic situations. In contrast, being in a good mood may inform the individual that his or her current situation is nonproblematic and may thus foster reliance on simple heuristic strategies. If so, we may expect individuals in a bad mood to be more likely to elaborate a message than individuals in a nonmanipulated mood, in particular because nonmanipulated moods are usually of a somewhat elevated quality (Bless & Schwarz, 1984; Matlin & Stang, 1978; Sommers, 1984), whereas individuals in a good mood are least likely to engage in message elaboration. Clearly, future research should attempt to induce good and bad moods at several levels of extremity to explore these issues.

Finally, we note that the current findings are consistent with results reported by Worth and Mackie (1987) on the basis of different experimental procedures. It therefore seems safe to conclude that the valence of the induced mood states, rather than any specific characteristics of the mood manipulations, drives the phenomena observed.

In conclusion, putting recipients in a good mood when we want to influence them may not always be a good idea. Specifically, when we have strong arguments to present in favor of our case, a good mood may reduce their impact by interfering with recipients' elaboration of the message, unless recipients are highly motivated for other reasons. This interference is particularly undesirable because attitude change via a central route of persuasion has been found to be more stable than attitude change via a peripheral route (Petty & Cacioppo, 1986a, 1986b). Thus, strong arguments are likely to be more persuasive when we deliver them to an audience that is in a neutral or slightly depressed mood. Weak arguments, in contrast, are more effective when recipients do not elaborate them. Therefore, if we have nothing compelling to say, putting the audience in a good mood may be a smart choice—much as many advertisers seem to have known for quite a while.

REFERENCES

Bless, H., & Schwarz, N. (1984). *Ist schlechte Stimmung die Ausnahme? Eine Metaanalyse von Stimmungsunter- suchengen* [Is bad mood the exception? A meta-analysis of mood studies]. Paper presented at the 26th Tagung experimentell arbeitender Psychologen, Nürnberg.
Bower, G. H. (1981). Mood and memory. *American Psychologist, 36,* 129–148.
Cacioppo, J. T., Harkins, S. G., & Petty, R. E. (1981). The nature of attitudes and cognitive responses and their relationship to behavior. In R. E. Petty, T. M. Ostrom, & T. C. Brock (Eds.), *Cognitive responses in persuasion* (pp. 31–54). Hillsdale, NJ: Lawrence Erlbaum.
Chaiken, S., Liberman, A., & Eagly, A. H. (1989). Heuristic and systematic information processing within and beyond the persuasion context. In J. S. Uleman & J. A. Bargh (Eds.), *Unintended thought: Limits of awareness, intention, and control* (pp. 212–252). New York: Guilford Press.
Fiedler, K. (1988). Emotional mood, cognitive style, and behavior regulation. In K. Fiedler & J. Forgas (Eds.), *Affect, cognition and social behavior* (pp. 100–119). Toronto: Hogrefe.
Hastie, R. (1984). Causes and effects of causal attribution. *Journal of Personality and Social Psychology, 46,* 44–56.
Isen, A. M. (1987). Positive affect, cognitive processes, and social behavior. In L. Berkowitz (Ed.), *Advances in experimental social psychology* (Vol. 20, pp. 203–253). Orlando, FL: Academic Press.
Matlin, M., & Stang, D. (1978). *The Pollyanna principle.* Cambridge, MA: Schenkman.
Murdock, B. B., Jr. (1982). Recognition memory. In C. R. Puff (Ed.), *Handbook of research methods on human memory and cognition.* Orlando, FL: Academic Press.
Peterson, C., & Seligman, M. E. P. (1984). Causal explanations as a risk factor for depression: Theory and evidence. *Psychological Review, 91,* 347–374.
Petty, R. E., & Brock, T. C. (1981). Thought disruption and persuasion: Assessing the validity of attitude change experiments. In R. E. Petty, T. M. Ostrom, & T. C. Brock (Eds.), *Cognitive responses in persuasion.* Hillsdale, NJ: Lawrence Erlbaum.
Petty, R. E., & Cacioppo, J. T. (1986a). *Communication and persuasion.* New York: Springer-Verlag.
Petty, R. E., & Cacioppo, J. T. (1986b). The elaboration likelihood model of persuasion. In L. Berkowitz (Ed.), *Advances in experimental social psychology* (Vol. 19). Orlando, FL: Academic Press.
Rosenbaum. M. (1980). A schedule for assessing self control behaviors: Preliminary findings. *Behavior Therapy, 11,* 109–121.
Rosenthal, R., & Rosnow, R. L. (1985). *Contrast analysis: Focused comparisons in the analysis of variance.* Cambridge: Cambridge University Press.
Schwarz, N. (1987). *Stimmung als Information: Untersuchungen zum Einfluß von Stimmungen auf die Bewertung des eigenen Lebens* [Mood as information]. Heidelberg: Springer-Verlag.
Schwarz, N. (1990). Feelings as information: Informational and motivational functions of affective states. In E. T. Higgins & R. Sorrentino (Eds.), *Handbook of motivation and cognition: Vol. 2. Foundations of social behavior* (pp. 527–561). New York: Guilford Press.

Schwarz, N., & Clore, G. L. (1988). How do I feel about it? Informative functions of affective stales. In K. Fiedler & J. Forgas (Eds.), *Affect, cognition, and social behavior.* Toronto: Hogrefe.

Sommers, S. (1984). Reported emotions and conventions of emotionality among college students. *Journal of Personality and Social Psychology, 46,* 207–215.

Weiner, B. (1985). "Spontaneous" causal thinking. *Psychological Bulletin, 97,* 74–84.

Worth, L. T., & Mackie, D. M. (1987). Cognitive mediation of positive affect in persuasion. *Social Cognition, 5,* 76–94.

Zimbardo, P. G., Snyder, M., Thomas, J., Gold, A., & Gurwitz, S. (1970). Modifying the impact of persuasive communications with external distraction. *Journal of Personality and Social Psychology, 16,* 669–680.

Emotions Effects on Others

Having considered a variety of ways in which emotional changes within an individual lead to social consequences, we now move on to consider how one person's emotional state more directly influences other people. One of the most important of these is *emotional contagion*, the spreading of an emotional state from one person to another. Emotional contagion is one of the oldest topics studied by social scientists, being one of the aspects of crowd behavior that was addressed by Gustav Le Bon in his 1896 book on the topic. The most detailed modern treatment of emotional contagion is the recent book by Hatfield, Cacioppo, and Rapson (1994), which presents convincing evidence that emotional contagion occurs. One of the studies they cite as evidence is the first reading presented in this section, James Coyne's (1976a) classic study of emotional contagion from depressed individuals. Coyne asked undergraduate women to make a 20-minute telephone call to a middle-aged woman. Unbeknownst to the students, these women were selected from one of three groups: depressed patients, nondepressed mental health patients, and nonpatients with no mental health diagnoses. The students who spoke with depressed patients reported feeling more depressed, anxious, and hostile after their telephone conversation than did either of the other two groups of students. In other words, the depressed patients' moods proved contagious to those speaking to them over the phone. These findings not only demonstrate the occurrence of emotional contagion, but also suggest a profound social problem facing depressed individuals, whose presence is aversive to others. Unless depressed individuals have the social skills to maintain social relationships despite the effects of their depression, Coyne argues, they will find themselves facing rejection by others.

In their book on emotional contagion, Hatfield and colleagues argue that quite a few mechanisms can give rise to emotional contagion, which therefore should not be thought of as a unified phenomenon. Their book focuses on two mechanisms, both quite low-level, which work together to produce emotional contagion. One mechanism is the tendency of people to mimic others, synchronizing with their movements, expressions, vocalizations, and postures. The other mechanism is the tendency for feedback from such movements to give rise to emotional feelings, either directly or via self-perception (Laird & Bresler, 1992; Larsen, Kasimatis, & Frey, 1992; Strack, Martin, & Stepper, 1988). Together, these mechanisms could produce emotional contagion. As interesting as this account is, one is naturally curious about other mechanisms. Surely some involve more cognitive aspects of social interaction.

In discussing his research findings, Coyne (1976a) speculates on mechanisms of a more cognitive sort. He points out that depressed patients were much more likely than others to bring up unhappy conversation topics, often inappropriately personal ones. The sheer unpleasantness of these topics may have been one source of emotional contagion. An implication of Coyne's research is that emotional contagion of depression creates a social environment that may contribute to maintaining the depression. If depression tends to elicit from others insincere and weak reassurance or, worse, rejection and withdrawal, it may tend to confirm or worsen the depressed individual's sense of aloneness, unattractiveness, or worthlessness. This may intensify the depression, and may lead to stronger attempts to elicit pity and help that make the depression even more contagious to others (Coyne, 1976b).

Emotional contagion is one way in which emotion affects others. Another is *social sharing*—talking with another person about an emotional experience. Our knowledge of social sharing of emotion is largely the result of a series of studies by social psychologist Bernard Rimé. His early research established that social sharing of emotions is extremely common—in one questionnaire study, about 90% of the emotions that were recalled had been shared with at least one person (Rimé, Mesquita, Phillippot, & Boca, 1991). The person with whom an emotion was shared was usually a relative, close friend, or romantic partner. These findings held true for a variety of emotions, and for people of a variety of ages and cultures. Subsequent studies demonstrated that this high rate of social sharing was genuine and not an artifact of memory bias.

In the paper reprinted below, Christophe and Rimé (1997) consider the effects of social sharing on the person with whom the emotion is shared. They gave a questionnaire to students in a social psychology class, asking for information about a time when someone had shared an emotional experience with them. As one would expect from research on emotional contagion, Christophe and Rimé found that being the recipient of a shared emotion is itself an emotion-inducing experience. Emotional contagion was not the only process at work, however, because the emotions of interest and surprise were rated as having the highest intensity, and these emotions were reactions to the news of the emotional event, not the emotion that was being shared. Another finding was that the vast majority of participants—66% to 78%—reported that they themselves subsequently shared this event with a third person. This percentage is apparently not reduced if the information is received in confidence, a fact one may wish to keep in mind if one truly wants the news of one's emotional experience not to spread around!

Other important social psychological research is related

to social sharing. Research by James Pennebaker demonstrates that social sharing of emotions, as well as nonsocial writing about emotions, has a number of physical and mental health benefits (Pennebaker, 1997; Petrie, Booth, & Pennebaker, 1998). Following up on this work, Finkenauer & Rimé (1998) have shown that the negative effects of emotional secrecy on physical health are due to the lack of social sharing per se, and cannot be accounted for by a general tendency to experience negative emotions.

REFERENCES

Christophe, V., & Rimé, B. (1997). Exposure to the social sharing of emotion: Emotional impact, listener responses and secondary social sharing. *European Journal of Social Psychology, 27*, 37–54.

Coyne, J. C. (1976a). Depression and the response of others. *Journal of Abnormal Psychology, 85*, 186–193.

Coyne, J. C. (1976b). Toward an interactional description of depression. *Psychiatry, 39*, 14–27.

Finkenauer, C., & Rimé, B. (1998). Keeping emotional memories secret: Health and subjective well-being when emotions are not shared. *Journal of Health Psychology, 3*, 47–58.

Hatfield, E., Cacioppo, J. T., & Rapson, R. L. (1994). *Emotional contagion*. Cambridge, England: Cambridge University Press.

Laird, J. D., & Bresler, C. (1992). The process of emotional experience: A self-perception theory. In In M. S. Clark (Ed.), *Review of personality and social psychology: Vol. 13. Emotion* (pp. 213–234). Newbury Park, CA: Sage.

Larsen, R. J., Kasimatis, M., & Frey, K. (1992). Facilitating the furrowed brow: An unobtrusive test of the facial feedback hypothesis applied to unpleasant affect. *Cognition and Emotion, 6*, 321–338.

Le Bon, G. (1896). *The crowd: A study of the popular mind.* London: Ernest Benn.

Pennebaker, J. W. (1997). Writing about emotional experiences as a therapeutic process. *Psychological Science, 8*, 162–166.

Petrie, K. J., Booth, R. J., & Pennebaker, J. W. (1998). The immunological effects of thought suppression. *Journal of Personality and Social Psychology, 75*, 1264–1272.

Rimé, B., Mesquita, B., Philippot, P., & Boca, S. (1991). Beyond the emotional event: Six studies on the social sharing of emotion. *Cognition and Emotion, 5*, 435–465.

Strack, F., Martin, L. L., & Stepper, S. (1988). Inhibiting and facilitating conditions of the human smile: A nonobtrusive test of the facial feedback hypothesis. *Journal of Personality and Social Psychology, 54*, 768–777.

Discussion Questions

1. What are some ways in which one person could come to experience another person's emotional state?
2. How might a depressed person's effect on others serve to perpetuate his or her depression? Do anxiety, happiness, irritability, or pride perpetuate themselves in an analogous fashion?
3. What effects does social sharing have on relationships?
4. What are some of the reasons why people share their emotional experiences with others? What functions might social sharing serve?

Suggested Readings

Hatfield, E., Cacioppo, J. T., & Rapson, R. L. (1994). *Emotional contagion*. Cambridge, England: Cambridge University Press. Readers who are interested in the phenomenon of emotional contagion will enjoy reading this book-length treatment. Written in a readable style, the authors review the evidence that emotional contagion occurs. They point out that this phenomenon is probably caused in a variety of ways, and they provide in-depth reviews of several of the most basic, low-level mechanisms. They expand the topic to include individual differences in the ability to transmit one's emotions and in the ability to be infected by others' emotions.

Pennebaker, J. W. (1997) *Opening up: The healing power of expressing emotions*. New York: Guilford. This book presents an overview of Pennebaker's research on the benefits of writing about emotions or sharing them with others. The benefits are both emotional and physical, and one theme of the book is the relation between mind and body.

Coyne, J. C. (1976). Toward an interactional description of depression. *Psychiatry, 39*, 14–27. In this article James Coyne presents an interpersonal theory of depression that grows out of the observations he reports in the article reprinted in the present volume. It characterizes the symptoms of depression as having a social basis, and suggests a way of applying the social psychology of emotion to understanding depression.

Strack, F., Martin, L. L., & Stepper, S. (1988). Inhibiting and facilitating conditions of the human smile: A nonobtrusive test of the facial feedback hypothesis. *Journal of Personality and Social Psychology, 54*, 768–777. ALSO Laird, J. D., & Bresler, C. (1992). The process of emotional experience: A self-perception theory. In M. S. Clark (Ed.), *Review of personality and social psychology: Vol. 13. Emotion* (pp. 213–234). Newbury Park, CA: Sage. The work of Hatfield and colleagues suggests that one mechanism of emotional contagion is that feedback bodily imitation produces emotional feelings. Whether bodily feedback affects emotion, and how it does so, is the topic of these two articles. The paper by Strack and colleagues reports a famous and ingenious test of what is called the "facial feedback hypothesis" that indeed finds evidence that facial movements influence emotional experience. These authors suggest that the effect is the inevitable results of hardwired nervous system activity, but the paper by Laird and Bresler proposes a different interpretation, that cognitive processes of self-perception are responsible.

Depression and the Response of Others

James C. Coyne • Miami University

Each of 43 normal subjects conversed on the telephone with either a depressed patient, a nondepressed patient, or a normal control. It was found that following the phone conversation, subjects who had spoken to depressed patients were themselves significantly more depressed, anxious, hostile, and rejecting. Measures of activity, approval responses, hope statements, and genuineness did not distinguish between subject groups or between target groups, but important differences were found in the subjects' perception of the patients. It was proposed that environmental response may play an important role in the maintenance of depressed behavior. Furthermore, special skills may be required of the depressed person to cope with the environment his behavior creates.

The possibility that the behaviors associated with depression might be interwoven and concatenated with a corresponding pattern in the response of others has seldom been explored (Coyne, 1976). The persistent assumption has been that the support and information available to depressed persons are incongruent with their depression and that, therefore, the continued display of symptoms is evidence of their distorted view of the environment.

The behavioral approach to depression, as formulated by Ferster (1973, 1974) and further developed by Lewinsohn (Lewinsohn, 1974; Libet & Lewinsohn, 1973; MacPhillamy & Lewinsohn, 1974), postulates that a low rate of response-contingent positive reinforcement is a sufficient explanation for depressed behavior. It would seem that such an approach would give extensive attention to the environment in which depressed behavior occurs. However, Ferster continues with traditional assumptions: "We cannot assume the depressed person actually sees very much of the features of the social world around him" (1973, p. 562). In his studies of the behavior of depressed persons in the home and in group therapy, Lewinsohn (Lewinsohn & Shaffer, 1971; Libet & Lewinsohn, 1913) has tended to attribute both the behavior of depressed persons and the contingencies they are offered to their lack of social skill. An alternative explanation for the apparent behavior deficits of depressed persons is that others are unwilling to interact with them and that depressed persons lack the special skills necessary to overcome this.

A number of writers have argued that depressed persons face aversive and unpredictable environments. Jacobson (1954) noted that depressed persons often make their whole environment feel guilty, and this provokes defensive aggression and even cruelty precisely when the depressed persons are most vulnerable. Weissman and Paykel (1974) summarized a number of studies examining the social relationships of depressed women and reported social disturbance extending into all roles of depressed women, whether as mother, wife, worker, or member of the community. Weissman and Paykel suggested that social consequences of depression may themselves be stressful and tend to perpetuate the disorder.

Describing the social interaction of depressed persons within a systems framework, Coyne (1976) argued that depressed persons and members of their environment become enmeshed in an emergent system of depressive symptom and response from others. The symptoms of depressed persons are aversive yet powerful in the ability to arouse guilt in others and to inhibit any direct expression of annoyance and hostility from others. Members of the social environment attempt to reduce the aversive behavior of depressed persons and alleviate guilt by manipulating them with nongenuine reassurance and support. At the same time, these same persons reject and void the depressed persons. As discrepancies between the reassurance of others and their actual behavior become apparent, the depressed persons are confirmed in their suspicion that they are not accepted and that further interactions cannot be assured. To maintain their increasingly uncertain security and to control the behavior of others, depressed persons display more symptoms and convey more distress, thereby further stimulating the depressive social process.

In a partial test of this model, the present study examined the reaction of others to the behavior of depressed persons. The general hypotheses were that (a) normal subjects respond differentially to the behavior of depressed patients, (b) this differential response is due to the fact that the target individuals are depressed, and not that they are patients, and (c) this pattern can be related to the symptomatology of depression. More specifically, it was hypothesized that depressed persons induce depression and hostility in others, and consequently are rejected socially. It was further hypothesized that behavioral and content analysis measures would reveal that subjects focused on the depressed persons and their difficulties in the interactions in unsuccessful and nongenuine attempts to deal with the patients' depression. Finally, social perception questions were provided to test the hypothesis that others perceive depressed persons as exaggerating their plight and that this perception is related to their overall response pattern.

Method

SUBJECTS

Serving as subjects were 45 Miami University female undergraduates. They were drawn from psychology classes as target individuals became available and were randomly assigned to treatment conditions.

SELECTION OF TARGET INDIVIDUALS

The Zung Self-Rating Depression Scale (SDS) was used to select patient target individuals. It does not provide for the differential diagnosis of depression as disorder but rather serves to measure the intensity of depression regardless of diagnosis. High scores, therefore, are not interpreted as diagnostic but rather as indicating the presence of clinically significant symptoms (Zung, 1965).

A cutoff score on the SDS of greater than 55 was used to designate depressed target individuals; a cutoff score of less than or equal to 40 was used to designate nondepressed patient individuals.

TARGET INDIVIDUALS

On the basis of SDS scores, 15 depressed and 15 nondepressed females were drawn from the Dayton, Ohio, Good Samaritan Mental Health Center outpatient population.

Fifteen normal control females were chosen from the Dayton-Middletown area. These individuals were drawn from members of a hospital auxiliary, supermarket employees and customers, and neighbors of Miami University branch campus students. All were screened for depression.

The mean age of target individuals was 41.8 years. An effort was made to control for age across groups and no significant differences occurred in the final sample.

PROCEDURE

Each subject was randomly paired with one target individual and talked with her on the telephone for 70 minutes. Both were under instructions that this was a study of the acquaintance process. It was explained that neither person would know anything about the other except that they were female, located, somewhere in Ohio, and had volunteered to participate in a study of acquaintance. The experiment was compared with the situation that would be encountered if a person were to strike up a conversation with a stranger seated next to her on the bus. It was explained that each person was free to discuss or withhold what information she saw fit, except that they were not to reveal their last name or their exact location. Subjects and target individuals were told that the conversation would be taped and a questionnaire would follow.

Following the phone conversations, both subjects and target individuals filled out questionnaires concerning mood, perception of the other, and willingness to interact again under varying conditions.

Tapes of the conversations were rated on a variety of measures by judges who were trained but blind with respect to hypotheses and target individual classification.

MEASURES

The Today Form of the Multiple Affect Adjective Check List (MAACL; Zuckerman & Lubin, 1965) was used to measure postconversation mood in both subject and target individuals.

Willingness to engage in future interaction was measured by a series of questions answered either affirmatively or negatively on a 6-point scale (e.g., "Would you like to meet this person?"). Situations sampled were meeting this person, asking her for advice, sitting next to her on a 3-hour bus trip, inviting her to the respondent's house, approving if a close relative were married to her, willingness to work with her on a job, and admitting her to the respondent's circle of friends.

Perception of the other participant was measured using two sets of scales. The first involved the question "How do you think this person would like you to see her?" which was followed by nine bipolar scales of the same general form as described above. The nine scales were sad–happy, pleasant–unpleasant, negative–positive, good–bad, comfortable–uncomfortable, strong–weak, cold–warm, high–low and active–passive. The second question "What do you think that this person would be like if you really got to know her?" was followed by the same nine scales.

Tapes of the conversation were scored for activity, other-self ratio, approval responses, hope statements, and genuineness. Activity of a participant was measured by simply timing the total amount of speech in a random 4-minute segment of tape.

An other-self ratio was obtained by taking the ratio of time spent talking about the other person and life space to the time spent talking about oneself and one's own life space in a randomly chosen 4-minute segment of tape. For the purpose of

data analysis, ratio scores were transformed to the form log (x + .01). Raters for this measure were obtained by training four undergraduates and then selecting the two showing greatest agreement. Subsequently, each of the two judges rated the same 4-minute segments of 15 tapes, and a reliability coefficient of .82 was obtained.

Approval responses were measured by simply counting the number of "hm-hmms," "yeahs," and "yeses" in a random 4-minute segment of tape. Reliability coefficients for four raters ranged from .92 to .98.

Hope statements were measured using a content analysis scale for verbal samples derived from that of Gottschalk (1974). Construct validation studies of Gottschalk's original scale indicated significant negative correlations between Hope scores and psychiatric ratings from the Brief Psychiatric Rating Scale (BPRS) depression and anergia factor scores and the Hamilton Depression Rating Scale factors of anxiety–depression and sleep disturbance. In the present study, Gottschalk's scoring system was applied to transcripts of 20 randomly selected declarative statements from each subject and each target individual. Scores were obtained by summing the ratings of each of the 20 statements. Two raters were obtained by selecting from four undergraduates the two showing greatest agreement. A reliability coefficient of .88 was subsequently obtained.

Genuineness was measured using the 5-point Carkhuff scale (Carkhuff, 1969; Carkhuff & Berenson, 1967). Essentially the scale measures the degree in which a person's verbalizations are related to what he appears otherwise to be feeling at the moment, the extent to which he is responding according to his prescribed role rather than expressing what he personally feels or means, and his impact on the recipient of the communication (Carkhuff, 1969). Three undergraduates were selected as raters from a class which was reviewing the practice of client-centered therapy, and these students were given further training with the specific scale. Reliabilities obtained after training ranged from .72 to .84.

Results

Since our interest is in the difference between the response to depressed patients and the response to the other target individuals, planned comparisons rather than overall analyses of variance were conducted. The general hypotheses that there are differences in the response to depressed patients, and that these differences are due to their depression and not their patients' status was tested using comparisons of the form of the following hypothesis: $2\mu_D - (\mu_C + \mu_p) = 0$ where μ_D is the mean response to depressed patients, μ_C the mean response to normal controls, and μ_p the mean response to nondepressed patients. A second planned comparison for all variables tested the general hypothesis that there are no differences between the response to normal controls and the response to nondepressed patients.

SUBJECT VARIABLES

As predicted, mood measures revealed subjects to be significantly more depressed, $F(1, 43) = 39.10$, $p < .001$, anxious, $F(1, 43) = 12.31$, $p < .001$, and hostile, $F(1, 43) = 45.81$, $p < .001$, following interactions with depressed patients than following interactions with nondepressed or normal controls. There were no significant differences between mood responses to nondepressed patients and normal target individuals. (See Table 13.1.)

There was a lack of significant results with regard to behavioral and content analysis measures of subject response. There were no significant differences in activity, approval responses, hope measures, or genuineness. The only significant difference found was with the other–self talking ratio. Subjects talked more about the target individuals relative to talking about themselves when the target individuals were depressed patients, $F(1, 43) = 8.39$, $p < .01$. A second planned comparison indicated that subjects had higher self–other scores for nondepressed patients than for normal controls, $F(1, 43) = 5.43$, $p < .05$.

TABLE 13.1. Subject Mood (Multiple Affect Adjective Check List) Scores

Group	Depression	Anxiety	Hostility
Patient			
Depressed			
M	14.80	7.73	7.40
SD	3.45	2.76	1.99
Nondepressed			
M	7.47	3.27	3.60
SD	4.98	2.01	1.69
Normal			
M	6.60	3.13	3.53
SD	3.08	1.69	1.80

Measures of willingness to engage in future interaction were combined in one overall willingness-to-interact score (corrected odd–even item correlation = .81). Subjects were significantly more rejecting of the depressed patients, $F(1, 43) = 5.07$, $p < .05$, on the overall measure, and on the specific measures of willingness to sit next to them on the bus, $F(1, 43) = 5.07$, $p < .05$, and willingness to ask for advice, $F(1, 43) = 5.07$, $p < .01$. A test difference in response to nondepressed patients versus normal controls proved nonsignificant.

In answer to "How do you think this person would like you to see her?" subjects perceived depressed patients as wishing to be seen as sadder, $F(1, 43) = 10.12$, $p < .01$, less pleasant, $F(1, 43) = 6.05$, $p < .05$ more negative, $F(1, 43) = 7.01$, $p < .05$, more uncomfortable, $F(1, 43) = 8.03$, $p < .05$, low, $F(1, 43) = 7.27$, $p < .05$, and passive, $F(1, 43) = 5.10$, $p < .05$. However, larger differences were found in response to the question "What do you think that this person would be like if you really got to know her?" Depressed patients were seen as sadder, $F(1, 43) = 25.70$, $p < .005$, more uncomfortable, $F(, 43) = 13.30$, $p < .005$, weaker, $F(,43) = 13.88$, $p < .005$, lower in mood, $F(1, 43) = 11.65$, $p < .005$, passive, $F(1, 43) = 5.10$, $p < .05$, and negative, $F(1, 43) = 5.50$, $p < .05$. Taking an overview, it seems that the subjects perceived the depressed patients as making somewhat less of an effort than other target individuals to maintain a socially desirable self-presentation but, nonetheless, in reality as being more depressed. The hypothesis that the depressed patients would be perceived as merely enacting a role performance, exaggerating their difficulties in order to receive sympathy, was clearly not supported.

Examination of the correlation matrix of subject variables (see Table 13.2) suggests that subject mood may be an important mediating variable in response to target individuals. As can be noted, there is a significant relation between subject mood, depression and rejection of opportunities for future interaction, with less significant relations between rejection and subject hostility and anxiety. The largest correlations between mood variables and perceptions of the target individuals were in answer to the question "What...this person would be like if you really got to know her?" Perceived sadness, weakness, discomfort, passivity, and low mood in target individuals were significantly correlated with subject mood.

Target individual variables. As would be ex-

TABLE 13.2. Correlations Among Subject Variables

Variable	Depression	Anxiety	Hostility
Mood			
Depression		.760****	.782****
Anxiety	.760****		.848****
Hostility	.782****	.848****	
Acceptance/rejection			
Willingness to			
meet	−.326*	ns	ns
seek advice from	−.295*	ns	ns
sit with on bus	−.520***	−.482***	−.527***
share apartment	−.371*	ns	ns
invite to home	ns	ns	ns
approve if relative married	ns	ns	ns
work with	−.300*	ns	ns
admit to circle of friends	ns	ns	ns
Overall willingness	−.406**	−.374**	−.343*
Perception of target self-presentation effort			
Target would like to be seen as			
sad–happy	ns	−.358*	−.345*
pleasant–unpleasant	ns	.381**	ns
negative–positive	−.372**	−.351*	−.335*
good–bad	ns	ns	ns
comfortable–uncomfortable	.308*	.466**	.408**
strong–weak	ns	.384**	.339*
cold–warm	ns	−.301*	ns
high–low	ns	.305*	.292*
active–passive	.305*	.402**	.365*
Perception of target "real" self			
Target individual would be if I really got to know her			
sad–happy	−.601****	−.482***	−.508***
pleasant–unpleasant	ns	ns	ns
negative–positive	ns	ns	−.351*
good–bad	ns	ns	ns
comfortable–uncomfortable	.362*	.410**	.394**
strong–weak	.474**	.408**	.363*
cold–warm	−.409**	−.461**	−.473***
high–low	.574****	.484***	.526***
active–passive	.606****	.418**	.485***

* $p < .05$.
** $p < .01$.
*** $p < .001$.
**** $p < .0001$.

pected, depressed patients scored as significantly more depressed, $F(1, 43) = 49.54$, $p < .001$, anxious, $F(1,43) = 24.39$, $p < .001$, and hostile, $F(1, 43) = 16.64$, $p < .001$, than nondepressed patients and normal controls on the postconversation questionnaires. Zuckerman and Lubin (1963) indicate that test–retest reliability coefficients are much higher for psychiatric patients ($r = .69$) than for normals ($r = .19$), suggesting that the patient mood scores are more indicative of chronic mood than the effects of specific experimental manipulations.

The mood scores of the patients therefore reflect their chronic mood state rather than the effects of the conversations. In fact, following the experiment many of the depressed patients commented on how pleasant it had been to talk about themselves for twenty minutes.

Behavioral and content analysis measures did not differentiate among the three target groups. There obviously were differences in behavior and verbal content, for subjects' social perception scores indicate clear differences. However, it appears that simply counting "hm-hmms" and timing activity do not capture these essential differences.

Across target groups, measures of willingness to engage in future interaction and social perception (i.e., perception *of* the subjects *by* the target individuals) measures all proved nonsignificant except that depressed patients were less willing to invite subjects to their homes, $F(1, 43) = 4.11, p < .05$.

Interrelations among subject and target variables. Correlations between target mood and subject variables are presented in Table 13.3. An examination of these correlations suggest that the mood depression of the depressed patients, and not their hostility, has the greatest effect on subject variables. Planned comparisons have indicated that depressed patients were significantly more hostile as well as more depressed than other target individuals. One might argue that it is the hostility of the depressed patients that results in subject mood changes and rejection. However, an examination of the correlation matrix in Table 13.3 shows the strongest relations are between target depression (mood) and subject mood and rejection. Target hostility and rejection by the subject are not significantly related, and neither are target hostility and subject depression. Other correlations of target hostility and subject mood variables can be explained by the high ($r = .509$) correlation of target hostility and target depression. Thus, it appears that it is the depression of the target individuals that has the greatest single impact on subject variables.

Other relations between subject and target individuals of interest include that between subject genuineness and target individual anxiety ($r = .31, p < .05$). The level of hope and number of approval statements emitted by target individuals were correlated with their perception of subjects as attempting to be seen as happy ($r = .40, p < .01$; $r = .36, p < .05$, respectively).

Discussion

The depressed patients induced negative affect in those with whom they interacted and were rejected. The interpersonal attraction literature suggests additional implications. An induction of negative affect has a powerful mediating effect between the stimulus behavior of an actor and the impact on the perceptions of an observer (Gouaux, Lamberth, & Friedrich, 1972; Byrne, 1971). Gouaux (1971) has argued that attraction responses are not simply a function of the qualities attributed to the person being evaluated but also a function of additional positive and negative internal states of the observer. Studies demonstrating this have typically employed a mood induction independent of the behavior of the actor. Since in the present study the mood induction was a direct result of some behavior of the depressed actor, the effect on interpersonal attraction could be expected to be even stronger. The mood induction by the depressed patients would seem to make them aversive and unattractive regardless of what other qualities they possess or any adaptive behavior they display.

The depressed patients in the present study induced negative affect in others and were accepted less without being lower in activity level or rate of positive response. This can be taken as support for an alternative interpretation of the Libet and Lewinsohn (1973) data; the depressed persons in their study were lower in activity, rate of positive response, and interpersonal range because few people were willing to interact with them. Perhaps a suitable reformulation of Libet and Lewinsohn's view that depressed persons have a deficit in response capability is that depressed persons lack the special social skills necessary to overcome the effects of their mood induction on others. Depressive behavior induces negative affect in others so that noncontingent punishment and unfavorable contingencies are offered to the depressed persons. For the depressed persons to maintain social relationships despite this would seem to require either a special set of relationships resistant to such disruptions or particularly skilled depressed persons. Such an interpretation avoids an inherent difficulty in the Libet and Lewinsohn view. If, as they postulate, the differences in the behavior of depressed persons are due to deficits in response capability, how can it be explained that they were at some time, most of their lives probably, nondepressed?

Despite the application of a number of behavioral and content analysis measures, the present study failed to uncover exactly what in the behavior of the depressed person led to mood induction in the subjects. That striking differences existed between the behavior of the depressed persons and that of the other target individuals is apparent from both the mood induction in the subjects and the highly significant differences in the perception of the depressed patients by the subjects.

TABLE 13.3. Correlations Between Target Mood and Subject Variables

Subject	Target Depression	Anxiety	Hostility
Mood			
Depression	.500****	.354*	ns
Anxiety	.643****	.454**	.469**
Hostility	.400**	.409**	.353*
Willingness to meet	ns	ns	ns
seek advice from	−.416**	ns	ns
sit with on bus	−.329*	ns	ns
share apartment	−.300*	ns	ns
invite to home	ns	ns	ns
approve if relative married	−.395**	−.326*	−.475***
work with	ns	ns	ns
admit to circle of friends	ns	ns	ns
overall willingness	−.432**	ns	ns
Target would like to be seen as			
sad–happy	−.384**	−.448**	−.456**
pleasant–unpleasant	ns	ns	ns
negative–positive	−.371	ns	ns
good–bad	ns	ns	ns
comfortable–uncomfortable	.391**	.436**	.442**
strong–weak	.391**	.517***	.420**
cold–warm	ns	ns	ns
high–low	ns	.315*	.308*
active–passive	.492***	.549****	.448**
Target would really be			
sad–happy	−.543****	−.367*	−.354*
pleasant–unpleasant	ns	ns	ns
negative–positive	−.339*	ns	−.363*
good–bad	ns	ns	ns
comfortable–uncomfortable	.453**	.435**	ns
strong–weak	ns	ns	ns
cold–warm	ns	ns	ns
high–low	.352*	ns	ns
active–passive	.319*	ns	ns

$*p < .05.$
$**p < .01.$
$***p < .001.$
$****p < .0001.$

It is likely that some measures of the appropriateness of self-disclosure would capture the important difference in the behavior the depressed persons. Contrary to Jourard's (1971) position that nondisclosure is healthy, Chaikin and Derlega (1971a) found that nondisclosure of intimate information was regarded as appropriate, and individuals disclosing intimate information to strangers were regarded as maladjusted. Chaikin Derlega (1974b) found also that nonreciprocal disclosure was rated as more inappropriate than reciprocated disclosure. Cozby (1973) has even suggested that self-disclosure curvilinearly related to mental health, with unusually low or high levels of disclosure being related to maladjustment. One could hypothesize that it is the nonreciprocal–high disclosure of intimate problems by depressed persons that induces the negative affect in others. Listening to the tapes from the study, one is impressed by the willingness of the depressed patients to discuss death, marital infidelities, hysterectomies, family strife, and a variety of other intensely personal matters. Some of these topics of conversation may have an inherently mood-inducing quality to them, and this may account for the mood of the subjects. Clearly, more research is needed.

In summary, the induction of negative affect in others by depressed persons found in the present study raises questions about reactive responses from the environment. Actual behavioral consequences remain to be fully demonstrated, but this mood induction may reduce the effects of adaptive, prosocial behaviors of depressed persons. To encourage more social behaviors without reducing the aversiveness of depressed persons may only further weaken their repertoires. As argued elsewhere (Coyne, 1976), the environmental conditions elicited by depressed behavior may come to have an existence, independent of subsequent behavior by depressed persons.

The present study leaves unanswered questions as to exactly what in the behavior of depressed persons induces mood changes in others, but the solution may lie in the nonreciprocal, high disclosure of intimate problems. Further research is needed to verify this and the related hypothesis that some of the inappropriate topics of conversation introduced by the depressed person have inherently depressing qualities.

Given that the present study used only female target individuals and subjects, it leaves questions concerning sex differences in relative response to depression unanswered. Because the handling of affective conversational material seems so central to this reaction, important sex differences may exist. Here, too, further research is needed.

REFERENCES

Byrne, D. (1971). *The attraction paradigm.* New York: Academic Press.

Carkhuff, R. R. (1969). *Helping and human relations*, Volume 2. New York: Holt, Rinehart & Winston.

Carkhuff, R. R., & Berenson, B. G. (1967). *Beyond counseling and psychotherapy.* New York: Holt, Rinehart & Winston.

Chaiken, A. L., & Derlega, V. J. (1974a). Liking for the norm-breaker in self-disclosure. *Journal of Personality, 42,* 117–129.

Chaiken, A. L., & Derlega, V. T. (1974b). Variables affecting the appropriateness of self-disclosure. *Journal of Consulting and Clinical Psychology, 42,* 588–593.

Coyne, J. C. (1976). Toward an interactional description of depression. *Psychiatry, 39,* 14-27.

Cozby, P. C. (1973). Self-disclosure: A literature review. *Psychological Bulletin, 79,* 73–91.

Ferster, C. B. A (1973). A function analysis of depression. *American Psychologist, 28,* 857–870.

Ferster, C. B. (1974). Behavioral approaches to depression. In R. J. Friedman & M. M. Katz (Eds.), *The psychology of depression.* New York: Wiley.

Gottschalk, L. (1974). A hope scale applicable to verbal samples. *Archives of General Psychiatry, 30,* 779–788.

Gouaux, C. (1971). Induced affective states and interpersonal attraction. *Journal of Personality and Social Psychology, 20,* 37–43.

Gouaux, C., Lamberth, J., & Friedrich, C. (1972). Affect and interpersonal attraction: A comparison of trait and state measures. *Journal of Personality and Social Psychology, 24,* 53–58.

Jacobson, E. (1954). Transference problems in the psychoanalytic treatment of severely depressed patients. *Journal of the American Psychoanalytic Association, 2,* 595–606.

Jourard, S. M. (1971). *The transparent self* (2nd ed.). Princeton, NJ.: Van Nostrand.

Lewinsohn, P. M. (1974). A behavioral approach to depression. In R. J. Friedman & M. M. Katz (Eds.), *The psychology of depression.* New York: Wiley.

Lewinsohn, P. M., & Shaffer, M. (1971). The use of home observations as an integral part of the treatment of depression: Preliminary report and case studies. *Journal of Consulting and Clinical Psychology, 37,* 87–94.

Libet, J. M., & Lewinsohn, P. M. (1973). Concept of social skill with special reference to the behavior of depressed persons. *Journal of Consulting and Clinical Psychology, 40,* 304–312.

MacPhillamy, D. J., & Lewinsohn, P. (1974). Depression as a function of levels of desired and obtained pleasure. *Journal of Abnormal Psychology, 83,* 651–657.

Weissman, M. M., & Paykel, E. S. (1974). *The depressed woman.* Chicago: Chicago Press.

Zuckerman, M., & Lubin, B. (1965). *Manual for the multiple affect adjective checklist.* San Diego: Educational Testing Service.

Zung, W. W. K. (1965). A self-rating depression scale. *Archives of General Psychiatry, 12,* 63.

Exposure to the Social Sharing of Emotion: Emotional Impact, Listener Responses and Secondary Social Sharing

Véronique Christophe • Labacolil, Université de Lille 3, France
Bernard Rimé • Université de Louvain, Louvain-la-Neuve, Belgique

In line with evidence showing that emotion involves a social sharing process in which the subject communicates about emotional experience, this article examines the impact of being exposed to such communications. First, it was predicted that being exposed to the social sharing of an emotion is emotion-inducing. Second, it was reasoned that if this holds true, then the listener should later engage in socially sharing with other persons the emotional narrative heard. Thus, a process of "secondary social sharing" was predicted. In two independent studies subjects recalled a situation in which someone had shared an emotional experience with them. They then rated emotions felt while exposed to the narrative, responses adopted toward the sharing person, and extent of secondary social sharing. The predictions were supported. Exposure to a social sharing situation was confirmed as itself emotion-inducing. Secondary social sharing was recorded in 66 percent of the cases in Study 1 and in 78 percent in Study 2. Both studies also showed that exposure to the sharing of highly intense emotional episodes elicited more repetitive secondary social sharing and a superior number of target persons than exposure to episodes of love or of moderate emotional intensity.

The cognitive-motor view of expression (Rimé, 1983, 1984; Rimé & Schiaratura, 1991) stresses that an important proportion of episodic information is encoded under nonverbal, dynamic forms. This information consists of (a) bodily movements involved in sensory receptors' orientation and tracking (e.g., Jacobson, 1930), (b) affect-related visceral and motor changes (e.g., Cacioppo & Petty, 1981; Lang, 1979), (c) anticipatory and actual adaptive bodily responses (e.g., Frijda, 1986; Lang, 1979), and (d) mimetic symbols capturing critical dynamic attributes of perceived objects, persons, or events (Jousse, 1955/1974; Michotte, 1948, 1950; Piaget, 1951; Werner & Kaplan, 1963). According to this theory, emotionally-arousing episodes are eliciting particularly dense nonverbal-dynamic encoding. Nonverbal-dynamic information is further assumed to remain mentally active and thus to be the focus of attention—under the form of mental images—as long as it fails to be assimilated together with corresponding verbalizations. When expressed under conceptual forms conforming to the rules of lexicon, syntax and logic in the unidimensional string of verbal communication, dynamic information progressively finds its way into and across long-term memory networks. A clear implication of this theory is that people who were exposed to an emotion will experience the need to talk about this episode.

Another line of reasoning leads to a similar prediction. Emotion is commonly defined as involving the interruption of goal-oriented processes which were active immediately prior to the emotional circumstances (e.g., Simon; 1967; Mandler, 1975). Such an interruption in the motivational process challenges people's anticipations. It may also question the wider plans which these anticipations were part of, as well as generalized assumptions underlying these plans. In extreme cases—major life events—fundamental beliefs about the self and the world have been evidenced as largely undermined and sometimes destroyed (Janoff-Bulman, 1992). Thus, a person just exposed to an emotion may be expected to experience the self as modified. Perceiving the self as modified can in turn be expected to elicit a powerful motivation to seek social contacts with significant others. Indeed, people's self-image and self-identify are by and large the product of how significant others perceive them and treat them (Mead, 1934). Experiencing the self as modified would thus stimulate the need to interact with significant others in order to either confirm or disconfirm changes in personal identity, or to help in reconstructing assumptions and beliefs. It is thus predicted that people who were exposed to emotion would be in need of interpersonal interaction.

The prediction that exposure to an emotion induces the need to undertake interpersonal interaction and to talk about the emotional experience was recently documented by studies on the social sharing of emotion. This refers to a process which takes place in the hours, days, weeks and sometimes months following the experience of an emotion. It usually happens under the form of conversations in which people openly communicate with some target person about the emotional circumstances and related feelings and reactions (Rimé, 1989; Rimé, Mesquita, Philippot, & Boca, 1991a). A good deal of empirical evidence supports the view that current life emotions, whether positive or negative, induce social sharing in a quite general manner. In several studies investigating the recall of recent emotional episodes, subjects reported having talked with people about these episodes in 90 to 96 percent of the cases (for a review, see Rimé, Philippot, Boca & Mesquita, 1992). Sharing an emotion socially was initiated

early after experiencing it and it was predominantly repetitive. Emotional episodes rated as more intense involved more frequent and more extended social sharing (Rimé et al., 1991a; Rimé, Noël & Philippot, 1991b). These findings were replicated across diary studies in which subjects had to report daily about the most emotional event of the day (Rimé, Philippot, Finkenauer, Legast, Moorkens, & Tornqvist, 1995), as well as across follow-up studies in which subjects were contacted first after exposure to some important emotion (e.g., traffic accident, child delivery . . .) and then again some weeks later (Boca, Rimé, & Arcuri, 1992; Rimé et al., 1995). Emotions induced in the laboratory have also been shown to set the social sharing process (Luminet, Bouts, Manstead & Rimé, 1995). Overall thus, the general notion seems to be well supported.

An important implication of these findings is that human beings are very frequently led to play the role of receiver or of partner for the social sharing initiated by some other person. In this context it is most noteworthy that Rimé et al. (1992) observed that for all age groups, these targets of social sharing are overwhelmingly recruited among intimates (i.e., parents, brothers, sisters, friends, or spouse/companion). From the above theory and findings new questions emerge. They concern the impact of the social sharing process on the target. What is the emotional effect of having listened to an emotional narrative? Will the target in turn also react with social sharing? These questions are at the heart of the two studies presented in this paper. Prior research already suggests that in effect the social sharing of an emotion has an emotional impact on target persons. Lazarus, Opton, Monikos and Rankin (1965) observed increased autonomic arousal among subjects listening to a distressed person. Archer and Berg (1978) observed heightened anxiety among subjects who listened to other people disclosing intimate aspects of themselves. Strack and Coyne (1983) observed that subjects, exposed to a 15-minute conversation with depressed persons, rated themselves as more anxious, more depressed and more hostile than subjects exposed to control persons. Shortt and Pennebaker (1992) showed college students videorecordings of disclosures of traumas experienced by Holocaust survivors, which differed in depth of disclosure. The deeper the revealed emotions, the more emotionally aroused were the viewers, as evidenced by a skin conductance measure.

If in effect exposure to the social sharing of an emotion is itself emotion-eliciting, it follows from our theory that the listener too would later engage in socially sharing the emotional narrative he or she had been exposed to with some third person. In other words, a process of "secondary social sharing" is likely to be manifested by the listener once the primary social sharing process has ended. However, as indicated earlier, socially sharing an emotional experience is generally viewed as a disclosure of intimate matters. It thus assumes confidentiality, an assumption supported by the fact that the addressee generally is an intimate person. Contrarily to common sense, our reasoning leads us to predict that in the domain of secondary social sharing of emotion, confidentiality may well be the exception rather than the rule.

The two studies reported in this paper were intended to test this proposition. More specifically, we tested the hypothesis that the more intense the socially shared emotion, the more the listener would evidence later manifestations of secondary social sharing.

The method used in both studies was a modified version of the retrospective or "recall" method in which subjects have to recall a recent emotional episode and then to answer questions about this episode (e.g., Scherer, Wallbott, & Summerfield, 1986; Shaver, Schwartz, Kirson, & O'Connor, 1987; Wallbott, & Scherer, 1994). In the modified version used here, subjects had to recall a recent episode in which someone socially shared an emotion with them. In Study 1, subjects freely selected such an episode and were post hoc grouped in three classes according to the level of emotionality they reported having felt when exposed to the narrative. In Study 2, subjects were randomly assigned to one of three conditions of emotional intensity of the socially shared episode they had to retrieve from memory. Dependent variables comprised the rating of basic emotions felt while exposed to the emotion narrative, responses adopted toward the sharing person, and the extent of secondary social sharing.

Study 1

Method

SUBJECTS

One hundred and thirty-four students, 42 males and 92 females, aged between 18 and 28 years (*M*

= 21.06) all enrolled in a social psychology class at the Department of Social and Economic Administration of the University of Lille 3, volunteered to participate.

PROCEDURE

The general purpose of the study was explained to the subjects in the classroom. They were asked to complete the questionnaire of the study at home and to hand it in after the lecture a week later. Confidentiality and anonymity were granted.

QUESTIONNAIRE

General Information. After having mentioned their age and gender, subjects were instructed to retrieve from their recent memories an episode in which someone had reported to them a personal experience involving an emotional state. Once such an episode was retrieved, subjects had to briefly specify what has happened to this person. They then answered questions on (a) how long ago did the social sharing situation happen, and (b) who was the person who socially shared the emotion (spouse or companion, close friend, family member, colleague, acquaintance, or stranger).

Felt Emotions. Subjects rated the intensity of the emotion they had felt when listening to the socially shared emotional episode. These ratings were collected on a 10-point scale anchored from "not at all upset" (*pas du tout bouleversé(e)*) to "very much upset" (*tout-à-fait bouleverse(e)*). They then rated the primary emotions felt in this situation by completing a modified version of the Differential Emotional Scale (Izard, 1977). Twelve primary emotions (anger, guilt, disgust, anxiety, interest, joy, contempt, fear, surprise, happiness, and sadness) were presented, each with a 7-point scale (not at all/very strongly).

Secondary Social Sharing. Subjects were asked if after their exposure to the social sharing situation, they themselves had happened to speak to some other person(s) about the episode to which they had listened ("secondary social sharing"). Answers were collected on five successive items: (a) yes or no, (b) if yes, with what delay after the social sharing situation did they talk about the told episode for the first time? (immediately after/the same day/the same week/the same month/later), (c) how often did they talk about it? (never/once or twice/three to four times/five to six times/more than six times), (d) with how many persons did they talk about it? (only one person/two persons/ three to four/five to six/more than six persons), (e) how often do they still talk about it now? (several times a day/once a day/once a week/once a month/never more).

Results

On average, the reported social sharing situations had taken place some 5.51 months ($S.D.$ = 7.39) before the time of the present investigation. The teller was a friend in 51.49 percent of the cases, a family member in 25.37 percent, the spouse or companion in 8.21 percent, and a non-intimate person in 14.93 percent. Consistent with the literature showing the exposure to the narrative of an emotion to be emotion-inducing, subjects' ratings of intensity of emotion felt when listening to the socially shared episode were generally quite high, with an average of 6.32 ($S.D.$ = 2.87) on the 10-point scale. Seven-point scale ratings of the primary emotions felt while listening evidenced elevated scores for interest (M = 6.09, $S.D.$ = 1.30) and for surprise (M = 4.52; $S.D.$ = 2.16).

Using subjects' ratings of intensity of emotion felt when listening to the socially shared episode, three groups were created. Subjects who scored in the lower quartile of the distribution of the emotional intensity scale constituted the low emotional intensity group (scores 1 to 4, N = 35). Those who scored in the higher quartile constituted the high emotional intensity group (scores 9 and 10, N = 37). Finally, subjects scoring in between these two extremes formed the moderate emotional intensity group (N = 62). These three groups were comparable for gender, $X^2(2, N = 134)$ = 4.06, $n.s.$, for age $F(2, 131)$ 1.36, $n.s.$, for time elapsed since the social sharing situation, $F(2, 131)$ = 1.68, $n.s.$, as well as for type of social relationship, $X^2(10, N = 134)$ = 17.48, $n.s.$ Yet, they differed very markedly on emotional intensity ratings, with M = 2.49 ($S.D.$ = 1.22) in the low intensity group, M = 6.52 ($S.D.$ = 1.16) in the moderate one, and M = 9.76 ($S.D.$ = 0.43) in the high intensity group, $F(2, 131)$ = 449.32, p = 0.0001.

FELT EMOTIONS

In order to specify in what respect the three groups differed, they were compared for primary emo-

tions felt when exposed to the social sharing. As can be seen from Table 14.1, strongly significant effects were found for most emotions, with only a few (guilt, contempt, and happiness) failing to discriminate between groups. Post hoc comparisons (Scheffé) showed most of these effects to be due to higher rated emotional feelings in the high emotional intensity group as compared to the two other ones, which generally did not differ from each other. Remarkably high ratings were observed for the emotion of interest in all three groups. In the high emotional intensity group in particular, the average rating of interest (6.73) was close to the endpoint of the scale.

SECONDARY SOCIAL SHARING

After the social sharing situation, subjects spoke about the shared episode to some third person in 66.4 percent of the cases. This high figure did not vary across the intensity groups, $X^2(2, N = 134)$<1. Yet, subjects in the high emotional intensity group talked about it later more recurrently than did subjects in the low and in the moderate emotional intensity groups which did not differ from each other on this variable, $F(2,131)$ = 5.39, p = 0.005 (see Figure 14.1). Similarly, subjects in the high emotional intensity group talked later about the socially shared episode with more different persons than in the two other groups, $F(2, 131)$ = 3.25, $p < 0.05$ (see Figure 14.1). Subjects talked for the first time during the day of the social sharing situation in 38.8 percent of the cases, and during the same week in 17.9 percent. Finally, 36.5 percent of all subjects still happen to talk about their received social sharing at the time they completed the questionnaire. On neither of these measures were there significant differences between the three intensity groups.

As subjects' gender was unevenly distributed, the question could be raised to what extent gender effects could account for the secondary social sharing process evidenced here. This was checked by comparing males and females for the three basic variables of secondary social sharing—rate, recurrence, and number of partners. Rate of social sharing evidenced a trend for females to develop secondary social sharing in a higher proportion (70.65 percent) than males (57.14 percent), but this difference failed to be significant, $X^2(2, N = 134)$ = 2.36, $n.s.$ As regards recurrence and number of partners, observed statistics were far from ap-

TABLE 14.1. Means and Standard Deviations for Primary Emotions Felt at Exposure to the initial Social Sharing Situation

Emotions felt	Intensity of shared episode			
	Low (*N* = 35)	Medium (*N* = 62)	High (*N* = 37)	$F(2,131)$
Anger	2.35$_a$ (1.89)	2.84$_a$ (2.08)	4.39$_b$ (2.44)	9.27****
Guilt	1.21 (0.83)	1.22 (0.89)	1.47 (1.42)	0.80
Disgust	2.67$_a$ (2.06)	3.13$_a$ (2.27)	4.70$_b$ (2.35)	8.48****
Anxiety	1.42$_a$ (0.77)	2.61$_b$ (1.81)	4.48$_c$ (2.04)	30.48***
Shame	1.00$_a$ (0.02)	1.04$_a$ (0.18)	1.44$_b$ (1.50)	3.64**
Interest	5.46$_a$ (1.70)	6.06$_a$ (1.18)	6.73$_b$ (0.56)	9.82****
Joy	2.97$_a$ (2.27)	2.26$_a$ (2.06)	1.12$_b$ (0.36)	9.46****
Contempt	1.37$_a$ (1.08)	1.91$_{ab}$ (1.88)	2.26$_b$ (2.10)	2.29
Fear	1.46$_a$ (0.91)	2.03$_a$ (1.46)	4.19$_b$ (2.09)	32.69****
Surprise	3.84$_a$ (2.02)	4.39$_{ab}$ (2.16)	5.39$_b$ (2.05)	5.15***
Happiness	1.94$_{ab}$ (1.88)	2.15$_a$ (2.12)	1.32$_b$ (1.27)	2.37*
Sadness	1.66$_a$ (1.06)	3.02$_b$ (2.00)	4.71$_c$ (2.06)	25.33****

Note. Means within a row with different subscripts were found reliably different from one another at the 0.05 level in Scheffé post hoc comparisons.
*$p < 0.10$; **$p < 0.05$; ***$p < 0.01$; ****$p < 0.001$.

proaching significance, $F(1,131) = 3.35$, *n.s.* and $F(1,131) = 2.74$, *n.s.*, respectively.

Discussion

Subjects' ratings of their emotions when exposed to the social sharing of an emotional episode confirmed that Listening to another person's emotion is an emotion-inducing situation. It triggers in particular the primary emotions of interest and of surprise. Episodes rated as globally more upsetting were also found to generally trigger negative emotions at a more intense level.

The puzzling prediction considered in the introduction of this paper was clearly confirmed. Contrarily to what common sense would expect, socially shared emotional episodes are in no way kept confidential by receivers. In spite of the fact that they were intimates of the original sharing person in 85 percent of the cases, receivers who participated in this study did undertake secondary social sharing in a vast majority of the cases. In about two-thirds of the collected episodes indeed, listeners acknowledged that they later talked about it to one or more persons. In spite of common sense illusions of confidentiality in this matter, listeners did so in a rather extensive manner, as secondary social sharing was reported by them as having occurred twice or more in 53 percent of all cases, and with two or more persons in 54 percent. However, the global rate of social sharing—66.4 percent of the cases—did not vary as a function of the intensity of the emotion they felt. It is thus possible that the mere fact that the episode listened to was perceived as involving emotion acted as a launching condition for secondary social sharing to take place later. Yet, the number of times secondary social sharing occurred and the number of persons with whom it occurred varied as a function of the emotional intensity felt by the original

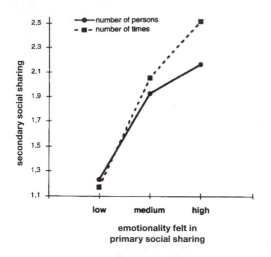

secondary social sharing

— number of persons
- ■ - number of times

low   medium   high

emotionality felt in
primary social sharing

FIGURE 14.1 ■ Frequency of secondary social and number of persons with whom secondary social sharing occurred as a function of the level of emotionality felt when exposed to the primary social sharing.

listener in the initial social sharing situation. The latter findings were thus in clear support of the hypothesis underlying the study.

However, the test conducted here was limited in one particular respect. The three groups were created from subjects' own ratings of the emotionality they had felt while listening to the episode that was socially shared with them. It is possible that subjects rated as more emotionally intense precisely those episodes that they had happened to talk about more often. Thus, the data from Study 1 should be considered as tentative and in need of replication with a tighter procedure.

Study 2

In this study, subjects had to retrieve from memory a situation in which someone socially shared with them an emotional episode resembling one from on a list of 20 events which they were given. Three such lists each comprising 20 emotional life events were used. They included respectively, low, moderate and high intensity emotional events. A between-subject design was created by randomly assigning each subject to one of these lists. Once subjects had retrieved the requested memory, they first had to describe briefly the emotional episode involved so that its correspondence with the list could later be checked by the investigators. Sub-

jects then completed the questionnaire covering the dependent measures.

Method

SUBJECTS

All psychology students ($N = 177$) attending an advanced psychology class at the Department of Psychology of the University of Louvain were distributed the questionnaire of this study. They were invited to complete it at home and to bring it back to the next lecture a week later. Of those contacted, 150 brought the form back within the requested period.

CONDITIONS

Instructions on the front page of the questionnaire served to assign subjects to conditions of intensity of the socially shared emotional experience. Randomly distributed across subjects, the front page of the questionnaire was varied by presenting one of three lists of 20 emotional events. One list was composed of 20 events which ranked at the lower end of the list of life events developed by Holmes and Rahe (1967) (e.g., quarrel with a friend, death of a pet, unhappy love affair) and was intended to form a list of low emotional intensity events. A second list comprised 20 events which ranked at the higher end of the Holmes and Rahe list (e.g., abortion, divorce, academic or professional failure) and represented a list of moderate emotional intensity events. A third list was made of 20 events taken out of those mentioned by Green (1990) as potential elicitors of post traumatic stress disorder (e.g., sudden death of someone they were close to, rape, exposure to disaster) and thus was constituted a list of high intensity emotional events.

Subjects were instructed to retrieve from their memories and briefly describe a situation in which someone had socially shared with them an emotional experience resembling one of those in the list they had received. The questionnaire then had to be completed with reference to this situation.

QUESTIONNAIRE

General Information. Subjects had to specify (a) the time elapsed since the social sharing situation took place, (b) their link with the person who told them the emotional experience (scale as in

Study 1), and (c) the intensity of the emotional upset elicited in them by listening to the reporting person (scale as in Study 1).

Listener Responses to the Social Sharing. This part of the questionnaire had been developed for the present study in a pilot study conducted on 56 volunteer psychology students of the University of Lille 3, 48 females and 8 males aged between 21 and 39 years (M = 24.04). These subjects all recalled a situation in which someone had socially shared an emotional experience with them. Referring to this memory, they then wrote open answers to questions regarding their (a) nonverbal displays (did you modify your voice, or face, or posture when listening to the narration), (b) verbal responses (what did you tell the other person?), (c) interpersonal gestures (did you address some gesture to the other person?). A cluster analysis was then conducted on the collected material with the purpose of grouping answers with equivalent content into the same cluster. The procedure resulted in 11 clusters. For the purpose of the present study, for each cluster three items were selected among representatives open answers collected in the pilot study. Each of the resulting 33 items was to be rated on a 7-point scale anchored from "not at all" to "very much".

Secondary Social Sharing. As in Study 1, subjects were asked if after their exposure to the social sharing situation, they themselves had happened to tell to some other persons about the episode to which they had listened ("secondary social sharing"). Answers were collected on five successive items: (a) yes or no, (b) if yes, with what delay after the social sharing situation did they talk about the episode they had listened to for the first time? (c) How often did they talk about it? (d) With how many persons did they talk about it? (e) How often do they still talk about it now? Scales were as in Study 1.

Results and Discussion

CONFORMITY TO INSTRUCTIONS AND COMPARABILITY OF CONDITIONS

When checking whether the episodes described by subjects as socially shared with them, corresponded to the list of emotional events of the conditions they were assigned to, this was not the case for 29 of them. Consequently this material was discarded leaving finally 121 subjects, 23 males

and 98 females aged between 18 and 55 years (M = 21.1), with 41 in the low intensity condition, 42 in the moderate, and 38 in the high intensity condition.

Comparability of the experimental conditions was then checked for (a) gender, (b) age, (c) time elapsed since the social sharing situation took place, and (d) type of link subjects had with the person who socially shared the emotion with them. Gender was homogeneously distributed across conditions, X^2 (2, N = 121) = 1.18, *n.s.*, as was age, $F(2,118)$ = 1.36, *n.s.* However, time elapsed since the episode elicited a significant effect, $F(2,118)$ = 7.33, p = 0.001. Consistent with the notion that high intensity emotional episodes are less common and thus less frequent (American Psychiatric Association, 1987), post hoc tests (Scheffé) showed that episodes in the high emotional intensity condition were less recent (M = 9.6 months, *S.D.* = 12.3) than was the case for the low and the moderate intensity conditions which did not differ significantly from each other (M = 2.8 months, *S.D.* = 4.1, and M = 4.4 months, *S.D.* = 6.2, respectively). Finally, homogeneity of conditions was recorded for type of link with the teller of the episode, X^2 (8, N = 121) = 9.17, *n.s.* Consistent with former observations (Rimé et al., 1991a, 1992), the teller was a friend in 61.2 percent of the cases, and either a family member or a spouse or companion in 27.2 percent, and only the remaining 11.6 percent were non-intimates.

ELICITED EMOTION

The extent to which the conditions actually differed in intensity of emotion elicited by the social sharing situation was then tested. A one-way ANOVA conducted on subjects' ratings evidenced a strongly significant effect, $F(2,118)$ = 8.91, p < 0.001. *Post hoc* comparisons (Scheffé) revealed that subjects in the low intensity condition had been significantly less emotionally aroused by their exposure to the socially sharing episode (M = 6.29, *S.D.* = 2.44) than both those in the moderate and in the high intensity condition (M = 7.83, *S.D.* = 1.75 and M = 8.08, *S.D.* = 1.92, respectively). The latter two conditions failed to differ significantly.

LISTENER RESPONSES

Data from the total pool of subjects for the 33-item questionnaire assessing listener responses were first submitted to a factor analysis in order to obtain empirically-based clusters. A Varimax solution accounting for 51.5 percent of the total variance resulted in five factors. Factor I (24.9 percent of the total variance) grouped manifestations of social support (e.g., attempts at comforting, or expressing unconditional support). Factor II (9.7 percent) comprised nonverbal comforting (e.g., hug, kiss, or touch). Factor III (6.3 percent) reflected later involvement, with some concrete action by the subject in favour of the teller (e.g., inviting them home, or to a distractive environment, or undertaking some helpful action). Factor IV (5.6 percent) consisted of de-dramatizing or of perspective taking. Factor V (5.0 percent) grouped further talking or verbalizing, (e.g., expressing the need to know more, asking for further details, or trying to clarify some aspects).

Subjects' ratings of listener response items were converted into five scores by averaging the various items having high loadings on the same factor. One-way ANOVAs showed that three out of the five types of listener response elicited differences between conditions (see Figure 14.2). They all discriminated the high emotional condition from the two other conditions which did not differ significantly from one another. Thus, subjects in the high emotional condition evidenced less verbal expression, $F(2,118) = 3.02$, $p = 0.05$, attempted less de-dramatizing. $F(2,118) = 2.94$, $p = 0.05$, and manifested much more nonverbal comforting, $F(2,118) = 7.58$, $p < 0.001$.

SECONDARY SOCIAL SHARING

Secondary social sharing was mentioned in 78.5 percent of the cases, and this figure was independent of conditions of intensity of the socially shared emotional episode, $X^2(2, N = 121) = 1.05$, n.s. The latency of initiation of secondary social sharing did not vary across conditions either. In 40.5 percent of cases, subjects initiated secondary social sharing during the day of the social sharing situation. However, replicating Study 1, the two measures of the extent of social sharing—frequency of secondary social sharing and number of persons with whom secondary social sharing occurred—evidenced significant differences as a function of the conditions of emotional intensity of the shared episode. As shown in Figure 14.3, subjects of the high intensity condition manifested secondary social sharing more often, $F(2,118) =$

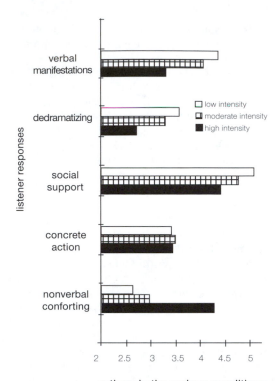

FIGURE 14.2 ■ Level of listener responses across conditions of intensity of the shared emotional episode.

3.12, $p < 0.05$, and with more persons, $F(2,118) = 3.17$, $p < 0.05$ than those who reported either moderate or low intensity conditions, these latter two groups failing to differ significantly.

Finally, 47.9 percent of the subjects answered that at present they still socially share the episode that was told to them. This happened at least once a day in 40.5 percent of cases, and at least once a week in 25.6 percent, but experimental conditions did not differ in this respect, $F(2,118) < 1$.

General Discussion

A first hypothesis predicted that more intense shared emotional episodes would induce more intense emotional responses in the listener. In Study 1, listener's ratings of their primary emotions evidenced two contrasting observations. First, regardless of the intensity of the emotional episode heard, the emotion of interest was always markedly preponderant, with average ratings close to the extreme anchor of the scale. Second, the more the emotional episode heard was rated as intense by listeners, the higher was the level of most of their rated negative emotions. In Study 2, this relationship was unambiguously confirmed using a procedure involving random assignment of subjects to conditions of emotional intensity of the episode. Thus, the first hypothesis was supported.

The contrasting observations of Study 1 deserve to be further considered. The findings regarding the emotion of interest suggest that not only strong emotional events, but even relatively mild ones do trigger positive feelings and approach motives among listeners. This is consistent with the general observation from current Life that emotionally-loaded materials are attractive to lay persons. The data further suggest that the attraction elicited by exposure to emotionally-loaded materials does not occur without a counterpart. As emotional upset increased among exposed persons, so did the level of most of their negative affects too. Thus, exposure to social sharing of an intense emotional episode is Likely to trigger an approach–avoidance conflict and high intensity episodes may eventually arouse strong avoidance responses. This was also observed by Pennebaker (1993) in a community recently struck by an earthquake. Some time after the disaster, people started wearing T-shirts reading "Thank you for not sharing with me your earthquake experience."

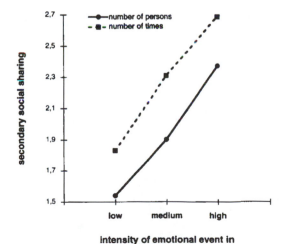

FIGURE 14.3 ■ Frequency of secondary social sharing and number of persons with whom secondary social sharing occurred as a function of intensity of the emotional event in the primary social sharing.

One may wonder why subjects in the present studies—especially those who reported intense emotional episodes—willingly lent themselves to social sharing in spite of the avoidance forces triggered by the narrative. A very plausible answer lies in their particular social relationship to the person who shared it with them. In an overwhelming majority—some 85 percent—listeners were in fact intimates, like parents, siblings, a companion or a spouse, or close friend. Such data replicated existing evidence that the social sharing of emotion develops with intimates (Rimé et al., 1991a, 1992). Non-intimates can escape a potentially painful or ego-threatening social sharing situation. As far as intimates are concerned, commitment is usually too strong and social bonds too robust. Altering them would cause important damage to the self of both parties. Therefore, lending oneself to the social sharing of emotion by an intimate is probably an inescapable situation.

It has been found that social responses when exposed to someone's misfortune often consist of minimizing the problem, of moderating the degree of disclosure, or even of discouraging open emotional expression (Lehman, Ellard, & Wortman, 1986; Dakoff & Taylor, 1990; Lehman & Hemphill, 1990; Pennebaker, 1993). Yet, such responses were in no manner evidenced here. In Study 2, as intensity increased, de-dramatizing responses and verbal manifestations by the listeners decreased. In a compensatory manner, intense episodes elicited much more nonverbal comforting behaviours than was the case for low and moderate intensity episodes. Thus, the social responses recorded here seemed characterized by tolerance, availability, and appropriate tuning of behaviours. This may be due to the fact that listeners in the present study were essentially intimates whereas in most cases former studies considered a wider social environment. Intimates may indeed be more tolerant to the victims' emotional expression. Another possibility might lie in the self-report character of the present investigation. Listeners may have been biasing their descriptions in a socially desirable direction. Lehman et al. (1986) showed that most people know intuitively how to provide support to others, but may not do so in order to protect themselves. Thus, future investigations should compare the actual social responses displayed by intimates and non-intimates when faced with the social sharing of emotional episodes differing in intensity.

The major hypothesis was that exposure to the social sharing of an emotion would in turn elicit secondary social sharing. The two reported studies offered clear support for this prediction and their data closely replicated one another. Secondary social sharing was recorded respectively in 66 percent (Study 1) and in 78 percent (Study 2) of cases, with no significant difference between the two. These data thus provide further evidence that emotion leads to social sharing. One may wonder to what extent the recall procedure used led to the overestimation of the rate of social sharing. This question was examined earlier on empirical grounds in studies about primary social sharing. Recall procedures (Rimé et al., 1991a) and diary recordings of an emotional event registered on the day of the event itself (Rimé et al., 1995) evidenced quite similar rates of immediate social sharing. Thus, it does not seem that the recall procedure induces bias in this respect.

A more basic question concerns the precise nature of the causes of secondary social sharing. Is it due to the emotional quality of the event itself, or could it be attributed to correlated variables like importance, unexpectedness, or novelty of the shared event? In this regard however, we feel it should be stressed that the latter are not variables "confounded" with emotionality. They each are, by definition, integral parts of the appraisal process involved in the elicitation of emotion (e.g., Scherer, 1982; Smith & Ellsworth, 1985; Frijda, 1986). The emotion itself thus necessarily rests upon some degree of appraised importance, unexpectedness, novelty, and the like. Therefore, the more relevant question is which of these appraisal dimensions impact more or less on social sharing and this question should definitely be addressed in future studies.

The various findings of these two studies on secondary social sharing were closely consistent with earlier findings on primary social sharing. Thus, both studies showed that exposure to the sharing of more intense emotion elicits more repetitive social sharing, as well as social sharing targeted at a superior number of persons (Rimé et al., 1991a, 1995). Also consistent with previous data (Rimé et al., 1991a), secondary social sharing was found here to be initiated on the day the episode was heard in 39 percent (Study 1) and 40 percent (Study 2) of cases. Finally, as regards perpetuation of social sharing (Rimé et al., 1995), 36 percent of subjects in Study 1 and 48 percent of those in Study 2 reported that they still talk about the episode which they had heard at the time of this investigation, which meant an average of several months after the original exposure.

Earlier in this paper we referred to a paradox of secondary social sharing. People—especially intimates—are not supposed to speak widely to others about the emotion they had heard about in confidence. Yet, the data showed that this happens in some two-thirds to three-quarters of cases. Such a finding was again recently obtained by Christophe and Di Giacomo (1995) who also investigated the extent to which subjects preserved the anonymity of the source while engaging in secondary social sharing. It was found that they do not at all. People reported having explicitly mentioned the name of the source in 78 percent of the cases investigated. Hence, if one does not want an emotional episode to be spread around, one should better not share it at all.

According to the theoretical perspective adopted in this paper, the motives for engaging in secondary social sharing are twofold. First, people store dense dynamic information while listening to the emotional episode of another person. This information remains present in the attentional channel in the form of mental images until it becomes thoroughly verbally processed. Second, aspects of the self are challenged by exposure to the emotional narrative. People would thus be inclined to restore or reconstruct these aspects, a task requiring interaction with significant others. However, personal motives may not be the sole reason underlying secondary social sharing. Interpersonal motives may be involved as well, because repeating exciting emotional narratives may enhance the teller's social visibility and social integration. Finally, collective interests may also be served by secondary social sharing as it contributes to the spreading of emotional knowledge within a community (Rimé, 1995). If emotional experiences are commonly shared socially and if social sharing of emotions elicits secondary social sharing, an extension and updating of the collective data base with new individual emotional scenarios would be continuous. This process offers an ideal source for elaborating and refining socially shared emotion prototypes and emotion scripts. These potential intrapersonal, interpersonal and collective contributions of secondary social sharing thus open many avenues for future research.

REFERENCES

Archer, R. L., & Berg, J. H. (1978). Disclosure reciprocity and its limits: A reactance analysis. *Journal of Experimental Social Psychology, 14,* 527–540.

American Psychiatric Association. (1987). *Diagnostic and Statistical Manual of Mental Disorders,* (3rd ed. revised). Washington, DC: American Psychiatric Association.

Boca, S., Rimé, B., & Arcuri, L. (1992, January). Uno studio longitudinale di eventi emotivamente traumatici. Paper presented at the *Incontro Annuale delle Emozioni,* University of Padova, Italy.

Cacioppo, J. T., & Petty, R. E. (1981). Electromyograms as measures of extent and affectivity of information processing. *American Psychologist, 36,* 441–456.

Christophe, V., & Di Giacomo, J. P. (1995). *Contenu du partage social secondaire suite à un épisode émotionnel négatif ou positif.* Unpublished manuscript.

Dakoff, G. A., & Taylor, S. E. (1990). Victim's perceptions of social support: What is helpful from whom? *Journal of Personality and Social Psychology, 58,* 80–90.

Frijda, N. (1986). *The emotions.* Cambridge: Cambridge University Press.

Green, B. L. (1990). Defining trauma: Terminology and generic stresser dimensions. *Journal of Applied Social Psychology, 20,* 1632–1642.

Holmes, T. S., & Rahe, R. H. (1967). The social readjustment scale. *Journal of Psychosomatic Research, 11,* 103–111.

Izard, C. E. (1977). *Human emotions.* New York: Plenum.

Jacobson, E. (1930). Electrical measurements of neuromuscular states during mental activities: IV. Evidence of contraction of specific muscles during imagination. *American Journal of Physiology, 95,* 243–259.

Janoff-Bulman, R. (1992). *Shattered assumptions. Towards a new psychology of trauma.* New York: Free Press.

Jousse, M. (1955/1974). *L'anthropologie due geste.* Paris: Gallimard.

Lang, P. J. (1979). A bio-informational theory of emotional imagery. *Psychophysiology, 16,* 495–512.

Lazarus, R. S., Opton, E. M., Monikos, M. S., & Rankin, N. O. (1965). The principle of short circuiting of threat: Further evidence. *Journal of Personality, 33,* 307–316.

Lehman, D. R., & Hemphill, K. J. (1990). Recipient's perceptions of support attempts and attributions for support attempts that fail. *Journal of Social and Personal Relationships, 7,* 563–574.

Lehman, D. R., Ellard, J. H., & Wortman, C. B. (1986). Social support for the bereaved: Recipients' and providers' perspectives on what is helpful. *Journal of Consulting and Clinical Psychology, 54*(4), 438–446.

Luminet, O., Bouts, P., Manstead, S. R., & Rimé, B. (1995). *Social sharing of emotion: Experimental evidence.* Unpublished manuscript. Louvain-la-Neuve, Belgium: University of Louvain.

Mandler, G. (1975). *Mind and emotion.* New York: Wiley.

Mead, G. H. (1934). *Mind, self and society* (posthumous; C. M. Morris, Ed.). Chicago: University of Chicago Press.

Michotte, A. (1948). Le caractère de réalité des projections cinématographique. *Revue Internationale de Filmologie, 1,* 249–261.

Michotte, A. (1950). The emotional significance of movement. In M. L. Reymert (Ed.), *Feelings and emotions.* New York: McGraw-Hill.

Pennebaker, J. W. (1993). Social mechanisms of constraint. In D. M. Wegner, & J. W. Pennebaker (Eds.), *Handbook of mental control* (pp. 200–219). Englewood Cliffs, New Jersey: Prentice Hall.

Piaget, J. (1951). *La formation du symbôle chez l'enfant.* Neufchâtel: Delachaux et Niestlé.

Rimé, B. (1983). Nonverbal communication or nonverbal behavior? Towards a cognitiv-emotor theory of nonverbal behavior. In W. Doise, & S. Moscovici (Eds.), *Current issues in European social psychology* (Vol. 1, pp. 85–141). Cambridge: Cambridge University Press.

Rimé, B. (1984). Langage et communication. In S. Moscovici (Ed.), *Psychologie sociale* (pp. 415–446). Paris: Presses Universitaires de France.

Rimé, B. (1989). Le partage social des emotions. In B. Rimé, & K. Scherer (Eds.), *Textes de base en psychologie: Les émotions* (pp. 27–303). Lausanne: Delachaux et Niestlé.

Rimé, B. (1995). The social sharing of emotional experience as a source for the social knowledge of emotion. In J. A. Russell, J. M. Fernandez-Dols, A. S. R. Manstead, & J. C. Wellenkamp (Eds.), *Everyday conceptions of emotions. An introduction to the psychology, anthropology and linguistics of emotion* (pp. 475–489). Doordrecht, The Netherlands: Kluwer.

Rimé, B., & Schiaratura, L. (1991). Speech and gestures. In R. S. Felman, & B. Rimé (Eds.), *Fundamentals of nonverbal behavior* (pp. 239–281). New York: Cambridge University Press.

Rimé, B., Mesquita, B., Philippot, P., & Boca. S. (1991a). Beyond the emotional event: Six studies on social sharing of emotion. *Cognition and Emotion, 5,* 435–465.

Rimé, B., Noël, M. P., & Philippot, P. (1991b). Episode émotionnel, réminiscences mentales et réminiscences sociales. *Cahiers Internationaux de Psychologie Sociale, 11,* 93–104.

Rimé, B., Philippot, P., Boca, S., & Mesquita, B. (1992). Long-lasting cognitive and social consequences of emotion: Social sharing and rumination. In W. Stroebe, & M. Hewstone (Eds.), *European Review of Social Psychology* (Vol. 3, pp. 225–258). Chichester: Wiley.

Rimé, B., Philippot, P., Finkenauer, C. Legast, S., Moorkens, P., & Tornqvist, J. (1995). Mental rumination and social sharing in current life emotion. Unpublished manuscript. Louvain-la-Neuve, Belgium: University of Louvain.

Scherer, K. R. (1983). Emotion as process: Function, origins and regulation. *Social Science Information, 21,* 555–570.

Scherer, K. R., Wallbott, H. G., & Summerfield, A. B. (Eds.). (1986). *Experiencing emotion. A cross-cultural study.* Cambridge: Cambridge University Press.

Shaver, P., Schwartz, J., Kirson, D., & O'Connor, C. (1987). Emotion knowledge: Further exploration of a prototype approach. *Journal of Personality and Social Psychology, 52,* 1061–1086.

Shortt, J. W., & Pennebaker, J. W. (1992). Talking versus hearing about the Holocaust experiences. *Basic and Applied Social Psychology, 1,* 165–170.

Simon, H. A. (1967). Motivational and emotional controls of cognition. *Psychological Review, 84,* 29–39.

Smith, C. A., & Ellsworth, P. C. (1985). Patterns of cognitive appraisals in emotion. *Journal of Personality and Social Psychology, 48,* 813–838.

Strack, S., & Coyne, J. C. (1983). Shared and private reaction to depression. *Journal of Personality and Social Psychology, 44,* 798–806.

Wallbott, H. G., & Scherer, K. R. (1994). Evidence for universality and cultural variation of differential emotion response patterning. *Journal of Personality and Social Psychology, 66,* 310–328.

Werner, H., & Kaplan, R. (1963). *Symbol formation.* New York: Wiley.

INTRODUCTION TO PART 8

Emotion and Facial Expressions

Facial expressions are the best-known examples of nonverbal behavior associated with emotions. The angry glare, the embarrassed aversion of gaze, the delighted brightening of expression—the face seems particularly able to express emotions. Expression of emotion implies communication of one's appraisal of a situation, of one's disposition to behave, of the mode of upcoming interaction. In short, one supremely social aspect of emotion is the facial expression and communication of emotion.

The face is not the only channel of emotional communication. Certainly posture, tone of voice, muscle tone, and other nonlinguistic cues can be evocative of emotion. And although we forever complain about the inadequacy of language, we manage to use words to express emotion as well. In social psychology, research has addressed all these ways of expressing and communicating emotion, but the most studied has been facial expressions.

The modern study of facial expressions of emotion began in 1872 with the publication of Charles Darwin's *The Expression of the Emotions in Man and Animals*. Darwin's account of the origins of emotional expressions is no longer believed by most psychologists—in fact, it is surprisingly "non-Darwinian" in the sense that it does not propose that emotional expressions evolved for the purpose of expressing emotion (Fridlund, 1994). Nevertheless, Darwin's acute observations marked the start of modern interest in nonverbal expression of emotion. Social psychological research has followed up on Darwin's evolutionary approach in numerous ways. One of the best known is research on the extent to which facial expressions are recognized across cultures. The research of Paul Ekman has been

251

particularly influential. In his most well-known study, Ekman and his collaborators found that members of a remote New Guinea tribe, when shown photographs of posed Western facial expressions, matched them to descriptions of emotion-eliciting events much as did members of Western cultures (Ekman & Friesen, 1971). To many psychologists, such evidence suggests that at least some aspects of facial expressions have an innate basis, although other interpretations of these data are possible (Russell, 1994).

Perhaps the central question about facial expressions in contemporary psychology concerns the relation between facial expressions and emotional states. The everyday phrase "facial expressions of emotion" suggests two related but separate claims: (a) that these expressions accompany emotions and (b) that their purpose is to express a person's emotional state. A scholarly dispute is now occurring between those researchers who basically accept these two claims and those who do not.

The former approach contends that facial expressions are a fundamental part of emotional reactions. On this account, the arousal of a basic emotion such as shame or anger necessarily includes neural stimulation of the facial muscles that produce a facial expression of shame or anger. This stimulation may be inhibited according to social conventions or motives to deceive, but it is intrinsic to emotion and the face therefore tends to mirror a person's emotional state (Ekman, 1972). This approach has been termed variously the "emotional expression view" (Manstead, Fischer, & Jakobs, 1999) or the "direct readout view" (Sabini, 1995, possibly following Buck, 1984) to highlight its emphasis on the direct correspondence between facial expressions and emotions.

The major alternative to the direct readout view has been termed variously the "behavioral ecology view" (Fridlund, 1994) or the "social communications view" (Sabini, 1995). On this account an emotion does not necessarily entail a facial expression at all. Rather, facial expressions are thought to occur for the purpose of communicating social intentions and requests. Facial expressions often occur during emotions because emotions often occur in social contexts where a motive exists to signal intentions and requests, but these expressions are not part of emotions. On this account, for example, a solitary person, or a person with motives to deceive, can experience emotions without exhibiting a facial expression "expressive" of that emotion.

The differences between these two views are sharp, and the debate over them is ongoing. This section therefore presents two articles, each representing one of these views of the relation between facial expressions and emotion. The first, by Ekman, Friesen, and Ancoli (1980), is a classic statement of research in the tradition of the direct readout view. (Note that the authors of this 1980 report carefully note the incongruence of their approach with the two-factor theory of Schachter.) In this experiment, participants watched films that were either pleasant or frightening/disgusting and rated their emotional reactions on a questionnaire. Their facial expressions were videotaped secretly and the movements of their facial muscles were painstakingly determined. One facial action, the pulling upwards of the corners of the lips, was found to correlate with ratings of happiness following the pleasant film. Several facial actions were correlated with self-reported intensity of negative emotions, and a subset of these was correlated more with disgust than with any other negative emotion. In sum, the article by Ekman,

Friesen, and Ancoli suggests a close relation between the intensity of subjective emotional experience and the intensity of facial expression of emotion.

The second article in this section is a classic statement of research in the tradition of the social communication view. In this research Fridlund (1991) addressed one of the key objections to the social communications view of facial expressions, namely, that people in fact do make facial expressions when they are alone. In defense of this view Fridlund proposes that people may imagine themselves in social situations even when they are physically alone, and that solitary facial expressions may reflect a social state of mind if not an actual social situation. To test this notion Fridlund showed participants an amusing videotape in one of four contexts. One context was clearly social—with a friend—whereas the other three were physically solitary but varying in the degree to which they encouraged a social frame of mind: believing that a friend was watching the same tape in another room, believing that a friend was in another room but doing something else, and participating alone without any reference to a friend. The intensity of the participants' smiling was found to vary in proportion to the sociality of the context, but their self-reported happiness did not.

Thus, one of our readings reports a close relation between facial expression and subjective emotional experience and the other one does not. Contemporary social psychologists are trying to reconcile these findings and the theoretical perspectives they support. There is not yet a clear resolution, but the trend in theory and research is toward acknowledging that both views capture important truths about facial expressions of emotion: they do seem linked to emotion, and they are much more prevalent in public than in private. The challenge is to develop a new theory that incorporates both insights without contradiction. One recent, interesting attempt to do so is the chapter by Manstead, Fischer, and Jakobs (1999), which provides an up-to-date review of the evidence and proposes a hybrid theory in which facial expressions serve both social and emotional functions.

REFERENCES

Buck, R. (1984). *The communication of emotion.* New York: Guilford.

Darwin, C. (1872). *The expression of the emotions in man and animals.* London: John Murray.

Ekman, P. (1972). Universals and cultural differences in facial expressions of emotion. In H. E. Howe, Jr. (Series Ed.) & J. Cole (Vol. Ed.), *Nebraska symposium on motivation: 1971* (Vol 19, 207–283). Lincoln, NE: University of Nebraska Press.

Ekman, P, & Friesen, W. V. (1971). Constants across culture in the face and emotion. *Journal of Personality and Social Psychology, 17,* 124–129.

Ekman, P., Friesen, W. V., & Ancoli, S. (1980). Facial signs of emotional experience. *Journal of Personality and Social Psychology, 39,* 1125–1134.

Fridlund, A. J. (1991). Sociality of solitary smiling: Potentiation by an implicit audience. *Journal of Personality and Social Psychology, 60,* 229–240.

Fridlund, A. J. (1994). *Human facial expression: An evolutionary view.* San Diego, CA: Academic Press.

Manstead, A. S. R., Fischer, A. H., & Jakobs, E. B. (1999). The social and emotional functions of facial displays. In P. Philippot, R. S. Feldman, & E. J. Coats (Eds.), *The social context of nonverbal behavior* (pp. 287–313). Cambridge, England: Cambridge University Press.

Russell, J. A. (1994). Is there universal recognition of emotion from facial expression? A review of the cross-cultural studies. *Psychological Bulletin, 115,* 102–141.

Sabini, J. (1995). *Social psychology* (2nd ed.). New York: Norton.

Discussion Questions

1. How many different facial expressions can communicate happiness, or fear, or anger? Do they each express the same emotion? Do they seem related to actions that are associated with the emotion they express?
2. How difficult is it to conceal the expression of an emotion that is being experienced, or to display the expression of an emotion that is not being experienced? How would the direct readout view explain your answer? How would the social communication view explain your answer?
3. Why do people make facial expressions when alone? Consider how both the direct readout view and the social communication view would address this issue.
4. The measurement of facial expressions is often accomplished using FACS or EMG data. What do these acronyms stand for, and how does each work?

Suggested Readings

Ekman, P., & Rosenberg, E. L. (1997). *What the face reveals: Basic and applied studies of spontaneous expression using the facial action coding system (FACS)*. New York: Oxford University Press. Reprinted in this volume are 22 research studies that used the FACS system for coding facial actions. Many of the chapters illustrate the direct readout view of facial expressions and emotion. The chapters on appeasement, lying, recognition, dyadic interactions, and psychotherapeutic interactions will especially interest social psychologists.

Fridlund, A. J. (1994). *Human facial expression: An evolutionary view*. San Diego, CA: Academic Press. This book vigorously challenges the direct readout view and articulates the social communications view. It includes one chapter by James Russell that questions the evidence for universal facial expressions of emotion.

Russell, J. A., & Fernández-Dols, J. M. (Eds.) (1997). *The psychology of facial expression*. Cambridge, England: Cambridge University Press. The challenges to the direct readout that were issued in the early 1990s helped stimulate a variety of new approaches and cross-fertilizations. The 16 chapters in this volume summarize many of these and provide a useful guide to a field that is presently in flux.

Kraut, R. E., & Johnston, R. E. (1979). Social and emotional messages of smiling: An ethological approach. *Journal of Personality and Social Psychology, 37*, 1539–1553. This classic series of experiments was one of the first to suggest limitations to the direct readout view. The ingenious methodology (which includes observing bowlers and hockey fans in natural settings) adds to this paper's appeal.

Ekman, P., & Friesen, W. V. (1971). Constants across culture in the face and emotion. *Journal of Personality and Social Psychology, 17*, 124–129. This classic paper reports the study in which members of the Fore tribe in New Guinea matched photographs of posed Western facial expressions with emotions.

Jakobs, E., Manstead, A. S. R., & Fischer, A. H. (1999). Social motives, emotional feelings, and smiling. *Cognition and Emotion, 13*, 321–345. This paper reports research in which variables relevant to both the direct readout view and the social communication view were manipulated. The complex interplay of variables that was observed suggests a possible direction for future theory and research: to find how social and emotional factors interact in influencing facial displays.

Facial Signs of Emotional Experience

Paul Ekman and Wallace V. Friesen • University of California, San Francisco
Sonia Ancoli • University of California, San Diego

Spontaneous facial expressions were found to provide accurate information about more specific aspects of emotional experience than just the pleasant versus unpleasant distinction. Videotape records were gathered while subjects viewed motion picture films and then reported on their subjective experience. A new technique for measuring facial movement isolated a particular type of smile that was related to differences in reported happiness between those who showed this action and those who did not, to the intensity of happiness, and to which of two happy experiences was reported as happiest. Those who showed a set of facial actions hypothesized to be signs of various negative affects reported experiencing more negative emotion than those who did not show these actions. How much these facial actions were shown was related to the reported intensity of negative affect. Specific facial actions associated with the experience of disgust were identified.

Current emotion theorists disagree about whether different emotions are characterized by distinctive bodily response system changes (e.g., autonomic nervous system [ANS] or facial expression patterning). Those who follow Schachter and Singer (1962) claim that cognitive expectations are the only important determinants of which emotion is subjectively experienced. ANS activity is not patterned but reflects the extent, not the type, of emotion that is aroused. This viewpoint has largely ignored the possibility that facial expressions might be a differentiated response system distinguishing among emotions. Those who disagree with Schachter and Singer do not share the same theory, but each has emphasized response system changes that are distinctive for each emotion: the ANS by Lazarus (1966) and facial expressions by Plutchik (1962) and Tomkins (1962, 1963).

If facial expressions are distinctive for each emotion, this would have important consequences both intrapersonally, coloring the subjective experience, and interpersonally, signaling to others how one feels. Although both roles have been recognized, those theorizing about the role of the face in the experience of emotion have emphasized intrapersonal functions. For example, Tomkins (1962) defined the subjective experience of emotion as the feedback from the facial muscular changes. Recent experiments have investigated how a subject's performance of different muscular movements influences his or her subjective experience of emotion (Izard, 1977: Laird, 1974; Tourangeau & Ellsworth, 1979). However, the face may also influence a person's emotional experience by providing signals to others about how the person feels. If B perceives A's facial expression of emotion, B's behavior toward A may change, and A's notice of this may influence or determine A's experience of emotion.

The viability of proposals that facial expression plays important, perhaps multiple, roles in the experience of emotion depends on the capability of the face to (a) show distinctive expressions for each of a number of emotions, such as fear, anger, disgust, happiness, and so forth, and (b) vary with the felt differences in the intensity of emotion. Such evidence does not exist for spontaneously occurring emotion. The data only show that the face can provide information about the much simpler, grosser distinction between whether an emotion is pleasant or unpleasant.

Much of the current renascence of interest in the face was generated by cross-cultural studies that found universality. Most of these experiments, however, did not examine spontaneous behavior. Instead people in different cultures were asked to label contrived expressions (Ekman & Friesen, 1971; Ekman, Sorenson, & Friesen, 1969; Izard, 1971). The one study that examined spontaneous facial expression in two cultures (Ekman, 1972) focused only on the gross distinction between pleasant and unpleasant emotions. Since then a number of studies within a single culture have documented but not extended the finding that the face can show whether an emotion is pleasant or unpleasant. (See review of such studies from 1970 to 1979 in Ekman & Oster, 1979, and of such studies from 1914 to 1970 in Ekman, Friesen, & Ellsworth, 1972, chapters 15 and 16.)

The primary purpose of the present experiment was to venture beyond the pleasant versus unpleasant dichotomy to determine whether spontaneous facial expressions can provide information about more specific aspects of emotional experience: Does facial behavior vary with the felt intensity of a pleasant or of an unpleasant emotion? Are subtle differences between pleasant experiences shown on the face? Is there one type of smile more than other smiles that relates to a pleasant experience? Can a particular negative emotion be read from the face, not just the more general information that the emotion is unpleasant? A second purpose of this study was to obtain evidence about how spontaneous facial actions might be related to a person's subjective experience of emotion. Most previous studies instead have focused on how spontaneous facial behavior varies with some manipulations in experimental condition, or signals information to others.

Either of two complementary methods could be used to score facial behavior: directly measuring facial actions when different emotions occur or asking observers to make emotion judgments when

viewing samples of such facial behavior. We chose direct measurement of facial actions to accomplish the third purpose of this experiment—to test hypotheses about the particular facial actions that signal particular aspects of emotion (e.g., Ekman & Friesen, 1975; Ekman, Friesen, & Tomkins, 1971; Izard, 1971). So far these formulations have been tested only in teas of their ability to identify contrived facial expressions, not spontaneously occurring emotion. We sought to provide a sounder basis about what different facial actions may signify.

Method

A new technique for measuring facial behavior, the Facial Action Coding System (Ekman & Friesen, 1976, 1978a), was applied to videotape records gathered while subjects viewed positive and stress-inducing motion picture films and then reported on their subjective experience.

SUBJECTS

Thirty-five right-handed, female Caucasians, ranging in age from 18 to 35 years ($M = 25.14$), volunteered as subjects. Subjects of only one gender were recruited, since Hall (1978) has shown some differences in facial encoding associated with gender. It was thought that female subjects might feel more comfortable than males with the female experimenter (S. A.). Through advertisements subjects were recruited to participate in an experiment on psychophysiology in which brain waves, heart rate, muscle tension, basal skin resistance (BSR), and respiration would be recorded while they watched films. They were not told that we were interested in emotion or that they would be videotaped. This information was withheld until after the experiment to avoid self-conscious behavior.

STIMULI

In the positive condition, subjects saw films intended to induce positive affect; in the negative condition, subjects saw a film intended to induce negative affect. The positive films consisted of three distinct 1-min. films produced by Ekman and Friesen (1974) that yielded similar self-reports of strong positive affect. One film showed a gorilla playing in zoo, another showed ocean waves, and the third showed a puppy playing with a flower.

The reactions to the ocean film are not reported, since this film was designed to yield little observable facial response; indeed, this was the case. Only seven of the subjects showed any facial response to the ocean film. This film had been included for the purpose of another investigation of the psychophysiological responses of these subjects (Ancoli, 1979). The three positive films were always shown in the same order, with a 10-sec blank period between each: gorilla, ocean, and then puppy.

The film intended to produce negative affect was an edited version of a workshop accident film first used in research by Birnbaum (1943). Other investigators (Lazarus, 1966; Ellsworth, personal communication, 1976) found that subjects reported experiencing fear and disgust. The film was edited to eliminate most of the scenes other than those directly leading to and showing two accidents: A man has the tip of his finger cut off by a saw, and a man dies after a plank of wood is thrust through his chest by a circular saw. These two scenes were always shown in the same order, with only a few scenes between them—first the finger cut, then the death.

SUBJECTIVE EXPERIENCE OF EMOTION

Subjects reported their emotional reactions on a questionnaire composed of a set of 9-point scales that previous studies (Ekman & Friesen, 1974) had found sensitive to differential reactions to the stimulus films. Separate scales were included for interest, anger, disgust, fear, happiness, pain, sadness, surprise, and arousal. Each scale was unipolar, with 0 representing no emotion and 8 the strongest feeling. Instructions explained that the

> strength of a feeling should be viewed as a combination of (a) the number of times you felt the emotion—its frequency; (b) the length of time you felt the emotion—its duration; and (c) how intense or extreme the emotions was—its intensity.

Only two of the emotion terms were explained. Pain was said to refer to the experience of empathetic pain. Arousal was said to be an index of the total emotional state.

PROCEDURE

Each subject was seen individually. She was seated in a 2 m × 2 m electrically shielded room. Leads for recording electroencephalogram, heart rate, respiration, BSR, and skeletal muscle electromyogram were attached. (Results on these autonomic measures are reported in Ancoli, 1979.) The videocamera was concealed. The lights were left on in the room, and the subject was told that she had been randomly selected to be in a bright-light condition in the experiment.

After the instructions, the subject was left alone in the room, and all further communication was by means of an audio-only intercom. There was a 20-min. baseline period in which the subject was instructed to relax. There was no video-recording during this period. The subject then was asked to fill out the emotion questionnaire to describe her feelings during the baseline period. Next, the subject was exposed to either the positive or negative film condition. The order of presenting the positive and negative conditions was counterbalanced among the subjects. The films were shown at eye level on a small screen, 18 × 30 cm, 60 cm away from the subject. At the conclusion of the first experimental condition, the subject filled out a second emotion questionnaire. If the first condition had been positive, she was required to fill out separate questionnaires to report her reactions to each film: gorilla, ocean, and puppy. If the first condition had been negative, she was required to fill out separate questionnaires to report her reactions to each of the two accidents. After the questionnaires had been answered, there was another 5-min. baseline period, followed by another questionnaire to report feelings. The second condition was then begun, followed by additional questionnaires to report reactions to the film(s).

In debriefing sessions, subjects were told about the videotaping. None reported having suspected that a camera was used. The subject was given the choice to either sign a second consent form for use of the video recording or have us destroy the video recording. All subjects consented.

FACIAL MEASUREMENT

The facial activity shown by each subject during the positive and negative conditions was measured with Ekman and Friesen's (1976, 1978a) Facial Action Coding System (FACS). This system was designed to measure all visible facial behavior, not just actions that might presumably be related to emotion. FACS distinguishes 44 *action units*. These are the minimal u... that are anatomically separate and visually distinguishable. Any facial movement can be described in terms of the particular action unit that singly or in combination with other units produced it. In addition to scoring the action units, FACS can be used to specify exactly when each movement begins and ends.

One person (S.A.) scored all the facial activity shown by the 35 subjects. A second person scored a sample of behavior that consisted of reactions in either the positive or negative conditions from 10 subjects and a 30-sec sample that was selected in a random fashion from each of the other 25 subjects. Intercoder reliability was evaluated by using a ratio in which the number of action units on which the two persons agreed was multiplied by two and was then divided by the total number of action units scored by the two persons. This agreement ratio was calculated for each event observed by one or both persons. The mean ratio across all events was .756, which is almost exactly the figure reported by Ekman and Friesen (1978b) for interceder reliability. Other techniques for evaluating intercoder reliability in the scoring of the videotapes in this experiment also suggested that reliability was acceptable (Ancoli, 1979).

Results

FACIAL SIGNS OF POSITIVE AFFECT

It might seem obvious that the smile is the sign of positive affect. Yet some observers (Birdwhistell, 1970; Klineberg, 1940; LaBarre, 1947; Leach, 1972) have claimed that the smile is often a sign of negative affect. This disagreement may occur in part because the term *smile* is too imprecise, concealing quite different behaviors. Some of those who have measured facial behavior (especially Blurton Jones, 1971; Brannigan & Humphries, 1972; Grant, 1969) have distinguished more than one type of smile, for example, upper smile, broad smile, tight smile, and so forth. To complicate matters, these students of the face do not always list the same number of varieties of smiling nor do they specify just which ones, if any, are signs of positive affect.

The Facial Action Coding System (Ekman & Friesen, 1978b) takes a different approach. It does not utilize the term *smile* but allows for description in nonaffective terms of all visibly distinctive facial actions. A smiling appearance, in which the lip corners are pulled upwards, to some extent can be produced by the action of zygomatic major, zygomatic minor, buccinator, risorious, or caninus muscles. FACS allows for scoring each of these actions, combinations of these actions, and combinations of these with still other facial actions. Quite separate from FACS descriptive measurement of facial activity, Ekman and Friesen (1978a) predicted which actions are signs of positive affect. Based on hunch and observation, and partially supported by the hunches of other observers (in particular, Darwin, 1872/1955, and Tomkins, 1962, 1963), Ekman and Friesen predicted that among the many smiling actions, only those produced by zygomatic major (which FACS scores as Action Unit 12) are signs of happiness. Furthermore, they hypothesized that when Action Unit 12 combines with any of the other smiling actions or with certain other facial movements, such as tightening, pressing, stretching, pursing, pushing up the lower lip, or raising the upper lip, the meaning of the expression is changed. It may be controlled happiness, simulated happiness, or an instance in which positive affect has blended with, comments on, or masks negative affect.

Happy or not. The first test of whether facial actions provide information about differences in the experience of positive affect—specifically of the hypotheses that Action Unit 12 is the sign of such positive affect—was to compare the happiness ratings of those who showed this action and those who did not. There were only seven subjects who never showed Action Unit 12 in either the gorilla or the puppy film. These people reported being less happy (mean happiness rating across the two films was 1.79) than those who showed Action Unit 12 ($M = 3.74$), $t(32) = 2.44$, $p < .02$. When the facial behavior and self-report were analyzed separately for each positive film, the same results were obtained for the reactions to the gorilla and the puppy films.

How happy. The next test of the hypotheses about Action Unit 12 was to determine if variation in the amount of Action Unit 12 was associated with variation in the subjective experience of happiness. Two analyses examined this question. One determined whether FACS scores were correlated with self-reports of the intensity of happiness. The other determined whether FACS scores would allow accurate prediction of which positive film the subject had reported liking most.

Three measures of Action Unit 12 were correlated with the self-report of happiness. One mea-

TABLE 15.1. Correlations Between Measures of Action Unit 12 and Reports of Happiness

Facial measure	Gorilla film (n = 20)		Puppy film (n = 23)	
	Raw score	Change score	Raw score	Change score
Frequency of Action Unit 12	−.08	−.01	.60***	.31**
Duration of Action Unit 12	.20	.35**	.21*	.16
Maximum intensity of Action Unit 12	.17	.34**	.04	.20

* $p = <.10$. ** $p = <.05$ *** $p = <.01$.

sure was the frequency and another was the duration of Action Unit 12 during a positive film. The third measure was the maximum intensity—slight, moderate, or extreme—that this action reached during a positive film. Subjects who showed no Action Unit 12 activity were excluded from this data analysis, as the previous analysis had established that they would anchor the low end of the facial activity and self-report variables.

Each of the three measures was correlated (taus; Nie, Hull, Jenkins, Steinbrenner, & Bent, 1970, chap. 18) with the self-reported happiness score for a positive film (raw score) and with the difference between that score and the happiness reported during the previous baseline period (change score). Table 15.1 shows that the amount of Action Unit 12 was generally correlated with variations in the self-report of happiness. Which particular measures were significantly correlated differed for the two films. It does not seem appropriate to attempt an explanation of variations in the magnitude of these correlations until these findings are replicated.

The second approach to the question of whether variation in Action Unit 12 was a sign of variation in the subjective experience of happiness was to determine whether the amount of Action Unit 12 would predict which of two happy experiences was the happier. Although there were no significant differences in the amount of happiness reported for the puppy and gorilla films, and the reports to each were correlated (Pearson $r = .41$, $p < 05$), most subjects had rated one or the other film as producing more happy feelings. For each subject, the amount of Action Unit 12 produced during the gorilla and puppy films was used to predict which film the subject subsequently rated as producing stronger happy feelings. This prediction was made separately on the basis of the three measures of Action Unit 12—frequency, duration, and maximum intensity. Subjects who did not differ between films in their use of Action Unit 12 on a particular measure were excluded from the data analysis. A prediction also was made utilizing all three measures (frequency, duration, and maximum intensity) and selecting as the happiest film the one on which at least two of the three measures agreed.

Table 15.2 shows that the facial measures accurately predicted which film a subject reported as producing more happiness. The analyses in Table 15.2 used the raw happiness reports. When change scores (differences from baseline) were analyzed in the same fashion, the same results were obtained.

Contrary to Ekman and Friesen's hypothesis, it is possible that when a person watches a pleasant film, any facial movement, not just Action Unit 12, might be related to reports of happiness. To check this possibility, frequency and duration scores for all facial activity other than Action Unit 12 were calculated. The scores included smiling

TABLE 15.2. T Tests Between Self-Reports of Happiness When the Face Showed More or Fewer Signs of Action Unit 12

Facial measure	n	Mean happy self-rating for film predicted on basis of facial measure to be		t	p
		Most happy	Least happy		
Frequency	24	3.95	3.29	1.35	.19
Duration	27	4.22	3.26	2.30	.03
Maximum intensity	21	4.29	3.19	2.18	.04
Combination of frequency, duration, and maximum intensity	24	4.33	2.96	3.27	.003

appearances produced by risorious, caninus, buccinator, and zygomatic minor muscles, as well as other facial actions in which the lip corners are not pulled up. These scores were not significantly correlated with happiness self-reports in either film and did not predict which films the subject had liked best.

To summarize, measurement of a specific facial action produced by the zygomatic major muscle, Action Unit 12, accurately differentiated reported differences in positive affective experience. The more Action Unit 12, the more happiness the subjects subsequently reported. The amount of Action Unit 12 predicted which of two films would be rated as having produced the strongest happy feelings. And subjects who never showed Action Unit 12 reported less happiness than those who did. Similar questions were asked about facial activity and negative affect.

FACIAL SIGNS OF NEGATIVE AFFECT

Unhappy or not. Among the variety of actions scored by FACS, there is a subset that Ekman and Friesen hypothesized as being signs of anger, fear, disgust, sadness, contempt, or blends of those emotions. Forty-one percent of the facial movements that occurred when the subjects watched the accident film involved such facial actions. The first test of the hypotheses about which facial actions show negative affect was whether those subjects who never showed such facial activity reported experiencing less negative affect than those who did show such facial actions. Twelve subjects never showed the facial actions hypothesized as negative affect signs. Most of these subjects showed facial behavior interpreted by Ekman and Friesen as positive or ambiguous. The affective self-reports averaged across the two accidents were compared for these 12 persons and 21 persons showing nega

tive facial actions. (Two more subjects, whose facial behavior was ambiguous, were excluded because negative action units were shown considerably before the appearance of the first accident.)

Table 15.3 shows that those who showed actions hypothesized as signs of negative affects reported significantly more fear, pain, sadness, surprise, and arousal than those who did not. The trend was in the predicted direction for reports of interest and disgust, but not for anger.

How unhappy. The next test of the hypotheses about those facial actions that show negative affect was to determine whether these actions correlated with the self-reports of intensity of specific negative emotions. Table 15.4 shows that these facial actions correlated with the self-reports (averaged across the two accidents) for some of the negative emotions as well as with the report of generalized arousal.

How disgusted. The next issue was whether the specific predictions about facial signs of particular negative emotions are correct. These hypotheses could be test by determining if variations in facial signs of a particular negative emotion were associated with variations in the subjective experience reported for that emotion. So, for example, actions predicted to be signs of disgust should correlate with the report of disgust more than with reports of sadness, fear, or pain; actions predicted to be signs of fear should correlate with the report of fear more than with the reports of disgust, sadness, or pain, and so forth. It was possible to test hypotheses only about disgust, since very few subjects showed action units relevant to any of the other negative emotions.

Thirteen subjects showed facial actions hypothesized as signs of disgust without showing actions relevant to any of the other negative emotions. (These appearances involve pulling upward the central portion of the upper lip, raising and stretch-

TABLE 15.3. Differences on Self-Reported Emotion Between Those Who Did and Did Not Show Negative Facial Actions

Facial action	Mean self-reports about the two accidents						
	Disgust	Surprise	Sadness	Fear	Pain	Arousal	Interest
Negative *M* (*n* = 21)	4.48	5.14	2.95	5.14	5.93	6.24	4.83
Nonnegative *M* (*n* = 12)	3.08	3.13	1.25	3.13	3.42	4.33	3.75
t	1.54	2.59	2.03	2.09	3.04	2.69	1.35
p	.067	.007	.026	.023	.002	.006	.185

Note. All tests are one-tailed except for anger and interest, which are two-tailed.

TABLE 15.4. Correlations Between the Sum of All Negative Facial Actions and Reports of Specific Emotions

Facial measure	Self-report					
	Disgust	Anger	Sadness	Fear	Pain	Arousal
Frequency scores	.21*	−.04	.14	.19*	.35***	.32***
Duration scores	.22**	−.10	.10	.12	.33***	.25***

Note. N = 35. * p < .10. ** p < .05. *** p < .01.

ing the nostril wings, and deepening the nasolabial fold. They are produced by levator labii superioris, caput infraorbitalis, Action Unit 10; and alaeque nasi, Action Unit 9, which also wrinkles the bridge and sides of the nose.) The top portion of Table 15.5 shows that these facial actions were correlated with the self-reports of disgust and not at all, or negatively, with the reports of anger and sadness. Contrary to predictions, one of the disgust facial action measures was significantly correlated with the report of fear, and there was a trend with the pain report. Suspecting that these findings on fear and pain might be due to general arousal rather than the specifics of these emotions, we calculated correlations partialing out the self-report of arousal. The middle rows in Table 15.5 show that the correlations between disgust facial actions and the self-report of disgust survived, whereas the relationship between these facial actions and the report of fear or of pain weakened. The pattern of partial correlation thus supports the

hypothesis that these particular facial actions are specific to the subjective experience of disgust.

It might be argued that when people watch an unpleasant film, any facial activity, not just Action Unit 9 or 10, would be associated with the experience of disgust. This was not the case. The bottom two rows of Table 15.5 show that the ambiguous facial actions correlated less with the report of disgust than did the disgust facial actions.

Discussion

Facial action was found to provide accurate information about a number of different aspects of the subjective experience of emotion. Variation in specified facial actions was related to the intensity of reported emotions, to the extent of happiness, and to the extent of unhappiness. Even when a person reported enjoying two experiences, facial measurement discriminated which was enjoyed most. And there was evidence to suggest that

TABLE 15.5. Partial Correlations Between Facial Actions and Reports of Specific Emotions, Controlling on the Self-Report of Arousal

Type of correlation	Facial measure	Self-report				
		Disgust	Anger	Sadness	Fear	Pain
Tau						
	Disgust frequency scores	.37**	−.35**	−.46**	.28	.16
	Disgust duration scores	.55***	−.23	−.20	.46**	.41*
Partial, controlling on arousal						
	Disgust frequency scores	.31	−.32	−.52	.05	−.11
	Disgust duration scores	.52	−.19	−.22	.31	.24
	Ambiguous frequency scores	.10				
	Ambiguous duration scores	.29				

Note. N = 35. * p < .10. ** p < .05. *** p < .01.

facial actions may be specific to each negative emotion.

Although others (e.g., Birdwhistell, 1970) have claimed that smiling occurs with negative as much as with positive emotions, this study supported Ekman and Friesen's hypothesis that a particular type of smile—Action Unit 12 produced by the zygomatic major muscle—is associated with the experience of happiness. Some support was also obtained for Ekman and Friesen's hypothesis that only this action is a positive sign. Smiling actions in which the upward curve of the lip corners is produced by risorious, buccinator, or zygomatic minor muscles (predicted to be signs of fear, contempt, and sadness) occurred almost exclusively during the accident film.

Since Action Unit 12 was not totally absent during the accident film, the argument could still be made that even this type of smile may be a sign of negative emotion. Although not conclusive, the evidence suggests this is not so. At least it would be a rare sign of negative emotion, for Action Unit 12 occurred only about one tenth as much during the accident as during the gorilla/puppy film. Furthermore, the occurrence of Action Unit 12 during the accident film was not related to the self-report of negative emotions or positive emotions.

Ekman and Friesen (1975, chapter 11) have outlined a number of reasons why Action Unit 12 may occur during negative affect, even though they maintain that this action is not a sign of negative affect. Quite the contrary. Signaling positive emotion, Action Unit 12 may be deployed in a number of negative contexts: to comment on the negative feeling (e.g., grin and bear it), if there is a blend of positive and negative feelings (e.g., scorn, bittersweet, etc.); to mask a negative feeling or to deliberately, falsely simulate the appearance of positive feeling. Two further findings about Action Unit 12 expressions during the accident film were consistent with these interpretations. First, almost half of them were part of expressions that also included actions that signify negative emotions. This virtually never occurred for Action Unit 12 expressions during the gorilla/puppy film. Second, preliminary analyses suggest that during the accident film, Action Unit 12 expressions were more asymmetric than during the gorilla/puppy film. This fits with other findings (Ekman, 1980; Lynn & Lynn, 1938; Ekman, Hager, & Friesen, 1981) that when Action Unit 12 is a sign of spontaneous happiness, it

is more symmetrical, and when it is deliberately performed, it is more asymmetrical.

Finally, it should be acknowledged that some of the Action Unit 12 expressions during the accident film could have been instances in which positive affect was felt. There are probably few experimental manipulations of negative affect that totally succeed for all subjects continuously and that do not strike at least a few, at least for a moment, as ridiculous or amusing. And, of course, subjects may at points show a happy expression in relief once they realize that the negative affect manipulation is not going to be as terrible as they feared.

The findings on the facial actions relevant to negative affect, and in particular for disgust, were encouraging. They are consistent with findings on the meaning of particular facial actions in studies of posed behavior. They should be replicated with other stimulus films and with other events apart from film as the source of negative affect. Similar research is needed also to test hypotheses about the facial actions signaling anger, fear, sadness pain, and surprise; variations in the intensity of each of these emotions; and blends of these emotions. To demonstrate more conclusively the specificity of the emotional information signified by a particular set of facial actions—that they are associated with one but not with another negative emotion—a comparison is needed that could not be made in this study. It is necessary to show not only that disgust actions correlate with disgust more than with anger reports (as found in this study) but also that anger actions correlate with anger more than with disgust reports. To make such a comparison, emotion-inducing stimuli would have to be used that would elicit facial actions relevant to anger and actions relevant to disgust.

More generally, this experiment demonstrated that facial expressions are differentiated for the spontaneous occurrence of particular emotions. It thus strengthens the empirical base of the theories of emotion that emphasized differentiated response systems, particularly those that dealt extensively with the face (Plutchik, 1962; Tomkins, 1962, 19631 and theorists who derive from Tomkins, such as Ekman, 1977, and Izard, 1977). These findings should challenge the cognitive theorists of emotion to expand their formulation to accommodate differentiated facial expressions of emotion and to consider measuring facial expressions in their experiments.

How important spontaneous facial expressions of emotion may be as social signals was not addressed in this study, although these findings raise such a possibility. Before presuming that facial expressions provide clues to others about how a person feels, let alone the further assumption that feedback of how others react may influence the expressor's experience, two research steps must be taken. First, it must be shown that people who observed expressions, such as those shown in this experiment, would be able to make the differentiations that were achieved by the fine-grained, slowed motion measurement with FACS. Second, it must be determined whether facial expression will remain as rich a source of differentiated information about emotion when the subject is not alone but in the presence of others. Ekman and Friesen (1969) have theorized that in social situations, people wittingly and unwittingly manage their facial expressions of emotions following culturally based display rules specifying who can show what emotion to whom and when. Friesen (1972) began such work by showing differences between Japanese and Americans when they watched stress-inducing films in the presence of another person. It is likely that in some social situations, at least some people may amplify while others may conceal or disguise their expressions, but this remains to be studied.

This experiment also served to show the utility of FACS. Since all observable facial behavior was measured, not just some actions presumed to signify emotion (as in Izard's, 1979, facial measurement technique), it was possible to test whether the presumptions were correct or not. Observers' global judgments of emotion, the most popular alternative for measuring information from the face, cannot isolate the particular actions that do and do not relate to a particular emotion.

REFERENCES

Ancoli, S. (1979). *Psychophysiological response patterns to emotions.* Unpublished doctoral dissertation, University of California, San Francisco.

Birdwhistell, R. L. (1970). *Kinesics and context.* Philadelphia: University of Pennsylvania Press.

Birnbaum, R. (1964). *Autonomic reaction to threat and confrontation conditions of psychological stress.* Unpublished doctoral dissertation, University of California, Berkeley.

Blurton Jones, N. G. (1971). Criteria for use in describing facial expression in children. *Human Biology, 41,* 365–413.

Brannigan, C. R., & Humphries, D. A. (1972). Human nonverbal behavior, a means of communication. In N. B. Blurton Jones (Ed.), *Ethological studies of child behavior.* London: Cambridge University Press.

Darwin, C. (1955). *The expression of the emotions in man and animals.* New York: Philosophical Library. (Originally published, 1872)

Ekman, P. (1972). Universals and cultural differences in facial expression of emotion. In J. Cole, (Ed.), *Nebraska Symposium on Motivation* (Vol. 19). Lincoln: University of Nebraska Press.

Ekman, P. (1977). Biological and cultural contributions to body and facial movement. In J. Blacking, (Ed.), *Anthropology of the body.* London: Academic Press.

Ekman, P. (1980). Asymmetry in facial expression. *Science, 209,* 833–834.

Ekman, P., & Friesen, W. V. (1969). The repertoire of nonverbal behavior: Categories, origins, usage, and coding. *Semiotica, 1*(1), 49–98.

Ekman, P., & Friesen, W. V. (1974). Constants across cultures in the face and emotion. *Journal of Personality and Social Psychology, 17,* 124–129.

Ekman, P., & Friesen, W. V. (1974). Detecting deception from the body or face. *Journal of Personality and Social Psychology, 29,* 288-298.

Ekman, P., & Friesen, W. V. (1975). *Unmasking the face.* Englewood Cliffs, NJ: Prentice-Hall.

Ekman, P., & Friesen, W. V. (1976). Measuring facial movement. *Environmental Psychology and Nonverbal Behavior, 1*(1).

Ekman, P., & Friesen, W. V. (1978a). *Investigator's Guide to the Facial Action Coding System, Part II.* Palo Alto, CA: Consulting Psychologists Press.

Ekman, P., & Friesen, W. V. (1978b). *Manual for the Facial Action Coding System.* Palo Alto, CA: Consulting Psychologists Press.

Ekman, P., Friesen, W. V., & Ellsworth, P. (1972). *Emotion in the human face: Guidelines for research and an integration of findings.* New York: Pergamon Press.

Ekman, P., Friesen, W. V., & Tomkins, S. S. (1971). Facial affect scoring technique (FAST): A first validity study. *Semiotica, 3*(1), 37–38.

Ekman, P., Hager, J. C., & Friesen, W. V. (1981). The symmetry of emotional and deliberate facial actions. *Psychophysiology, 18,* 101–106.

Ekman, P., & Oster, H. (1979). Facial expressions of emotion. *Annual Review of Psychology, 30,* 527–554.

Ekman, P., Sorenson, E. R., & Friesen, W. V. (1969). Pancultural elements in facial displays of emotions. *Science, 164*(3875), 86–88.

Friesen, W. V. (1972). *Cultural differences in facial expressions in a social situation: An experimental test of the concept of display rules.* Unpublished doctoral dissertation, University of California, San Francisco.

Grant, N. G. (1969). Human facial expression. *Man, 4,* 525–536.

Hall, J. (1978). Gender effects in decoding nonverbal cues. *Psychological Bulletin, 85,* 845–857.

Izard, C. (1971). *The face of emotion.* New York: Appleton-Century-Crofts.

Izard, C. (1977). *Human emotions.* New York: Plenum Press.

Izard, C. (1979). *The maximally discriminative facial movement coding system.* Unpublished manuscript, Instructional Resources Center, University of Delaware.

Klineberg, O. (1940). *Social psychology.* New York: Holt.

Laird, J. D. (1974). Self-attribution of emotion: The effects of expressive behavior on the quality of emotion experience. *Journal of Personality and Social Psychology, 29,* 475–486.

LaBarre, W. (1947). The cultural basis of emotions and gestures. *Journal of Personality, 16,* 49–68.

Lazarus, R. S. (1966). *Psychological stress and the coping process.* New York: McGraw-Hill.

Leach, E. (1972). The influence of cultural context on nonverbal communication in man. In R. Hinde (Ed.), *Nonverbal communication.* London: Cambridge University Press.

Lynn, J. G., & Lynn, D. R. (1938). Face–hand laterality in relation to personality. *Journal of Abnormal and Social Psychology, 13,* 291.

Nie, N., Hull, C. H., Jenkins, J., Steinbrenner, K., & Bent, D. (1962). *Statistical package for the social sciences* (2nd ed.). New York: McGraw-Hill.

Plutchik, R. (1962). *The emotions.* New York: Random House.

Schachter, W., & Singer, J. E. (1962). Cognitive, social, and physiological determinants of emotional state. *Psychological Review, 69,* 379–399.

Tourangeau, R., & Ellsworth, P. C. (1979). The role of facial response in the experience of emotion. *Journal of Personality and Social Psychology, 37,* 1519–1531.

Tomkins, S. S. (1962). *Affect, imagery, consciousness: Vol. 1. The positive affects.* New York: Springer.

Tomkins, S. S. (1963). *Affect, imagery, consciousness: Vol. 2. The negative affects.* New York: Springer.

Sociality of Solitary Smiling: Potentiation by an Implicit Audience

Alan J. Fridlund • University of California, Santa Barbara

Subjects viewed a pleasant videotape either: (a) alone, (b) alone but with the belief that a friend nearby was otherwise engaged, (c) alone but with the belief that a friend was viewing the same videotape in another room, or (d) when a friend was present. Subject's smiling, as estimated by facial electromyography, varied monotonically with the sociality of viewing but not with reported emotion. The findings confirm audience effects for human smiles, demonstrate that the effects do not depend upon the presence of the interactant, and indicate that the smiles are better predicted by social context than by emotion. Both naive and expert independent raters given descriptions of the study made predictions that conformed to previous emotion-based accounts of faces but departed from the findings. The results suggest that some solitary faces may be implicitly social, a view consistent with both contemporary ethology, and role and impression-management theories of behavior.

People make faces when they are alone. This curious fact may have been crucial in shaping the most popular contemporary theories of facial expression. These generally hold that whereas some faces reflect social convention, others are quasi-reflexive released displays of felt emotion (Buck, 1984; Darwin, 1872; Ekman, 1972, 1973, 1977, 1984; Ekman & Friesen, 1969, 1975, 1982; Frijda, 1986; Izard & Malatesta, 1987; Lorenz, 1970, 1973; Plutchik, 1981; Tinbergen, 1952; Tomkins, 1962, 1963; Vaughan & Lanzetta, 1980). Solitary faces are usually considered the "purest" expressions of emotion, because in solitude one should be minimally constrained by social demands (Buck, 1984; Ekman, 1984; Ekman, Davidson, & Friesen, 1990).

There is, however, another interpretation of solitary faces that would propose a role for implicit sociality. When we are alone, we often imagine social interactants. We see our partner's smiling face in our "mind's eye," and we find ourselves affiliatively returning the smile. We remember disciplining a child, and we find ourselves making a scowl. If many of the faces we make in solitude actually reflect imaginary interaction, then these private faces might be as conventional as our public ones.[1]

That sociality could mediate both public and

---

[1]Fridlund (1991) outlined five examples of ways in which we may be imaginally or implicitly social although actually alone: (a) when we treat ourselves as social interactants (e.g., talking to ourselves, hitting ourselves, or patting ourselves on the back), (b) acting as though others are present when they are not (e.g., speaking to someone who has in fact left the room), (c) imagining that others are present when they are not (e.g., recalling a pleasant moment with a lost love), (d) forecasting interactions with others who are not immediately present (e.g., smiling just before entering the office in the morning), (e) anthropomorphizing nonhuman animals, or animate or inanimate objects, as interactants (e.g., talking to pets, dolls, stuffed animals, houseplants, or errant golf balls).

private faces would be compatible with more traditional role and impression-management theories
of behavior, which hold that expressions are a
means "to control images that are projected in real
or imagined social interactions" (Schlenker, 1980,
p. 6; see also Baldwin & Holmes, 1987; Greenwald
& Breckler, 1985; Schlenker, 1985; Schlenker &
Weigold, 1989; Snyder, 1979). Thus, smiling and
scowling are faces conventionally made in affiliation and discipline; they should be seen whether
the interaction takes place in the world or "in our
heads." Social mediation would also dovetail with
contemporary ethology, which now emphasizes
types of social interaction more than reflex-like
emotions in accounting for both nonhuman displays and human facial expressions (Cheney,
Seyfarth, & Smuts, 1986; Hinde, 1985a, 1985b;
Krebs & Dawkins, 1984; Marler & Mitani, 1988;
Provine & Fischer, 1989; Smith, 1977; see also
Fridlund, 1991, for review of studies).

Positing that implicit interaction mediates solitary faces first requires evidence that in vivo interaction mediates public faces. We know intuitively that the faces we make depend greatly on
those around us. Several experimental demonstra-
tions of such *direct audience effects* show that sociality, especially eye contact, mediates the faces
people make when they are (a) scoring strikes in
bowling, watching hockey games, and discussing
the weather (Kraut & Johnston, 1979), (b) being
interviewed during film viewing (Friesen, 1972),
(c) tasting and smelling (Brightman, Segal,
Werther, & Steiner, 1977; Gilbert, Fridlund, &
Sabini, 1987; Kraut, 1982), (d) in pain (Kleck et
al., 1976), (e) watching another in pain (Bavelas,
Black, Lemery, & Mullett, 1986), (f) being exposed to humorous material (Bainum, Lounsbury,
& Pollio, 1984; Chapman, 1973, 1975; Chapman
& Wright, 1976; Freedman & Perlick, 1979), and
(g) have reached as little as 10–18 months of age
(Jones & Raag, 1989).

Although direct audience effects on faces are
well documented, I know of no published research
on *implicit audience effects* on faces—that is, instances in which we find ourselves making faces
when our interactants are elsewhere or are simply
the products of our imagination (but see Fridlund
et al., 1990, for an indirect test using affective
imagery). Experimentally determining these implicit audience effects would itself be important

for understanding the role of sociality in solitary
faces.[2]

I thus sought to explore both explicit and implicit audience effects on faces. I wished to study
smiles specifically, because they are measured so
economically—by means of the actions of one
muscle, the *zygomatic major*, which runs from the
lip corner to the top and front of the ear (Fridlund
& Cacioppo, 1986).

In four conditions differing in sociality, subjects
viewed a pleasant videotape specifically intended
to elicit smiles. Some viewed the videotape with a
friend; others viewed entirely alone. The remaining subjects viewed alone, but the situation was
implicitly social: They believed that a friend in
another room was either viewing the same videotape or performing an irrelevant task. These conditions could allow determining whether facial
behavior was affected by viewing with a friend (a
direct audience effect), as well as by simply believing that a friend was nearby (an implicit audience effect). By contrasting the two implicit-soci-
ality conditions (i.e., those in which subjects
believed that friends were either coviewing or otherwise engaged), it could be ascertained whether
any implicit audience effects were influenced by
the activities of the imagined friend.

Finally, by measuring emotional self-report, an
estimate could be obtained of the extent to which
any effects of direct or implicit sociality were
mediated through the differential in induction of
felt emotion. It seemed that if emotion had a major role in solitary faces (i.e., happier people should
smile more; cf. Cacioppo, Petty, Losch, & Kim,
1986; Ekman, Friesen, & Ancoli, 1980; Ekman et
al., 1990), then in the three videotape conditions

---

[2]One study (Chapman, 1974) examined *frontalis* (forehead)
region EMG signals in subjects exposed to a direct audience,
a concealed audience, and alone. In all conditions, subjects
were hooked to electrodes while they read a dramatic passage
in fully prone position. I share concerns expressed by previous
authors (see Moore & Baron, 1983) that (a) this
unconventional manipulation may have embarrassed subjects
and (b) the EMG signals may have measured ocular muscle
tension associated with differential compliance with
instructions to keep the eyes open (or, indeed, anxiety; see
Fridlund, Cottam, & Fowler, 1982; Fridlund, Hatfield, Cottam,
& Fowler, 1986). Implicit audiences have been used frequently
in the social impact literature (e.g., Latané, 1981), but these
studies have assessed variables such as group task
performance, not facial behavior.

in which viewers sat alone, felt happiness would parallel smiling both within and across these conditions. Any group differences in smiling would result from effects on happiness due to assignment to the conditions (i.e., arriving to the experiment alone vs. being separated from the friend, etc.).

In the frankly social, actual coviewing condition, social demands might produce enhancement of total smiling, and as a consequence of such dissimulation, this smiling would show the poorest correlation with felt happiness (cf. Buck, 1984; Ekman, 1972, 1977, 1984; Friesen, 1972); alternatively, concern or apprehensiveness among some subjects about being emotional in the presence of another might result in reduced smiling. This was assessed by asking for self-reports of dysphoria as well as happiness and by measuring not only subjects' smiling but also their brow knitting (contractions of the *corrugator supercilii* muscle, which typically indicate concentration or disturbance).

If implicit sociality mediated even the smiling issued in solitude, then given the existing evidence that direct audience effects on smiles are potentiating (studies cited earlier), smiling should thus increase with the sociality of viewing, implicit or explicit. Specifically, smiling should show increments over the four experimental conditions: (a) viewing with no implicit friend, (b) viewing alone but with the belief that a friend was otherwise occupied, (c) viewing alone but with the belief that a friend was simultaneously viewing elsewhere, and (d) viewing with the friend physically present.

Subjects' facial behavior was measured with surface facial electromyographic (EMG) signals, using recording sites directly over the facial muscles responsible for smiling. The facial EMG method samples the electrical discharges created by contracting muscle tissue. Consequently, it provides a sensitive and precise measure of muscular contraction and enables reliable quantification of facial actions (see Fridlund & Cacioppo, 1986, for methods and standards).

Finally, I sought to discover what findings would be predicted from common intuitions and by experts on the face and emotion. I thus conducted a second, *Gedanken* (thought) experiment. The videotape study was described to naive and expert raters, who then predicted the subjects' smiling and felt emotion. The actual viewer data are reported first, followed by the *Gedanken* experiment results.

Experiment 1: Test of Direct and Implicit Audience Effects

Method

SUBJECTS

Sixty-four undergraduate volunteers, 32 men and 32 women, provided their informed consent to participate for course credit in a study advertised as measuring "unconscious physiological activity while watching videotapes." Forty-eight of the 64 volunteers were asked to bring same-sex friends to the experimental session; 16 were asked to arrive alone.

EXPERIMENTAL CONDITIONS

Participants were divided evenly among four experimental conditions that involved presentation of a pleasant videotape and measurement of both smiling and emotional experience. The conditions, detailed next, varied the social context of videotape viewing. Eight men and 8 women participated in each condition. The 16 subjects recruited alone were assigned to the solitary participation condition, and the 48 who arrived with same-sex friends were assigned to one of the three remaining conditions. Subjects were recruited alone in the first condition to minimize the sociality of videotape viewing.

Condition 1: solitary participation. The participant arrived for the experiment and viewed the videotape alone.

Condition 2: implicit irrelevant task. Participants were informed that the television room had monitoring equipment for only one viewer and that whoever did not view the tape would be asked to assist in a second study "down the hall" involving completion of "psychological tests of coping styles." A coin toss determined who remained to view the videotape. In actuality, whoever drew the coping styles test was merely escorted from the laboratory, debriefed immediately, and allowed to return to the soundproofed laboratory control room to watch the progress of the experiment. The deception was left intact for the actual viewer until the end of the experiment.

Condition 3: implicit coviewing. Participants were informed that both would view the videotape but because the viewing room had monitoring equipment for only one viewer, the other would watch down the hall in an identical viewing room. Both participants were informed that they would watch the same videotape, just on different television screens. A coin toss determined whether subject or friend stayed to view the videotape. The same procedure used in the previous condition was followed for those chosen to view the videotape "down the hall," and as before, the deception remained intact for the actual viewer until the end of the experiment.

Condition 4: explicit coviewing. Participants were seated next to each other facing a video monitor and viewed the videotape together. They were instructed to refrain from talking and to look at the television monitor but not at each other. Only one of the coviewers was selected for facial EMG monitoring; selection was performed by means of a coin toss.

All 64 participants (either individuals or pairs) were recruited and assigned to conditions on a rotating basis. Subjects were tested over a 4-month period, during all times of the day and days of the week; thus the rotation of group assignment provided de facto counterbalancing of these factors. For purposes of clarity, the participant selected for EMG monitoring is henceforth denoted the subject, and the participant who was either escorted from the lab (Conditions 2 and 3) or coviewed the videotape (Condition 4) is denoted the friend.

RECORDING PROCEDURE

Depending on the experimental condition, the subjects (and in Condition 4, the friends as well) were seated in a soundproofed room 2.5 m from a 13-in. color television monitor. Surface EMG electrodes were then affixed on the subject's face over three major mimetic muscles (Fridlund & Izard, 1983; Schwartz, Fair, Salt, Mandel, & Klerman, 1976). In the explicit coviewing condition, in which participants sat beside each other, EMG monitoring was performed only on one (again, the subject), with selection determined by a coin toss.

To detect smiling, differential integrated EMG recordings were obtained from left and right cheek sites directly over the *zygomatic major* muscles, which retract the lips corners to form the smile (Ekman & Friesen, 1978; Fridlund. Ekman. & Oster, 1987; Izard, 1979). The facial EMG technique does not sample muscular behavior strictly confined to the single muscle underlying the elec-

trodes (e.g., the *zygomatic major*). The detection region is diffuse and susceptible to the actions of adjacent muscles (Fridlund & Fowler, 1978). However, the cheek site is very sensitive to *zygomatic major* contractions (Tassinary, Cacioppo, & Geen, 1989), and this experiment used a specific stimulus unlikely to induce appreciable facial behavior other than smiling (cf. Ekman et al., 1980). These factors lend credence to the inference that the bilateral *zygomatic major* site EMG activity in this study probably did substantially reflect subjects' smiling (also see footnote 5).

EMG activity was also obtained from a site overlying the left *corrugator supercilii,* which furrows the brow when one concentrates, signals disturbance, and so on (Darwin, 1872; Ekman, 1979; Fridlund, 1991). Activity from the *corrugator supercilii* site was used to assess whether subjects' viewing condition made them differentially attentive or dysphoric. Because its contractions are unrelated, or sometimes reciprocal to smiles, activity from this site could also control for the possibility that *zygomatic major* site EMG signals might reflect the viewer's muscular activity generally and not smiles specifically. Posed faces obtained using pilot subjects indicated negligible electrical cross talk between cheek and brow EMG sites that would otherwise obviate the use of the *corrugator supercilii* site as a control.

Three steps were taken to minimize both participants' self-consciousness about the electrodes and their tendency to make faces consistent with their expectations about the experiment. First, dummy electrodes were affixed atop the head and to the dorsum of the hand. Viewers were informed that face and head electrodes detected "brain wave activity, especially from the frontal part of the brain," whereas the hand electrode detected "heart rate and sweat gland response." Second, the rationale provided during recruitment was repeated— that is, viewers were instructed that these responses were purely physiological, unconscious, not amenable to voluntary control, and thus it "really didn't matter" what they consciously thought or how they behaved during the experiment.

A third technique assessed experimental demand by certifying the intactness of the cover story. At the conclusion of the experiment, viewers completed "guess sheets" that challenged them to state the experimental hypotheses. No subject in either implicit condition guessed that his or her friend's participation was illusory, and nearly all subjects appeared surprised when informed of the deception and greeted by their friends at the end of the experiment. No one guessed that the sociality of viewing was being investigated. Five of the 64 subjects (2 who viewed with friends, and 1 in each of the remaining three viewing conditions) mentioned "smiling," "laughing," or "movements" among their guesses about the purpose of the experiment. Their data were unremarkable and thus were retained for analysis.

VIDEOTAPE STIMULUS

After connection of the recording electrodes, viewers were asked to relax for 60 s to provide a prestimulus baseline. They then watched a videotape that ran 13 min, 15 s in length and contained five segments intended to elicit smiles across a range of undergraduate subjects. The segments and their respective lengths were as follows: (a) cute babies playing with rattles (1 min, 50 s), (b) a dog playing in the yard with a flower (45 s), (c) cute babies playing peek-a-boo (3 min, 20 s), (d) sea otters playing in an aquarium (35 s), and (e) the Steve Martin "Common Knowledge" skit (a spoof of the game show "Jeopardy") from "Saturday Night Live" (6 min, 45 s).

EMOTION RATINGS

Immediately before the videotape, viewers completed a modified version of the Differential Emotions Scale (DES; Izard. 1972), a measure of self-reported emotion used in previous affective imagery studies (e.g., Schwartz et al., 1976; Fridlund, Schwartz, & Fowler, 1984). The scale requested self-report of emotional state along 10 hedonic dimensions. At the conclusion of the videotape, viewers reported their experience during the videotape by again completing the modified DES.[3]

The two scales were labeled Ratings Sheet 1 and Ratings Sheet 2. Each form asked subjects to indicate with an X on unanchored 0–100 scales the extent to which they felt each of the following 12 states: hunger, thirst, anger, fatigue, fear, surprise, happiness, disgust, contempt, interest, curiosity, and sadness. Lines were 100 mm long, were calibrated in millimeters from 0 to 100, and were numbered at each centimeter. The ratings sheets were headed by the instructions, "Please make an X on each line to show how strongly you" (a) "feel

each of the following RIGHT NOW" (Ratings Sheet 1) and (b) "felt each of the following DURING THE VIDEOTAPE" (Ratings Sheet 2). The two forms were otherwise identical.

Results

EMG DATA

To analyze viewers' cheek- and brow-site EMG activity, arithmetic means were computed for each site; these are reliable measures of overall muscle contraction (cf. Cacioppo, Tassinary, & Fridlund, 1990). In accordance with standard statistical practice (Hildebrand, 1986) and consistent with previous studies (e.g., Fridlund, Cottam, & Fowler, 1982; Fridlund et al., 1984; Fridlund, et al., 1986),

---

[3]There are potential objections to the use of one global rating to assess happiness during the videotape. One objection is that global ratings may be insensitive to subjects' reactions to different portions of the videotape. I chose global ratings rather than periodic or episodic samples throughout the videotape because it seemed that sequential ratings would place subjects in a judgmental, vigilant set that would curtail further subjects' spontaneity.

An additional objection is that subjects may have showed higher cheek-site electromyography levels because they found the videotape amusing, even though it made them feel no happier. Such hermeneutical variations on happiness were omitted in this study because I presumed that subjects who found the tape funny would alter their happiness ratings accordingly when this dimension was the closest by forced choice. The presumption was confirmed in piloting for a related experiment. Amusement and contentment categories were added to rating sheets for 12 pilot subjects shown the same videotape. The subjects who reported being more amused also rated themselves happier ($r = .87$, $p = .0018$) as well as more content ($r = .79$, $p = .002$). Thus subjects' happiness ratings quite likely captured their amusement.

Despite these standard objections, previous studies of faces made during imagery or videotape viewing have usually found that global happiness ratings correlated with smiling. Regrettably, nearly all such studies used social stimuli (imaginary or viewed on film or videotape) as elicitors of emotion, and it may be questioned whether any correlations would be sustained if differences in sociality were controlled. Corroborating this speculation was a widely cited study of solitary subjects exposed to three videotape segments: a monkey playing, an ocean scene, and the dog-playing-with-flower segment used in this study (Ancoli, 1979). The three segments produced equivalent happiness ratings. However. subjects smiled substantially to the social stimuli (monkey and dog play behavior) but negligibly to the canonically asocial ocean stimulus. The smiling and happiness data for the ocean stimulus were omitted from the final report (Ekman, Friesen, & Ancoli, 1980).

means were log transformed [$\log_{10}(EMG + 1)$] to minimize skewness and heteroscedasticity. Skewness was determined by direct moment computation; heteroscedasticity was determined by correlating means with variances across the four viewing conditions.

Because of their correlated actions, and because the theoretical import of left–right imbalances in facial EMG signals is unclear (Fridlund, 1988), left and right cheek sites were considered paired dependent measures under multivariate analysis of variance (MANOVA); the resulting Wilks's lambda statistics were referred to the F distribution. The brow site (overlying the left *corrugator supercilii*) was analyzed using separate, univariate analysis of variance (ANOVA). In accordance with the experimental hypotheses and based on previous studies of audience effects on smiles, tests of cheek-site EMG activity among viewing conditions were one-tailed except as noted. Tests of self-report were two-tailed.

I first validated the videotape's efficacy in eliciting cheek-site EMG activity over baseline levels. As Figure 16.1A indicates, EMG activity in the cheek (*zygomatic major* region) sites showed marked increments over baseline, $F(2, 60) = 55.66$, $p < 10^{-6}$, with increments occurring in all conditions, all $Fs(2, 14) > 6.59, p < .005$. The videotape thus worked as intended. The increments were not due to carryover from unequal prevideotape baselines; baseline levels of left and right cheek-site EMG activity did not differ among viewing conditions, $F(6, 118) = .626, p > .70$, or between the participate alone and the three remaining conditions, $F(2, 59) = .817, p < .45$. This equivalence also allays concerns that the responses of those participating alone versus with friends were influenced by subject selection or assignment to viewing condition. There were no sex differences in cheek-site EMG levels either across conditions, $F(2, 55) = 1.63, p < .21$, or as a function of condition, $F(6,110) = 1.59, p < .17$. All EMG data were therefore collapsed across men and women.

Figure 16.1A shows the EMG activity for the four viewing conditions in the left and right cheek sites and the brow (*corrugator supercilii* region) control site. Among subjects who participated alone or who believed that their friends were completing tests, the cheek-site EMG levels suggested weak but visible smiling (see Fridlund et al., 1984). Among subjects who coviewed with a friend or who believed that their friend was coviewing else-

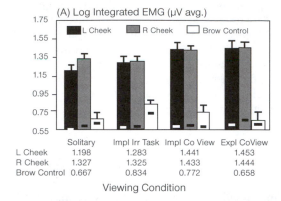

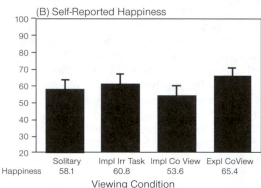

FIGURE 16.1 ■ (A) Cheek-site electromyography (EMG) activity [$\log_{10}(X + 1.0)$] over the left (L) and right (R) *zygomatic major* muscles responsible for smiling (left and middle bars, respectively), with left *corrugator supercilii* (brow) control site (right bar), as a function of videotape viewing condition. Contrasting inset bars for cheek sites denote prevideotape levels; brow-site levels during viewing did not change appreciably from prevideotape levels. (B) Reports of happiness as a function of videotape viewing condition. Solitary = solitary participation; Impl Irr Task = implicit irrelevant task; Impl CoView = implicit coviewing; Expl CoView = explicit coviewing. Error bars depict standard errors of the mean.

where, these EMG levels are consistent with moderate to strong smiling. The low brow-site EMG amplitudes suggest brow knitting at or below the threshold of visibility.

Discovering any direct or implicit audience effects required testing whether the social context of viewing influenced cheek-site EMG activity. Audience effects were confirmed. Not only did cheek-site EMG levels vary with viewing condition (Figure 16.1A), $F(6, 118) = 2.22$, $p < .046$, two-tailed, but a test for linear trend over the four viewing conditions was also significant (polynomial weights $-3, -1, 1, 3$), $F(2, 59) = 5.72$, $p <.003$, quadratic and cubic components, *ns*. Among just those subjects who viewed the tape alone (i.e., those in the participate alone and the two implicit conditions), a test for linear trend was significant (polynomial weights $-1, 0, 1$), $F(2, 44) = 4.25$, $p <.02$, quadratic component, *ns*. Because the four viewing conditions may not represent equal increments in sociality, the linear trends are more properly considered tests of monotonicity. Thus, cheek-site EMG activity varied monotonically with the sociality of viewing.

These EMG-level differences signify cheek-site activity specifically and not just general changes in facial muscular tension, as shown by the poor relationship between EMG activity in the left brow control site with viewing condition (see Figure 16.1A), $F(3, 60) = 1.93$, $p < .15$, two-tailed. Nor did brow-site EMG levels show a monotonic trend over viewing conditions like that exhibited by the cheek sites (polynomial weights $-3, -1, 1, 3$), $F(1, 60) = .10$, $p < .39$, one-tailed. Multivariate analysis of covariance (MANCOVA) was then used to remove the control-site amplitudes from the test of cheek-site EMG over viewing conditions. The differences resulting from this statistical control were negligible (MANCOVA on cheek-site EMG levels over conditions, $F(6, 118) = 2.22$, $p < .047$, two-tailed. The control-site tests also suggest that cheek-site EMG differences were not due to viewers' differential concentration on, or negative reactions to, the videotape. They further suggest that subjects with friends physically present did not inhibit smiling because they were embarrassed or otherwise disturbed by the measurement apparatus.

Given the overall effect for sociality of viewing on cheek-site EMG activity, multivariate contrasts allowed comparisons among individual conditions. Direct audience effects were confirmed: Subjects who viewed with friends physically present exhibited higher cheek-site levels than those who participated alone, $F(2, 59) = 4.65$, $p < .007$. The physical presence of the friend was not necessary to potentiate cheek-site activity. EMG levels in subjects with friends physically present did not differ from that seen when subjects simply believed that friends were simultaneously viewing elsewhere, $F(6, 118) = 0.012$, $p < .50$. Implicit audience effects were also confirmed: Subjects who

believed that their friends were coviewers exhibited much higher cheek-site EMG levels than those who participated alone, $F(2, 59) = 4.32$, $p < .01$. This comparison was especially interesting given that subjects were physically alone in both conditions.

I next wanted to ascertain whether the activity purportedly engaged in by friends in the implicit conditions (either taking tests or coviewing) affected subjects' EMG activity. Subjects who believed that their friend was viewing elsewhere tended to show more cheek-site activity than those who believed their friend was completing tests, $F(2, 59) = 1.53$, $p < .13$. Finally, subjects who believed that their friend was completing tests tended to show higher cheek-site EMG levels than subjects who participated alone, $F(2, 59) = 1.50$, $p < .13$. Although they are consistent with predictions that are based on a role for implicit sociality, I am nonetheless cautious about these marginal effects.

EMOTION RATINGS

After finding that subjects' cheek-site EMG activity varied monotonically with the sociality of viewing, it was important to ascertain the relative contribution of subjects' reported emotional state during the videotape. Their cheek-site EMG activity was thus analyzed as a function of their happiness ratings. Because the ratings showed distributions that approximated normality, no transformation was required.[4]

I first assessed whether subjects' happiness ratings differed with viewing condition. These ratings are depicted in Figure 16.1. To the extent that happiness determined cheek-site EMG levels, happiness differences should parallel the EMG differences, at least among subjects who viewed alone (i.e., the participate alone and the two implicit

[4] Analyses of self-report data by sex showed initial differences on overall ratings, $F(11, 46) = 2.65$, $p = .009$, that did not interact with viewing condition, $F(36, 133) = 1.20$, $p = .23$. This effect was chiefly due to women's greater initial curiosity, $F(1, 56) = 4.75$, $p = .034$, but lower surprise, $F(1, 56) = 6.43$, $p = .014$. I cannot explain this odd result. Following videotape presentation, the sex differences in happiness ratings disappeared, $F(1, 56) = 1.56$, $p = .22$, as did those on the remaining 11 dimensions, $F(12, 45) = 1.69$, $p = .11$. This latter marginal effect was due largely to men's greater hunger by the end of the experiment (the difference in hunger did not interact with condition). Self-report data were thus collapsed across men and women.

conditions). This was not found. When subjects' happiness ratings for videotape viewing were analyzed, using a univariate ANOVA, there were no differences among viewing conditions, $F(3, 56) = 0.65$, $p > .58$. Self-report differences before videotape viewing could potentially have carried over and obscured differences during viewing, but prevideotape happiness ratings did not differ among viewing conditions, $F(3, 56) = 1.33$, $p < .28$, or on the 11 remaining self-report dimensions, $F(33, 136) = 1.14$, $p < .31$. Nor did prevideotape ratings of subjects who participated alone (Condition 1) differ from those who arrived with a friend (Conditions 2–4), either on happiness, $F(1, 60) = .01$, $p > .93$, or on the remaining 11 dimensions, $F(11, 50) = 1.33$, $p < .24$. Like the prevideotape EMG levels, the equivalence in prevideotape ratings counters concerns that responses of those who participated alone versus with friends reflected artifacts of initial subject selection. Taken together, these self-report findings suggest that viewing condition did not affect cheek-site EMG levels through the differential experience of happiness during the videotape.

Having ruled out differences in felt happiness during viewing, it was still possible that some other emotion or combination of emotions could have produced a pattern congruent with that found for the cheek-site EMG levels. For example, subjects might have been differentially inhibited, angry, and so on across the viewing conditions and their EMG levels might have been attenuated. Given that brow-site activity (which would signal any disturbance) did not differ across viewing conditions and did not parallel the differences in cheek-site EMG levels, this was unlikely. I nonetheless used a global MANOVA to analyze the remaining 11 self-report measures collectively. No clear differences emerged, $F(33, 136) = 1.33$, $p < .14$. The marginal effect for viewing condition was due largely to differences in reported hunger and fatigue. The pattern of means, however, did not explain the differences in cheek-site activity, nor did ratings of fear, anger, sadness, disgust, and contempt. These findings discount explanations relating the cheek-site EMG differences to inhibition or discomfiture in one or more viewing conditions (all Fs <1.45, $p < .25$).

It was also conceivable that although overall reported happiness did not differ across viewing conditions, individual subjects (or at least those who viewed alone) who exhibited the highest cheek-site EMG levels might still report being the happiest. This hypothesis was tested first by regressing left/right cheek-site EMG amplitudes on happiness ratings of the 64 subjects pooled across all viewing conditions. Relationships between subjects' EMG levels and their own happiness ratings were negligible, $F(2, 61) = 1.52$, $p < .24$. The levels and variances of both EMG activity and reported happiness did not suggest that low correlations resulted from restriction of range.

Regressions of cheek-site EMG activity on postvideotape ratings within each condition were all nonsignificant but were most predictive when subjects sat with a friend; regression Fs were for actual coviewers, $F(2, 13) = 2.99$, $p < .10$; for subjects who participated alone, $F(2, 13) = .21$, $p > .80$, for those whose friend "completed tests," $F(2, 13) = .32$, $p > .72$, and for those whose friend "watched elsewhere," $F(2, 13) = .04$, $p > .95$. These results countered the interpretation that differences among cheek-site EMG amplitudes of subjects who participated alone should most reflect differences in happiness, whereas those of actual coviewers should be most dissimulative and least related to happiness. The regression of left and right cheek sites on initial ratings was nonsignificant and thus did not bias the preceding regression by means of carryover effects, regression $F(2, 61) = .35$, $p > .70$.

The global postvideotape ratings were potentially susceptible to primacy or recency effects for portions of the videotape presentation; either could weaken the regressions of the subjects' cheek-site EMG amplitudes on their self-report. Neither effect was observed when discrete portions of the videotape (babies, animals, and the comedy sketch) were regressed on postvideotape happiness ratings. All of these regressions were nonsignificant.

Finally, I wished to examine the relative importance of viewing condition versus self-reported happiness in accounting for variations in subjects' cheek-site EMG amplitudes. Separate regressions were conducted of viewing condition and happiness ratings on left and right cheek-site EMG levels across the 64 subjects. These analyses showed that viewing condition accounted significantly for subjects' EMG levels, regression $F(2, 61) = 5.81$, $p < .006$, but as reported, rated happiness did not —again, regression $F(2, 61) = 1.52$, $p < .24$. I then analyzed only subjects who viewed alone (i.e., the explicit coviewing subjects were excluded) and should have been least impacted by sociality. The findings were similar. Viewing condition accounted significantly for cheek-site EMG levels, regression $F(2, 45) = 4.34, p < .02$, but rated happiness did not, regression $F(2, 45) = .27, p > .75$.

Experiment 2: Demand Characteristics Control

Although the finding of direct audience effects might reasonably have been expected, it was a novel result that believing that a friend was a coviewer elsewhere would produce potentiation in *zygomatic major* region EMG activity equal to the friend's physical presence. The finding that the potentiation of EMG activity by both explicit and implicit audiences was unaccompanied by increases in reported happiness was equally surprising. These findings did not accord with common intuitions about the face and emotion or most scientific accounts of smiles. I sought to establish this empirically by recruiting groups of raters and asking them to indicate how subjects would respond to the experimental manipulations.

This *Gedanken* experiment was an adaptation of the demand characteristics control group, or pseudoexperiment, technique typically used in mental-imagery-scanning studies to establish how experimental demand might bias subjects (cf. Kosslyn, Pinker, Smith, & Schwartz, 1979; after Milgram, 1974; Orne, 1962). Its present purpose was to determine the outcome most people would expect from the first experiment.

Method

I recruited 24 advanced undergraduates from a class in personality psychology. All students had taken previous classes in introductory psychology that included discussions of emotion and facial expressions but had received no formal training in either. Their predictions could thus be taken as reflecting common intuitions about emotions and faces.

I also obtained predictions from a small sample ($n = 5$) of advanced graduate students and doctoral candidates studying the face and emotion at a major northeastern university (several have now entered the field). Because these students had received formal training, their predictions could be taken as theoretically informed.

All raters were provided a 1½-page description of the experiment that summarized the content of the videotape and detailed the four viewing conditions. The description was an accurate summary of the exact procedures in the study, except for the omission of the EMG monitoring and the deception used in the two implicit conditions (i.e., raters believed, as the actual subjects did, that friends actually completed tests or coviewed elsewhere).

For each of the four viewing conditions, raters were asked to predict the following: (a) How happy people in each group would say they were during the videotape after they viewed it, and (b) how much subjects in each group would smile while they watched the videotape. Raters recorded their smiling and happiness predictions by providing 0–100 numerical ratings for the happiness and smiling subjects would report and show in each condition. After completing their predictions, raters were asked to provide rationales for their responses.

Results

Summaries of predictions by both the undergraduate and graduate students are depicted in Figure 16.2 (panels A and B indicate smiling and happiness predictions, respectively).

UNDERGRADUATE PSEUDOSUBJECTS

The undergraduates' predictions were analyzed with one-way repeated measures ANOVAs, using the multivariate approach (O'Brien & Kaiser, 1985). As Figure 16.2A shows, the undergraduates predicted large differences in smiling among viewing conditions, $F(3, 21) = 9.02, p <.001$. However, step-down F tests of the predictions showed that they were wholly discrepant from the actual EMG findings.

According to the undergraduates, subjects who viewed with a friend would smile more than subjects in all other conditions, $F(1, 23) = 27.3, p < .001$, and they would also smile more than subjects who believed a friend was viewing elsewhere, $F(1, 23) = 17.8, p < .001$. These latter subjects would, in turn, smile more than those who believed their friend was completing tests, $F(1, 23) = 10.6$, $p < .005$, and those who participated alone, $F(1, 23) = 7.84, p < .011$ .Subjects who believed that their friend was completing tests would show smiling equal to that of subjects who participated alone, $F(1, 23) = .29, p > .60$.

Figure 16.2B shows the undergraduates' predictions about subjects' emotional reports. These raters predicted large differences among viewing conditions in reported happiness, $F(3, 21) = 13.6, p < .001$. Unlike the experimental subjects, the hypothetical subjects conformed to the commonplace presumption that smiles must express felt happiness.

Predicted Smiling and Happiness

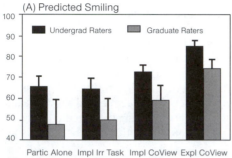

(A) Predicted Smiling

Viewing Condition	Partic Alone	Impl Irr Task	Impl CoView	Expl CoView
Undergrd Raters	66.1	64.6	72.5	84.8
Graduate Raters	48	50	59	74

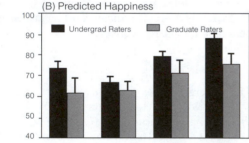

(B) Predicted Happiness

Viewing Condition	Partic Alone	Impl Irr Task	Impl CoView	Expl CoView
Undergrd Raters	73.9	69.3	78.6	86.9
Graduate Raters	62	63	70.6	73

FIGURE 16.2 ■ (A) Smiling and (B) happiness ratings of hypothetical subjects predicted by independent raters given a detailed description of experimental procedures; raters were advanced undergraduates ($n = 24$; left bars), and advanced graduate students and doctoral candidates ($n = 5$) studying the face and emotion (right bars). (Videotape viewing conditions are abbreviated as follows: Partic Alone = subjects participated and viewed alone; Impl Irr Task = subjects viewed alone, under the belief that a friend was nearby, engaged in an irrelevant task—"completing psychological tests"; Impl CoView = subjects viewed alone, under the belief that a friend was also viewing nearby; Expl CoView = subject and friend viewed the videotape together. To facilitate comparisons, ordinate scaling was adjusted for visual equivalence of participate alone levels. Error bars depict standard errors of the mean.)

First, the undergraduates' predictions were consistent with the belief that over viewing conditions, smiling would parallel rated happiness. Subjects viewing with a friend would rate themselves happier than subjects in all other conditions, $F(1, 23) = 40.6, p < .001$, and they would also report greater happiness than just those subjects who believed that a friend was viewing elsewhere, $F(1, 23) = 37.3, p < .001$. These latter subjects would, in turn, report being happier than those who believed that their friend was completing tests, $F(1, 23) = 18.5, p < .001$, and those who participated alone, $F(1, 23) = 10.3, p < .005$. Subjects who believed that their friend was completing tests should tend to report being happier than those who participated alone, $F(1, 23) = 3.77, p < .066$.

Second, within each viewing condition, the undergraduates predicted that subjects' smiling would show uniformly high correlations with happiness ratings. These within-condition analyses regarded each rater's prediction as, in effect, a subject in the pseudoexperiment. The Pearson correlations for the four conditions were subjects participating alone, $r(24) = .79, p < .001$; subjects who believed that friends were completing tests, $r(24) = .50, p < .014$; subjects who believed that friends were viewing elsewhere, $r(24) = .72, p < .001$; and subjects viewing with a friend physically present, $r(24) = .74, p < .001$. Results from the actual subjects showed negligible correlations, belying the raters' implicit assumption about the relationship of smiling to happiness.

The rationales the undergraduates provided clarified the bases for their predictions. Almost without exception, these rationales emphasized how the four viewing conditions would affect emotional state, under the assumption that smiling would follow automatically. "People are happier and smile more when they are with friends" stated one. "Naturally, happier people smile more" responded another. In dissecting her differential predictions about the viewing conditions, one rater stated schematically, "Assume individuals enjoyed sharing video w/others. Assume would rather watch video than take psychological test. Assume smile = happiness. Assume happiness caused by videotape canceled out by anxiety caused by 'test'." None of the rationales provided by the undergraduates included any idea that happiness and smiling were dissociable under these experimental conditions.

GRADUATE STUDENT PSEUDOSUBJECTS

The graduate students' predictions coincided over-all with those of the undergraduate sample. These raters predicted direct audience effects but under-estimated implicit audience effects considerably. Their predicted means for smiling (using a 0–100 scale) were as follows (and see Figure 16.2A): sub-jects who participated alone, 48; subjects who believed friends were completing tests, 50; sub-jects who believed friends were viewing elsewhere, 59; and subjects with friends physically present, 74. Predicted happiness ratings (0–100 scale; Fig-ure 16.2B) for the four viewing conditions were, respectively, 62, 63, 70.6, and 73. Thus the gradu-ate students as well as the undergraduates believed that smiles would vary directly with happiness.

Like the undergraduates, the graduate students also predicted that within viewing conditions, sub-jects' smiling would be strongly associated with reported happiness. Unlike the undergraduates, however, they predicted that the strongest and weakest correlations between rated happiness and smiling would occur, respectively, among those subjects who participated alone, $r(5) = .94$, $p < .017$, and those who viewed with friends physi-cally present, $r(5) = -.02$, $p > .96$. Predicted corre-lations for the remaining groups were intermedi-ate (for hypothetical subjects who believed friends were completing tests, $r(5) = .93$, $p < .025$, for those who believed friends were viewing elsewhere, $r(5) = .61$, $p < .29$. These predictions would be expected from an interpretation that sociality substantially mediates only public faces.

The graduate students' rationales for their pre-dictions illustrated this interpretation. One student wrote, "The differences that I would expect have to do with feeling rules and display rules." An-other stated, "Subjects [with actual coviewers] should react most strongly, but the difference should be greater for their expressive behavior than the self reports [which are due to] culture-specific ideas about the videotape and the kind of reaction one should show." Still other explanations were invoked, with these students adducing constructs and mechanisms such as attribution, cultural speci-ficity, display rules, facial feedback, feeling rules, motor mimicry, social comparison, social conta-gion, social facilitation, and social inhibition.

In summary, both groups of students predicted direct audience effects but substantially underes-timated implicit audience effects. When audience effects were predicted, they were always accom-panied by parallel differences in happiness (Fig-ure 16.2). Within each condition, both groups of raters predicted that happiness would be intimately related to smiling. One exception was provided by the graduate students, who predicted that smil-ing would dissociate from happiness only in the actual coviewing condition. The undergraduates' rationales were often explicit in their equation of happiness with smiling; those provided by the graduate students allowed for some dissociation of smiling from happiness by viewing condition. Despite the great differences in their rationales, the two sets of raters generated largely concordant predictions. These were discrepant from the ac-tual findings.

Discussion

Our findings demonstrate that while viewing a pleasant videotape, the presence of a friendly coviewer potentiates bilateral EMG activity in cheek sites directly overlying the *zygomatic ma-jor* muscles responsible for smiling.[5] However, the coviewer need not be physically present; equal enhancement occurs in the mere psychological presence of a coviewer. The enhanced cheek-site EMG levels observed with just the psychological presence of a coviewer was dramatic when con-trasted with that of subjects who participated alone, considering that in both of these conditions, sub-jects viewed in solitude. Across all four videotape-viewing conditions, subjects' cheek-site EMG ac-tivity varied as a positive, monotonic function of the sociality of viewing.

These findings indicate both direct and implicit audience effects for smiles. Furthermore, the equivalence of self-report across the four viewing conditions implies that these audience effects were not measurably mediated by the differential induc-tion of felt emotion. Our data also suggest that implicit audience effects may depend on the ac-tions of the imagined other (we are guarded about the latter inference, given the marginal effects).

---

[5]Mean EMG levels were derived for the entire viewing epoch. Thus it is unknown whether subjects smiled more frequently, more intensely, or both. Such determination would require visible facial coding by means of systems like FACS (Ekman & Friesen, 1978) or MAX (Izard, 1979) or more microanalytic study of the second-to-second EMG signals (e.g., Fridlund et al., 1984, 1986).

The differences in cheek-site EMG amplitudes did not appear to result from dysphoria in subjects who participated alone or from embarrassment, inhibition, or dissimulative production of smiles in subjects who viewed with friends. Mitigating these accounts were two lines of evidence: (a) EMG activity in the brow site (overlying the *corrugator supercilii*, which typically indicates disturbance) did not differ across viewing conditions and did not parallel the cheek-site changes, and (b) emotional self-report indicated no differential incidence of emotions such as fear, anger, sadness, contempt, or disgust.

In the second, *Gedanken* experiment, predictions by both undergraduates and graduate student experts in emotion and facial expressions indicate that these findings run counter both to intuition and common theory about faces. In accordance with the induction that smiles imply felt happiness, both groups of raters considerably underestimated implicit audience effects and predicted that smiling would parallel reported happiness. The undergraduates' predictions about smiling were based on the emotionality these raters believed would be engendered by each viewing condition. Graduate student experts made predictions similar to those of the undergraduates but provided more complex rationales that allowed that viewing condition (chiefly, explicit coviewing) could dissociate smiles from happiness.

The results ran contrary to the raters' predictions and to the view that emotion is necessarily deducible from either public or private smiling. Subjects' cheek-site EMG levels varied monotonically with perceived sociality and negligibly with felt emotion. This finding pointed to an interactional account of the inferred smiling that was based on the actual or implicit social context of viewing. The interactional account derives from role and impression-management theories that maintain that we assume roles consistent with our audiences, whether they are real or imaginary (Goffman, 1959; Greenwald & Breckler, 1985; Mead, 1934; Schlenker, 1980; Schlenker & Wiegold, 1989; for relevant views of faces, see Birdwhistell, 1970; Kendon, 1975; Mandler, 1975; and Patterson, 1983; note that this use of the word role implies no necessary perfidy or inauthenticity).

In this interactional account, the implicit and explicit coviewing subjects were both cast as friendly associates in a pleasant experience (watch-

ing the videotape), and this kind of situation calls for frequent reciprocation of affiliative smiles (e.g., parents viewing their child's school play). In contrast, friends doing different things in each other's presence usually just give off occasional acknowledgment smiles (e.g., two passersby in an office; see Goffman, 1967, 1971). The subjects who viewed while believing that their friends were completing psychological tests were cast in a situation with no shared activity, and thus they tended to exhibit lower cheek-site EMG levels; subjects with no friends in the proximal experimental context showed the lowest EMG levels of all.

These data are indeterminate with regard to the mechanism that accounts for these audience effects. My conjecture, anticipated by the "imaginary objects" accounts of Piderit (1886) and Gratiolet (1865/1990), is that subjects' smiling was mediated by visual imagery. Like the everyday experiences of finding ourselves smiling while imagining our partner's smiling face or scowling when imagining disciplining a child, subjects who arrived with friends but viewed the videotape alone may conceivably have conjured visually their friend and then made faces toward him or her.[6] They may also have imagined sharing their experiences with their friends after the experiment (cf. Schlenker & Weigold, 1989); in fact, perceptual studies show that people spontaneously imagine what they expect to see (Finke & Shepard, 1986).

Mediation by visual imagery, as well as being intuitively compelling, is suggested by (a) the dependency on in vivo visual contact seen by Kraut and Johnston (1979), Jones and Raag (1989), Brightman et al. (1977), and Bavelas et al. (1986), (b) the shaping of judgments of written material, and evaluations of oneself under failure, by visual imagery priming of different "salient private audiences" (Baldwin & Holmes, 1987), and (c) the observation that controlling for self-reported happiness, highly social imagery occasioned more smiling than imagery than was less social (Fridlund et al., 1990). Other mechanisms may reasonably mediate implicit audience effects. Our staging of the experimental conditions may have produced role-appropriate behavior strictly out of habit,

---

[6] This prediction was first stated by Cooley (1902): "People differ much in the vividness of their imaginative sociability. The more simple, concrete, dramatic, their habit of mind is, the more their thinking is carried on in terms of actual conversation with a visible and audible interlocutor" (p. 95).

without the necessary involvement of visual imagery (see Stanislavski, 1965).

I hasten to mention possible objections to the social role formulation: (a) that the above-baseline cheek-site EMG levels in subjects who participated alone mitigates the exhaustiveness of an implicit-audience account, (b) that the audience effects were due merely to social facilitation, and (c) that the cheek-site EMG levels of the solitary viewers reflected "display rules." To elaborate on each:

1. Subjects who participated alone clearly showed more cheek-site EMG activity during the videotape than preceding it, but the social context for these subjects would seem nonexistent. The observed EMG activity should then be primarily emotional by default. This position is certainly plausible. It is nonetheless problematic given that the cheek-site EMG levels of subjects who participated alone bore no relationship to their happiness ratings. More critically, it necessarily assumes that the solitary subjects had no implicit audience because one was not contrived experimentally. Their audience may simply have been outside the experimental context (e.g., a friend who did not accompany the subject to the experiment) or was evoked by their associations to the film (i.e., segments of the videotape invoked recall of past in vivo social interactions). It is also questionable nowadays whether any subjects placed alone in a psychology laboratory are certain that they are unobserved. As a consequence, the experimenter and the measurement devices may have constituted an ancillary implicit audience in all viewing conditions. Establishing the "ground truth" on the relation of any faces to felt emotion would require controlling for such unintended sociality.

2. The audience effects might ostensibly reflect social facilitation by means of Hullian drive induction (Geen & Gange, 1977; Moore & Baron, 1983). I do not believe that this mechanism plausibly explains the data for three reasons. First, increments in generalized drive produced by others should have occasioned parallel changes in both cheek-site EMG amplitudes and reported happiness and perhaps even activity from the brow site (assuming that these responses have the greatest habit strength). The data did not conform with this pattern. Second, a coviewer's physical presence should have effected dramatic potentiation of cheek-site EMG levels and happiness as compared with an implicit coviewer, but EMG amplitudes and reported happiness were equivalent in the two

conditions. Third, a drive induction account would not predict the tendency of subjects' cheek-site EMG levels to differ with the actions of the implicit other (but, again, I am guarded about this finding given the marginal effects).

3. It might be argued that solitary subjects' cheek-site EMG levels reflected smiling that was due simply to overlearned display rules governing in vivo social behavior (display rules are putative conventions for attenuating, histrionically intensifying, or masking involuntary emotional faces in public; see Ekman, 1972). Invoking display rules to explain solitary faces is difficult to defend because it is self-contradictory: The pivotal experiment held to demonstrate them used solitary subjects as controls, under the assumption that their faces were most purely emotional (Ekman, 1972, 1973, 1984; see reanalysis of display rules study by Fridlund, 1991). As the data show, correlations between cheek-site EMG levels and reported happiness were low in all conditions. They were not demonstrably higher in subjects who participated alone, when the facial behavior was ostensibly the least social. In fact, the correlation between cheek-site EMG levels and reported happiness was the highest for the subjects who viewed the videotape in the physical presence of a friend.[7]

Thus, such explanations do not seem tenable. An implicit sociality account of these audience effects is nonetheless open to criticism on two more general grounds: (a) that it is solipsistic and (b) that it is not disconfirmable. To consider each:

1. Casting solitary viewers' facial activity as social role behavior before audiences of their own making may at first seem absurdly solipsistic. It nonetheless accords with everyday experience. We mutter to ourselves and hear ourselves respond, we praise or scold ourselves and enjoy or suffer the consequences, and we rehearse what we will say to others and foresee their likely reactions. People can blush with embarrassment when alone

---

[7] Within-condition correlations, even if there were no contribution of sociality, should not approach unity given differences among subjects within each condition in facial muscle size and conformation, placement of detection electrodes, moduli used while rating emotions (cf. Stevens, 1956), and interpretation of emotion terms on the ratings scales. The quasi-random subject assignment to viewing condition controls for these factors in group analyses, and thus between-groups inspection of mean levels and differences among the within-group correlations are probably more informative.

(B. Apfelbaum, personal communication, July 1989; Goffman, 1959; Ribot, 1897), and they often respond sexually to idealized partners during highly visual seduction fantasies (Masters, Johnson, & Kolodny, 1985). These episodes are difficult to explain without invoking concepts of role and audience. In fact, viewing private behavior as role behavior accords entirely with traditional conceptions of thinking as dialogical and the self as a creation of public interaction (Cooley, 1902; Goffman, 1979; Mead, 1934; Vygotsky, 1962; see also Skinner, 1957).

2. Explaining solitary faces by appeal to implicit sociality, it might be contended, is impossible to disconfirm because implicit or imaginal interactants can never be ruled out completely. It may be that this theory, like many others, is untestable in extremis, but as the present findings suggest, it can be exposed to falsification using experimentally manipulable ranges of sociality.

Finally, in offering these findings, I must voice appropriate caution about their limitations. Subjects reported being equivalently happy across viewing conditions, and thus emotional mediation of facial behavior may have been systematic (i.e., invariant), a proposition weakened but not vitiated by the poor happiness–EMG associations within viewing conditions. These results thus do not exclude a role for emotion in the instigation of public or private faces, but they do warrant caution in deducing emotion from either. The interactional explanation of solitary faces obviously depends on confirmation with evocations other than videotapes, with emotions other than happiness, and with expressions other than smiling. Such research will map the extent of both direct and implicit human audience effects.

I began this study by questioning why people make faces when they are alone. These initial findings lead me to believe that solitary faces occur for the same reasons as public ones, if only because when we are alone we create social interactions in our imaginations. They suggest the possibility that sociality may play a major role in the mediation of solitary faces. At minimum, these findings suggest that implicit sociality must be controlled before solitary facial behavior is ascribed to emotion.

REFERENCES

Ancoli, S. (1979). *Psychophysiological response patterns to emotions.* Unpublished doctoral dissertation, University of California, San Francisco.

Bainum, C. K., Lounsbury, K. R., & Pollio, H. R. (1984). The development of laughing and smiling in nursery school children. *Child Development, 55,* 1946–1957.

Baldwin, M. W., & Holmes, J. G. (1987). Salient private audiences and awareness of the self. *Journal of Personality and Social Psychology, 52,* 1087–1098.

Bavelas, J. B., Black, A., Lemery, C. R., & Mullett, J. (1986). "I show how you feel." Motor mimicry as a communicative act. *Journal of Personality and Social Psychology, 50,* 322–329.

Birdwhistell, R. L. (1970). *Kinesics and context.* Philadelphia: University of Pennsylvania Press.

Brightman, V. J., Segal, A. L., Werther, P, & Steiner, J. (1977). Facial expression and hedonic response to taste stimuli. *Journal of Dental Research, 56,* B161 (Abstract).

Buck, R. (1984). *The communication of emotion.* New York: Guilford Press.

Cacioppo, J. T., Petty, R. E., Losch, M. E/, & Kim, H. S. (1986). Electromyographic activity over facial muscle regions can differentiate the valence and intensity of affective reactions. *Journal of Personality and Social Psychology, 50,* 260–268.

Cacioppo, J. T, Tassinary, L. G., & Fridlund, A. J. (1990). The skeleto-motor system. In J. T. Cacioppo & L. G. Tassinary (Eds.), *Principles of psychophysiology, 50,* (pp. 325–384). New York: Cambridge University Press.

Chapman, A. J. (1973). Social facilitation of laughter in children. *Journal of Experimental Social Psychology, 9,* 528–541.

Chapman, A. J. (1974). An electromyographic study of social facilitation: A test of the "mere presence" hypothesis. *British Journal of Psychology, 65,* 123–128.

Chapman, A. J. (1975). Humorous laughter in children. *Journal of Personality and Social Psychology, 31,* 42-49.

Chapman, A. J., & Wright, D. S. (1976). Social enhancement of laughter: An experimental analysis of some companion variables. *Journal of Experimental Child Psychology, 21,* 201–218.

Cheney, D. L., Seyfarth, R. M., & Smuts, B. (1986). Social relationships and social cognition in nonhuman primates. *Science, 234,* 1361–1366.

Cooley, C. H. (1902). *Human nature and the social order.* New York: Scribner.

Darwin, C. (1872). *The expression of the emotions in man and animals.* London: Albemarle.

Ekman, P. (1972). Universals and cultural differences in facial expressions of emotion. In J. Cole (Ed.), *Nebraska symposium on motivation* (Vol. 19). Lincoln: University of Nebraska Press.

Ekman, P (1973). Cross-cultural studies of facial expressions. In P. Ekman (Ed.), *Darwin and facial expression* (pp. 169–229). San Diego, CA: Academic Press.

Ekman, P. (1977). Biological and cultural contributions to body and facial movement. In J. Blacking (Ed.), *The anthropology of the body.* San Diego, CA: Academic Press.

Ekman, P. (1979). About brows: Emotional and conversational signals. In J. Aschoff, M. von Cranach, K. Foppa, W

Lepenies, & D. Ploog (Eds.), *Human ethology*. Cambridge, England: Cambridge University Press.

Ekman, P. (1984). Expression and the nature of emotion. In P. Ekman & K. Scherer (Eds.), *Approaches to emotion* (pp. 319–343). Hillsdale, NJ: Erlbaum.

Ekman, P., Davidson, R. J., & Friesen, W. V. (1990). The Duchenne smile: Emotional expression and brain physiology II. *Journal of Personality and Social Psychology, 58,* 342–353.

Ekman, P., & Friesen, W. V. (1969). The repertoire of nonverbal behavior: Categories, origins, usage, and coding. *Semiotica, 1,* 49–98.

Ekman, P., & Friesen, W. V. (1975). *Unmasking the face.* Englewood Cliffs, NJ: Prentice-Hail.

Ekman, P., & Friesen, W. V. (1978). *The Facial Action Coding System.* Palo Alto, CA: Consulting Psychologists Press.

Ekman, P., & Friesen, W. V. (l982). Felt, false, and miserable smiles. *Journal of Nonverbal Behavior, 6,* 238–252.

Ekman, P., Friesen, W. V., & Ancoli, S. (1980). Facial signs of emotional experience. *Journal of Personality and Social Psychology, 39,* 1125–1134.

Finke, R. A., & Shepard, R. N. (1986). Visual functions of mental imagery. In K. R. Boff, L. Kaufman, & J. P. Thomas (Eds.), *Handbook of perception and human performance: Vol. II. Cognitive processes and performance* (pp. 37-1 to 37-55). New York: Wiley.

Freedman, J. L., & Perlick, D. (1979). Crowding, contagion, and laughter. *Journal of Experimental Social Psychology, 15,* 295–303.

Fridlund, A. J. (1988). What can asymmetry and laterality in facial EMG tell us about the face and brain? *International Journal of Neuroscience, 39,* 53–69.

Fridlund, A. J. (1991). Evolution and facial action in reflex, social motive, and paralanguage. *Biological Psychology, 32,* 3–100.

Fridlund, A. J., & Cacioppo, J. T. (1986). Guidelines for human electromyographic research. *Psychophysiology, 23,* 567–589.

Fridlund, A. J., Cottam, G. L., & Fowler, S. C. (1982). In search of the general tension factor: Tensional patterning during auditory stimulation. *Psychophysiology, 19,* 136–145.

Fridlund, A. J., Ekman, P., & Oster, H. (1987). Facial expressions of emotion. In A. Siegman & S. Feldstein (Eds.), *Nonverbal behavior and communication* (pp. 143–224). Hillsdale, NJ: Erlbaum.

Fridlund, A. J., & Fowler, S. C. (1978). An eight-channel computer-controlled scanning electromyograph. *Behavior Research Methods & Instrumentation, 10,* 652–662.

Fridlund, A. J., Hatfield, M. E., Cottam, G. L., & Fowler, S. C. (1986). Anxiety and striate-muscle activation: Evidence from EMG pattern analysis. *Journal Abnormal Psychology, 95,* 228–236.

Fridlund, A. J., & Izard, C. E. (1983). Electromyographic studies of facial expressions of emotions and patterns of emotions. In J. T. Cacioppo & R. E. Petty (Eds.), *Social psychophysiology: A sourcebook* (pp. 243–286). New York: Guilford Press.

Fridlund, A. J., Sabini, J. P., Hedlund, L. E., Schaut, J. A., Shenker, J. I., & Knauer, M. J. (1990). Social determinants of facial expressions during affective imagery: Displaying

to the people in your head. *Journal of Nonverbal Behavior, 14,* 113–137.

Fridlund, A. J., Schwartz, G. E., & Fowler, S. C. (1984). Pattern-recognition of self-reported emotional state from multiple-site facial EMG activity during affective imagery. *Psychophysiology, 21,* 622–637.

Friesen, W. V. (1972). *Cultural differences in facial expressions in a social situation: An experimental test of the concept of display rules.* Unpublished doctoral dissertation, University of California. San Francisco: University of California Microfilm Archives.

Frijda, N. (1986). *The emotions.* Cambridge, England: Cambridge University Press.

Geen, R. G., & Gange, J. J. (1977). Drive theory of social facilitation: Twelve years of theory and research. *Psychological Bulletin, 84,* 1267–1288.

Gilbert, A. N., Fridlund, A. J., & Sabini, J. (1987). Hedonic and social determinants of facial displays to odors. *Chemical Senses, 12,* 355–363.

Goffman, E. (1959). *The presentation of self in everyday life.* New York: Anchor.

Goffman, E. (1967). *Interaction ritual.* New York: Anchor.

Goffman, E. (1971). *Relations in public.* New York: Harper & Row.

Goffman, E. (1979). Response cries. In M. von Cranach, K. Foppa, W. Lepenies, & D. Ploog (Eds.), *Human ethology* (pp. 203–240). Cambridge, England: Cambridge University Press.

Gratiolet, P. (1990). *On physiognomy and the movements of expression.* A. J. Fridlund (Ed.) & C. Nivet (Ed. & Trans.). Manuscript in preparation. (Original work published 1865)

Greenwald, A. G., & Breckler, S. J. (1985). To whom is the self presented? In B. R. Schlenker (Ed.), *The self and social life.* New York: McGraw-Hill.

Hildebrand, D. K. (1986). *Statistical thinking for behavioral scientists.* Boston: Duxbury.

Hinde, R. A. (1985a). Expression and negotiation. In G. Zivin (Ed.), *The development of expressive behavior* (pp. 103–116). San Diego, CA: Academic Press.

Hinde, R. A. (1985b). Was "the expression of the emotions" a misleading phrase? *Animal Behaviour, 33,* 985–992.

Izard, C. E. (1972). *Patterns of emotion. A new analysis of anxiety and depression.* San Diego, CA: Academic Press.

Izard, C. E. (1979). *The Maximally Discriminative Facial Movement Coding System.* Newark: University of Delaware, Instructional Resources Center.

Izard, C. E., & Malatesta, C. Z. (1987). Perspectives on emotional development: I. Differential emotions theory of early emotional development. In J. Osofsky (Ed.), *Handbook of infant development* (Rev. ed., pp. 494–559). New York: Wiley-Interscience.

Jones, S. S., & Raag, T. (1989). Smile production in older infants: The importance of a social recipient for the facial signal. *Child Development, 60,* 811–818.

Kendon, A. (1975). Some functions of the face in a kissing round. *Semiotica, 15,* 299–334.

Kleck, R. E., Vaughan, R. C., Cartwright-Smith, J., Vaughan, K. B., Colby, C. Z., & Lanzetta, J. T. (1976). Effects of being observed on expressive, subjective, and physiological responses to painful stimuli. *Journal of Personality and Social Psychology, 334,* 1211–1218.

Kosslyn, S. M., Pinker, S., Smith, G. E., & Schwartz, S. P (1979). On the demystification of mental imagery. *Behavioral and Brain Sciences, 2,* 535–581.

Kraut, R. E. (1982). Social presence, facial feedback, and emotion. *Journal of Personality and Social Psychology, 42,* 853-863.

Kraut, R. E., & Johnston, R. E. (1979). Social and emotional messages of smiling: An ethological approach. *Journal of Personality and Social Psychology, 37,* 1539–1553.

Krebs, J. R., & Dawkins, R. (1984). Animal signals: Mind-reading and manipulation. In J. R. Krebs & N. B. Davies (Eds.), *Behavioural ecology* (2nd ed., pp. 380–402). Oxford, England: Basil Blackwell.

Latané, B. (1981). The psychology of social impact. *American Psychologist, 36,* 343–356.

Lorenz, K. Z. (1970). *Studies on animal and human behavior* (Vols. I and 2). Cambridge, MA: Harvard University Press.

Lorenz, K. Z. (1973). The biology of expression and impression. In K. Z. Lorenz & P. Leyhausen (Eds.), *Motivation of human and animal behavior: An ethological view.* New York: Van Nostrand Reinhold.

Mandler, G. (1975). *Mind and emotion.* New York: Wiley.

Marler, P., & Mitani, J. (1988). Vocal communication in primates and birds: Parallels and contrasts. In D. Todt, P. Goedeking, & D. Symmes (Eds.), *Primate vocal communication* (pp. 3–14). West Berlin, Federal Republic of Germany: Springer-Verlag.

Masters, W. H., Johnson, V. E., & Kolodny, R. C. (1985). *Human sexuality* (2nd ed.). Boston: Little, Brown.

Mead, G. H. (1934). *Mind, self, and society from the standpoint of a social behaviorist.* Chicago: University of Chicago Press.

Milgram, S. (1974). *Obedience to authority.* New York: Harper & Row.

Moore, D. L., & Baron, R. S. (1983). Social facilitation: A psychophysiological analysis. In J. T. Cacioppo & R. E. Petty (Eds.), *Social psychophysiology: A sourcebook* (pp. 434–466). New York: Guilford Press.

O'Brien, R. G., & Kaiser, M. (1985). MANOVA method for analyzing repeated measures designs: An extensive primer. *Psychological Bulletin, 97,* 316–331.

Orne, M. T. (1962). On the social psychology of the psychological experiment: With particular reference to demand characteristics and their implication. *American Psychologist, 17,* 776-783.

Patterson, M. (1983). *Nonverbal behavior: A functional perspective.* New York: Springer-Verlag.

Piderit, T. (1886). *Expression and physiognomy.* In A. J. Fridlund (Ed.) & L. H. W. Fajardo (Trans.). Manuscript in preparation. (Original work published 1886)

Plutchik, R. (1981). *Emotion: A psychoevolutionary synthesis.* New York: Harper & Row.

Provine, R. R., & Fischer K. R. (1989). Laughing, smiling, and talking: Relation to sleeping and social context in humans. *Ethology, 83,* 295–305.

Ribot, T. (1897). *The psychology of the emotions.* London: Scott.

Schlenker, B. R. (1980). *Impression management.* Monterey, CA: Brooks-Cole.

Schlenker, B. R. (Ed.). (1985). *The self and social life.* New York: McGraw Hill.

Schlenker, B. R., & Weigold, M. F. (1989). Goals and the self-identification process: Constructing desired identities. In L. A. Pervin (Ed.), *Goal concepts in personality and social psychology.* Hillsdale, NJ: Erlbaum.

Schwartz, G. E., Fair, P. L., Salt, P., Mandel, M. R., & Klerman, G. L. (1976). Facial muscle patterning to affective imagery in depressed and nondepressed subjects. *Science, 192,* 489.

Skinner, B. F. (1957). *Verbal behavior.* New York: Appleton-Century-Crofts.

Smith, W. J. (1977). *The behavior of communicating.* Cambridge, MA: Harvard University Press.

Snyder, M. (1979). Self-monitoring processes. In L. Berkowitz (Ed.), *Advances in experimental social psychology* (Vol. 12, pp. 85–128). San Diego, CA: Academic Press.

Stanislavski, K. S. (1965). *Creating a role.* (H. I. Popper, Ed., & E. R. Hapgood, Trans.). New York: Theatre Arts.

Stevens, S. S. (1956). The direct estimation of sensory magnitudes—Loudness. *American Journal of Psychology, 69,* 1–25.

Tassinary, L. G., Cacioppo, J. T., & Geen, T. R. (1989). A psychometric study of surface electrode placements for facial electromyographic recording: I. The brow and cheek muscle regions. *Psychophysiology, 26,* 1–16.

Tinbergen, N. (1952). "Derived" activities: Their causation, biological significance, origin and emancipation during evolution. *Quarterly Review of Biology, 27,* 1–32.

Tomkins, S. S. (1962). *Affect, imagery, consciousness: Vol. I. The positive affects.* New York: Springer.

Tomkins, S. S. (1963). *Affect, imagery, consciousness: Vol. 2. The negative affects.* New York: Springer.

Vaughan, K. B., & Lanzetta, J. T. (1980). Vicarious instigation and conditioning of facial expressive and autonomic responses to a model's expressive display of pain. *Journal of Personality and Social Psychology, 38,* 909–923.

Vygotsky, L. S. (1962). *Thought and language.* Cambridge, MA: MIT Press.

Shame, Guilt, Envy, and Jealousy

Up to this point, the articles in this book have tended to address emotions collectively. The emphasis has been upon emotion as a general phenomenon, or upon what is generally true of a diverse group of emotions. A few articles have focused on a particular emotion, such as jealousy in the case of sex differences, or embarrassment in the case of social function, or depression in the case of social contagion, but the emphasis has been on the general category of emotion. The final two parts of this book break away from this generalization to focus on specific emotions.

The number of specific emotions that interest social psychologists is very large. The overview chapter in this volume provided some idea of the range and scope of emotions that affect social life. In the remaining two sections of this book it is possible only to sample some of the most important, interesting, and well-studied emotions. One of these, anger, will be the topic of the concluding section. In this penultimate section are three articles that examine four emotions that are particularly interesting from a social point of view: shame, guilt, envy, and jealousy.

In the first article, Tangney, Wagner, Fletcher, and Gramzow (1992) examine how shame and guilt might be linked to anger, hostility, and aggression. June Tangney's research has been at the forefront of a movement to investigate the nature of shame and guilt and examine how they are related to other social phenomena. In the two studies reported in this article, individual-differences methodology is used to assess the relation between shame and guilt with anger and hostility. That is, the research asks whether people who tend to experience shame or tend to experience guilt also tend to exhibit anger, hostility, and aggression. The results suggest that shame-proneness is positively correlated with the tendencies to experience anger and hostility, although not with aggression. Guilt-proneness, in contrast, was not so correlated, and in fact tended to exhibit a slight negative correlation with all these constructs.

Two aspects of this article have influenced later research. The first has to do with the functions of shame and guilt. The implication of this and other research by Tangney (1991) is that guilt plays a useful function by increasing interpersonal empathy and motivating repair of any harm that was done, whereas shame is less useful motivating social withdrawal, self-contempt, and socially dangerous anger and hostility. This implication has attracted the interest of many researchers. For example, Kitayama, Markus, and Matsumoto (1995) have proposed that shame may function quite differently in a more inter-dependent culture such as that of Japan. And numerous researchers have suggested that even in Western cultures shame and guilt can function adaptively or maladaptively depending on a subtle variety of factors (e.g., Lindsay-Hartz, de Rivera, & Mascolo, 1995; Sabini & Silver, 1997).

The second important issue raised by this article is the difficulty of defining these complex social emotions. There is considerable disagreement among psychologists about just how to define shame and guilt: what appraisals lead to them, how to they affect people's thoughts, feelings, motivations, and behavior? Tangney adheres to an approach originating in the mid-twentieth-century that distinguishes shame from guilt largely based on the focus of the appraisal: shame concerns the whole self, whereas guilt concerns a particular action or effect one is responsible for. This definition has a number of advan-tages, but it is not the only possible one. An older distinction, for example, construed shame as a reaction to others' disapproval, and guilt as a reaction of one's own inner conscience. It is important to study groups of easily confused emotions, such as shame and guilt, so that the advantages of different definitions can be considered.

The second article in this section, by Baumeister, Stillwell, and Heatherton (1995), proposes that important aspects of guilt can be appreciated only by considering the social nature of guilt. These authors do not dispute the distinction between guilt and shame used by Tangney, but they do dispute the completeness of an intrapsychic account of this emotion. Guilt, they point out, occurs primarily in the context of ongoing relationships. It may be triggered by a failure to meet another's standards or expectations, or merely by inequities that favor oneself or accidents that harm another. Guilt plays a role in inter-personal dynamics and strategic positioning within rela-tionships, as shown people's attempting to manipulate guilt feelings in others. Furthermore, guilt has a number of effects that tend to heal relationships. The authors build a strong case for the social nature of guilt. The tension be-tween intropsychic and social accounts of emotions that these readings demonstrate for guilt is a general theme in the psychology of emotion. In the next section of this book we will see that anger can be understood in both ways too.

To gather information about the nature of guilt, Baumeister, Stillwell, and Heatherton used the technique of autobiographical narrative. Asking people to remember and describe a personal experience of an emotion is a useful technique for learning about emotions that cannot, for pragmatic or ethical reasons, be elicited in the laboratory. It is also useful for learning about emotions in their natural context. The technique usually involves collecting accounts of more than one type so that they can be compared. In the first study reported, memories of transgressions leading to guilt were compared to memories of transgressions not leading to guilt; in the second stuy, memories of being made to feel guilty were compared to memories of making another person feel guilty. Subsequent readings in this volume will provide further examples of this technique: The next reading in this section compares memories of envy with those of jealousy, and one article in the next section of this book (Reading 21) compares being angry at someone with being the target of someone's anger. In all these cases one should keep in mind that the technique has limitations as well as advantages. Autobiographical memories often involve a mix of emotions, and they often vary in more ways than would be the case in a controlled experiment. The memories that are recalled are not always of the type that was requested. The data consists of people's recollections of emotions, so distortions and omissions may be present. Nevertheless, autobiographical narratives allow researchers an opportunity to study the rich tapestry of emotions that occur in actual social life.

The final article in this section (Parrott, 1991) addresses two other emotions that are often confused: envy and jealousy. One point made in this article is that the envy and jealousy can be distinguished from each other both in terms of the situations that lead to them and in terms of the emotional experiences themselves. Envy occurs in situations where a person longs for something that someone else has but the envious person lacks. A quite different situation gives rise to jealousy: A person is threatened with the loss of an important relationship to a rival. The article presents evidence that envy and jealousy are experienced differently as well. One reason for the confusion of these emotions is that the English word "jealousy" can be applied to both emotions. Calling the former "envy" and the latter "jealousy" helps clarify matters a bit.

A second point made in this article is that neither envy nor jealousy consists of a single, invarient emotion. Rather, there are subtypes of both envy and jealousy, and the article sets out a number of important ones. Envy can come in both hostile and nonhostile forms. Jealousy can occur in response to threats that are only suspected, as well as to threats that are fully realized and have resulted in the loss of the relationship. Each of the subtypes involves several component feelings. The idea that emotion words do not correspond in a one-to-one fashion with emotional states is an important one that can be fruitfully applied to other emotions as well.

Finally, like the articles on shame and guilt, this one places envy and jealousy in their social context. Both have social origins: envy in social comparison, jealousy in relationships. Both, in their hurtful ways, demonstrate the social origins of our sense of self. In contrast to the articles on sexual jealousy (Readings 6 & 7), this article makes clear that jealousy occurs in a variety of relationships and involves a rich and varied emotional experience. Finally, like shame and guilt, envy and jealousy play a rich and varied role in our social and moral lives.

REFERENCES

Baumeister, R. F., Stillwell, A. M., & Heatherton, T. F. (1995). Interpersonal aspect of guilt: Evidence from narrative studies. J. P. Tangney & K. W. Fischer (Eds), Self-conscioius emotions: The psychology of shame, guilt, embarrassment, and pride (pp. 255–273). New York: Guilford.

Kitayama, S., Markus, H. R., & Matsumoto, H. (1995). Culture, self, and emotion: A cultural perspective on "self-conscious" emotions. In J. P. Tangney & K. W. Fischer (Eds.), *Self-conscious emotions: The psychology of shame, guilt, embarrassment, and pride* (pp. 439–464). New York: Guilford.

Lindsay-Hartz, J., de Rivera, J., & Mascolo, M. F. (1995). Differentiating guilt and shame and their effects on motivation. In J. P. Tangney & K. W. Fischer (Eds.), *Self-con-scious emotions: The psychology of shame, guilt, embarrassment, and pride* (pp. 274–300). New York: Guilford.

Parrott, W. G. (1991). The emotional experiences of envy and jealousy. In P. Salovey (Ed.), *The psychology of jealousy and envy* (pp. 3–30). New York: Guilford.

Sabini, J., & Silver, M. (1997). In defense of shame: Shame in the context of guilt and embarrassment. *Journal for the Theory of Social Behaviour, 27*, 1–15.

Tangney, J. P. (1991). Moral affect: The good, the bad, and the ugly. *Journal of Personality and Social Psychology, 61*, 598–607.

Tangney, J. P., Wagner, P., Fletcher, C., & Gramzow, R. (1992). Shamed into anger? The relation of shame and guilt to anger and self-reported aggression. *Journal of Personality and Social Psychology, 62*, 669–675.

Discussion Questions

1. Discuss what the words "shame" and "guilt" mean in everyday life. How do the everyday meanings compare with the academic approaches you have read?
2. It is sometimes said in the United States that various national problems have arisen because the nation has "lost its sense of shame." What is meant by that explanation, and how does it pertain to research findings on the function or dysfunction of shame and guilt?
3. What are communal and exchange relationships, and how do they apply to the experience and function of guilt?
4. In Western cultures we have become used to thinking of emotions as intrapsychic phenomena, as happening inside of a single person. But in other cultures, and increasingly in psychology, emotions are viewed as occurring between people, or to relationships. How might guilt or anger be understood as something that happens within a social relationship?

Suggested Readings

Tangney, J. P. & Fischer, K. W. (Eds.). (1995). *Self-conscious emotions: The psychology of shame, guilt, embarrassment, and pride*. New York: Guilford. Readers wanting to learn about a variety of contemporary approaches to self-conscious emotions would do well to start with this book, from which the reading by Baumeister, Stillwell, and Heatherton was taken. It includes chapters by many of the leading researchers in social and developmental psychology.

Miller, R. S. (1996). *Embarrassment: Poise and peril in everyday life.* New York: Guilford. Embarrassment arguably has a much greater impact on everyday life than it is usually given credit for. This readable book provides an interesting and accessible introduction.

De Rivera, J. (1984). The structure of emotional relationships. In P. Shaver (Ed.), *Review of personality and social psychology, Vol. 5: Emotions, relationships, and health* (pp. 116–145). Beverly Hills, CA: Sage. Those interested in understanding the sense in which emotions occur beyond the individual psyche may find this chapter by Joseph de Rivera to be helpful. It sets out some of the assumptions behind what some find to be a counterintuitive idea.

Salovey, P. (Ed.) (1991). *The psychology of jealousy and envy.* New York: Guilford. Most of the leading social psychologists doing research on envy or jealousy contributed a chapter to this volume, which therefore makes a good resource for those wishing to learn more about these emotions.

Schoeck, H. (1969). *Envy: A theory of social behaviour* (M. Glenny & B. Ross, Trans). Indianapolis, IN: Liberty Press. (Original work published 1966) This book surveys envy in all its aspects, drawing on all the social sciences and humanities. Helmut Schoeck is a sociologist, who advances the interesting (if controversial) thesis that cultural differences in permitting or punishing expressions of envy impact a society's productivity and innovation by holding back or liberating that society's most talented members. This thesis is a good example of examining the functions of emotions at the cultural level of analysis (see Reading 9).

Salovey, P., & Rodin, J. (1984). Some antecedents and consequences of social-comparison jealousy. *Journal of Personality and Social Psychology, 47,* 780–792. Emotions such as envy, jealousy, shame, and guilt are difficult to study in the laboratory, but this experiment proves that it can be done. This carefully designed experiment investigated the eliciting conditions for envy. The findings suggest that envy occurs only when one is inferior to another person in a domain that is particularly self-defining.

Shamed Into Anger? The Relation of Shame and Guilt to Anger and Self-Reported Aggression

June Price Tangney, Patricia Wagner, Carey Fletcher, and Richard Gramzow
• George Mason University

The relation of shame and guilt to anger and aggression has been the focus of considerable theoretical discussion, but empirical findings have been inconsistent. Two recently developed measures of affective style were used to examine whether shame-proneness and guilt-proneness are differentially related to anger, hostility, and aggression. In 2 studies, 243 and 252 undergraduates completed the Self-Conscious Affect and Attribution Inventory, the Symptom Checklist 90, and the Spielberger Trait Anger Scale. Study 2 also included the Test of Self-Conscious Affect and the Buss-Durkee Hostility Inventory. Shame-proneness was consistently correlated with anger arousal, suspiciousness, resentment, irritability, a tendency to blame others for negative events, and indirect (but not direct) expressions of hostility. Proneness to "shame-free" guilt was inversely related to externalization of blame and some indices of anger, hostility and resentment.

Shame and guilt are often mentioned in the same breath as moral emotions that each motivate self-regulatory processes, including the regulation of hostility and aggression (Ausubel, 1955; Damon, 1988). Whether conceptualized as super-ego derivatives or as self-mediated punishment, these negative emotions are generally presumed to inhibit the expression of socially and morally unacceptable impulses, most notably in the domains of sex and aggression.

It is surprising, then, that little empirical work has been conducted to examine the relation of shame and guilt to anger, hostility and aggression. The few extant studies have, for the most part, focused on guilt. Using the Hostility–Guilt subscale from the Mosher Forced-Choice Guilt Inventory (Mosher, 1966), a number of investigations have provided evidence of an inverse relationship between guilt and hostility and aggression (Abramson, Mosher, Abramson, & Woychowski,

1977; Ackerman, McMahon, & Fehr, 1984; Fehr, 1979; Mosher, Mortimer, & Grebel, 1968; Schill, 1972; Schill & Schneider, 1970). The Hostility–Guilt scale, however, can be viewed more specifically as an index of aggression anxiety. Findings involving Morality–Conscience, a more general guilt subscale derived from the Mosher Inventory, have been less consistent (e.g., Abramson et al., 1977). Similarly, the Guilt scale derived from the Buss-Durkee Hostility Inventory appears generally unrelated to indices of overt aggression and covert hostility (Buss & Durkee, 1957). And in a more recent study using the Personal Feelings Questionnaire (Harder & Lewis, 1986), both the Guilt and the Shame scales were positively correlated with the Multiple Affect Adjective Check List (MAACL) Hostility scale.

The lack of consistency in the empirical literature dealing with guilt and hostility–aggression may exist partly because psychologists often fail to make a distinction between shame and guilt. The Buss-Durkee Guilt scale, for example, explicitly includes both shame and guilt items, and the Mosher Morality–Conscience scale similarly can be viewed as an index of shame–guilt. Although Harder and Lewis (1986) have attempted to differentiate between proneness to shame and proneness to guilt with their Personal Feelings Questionnaire (PFQ), there is some question whether the measurement approach used in the PFQ (global ratings of the self's general affective experience) is more appropriate to the assessment of shame than of guilt (Tangney, Wagner, & Gramzow, 1992).

The distinction between shame and guilt is an important one. A growing theoretical and empirical literature underlines important differences in the phenomenology of these two emotions (DeRivera, 1977; Lewis, 1971; Lindsay-Hartz, 1984; Tangney, 1989; Weiner, 1985; Wicker, Payne, & Morgan, 1983)—differences that may have differential implications for the experience and regulation of hostility and aggression. In summary, shame and guilt both involve negative affect, but the focus of the negative affect differs, leading to distinct phenomenological experiences. In guilt, the object of concern is some specific action (or failure to act). Thus, in guilt, behavior is evaluated somewhat apart from the self. There is remorse or regret over the "bad thing" that was done and a sense of tension that often serves to motivate reparative action.

The tension, remorse, and regret of guilt can be quite uncomfortable, particularly when reparation is blocked for one reason or another. Nonetheless, the shame experience is far more painful and devastating. In shame, the object of concern is the entire self. The "bad thing" is experienced as a reflection of a "bad self," and the entire self is painfully scrutinized and negatively evaluated. With this painful scrutiny of the self, there is a corresponding sense of shrinking, of being small, and of being worthless and powerless. Shame also involves a sense of exposure. In introducing the notion of an "internalized other" Lewis (1971) extended the definition of shame beyond an affective reaction to public disapproval. But there is typically the imagery of an explicit or implicit disapproving other. Even when alone, the disapproving self imagines how the self (as disapproved object) might look to another. Thus, it is not surprising that the person in the midst of the shame experi-

ence often wants to hide from others generally, and more specifically to remove himself or herself from any interpersonal situation that may have given rise to this experience.

One of the many consistent findings reported in these phenomenological studies (Lewis, 1971; Lindsay-Hartz, 1984; Tangney, 1989; Wicker, Payne, & Morgan, 1983) is that the motivational components of shame stand in sharp contrast to those of guilt. Whereas guilt motivates a desire to repair, to confess, apologize, or make amends, shame motivates a desire to hide—to sink into the floor and disappear.

There are also suggestions in the theoretical and clinical literature that shame can motivate anger as well—in particular, a kind of hostile, humiliated fury. Lewis (1971) first noted this link between shame and humiliated fury in her clinical case studies. According to Lewis, in shame, hostility is initially directed toward the self. But because shame also involves the imagery of a rejecting, disapproving other, this hostility is easily redirected in retaliation toward the rejecting other. Lewis sees this as a defensive maneuver—an attempt to turn the tables and to right the self, which has been impaired in the shame experience. It is an ill-fated defense, however. At some level, the shamed individual recognizes this humiliated fury as inappropriate or unjust (Lewis, 1987), and this recognition may lead to further shame or guilt.

In an independent series of case studies, Miller (1985) identified two types of shame-anger interactions. When initially angered, one can become ashamed of the anger. More often, an initial sense of shame can lead to subsequent anger toward a shaming other. Miller views both types of affective interactions as essentially defensive in nature. In the anger-to-shame sequence, the individual moves from an active stance to a passive state, taking refuge in the passive and disabling shame experience, escaping aggression by dismantling the active self. In the shame-to-anger sequence, the process is reversed. From the initial passive and disabling experience of shame, the individual attempts to mobilize the self and gain control through active anger and aggression.

The consistent theme emerging from these and other case studies and clinical observations (e.g., Kinston, 1987; Nathanson 1987; Retzinger, 1987; Scheff, 1987) is that, rather than curbing hostile and aggressive impulses, shame tends to *initiate* a particular type of anger episode, namely, an irrational and generally counterproductive rage reaction.

Shame has not been considered explicitly in the vast empirical literature on aggression, but the results from several lines of inquiry are suggestive. In many of the frustration-aggression studies, for example (e.g., Geen & Berkowitz, 1967), it was not frustration per se that led to aggression, but frustration in conjunction with arbitrary and unwarranted provocation. These latter manipulations often represented efforts at humiliation and embarrassment—in a word, *shame*. It was the apparently shamed participants who exhibited elevated levels of aggression. At a more general level, Berkowitz's (1983, 1989) studies linking negative affect to anger and aggression are also relevant. Numerous studies have indicated that shame is an acutely painful affective experience (Lindsay-Hartz, 1984; Tangney, 1989; Wicker Payne, & Morgan, 1983). Thus, the pain of shame, itself, may foster anger and perhaps aggression.

Perhaps the most direct empirical evidence linking shame to anger come from studies by Averill (1982), Wicker, Payne, and Morgan (1983), Harder and Lewis (1986), and Tangney (1990). In Averill's studies, participants' descriptions of anger experiences indicated that a common cause of anger is a "loss of personal pride" or loss of self-esteem—very likely shame-related experiences. In Wicker et al.'s (1983) study, participants' ratings of shame experiences indicated that shame led not only to a desire to hide, but also to a desire to punish others. In Harder and Lewis's (1986) study, shame-proneness, as assessed by the PFQ, was positively correlated with the MAACL Hostility scale. Finally, in four independent studies of adults, Tangney (1990) reported a consistent positive relationship between proneness to shame and a tendency to externalize blame, in contrast to negative or negligible correlations between externalization and proneness to guilt. Such externalization of blame may ameliorate the pain of shame in the short run, but it can lead either to subsequent withdrawal from the blamed person or to an exacerbation of the hostile, humiliated fury described by Lewis (1971) and Scheff (1987).

In summary, there has been little systematic empirical effort to delineate the differential relation of shame and guilt to anger and aggression. Nonetheless, psychological theory, clinical observations, and some empirical evidence suggest a positive link between shame and anger and aggression. In contrast, although the empirical evidence is mixed, psychological theory suggests an inverse relationship between guilt and anger and aggression.

In the current two studies, we used the recently developed Self-Conscious Affect and Attribution Inventory (SCAAI; Tangney, Burggraf, Hamme, & Domingos, 1988), a scenario-based measure of proneness to shame, proneness to guilt, and externalization of blame, to more directly examine the differential relation of shame and guilt to anger, hostility, and aggression. In Study 1, participants completed the SCAAI, the Trait Anger Scale (TAS; Spielberger, Jacobs, Russell, & Crane, 1983), and the Symptom Checklist 90 (SCL-90; Derogatis, Lipman, & Covi, 1973). The SCL-90 provides two subscales that are particularly relevant here: Anger–Hostility (assessing the frequency and degree to which respondents experience and express anger, hostility, and annoyance) and Paranoid Ideation (assessing feelings of distrust, but also externalization of blame and the imagery of exposure).

In Study 2, we expanded our assessment of shame and guilt, as well as anger, hostility, and aggression. In addition to the SCAAI, participants completed the Test of Self-Conscious Affect (TOSCA), a revised version of the SCAAI constructed from subject-generated scenarios and responses. As in the previous study, participants completed the TAS and the SCL-90. In addition, they were administered the Buss-Durkee Hostility Inventory (Buss & Durkee, 1957), which provides a variety of indices of hostility and self-reported aggression.

We expected to replicate the previous finding of a link between shame and externalization of blame (Tangney, 1990), and we anticipated a substantial positive relationship between proneness to shame and anger, hostility, and self-reported aggression, consistent with the theoretical and clinical literature on shame. In contrast, we expected guilt-proneness to be inversely related to indices of externalization of blame, anger, hostility, and self-reported aggression.

Method

PARTICIPANTS

Participants in Study 1 were 243 undergraduates attending a large east-coast state university who received credit toward an undergraduate course requirement in return for their participation. The students ranged in age from 18 to 55 years old ($M = 21.1$); 71% were female; 77% were White, 5% were Black, 13% were Asian, and 6% had some other ethnic background. In regard to religious affiliation in childhood, 39% reported it as Catholic, 32% Protestant, 4% Jewish, 13% other, and 12% no affiliation.

Participants in Study 2 were 252 undergraduates attending a large east-coast state university who received credit toward an undergraduate course requirement in return for their participation. The students ranged in age from 17 to 35 years old ($M = 19.4$); 71% were female; 81% were White, 6% were Black, 9% were Asian, and 4% had some other ethnic background. In regard to religious affiliation in childhood, 36% reported it as Catholic, 22% Protestant, 3% Jewish, 22% other, and 16% no affiliation.

MEASURES AND PROCEDURES

The data reported here were collected as part of two larger investigations of the personality and cognitive correlates of proneness to shame and proneness to guilt. Students in Study 1 participated in two sessions and students in Study 2 participated in four sessions. The sessions lasted from 30 to 60 min each and were conducted on separate days. At the beginning of the studies, informed consent forms were distributed that described the general nature of the procedures. Participants were advised that the investigation was "a psychological study to learn more about emotions, perceptions, and styles of thinking among normal, young adults." The voluntary, confidential, and anonymous nature of the study was emphasized, and students were asked not to write their names on any of the study questionnaires.

Questionnaires were coded with unique ID numbers in advance. At the end of each session, participants were asked to write on a Post-it Note a unique and easily remembered pseudonym. The Post-it Note was affixed to the questionnaire packet for the subsequent session. On their return for a subsequent session, participants were asked to recall their pseudonym, and the Post-it Note was removed, leaving the questionnaires indexed by ID numbers only. In this way, it was possible to link questionnaires across sessions while preserving participants' anonymity. In only one case was

a participant unable to recall his pseudonym. This participant from Study 2 was excused from subsequent sessions. The following were among the measures completed by participants.

Self-Conscious Affect and Attribution Inventory (SCAAI; Tangney, et al., 1988). The SCAAI is designed to assess characteristic affective, cognitive, and behavioral responses associated with shame, guilt, externalization of blame, detachment–unconcern, and pride. The SCAAI is a paper-and-pencil measure composed of 13 brief scenarios that college students would be likely to encounter in day-to-day life. The 10 negatively valenced scenarios are followed, in random order, by responses indicating shame, guilt, externalization, and detachment–unconcern. Three positively valenced scenarios are followed by responses indicating shame, guilt, externalization, alpha pride (pride in self), and beta pride (pride in behavior). The SCAAI is not a forced-choice measure. Subjects rate, on a 5-point scale, their likelihood of responding in each of the manners indicated. Relevant items are summed across scenarios to create indices of shame-proneness, guilt-proneness, externalization, detachment–unconcern, alpha pride, and beta pride. In previous reports, we have presented data supporting the reliability and construct validity of the central scales of the SCA/A I (Tangney, 1990, 1991; Tangney, et al., 1988). Shame and Guilt scales demonstrated satisfactory reliability, as indicated by analyses of their internal consistency (.60–.82 across four studies) and test-retest stability (.79 for shame and .73 for guilt). Regarding validity, the interrelationship among SCAAI subscales and their relation to other measures of shame and guilt indicate that the SCAAI yields related, but functionally distinct indices of proneness to shame and proneness to guilt in a way that other measures have not. Moreover, across several independent studies, shame has been consistently linked to low self-esteem, numerous indices of psychopathology, an impaired capacity for empathy, and dysfunctional family relationships (Burggraf & Tangney, 1989; Hamme, 1990; Tangney, 1991; Tangney, Wagner, & Gramzow, 1992). Guilt, on the other hand, has been consistently positively related to interpersonal empathy and negatively related to a detached–unconcerned attitude toward negative interpersonal events and a hostile sense of humor, which is found particularly when the unique variance in guilt is considered (Gessner & Tangney, 1990; Tangney, 1990, 1991).

In Study 1, estimates of internal consistency (Cronbach's alpha) for the SCAAI Shame and Guilt scales were .75 and .65, respectively. In Study 2, estimates of internal consistency for the SCAAI Shame and Guilt scales were .78 and .70, respectively.

Test of Self-Conscious Affect (TOSCA; Tangney, et al., 1989). The TOSCA was modeled after the SCAAI. The TOSCA also consists of a series of brief scenarios (10 negative and 5 positive) and associated responses, yielding indices of shame-proneness, guilt-proneness, externalization, detachment-unconcern, alpha pride, and beta pride. This entirely new set of scenarios was drawn from written accounts of personal shame, guilt, and pride experiences provided by a sample of several hundred college students and adults not attending college. The new responses were drawn from a much larger pool of affective, cognitive, and behavioral responses provided by a second sample of adults not attending college. The TOSCA has several advantages over the original SCAAI. First, the items were subject generated rather than experimenter generated, enhancing the ecological validity of the measure. Second, the items am appropriate for adults of all ages, not specifically college students. Third, in terms of reliability and validity, our preliminary analyses indicate that the TOSCA is equivalent to, and in some respects more psychometrically sound than, the SCAAI. For example, test-retest reliability in a previous sample of 44 undergraduates was .85 and .74 for shame and guilt, respectively.

The TOSCA was administered to participants in Study 2 only. Estimates of internal consistency (Cronbach's alpha) for the TOSCA Shame and Guilt scales were .76 and .66, respectively.[1]

Symptom Checklist 90 (SCL-90; Derogatis, et al., 1973). The SCL-90 is a self-report clinical rating scale composed of 90 symptoms. Participants rate each item on a 5-point scale to indicate absence or intensity. The SCL-90 is a widely used rating scale, appropriate for psychiatric outpatients as well as for screening nonclinical populations. Two of the nine clinical subscales am particularly relevant to the question of anger and aggression—the Hostility scale and the Paranoid Ideation scale. Numerous studies support the reliability and validity of the SCL-90 (e.g., Derogatis, 1989; Derogatis & Cleary, 1977; Derogatis, Rickels, & Rock, 1976). In both of the current studies, estimates of internal consistency (Cronbach's alpha)

for the Hostility subscale were .82. Estimates of internal consistency (Cronbach's alpha) for the Paranoid Ideation subscale were .66 and .76 for Study 1 and Study 2, respectively.

Trait Anger Scale (TAS; Spielberger et al., 1983). The TAS is composed of 15 items, each rated on a 4-point scale. Two four-item subscales, Anger Temperament and Anger Reactivity, can also be derived from the TAS. Spielberger et al. (1983) presented data supporting the reliability and validity of this measure. In the current studies, estimates of internal consistency (Cronbach's alpha) for the Anger Temperament and Anger Reactivity subscales ranged from .65 to .88 ($M = .78$). Estimates of internal consistency (Cronbach's alpha) for the total TAS were .89 and .85 for Study 1 and Study 2, respectively.

Buss-Durkee Hostility Inventory (Buss & Durkee, 1957). The Buss-Durkee Hostility Inventory, one of the most widely used, well-validated measures of hostility, is composed of 75 items. In the current study, participants rated each item on a 5-point scale. The inventory yields seven hostility scales: Assault (a direct physical aggression scale assessing physical violence against others), Verbal Hostility (assessing direct verbal aggression), Indirect Hostility (assessing indirect and undirected hostility), Irritability (e.g., grouchiness, exasperation, and rudeness), Negativism (assessing passive and active oppositional behavior), Resentment (assessing anger over real or imagined mistreatment), and Suspicion (assessing mistrust and projection of hostility onto others). The inventory also yields a nine-item Guilt scale that assesses feelings of guilt and remorse, as well as feelings of shame. As noted above, the Buss-Durkee Guilt scale might be more correctly labeled a measure of guilt-shame.

The Buss-Durkee Hostility Inventory was administered to participants in Study 2 only. Estimates of internal consistency (Cronbach's alpha) for the inventory subscales ranged from .57 for Indirect Hostility to .78 for Assault ($M = .68$).

In Study 1, participants completed the SCAAI and the SCL-90 in Session 1 and the TAS in Ses-

---

[1] The Study 2 sample was initially randomly split, and item analyses were conducted on one half to select the final 15 TOSCA scenarios from a larger pool of scenarios. Thus, the reliability estimates reported here are based only on the second half of the sample. (Item analyses involved only the TOSCA items; none of the other measures used in the study were considered in the preliminary analyses of the TOSCA.)

sion 2. In Study 2, participants completed the TOSCA in Session 1 and the SCAAI, the SCL-90, the TAS, and the Buss-Durkee Inventory in Session 2.

Results

SHAME-PRONENESS, GUILT-PRONENESS, AND EXTERNALIZATION

Table 17.1 presents the correlations of proneness to shame and proneness to guilt with externalization of blame from Study 1 and Study 2. In Study 2, correlations are presented for both the SCAAI and the TOSCA. In both studies, the tendency to experience shame across a range of situations was strongly correlated with a tendency to externalize cause or blame. In contrast, the bivariate correlations indicate that proneness to guilt is essentially orthogonal to externalization.

Across numerous studies, we have found a substantial positive correlation between shame-proneness and guilt-proneness as assessed by the SCAAI (Tangney, 1990). This covariation between measures of shame and guilt no doubt reflects the fact that shame and guilt share a number of features in common (e.g., both are dysphoric affects that involve internal attributions of one sort or another) and that these affects can be experienced in tandem (Lewis, 1971). In the current studies, SCAAI shame and guilt were correlated .46 and .63[2] (Studies 1 and 2, respectively) and TOSCA shame and guilt were correlated .45. To further refine our analyses, we conducted part correlations, factoring out shame from guilt and vice versa.

The part correlations show an even clearer pattern of results, replicating our previous findings (Tangney, 1990). Across both studies and both measures, shame residuals were consistently posi-

tively correlated with externalization. Guilt residuals were consistently negatively correlated with externalization. Thus, individuals who tend to experience "shame-free" guilt are not prone to externalize blame. Rather, they appear to accept responsibility for negative interpersonal events. On the other hand, shame-prone individuals appear generally disposed to feel badly about themselves while also blaming others for negative events, perhaps as a means of defending against the overwhelming global experience of shame. This pattern of results raises the question of whether shame-prone individuals are also more prone to anger and other-directed hostility.

SHAME-PRONENESS AND GUILT-PRONENESS AND ANGER, HOSTILITY AND AGGRESSION

Table 17.2 presents the Study 1 correlations of proneness to shame and proneness to guilt with the TAS and the Anger-Hostility and Paranoid Ideation scales from the SCL-90. Considering the bivariate correlations, shame-proneness was positively related to all indices of anger and hostility, with the exception of the Anger Temperament subscale, for which the correlation was negligible. On the other hand, guilt-proneness was generally orthogonal to measures of anger and hostility. There was a statistically significant positive bivariate correlation between Guilt and Paranoid Ideation, but part correlational analyses revealed that this moderate correlation was entirely due to the shared variance between shame and guilt. Indeed, when considering the part correlations, guilt residuals were significantly negatively correlated with trait anger.

Table 17.3 presents the Study 2 correlations of proneness to shame and proneness to guilt with indices of anger, hostility, and aggression, including those derived from the Buss-Durkee Inventory. Correlations involving the SCAAI Shame and Guilt scales appear below those involving the

TABLE 17.1. Relation of Shame-Proneness and Guilt-Proneness to Externalization of Blame

| Externalization | Bivariate correlation | | Part correlation | |
	Shame	Guilt	Shame residual	Guilt residual
Study 1—SCAAI	.21***	−.06	.27***	−.18**
Study 2—SCAAI	.32***	.02	.40***	−.24**
Study 2—TOSCA	.40***	.07	.41***	−.12*

Note. Ns = 243–251. SCAAI = Self-Conscious Affect and Attribution Inventory; TOSCA = Test of Self-Conscious Affect.
*p < .05. **p < .01. ***p < .001.

[2] The correlation between the SCAAI shame and guilt measures in Study 2 was substantially higher than expected. In five previous studies using the SCAAI, shame-guilt correlations have ranged from .43 to .48. An inspection of the joint distribution for Study 2 revealed 5 outliers. These 5 participants had responded rather idiosyncratically to the SCAAI, primarily making use of the extreme ends of the 5-point rating scale. Apart from these 5 outliers, the Study 2 sample often substantial nonshared shame and guilt variance as observed in previous samples.

TABLE 17.2. Relation of Anger-Hostility to Shame-Proneness and Guilt-Proneness: Study 1

Measure	Bivariate correlation		Part correlation	
	Shame	Guilt	Shame residual	Guilt residual
Trait Anger Scale				
Trait Anger	.17*	−.04	.21**	−.13*
Anger Temperament	.03	−.07	.06	−.09
Anger Reactivity	.15*	.04	.14*	−.03
SCL-90				
Anger–Hostility	.13*	.02	.13*	−.04
Paranoid Ideation	.23***	.14*	.19**	.04

Note: Ns = 228–242. SCL-90 = Symptom Checklist 90.
*p < .05. **p < .01. ***p < .001.

TOSCA Shame and Guilt scales. The results of study 2 replicate and extend those of Study 1. Shame-proneness was consistently and substantially correlated with indices of anger, hostility, irritability, resentment, suspiciousness, and paranoid ideation. This held true for shame scales derived from both the SCAAI and TOSCA measures and when both bivariate and part correlations (when guilt was factored out from shame) were considered. In contrast, when the bivariate correlations were considered, guilt-proneness showed little consistent relationship to these measures. Part correlational analyses revealed that the occasional modest positive correlation between guilt and anger or suspiciousness was entirely due to the shared variance between shame and guilt. As in Study 1, results involving the guilt residuals indicate that, in fact, shame-free guilt is inversely related to anger, resentment, and suspiciousness, particularly as assessed by the SCL-90 and Buss-Durkee scales.

In considering Study 2's expanded assessment of anger, hostility, and self-reported aggression, there is one intriguing exception to the differential relationship of shame and guilt to these measures. Shame-proneness was positively correlated with measures of anger arousal, irritability, and indirect hostility. But shame was not related to measures of more direct aggression. The Buss-Durkee Assault scale (an index of direct physical aggression) was orthogonal to shame, and the Verbal Hostility scale (an index of direct verbal aggression) was negatively correlated with the TOSCA Shame scale.

Finally, the results involving the Buss-Durkee Guilt scale are consistent with the notion that this measure is actually an undifferentiated index of shame-guilt. The Buss-Durkee Guilt scale was positively correlated with both shame and guilt scales derived from the SCAAI and TOSCA inventories.

Discussion

The results of two independent studies of undergraduates underline that shame and guilt are distinct affective experiences that have different implications for the experience of anger and hostility. Shame-proneness was consistently positively correlated with anger arousal, suspiciousness: resentment, irritability, a tendency to blame others for negative events, and indirect (but not direct) expressions of hostility. Proneness to "shame-free" guilt, on the other hand, was inversely related to externalization of blame and some indices of anger, hostility, and resentment.

The current studies were correlational, assessing fairly global dispositions to experience shame, guilt, anger, and related states. Thus, the findings cannot speak directly to the causal links among these affective states. The positive correlation between shame and anger, for example, may reflect two distinct processes (or some combination of both). As noted by Miller (1985), one possibility is that once initially angered, an individual may become ashamed of the anger, particularly if it engenders hostile and aggressive behavior toward others. This anger-to-shame linkage seems somewhat less likely in light of the fact that shame-proneness was consistently linked to indices of anger arousal and indirect hostility but not to measures of more direct verbal and physical aggression. Nonetheless, some individuals may subscribe to the belief that anger—expressed or unexpressed—is socially and morally unacceptable and hence shameful.

A second possibility, one favored by the current authors, is that an initial sense of shame fosters subsequent anger and hostility. Such a shame-to-anger linkage is consistent with numerous clinical observations leg., Kinston, 1987; Lewis, 1971; Nathanson, 1987; Retzinger, 1987; Scheff, 1987), as well as with empirical studies suggesting that anger is likely to be engendered by negative affect, generally (Berkowitz, 1989), and more specifically by threats to one's self-esteem (Averill, 1982). Shame is a very painful emotion that involves a negative evaluation of the global self. Thus, the pain of shame, and its resulting (if only temporary) loss of self-esteem, may give rise to

Table 17.3. Relation of Anger-Hostility to Shame-Proneness and Guilt-Proneness: Study 2

Scale	Bivariate correlation		Part correlation	
	Shame	Guilt	Shame residual	Guilt residual
Trait Anger Scale				
Trait Anger	.33***	.14*	.30***	−.01
	.19**	.08	.18**	−.05
Anger Temperament	.13*	.04	.13*	−.03
	.03	−.02	.05	−.05
Anger Reactivity	.26***	.09	.24***	−.03
	.16**	.11*	.12*	.01
SCL-90				
Anger–Hostility	.20**	−.05	.24***	−.15**
	.19**	.01	.23***	−.14*
Paranoid Ideation	.35***	.08	.35***	−.09
	.40***	.17**	.38***	−.11*
Buss–Durkee Hostility Inventory				
Indirect Hostility	.18**	.06	.17**	−.02
	.16**	.03	.17**	−.08
Irritability	.36***	.10	.36***	−.08
	.30***	.11*	.30***	−.10
Negativism	.20**	.01	.21***	−.09
	.07	−.07	.15*	−.15*
Resentment	.42***	.05	.45***	−.16**
	.37***	.07	.42***	−.21***
Suspicion	.40***	.13*	.39***	−.06
	.39***	.15*	.38***	−.12*
Assault	.03	−.06	.07	−.09
	−.07	−.15*	.03	−.13*
Verbal Hostility	−.00	−.02	.01	−.02
	−.12*	−.16**	−.02	−.11*
Guilt (Guilt-Shame)	.45***	.36***	.32***	.18**
	.52***	.43***	.33***	.13*

Note. Correlations involving the Self-Conscious Affect and Attribution Inventory (SCAAI) appear below those of involving the Test of Self-Conscious Affect (TOSCA). TOSCA Ns = 226–230. SCAAI Ns = 222–225. SCL-90 = Symptom Checklist 90.
*p < .05. **p < .01. ***p < .001.

unfocused anger and hostility. Such shame-based anger can then be easily directed toward others, because shame typically involves the imagery of a real or imagined disapproving other (Lewis, 1971; Lindsay-Hartz, 1984). Moreover, because shame is such a sweeping negative affective experience, denouncing the global self, it is often experienced as disproportionate with the seriousness of the eliciting situation—as an "unfair" affective response. Rather than construing this overblown affective reaction as internally generated, the shamed individual may attribute this "unfair" experience to others involved in the eliciting situation and thus become angry. Finally, the defensive potential of anger and hostility may further contribute to the shame-anger link. Shame is an overwhelmingly painful experience that involves a clear threat to one's sense of self-worth and self-efficacy. As sug-

gested by Lewis (1971) and Miller (1985), shamed individuals may be motivated to anger because such anger is likely to provide some relief (albeit temporary) from the global, self-condemning, and debilitating experience of shame. In directing hostility outward and blaming others, the individual mobilizes the impaired self, while at the same time sparing the self from further condemnation.

As in previous studies (Tangney, 1990, 1991) guilt-proneness emerged as the apparently more adaptive disposition. Consistent with the theoretical and phenomenological literature, our findings suggest that the experience of "shame-free" guilt fosters an acceptance of responsibility rather than a tendency to blame others for negative interpersonal events. And such "shame-free" guilt appears moderately negatively correlated with anger arousal, hostility, and resentment. Perhaps because guilt involves a negative evaluation of specific behaviors somewhat apart from the global self, the experience of guilt is less threatening and therefore less likely to invoke defensive maneuvers akin to externalization of blame and other-directed anger. Moreover, because guilt is uncomfortable but not overwhelming (that is, the affective response is likely to be proportionate with the seriousness of the eliciting situation), an individual in the midst of the guilt experience may be more likely to view this affective response as "justified" and thus own the negative affective consequences. Finally, previous studies (Tangney, 1991) indicate a positive link between guilt and empathy. Thus, in cases of interpersonal harm, the guilt-prone individual's response is likely to be modulated by interpersonal empathy and concern, diffusing the potential for anger and hostility that is so prominent in the case of shame. In a number of respects, then, guilt—not shame—appears to be the more "moral" emotion.

Last, our findings underline the importance of carefully considering measurement issues when studying shame and guilt. As noted above, many of the older measures of guilt may be mislabeled; that is, they appear to tap features associated with both shame and guilt. The use of such confounded or multidimensional measures may obscure some very interesting differential relationships of shame and guilt to other constructs of interest. In effect, such differential relationships may cancel each other out, leading researchers to believe that shame and guilt are not very important to the domain of study at hand.

The Buss-Durkee Guilt scale is a good case in point. An examination of the item content of the Buss-Durkee Guilt scale, as well as its relationship to the SCAAI and TOSCA Shame and Guilt scales, indicates that the former scale is a confounded measure of shame-guilt. In previous studies (including our own), the Buss-Durkee Guilt scale has been only very modestly correlated with measures of anger and hostility, likely because effects due to shame and guilt have canceled each other out. One wonders how many researchers over the years have more or less dismissed the construct of guilt as a result; for it is only when we assess *and differentiate* shame and guilt that we find this quite intriguing differential pattern of results, suggesting that shame and guilt have quite different implications for interpersonal processes, including anger and hostility.

REFERENCES

Abramson, P. R., Mosher, D. L., Abramson, L. M., & Woychowski, B. (1977). Personality correlates of the Mosher Guilt Scales. *Journal of Personality Assessment, 41,* 373–382.

Ackerman, A. M., McMahon, P. M., & Fehr, L. A. (1984). Mock trial jury decisions as a function of adolescent juror guilt and hostility. *Journal of Genetic Psychology 144,* 195–201.

Ausubel, D. P. (1955). Relationships between shame and guilt in the socializing process. *Psychological Review, 62,* 378–390.

Averill, J. R. (1982). *Anger and aggression: An essay on emotion.* New York: Springer-Verlag.

Berkowitz, L. (1983). The experience of anger as a parallel process in the display of impulsive "angry" aggression. In R. G. Geen & E. I. Donnerstein (Eds.), *Aggression: Theoretical and empirical reviews* (pp. 103–133). San Diego, CA: Academic Press.

Berkowitz, L. (1989). Frustration-aggression hypothesis: Examination and reformulation. *Psychological Bulletin, 106,* 59–73.

Burggraf, S. A., & Tangney, J. P. (1989, June). *Proneness to shame, proneness to guilt, and self-concept.* Poster presented at the meetings of the American Psychological Society, Alexandria, VA.

Buss, A. H., & Durkee, A. (1957). An inventory for assessing different kinds of hostility in clinical situations. *Journal of Consulting Psychology, 21,* 343–348.

Damon, W. (1988). *The moral child: Nurturing children's natural moral growth.* New York: Free Press.

DeRivera, J. (1977). *A structural theory of emotions.* New York: International Universities Press.

Derogatis, L. R. (1989). *Description and bibliography for the SCL-90-R and other instruments of the psychopathology rating scale series.* Riderwood, MD: Clinical Psychometric Research, Inc.

Derogatis, L. R., & Cleary, P (1977). Confirmation of the dimensional structure of the SCL-90: A study in construct validation. *Journal of Clinical Psychology, 33,* 981–989.

Derogatis, L. R., Lipman, R. S., & Covi, L. (1973). SCL90: An outpatient psychiatric ratings scale—Preliminary report. *Psychopharmacology Bulletin, 9,* 13–28.

Derogatis, L. R., Rickels, K., & Rock, A. (1976). The SCL-90 and the MMPI: A step in the validation of a new self-report scale. *British Journal of Psychiatry, 128,* 280–289.

Fehr, L. A. (1979). Media violence and catharsis in college females. *Journal of Social Psychology, 109,* 307–308.

Geen, R. G., & Berkowitz, L. (1967). Some conditions facilitating the occurrence of aggression after the observation of violence. *Journal of Personality. 35,* 666–676.

Gessner, T. L., & Tangney, J. P. (1990, March). *Personality and adjustment correlates of wit and witticism.* Poster presented at the meetings of the Eastern Psychological Association, Philadelphia, PA.

Hamme, H. (1990). *Family correlates of proneness to shame and proneness to guilt.* Unpublished doctoral dissertation, Bryn Mawr College, Bryn Mawr, PA.

Harder, D. W., & Lewis, S. J. (1986). The assessment of shame and guilt. In J. N. Butcher & C. D. Spielberger (Eds.), *Advances in personality assessment* (Vol. 6, pp. 89–114). Hillsdale, NJ: Erlbaum.

Kinston, W. (1987). The shame of narcissism. In D. L.

Nathanson (Ed.), *The many faces of shame* (pp. 214–245). New York: Guilford Press.

Lewis, H. B. (1971). *Shame and guilt in neurosis.* New York: International Universities Press.

Lewis, H. B. (1987). Shame and the narcissistic personality. In D. L. Nathanson (Ed.), *The many faces of shame* (pp. 93–132). New York: Guilford Press.

Lindsay-Hartz, J. (1984). Contrasting experiences of shame and guilt. *American Behavioral Scientist, 27,* 689–704.

Miller, S. (1985). *The shame experience.* Hillsdale, NJ: Erlbaum.

Mosher, D. L. (1966). The development and multitrait-multimethod matrix analysis of three measures of three aspects of guilt. *Journal of Consulting and Clinical Psychology, 30,* 25–29.

Mosher, D. L., Mortimer, R. L., & Grebel, M. (1968). Verbal aggressive behavior in delinquent boys. *Journal of Abnormal Psychology, 73,* 454–460.

Nathanson, D. L. (1987). A timetable for shame. In D. L. Nathanson (Ed.), *The many faces of shame* (pp. 1–63). New York: Guilford Press.

Retzinger, S. R. (1987). Resentment and laughter: Video studies of the shame-rage spiral. In H. B. Lewis (Ed.), *The role of shame in symptom formation* (pp. 151–181). Hillsdale, NJ: Erlbaum.

Scheff, T. J. (1987). The shame-rage spiral: A case study of an interminable quarrel. In H. B. Lewis (Ed.), *The role of shame in symptom formation* (pp. 109–149). Hillsdale, NJ: Erlbaum.

Schill, T. R. (1972). Aggression and blood pressure responses of high and low guilt subjects following frustration. *Journal of Consulting and Clinical Psychology, 38,* 461.

Schill, T. R., & Schneider, L. (1970). Relationship between hostility guilt and several measures of hostility. *Psychological Reports, 27,* 967–970.

Spielberger, C. D., Jacobs, G., Russell, S., & Crane, R. S. (1983). Assessment of anger: The State-Trait Anger Scale. In J. N. Butcher & C. D. Spielberger (Eds.), *Advances in personality assessment* (pp. 161–189). Hillsdale, NJ: Erlbaum.

Tangney, J. P. (1989, August). *A quantitative assessment of phenomenological differences between shame and guilt.* Poster presented at the 97th Annual Convention of the American Psychological Association, New Orleans, LA.

Tangney, J. P. (1990). Assessing individual differences in proneness to shame and guilt: Development of the Self-Conscious Affect and Attribution Inventory. *Journal of Personality and Social Psychology, 59,* 102–111.

Tangney, J. P. (1991). Moral affect: The good, the bad, and the ugly. *Journal of Personality and Social Psychology, 61,* 598-607.

Tangney, J. P, Burggraf, S. A., Hamme, H., & Domingos, B. (1988, March). *Assessing individual differences in proneness to shame and guilt: The Self-Conscious Affect and Attribution Inventory.* Poster presented at the meetings of the Eastern Psychological Association, Buffalo, NY.

Tangney, J. P., Wagner, P., & Gramzow, R. (1989). *The Test of Self-Conscious Affect.* Unpublished measure, George Mason University, Fairfax, VA.

Tangney, J. P., Wagner, P., & Gramzow, R. (1992). Proneness to shame, proneness to guilt, and psychopathology. *Journal of Abnormal Psychology, 103,* 469–478.

Weiner, B. (1985). An attributional theory of achievement and emotion. *Psychological Review, 92,* 548–573.

Wicker, F. W., Payne, G. C., & Morgan, R. D. (1983). Participant descriptions of guilt and shame. *Motivation and Emotion, 7,* 25–39.

Interpersonal Aspects of Guilt: Evidence from Narrative Studies

Roy F. Baumeister, Arlene M. Stillwell, and Todd F. Heatherton

Psychologists have discussed guilt for decades, but solid and reliable conclusions have not emerged. Theoretical difficulties and methodological obstacles have plagued empirical work, resulting in a scarcity of data. *The Journal of Personality and Social Psychology* contained only three titles that referred to guilt in the entire decade of the 1980s (plus a couple more on sex guilt). In that same decade, the *Annual Review of Psychology* volume indices listed only three pages on which the word "guilt" appeared. Many textbooks on emotion and motivation do not cover guilt at all.

The 1990s have begun with a renewed or, reborn interest in guilt. Tangney (1990, 1991; see also Tangney, Wagner, Fletcher, & Gramzow, 1992) has shown that it is possible to distinguish guilt from shame and to study the behavioral consequences of each. Zahn-Waxler and Kochanska (1990) have demonstrated that developmental psychologists have slowly built up an enlightening collection of guilt-related empirical finding, and they have called for new theories to integrate these findings and shape further research.

Responding to that call, we have outlined a theory of the interpersonal aspects of guilt (Baumeister, Stillwell, & Heatherton, 1994). Our argument may be summarized briefly as follows. Whereas traditional theories have depicted guilt as a largely intrapsychic phenomenon based on self-judgment, we regard guilt as an interpersonal phenomenon based in close relationships, espe-cially in certain interactions with intimate partners. To some extent, this is merely a shift in emphasis—a shift toward considering self-judgment the derivative phenomenon and interpersonal dynamics the main foundation. Still, we do reject the strongest assertions of intrapsychic theories, such as that of Lewis (1971), who asserted that "guilt is evoked only from within the self" (p. 85) and "the imagery of the self vis-a-vis the 'other' is absent in guilt" (p. 251).

Interpersonal Function of Guilt

Our contention is that guilt serves to protect and strengthen interpersonal relationships. The prototype cause of guilt is hurting a relationship partner. (We use the term "relationship partner" in a broad sense, referring to the other person involved in any type of relationship, and thus not just a romantic partner.) Generally, people will feel guilty when they benefit inequitably at a partner's expense or inflict harm, loss, distress, disappointment, or other misfortune on a significant other person. Subjectively, guilt is an unpleasant emotional state, and we suggest two affective bases for it—namely, empathic distress over the suffering of one's partner and victim (e.g., Hoffman, 1982), and separation or exclusion anxiety over the possible loss or damage to the relationship that may be caused by one's transgression (see Baumeister & Tice, 1990; Bowlby, 1969, 1973).

Three main specific functions of guilt can be identified.

The first is that guilt directly contributes to good relationships by promoting behaviors that benefit relationships and by serving as a symbolic affirmation of the relationship. Guilt causes people to act in ways that will be beneficial to relationships, such as expressing affection, paying attention, and refraining from transgressions. Furthermore, relationships may be threatened by even seemingly mild transgressions, because such actions symbolically convey that the transgressor does not care enough about the partner or the relationship to behave as the other wishes. By feeling guilty (and showing it), the transgressor can then erase the symbolic damage to the relationship, because the presence of guilt indicates that the transgressor really does care.

The second function of guilt is as an influence technique. One person may get his or her way by making the other feel guilty. To use guilt as an influence technique, the influencer communicates to the partner that some action or inaction will hurt the influencer in some fashion (including disappointing, distressing, or harming him or her). That action or inaction will therefore make the partner feel guilty because it entails hurting the influencer. To avoid the aversive state of guilt, the partner avoids that action or inaction. In this case, merely the threat of impending guilt is enough to keep the potentially offending partner from acting in the undesirable fashion. Guilt may thus operate either as a deterrent (before the fact) or as an impetus for desired behavior change (after the fact).

Guilt is an influence technique that operates in the absence of formal, objective, status-based, or physical power; indeed, it may be especially useful to the less powerful partners in relationships. As such, guilt serves to equalize the balance of power. It also emphasizes the relationship bond and should therefore be far more effective for influencing intimate partners than for influencing casual acquaintances or strangers. Although guilt may be an effective influence technique, its use may involve significant costs, one of which is a partner's resentment (despite compliance). Another potential cost is "metaguilt"—that is, guilt over inducing guilt. Guilt results from hurting a partner, and making the partner feel guilty is a form of hurting so some people could conceivably feel guilty over making intimate partners feel guilty.

The third function of guilt is to redistribute emotional distress. Transgressions may create affective inequities, because one person did what he or she wanted and therefore may feel good, while the victim suffers the negative consequences. Such affective inequities are bad for relationships and hamper effective communication and interaction (e.g., Locke & Horowitz, 1990). Guilt, however, reduces the benefits of the transgressor. Moreover, the transgressor's guilt may make the victim feel better. The net effect of guilt is therefore to reduce the negative affect of the victim and increase that of the transgressor, as if transferring the negative affect from the victim to the transgressor—who, after all, is its rightful owner in the sense of being the person who has caused it.

Why might victims feel better when they see that transgressors feel guilty? At least two sets of reasons can be offered. First, a transgressor's guilt already helps rectify the inequity, because the transgressor can be seen as suffering for his or her misdeed rather than enjoying his or her ill-gotten gains, so to speak. Second, as noted earlier, the guilt feelings may serve as evidence that the transgressor cares about the relationship and about the victim, and this affirmation of the social bond may be reassuring to the victim. In other words, feeling guilty may be an effective way of communicating the existence of affectional ties.

Autobiographical Narratives

The research we conducted (Baumeister, Stillwell, & Heatherton, 1995; see also Baumeister, Reis, & Delespaul, 1995) was not explicitly designed to test these assertions about guilt. Rather, it was designed to explore in a broad way the interpersonal transactions and contexts of guilt. Both studies used autobiographical-narrative methodology, which in recent years has been particularly useful in shedding light on guilt (e.g., McGraw, 1987; Tangney, 1992).

As suggested earlier methodological and ethical difficulties have plagued and retarded the empirical study of guilt. Experimental studies have mainly relied on accidental transgressions, because it is nearly impossible to induce subjects systematically or reliably to commit intentional transgressions in he laboratory. Even if it were possible to induce subjects to act in highly immoral ways, it would not be ethical to do so. McGraw (1987) has noted that accidental transgressions do not necessarily produce the same effects as intentional transgressions, and it is very difficult to elicit the latter in the laboratory. Moreover, our emphasis on the interpersonal context suggests that empirical studies of guilt should focus on transgressions within intimate relationships, but it seems highly unethical to use laboratory procedures to induce serious intentional transgressions (or indeed guilt of any sort) within important relationships.

Our empirical approach has thus made use of autobiographical narratives, a methodology that has become increasingly available to personality and social psychologists in recent years (Gergen & Gergen, 1988; Harvey, Weber, & Orbuch, 1990; McAdams, 1985; Ross & Holmberg, 1990). It has proven particularly useful in exploring topics that resist conventional laboratory methods, such as the termination of intimate relationships (Harvey, Flanary, & Morgan, 1988; Harvey, Weber, Galvin, Huszti, & Garnick, 1986; Vaughan, 1986), unrequited love (Baumeister & Wotman, 1992), criminal and antisocial activity (J. Katz, 1988), the interpersonal genesis of anger (Baumeister, Stillwell, & Wotman, 1990), lay understanding of emotion (Shaver, Schwarz, Kirson, & O'Connor, 1987), and sexual masochism (Baumeister, 1988a, 1988b, 1989). Guilt falls into this category of theoretically important but empirically elusive phenomena, and so it seems a prime candidate for this methodology (Brooke, 1985; 1987; Tangney, 1992).

In essence, the method relies on having people relate significant stories from their own lives pertaining to a particular theme (which is defined by the topic of study). The stories are then coded for content on dimensions relevant to the hypotheses. Our approach has generally relied on comparisons between two sets of stories. Thus, in previous research we have compared male against female accounts of masochistic experiences (Baumeister, 1988b), and compared perpetrators' and victims' accounts of interpersonal transgressions (Baumeister et al., 1990). In our first study on guilt, we compared interpersonal transgressions that led to guilt with transgressions that did not lead to guilt. In a second one, we compared accounts of being made to feel guilty with accounts of making someone else feel guilty (Baumeister, Stillwell, & Heatherton, 1995).

The methodological implications and limitations of autobiographical narratives are discussed elsewhere (see, e.g., Baumeister et al., 1990;

Baumeister & Stillwell, 1992). Briefly, autobiographical narratives sacrifice some of the precision, control, and homogeneity that are obtainable with laboratory experimentation. The benefits include an increase in external validity (because of using real stories from actual lives rather than laboratory simulations) and, most important, the capacity to study topics that resist laboratory methods. As noted elsewhere, we regard laboratory experimentation as the best methodology when viable, but the inability of laboratory experimentation to provide a thorough understanding of guilt has encouraged us to pursue this alternative method (see also Brooke, 1985; McGraw, 1987).

Guilt or No Guilt?

Our first investigation in this line of research (Baumeister, Stillwell, & Heatherton, 1995, Study 1) was an attempt to explore the factors related to feeling guilty over a transgression. We collected first-person accounts of transgressions, specifying that these had to be things about which the person later felt guilty. To furnish a basis for comparison, we also collected accounts of transgressions that did not lead to guilt. In order to define the transgression in a comparable way, the instructions for all stories requested each subject to relate an incident in which he or she had done something that made someone else angry. Using anger as a criterion is an effective way of eliciting stories about interpersonal transgressions (cf. Baumeister et al., 1990), but of course it may not cover the full range of guilt-inducing episodes. Thus, every subject wrote two stories about transgressions that he or she had committed—one chosen so that the transgressor did not feel guilty, and the other so that the transgressor did feel guilty. In other respects the instructions for the two stories were identical; thus the two sets of stories were comparable in terms of another person's condemnation and disapproval of the subject's actions, and they differed as to whether the subject felt guilty afterwards.

The stories were provided by upper-level college students. We randomly varied the order in which each subject wrote the two stories, but there did not seem to be any effect of which one the person wrote first. Subjects were assured of confidentiality and asked not to identify themselves or anyone else in the stories. A secretary then typed the stories, and a judge coded them along a series of dimensions. We used a dichotomous coding system, in Which the coder simply made a series of binary judgments as to whether the story contained a given feature or not (e.g., "Did the transgressor apologize in the story?"). Table 18.1 summarizes the main results.

The first issue that concerned us was whether guilt is linked to dose or otherwise special relationships. To examine this, we looked for differences in the relationship between transgressor and victim in the guilty stories as opposed to the not-guilty stories. Consistent with the interpersonal view of guilt, people were significantly more likely to express high esteem for the other (angry) person in the guilty stories than in the not-guilty stories. More specifically, 85% of the guilty stories expressed some high or positive regard for the partner, as compared to only 37% of the not-guilty stories. This pattern fits the view that guilt is characteristic of offenses within the context of valued relationships. People apparently feel less guilty about their transgressions against people whom they dislike or disrespect.

As examples, many episodes referred to partners in intimate relationships. Others described close friends and emphasized that the guilt was linked to remorse over potential damage to the relationship. In one subject's words, "We had been really good friends during the year. . . . I felt bad that our friendship had gone bad." One woman's story indicated that her rising esteem for the partner produced the guilt. She had been dating several men innocently, but when she fell in love with one of them she felt guilty over having dated the others, even though she stopped seeing them. Another wrote of leaving for the summer without saying goodbye to a close friend.

It must be kept in mind that these results are correlational. There is no way of assessing whether the disrespect eliminated the guilt or whether the lack of guilt led to disrespect, although the former seems far more plausible. Our results do suggest, however, that derogating a victim would be an effective way of minimizing guilt. Previous studies have shown tendency for people to derogate their victims (Lerner & Matthews, 1967). Such derogation may accomplish the result of making one's relationship to the victim trivial, expendable, or undesirable. By thus severing the social bond, one removes an important basis for guilt. It is also noteworthy that Noel (1973) failed to replicate the standard finding that people become more helpful and compliant after committing a (usually accidental) transgression. In Noel's study, the transgression involved derogating another person; possibly the derogation of the victim removed the guilt that often mediate subsequent altruistic behavior.

An experimental study by I. Katz, Glass, and Cohen (1973) is also relevant to the implication that derogation may reduce guilt. In that study, white subjects derogated black victims more than white victims, which seems to suggest that severing the tie of fellow-feeling is easier when one's victim is from another race. This suggestion seems to fit several observational studies, which have proposed that perpetrators of crimes and atrocities tend to derogate their victims to remove any sense of fellow-feeling; perpetrators even sometimes regard their victims as subhuman, especially when the victims belong to some ethnic or social group that can be clearly separated from their own (Conquest, 1986; Lifton, 1986).

Taken together with these past conclusions, our work thus seems to suggest that a positive relationship context is an important foundation for guilt. People feel guilty about offenses against esteemed others. Such transgressions may pose a risk to a valued relationship, and so the resultant guilt may well be regarded as an adaptive reaction if guilt is indeed (as we have suggested) a relationship-enhancing pattern born out of positive concern over a desired relationship.

Our theory has suggested further that guilt has relationship-enhancing functions. Because the interpersonal relationships varied systematically

TABLE 18.1. Comparison of Stories in Which the Author Did versus Did Not Feel Guilty

Coding dimension	Percentage coded yes	
	Guilty	Not guilty
Lesson learned	40.4	0.0
Mitigating circumstances	46.8	80.4
Perpetrator regards victim highly	85.1	36.9
Apology given	36.1	6.5
Author still feels bad	21.3	2.1
Perpetrator was selfish	42.5	8.7
Perpetrator's actions were justified	27.6	97.8
Victim helped provoke incident	44.6	82.6
Perpetrator confessed misdeed	8.5	0.0
Perpetrator happy with outcome	8.5	56.5
Perpetrator's behavior changed	21.3	2.1
Things now back to normal	44.6	69.5
Perpetrator foresaw outcome	29.7	78.2

Note. n = 86–93 stories.

between the two sets of stories (as our first finding indicated), it was not feasible to code the stories for comparative relationship outcomes. One dimension that could be effectively coded, however, was whether the narrator indicated having learned a lesson or changed subsequent behavior patterns as a result of this. To be sure, anger may be understood generally as an objection to another's actions (e.g., Averill, 1982), so one might expect all incidents to lead to behavior change. But we found that guilt feelings were apparently a powerful mediator of such changes. Only one not-guilty story referred to behavior change, whereas 21.3% of the guilty stories did, and the difference was significant. An even stronger finding was obtained by coding whether subjects indicated that they had learned a lesson or changed in any positive fashion. Forty percent of the guilty stories contained some indication of having learned or changed, whereas none of the not-guilty stories contained such an indication.

Several examples are useful to illustrate these lessons. One subject described an argument and looked back with regret: "If I had to do it over again, I would have tried to be more tactful. As a matter of fact, if I ever see that guy and his truck, I do plan to apologize to him." Insight into self was often mentioned, as in this example: "I regretted treating my friend badly and I decided to apologize to her. I explained to her why I did what I did, and it really helped me understand my feelings." Other lessons pertained to relationship partners, as in the case of the woman who had a summer romantic fling while away from her boyfriend, who was quite upset by the affair: "I never realized how fragile he was, and I wish to God I had thought things through first." Yet other lessons referred to improvements in interpersonal relationships, as in the following example: "Some good came out of this, however. We agreed from then on that if we ever got into a dumb argument on the phone, we won't let it escalate; instead, we will wait until we see each other and can talk it over in a civilized manner." These results are nicely consistent with suggestions that guilt is an effective internal mechanism for adaptation and self-control (e.g., Freud, 1930; Wertheim & Schwarz, 1983). Although some studies have suggested that people who feel guilty are better socialized and more responsible than people like sociopaths, who are relatively immune to guilt feelings (e.g., Zahn-Waxler & Kochanska, 1990), our results extend

that argument by replicating the effect within subjects. All our subjects (except one) wrote both a guilty story and a not-guilty story, and as a general pattern they learned and changed more when they had felt guilty. In other words, guilt is linked with learning and changing in socially desirable ways, and this link obtains both in comparisons of guilty versus not-guilty people and in comparisons of guilty versus not-guilty episodes within the same individual's experience.

The fact that guilt leads to behavior change is of course particularly important in laying the foundation for the influence function we have proposed. That is, guilt will only serve as an effective influence technique if it does cause people to alter their behavior. Study 2 has examined the interpersonal manipulation of guilt feelings directly.

Several findings of lesser importance can be briefly mentioned. As compared with the not-guilty stories, guilty stories were more likely to suggest that the author still felt bad about the incident, more likely to include having apologized, less likely to cite mitigating circumstances, less likely to place some causal blame or responsibility on the other person, less likely to contain self-justifications, more likely to portray the author's action as selfish, less likely to portray the author as happy with the outcome, less likely to indicate that things had gotten back to normal, and less likely to suggest that the author had foreseen the outcome. The last point corroborates McGraw's (1987) ironic finding that people tend to report more guilt about unintended actions or unforeseen consequences.

Making Someone Feel Guilty

Our second study (Baumeister, Stillwell, a Heatherton, 1995, Study 2) was directly concerned with the interpersonal manipulation of guilt. Specifically, we asked people to describe incidents in which they caused someone to feel guilty or in which someone made them feel guilty. The sample for this study was comprised of adults of all ages, as most of them were drawn from among visitors to the Ontario Science Centre. (Others came from an upper-level psychology course.) Most of our results involved comparing the two sets of accounts based on the two situational roles: guilt inducers and their targets. Comparing accounts based on different situational roles has been a standard way of using this methodology (e.g., Baumeister et al.,

1990; Baumeister, Wotman, & Stillwell, 1993). Table 18.2 presents the main comparisons.

A set of hypotheses about the interpersonal manipulation of guilt follows directly from our theoretical exposition. When one person harms, frustrates, upsets, or disappoints another, the latter may be motivated to make the former feel guilty, especially because of the relationship-enhancing effects of guilt. Making the other feel guilty should involve displaying one's suffering or misfortune and emphasizing the other's responsibility for it. Simple disclosure may be enough, but people may understandably be tempted to facilitate the induction of guilt by exaggerating their suffering. Thus, one person portrays a vivid or enhanced image of one's suffering to the other and then relies on the other's concern to induce guilt. The attempted induction of guilt should ostensibly serve some relationship-enhancing function, particularly getting the other to affirm his or her commitment to the relationship.

Successful guilt induction should have several consequences. It should lead to behavior change on the part of the guilty person. It should make the victim/manipulator feel better in some way, thereby redistributing the negative affect (i.e., transferring it from victim to transgressor). In some cases, however, the affective improvement may be

TABLE 18.2. Comparison of Guilt Induction Stories Written by Reproachers and Targets

Category	Percentage coded yes	
	Target	Reproacher
Reference to other's standards	55.1	13.0
Metaguilt	0.0	21.2
Target did something wrong	22.7	52.9
Target failed to act (sin of omission)	70.2	53.1
Target resents	37.2	1.9
Interpersonal neglect as offense	58.7	32.7
Self-justifying statements	62.5	60.4
Self-blame	34.8	19.2
Reproacher was frankly manipulative	14.6	32.7
Differing expectations as cause	49.0	29.1
Target apologizes, regret	20.8	46.3
Reproacher used past	18.4	37.0
Reproacher lied or falsified	0.0	16.4
Reproacher felt better afterward	4.7	44.0
Target felt bad	49.0	67.3
Target overreacted	4.1	5.6
Reproacher overreacted	44.9	16.7

Note. n = 93–104 stories.

tempered by "metaguilt"—that is, guilt over inducing guilt. Also, in some cases guilt may succeed in eliciting behavioral compliance but may generate resentment or other negative reactions, which should be more apparent to the person who is made to feel guilty than to the manipulator.

Before we proceed to described how the accounts by inducers differed from those of their targets, we want to emphasize a basic issue that was already raised in our previous study—namely, the relationship context of guilt. We wanted to see whether guilt induction would be linked to close relationships as clearly as simple accounts of feeling guilty (in Study 1) were. And they were. Although subjects were free to describe episodes of guilt induction between themselves and strangers, they overwhelmingly chose instead to describe incidents between themselves and intimate partners such as family members, lovers, and close friends. We coded whether the other person in the guilt story was (1) an intimate, such as a relative, lover, or close friend; (2) a casual acquaintance or work/business associate; (3) a stranger to whom the author had some role relationship; or (4) a stranger with whom the author had no relationship. The fourth category was completely empty. Only one incident fell into the third category, and that incident involved a lifeguard making a child feel guilty for heedless behavior that might have hurt someone. Six incidents fell into the second category; these involved four teacher-student relationships, one coach-athlete relationship, and one relationship of a businessman to a long-term client. The remaining 95 (not counting two ambiguous ones, which also seemed to suggest long-term relationships) fell into the first category because of overt references to close relationships. Apparently those whom people deliberately cause to feel guilty are mainly friends, relatives, and lovers.

Guilt may therefore be considered an influence technique that is particularly suited to close relationships. There are several possible reasons for this. First of all, many influence techniques are exploitative or coercive, or may rely on deceptive manipulations that cannot be repeated or sustained indefinitely (see Cialdini, 1984), and so these may not be suitable for long-term relationships. Indeed, explicit coercion may be sustained in a relationship if one person is clearly more powerful, but the greater the assumptions of equity and equality, the more costly direct coercion becomes. Guilt may seem preferable to coercion because the other person seemingly complies freely rather than under duress, although, as we have suggested, this is probably an illusion; guilt has its costs, but they are simply hidden. Guilt is also available to the person with less power in the relationship. Perhaps most importantly, guilt depends on empathy and on the mutual commitment to the relationship, and so it is really most viable in the context of a long-term, emotionally intense relationship.

The first function of guilt we have described is to motivate people to affirm their social bonds by expressing commitment or affection, or at least paying attention to relationship partners. Consistent with the hypothesis that guilt serves this function, the single biggest category of causes of interpersonal guilt induction was neglecting one's partner. Although this was substantial in both samples, it was more common in the accounts of the targets than in those of the reproachers. Targets may have preferred to describe such incidents because there was little moral wrongdoing on their part and because many of them were able to justify having neglected others because of devoting themselves to their work or other preoccupations. Still, it is apparent that people are quite aware of being made to feel guilty for not paying enough attention to others.

Neglecting to attend to someone is a sin of omission rather than a sin of commission, which is of particular interest, insofar as previous studies have largely focused on sins of commission (as noted by Zahn-Waxler & Kochanska, 1990). Indeed, Tangney (1992) has suggested that guilt is overwhelmingly associated with sins of commission rather than omission. Our results differed from that view, however: Over half the reproachers' accounts and two-thirds of the targets' accounts referred to sins of omission. It appears that the interpersonal manipulation of guilt is often associated with failure to act rather than with actions. Possibly when people are asked to recall an incident that evoked guilt, they recall a sin of commission, but when they are asked to recall an interpersonal induction of guilt, the sins of omission come more readily to mind.

Our model suggests that people may sometimes be tempted to exaggerate their suffering in order to generate guilt in others, and these accounts confirmed that pattern. A significant minority of reproachers referred to bare-faced attempts to make others feel guilty, and some even acknowledged having dissembled, distorted, misled, or used falsehoods in order to generate guilt. In this sample, none of the targets' accounts referred to such bare-faced or hypocritical tactics in the attempt to generate guilt, although many targets did feel that the reproachers had overreacted (which could have a similar meaning). These findings suggest that people sometimes do successfully deceive others, such as by exaggerating or misrepresenting their suffering, to make others feel guilty.

Negative reactions by the target have been proposed as one potential cost of the use of guilt as an influence technique. The most important among these reactions may be resentment, which was apparent in our sample. Target resentment was significantly more common in the targets' own accounts than in the reproachers' accounts. This suggests that many targets may keep their resentment more or less to themselves, indeed often complying overtly with the wishes of the reproachers. The lack of references to resentment among the reproachers' accounts suggests that they may often be unaware of (or choose to ignore) this negative reaction among the people they manipulate with guilt. This important cost of guilt as an influence technique may not be immediately apparent to guilt inducers.

A second possible cost of using guilt as an influence technique is metaguilt—that is, feeling guilty over making others feel guilty. This cost was also apparent in our sample, although, like resentment, it was only apparent in one of the two sets of accounts. Although the targets' accounts made no reference to the notion that reproachers might feel guilty, a significant minority of reproachers did indicate that they felt guilty about their manipulation.

The fact that some reproachers felt guilty about inducing guilt helps to explain one surprising result, which was that both groups of authors included self-justificatory statements at approximately the same rate. One might assume that people who feel guilty would be moved to justify themselves, and thus that statements of self-justification would be more common in the targets' accounts, but many reproachers felt it necessary to justify their actions too. Apparently, deliberately making someone feel guilty violates some norms (especially norms of not making others feel bad), and so inducers had to justify what they did.

Our third hypothesized interpersonal function of guilt is the redistribution of negative affect, and this too was apparent in our sample. Not surprisingly, targets generally were made to feel bad and feel guilty as a result of the reproachers' efforts. Of greater interest is the finding of significant affect improvements by the reproachers: Almost half the reproachers' accounts indicated that they felt better after the incident. These affective improvements suggest that a transfer model describes guilt induction better than a contagion model; because the contagion model would entail that one person would feel worse and the other would continue feeling bad. Instead, we found that one's feeling worse was linked to the other's feeling better, as if some of the negative affect had been transferred out of one person and into the other.

Furthermore, we have reasoned that one cause of a reproacher's affective improvement would be the positive expressions of guilt and remorse by the partner, whose visible remorse should presumably operate as a symbolic indication of his or her commitment to the relationship and caring about the other. Consistent with this finding, a significant number of accounts included references to the targets' remorse or overt apologies. What was especially striking was that thee references were more common in the reproachers' accounts than in the targets' own accounts. In a recent study of accounts involving anger, offenders were far more likely than their victims to mention-apologies (Baumeister et al., 1990). That pattern also conforms to a more general property of autobiographical narratives, which is that people refer to their own feelings and actions more than to those of other people. Yet in the present study the opposite pattern emerged: Reproachers' accounts featured the apologies of their targets more than the targets' own accounts did.

One plausible explanation for this remarkable salience of the apology to its recipient is, again, the relationship-enhancing message that it conveyed. If a reproacher were indeed to feel better as a result of the guilt induction and the other's guilty affirmation of the relationship, then that would explain why the apology would be sufficiently important as to be included in many reproachers' accounts. A related reason was that reproachers were describing their efforts to make someone feel guilty, and so the targets' apologies were a form of proof that their efforts had been successful.

It is also worth mentioning that targets' accounts had a relatively high number of references to differing expectations and to the other persons' (i.e., the reproachers') standards. Such discrepancies between one's own standards or expectations and the other person's may be especially salient to a target, for they form the basis for the guilt induction. Furthermore, appealing to such discrepancies may allow the target to feel justified and decent while still acknowledging that another made him or her feel guilty, as if the target were to say that his or her behavior was objectionable in another's view but nonetheless correct in his or her own estimation. This finding underscores our argument that guilt is not necessarily or even primarily a result of a self-evaluation process. Contrary to Mosher's (1965) exclusive focus on one's own internalized standards, it is quite apparent that people do feel guilty in response to the standards of others, and even feel guilty despite discrepancies between their standards and others' standards. Indeed, Mosher's hypothesis that guilt is an expectancy of self-mediated punishment (1965, p. 162) received no support in either of these two studies, for no subject referred to an expectancy of self-mediated punishment.

Following Locke and Horowitz (1990), we have suggested (Baumeister et al., 1994) that part of the value of redistributing negative affect is that it brings the partners into similar emotional states, which facilitates communication between them; and of course the improved communication may be beneficial for the relationship. Our data cannot assess relationship outcomes in any systematic fashion, but there were some indications that guilt inductions did have that effect. Here is a good example stating explicitly that guilt induction helped the two people communicate better:

> When I was about 18–19 years old, I was still living at home with my patents and I stayed out all night at a party—got home 8–9 A.M. the next day. I didn't call—it didn't even cross my mind to call home. When I did get home, kind of hung-over, tired—my mother was waiting for me with the biggest guilt trip known to man. She started the "you don't love me—you make me worry so much—I though you were dead" routine. She told me—worst of all—that she was disappointed in me! This is my mother, who fawned over every little achievement I had from kindergarten to getting my driver's license. The way she made me feel stuck with me. We made up, of course, after lots of crying and explaining. But, to this day, I can still picture the look of disappointment on her face and the tone of her voice. I hope to God I never make her feel like that again.

Thus, this story about guilt testifies to redistribution of negative affect, to improved communication, and to positive and lasting behavior change.

Guilt, Other Emotions, and Interpersonal Relations

The studies we have described shed light on the likely interpersonal dynamics of guilt, but they were not designed to address the basic question of how interpersonal a phenomenon guilt is. The instructions in the preceding studies specifically asked people to describe interpersonal incidents, and so episodes of solitary guilt would be left out. To be sure, there was no pressure to describe incidents involving close relationships, and the high frequency of such relationships in these samples of stories does suggest that guilt is mainly linked to them, but there remains the possibility that guilt is often felt in connection with solitary transgressions and reflections.

One of us participated in some research that was directly concerned with examining the solitary versus interpersonal nature of guilt (Baumeister, Reis, & Delespaul, in press). In one of the studies in that project, subjects were asked to provide the most recent incident in which they had felt guilty. They were also asked to describe their most recent experiences of anxiety, sadness, frustration, fear, and anger or irritation (the sequence was varied). These were then coded for whether the episode was solitary versus interpersonal. In this way, guilt could be compared with other emotions with regard to its "interpersonalness"; after all, even if most incidents of guilt were found to be interpersonal, this might be trivial if most reports of incidents involving any other emotion were equally interpersonal.

The results of that study indicated, however, that guilt seems to be one of the more interpersonal emotions. Indeed, among the six emotions included in the study, guilt ranked the highest on interpersonalness. There were fewer solitary guilt episodes than episodes of any of the other emotions, and the degree of close or intimate relatedness was higher in the guilt stories than in any of the other emotion stories. Sadness was the only emotion to score close to guilt on interpersonalness. Frustration, anxiety, and fear were often associated with being alone.

In that study, the stories were also subjected to content analysis, in order to determine what sorts of things led to guilt. Consistent with the evidence we have already reported, this study found that neglecting a relationship partner was the single largest category of incidents that caused guilt. Failing to live up to an interpersonal obligation was another large category (indeed, these two categories combined accounted for about a third of the total causes of guilt in this sample). Romantic infidelities and other betrayals also accounted for quite a few of the stories. Thus, transgressions against close relationships predominated.

To be sure, a number of solitary transgressions were reported, and so it would be excessive to claim that other people are always centrally involved in guilt. People reported guilt over neglecting their studies (especially for procrastinating on an assignment) failing to exercise, and overeating (especially breaking a diet). Although there may have been some interpersonal concerns in the background of these incidents, such as the feeling that one is letting one's parents down by not studying, these do seem to indicate that guilt can be felt on a fairly solitary basis. Still, cases of solitary guilt appear to constitute a small minority. Most guilt is interpersonal.

Further light on the interpersonal nature of guilt was shed by the other study in this investigation (Baumeister, Reis & Delespaul, 1995). This study used an experience-sampling methodology: Subjects carried a beeper that went off at random intervals, and they were instructed to stop and record their thoughts, feelings, and activities whenever they were beeped. This study found that people often happened to be alone when they felt guilty— but that the guilt usually referred to interpersonal problems or concerns.

One of the beeper study's analyses looked at the relation between the subjects' thoughts and feelings and their reporting of guilt. It was surprising how little relation there was; evidently, subjects could feel guilty when engaged in almost any activity or thinking about almost any topic. Forty-five large categories of thoughts and activities were constructed, and the frequency of guilt reports in each of them was computed. Only one of these categories departed from the overall mean (using a 1% confidence interval) frequency of guilt: People were especially likely to feel guilty when they were thinking about themselves in relation to other people. In other words, there is almost no relation between what a person is doing or thinking and the likelihood that the person may feel guilty—with one big exception: namely, that people are extra likely to feel guilty when thinking about themselves in relation to others. The fact that this exception stood out from the typical pattern seems very consistent with the hypothesis that guilt is rooted in interpersonal relatedness.

Concluding Remarks

We have suggested that guilt should be understood as something that happens between people as much as it happens inside them. Instead of studying guilt by examining how people judge their own actions, we propose studying guilt by examining the exchanges within close relationships. Inequities and transgressions can cause guilt, and if the transgressor does not stem to feel guilty enough, the partner may do or say things to stimulate and increase guilt feelings. By manipulating the target's feelings of guilt, the partner seeks and often finds confirmation of the target's continuing investment in the relationship.

The need for an interpersonal understanding of guilt is supported by recent accumulating evidence. Hoffman (1982) has argued that guilt is based in empathic distress, which is an affective response to another person's suffering. Tangney (1992) concluded that all categories of guilt-inducing incidents she examined were interpersonal except one—namely, breaking a diet. We would even question that one exception; dieting, after all, is guided and motivated by interpersonal concerns (such as being attractive to others), and we doubt that people living in extreme solitude would be dieters. Lastly, our own data attest to the importance of the relationship bond for causing guilt. In our work, transgressions that led to guilt were linked to important social bonds, whereas transgressions toward unimportant other people were less likely to cause guilt. In addition, reports of making someone else feel guilty were overwhelmingly presented in the context of close relationships.

Three interpersonal functions of guilt have been suggested. The research we have described provided some support for each of them. The first function is that guilt directly strengthens relationships by stimulating relationship-enhancing patterns of behavior. Guilt makes people learn lessons and change their behavior so as to avoid doing

things that will threaten their social attachments, such as hurting, distressing, or upsetting partners in relationships. Guilt also apparently functions as a form of pressure to make people pay positive attention to their partners, which presumably will benefit a relationship. It would be foolish to contend that guilt is invariably effective, but its general function seems to be to make people know not to repeat actions that have hurt, disappointed, or distressed an intimate partner.

The second function of guilt is as an influence technique. People make use of others' capacity for guilt in order to get their way. The apparently high rate of behavior change following guilt confirms that guilt induction can be an effective way of altering a partner's behavior. It is apparent that people sometimes exaggerate their suffering or distress in order to increase a partner's guilt feelings, presumably with the goal of altering that person's future behavior.

The third function of guilt is to redistribute emotional distress within the dyad. We have described evidence that guilt makes the transgressor feel worse and the victim feel better, thus effectively transferring the negative affect from the victim to the transgressor (who was responsible for causing it in the first place). We have also provided some evidence that interpersonal guilt manipulations sometimes bring people into similar emotional states, thereby facilitating communication and enhancing the relationship (cf. Locke & Horowitz, 1990).

Further research is needed to illuminate the interpersonal implications of guilt. A particularly fruitful area may be the negotiation of guilt over long periods of time in close relationships; one may speculate that transgressions and inequities are tracked by bath partners, resulting in a kind of guilt accounting. A return to the laboratory study of guilt would also be desirable, once the underlying mechanisms that result in guilt are better understood. More data on metaguilt would also be valuable.

For the present, however, it appears that guilt does serve important functions for strengthening and maintaining dose relationships. The undeniable importance of maintaining close relationships in human social life may help explain why our society continues to cultivate people's capacity for feeling guilty. Psychological theory may gain a better understanding of guilt by analyzing the interpersonal context in which guilt is created, negotiated, and resolved.

REFERENCES

Averill, J. (1982). *Anger and aggression: An essay on emotion.* New York: Springer-Verlag.

Baumeister, R. F. (1988a). Masochism as escape from self. *Journal of Sex Research, 25,* 28–59.

Baumeister, R. F. (1988b). Gender differences in masochistic scripts. *Journal of Sex Research, 25,* 478–499.

Baumeister; R. F. (1989). *Masochism and the self.* Hillsdale, NJ: Erlbaum.

Baumeister, R. F., Reis, H. T., & Delespaul, P. (1995). Subjective and experiential correlates of guilt in daily life. *Personality and Social Psychology Bulletin, 21:* 1256–1268.

Baumeister, R. F., & Stillwell, A. M. (1992). Autobiographical accounts, situational roles, and motivated biases: When stories don't match up. In J. Harvey, T. Orbuch, & A. Weber (Eds.), *Accounts, attributions, and close relationships* (pp. 52–70). New York: Springer-Verlag.

Baumeister, R. F., Stillwell, A. M., & Heatherton, T. F. (1994). Guilt: An interpersonal approach. *Psychological Bulletin, 115,* 243–267.

Baumeister, R. F., Stillwell, A. M., & Heatherton, T. F. (1995). Personal narratives about guilt: Role in action control and interpersonal relationships. *Basic and Applied Social Psychology, 17,* 173–198.

Baumeister, R. F., Stillwell, A. M., & Wotman, S. R. (1990). Victim and perpetrator accounts of interpersonal conflict: Autobiographical narratives about anger. *Journal of Personality and Social Psychology, 59,* 994–1005.

Baumeister, R. F., & Tice, D. M. (1990). Anxiety and social exclusion. *Journal of Social and Clinical Psychology, 9,* 165–195.

Baumeister, R. F., & Wotman, S. R. (1992). *Breaking hearts: The two sides of unrequited love.* New York: Guilford Press.

Baumeister, R. F., Wotman, S. R., & Stillwell, A. M. (1993). Unrequited love: On heartbreak, anger, guilt, scriptlessness, and humiliation. *Journal of Personality and Social Psychology, 64,* 377–394.

Bowlby, J. (1969). *Attachment and loss: Vol. 1. Attachment.* New York: Basic Books.

Bowlby, J. (1973). *Attachment and loss: Vol. 2. Separation: Anxiety and anger.* New York: Basic Books.

Brooke, R. J. (1985). What is guilt? *Journal of Phenomenological Psychology, 16,* 31–46.

Cialdini, R. B. (1984). *Influence: How and why people agree to things.* New York: Morrow.

Conquest, R. (1986). *The harvest of sorrow: Soviet collectivization and the terror-famine.* New York: Oxford University Press.

Freud, S. (1930). *Civilization and its discontents* (J. Riviere, Trans.). London: Hogarth Press.

Gergen, K. J., & Gergen, M. (1988). Narrative and the self as relationship. In L. Berkowitz (Ed.), *Advances in experimental social psychology* (Vol. 21, pp. 17–56). San Diego: Academic Press.

Harvey, J. H., Flanary, R., & Morgan, M. (1988). Vivid memories of vivid loves gone by. *Journal of Social and Personal Relationships, 3,* 359–373.

Harvey, J. H., Weber, A. L., Galvin, K. S., Huszti, H. C., & Garnick, N. N. (1986). Attribution in the termination of close relationships: A special focus on the account. In R. Gilmour & S. Duck (Eds.), *The emerging field of personal relationships* (pp. 189–201). Hillsdale, NJ: Erlbaum.

Harvey, J. H., Weber, A. L., & Orbuch, T. L. (1990). *Interpersonal accounts: A social-psychological perspective.* Oxford:

Basil Blackwell.

Hoffman, M. L. (1982). Development of prosocial motivation: Empathy and guilt. In N. Eisenberg (Ed.), *Development of prosocial behavior* (pp. 281–313). New York: Academic Press.

Katz, I., Glass, D. C., & Cohen, S. (1973). Ambivalence, guilt, and the scapegoating of minority group victims. *Journal of Experimental Social Psychology, 9,* 423–436.

Katz, J. (1988). *Seductions of crime: The moral and sensual attractions of doing evil.* New York: Basic Books.

Lerner, M. J., & Matthews, G. (1967). Reactions to suffering of others under conditions of indirect responsibility. *Journal of Personality and Social Psychology, 5,* 319–325.

Lewis, H. B. (1971). *Shame and guilt in neurosis.* New York: International Universities Press.

Lifton, R. J. (1986). *The Nazi doctors: Medical killing and the psychology of genocide.* New York: Basic Books.

Locke, K. D., & Horowitz, L. M. (1990). Satisfaction in interpersonal interactions as a function of similarity in level of dysphoria. *Journal of Personality and Social Psychology, 58,* 823–831.

McAdams, D. P. (1985). *Power, intimacy and the life story: Personological inquiries into identity.* Homewood, IL: Dorsey Press.

McGraw, K. M. (1987). Guilt following transgression: An attribution of responsibility approach. *Journal of Personality and Social Psychology, 53,* 247–256.

Mosher, D. L. (1965). Interaction of fear and guilt in inhibiting unacceptable behavior. *Journal of Consulting Psychology, 29,* 161–167.

Noel, R. C. (1973). Transgression–compliance: A failure to confirm. *Journal of Personality and Social Psychology, 27,* 151–153.

Ross, M., & Holmberg, D. (1990). Recounting the past: Gender differences in the recall of events in the history of a close relationship. In J. M. Olson & M. P. Zanna (Eds.), *The Ontario Symposium: Vol. 6. Self-inference processes* (pp. 135–152). Hillsdale, NJ: Erlbaum.

Shaver, P., Schwartz, J., Kirson, D., & O'Connor, C. (1987). Emotion knowledge: Further exploration of a prototype approach. *Journal of Personality and Social Psychology, 52,* 1061–1086.

Tangney, J. P. (1990). Assessing individual differences in proneness to shame and guilt: Development of the Self-Conscious Affect and Attribution Inventory. *Journal of Personality and Social Psychology, 59,* 102–111.

Tangney, J. P. (1991). Moral affect: The good, the bad, and the ugly. *Journal of Personality and Social Psychology, 61,* 598–607.

Tangney, J. P. (1992). Situational determinants of shame and guilt in young adulthood. *Personality and Social Psychology Bulletin, 18,* 199–206.

Tangney, J. P., Wagner, P. E., Fletcher, C., & Gramzow, R. (1992). Shamed into anger? The relation of shame and guilt to anger and self-reported aggression. *Journal of Personality and Social Psychology, 62,* 669–675.

Vaughan, D. (1986). *Uncoupling.* New York: Oxford University Press.

Wertheim, E. H., & Schwartz, J. C. (1983). Depression, guilt, and self-management of pleasant and unpleasant events. *Journal of Personality and Social Psychology, 45,* 884–889.

Zahn-Waxler, C., & Kochanska, G. (1990). The origins of guilt. In R. A. Thompson (Ed.), *Nebraska Symposium on Motivation: Vol. 36. Socioemotional development* (pp. 182–258). Lincoln: University of Nebraska Press.

The Emotional Experiences of Envy and Jealousy

W. Gerrod Parrott • Georgetown University

The principal task of this chapter is to present an account of the ways in which envy and jealousy are experienced. Both envy and jealousy can occur in several forms, which can be distinguished by the assessments and attentions of the person having the emotion. I contend that there is little that can be said in general about the experience of envy or jealousy. Envy and jealousy do not map as neatly onto the terms of emotion theory as do, say, sadness or fear; envy and jealousy exhibit greater variation in the conditions that elicit them and in the ways that people experience them. In order to speak clearly about these emotions, it is necessary to distinguish the important subtypes.

My analysis draws on a set of data being studied by Richard Smith and myself. We have collected several hundred detailed, first-person accounts of actual experiences of envy and jealousy, from subjects who were then asked to rate their experience on a number of scales. Analysis of these stories and of the data that accompany them has informed much of the account I present in this chapter, and I occasionally summarize the results of this research in support of my claims.

Underlying such an analysis of envy and jealousy are a number of conceptual issues concerning emotion, the relation between emotion and conscious experience, and the sources of emotional "feelings." These general issues need to be addressed prior to discussing envy and jealousy in particular.

Emotion and Emotional Experience

When people are asked to describe an actual experience of envy or jealousy, they usually provide a narrative of what I call an "emotional episode." An emotional episode includes the circumstances that lead up to an emotion or sequence of emotions, the emotions themselves, any attempts at self-regulation or coping that occur, subsequent events and actions, and the resolution or present status quo. In short, an emotional episode is the story of an emotional event, and it seems a natural unit of analysis for understanding human emotions. Most of the concepts in psychological theories of emotion are abstractions from the emotional episode: appraisals, "basic emotions," feelings, coping, display rules, effects of mood on cognition, cultural norms, and so on. These aspects may legitimately be studied in their own right, but to be properly understood, they must be returned to the context of the emotional episodes in which they occur (cf. Lazarus, Kanner, & Folkman, 1980; White, 1981).

Part of the difficulty in understanding envy and jealousy is in seeing how they map onto these narrower categories. Traditionally, the two are defined in terms that include the beliefs, motives, and emotional reactions of the emotional person, as well as the situations that evoke these responses (Parrott, 1988b). Envy may be said to occur when a person lacks what another has and either desires it or wishes that the other did not have it. It occurs when the superior qualities, achievements, or possessions of another are perceived as reflecting badly on the self. Envy is typically experienced as feelings of inferiority, longing, or ill will toward the envied person (Neu, 1980; Salovey & Rodin, 1984). Jealousy, on the other hand, may be said to occur when a person either fears losing or has already lost an important relationship with another person to a rival. Jealousy may be experienced in a number of ways, but typically these are thought to include fear of loss, anger over betrayal, and insecurity (Hupka, 1984; Mathes, Adams, & Davies, 1985). In analyzing envy and jealousy, I assume that the emotion people *experience* is determined by the cognitive appraisals that they make and by the aspects of those appraisals on which they focus their attention. This assumption is common to most cognitive approaches to emotion (for a review, see Smith & Ellsworth, 1985; for arguments concerning the consciousness of emotions and the role of attentional focus, see Ortony, Clore, & Collins, 1988.

Emotions, however, are not simply "feelings" or conscious experiences. Psychologists' conceptions of emotions include other elements in addition to experience, such as cognitive appraisals, social conventions, and physiological responses. These elements are conceptually distinct from conscious experience, even though they may in fact contribute to such experiences. Furthermore, as I discuss below, conscious experience is not always relevant to our use of emotion words, as when observers attribute envy or jealousy to others who do not believe themselves to be envious or jealous. Nevertheless, having certain experiences or "feelings" is often part of what is meant when a person is said to have a certain emotion, and it is sensible to speak of a person's having "feelings" of envy or jealousy. In this chapter I present a typology of these experiences.

Emotional experiences or "feelings" may result, in part, from changes in the body or from the activation of "primitive" or "noncognitive" areas of the brain, as some theorists have posited; however, it is important to note that emotional feelings can result from other sources as well. Feeling, as the term is used in speaking of emotion, may result from many high-level cognitive activities, such as having attention drawn to certain aspects of a situation, doubting, thinking hurriedly, and so forth (Parrott, 1988a). In addressing the experiences of envy and jealousy, I mean to include these aspects of experience, as well as those addressed by biologically oriented emotion theorists. I view emotional experience as inextricably bound up with such types of cognitive activity (Parrott, 1988a; Parrott & Sabini, 1989). This chapter concentrates on the perspective of people experiencing emotion: the manner in which they construe the situation, the aspects of the situation that they focus on, their evaluations of the situation, and their reactions to their own evaluations. These elements contribute to the emotional experience of envy and jealousy, just as limbic system activity or feedback from the body's periphery does (see also Frijda, 1986).

In focusing on emotional experience, I must distinguish those cases in which people are aware of being envious or jealous from those cases in which they are motivated by envy or jealousy yet do not know it. One important use of emotion words in everyday life is to explain a person's behavior (Peters, 1972). Both "envy" and "jealousy" can be used in this way: People may be said to be envious or jealous if their behavior is seen by others as being motivated by envy or jealousy. When envy or jealousy is meant in this way, no claim at all is made about the manner in which envious or jealous people are experiencing the situation—they may or may not realize that they are envious or jealous, and their feelings are irrelevant to the claim that envy or jealousy is the motive for their actions (Silver & Sabini, 1978b). In fact, it is easy to imagine situations in which an envious or jealous person is the *last* person to know that envy or jealousy motivates his or her actions. [. . .]

Envy

Of the two emotions that are the subject of this chapter, envy is presently the less studied. This contrasts with the past, when envy was widely discussed as a perennial problem of human nature. For example, the well-known *Maxims* of La Rochefoucauld (1678/1959) include more on envy than on jealousy; a later, similar collection by British essayist William Hazlitt (1823/1932) contains numerous aphorisms about envy while neglecting jealousy almost entirely. In recent times, envy has been mentioned less often, and in fact the word "jealousy" has now come to be used frequently in its place, although the two emotions are quite distinct. The sociologist Helmut Schoeck (1966/1969) argued that the concept of envy has been actively repressed in the social sciences and in moral philosophy since the turn of the century, possibly because it is unpleasant to admit to. Yet Schoeck's thesis is that envy has an important role in all societies—that there are crimes of envy, politics based on envy, institutions designed to regulate envy, and powerful motives for avoiding being envied by others. Neglecting envy costs us a complete understanding of many interesting phenomena, so let us try to give envy its due.

At the heart of envy is social comparison, a common and powerful influence on the self-concept (Festinger, 1954; Heider, 1958). Much of our self-esteem comes from comparison with others (Morse & Gergen, 1970; Tesser & Campbell, 1980). When one's abilities, achievements, or possessions compare poorly with those of another, there is the potential for a decrease in one's self-esteem and public stature, and surely this is one route to envy (Heider, 1958; Silver & Sabini, 1978a; see also Salovey & Rothman, 1991). Yet social comparison can lead to envy in other ways that have not been discussed as much. Social comparison can also stir up envy simply by heightening one's awareness of one's own deprivation, and it can promote envy by making salient the fact that one's own suffering is not shared by all.

Not all negative social comparisons lead to envy, however. Aristotle, in the *Nichomachean Ethics* and the *Rhetoric*, points out that envy is felt chiefly toward those who are our peers, for reasons having to do with notions of justice (Barnes, 1984). Spinoza (1677/1949, Part 3, Proposition 55) also noted this tendency, and attributed it to limits in what a person will desire. Contemporary research by Silver and Sabini (1978a) suggests that there are self-presentational reasons for this fact. People do not necessarily envy the Rockefellers' wealth, because the discrepancy does not reflect badly on them. It is only when the discrepancy between someone else's success and one's own failure serves to demonstrate or call attention to one's shortcomings that envy results.

Clearly, what Silver and Sabini demonstrated for public stature must be true for private self-esteem as well. A discrepancy between ourselves and dissimilar others does not suggest to us that we are inferior, whereas a discrepancy with persons who are comparable to ourselves in relevant respects provides strong evidence that our inferiority, not other factors, is the source of the discrepancy. This point was demonstrated experimentally in a study by Salovey and Rodin (1984), in which these factors were manipulated orthogonally in the laboratory. Undergraduates received either positive or negative feedback about a trait that was either high or low in relevance to their self-concept, after which they anticipated interacting with another student who had performed well in an area that was either related or not related to a subject's own aspirations. The results suggested that symptoms of envy occurred in only one of the eight conditions—the one in which students received negative feedback about their abilities in a domain that was central to their self-concept, and then faced interaction with a student who excelled in the same domain. Other studies suggest that young children may experience envy with less regard to the self-relevance of the aspects being compared. Bers and Rodin (1984) found that envy was more associated with self-relevance of comparison in children 10–11 years of age than in children 6–7 years of age.

It is a fact of life that people are unequal. Certainly some inequalities stem for injustice, but even in a just world some people would be born with more beauty than others, some would receive more of a given talent than others, some would fairly come to acquire more possessions than others, and so forth. It is difficult to imagine that these differences among peers could be made not to matter. When one contemplates how common the situations promoting envy are, one appreciates envy's potential ubiquity and influence.

Nevertheless nonsituational variables also influence the occurrence of envy. The qualities that were once called "character" (and that social scientists might today refer to as "personality variables") strongly influence whether d person succumbs to envy, even under the optimal conditions described above. Only if a person confronted with superiority is predisposed to feel inferior and resentful, rather than inspired and motivated to improve—only if a person construes another's success as a personal loss, rather than as a gain of a larger whole of which he or she is a part—will envy be provoked by the circumstances outlined above. On the whole, little is known about individual differences in susceptibility to envy. Heider (1958) discussed some possibilities, including the ability to make comparisons without inferring evaluations, the ability to join oneself with the other in a "we-group," and the ability to avoid the comparison of lots altogether. We (Smith, Parrott, Diener, Hoyle, & Kim, 1999) have constructed a scale designed to measure the propensity to become envious, and have demonstrated that it successfully predicts envy both in the laboratory and in everyday life. [. . .] Further research on the characterological determinants of envy clearly remains to be done, however.

Malicious and Nonmalicious Envy

Once the conditions for eliciting envy are met, the emotion can take several forms. I propose that at least six distinguishable emotions can be experienced as part of envy. This variety of envious experience can best be introduced by starting with a more general distinction, one between a sense of envy that is morally acceptable and one that is morally reprehensible. Since ancient times, authors have distinguished what I call "nonmalicious envy" from "malicious envy." The history of this distinction goes back to Aristotle, who distinguished envy from what he called "emulation." Modern authors continue to make similar distinctions. For example, Neu (1980) distinguishes "admiring envy" from "malicious envy"; Taylor (1988) distinguishes "admiring envy," "emulating envy, and "malicious envy"; and Rawls (1971) distinguishes "benign envy" and "emulative envy" from "envy proper." In inventing the term "nonmalicious envy" my aim is not to clutter the literature with additional terminology, but rather to reflect that Aristotle's emulation is not quite the same thing as modern conceptions of nonmalicious envy, and that such terms as "admiring envy" can be confusing. Aristotle distinguished emulation from envy by defining emulation as a longing, dissatisfaction, or angst

caused by seeing the presence, in persons whose nature is like our own, of good things that are highly valued and are possible for ourselves to acquire; but it is felt not because others have these goods, but because we have not got them ourselves. It is therefore a good feeling felt by good persons, whereas [malicious] envy is a bad feeling felt by bad persons. Emulation makes us take steps to secure the good things in question, envy makes us take steps to stop our neighbour having them. (Barnes, 1984, p. 2212)

Aristotle's emphasis was that some forms of envy ("emulation") motivate people to improve themselves, whereas others motivate people to take good things away from others. When a modern writer such as Neu adopts such a distinction, much of Aristotle's meaning is retained, but the emphasis is altered to focus more on the roles of self-esteem and feelings of inferiority—notions that did not much concern Aristotle. An additional problem is that the term "admiring envy" is confusing, since admiration need not be present in it at all. For both these reasons, I think that "nonmalicious envy" is a preferable term for those varieties of envy that are, after all, distinguished primarily by their contrast with "malicious envy." Some authors do not consider nonmalicious envy to be envy at all. Aristotle did not, and neither do Schoeck (1966/1969), Rawls (1971), or Silver and Sabini (1978b); however, many authors do (e.g., Neu, 1980; Taylor, 1988). I follow this broader usage, in part because it is clear from my data that in everyday usage people mean the word "envy" to encompass both senses.

The focus of nonmalicious envy is "I wish I had what you have." It may be experienced in a variety of ways: as inferiority to the envied person, longing for what the other has, despair of ever having it, determination to improve oneself, or admiration of the envied person. The focus of malicious envy, on the other hand, is "I wish you did not have what you do" (Neu, 1980). Both varieties of envy are unpleasant, but only one seems worthy of envy's membership among the seven deadly sins: It is the malicious variety that earned envy that distinction. The focus of malicious envy is the removal or destruction of the envied object or quality. To the person suffering malicious envy, the marvelous car should be stolen or damaged, the virtuous person corrupted or killed, the beautiful face covered or disfigured. In malicious envy it is not necessary to desire what the other has—only to desire that it be taken away from the other. Nor is it necessary that the good fortune of the envied person be at the expense of the envier (consider envy of another's virtue). Malicious envy, however, may involve the delusion that the other is somehow the cause of one's inferiority, and thus of one's unhappiness (see Smith, 1991). It thus may be experienced as anger or resentment over some alleged unfairness, and may be generalized to become hatred of the envied person. As Chesterfield said, "People hate those who make them feel their own inferiority" (Mahon, 1845, p. 9). It is this malicious form of envy that is considered a sin. For Aristotle, the evil of this envy was its desire to lessen the amount of goodness in the world, or, obversely, to experience joy at another's misfortune (an emotion for which there is no good word in English, but for which the Germans have a lovely word, *Schadenfreude*).

It should be apparent that there are strong similarities between malicious envy and anger. In fact, the distinction between the two rests primarily on whether the hostility is justified—a fact that illustrates the importance of including cognition and social standards in one's conception of emotion (see Fortenbaugh, 1975, for a discussion of Aristotle's position on this issue). If the superiority of the envied person results from what can reasonably be construed as unfair or unjustified actions (i.e., a transgression), then the anger it elicits may be considered to be justified, and may be called "righteous indignation" or "resentment" (the latter term was proposed by Rawls, 1971, to distinguish it from malicious envy). If, on the other hand, the superiority is not the result of injustice, then the anger is inappropriate and may be termed "malicious envy" (Silver & Sabini, 1978a).

The distinction between resentment and malicious envy is one that is made using the objective facts of the social world; in clear cases there will be agreement, whereas in ambiguous cases there will be debate (Sabini & Silver, 1982). At the moment an emotion occurs, however, a person may be wrong about whether anger is justified or not, and the distinction (mentioned above) between the explanatory and experiential meanings of emotion words may become relevant. In some cases judged by objective viewers as malicious envy, envious people may perceive themselves to be righteously indignant, not envious. They will be wrong in one sense, since the objective social facts will not support their claims of transgression or injustice; however, in such cases they will see themselves as justifiably angry or irritated, not as envious. In other cases of malicious envy, envious people may realize (to some extent, at least) that the anger felt toward the envied persons is unjustified. The perceptions of transgression that dominate their awareness and fuel their anger are not felt with total conviction, and are undermined to some extent by knowledge that their friends (or the judicial system) will not recognize their charges as valid. As much as one may *want* to believe that

the person given the lead in the play is the pet of the drama coach, as much as one may *feel* that the newspaper reporter has been biased in giving so many more words to one's teammate, there may also be awareness of the self-protective function such thoughts can have and of the reasons to be skeptical about them. This awareness reduces the malevolence of the envy, or at least inhibits the envious person from acting on it. It may also bring on some guilt about unjustified ill will.

Awareness that anger is unjustified may also lead to a resentment that has as its object not the envied person, but rather the unfairness of life itself. One may feel angry at the fates for making some people beautiful without feeling angry at beautiful people for being beautiful; one may feel resentful of the fact that some children are born into families that have intact marriages or lots of money without blaming the children who come from such families. As William Hazlitt (1823/1932) observed, "Envy, among other ingredients, has a mixture of the love of justice in it. We are more angry at undeserved than at deserved goodfortune" (p. 169). Nietzsche (1880/1911) likewise noted the existence of what he called envy's "nobler sister":

> In a condition of equality there arises indignation if A. is prosperous above and B. unfortunate beneath their deserts and equality. These . . . are emotions of nobler natures. They feel the want of justice and equity in things that are independent of the arbitrary choice of men—or, in other words, they desire the equality recognized by man to be recognized as well by Nature and chance. They are angry that men of equal merits should not have equal fortune. (p. 209)

The Varieties of Envious Experience

Distinguishing malicious from nonmalicious envy illustrates how our concept of envy, in an important way, requires us to think in terms of emotional episodes, for in making this distinction we already are depicting envy as unfolding in time. Both malicious and nonmalicious envy start with social comparison—with the realization that there is someone who is superior to oneself in a respect that is of importance to oneself. From this point, a focus on oneself and one's shortcomings leads to some form of nonmalicious envy. At this point, one may also come to resent the unfairness of one's fate.

If, however, there is a focus on the envied person as a cause of one's shortcoming, the hostility and hatred of malicious envy will result. It is plausible in at least some cases to consider malicious envy to be the result of a defensive reappraisal of the circumstances, motivated by the desire to avoid feeling inferior. This possibility was advanced in the writings of Nietzsche (1887/1967), and can be seen in analyses ranging from José Ortega y Gasset's (1914/1961) discussion of failures in seeking truth ("Rancor emanates from a sense of inferiority," p. 35) to H. L. Mencken's (1922) essay on the antagonism of artists toward their critics ("Injustice is relatively easy to bear; it is justice that hurts," p. 101).

Such malicious envy may then be countered following consideration of the objective bases of one's interpretation, and feelings of guilt and shame may follow along with reappraisal of the situation. If malicious envy remains unchecked by any such objective reappraisal, the envious person will *experience* righteous resentment, not envy; this is the special case described above, which from an objective perspective may be called envy but from the subjective perspective of the emotional person will not be experienced as envy. Envy evolves over time; like many emotions, it does not hold still for the emotion theorist. Our concept of envy as an emotion refers to this set of objectively evaluated reactions—not to any single moment of experience, nor to any single sequence of experiences.

According to this analysis, we can distinguish at least six emotions that can be experienced as part of envy. This list is not meant to be exhaustive, but it does describe a substantial proportion of cases. Analysis of several hundred first-person accounts of envy confirms that emotional episodes of envy contain one or more of these six types of envious experiences.

First, envy usually includes an intense longing for what the other has. This longing is brought on by focusing on the desired object or quality, by being aware of how much it is desired, and by being frustrated in this desire both by lacking it and by knowing that another person has been able to possess it.

Second, when envious people focus on their own shortcomings relative to the envied persons, their thoughts include awareness of their inferiority and of the implications for their self-concept and their public stature. The "feelings of inferiority" resulting from such a cognitive focus include distress and sadness (due to the appraisal of shortcoming and inferiority) and anxiety (due to the prospect of undesirable future events and uncertainty about one's self). Interestingly, in the experiment by Salovey and Rodin (1984) described above, depression and anxiety were significantly greater in the envy condition than in other conditions.

When an envious person construes another's superiority as the result of a specific, objective unfairness, he or she may see the envied individual (or others) as guilty of a transgression that has caused this individual to be able to enjoy undeserved advantages that may rightfully belong to the envious person. Such a construing may well lead to anger or resentment over the transgression, and, quite possibly, to hatred of the envied person. I call this type of experience "agent-focused resentment," because it is a resentment of a specific unfairness for which a person or group of persons is perceived as responsible. Whether this type of

TABLE 19.1. Emotional Experiences that Can Be Part of Envy

Emotional experience	Description
Longing	Longing for what another person has; frustrated desire
Inferiority	Sadness or distress over one's shortcomings or over inferiority to the envied person; anxiety over one's status; despair of ever obtaining what the envied person has
Agent-focused resentment	Resentment of a specific person or group; displeasure over their superiority; anger and hatred of those deemed responsible
Global resentment	Resentment of unfairness of circumstances or fate
Guilt	Guilt over ill will; belief that rancor is wrong; "enlightened malicious envy"
Admiration	Admiration; emulation

experience can accurately be called "envy" depends on the correctness of the accusation from which it follows. If the resentful person is correct about the transgression that has occurred, then the person should not be considered envious, but rather righteously angry or justifiably resentful (Rawls, 1971). If, on the other hand, the accusation is unjustified, then this experience would be an example of "malicious envy."

When envious people focus on the unfairness of life itself, of the circumstances in which fate has placed them, then their experience is also one of anger and resentment. There is a difference in the object of the emotion, however, so this resentment is of a different type than agent-focused resentment—what I call "global resentment." Global resentment is experienced as anger about the unfairness of life itself—at the unfairness that mere luck can cause another person to possess qualities or objects that one desires for oneself. Global resentment is marked by an awareness that the envied person is not to blame for his or her superiority; that no one else is directly responsible either; and that if one were oneself blessed with this advantage, one would not be wrong to enjoy it as well.

A fifth way in which envy can be experienced follows from the knowledge that the ill will produced by agent-focused resentment is not warranted. In reaction to such resentment, the envious person may then feel guilty or shameful (cf. Mayer & Gaschke, 1988). This type of experience is characteristic of the moral struggle envious people may have with themselves. For guilt to occur, envious people must realize that their malicious thoughts are wrong or sinful. The occurrence of guilt often accompanies the beginning of attempts to inhibit malicious envy and to replace it with something more worthy of a good person. Agent-focused resentment that is accompanied by guilt about this ill will might be called "enlightened malicious envy." In contrast, malicious envy that is unaccompanied by guilt or other awareness of inappropriateness—that is, anger that is experienced as righteous anger but objectively deemed envy—might be called "unenlightened malicious envy." A final form of envious experience is admiration, an appreciation of the envied person's good qualities. "Admiration is happy self-surrender; envy is unhappy self-assertion," wrote Kierkegaard (1849/1954, p. 217) in distinguishing the two. Al-

though this type of experience does not fit the prototype (or definition) of envy, it does occur as part of episodes of envy. People whose envy has included feelings of inferiority and global resentment may experience admiration when they switch their attention from their own deficiencies and the unfairness of having them to the qualities of the person whose example has brought on these other experiences. Admiration is part of Aristotle's emulation—the reaction that Aristotle deemed the desirable one, the one that naturally occurs in the person of good character. Admiration may lead envious people to try to improve themselves, using the envied person as an example. So admiration has a place in a list of envious experiences.

Actual episodes of envy are hypothesized to consist of one or more of the above-described types of experiences. What experiences will occur will depend on how the situation is interpreted and what aspects of the situation are focused on. In principle, a particular episode of envy may consist of any combination of these six types of experience; in practice, certain combinations will prove more common than others, since certain of these experiences imply incompatible interpretations of the situation. For example, admiring and resenting the envied person would be expected to be relatively uncommon, while admiring and feeling inferior to the envied person would be expected to be relatively more common. These combinations can be examined empirically, either by having coders rate accounts of envy or by having subjects rate their own accounts. With either method, what I have consistently found is that inferiority and admiration tend to occur most frequently when agent-focused resentment is absent, and vice versa. Global resentment and longing seem to be consistent either with inferiority or with agent-focused resentment. Reports of intense guilt about ill will do occur, but are fairly uncommon.

These findings suggest that two basic determinants of the quality of an envious experience are whether one believes one has been unfairly treated and whether one believes that one's disadvantage is one's own fault. Our data suggest that when one's own qualities are seen as being responsible for one's poor showing by comparison with another, the most salient responses are those concerning feelings of inferiority as well as motivation to improve oneself. When unfair treatment is perceived, feelings of anger and resentment predominate.

Jealousy

Jealousy is an emotion experienced when a person is threatened by the loss of an important relationship with another person (the "partner") to a "rival" (usually another person, but not necessarily so). A loss that does not involve the partner's starting up an analogous relationship with a rival does not produce jealousy. One does not become jealous when one's partner dies, or moves across the country; not would one be said to be jealous if one were *rejected* by the partner without the partner's taking up a new relationship with anyone else (Mathes et al., 1985). The threat must involve the loss of the relationship *to a rival*, whether this loss is feared, is actual and present, or is a fact of the past. This latter point is often described, but rarely explained. Mathes et al. (1985) attribute the distinction between rejection and jealousy to "social custom." [. . .]

The commonest examples of jealousy involve romantic relationships, so it is important to realize that jealousy occurs in other types of relationships as well. Sibling jealousy is well known, and jealousy may also occur between friends, employees with the same boss, students of the same teacher, and so forth. The relationship need not involve love, and the rival need not even be a person: A man may be jealous of his wife's love of law school, a woman of her husband's new car (Tov-Ruach, 1980). What is always true is that jealousy involves a triangle of relations. One side of this triangle represents the relationship between two people, the jealous person and the partner; another side represents the relationship between the partner and the rival; the third side, the attitudes of the jealous person toward the rival.

Given the variety of relationships and rivals that can generate jealousy, it has proved to be something of a challenge to characterize just what threat they all have in common. It is not the loss of romantic love, since jealousy occurs in nonromantic relationships; it is not the loss of the public appearance of a relationship, since jealousy can occur if a partner is known to be attracted to another yet decides not to act on this attraction. One attractive characterization is that the threat of jealousy is the loss of another's attention—a hypothesis developed by Neu (1980) and especially Tov-Ruach (1980). Not just any loss of attention produces jealousy (one does not usually become jealous when the switchboard operator puts one on hold); it is a loss of what Tov-Ruach called "formative attention" that results in jealousy. Formative attention is attention that sustains part of one's self-concept. For example, if my regular chess partner begins playing chess with another player, I would not become jealous of the new partner unless my partner's regular company has been formative to me in some way. Perhaps his enjoyment of my play sustains my view of myself as an interesting, worthy opponent; perhaps some quality of my partner has helped me develop as a chess player; perhaps my partner's choosing me as his or her preferred opponent has allowed me to think that I have desirable qualities as an opponent that few others offer; perhaps my partner has a certain status among local chess players that has been conferred on me by merit of being his or her customary partner. It is because relationships with others can be formative in these ways that the threat of losing such a relationship can be so devastating to one's self.

One might say, then, that at the heart of jealousy is a *need to be needed*. This need exists because relationships with other persons create and confirm certain aspects of our selves. Certain aspects of the self are intrinsically interpersonal (Tov-Ruach, 1980). We think of ourselves as being fun to be with, sexually attractive, humorous, or worthy opponents. These concepts are meaningless when applied to a person who does not interact with others: There is no "fun to be with" without others to be fun with, no "sexually attractive" without someone to be attracted, no "humorous" without a laughing audience, no "worthy opponent" without another opponent. We need others not only to confirm these aspects of ourselves, but, in a real sense, to *create* these aspects of ourselves. A steady relationship involving these sorts of interactions is, among other things, a constant source of self-definition. The threat of the loss of such a relationship is therefore the threat of a loss of self, not the loss of "property," as some have mistakenly claimed (e.g., Davis, 1936).

The fact that the prototypical cases of jealousy involve romantic love can be explained by the importance of the aspects of the self that are supported by this type of relationship in our culture. If one is jealous of one's chess opponent's interest in another player, the aspects of one's self that are threatened are not a central or substantial part of the self-concept (for most of us). On the other hand, if one is jealous of one's lover's interest in a romantic rival, the aspects of one's self that are threatened are both central and significant (for most of us). Interestingly, the most powerful jealousy of youth is sibling jealousy, and the relationship that appears threatened is the one that is most important—namely, that with one's parents. Surely one reason for the decline of sibling jealousy in adolescence and the ascent of romantic jealousy is the decline of parents and the ascent of romantic partners in sustaining the most important aspects of the self.

One approach to understanding the experience of jealousy is to define jealousy fairly narrowly, restricting it to a certain type of emotional experience. The advantage of this approach is that it will provide a fairly coherent category of emotional experience. The disadvantage is that in everyday parlance the word "jealousy" is used quite broadly, so a narrow definition will be useful as a technical term but will apply to only some of what is commonly called jealousy. Another approach is to define jealousy more broadly, which provides the advantage of including all usages of the term but also the disadvantage of conceptual looseness. The problem is that the situations that are said to cause jealousy tend to produce a variety of powerful emotions. If jealousy is defined broadly, as all of the emotions that tend to occur in these situations, then there will appear to be a bewildering variety of ways to experience jealousy. (I have found it convenient to define envy broadly in the preceding section only because the variety of experiences is tolerably small.) If jealousy is defined narrowly, then it will typically be only one of a variety of emotions that are experienced in the situations that produce jealousy. Below, I present one solution of each type. I find both to be useful—the narrower definition of jealousy because of its conceptual clarity; the broader one because of its usefulness in understanding the rich variety of experiences that occur during emotional episodes of jealousy.

An Emotional Experience Characteristic of Jealousy

If jealousy were to be defined narrowly as a single type of emotional experience, I would propose that it be defined as a type of anxious insecurity following from the perception of threat to a relationship that provides formative attention. Perceiving such a threat makes a person feel insecure about the status of the relationship, and also about the aspects of the self sustained by the relationship. What distinguishes this anxiety from other anxieties is that it is at once a fear of losing a relationship and of losing one's self. If there is a unique experience corresponding to jealousy, whether romantic, sibling, or otherwise, it seems likely to be this feeling of fear and insecurity.

When jealousy is defined so narrowly, emotional episodes involving jealousy must often be said to include other emotional experiences as well. When the narrow definition is used, these experiences are best considered separate emotions that occur when the jealous person shifts the focus of attention to other aspects of the situation besides the threat of loss. On this account, jealous people are often also angry people, hurt people, depressed people, and even disgusted or happy people (Hupka, 1984), but when we speak of their being jealous we emphasize their fear of loss. The word "jealousy" is often meant in a broader sense, so the narrow definition is suggested primarily as a technical term that calls attention to an experience common to the many varieties of jealousy. An additional reason for considering this narrow sense to be central is that it is often the source of many of the other emotional responses that occur in jealous episodes.

Suspicious Jealousy and Fait Accompli Jealousy

If the experience of jealousy were to be defined broadly, as a characteristic constellation of emotional experiences, then it would appear to take on a variety of forms. In order to make sense of this variety, several distinctions must be made between types of jealousy-inducing situations. The most important distinction concerns the nature of the threat to the relationship. Jealousy may occur when the threat is only suspected and its nature is unclear, or it may occur when the threat is unambiguously real and its effects on the relationship are known and achieved. When the threat is unclear or only suspected, we may call the resulting jealousy "suspicious jealousy," since the predominant reactions concern fears and uncertainties. When the threat to the relationship is unambiguous and damaging, we may term the resulting jealousy "*fait accompli* jealousy," since the threat is an accomplished fact, a thing that is known to be already done. In each of these situations jealousy may be experienced in a number of ways, but each situation is characterized by a different constellation of alternatives. This distinction is similar to one made by Hupka (1989, 1991), who has recently proposed that different experiences of jealousy follow from different levels of threat. Hupka distinguishes low, intermediate, and high levels of threat. His categories of low and intermediate threat correspond roughly to what I call suspicious jealousy; his category of high threat corresponds roughly to fait accompli jealousy. Hupka's emphasis on quantitative differences in level of threat differs from my emphasis on qualitative differences in the appraisals, motives, and concerns of people in these situations. Nevertheless, I consider his approach to be compatible with my own.

Suspicious jealousy occurs when a person believes that a partner may be transferring to a rival the type of attention that is formative in the relationship. The characteristic experience of this form of jealousy is that of anxiety and insecurity—the narrow sense of jealousy defined above. The importance of the relationship, the uncertainty concerning its status, and the jealous person's insecurity about the self create the anxiety, and this insecurity motivates the person to find out whether these fears are warranted. This motive, in turn, is responsible for a variety of cognitive symptoms that characterize the jealous person, including suspiciousness, inability to concentrate on other matters, ruminations and preoccupations, fantasies of the partner and rival enjoying a wonderful relationship, and an oversensitivity to slights or hints of dissatisfaction by the partner. These cognitive symptoms, I contend, are as much a part of the experience of suspicious jealousy as are the other aspects of anxiety (Parrott, 1988a). Other emotions may occur as well. It is not uncommon that the jealous person knows the rival, and focusing on that relationship may produce other emotional states; puzzlement, alarm, envy, anger, and hurt are commonly directed at the rival. I consider suspicious jealousy to be the prototype of jealousy. It accounts for the etymological relationship between "jealous" and "zealous," and it is most consistent with the usage of nonpsychologists (Hupka, 1989) and with historical usage. One of La Rochefoucauld's (1678/1959) *Maxims*, for example, is as follows: "Jealousy feeds on suspicion,

and it turns into fury or it ends as soon as we pass from suspicion to certainty" (p. 41).

Fait accompli jealousy, on the other hand, is relatively free of anxiety concerning the status of the relationship—that much, at least, is usually clear. The characteristic experiences of this form of jealousy depend on the focus of attention. When the focus is on the loss of the relationship, the experience is one of sadness; when the focus is on the wrongdoing or betrayal of the partner or the rival, the experience is one of anger or hurt; when the focus is on one's inadequacy, the experience is one of depression and anxiety; when the focus is on the stress of coping with new social status, the experience is one of anxiety; and, let us not forget, when the focus is on the superiority of the rival, the experience can be one of envy (a point that has never been made more clearly than by Spinoza, 1677/1949, Part 3, Proposition 35). These are some of the common experiences found in our data, but they do not exhaust the possibilities by any means. Disgust, and even happiness or relief, can result from the proper focus of concern (Hupka, 1984).

One experience found in our data that is not much discussed in the literature is envy of the former partner. In fait accompli jealousy, people frequently see their former partners as being happy in their new relationships. They compare their own loneliness to the apparent happiness of their ex-partners; they compare the dependence and yearning they continue to feel for their ex-partners to the ex-partners' apparent lack of such need for them.

Under some conditions, it should be noted, suspicious jealousy can result in experiences similar to fait accompli jealousy. During episodes of suspicious jealousy, people vacillate between doubt and certainty that their suspicions are true. They usually feel unsure about what is true, but at some moments they believe their worst suspicions to be true, whereas at others they think these suspicions are most likely groundless and are the products of an overactive imagination. It stands to reason that when jealous people are feeling most certain that their relationships are actually threatened, their experience will most resemble that of fait accompli jealousy. Their beliefs may still have something of a provisional nature, because there may still be a lack of evidence, or because their partners may still insist that nothing has changed; but to the extent that the suspicions seem warranted, jealous people will tend to react to the likely loss of relationships in the ways that characterize fair accompli jealousy. The true distinction between these two forms of jealousy, then, is best described as a jealous person's subjective assessment of the threat, rather than the objective nature of the threat.

In our data, cases of suspicious jealousy are characterized by a greater salience of suspicion and distrust; by more fear, apprehension, anxiety, and worry; and by more intense feelings of being threatened and fearing loss. Cases of fait accompli jealousy, on the other hand, are characterized by more longing for what another has, and by more guilt about ill will toward others, both of which are symptoms of the envy that is often a component of this type of jealousy. [...]

Are Envy and Jealousy Experienced Differently?

In the analyses above, it has been taken for granted that the experiences of envy and jealousy are qualitatively distinct. There is considerable precedent for doing so. Philosophers, going back at least to Cicero's *Tusculan Disputations* (written in 45 B.C.), have argued that the two emotions are quite distinct. Recent arguments for their differentiation have been made by Sullivan (1953), Schoeck (1966/1969), Neu (1980), and Taylor (1988). These authors all agree on two things: (1) that envy and jealousy should be distinguished, and (2) that people frequently fail to do so. Let us consider each of these points in turn.

The arguments for distinguishing envy and jealousy are many. Envy occurs when another has what one lacks oneself, whereas jealousy is concerned with the loss of a relationship one has. Jealousy concerns relationships with other people, whereas envy extends to characteristics and possessions. In envy the rival's gain need not be at one's own expense; in jealousy one's own loss is someone else's gain. The most typical experiences of jealousy are fear of loss, suspicion, distrust, and anger; those of envy are inferiority, longing, and ill will. The hostility that accompanies envy is not socially sanctioned, whereas that accompanying jealousy often is, so the envious person's ill will may be accompanied by the belief that this hostility is unjustified and wrong.

Why these two emotions should be so readily conflated is best understood by considering some similarities between them. Both may involve hostility, although (as noted above) the betrayal of jealousy is frequently a legitimate transgression, whereas the resentment of envy is unsanctioned. Both also involve losses of self-esteem stemming from social comparison, although here too there are differences. As noted above, in envy the social comparison is made by the envious person, whereas in jealousy it is presumed to be made by the partner. Thus, in accounts of jealousy one often finds the jealous person wondering what in the world the partner sees in the rival; by contrast, the envious person *knows* what is superior about the rival. Nevertheless, the result is quite similar—a loss of self-esteem. Finally, jealousy and envy may frequently co-occur. Envy is frequently part of episodes of jealousy, and each of these emotions may lead to the other. The conditions that precipitate jealousy of one's partner may encourage comparisons with the rival, leading to envy. Furthermore, envy of a person may lead to thinking of that person as a rival for one's partner, and thus to the anxious insecurity of jealousy.

Given these similarities, one might wonder whether the average person makes distinctions between envy and jealousy. It seems increasingly common for the word "jealous" to mean *either* jealous or envious (Schoeck, 1966/1969). It would be permissible, for example, for a baseball player to say that he is jealous of his wife's attention to a handsome new rookie, and also for him to say that he is jealous of Nolan Ryan's fastball. The former situation fits the classic definition of jealousy, the latter that of envy, and yet the word "jealous" happily fits them both. Thus, people may not make much of a distinction between jealousy and envy.

In one study, my colleagues and I empirically investigated this possibility (Smith, Kim, & Parrott, 1988). Subjects were first asked to write a description of a situation in which they had felt either strong envy or strong jealousy; afterwards, they were asked to describe a situation in which they had felt whichever emotion they were not asked about initially. Raters then coded these descriptions for whether they best fit the traditional definition of envy or that of jealousy. When asked initially for envy, subjects by and large (93%) described envy, but when asked for jealousy they were less consistent, describing jealousy 75% of the time and envy the rest. Thus, the word "envy" seems to have a fairly fixed meaning, whereas the word "jealousy" seems to be capable of having a broader range of meanings. This interpretation received further support from the second set of descriptions subjects wrote. When subjects had initially written about jealousy, their subsequent accounts of "envy" mostly corresponded to the traditional definition (91%), just as with the first set of descriptions; however, when subjects initially wrote about envy, a large proportion of their subsequent accounts of "jealousy" (41%) were also about envy. This shows that the term "jealousy" did not necessarily *contrast* with the envy situations previously described, whereas "envy" did seem to imply a contrast with the jealousy situations previously described.

This study helps to clarify what ordinary people think about the sort of situations referred to by "envy" and "jealousy." Their conceptions matched those of scholars fairly well. The word "envy" evoked descriptions of situations in which one's personal qualities did not measure up to those of another; the word "jealousy" evoked some situations like this as well, but mostly descriptions of times when an actual or desired relationship (usually a romantic relationship) was threatened by another.

What about the affective experiences evoked in such situations? Do ordinary people share scholars' ideas about those as well? To find out, we gave subjects a list of affective states that have been theorized to be typical of envy and/or jealousy, and asked them to indicate for each whether it was more characteristic of envy or of jealousy. Subjects reliably rated most of these attributes as being more characteristic of one affect or the other. Envy was believed to be characterized by motivation to improve, longing, inferiority, and self-criticism. Judged as more characteristic of jealousy were suspicion, rejection, anger, hurt, fear of loss, desire to get even, and overall intensity. A number of basic affects such as anxiousness and sadness were among the several items that produced no reliable preference (Smith et al., 1988).

Thus, people do appear to distinguish between envy and jealousy, both in terms of the situations that produce them and in terms of the feelings that characterize them. There is a difference, though, between what subjects *say* they feel when envious or jealous and what they *actually* feel. In one published paper investigating differences in actual experiences of envy and jealousy, Salovey and Rodin (1986) reported a series of three experiments in which they looked for different patterns of emo-

tions or thought in the two. Surprisingly, the most they ever found was that jealousy seemed much more intense than envy. Otherwise, envy and jealousy seemed to be experienced in basically the same way. The differences seemed more quantitative than qualitative.

Such a comparison presupposes, of course, that envy and jealousy can be addressed as coherent entities. The analyses I have provided above suggest that this is not entirely the case, and that one might be justified in asking "Which envy?" and "Which jealousy?" A global comparison of the experiences of envy and jealousy requires that certain assumptions be made about whether the types of envy and jealousy represented are typical of those experienced in real life, and whether it is informative to average across the various subtypes of envy and jealousy. Nevertheless, Salovey and Rodin's finding seems quite puzzling in light of the differences that have been postulated to exist.

There could be several explanations for this puzzling finding. One, suggested by Salovey and Rodin, is that "envy" and "jealousy" refer to different situations that both produce essentially the same sort of experience. Another possibility is that envy and jealousy co-occur much of the time, so empirical measures of one will be confounded by the presence of the other. Finally, it seems possible that the greater *intensity* of jealousy may serve to obscure differences in the *quality* of the two. Given that the typical case of jealousy seems to be so much more intense than the typical case of envy, comparing subjects' ratings of the two will show that jealousy swamps envy on most measures. But our notion of the *quality* of an affective experience is less closely related to the *absolute values* of the various affective components than it is to the *relative salience* of the components—the "affective profile" of the experience.

The accounts of envy and jealousy that I have collected represent a sample of real-life experiences. Subjects ($N = 149$) rated their experiences on scales designed to capture the differences between envy and jealousy (as well as their shared qualities). Examining these ratings of actual experiences of envy and jealousy clarifies these issues considerably (Parrott & Smith, 1993).

If one simply compares the ratings of envy and jealousy on these items, one finds a convincing replication of one of Salovey and Rodin's (1986) findings—namely, that jealousy produces more intense affective reactions than does envy. Of the

59 items, 32 were significantly greater for jealousy than for envy, while only 1 was significantly greater for envy (that item was "Others would disapprove if they knew what I was feeling").

In order to pursue the idea about relative salience, we equated the subjects' ratings for intensity by subtracting the mean of each subject's rating across all 59 items from each of his or her individual ratings. With these transformed ratings, one can again ask whether the envy and jealousy groups differ. If the same items are salient in both envy and jealousy, there should be no differences between the two groups on these transformed scores. On the other hand, any differences would suggest that there are qualitative differences between envy and jealousy that are not attributable to differences in intensity. What we found was strong evidence of the latter: qualitative differences. Overall, of the 59 items, 26 differed ($p <$ .10); envy and jealousy were each greater in magnitude for 13 of these 26 (see Table 19.2). Feelings of inferiority, longing, resentment, and motivation to improve were more salient for envy than for jealousy. In addition, feelings of guilt about feeling ill will toward others and beliefs that one's feelings are unjustified were also more salient to the experience of envy. Jealousy, on the other hand, was characterized by a greater salience of distrust, fear of loss, self-doubt, and anxiety. So this analysis found some qualities to be more salient for envy than for jealousy, and others to be more salient for jealousy than for envy. To a remarkable extent, these differences correspond to those proposed by traditional definitions.

These results may offer a new insight or two as well. It is intriguing to note that three of the items, "inferior," "self-doubt," and "insecure," appear to have fairly similar meanings; however, the first was more salient for envy, whereas the latter two were more salient for jealousy. This finding suggests that a distinction might be made between different types of self-esteem, or between different routes to lowering self-esteem. "Inferior" implies that one evaluates oneself as comparing poorly with others, whereas "insecure" and "self-doubt" imply insecurities regarding getting along with others once they have judged one negatively. Thus, the data seem to confirm a point made above regarding the difference between envy and jealousy. In envy, one's own appraisal leads to dissatisfaction with oneself. In jealousy, the reflected appraisal of another leads to a lack of security and confidence.

Conclusion

In what is perhaps the oldest recorded myth, the Egyptian myth of Osiris, both envy and jealousy figure as motives. In this myth, the god Osiris, tall, slender, and handsome, becomes king of Egypt. He marries his beautiful sister, and brings prosperity and civilization first to Egypt and then the rest of the world. However, Osiris has an ugly and evil younger brother named Seth, who hates him. Seth envies the attractiveness, power, and success of his older brother. Seth also has reason to be jealous of Osiris, since Seth's wife becomes so at-

TABLE 19.2. Questionnaire Items that Distinguish Envy and Jealousy (When Transformed to Equate for Intensity)

Envy	Jealousy
Feeling inferior	Afraid of a possible loss
Privately ashamed of myself	Threatened
Feeling unfairly treated by life	Rejected
Frustration	Worried
Bitter	Suspicious
Feeling wishful	Betrayed
Longing for what another has	Self-doubt
Others would disapprove if they knew what I was feeling	Lonely
	Uncertain
Embarrassing to admit to	Feeling degraded
Guilt over feeling ill will toward someone	Self-conscious
Feeling sinful	Insecure
At first denied to myself that I felt this emotion	Intense feeling
Motivated to improve myself	

tracted to Osiris that she tricks him into sleeping with her and bears a child by him. Motivated by envy and jealousy, Seth sets a trap for Osiris and kills him (Griffiths, l970). Envy and jealousy are as old as humanity, and apparently will remain. Their durable hold on us, and the problems they create for us, are what motivate us to try to understand them.

REFERENCES

Barnes, J. (Ed.). (1984). *The complete works of Aristotle* (Vol. 2). Princeton, NJ: Princeton University Press.

Bers, S. A., & Rodin, J. (1984). Social-comparison jealousy: A developmental and motivational study. *Journal of Personality and Social Psychology, 47,* 766–779.

Davis, L. (1936). Jealousy and sexual property. *Social Forces, 14,* 395–405.

Festinger, L. (1954). A theory of social comparison processes. *Human Relations, 7,* 117–140.

Fortenbaugh, W. W. (1975). *Aristotle on emotion.* New York: Barnes & Noble.

Frijda, N. (1986). *The emotions.* New York: Cambridge University Press.

Griffiths, J. G. (1970). *Plutarch's de Iside et Osiride.* Cambridge, England: University of Wales Press.

Hazlitt, W. (1932). Characteristics: In the manner of Rochefoucault's Maxims. In P. P. Howe (Ed.), *The complete works of William Hazlitt* (Vol. 9, pp. 163–229). London: Dent. (Original work published 1823)

Heider, F. (1958). *The psychology of interpersonal relations.* New York: Wiley.

Hupka, R. B. (1984). Jealousy: Compound emotion or label for a particular situation? *Motivation and Emotion, 8,* 141–155.

Hupka, R. B. (1989, May). Components of the typical response to romantic jealousy situations. In G. L. White (Chair), *Themes for progress in jealousy research.* Symposium conducted at the Second Iowa Conference on Personal Relationships, Iowa City.

Hupka, R. B. (1991). The motive for the arousal of romantic jealousy: Its cultural origin. In P. Salovey (Ed.), *The psychology of jealousy and envy* (pp. 252–270). New York: Guilford.

Kierkegaard, S. (1954). The sickness unto death. In W. Lowrie (Ed. and Trans.), *Fear and trembling and the sickness unto death* (pp. 131–262). Princeton, NJ: Princeton University Press. (Original work published 1849)

La Rochefoucauld, F. (1959). *Maxims* (L. Tancock, Trans.). Harmondsworth, England: Penguin. (Original work published 1678)

Lazarus, R. S., Kanner, A. D., & Folkman, S. (1980). Emotions: A cognitive-phenomenological analysis. In R. Plutchik & H. Kellerman (Eds.), *Emotion: Theory, research, and experience* (Vol. 1, pp. 189–217). New York: Academic Press.

Mahon, L. (Ed.). (1845). *The letters of Philip Dormer Stanhope, Earl of Chesterfield* (Vol. 2). London: S. & J. Bentley, Wilson, and Fley.

Mathes, E. W., Adams, H. E., & Davies, R. M. (1985). Jealousy: Loss of relationship rewards, loss of self-esteem, depression, anxiety, and anger. *Journal of Personality and Social Psychology, 48,* 1552–1561.

Mayer, J. D., & Gaschke, Y. N. (1988). The experience and meta-experience of mood. *Journal of Personality and Social Psychology, 55,* 102–111.

Mencken, H. L. (1922). *Prejudices: Third series.* New York: Knopf.

Morse, S. J., & Gergen, K. J. (1970). Social comparison, self-consistency, and the concept of self. *Journal of Personality and Social Psychology, 16,* 149–156.

Neu, J. (1980). Jealous thoughts. In A. O. Rorty (Ed.), *Explaining emotions* (pp. 425–463). Berkeley: University of California Press.

Nietzsche, F. (1911). The wanderer and his shadow (P. V. Cohn, Trans.). In O. Levy (Ed.), *The complete works of Friedrich Nietzsche: Vol. 7. Human all-too-human (Part II)* (pp. 179–366). London: George Allen & Unwin. (Original work published 1880)

Nietzsche, F (1967). *On the genealogy of morals* (W. Kaufmann & R. J. Hollingdale, Trans.). New York: Vintage Books. (Original work published 1887)

Ortega y Gassett, J. (1961). *Meditations on Quixote* (E. Rugg & D. Marín, Trans.). New York: Norton. (Original work published 1914)

Ortony, A., Clore, G. L., & Collins, A. (1988). *The cognitive structure of emotions.* Cambridge, England: Cambridge University Press.

Parrott, W. G. (1988a). The role of cognition in emotional experience. In W. J. Baker, L. P Mos, H. V. Rappard, & H. J. Stam (Eds.), *Recent trends in theoretical psychology* (pp. 327–337). New York: Springer-Verlag.

Parrott, W. G. (1988b, August). Understanding envy and jealousy. In W. G. Parrott (Chair), *Envy and jealousy: Experiencing and coping with negative social emotions.* Symposium conducted at the meeting of the American Psychological Association, Atlanta.

Parrott, W. G., & Sabini, J. (1989). On the "emotional" qualities of certain types of cognition: A reply to arguments for the independence of cognition and affect. *Cognitive Therapy and Research, 13,* 49–65.

Parrott, W. G., & Smith, R. H. (1993). Distinguishing the experiences of envy and jealousy. *Journal of Personality and Social Psychology, 64,* 906–920.

Peters, R. S. (1972). The education of the emotions. In R. R. Dearden, P. H. Hirst, & R. S. Peters (Eds.), *Education and the development of reason* (pp. 466–483). London: Routledge & Kegan Paul.

Rawls, J. (1971). *A theory of justice.* Cambridge, MA: Harvard University Press.

Sabini, J., & Silver, M. (1982). *Moralities of everyday life.* New York: Oxford University Press.

Salovey, P., & Rodin, J. (1984). Some antecedents and consequences of social-comparison jealousy. *Journal of Personality and Social Psychology, 47,* 780–792.

Salovey, P., & Rodin, J. (1986). The differentiation of social-comparison jealousy and romantic jealousy. *Journal of Personality and Social Psychology, 50,* 1100–1112.

Salovey, P., & Rothman, A. (1991). Envy and jealousy: Self and society. In P. Salovey (Ed.), *The psychology of envy* (pp. 271–286). New York: Guilford.

Schoeck, H. (1969). *Envy: A theory of social behaviour* (M. Glenny & B. Ross, Trans.). Indianapolis, IN: Liberty Press. (Original work published 1966)

Silver, M., & Sabini, J. (1978a). The perception of envy. *Social Psychology, 41,* 105–117.

Silver, M., & Sabini, J. (1978b). The social construction of envy. *Journal for the Theory of Social Behaviour, 8,* 313–332.

Smith, C. A., & Ellsworth, P. C. (1985). Patterns of cognitive appraisal in emotion. *Journal of Personality and Social Psychology, 48,* 813–838.

Smith, R. H. (1991). Envy and the sense of injustice. In P. Salovey (Ed.), *The psychology of jealousy and envy* (pp. 79–99). New York: Guilford

Smith, R. H., Kim, S. H., & Parrott, W. G. (1988). Envy and jealousy: Semantic problems and experiential distinctions. *Personality and Social Psychology Bulletin, 14,* 401–409.

Smith, R. H., Parrott, W. G., Diener, E. F., Hoyle, R. H., &

Kim, S. H. (1999). Dispositional envy. *Personality and Social Psychology Bulletin, 25,* 1007–1020.

Spinoza, B. (1949). *Ethics* (J. Gutman, Ed.). New York: Hafner. (Original work published 1677)

Sullivan, H. S. (1953). *The interpersonal theory of psychiatry.* New York: Norton.

Taylor, G. (1988). Envy and jealousy: Emotions and vices. *Midwest Studies in Philosophy, 13,* 233–249.

Tesser, A., & Campbell, J. (1980). Self-definition: The impact of the relative performance and similarity of others. *Social Psychology Quarterly, 43,* 341–347.

Tov-Ruach, L. (1980). Jealousy, attention, and loss. In A. O. Rorty (Ed.), *Explaining emotions* (pp. 465–488). Berkeley: University of California Press.

White, G. L. (1981). A model of romantic jealousy. *Motivation and Emotion, 5,* 295–310.

Anger and the Explanation of Emotion

Anger, along with its behavioral cousin aggression, has been the subject of more research by social psychologists than any other emotion. For that reason anger is the topic of this book's final section. The two articles reprinted here have been selected not only to provide a range of insights into anger, but also to address a more general point about our understanding of emotion, namely, the types of explanation that can be given for why emotions occur.

Explanations of human behavior offered by social psychologists may include either of two sorts of accounts: causes or reasons (Harré & Secord, 1972; Moghaddam, 1998). Causal explanations present social phenomena as arising similarly to events in physics—a force is applied to a body, which responds in an automatic, mechanical fashion. Explanations based on reasons present social phenomena quite differently, as resulting from the choice of a person who has interpreted the meaning of a situation according to the norms of the local culture. Both types of explanation can apply to human beings, but they yield different pictures of human nature. When seen as caused, social phenomena appear to be determined, but when seen as based on reasons, they appear to be chosen based on meanings, rules, and norms (Harré, Clarke, & De Carlo, 1985). There is a complex philosophical literature on how these explanatory types apply in the social sciences. Its relevance to understanding emotion may not be so obvious in the abstract, but in the context of a specific emotion its importance becomes immediately salient. Anger makes a perfect case study.

In the first reading, Leonard Berkowitz (1990) presents his influential theory of anger, which is based on understanding this emotion in terms of its causes.

Berkowitz proposes that all aversive events cause some feelings of anger. This proposal integrates several older theories that posit more specific causes of anger, such as frustration, unpleasant temperatures, or pain. Berkowitz's theory posits that a network of associations links all aversive feelings with anger-related reactions. Activation of associations spreads in an auto-matic, mechanical fashion, just like the associative net-works that have been posited to account for the effects of emotion on subsequent cognition (see Reading 11). Berkowitz explicitly denies that the reasons people typically give for their anger have any actual, explanatory role. He suggests instead that complex thinking influences anger at a later stage, after primitive anger has already been aroused. Thus, for Berkowitz, anger is an irrational flash that occurs in automatic response to unpleasant feelings.

Berkowitz's approach contrasts sharply with that presented in the second article, by James Averill (1983). Of the approaches to emotion presented elsewhere in this volume, Averill's is closest to the cultural approach of Markus and Kitayama (Reading 5). He espouses the approach known as *social constructivism*, which maintains that human emotions exist within a culture's social practices, and cannot be fully understood if they are abstracted from their cultural matrix. Averill is the author of general statements of the social constructivist approach to emotions (Averill, 1980), as well as of critiques of attempts to reduce emotions to the level of biology or primitive responses (Averill, 1974). In the article reprinted here, Averill presents the constructivist approach in the context of his research on anger. He finds that, in American culture, anger leads people to work out the problems that have arisen in their relationships. He understands anger not in causal terms, but in terms of social standards and norms. He views the origins of anger not as mechanical but as based on understanding: anger

results from a judgment of blameworthiness.

The paradox of these two articles is that their modes of explanation seem incompatible, yet it is possible to view anger from each point of view. Both reasons and causes have a place in understanding anger. The problem is how to reconcile the two views. Part of the problem is definitional. Note how Averill carefully distinguishes anger from annoyance, whereas Berkowitz blurs both as variations on a single, basic feeling. Note how Averill does not think that other cultures have an emotion exactly like anger, whereas Berkowitz's approach applies not only cross-culturally but likely to other mammalian species as well. There is more than just definition at stake, however. Berkowitz maintains that anger is precognitive, Averill that it is postcognitive. This difference is one of several that parallel the debate between Zajonc and Lazarus over the role of cognition in emotion. As in that previous debate, understanding how cognition can be uncontrollable and unconscious makes the cognitive approach more plausible (see the Overview chapter on the debate between Zajonc and Lazarus).

Another difference concerns the notion of blameworthi-ness. Berkowitz maintains that people become angry at events that are not blameworthy. But from whose point of view, and at what point in time? People who experience envy sometimes feel anger when life seems unfair even though no one is to blame—this has been called "global resentment" (see Reading 19). Objectively, no one is to blame, but subjectively, it seems that someone or something ought to be blamed—the gods, or life itself. Thus, there may be subjective unfairness even when there is no objective unfairness (Smith, 1991), and thus an appraisal of blame may be present with anger even when it seems to be inappropriate.

One way to understand these two approaches is that they differ in their conception of what a scientific explanation ought to be like. Berkowitz takes a causal approach partly because it yields a set of broad objective laws predicting when anger will occur. Averill's approach, based on norms and reasons, cannot produce broad objective laws because it grounds anger in a rich context of social conventions, particular situations, and social relationships. To some, Averill's approach will seem utterly unscientific, but to others, general causal laws of the sort proposed by Berkowitz seem inappropriate as explanations of human action (Parrott, 1993). The approach that works in physics may not be best for understanding people.

REFERENCES

Averill, J. R. (1974). An analysis of psychophysiological symbolism and its influence on theories of emotion. *Journal for the Theory of Social Behaviour, 4*, 147–190.

Averill, J. R. (1980). A constructivist view of emotion. In R. Plutchik & H. Kellerman (Eds.), *Theories of emotion*. New York: Academic Press.

Averill, J. R. (1983). Studies on anger and aggression: Implications for theories of emotion. *American Psychologist, 38*, 1145–1160.

Berkowitz, L. (1990). On the formation and regulation of anger and aggression: A cognitive-neoassociationistic analysis. *American Psychologist, 45*, 494–503.

Harré, R., Clarke, D., & De Carlo, N. (1985). *Motives and mechanisms: An introduction to the psychology of action*. London: Methuen.

Harré, R., & Secord, P. F. (1972). *The explanation of social behaviour*. Totowa, NJ: Rowman and Littlefield.

Moghaddam, F. M. (1998). *Social psychology: Exploring universals across cultures*. New York: Freeman.

Parrott, W. G. (1993). On the scientific study of angry organisms. In R. S. Wyer, Jr. & T. K. Srull (Eds.), *Perspectives on Anger and Emotion: Advances in Social Cognition* (Vol. VI, pp. 167–177). Hillsdale, NJ: Erlbaum.

Smith, R. H. (1991). Envy and the sense of injustice. In P. Salovey (Ed.), *The psychology of jealousy and envy* (pp. 79–99). New York: Guilford.

Discussion Questions

1. Why does Berkowitz term his theory a "cognitive-neoassociationistic analysis"?
2. Averill's finding that only a small proportion of people become angry when no blameworthy action has occurred is discussed by both Berkowitz and Averill. What interpretation does each author place on this finding, and why?
3. What is the relation between emotion in humans and "emotion" in animals according to Averill? What relation do you think Berkowitz would propose?
4. Compare the articles by Berkowitz and Averill to other debates about the nature of emotion, such as the debate between Zajonc and Lazarus over the role of cognition (see the Overview chapter). What parallels can be drawn?

Suggested Readings

Averill, J. R. (1982). *Anger and aggression: An essay on emotion*. New York: Springer-Verlag. The findings and arguments Averill presents in Reading 21 were drawn from this book, which is a good resource for those wanting to learn more about his approach. The research on everyday accounts of anger is supplemented by insights from philosophy, law, and social constructivism.

Wyer, R. S., & Srull, T. K. (Eds.). (1993). *Perspectives on anger and emotion: Advances in Social Cognition* (Vol. VI). Hillsdale, NJ: Erlbaum. This volume consists of a lead article by Leonard Berkowitz that is followed by a series of commentaries written by emotion researchers from a variety of perspectives. It provides more information about Berkowitz's approach. With the commentaries, plus a rebuttal from Berkowitz, it is very useful for understanding the range of approaches that are applied to anger in academic psychology.

Stearns, C. Z., & Stearns, P. N. (1986). *Anger: The struggle for emotional control in America's history*. Chicago: University of Chicago Press. This book is a social history of how American conventions about the display of anger have changed from the colonial period to the present. It draws on diaries and popular advice across more than two centuries for its data, and nicely demonstrates the role of social conventions in guiding emotions.

Smith, R. H. (1991). Envy and the sense of injustice. In P. Salovey (Ed.), *The psychology of jealousy and envy* (pp. 79–99). New York: Guilford. Those interested in exploring the link between anger and envy would do well to start with this fine chapter. It introduces the distinctions between the objective and subjective sense of unfairness, and draws on both psychology and literature to explore the relation between envy and anger.

Kulik, J. A., & Brown, R. (1979). Frustration, attribution of blame, and aggression. *Journal of Experimental Social Psychology, 15*, 183–194. This experiment is notable for manipulating variables drawn from both the causal (frustration) and the rational (blame) traditions. The results, interestingly, provide some support for both traditions.

Baumeister, R. F., Stillwell, A., & Wotman, S. R. (1990). Victim and perpetrator accounts of interpersonal conflict: Autobiographical narratives about anger. *Journal of Personality and Social Psychology, 59*, 994–1005. This innovative and thought-provoking study of anger follows in the tradition of Averill, both in its use of autobiographical narrative and in its exploration of the different perspectives of the angry person and the person at whom the anger is directed. The differences in perspective that Baumeister and colleagues document provide many insights into the interpersonal nature of anger.

On the Formation and Regulation of Anger and Aggression: A Cognitive-Neoassociationisitic Analysis

Leonard Berkowitz • University of Wisconsin–Madison

Noting that a wide variety of unpleasant feelings, including sadness and depression, apparently can give rise to anger and aggression, I propose a cognitive–neoassociationistic model to account for the effects of negative affect on the development of angry feelings and the display of emotional aggression. Negative affect tends to activate ideas, memories, and expressive–motor reactions associated with anger and aggression as well as rudimentary angry feelings. Subsequent thought involving attributions, appraisals, and schematic conceptions can then intensify, suppress, enrich, or differentiate the initial reactions. Bodily reactions as well as emotion-relevant thoughts can activate the other components of the particular emotion network to which they are linked. Research findings consistent with the model are summarized. Experimental findings are also reported indicating that attention to one's negative feelings can lead to a regulation of the overt effects of the negative affect. I argue that the model can integrate the core aspect of the James–Lange theory with the newer cognitive theories of emotion.

Most people, psychologists and non psychologists alike, are fairly confident about when people will be prompted to become angry and attack an available target. Anger arises and aggression occurs, it is widely assumed, as a result of a perceived threat or the belief that one has been intentionally mistreated or even because of some frustration. However, there may well be more to the origin of aggression than is commonly supposed. Mounting evidence indicates that aggression can also be produced by a remarkably broad range of unpleasant occurrences that are not intentionally or unfairly produced by a human agent. Foul odors, high temperatures, exposure to painfully cold water, and even disgusting scenes can also heighten the hostility displayed, or the aggression that is directed toward another person, even when that individual cannot possibly be blamed for the unpleasantness and the aggression cannot alleviate the negative state of affairs (Anderson, 1989; Berkowitz, 1983, 1989). It is not especially profound to maintain that these aversive events can also create considerable irritation, annoyance, and even anger. Not infrequently, people say that they feel irritated or annoyed, and sometimes even that they are angry, when they are not feeling well or have been afflicted by some unpleasant occurrence.

These observations will serve as the starting point for the present analysis. The core notion in this model is that negative affect is the basic source of anger and angry aggression (Berkowitz, 1983,

1989). It is clear, of course, that cognitions can also influence the formation of angry feelings. However, cognitive processes need not operate only in the ways specified by conventional cognitive/appraisal/attributional formulations of emotion. For example, compare the formulation advanced by Leventhal (1984), whose thinking has greatly influenced my theorizing, with Weiner's (1985) attributional analysis. In this article, I suggest how anger can also be affected by both the associative linkages connecting negative affect with aggression-related ideas, memories, and expressive-motor reactions and also by people's schemas regarding the nature of anger.

Before proceeding further, however, it is advisable to make several introductory points. First, the term anger can be understood in many different ways—as feelings or a class of expressive-motor or physiological reactions or as a set of behaviors or a combination of all of these things. As an example, Averill (1982) viewed anger as a syndrome encompassing all of the different components just mentioned. I refer to anger only as a feeling, or more generally, as an experience, much as many psychologists, from William James to Howard Leventhal, have favored emphasizing the emotional experience in the study of emotions. This definition sidesteps the question of what is an emotion, and no claim is made that the type of feeling of interest to us here has all of the qualities that many psychologists maintain emotions must possess.

In this connection, some critics might argue that the present formulation deals only with diffuse feelings of irritation and annoyance rather than a focused anger. My answer is that although it certainly is possible to draw some distinctions among irritation, anger, and annoyance, we do not know whether these differences are all-important and lead to entirely different consequences. Indeed, many of the subjects exposed to the aversive treatments in the research summarized here rated themselves as feeling somewhat angry as well as irritated and annoyed (although not at the same level), and these self-reports of irritation, annoyance, and anger were often highly correlated. All in all, it could be argued, the differences among these feelings in what people experience largely reflect only differences in intensity, although some of the specific details may also be influenced by the amount and nature of the thought given to the feelings. Moreover, in the research my students and I have carried out, measures of these feelings tend to have

many of the same relations with overt behaviors. For good reason, then, in accordance with Bower (Bower & Cohen, 1982), in my analysis I view irritation, annoyance, and anger as members of the same class of feelings, and I use the term anger to refer to all of them.

Second, the formulation being offered here is basically only a micro-analysis of what psychological (not neural or physiological) processes may be at the root of the anger experience. Concentrating on the fine details of what may be at work in the production of this experience, the model has nothing to say about the kinds of interpersonal relationships that give rise to angry feelings even though these interpersonal relationships are the source of much of the anger that occurs in everyday life (Scherer & Tannenbaum, 1986). Space limitations do not permit a careful and detailed examination of all of the issues that are relevant to the present analysis, and this article only skims the surface of several of these matters. Nonetheless, with all of these shortcomings, the cognitive-neoassociationistic conception offered here can make a number of contributions to our understanding of anger and aggression. At the very least, the model suggests what frustrations, negative appraisals, and unpleasant environmental conditions have in common and why so many different kinds of aversive events give rise to anger and aggression. This proposal can also help to account for a number of seemingly unusual observations, observations that are not explained by most contemporary theories. Sadness, grief, and depression are certainly different in many ways from anger; they feel very different. Yet it is not at all unusual for sad, grieving, and depressed persons to show anger and even aggression when no one can be blamed. Any truly comprehensive analysis of anger and aggression must be able to explain theoretically why this happens.

The formulation goes further than this, however, and has implications for the analysis of emotions generally. At the broadest level, it attempts to integrate conceptions focusing on relatively automatic and nonthoughtful processes with other theories emphasizing higher order cognitive concepts such as appraisals and attributions. But, more specifically, in proposing this integration, the model enables us to bring together the fundamental core of the classic James–Lange (James, 1890) theory with the newer insights of contemporary cognitive approaches.

Are Cognitions Necessary?

I noted earlier that a wide variety of unpleasant occurrences can instigate aggressive reactions: immersion in cold water, exposure to high temperatures, foul odors, the sight of morally repugnant scenes, and so on. All of these conditions are aversive, and all generate negative affect. It is this unpleasant feeling that presumably produces the aggressive inclinations and the accompanying angry feelings. A major question, however, is whether these reactions are due to the negative affect alone. More specifically, one might ask, does the suffering person also have to have certain types of beliefs about the aversive event or its consequences before she or he will experience anger?

Anger in the Absence of the Supposedly Requisite Beliefs

Nearly every cognitive account of the origin of anger maintains that certain kinds of beliefs are necessary if this feeling is to arise (although the theorists taking this stance are not agreed as to whether these beliefs should be called appraisals or attributions). To take only two examples, Weiner (1985) has held that people will not be angered by unpleasant conditions unless these events are attributed to someone's intentional and controllable misdeed, whereas Lazarus (Lazarus, Averill, & Opton, 1970) has maintained that individuals must view the negative occurrences as threats to their well-being. The present model accepts a weak version of this thesis: Certain kinds of appraisal or attributional beliefs can intensify or weaken the anger experience. A frustration is especially bothersome when it blocks the attainment of personally significant goals and is attributed to another person's deliberate misbehavior, but it is less disturbing when unimportant strivings are thwarted and the interference is viewed as only an accidental occurrence. What the model questions is the strong version of the cognitive analysis maintaining that these beliefs are necessary if the aversive occurrence is to generate anger.

Contrary to such a statement, available evidence indicates that anger can arise even when the negative event is not regarded as a personal threat and is not blamed on someone's unjustified action. This can be seen in some of the studies alluded to earlier (cf. Berkowitz, 1983, 1989) and also in naturalistic, nonexperimental investigations of the arousal of anger in everyday life. Averill's (1982) study is a relatively recent case in point, although other, similar investigations dating back 50 years or more could also be cited. A small proportion of the community residents and university students in Averill's sample said they had become angry when someone had kept them from getting what they wanted, even though this individual had acted in accord with social rules or even when they had met with a negative but unavoidable occurrence.

Stein and Levine (1989) have also made some interesting observations along these lines. They asked their subjects—preschoolers, first graders, and university students—to indicate what emotions would be experienced by the protagonist in various kinds of incidents described to them. Although the participants were most likely to say that the protagonist was angry when this person had been intentionally harmed, Stein and Levine found that 60% of the subjects believed that the victim of an unpleasant event might well become angry even when the negative occurrence was only accidental or was produced by natural forces rather than some human agent. In these people's experience, then, it was not necessary for the aversive event to have been controllable or intentionally aimed at the victim for it to produce anger.

If these causal attributions are not always involved in the production of anger, does this emotion require other kinds of beliefs? Theorists have raised several possibilities, generally having to do with expectations of a threat or harm to oneself or with anticipations of future events. According to Stein and Levine (1989), for example, anger arises primarily when there is hope that a lost outcome will be regained. But this belief in the possibility of some remedy may only influence the strength of the anger experience without being necessary for it to occur. As learned helplessness theory tells us (Seligman, 1975), people with little hope that they can get what they want are likely to become passive and even depressed. The intense depression they feel might mask whatever anger is also present. Nevertheless, anger can occur even when there is little expectation that a desired state of affairs will be restored.

Anger with Sadness or Depression

There is evidence for this contention in the way anger is often blended together with sadness and depression in everyday life (see, e.g., Scherer &

Tannenbaum, 1986). As a matter of fact, sadness may well be more closely linked to anger than is commonly realized. Termine and Izard (1988) have recently noted that "situations or conditions eliciting sadness frequently elicit anger" so that, among other things, "infants respond to pain and separation by displaying both sadness and anger expressions" (p. 228). Similarly, people who are asked to show sadness in their facial expressions often display angry expressions as well.

The psychological literature on mourning and bereavement also testifies to the connection between sadness and anger. This literature is replete with reports of anger in those grieving over the death of a loved one, and Rosenblatt, Jackson, and Walsh (1972) have commented that "it is not uncommon for people who are bereaved to be angry and even to engage in violent acts" (p. 271). In many of these instances the mourners could not blame the death on someone's misdeed or even on a human agent, and there also was no possibility that the loved person would be restored to them. Yet they were angry. To take an example from the literature about anger among the bereaved, one article by Meyers and Pitt (1976) described how the young students in a parochial school displayed aggressive, acting-out behavior after two of their schoolmates were killed in separate accidents during the school vacation period and how the teachers experienced not only guilt and sadness when they thought about the deaths but also anger.

The research linking depression and anger is even more impressive. Here, too, the clinical literature abounds with reports of the hostility and anger displayed by depressed persons, children as well as adults (Berkowitz, 1983). Moreover, whereas psychoanalytic theorists generally view the depression as being caused by anger (e.g., Abraham, 1960), some researchers have demonstrated that the experimental induction of depressive feelings can also generate hostility and anger (Finman & Berkowitz, 1989; Miller & Norman, 1979). There is a very good possibility, then, that the depressed mood in itself produces angry feelings and hostile inclinations.

A Cognitive-Neoassociationistic Model of Anger Formation

To account for these observations, I (Berkowitz, 1983, 1989; Berkowitz & Heimer, 1989) have ad-

vanced a theoretical model that attempts to spell out the relation between the initial negative affect and the resulting angry feelings. Along with several other recent formulations (e.g., Bower & Cohen, 1982; Lang, 1979; Leventhal, 1984), this conception assumes that associative networks link specific types of feelings with particular thoughts and memories and also with certain kinds of expressive-motor and physiological reactions. Also with these other analyses, the model maintains that the activation of any one of the components in the network tends to activate the other parts as well. But this formulation also has some relatively unique features.

Most notably, according to this model, there is an associative connection between negative affect and anger-related feelings, ideas, and memories, and also with aggressive inclinations. It is because of these associations that persons who feel bad for one reason or another—whether they have a toothache, are very hot, are exposed to foul smells or an unpleasant noise, or are just very sad or depressed—are likely to be angry, have hostile ideas and memories, and to be aggressively disposed. More specifically, according to this formulation, the negative affect generated by the aversive occurrence automatically gives rise to at least two sets of reactions at the same time: bodily changes, feelings, ideas, and memories associated with escape from the unpleasant stimulation and also bodily reactions, feelings, thoughts, and memories associated with aggression. A variety of factors—genetic, learned, and situational—supposedly determine the relative strengths of these two response classes.

The basic fear experience presumably develops from the person's conscious and preconscious awareness of the initial escape-associated reactions, whereas awareness of the first aggression-associated feelings, thoughts, memories, and expressive-motor responses theoretically produces a rudimentary anger experience. In other words, from this perspective the rudimentary fear and anger experiences do not in themselves produce fearful and aggressive behavior but only parallel the escape and aggressive motor tendencies evoked by the negative affect.

But people do not always report being angry or afraid when an unpleasant event takes place. They might describe themselves as anxious, depressed, envious, guilty, or something else, but frequently they say little about being angry. I do not claim that this absence of reported anger is necessarily due only to a denial of these feelings. The negatively afflicted persons may actually not be consciously aware of any anger soon after they encounter the aversive stimulus because other emotional states have arisen and command their attention. The model contends that these other relatively complicated emotional experiences usually develop after the basic, primary reactions to the negative event. Positing a series of stages in the formation of emotions, the model assumes that relatively automatic associative processes are dominant at first and govern the initial primitive reactions. Complicated thoughts of the type postulated by cognitive theorists theoretically play only a small role at this early stage, except for the fairly simple initial appraisal of the incident as unpleasant. A fraction of time afterward, however, other, higher order cognitive processes begin to operate, particularly as thought is given to what has happened and its possible consequences.

It is in these later stages that the affected person makes appraisals and causal attributions and considers what feelings and actions are appropriate under the particular circumstances. This additional thought leads to the differentiation, intensification, suppression, or elaboration of the early rudimentary experiences. If the afflicted persons' arousal level is weak, for example, they may decide at this time that they are irritated or annoyed rather than angry. Or as cognitive/attributional theorizing proposes, afflicted persons may come to believe that they are, for example, sad and not angry, because they believe that one does not feel anger in this particular situation. They may even develop relatively complicated emotional experiences such as anxiety, contempt, envy, guilt, and even depression. The present formulation maintains that these later, more developed emotional experiences are essentially constructed as the mind brings together various sensory, ideational, and memorial inputs from all of those available, guided by the individual's prototypic conception of what the specific emotion is like (Leventhal, 1984, has also raised this possibility).

Another important assumption in this model is that the higher order cognitive processing governing the full development of the anger experience does not necessarily always go into operation. The aversively stimulated persons may have to be motivated to think more extensively and deeper about the various kinds of information they have received

(Showers & Cantor, 1985). Once they engage in this higher order processing, however, they consider the perceived causes of their arousal, the possible consequences of any action they might undertake, the goals they would like to attain, and also what sensations they are feeling and what ideas and memories have just occurred to them.

Research Support for the Model

The key proposition in my analysis, then, is that negative affect of any kind will first activate anger-related feelings, action tendencies, and thoughts and memories. Several published studies can be cited in support of this contention. In one, Baron (1984) showed that deliberately provoked subjects became less hostile toward their tormentor after they had an irrelevant pleasant experience. It is as if the pleasant feelings had lessened the negative affect-generated aggressive inclinations. In another experiment, Rule, Taylor, and Dobbs (1987) demonstrated that aversive events tend to heighten the accessibility of anger-related thoughts, even when the unpleasant stimulation is delivered to the subjects in keeping with approved social rules. In this investigation those participants who were exposed to scientifically legitimate but highly uncomfortable heat used more hostile ideas in constructing emotion-related stories than did the control subjects under a more comfortable temperature.

Findings from Recent Research

Research carried out at the University of Wisconsin (Monteith, Berkowitz, Kruglanski, & Blair, 1990, Note 2) has also yielded results in accord with my conception of an associative network linking negative affect, anger-related feelings, and anger-related thoughts. The first experiment along these lines explored whether both physical discomfort and thoughts of unpleasant occurrences would activate anger-related feelings and ideas. Some of the subjects were asked to imagine themselves being frustrated in a certain way (being caught in a traffic jam while driving to an important appointment), others were to think of themselves in a particular anxiety-provoking situation (being alone in an elevator stopped between floors in a deserted office building at night), and the last group had to imagine being in a neutral situation (doing grocery shopping). We assumed here that the thought of either of the aversive incidents would prime negative affect-related ideas and memories and that these, in turn, would activate the anger-related feelings and thoughts. However, we also believed that the people imagining themselves being frustrated would have more of these anger-related feelings and ideas because frustrating events are often associated with anger and aggression. Finally, we also expected that the negative affect produced by physical discomfort would heighten these effects.

The experiment designed to test this reasoning first established differences in physical discomfort. The individual male and female subjects extended their nondominant arm throughout the six-minute experimental procedure, either resting the arm on the table (in the low discomfort group) or holding it outward and unsupported (in the high discomfort condition). After the subjects' arms had been in the specified position for about three minutes, the experimenter asked the participants to think of themselves in one of the previously described situations and then relate how they would feel on that occasion. Three minutes later, at the completion of this task, and with their arm still in this position, they rated their present feelings on a series of mood items.

The tape-recorded stories told by the subjects were coded for the number of explicit references to anger and fear feelings. As can be seen in Table 20.1, the findings in the low discomfort condition demonstrated that the incidents had the desired effects on the subjects' emotional thoughts. The people telling the anxiety story expressed the greatest number of fear-related ideas, whereas those talking about the frustrating event voiced the greatest number of anger-related ideas. The high discomfort condition is more interesting. As the table shows, the high discomfort group had the highest number of anger-related thoughts in the frustra-

tion situation, significantly greater than the number of such ideas in the high discomfort group for the anxiety and neutral situations (although the mean for the frustration situation was not significantly greater than the mean for the frustration situation under low discomfort). Also as we had expected, those in the high discomfort group imagining the anxiety-provoking event mentioned anger-related ideas reliably more often than did their counterparts thinking of the neutral situation. What is especially noteworthy is the effect of the high physical discomfort on the expression of anger versus fear in response to the anxiety-provoking incident. The number of fear-related thoughts dropped significantly from low to high discomfort, whereas there was a corresponding significant increase in anger-related thoughts from the low to the high discomfort condition.

Putting all of the findings together, the results indicated that physical discomfort tends to activate both ideas and feelings related to anger. Moreover, consistent with the associative network model presented in this article, even thoughts of being in an unpleasant situation served to heighten the availability of these anger-related ideas. Finally, as expected, the subjects exposed to both discomfort and unpleasant thoughts—especially those in the high discomfort group exposed to frustration—reported the highest level of angry feelings and made the greatest number of references to anger-related ideas.

In another experiment, Monteith et al. (1990) demonstrated that physical discomfort can influence memory as well as thoughts and feelings. In a preexperimental phase, each female subject rated her attitudes toward three people: her mother, her boyfriend, and a neutral individual (someone well known to them but not especially close to them personally). Several weeks later, each woman was then brought to the laboratory and was placed in

TABLE 20.1. Effects of Discomfort Level and Imagined Incident on Number of Explicit References to Anger and Fear Feelings

	Situation in the low discomfort condition			Situation in the high discomfort condition		
Feeling reported	Frustration	Anxiety	Neutral	Frustration	Anxiety	Neutral
References to anger	3.6	1.0	.3	4.0	2.1	.4
References to fear	3.0	5.8	.3	3.4	3.1	.4

Note. The scores reported are the mean number of times the subjects made an explicit reference to feeling anger or fear as they imagined themselves being in the indicated situation. Although the subjects were encouraged to talk for three minutes, most said relatively little throughout this period. Data are from "The Influence of Physical Discomfort on Experienced Anger and Anger-Related Ideas" by M. Monteith, L. Berkowitz, A. Kruglanski, and C. Blair, 1990, unpublished manuscript.

TABLE 20.2. Effects of Discomfort Level on Recall of Conflict and Expressed Judgments

Subjects' responses	Low discomfort condition			High discomfort condition		
	Mother	Boyfriend	Neutral person	Mother	Boyfriend	Neutral person
Number of references to conflict in statement	.9	.7	.3	1.2	2.1	1.3
Negative judgment about target person	7.6	9.5	8.1	7.4	10.7	11.3

Note. The recalled conflict scores refer to the number of times there was a reference to conflict with the given target person in the recollection of a significant incident involving that target person. The negative judgment means reported were adjusted, by covariance analysis, for the initial ratings made at the time of pretesting. Data are from "The Influence of Physical Discomfort on Experienced Anger and Anger-Related Ideas" by M. Monteith, L. Berkowitz, A. Kruglanski, and C. Blair, 1990, unpublished manuscript.

either a low or high discomfort condition, again using the extended arm procedure. In a Latin Square design varying the order of presentation, the subject was asked to recall a significant incident involving one of the three target persons, and then she talked for three minutes about this person at the time of this particular incident. At the end of this period, and with her arm still in the same position, she rated the target person on the same items used in the pretesting phase. The procedure was then repeated with each of the other two targets.

The physical discomfort manipulation had a significant influence on the subjects' ratings of how irritated, annoyed, and angry they were at that time their arm was extended. More important, however, the discomfort also affected the participants' recollections of their relationship with the target persons as well as their expressed attitudes toward these individuals. Assuming that the negative affect would heighten the accessibility of memories associated with hostility, including memories of conflict, the womens' stories were coded for explicit references to conflict with the target person in the remembered incident. There was a significant main effect for discomfort on these recollections, as can be seen in Table 20.2. However, as an inspection of the table also reveals, the significant increase was primarily in their recall of a conflictful relationship with their boyfriends and with the neutral person but not in their memory of any conflict involving their mothers.

Discomfort level also influenced their expressed judgments of the targets. Carrying out a covariance analysis in order to control for the subjects' initial attitudes toward each target (as rated in the preexperimental session), we found that the women were significantly harsher in their stated views of the neutral person under high rather than low physical discomfort, but there were no such differences in the evaluations of the mother and boyfriend. Of course, it is possible that the uncomfortable women were reluctant to say anything clearly negative about these two very important people. (The adjusted means in each of the conditions are reported in Table 20.2.)

Findings from Earlier Research

Taken together, then, the two experiments just summarized have shown that negative affect tends to prime anger-related thoughts, which may then be employed in emotionally relevant situations and can also produce relatively unfavorable judgments of ambiguous targets. Other findings that my colleagues and I obtained in our Wisconsin laboratory also indicate that negative affect and aggression-related ideas combine to intensify anger-related feelings. In most of these other experiments (see Berkowitz & Heimer, 1989), the subjects were exposed to a physical treatment that was either slightly or very painful, and at the same time the subjects wrote essays that presumably primed few or many aggression-related ideas (essays that justified the use of punishment when disciplining someone). When the participants rated their feelings soon afterward, those given the physically painful treatment who wrote on aggression-related topics tended to report the strongest feelings of irritation, annoyance, and anger.

These results are supported by the findings in an earlier Wisconsin experiment (Berkowitz, Cochran, & Embree, 1981). Supposedly because we were investigating the effects of harsh environmental conditions on supervision, the participants had to keep one of their hands in water that was either at room temperature or was painfully cold as they administered rewards and punishments to a fellow student in evaluation of this person's work. Because aggression involves the intentional injury of another, we primed aggression-related ideas in half of the subjects by telling them beforehand that whatever punishment they gave the worker would hurt this person's performance. In delivering any punishment, therefore, they would be deliberately harming the worker and would presumably think of themselves as acting aggressively. These thoughts in turn were expected to activate still other aggression-related ideas and feelings. By contrast, the others were informed at the outset that any punishment they gave would actually help the worker (by motivating that person to do better), and thus they presumably were less likely to think of aggression.

The results are summarized in Table 20.3. The subjects in the very cold water-punishment hurts conditions tended to be relatively punitive to the worker and also rated themselves as having the strongest feelings of irritation and annoyance (anger was not rated). In sum, in this experiment as in the later studies reported by Berkowitz and Heimer (1989), aggression-related thoughts combined with negative affect to produce a fairly strong level of anger-related feelings and aggressive behavior.

Bodily Reactions in the Experience of Anger

In positing associative linkages between the various components of any given emotion—bodily

TABLE 20.3. Effects of Unpleasant Water Temperature on Anger-Related Feelings and Hostile Behavior

	Water temperature			
	Very cold		Moderate	
	Supposed effect of punishment			
	Hurts	Helps	Hurts	Helps
Water unpleasantness	7.6	7.7	4.4	4.3
Irritable-annoyed	6.5	5.6	3.8	4.4
Number of rewards– number of punishments	20.3	25.3	35.2	26.2

Note. The ratings are on a 9-step scale ranging from 1 (not very much) to 9 (very much). On the number of rewards–number of punishments measure, the lower the score the more hostile is the evaluation. Data are from "Physical Pain and the Goal of Aversively Stimulated Aggression" by L. Berkowitz, S. Cochran, and M. Embree, 1981. *Journal of Personality and Social Psychology, 40*, pp. 687–700. Copyright 1981 by the American Psychological Association.

reactions as well as ideas, memories, and feelings, the cognitive-neoassociationistic model, in accord with James (1890), Izard (1977), and Tomkins (1962), shows that specific bodily reactions can contribute to the emotional experience. The performance of these particular expressive–motor responses presumably activates to some degree the other components in the network to which they are linked. An increasing body of research supports this contention (see, e.g., Adelmann & Zajonc, 1989; Ekman & Oster, 1979; Leventhal & Tomarken, 1986), although there has been some contrary evidence (Tourangeau & Ellsworth, 1979). Unlike some other interpretations of these bodily feedback effects (e.g., Buck, 1980; Laird, 1974; Riskind & Gotay, 1982), however, the model regards this influence as occurring at a fairly automatic, associative level without necessarily being mediated by self-perceptions. It should be recognized, nevertheless, that the performance of the requisite motor responses usually does not lead to strong emotional feelings (see Leventhal & Tomarken, 1986) because any given emotional network has a number of different components, and these other parts are not set into full operation by the bodily reactions.

Higher Order Processing and Anger

The emphasis on associative processes up to this point does not mean that cognitive processes do not intervene to influence the anger experience. According to my analysis, the feeling of anger is shaped by relatively high level information processing as well as by lower level associations, especially after the initial, rudimentary emotional reactions. At this higher level, cognitive processing has to do with more than the introduction of attributions and expectations into the developing experience. Cognitions can also affect the way bodily reactions contribute to the forming experience.

Prototype-guided integration of "inputs." Several theorists have now pointed out that most persons have a fairly definite conception of each of the primary emotions and that these emotional schemas are in many respects similar to other prototypes (e.g., Shaver, Schwartz, Kirson, & O'Connor, 1987). According to cognitive–neoassociationistic model, once the higher order processing is in operation these prototypes determine how the various inputs (sensations, thoughts, memories, etc.) are combined to shape the subsequent emotional experience. It is at this time that anger becomes more fully differentiated from sadness or the other negative emotions.

One of the key differences between the prototypes of anger and sadness, according to several studies, has to do with the level of muscular tension that is felt (e.g., Scherer & Tannenbaum, 1986, p. 311; Shaver et al., 1987). For example, Shaver and his associates found that fist clenching is involved in the anger prototype, whereas sadness is typically accompanied by inactivity, lethargy, and a low energy level. Jo and I (1990) confirmed this difference in a questionnaire study we carried out.

We also reasoned that if the construction of the anger experience was guided by the anger prototype, fist clenching might well intensify the anger felt by those exposed to an anger-activating occurrence but would not increase the sadness of people given a sadness-activating treatment. To test this argument, we asked women undergraduates to recall and talk about a certain kind of incident—either of an angry, sad, happy, or neutral nature—while they squeezed a hand dynamometer at either a weak level (1 kg of force) or with much more force (7 kg). They were stopped after four minutes and, with the dynamometer still squeezed, they rated their feelings at that time on a series of adjective scales. Two measures derived from a factor analysis of these ratings are of special interest, one clearly related to anger and the other more indicative of sadness and depression (see Table 20.4).

The analyses of variance of these two indices produced different results. As we expected, the women recalling the anger-provoking incident while contracting their hand muscles with considerable tension reported the strongest angry feelings, significantly greater than the anger reported in the two sad groups. By contrast, the highest ratings on the sadness depression index were made by those talking about the sad event *who were not squeezing hard on the hand dynamometer*. Indeed, whereas those recalling the sad incident under high muscular tension were no sadder than the two groups talking about the anger-provoking event, the women recalling the sad occurrence under low muscular tension rated themselves as significantly sadder than any other group. (The means are given in Table 20.4.)

Multiple regression analyses carried out to determine what measures contributed significantly to the prediction of the two emotional indices further corroborate the model. Scores on the anger index were significantly affected by the number of anger-related ideas the subjects expressed in describing their emotional incident and also by the rated intensity of muscular tension they felt as they squeezed the hand dynamometer. There were different findings for the sadness/depression index. Scores on this feelings measure were significantly affected by the number of angry and sad ideas voiced in talking about the emotional incident, but not by the felt muscular tension. Thus, very much in keeping with the model, the muscular tension that the subjects felt helped determine their anger experience but not how sad/depressed they believed they were.

The James-Lange theory revisited. These results are clearly consistent with the central idea in the James–Lange theory of emotions. Along with this well-known and classic formulation, the expressive–motor feedback studies of the past two de-

TABLE 20.4. Effects of Muscular Tension and Recalled Incident on Reported Feelings

	Nature of recalled incident							
	Angry		Sad		Happy		Neutral	
	Induced muscular tension							
Feeling index	High	Low	High	Low	High	Low	High	Low
Anger	5.7	5.3	4.6	4.4	3.5	2.3	3.3	3.4
Sadness/ depression	4.0	3.8	4.3	5.4	2.7	2.2	2.8	2.6
Anxiety	3.0	2.6	3.3	3.4	2.1	2.3	2.4	2.3

Note. Each of the indices has a high level of internal consistency as determined by Cronbach's Alpha. The means reported here are the adjusted means, holding constant the premanipulation scores on the indices. For each index the higher the score the stronger were the reported feelings on the relevant 9-step scales. Data are from "The Prototypically-Guided Influence of Muscular Tension on Experienced Anger and Sadness" by E. Jo and L. Berkowitz, 1990, unpublished manuscript.

cades as well as the present findings demonstrate that muscular changes can contribute to emotional feelings. However, we can now go beyond these other conceptions. According to the analysis offered here, expressive–motor feedback influences the emotional experience in at least two ways: (a) by activating the other components in the particular emotional network in a relatively automatic manner and (b) presumably after some thought and attention are given to one's feelings, by being schematically combined with other sensory and ideational inputs in a constructed perceptual experience.

The Regulation of Emotional Effects

The cognitive–neoassociationistic model offered here goes beyond the development of the emotional experience and also deals with the behavioral effects of the emotion arousal. In general, what people say and do when they are emotionally aroused can also be influenced by both associative and cognitive processes. This observation is especially pertinent to the behavioral consequences of negative affect. Even though we are usually inclined to be hostile and even aggressive toward others when we are feeling bad, the hostility and aggression are not always apparent. Rather than lashing out at someone, we often act in a nonaggressive manner because we are more concerned with improving our mood or escaping from the unpleasant situation than with attacking an available target, and, of course, sometimes we do not want to do anything. The angry feelings and aggressive tendencies generated by the negative affect are not necessarily stronger than the other feelings and inclinations that also arise and are frequently masked by these other reactions.

Conscious anticipations of punishment obviously can suppress the aversively stimulated aggression. But what is more interesting is that we sometimes also hold back and do not display the hostility or aggression we are inclined to show because of the operation of a self-regulatory mechanism operating at a preconscious level. It is not altogether clear just what is involved in this self-regulation and exactly what activates it. However, five separate experiments conducted in my laboratory leave me with little doubt that this self-regulation of the effects of a bad mood is a fairly reliable phenomenon and that it seems to occur when attention is focused on the unpleasant feelings (Berkowitz & Troccoli, 1990; Finman & Berkowitz, 1989).

My theory is that when people become aware of their moderately negative feelings as a consequence of this attention, they are somewhat surprised or disturbed, and this prompts a relatively high level of cognitive activity. They think about the possible causes of their feelings and even consider what may be the best way to act. These considerations then steer their behavior. Otherwise, in the absence of this awareness-produced high level of cognitive activity, the hostile and aggressive tendencies created by the negative mood are less likely to be restrained and are likely to be expressed openly in a harsh treatment of the available target.

Space limitations do not allow a comprehensive description of the diverse investigations we have conducted on this matter, and I can only say that we have used both male and female subjects who were exposed to a variety of aversive treatments and displayed their negative judgments on different kinds of measures. In the most recent experiment along these lines (Berkowitz & Troccoli, 1990), differences in physical discomfort were again established using the extended arm procedure, and then half of the subjects (university women) were led to be highly aware of their feelings by being asked to rate their feelings at this time. The other subjects were given an equally long distracting task to carry out. After this was done, all of the participants listened to a recorded autobiographical statement made by a job applicant and then indicated their judgment of the applicant, all of this while keeping their arm in the specified position. Our principal dependent measure here was the number of socially unfavorable personality traits that subjects attributed to the applicant.

The analysis of variance of these scores yielded, among other things, a significant Discomfort Level × Direction of Attention interaction. As is shown in Table 20.5, the physically uncomfortable subjects whose attention had been diverted from their feelings expressed the most negative judgments of the target. Interestingly, the other uncomfortable subjects who had attended to their feelings actually voiced the least unfavorable judgments of the applicant as if they had tried harder to keep their negative mood from influencing what they said. These findings are supported by a multiple

TABLE 20.5. Mean Number of Bad Traits Attributed to a Job Applicant as Affected by Discomfort Level and Attention Direction

Low discomfort		High discomfort	
Aware	Distracted	Aware	Distracted
11.3	11.4	8.1	13.4

Note. The higher the score, the more unfavorable was the expressed judgment of the applicant. Data are from "Feelings, Direction of Attention, and Expressed Evaluation of Others" by L. Berkowitz and B. T. Troccoli. 1990. Experiment 2, unpublished manuscript.

regression analysis of what variables predicted scores on the negative judgments measure. In accord with the ANOVA results, there was a significant interaction of the feelings attention manipulation with the subjects' self-reported feelings of discomfort, again demonstrating that focusing attention on one's negative feelings moderated the influence of the felt displeasure on the expressed evaluations.

Related observations from clinical psychology. These reliable findings are consistent with observations reported by a number of clinical psychologists. Although I cannot review this literature here, it is worth noting the recent theorizing advanced by Brewin (1989) that seems closely related to this analysis. In his attempt to bring concepts from cognitive psychology to bear on clinical problems, Brewin suggested that

> the awareness of unwanted or unpleasant emotions . . . [will] trigger a number of specific subroutines, beginning with a deliberate search of memory and other available sources of information . . . to label or classify the experience, to locate the responsible causal agents, and to assess future severity. . . . Where appropriate there will be a further search to generate suitable coping options. (p. 384)

In the Wisconsin experiments I have mentioned, the subjects induced to be aware of their feelings generated "suitable coping options" by considering the relevant social standards, and they did not let their bad mood lead to openly harsh evaluations of the target.

Conclusion

Although the model presented in this article has concentrated on the relatively small details of the relation between negative affect and anger and aggression, there are some general lessons that can be drawn from the relevant research. Basically, I argue that suffering is seldom ennobling. It is the unusual individual whose character is improved as a result of undergoing painful or even merely unpleasant experiences. Religion sometimes tries to comfort us by suggesting that our sorrows can make us better people, but astute observers of humankind know better. The English novelist Somerset Maugham (1919/1977) once remarked that "it is not true that suffering ennobles the character... it makes men petty and vindictive." When people feel bad, they are all too likely to have angry feelings, hostile thoughts and memories, and aggressive inclinations.

But there is also reason for some hope, even though pain and suffering are widespread and displeasure is inevitable. For one thing, people are often drawn to others who are undergoing the same unpleasant conditions and share their unhappiness. We do not know precisely why this happens, but the tendency for people in misery to love others also in misery seems to limit the ill effects of negative feelings. Perhaps more important, the relatively primitive associative processes producing these ill effects can be countered by higher-level cognitive processes. Afflicted persons can restrain their hostile and aggressive tendencies, perhaps as a result of becoming aware of their feelings and seeing clearly that it is wrong for them to blame or attack others. Here as in so many other ways, it is thought and not suffering that makes us better.

REFERENCES

Abraham, K. (1960). *Selected papers on psychoanalysis.* New York: Basic Books.

Adelmann, P. K., & Zajonc, R. B. (1989). Facial efference and the experience of emotion. *Annual Review of Psychology, 40,* 249–280.

Anderson, C. A. (1989). Temperature and aggression: Ubiquitous effects of heat on occurrence of human violence. *Psychological Bulletin, 106,* 74–96.

Averill, J. (1982). *Anger and aggression. An essay on emotion.* New York: Springer-Verlag.

Baron R. (1984). Reducing organizational conflict: An incompatible response approach. *Journal of Applied Psychology, 69,* 272–279.

Berkowitz, L. (1983). Aversively stimulated aggression: Some parallels and differences in research with animals and humans. *American Psychologist, 38,* 1135–1144.

Berkowitz, L. (1989). Frustration-aggression hypothesis: Examination and reformulation. *Psychological Bulletin, 106,* 59–73.

Berkowitz, L., Cochran, S., & Embree, M. (1981). Physical pain and the goal of aversively stimulated aggression. *Journal of Personality and Social Psychology, 40,* 687–700.

Berkowitz, L., & Heimer, K. (1989). On the construction of the anger experience: Aversive events and negative priming in the formation of feelings. In L. Berkowitz (Ed.), *Advances in experimental social psychology* (Vol. 22, pp. 1–37). New York: Academic Press.

Berkowitz, L., & Troccoli, B. T. (1990). Feelings, direction of attention, and expressed evaluations of others. *Cognition and Emotion, 4,* 305–325.

Bower, G., & Cohen, P. (1982). Emotional influences in memory and thinking: Data and theory. In M. Clark & S. Fiske (Eds.), *Affect and cognition* (pp. 291–331). Hillsdale, NJ: Erlbaum.

Brewin, C. R. (1989). Cognitive change processes in psychotherapy. *Psychological Review, 96,* 379–394.

Buck, R. (1980). Nonverbal behavior and the theory of emotion: The facial feedback hypothesis. *Journal of Personality and Social Psychology, 38,* 811–824.

Ekman, P, & Oster, H. (1979). Facial expressions of emotion. *Annual Review of Psychology, 30,* 527–554.

Finman, R., & Berkowitz, L. (1989). Some factors influencing the effect of depressed mood on anger and overt hostility toward another. *Journal of Research in Personality, 23,* 70–84.

Izard, C. (1977). *Human emotions.* New York: Plenum Press.

James, W. (1890). *The principles of psychology* (Vol. 2). New York: Holt.

Jo, E., & Berkowitz, L. (1990). *The prototypically-guided influence of muscular tension on experienced anger and sadness.* Unpublished manuscript.

Laird, J. D. (1974). Self-attribution of emotion: The effects of expressive behavior on the quality of emotional experience. *Journal of Personality and Social Psychology, 29,* 475–486.

Lang, P. (1979). A bio-informational theory of emotional imagery. *Psychophysiology, 16,* 495–512.

Lazarus, R. S., Averill, J. R., & Opton, E. M., Jr. (1970). Toward a cognitive theory of emotions. In M. Arnold (Ed.), *Feelings and emotions.* New York: Academic Press.

Leventhal, H. (1984). A perceptual-motor theory of emotion. In L. Berkowitz (Ed.), *Advances in experimental social psychology* (Vol. 17, pp. 117–182). New York: Academic Press.

Leventhal, H., & Tomarken, A. J. (1986). Emotion: Today's problems. *Annual Review of Psychology, 37,* 565–610.

Maugham, S. W. (1977). *The moon and sixpence.* Salem, NH: Ayers. (Original work published 1919)

Meyers, J., & Pitt, N. W. (1976). A consultation approach to help a school cope with the bereavement process. *Professional Psychology, 7,* 559–564.

Miller, I., & Norman, W. (1979). Learned helplessness in humans: A review and attribution theory model. *Psychological Bulletin, 86,* 93–118.

Monteith, M., Berkowitz, L., Kruglanski, A., & Blair, C. (1990). *The influence of physical discomfort on experienced anger and anger-related ideas, judgments, and memories.* Unpublished manuscript.

Riskind, J. H., & Gotay, C. C. (1982). Physical posture: Could it have regulatory or feedback effects on motivation and emotion? *Motivation and Emotion, 6,* 273–298.

Rosenblatt, P. C., Jackson, D. A., & Walsh, R. P. (1972). Coping with anger and aggression in mourning. *Omega: Journal of Death and Dying, 3,* 271–284.

Rule, B. G., Taylor, B., & Dobbs, A. R. (1987). Priming effects of heat on aggressive thoughts. *Social Cognition, 5,* 131–144.

Scherer, K. R., & Tannenbaum, P. H. (1986). Emotional experiences in everyday life: A survey approach. *Motivation and Emotion, 10,* 295–314.

Seligman, M. E. P. (1975). *Helplessness.* San Francisco: Freeman.

Shaver, P., Schwartz, J., Kinon, D., & O'Connor, C. (1987). Emotion knowledge: Further exploration of a prototype approach. *Journal of Personality and Social Psychology, 52,* 1061–1086.

Showers, C., & Cantor, N. (1985). Social cognition: A look at motivated strategies. *Annual Review of Psychology, 36,* 275–305.

Stein, N. L., & Levine, L. J. (1989). The causal organization of emotional knowledge: A developmental study. *Cognition and Emotion, 3,* 343–378.

Termine, N. T., & Izard, C. E. (1988). Infants' responses to their mothers' expressions of joy and sadness. *Developmental Psychology, 24,* 223–229.

Tomkins, S. S. (1962). *Affect, imagery, consciousness: 1. The positive affects.* New York: Springer Verlag.

Tourangeau, R., & Ellsworth, P. C. (1979). The role of facial response in the experience of emotion. *Journal of Personality and Social Psychology, 40,* 355–357.

Weiner, B. (1985). An attributional theory of achievement motivation and emotion. *Psychological Review, 92,* 548–573.

READING 21

Studies on Anger and Aggression: Implications for Theories of Emotion

James R. Averill • University of Massachusetts, Amherst

A series of surveys on the everyday experience of anger is described, and a sample of data from these surveys is used to address a number of issues related to the social bases of anger. These issues include the connection between anger and aggression; the targets, instigations, and consequences of typical episodes of anger; the differences between anger and annoyance; and possible sex differences in the experience and/or expression of anger. In a larger sense, however, the primary focus of the paper is not on anger and aggression. Rather, anger is used as a paradigm case to explore a number of issues in the study of emotion, including the advantages and limitations of laboratory research, the use of self-reports, the proper unit of analysis for the study of emotion, the relationship between human and animal emotion, and the authenticity of socially constituted emotional responses.

The history of theories of emotion during the 20th century appears to be a welter of crosscurrents and conflicting trends. Yet, against the background, a certain periodicity can be discerned. Particular themes well up, become dominant for a time, and sink back into the general stream of thought. Each wave seems to endure for roughly 20 years, as illustrated in Figure 21.1.[1]

The first wave depicted in Figure 21.1 represents the psychophysiological theories stemming from the earlier speculations of James (1890) and Dewey (1895). This wave crested around 1910 and was on the decline by the end of the decade, in part because of Cannon's (1914) influential criticisms. The next wave represents the ascendency of the behaviorist tradition, as represented, for example, by Watson (1924) and Tolman (1923). Neobehaviorism followed, in which emotions were defined less as overt responses than as intervening variables. This third wave is epitomized by Brown and Farber (1951), who worked within the

Hull-Spence tradition, and by Lindsley (1951), who provided a physiological locus (the reticular activating system) for emotional activation or drive. The 1960s saw the beginnings of the cognitive "revolution," with the work of Arnold (1960),

---

[1] These 20-year epochs should be taken very loosely. They are meant to illustrate general trends, and I do not want to imply strict historical accuracy. Obviously, each wave had its antecedents in preceding periods, and its influence continued to be felt in subsequent epochs. (To take but one example, Schachter's cognitive theory is, by his own account, "neo-Jamesian.") The reader should also note other theoretical traditions not mentioned in Figure 21.1—for example, dimensional theories, stemming from Wundt; ethological (evolutionary) theories, stemming from Darwin; central-neural theories, stemming from Cannon; and psychoanalytical theories, stemming from Freud. These approaches have provided a consistent background input, and critique, the cumulative effect of which has been extremely important. However, they have never come to dominate the field at any given time as have the four types of theories mentioned in Figure 21.1. For a detailed history of theories of emotions during the 20th century, see Mandler (1979).

337

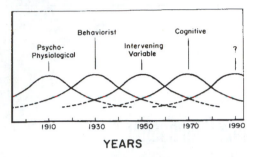

FIGURE 21.1 ■ Historical trends in theories of emotion during the 20th century.

Schachter (1964), and Lazarus (1966) deserving special mention. There are now signs that this cognitive wave is on the wane.[2]

What will the next wave be like? It is difficult to say, for the field is in a state of flux. Biologically based theories, with an emphasis on expressive reactions as opposed to physiological changes, have articulate advocates in Tomkins (1980), Izard (1977), and Plutchik (l980). My bet, however, is that the next wave of theories will have more of a social than a biological orientation. One of the objectives of the present essay is to help make this prediction a self-fulfilling prophecy.

Assumptions of a Constructivist View of Emotion

Let me begin by outlining briefly the basic assumptions of a social constructivist view of emotion. The term *constructivism* is used frequently in psychology to refer to the imposition of meaning or structure on events, for example, during perception or memory. The emotions are constructivist in this sense. But the way I am using the term, the connotation is more social than cognitive; that is, emotions are social constructions, not biological givens or the products of strictly intrapsychic processes.

---

[2] The demise of the cognitive revolution is difficult to document briefly. Like many revolutions, it is a victim of its own success. Much of psychology has become cognitive in a broad sense, but within that broad domain, old distinctions are beginning to reemerge (cf. Lazarus, Coyne, & Folkman, 1982; Marshall & Zimbardo, 1979; Maslach, 1979; Robinson, 1979, chap. 4; Zajonc, 1980). As yet, the various critiques do not provide any "united front," but they do suggest that the hegemony of cognition over affect is coming to an end.

A social-constructivist view (hereafter, I will drop the qualifying adjective *social*) rests on four major assumptions. First, emotions are responses of the whole person, and hence cannot be defined in terms of subclasses of responses (e.g., physiological or expressive reactions, cognitive appraisals, instrumental acts, or subjective experience). Second, emotions are complex, polythetic syndromes; that is, no subset of elements or kind of response is a necessary or sufficient condition for the whole. Third, the rules that govern the organization of the various elements of the syndrome are primarily social in origin. Fourth, emotions serve a function within the social system, or at least are correlated with other behaviors that have a social function.

It follows from these assumptions that emotions are social constructions (although I am omitting numerous details of the argument; see Averill, 1974, 1976, 1980a, 1980b, 1982). It does not follow from a constructivist view that genetically determined reactions are never incorporated into emotional syndromes or that the rules governing the whole are completely free of biological constraints. That is probably never true of any complex behavior, whether emotional or nonemotional. However, a constructivist view does suggest that the traditional search for the meaning of emotional syndromes in biological as opposed to social evolution is fundamentally misguided, as is any attempt to define emotions primarily in physiological or cognitive terms.

Studies on Anger and Aggression

Anger provides a particularly good paradigm case for assessing the viability of a constructivist view of emotion. Depending on how records are kept, most people report becoming mildly to moderately angry anywhere from several times a day to several times a week (Anastasi, Cohen, & Spate, 1948; Averill, 1979, 1982; Gates, 1926; Meltzer, 1933; Richardson, 1918). This frequency not only provides ample opportunity for study, it also raises interesting theoretical questions. Anger is a negative emotion both in terms of subjective experience and social evaluation. Young children are typically punished when they become angry (e.g., at parents or teachers), and adults who become angry too readily may be labeled childish. Why, in view of all this negative reinforcement, is anger so common? The answer typically given is that anger had, at one time during the evolution of the species, an adaptive function. Anger is a residue of our biological past, which under more civilized circumstances we can control only imperfectly.

This biological argument contrasts sharply with a constructivist point of view, which suggests that anger is a socially constituted syndrome that is maintained because of (not in spite of) its consequences.

Over the past several years I have been conducting a series of studies on the everyday experience of anger, the goal of which is to explore the extent to which this emotion is congruent with a constructivist point of view. These studies are based on written surveys in which subjects were asked to describe in detail a recent experience of anger—preferably one that occurred within the previous week. The complete results of these studies are presented elsewhere (Averill, 1982). For my present purposes, I have selected only a small sample of data for presentation. These data are not noteworthy because they represent new and innovative discoveries; rather, I have selected them because of the conceptual and methodological issues that they raise.

The data reported below are based on the responses of four groups of subjects. Two of these groups (80 students and 80 community residents) described their own experiences of anger. A third group (80 students) described their experiences as the target of another person's anger. In each case, subjects were asked to recall the most intense episode of anger during the previous week, or the most recent episode prior to that (no matter how mild it may have been). A fourth group of subjects (48 students) kept daily records of their experiences of anger and annoyance, and then completed detailed questionnaires comparing representative instances of each kind of emotion.

The community residents were selected at random from the telephone directory and were contacted by phone and letter. Of those eligible to participate (i.e., native-born Americans between the ages of 21 and 60), 54% returned usable questionnaires. The majority of these (57%) had no education beyond high school. The student subjects were recruited in the typical manner from psychology courses at a large state university. In all of these samples, half of the subjects were men and half were women.

The questionnaires used in these studies consisted of a mixture of forced-choice and open-ended items (approximately 90 items altogether). Nearly all aspects of an angry episode were covered: the nature of the instigation; relationship between the angry person and the target; thoughts, feelings, and responses during the episode; and the short-term and long-term consequences.

As already mentioned, I will present only a small sample of data (see Averill, 1982, for a complete report). My purpose is to raise certain issues of methodological and theoretical interest, not to present an exhaustive, empirical analysis of anger. In this section, I will address briefly the following six questions.

1. What is the connection between anger and aggression?
2. At whom do people typically become angry?
3. What are the causes of anger?
4. What are the consequences of anger?
5. How does anger differ from annoyance?
6. Are women less able than men to experience or express their anger?

Two answers will be offered to each question. The first answer reflects conventional psychological wisdom as might be found in an introductory textbook. Since no theorist would be likely to endorse this answer exactly as offered, the spokesperson for the conventional position will be labeled the *straw person*. To provide an alternative answer, I will call upon the *person in the street*. This is appropriate because the data to be presented are based on the way people describe their everyday experiences of anger. Let us begin with the first question.

What Is the Connection Between Anger and Aggression?

Straw person. Anger is the drive or motive behind many, if not most, forms of aggression. Alternatively (by more phenomenologically oriented psychologists), anger is the subjective experience that accompanies aggressive impulses.

This answer requires brief elaboration. All theorists recognize (a) that some forms of aggression (e.g., a professional killing) may be done without a trace of anger and (b) that people often become angry without becoming aggressive. However, with regard to the first point, "instrumental" aggression is typically distinguished from angry or hostile aggression and hence has not greatly influenced theories of emotion.[3] With regard to the second point, that people often do not become aggressive when angry, this is typically attributed to such factors as the inhibition, transformation, displacement, or sublimation of the aggressive response.

The presumed link between anger and aggression is most evident in biologically oriented theory and research (e.g., Plutchik, 1980). This is to be expected, because aggression is readily observable in animals, whereas anger involves a questionable inference. Nevertheless, generalizations from animal aggression to human anger are common. A link between anger and aggression is also implicit in much social psychological research. In most experiments on human aggression, for example, anger is manipulated as part of the experimental design. Yet, anger is seldom discussed as a substantive issue in its own right. The implicit assumption seems to be that anger is important only if it leads to aggression.[4]

Person in the street. Given an adequate provocation, nearly any response, and even no response, can count as a manifestation of anger. The possibilities include a pun or witticism, the withdrawal of affection, a request for an explanation, sulking and so on. Being unusually kind to or solicitous of the instigator is not even uncommon during anger.

Because behavior may vary almost indefinitely as a function of the person and the situation, it is not possible to describe a "typical" angry response. Recognizing this fact, Table 21.1 presents *one* possible breakdown of angry responses, and the percentage of episodes in which subjects (80, students and 80 community residents) said that they either felt like or actually did engage in a particular kind of response. (Because a person could, and typically did, engage in a variety of different responses during any given episode, the columns in Table 21.1 add to more than 100%.)

Consider first the right-hand column of figures, the responses that subjects said they actually made while angry. The major thing to note is that the most frequent responses were nonaggressive: engaging in calming activities (in 60% of the episodes) and talking the incident over with the instigator (in 59% of the episodes). Aggression, when it did occur, was primarily verbal or symbolic (in 49% of the episodes). The denial or removal of some benefit customarily enjoyed by the instigator (which might be considered, in some instances

TABLE 21.1. Aggressive and Nonaggressive Responses Characteristic of Anger

Response type	Impulses felt[a]	Responses made[a]
Direct aggression		
Verbal or symbolic aggression	82	49
Denial or removal of some benefit	59	41
Physical aggression or punishment	40	10
Indirect aggression		
Telling a third party in order to get back at the instigator (malediction)	42	34
Harming something important to the instigator	25	9
Displaced aggression		
Against a nonhuman object	32	28
Against a person	24	25
Nonaggressive responses		
Engaging in calming activities	60	60
Talking the incident over with a neutral party; no intent to harm the offender	59	59
Talking the incident over with the offender without exhibiting hostility	52	39
Engaging in activities opposite to the instigation of anger	14	19

[a] Expressed as percentage of episodes ($N = 160$) in which response occurred "somewhat" or "very much."

at least, as a form of passive aggression) occurred in 41% of the episodes.

Direct physical aggression or punishment occurred in only 10% of the episodes. "Contrary reactions"—that is, activities opposite to the instigation of anger, such as being extra friendly to the

---

[3] Although useful for some purposes, the distinction between instrumental and angry or hostile aggression is also somewhat misleading (see Bandura, 1973; Zillmann, 1979). Anger can be instrumental in achieving a wide variety of goals. The problem is to distinguish among goals that are intrinsic to anger (i.e., that are part of the legitimation of anger) and goals that an extrinsic (Averill, 1982).

[4] There are, of course, exceptions to this generalization (e.g., Novaco, 1975; Rule & Nesdale, 1976). Nevertheless, discussions of anger in the psychological literature are most conspicuous by their absence. Anger is, however a popular topic among trade books aimed at the general population. Some sample titles are: *The Angry Book* (Rubin, 1969), *Creative Aggression* (Bach & Goldberg, 1974), *How to Get Angry Without Feeling Guilty* (Bry, 1977), *How to Live With and Without Anger* (Ellis, 1977), and *Anger: The Misunderstood Emotion* (Tavris, 1982).

instigator—were about twice as frequent (in 19% of the episodes) as direct physical aggression. Moreover, in approximately one third of the episodes in which direct physical aggression did occur, the "aggression" (e.g., a spank) involved the punishment of a child. The intent was to deter, not to hurt. Physical aggression directed against adults was similarly mild, and as often as not was constructively motivated.

In short, the typical episode of anger is not particularly aggressive. When we turn to impulses felt, rather than responses made, aggressive tendencies become more apparent. Thus, referring to the first column of figures in Table 21.1, subjects felt like aggressing verbally in 82% of the episodes. The impulse toward physical aggression was not, however, particularly common (in 40% of the episodes). Indeed, the impulse toward physical aggression was less common than the desire to talk things over, either with the instigator (in 59% of the episodes) or with a neutral third party (in 52% of the episodes).

The data presented in Table 21.1 can be interpreted in several ways. The first, which is in keeping with the conventional view presented by our straw person, is that anger is an impulse toward aggression, but that this impulse is maybe inhibited, transformed (often beyond recognition, even by the angry person), or even turned into its opposite. The second interpretation, which accords more with the views of the person in the street, maintains that anger is compatible with a wide variety of different impulses and behaviors. It is impossible on the basis of available evidence to prove either interpretation. Indeed, that is not even the issue, for both interpretations may be correct under particular circumstances. The issue is one of generalization. Rather than assuming that the first (conventional) interpretation is correct in all or most instances of anger, let us take the person in the street at his or her word and see where it leads.

At Whom Do People Typically Become Angry?

Straw person. Anger is related to hatred, that is, we tend to become angry at people whom we dislike. This answer follows, in part, from the presumed link between anger and aggression. The reasoning goes somewhat as follows: Aggression involves, by definition, the infliction of harm upon another; we typically do not wish to harm those

we like; therefore, the target of anger should be someone who is disliked, or even hated.

Person in the street. The answer of the person in the street is presented in Table 21.2, which contains the distribution of angry episodes according to the relationship between the angry person and the target, and the sex of the target. Table 21.2 is based on descriptions provided by persons of their own anger; it includes only those episodes (116 out of a total of 160) in which the primary target was another person. Combining the data for male and female targets, in over half of the episodes the target was either a loved one (29%) or someone well-known and liked (24%). Acquaintances accounted for another 25% of the episodes. In only 8% of the episodes was the target someone who was well-known and disliked, and in another 13% of the episodes the target was a stranger.

There are, of course, a variety of reasons why people are more likely to become angry at friends and loved ones than at strangers and disliked others: For example, we are in more frequent contact with friends and loved ones; we can be more easily hurt by their actions; and we know how a friend or loved one is likely to respond to our anger. But whatever the reasons, the mere fact that the typical target of anger is a friend or loved one requires a reexamination of some commonly held assumptions, in addition to the presumed link between anger and hatred. Consider the frequently reported finding that men are more likely to be the target of anger and aggression than are women (see Baron,

TABLE 21.2. Anger Episodes × Target

	Episodes	
Target	*n*	%
Loved one		
M	15	13
F	19	16
Well-known & liked		
M	15	13
F	13	11
Well-known & disliked		
M	6	5
F	4	3
Acquaintance		
M	22	19
F	7	6
Stranger		
M	14	12
F	1	1

Note. Total number of episodes = 116. M = male, F = female.

1977, p. 221; Frodi, Macaulay, & Theme, 1977). As Table 21.2 indicates, this generalization is true only when the target is a stranger or acquaintance (as is typical in most psychological research). When anger is between loved ones or friends, which includes the majority of episodes in everyday affairs, both men and women are equally likely to be targets.[5]

Some comment should also be made about the fact that the data of only 116 out of 160 subjects are reported in Table 21.2. What about the remaining 44 subjects (28% of the total)? In 21 of the 44 episodes reported by these subjects the target was either the self, a group of two or more persons, or an institution. In another 14 episodes the primary target was an inanimate object, with another person being secondarily involved. Only 9 episodes (6% of the total) did not involve a human target, either directly or indirectly. And even in these 9 episodes there was a strong tendency to personify the target and imbue it with human characteristics.

In short, anger is a highly interpersonal emotion. It cannot be fully understood apart from the social context in which it occurs; and, as Table 21.2 illustrates, that context typically involves a close affectional relationship between the angry person and the target.

What Are The Causes of Anger?

Straw person. No single answer to this question is widely accepted by psychologists. Instead, a whole family of straw persons may be called upon to answer. The granddaddy of them all asserts that frustration is the primary cause of anger (Dollard, Doob, Miller, Mowrer, & Sears, 1939). Like many elders, this straw person no longer commands the attention that it once did, although it still occupies an honored place in many textbooks. Other members of the straw family assert that anger results when unexplained arousal (from whatever source, not just frustration) is attributed to some provocative circumstance. Incidental aggressive cues (e.g., the presence of a weapon) have also been given prominence as a contributory cause of angry (impulsive) aggression, especially if the person has been previously frustrated or aroused. Other members of the straw family include such factors as aversive stimuli, modeling, disinhibition, and deindividuation. What unites this rather diverse group into a single family is the tendency to treat

as interlopers the reasons that people typically offer for their own behavior.[6]

Person in the street. I will not attempt to describe the specific kinds of instigations to anger reported by the person in the street. Frustration (defined as the interruption of some planned or ongoing activity) is important, as are the loss of pride or self-esteem and the violation of personal wishes and accepted social norms. But the major issue for the person in the street is not the specific nature of the instigating event; it is the perceived *justification* for the instigator's behavior. Anger, for the person in the street, is an accusation. This is illustrated in Table 21.3.

Table 21.3 contains data from two groups of subjects: angry persons and the targets of another person's anger. Different episodes are involved (i.e., the angry persons and the targets were not describing the same set of incidents.[7] Over 85% of the episodes described by the angry persons involved either an act that they considered voluntary and unjustified (59%), or else a potentially avoidable accident (e.g., due to negligence or lack of foresight, 28%). About 50% of the instigations reported by targets also fall into one or the other of these two categories.

---

[5]As discussed earlier, psychological research and theoretical formulations often do not allow a clear distinction between anger and aggression. With regard to the issue at hand, it might be argued that men and women are equally likely to become the targets of anger but that the aggressive response is inhibited when the target is a woman. That, however, cannot be the entire story. The present data suggest that anger, as well as aggression, varies as a function of the sex of the target and the nature of the relationship. For the sake of completeness, it should also be noted that there are conditions, such as viewing certain kinds of pornography, that will considerably enhance the likelihood that a woman will become the target of aggression, even in the absence of an anger-inducing provocation (Donnerstein & Berkowitz, 1981).

[6] The shift in terminology in this paragraph from "causes" to "reasons" is deliberate. The logical distinction between these two classes of explanatory variables has been the subject of much debate (e.g., Harris & Secord, 1972; Locke & Pennington, 1982), the details of which need not concern us here. Suffice it to note that the difference between the type of explanation attributed here to the straw persons of psychology and the type of explanation preferred by the person in the street corresponds roughly to the distinction between the causes of and the reasons for behavior.

[7]Because the targets could only describe episodes in which they were aware of the other person's anger, a similar restriction was placed on the episodes described by the angry persons. That is, all the instigations reported in Table 21.3 resulted in the communication of anger.

TABLE 21.3. Perception of the Instigation by Angry Persons and by Targets

Perception of the instigation	Angry person[a]	Target[b]	Significance of the difference
A voluntary and unjustified act	59%	21%	<.01
A potentially avoidable accident or event	28%	28%	ns
A voluntary and justified act	12%	35%	<.01
An unavoidable accident or event	2%	15%	<.01

[a]n =102. [b]n = 80.

The differences between the appraised instigations by angry persons and targets are not surprising; it is easier to cast than to accept blame. However, the figures presented in Table 21.3 actually underestimate the accusatory nature of anger, at least as far as the responses of the targets are concerned. In their open-ended comments, more than half of the targets who denied any wrongdoing (i.e., by claiming that the instigation was either justified or an unavoidable accident) also made reference to the imputation of blame inherent ·in the other person's anger. Two common explanations offered by these "innocent" targets could be paraphrased as follows: "I understand why this person became angry, but I still had a right to do what I did," or, "It couldn't be helped."

In short, anger is a response to some perceived misdeed. This is perhaps the most important fact about anger. To many, the fact may seem trivially obvious, but we should not conclude that it is therefore trivial in a theoretical sense. For example, a representative of our straw family might contend that the *real* cause of a person's anger is frustration, arousal, or the like and that' subjects in the present studies were simply giving reasons (based on intuitive or naive "theories" of anger) to rationalize their behavior. This contention could be meant in several ways. It might mean that the reasons subjects offered for their behavior were mere rationalizations (e.g., reflecting social desirability). If this is the implication, then the contention is surely wrong (because, among other things, it could not account for the frequency with which targets accepted blame for the incidents they reported). On the other hand, the contention might mean that the reasons subjects offered for their behavior have little explanatory power and hence can be ignored from a scientific point of view. But

that cannot be true either. Whatever the logical status of reasons versus (other) causes, two things are clear: First, people do not behave independently of the way they conceptualize their behavior. Second, an important task of psychology is to account for the origins and functions of the relevant conceptualizations.

To summarize, the typical instigation to anger is a value judgment. More than anything else, anger is an attribution of blame. The attribution may not always be correct or free from self-serving biases, and it may be influenced by a host of factors (e.g., frustration, arousal, stimulus–response associations, anonymity) that are in themselves value neutral. The problem with many of the current accounts of anger—as represented by our straw family—is not that they are wrong. The problem is, rather, one of emphasis.[8]

What Are the Consequences of Anger?

Straw person. Although this question is seldom addressed explicitly in psychological research, the implicit assumption is that anger has largely negative consequences for the individual and for society at large. As described earlier, this assumption is one reason why many psychologists have postulated a biological or innate basis for angerlike tendencies. That is, anger is maintained in the behavioral repertoire in spite of its negative consequences because it is a product of natural selection.

Person in the street. When subjects and targets were asked to evaluate the overall consequences of the angry episodes that they had experienced, the ratio of beneficial to harmful consequences was about 3 to 1 for angry persons and 2.5 to 1 for targets. This does not mean that the experiences were somehow found pleasant or desirable. Few people find pleasure in their own anger, and to be the target of another's anger is even more unpleasant: But in spite of the unpleasantness, the consequences of most episodes of anger are evaluated positively.

Of course, angry persons might be expected to rationalize their own anger, and thus say it was for

---

[8]This is hardly an original observation. Many others have pointed out that anger involves a normative judgement, an attribution of blame (see Pepitone, 1976; Rule & Nesdale, 1976, for two recent examples). For the most part, however, psychological theories have had difficulty accommodating this fact.

the good. Therefore, the target's perceptions are more interesting in this regard. Table 21.4 presents a list of possible consequences, and the percentage of episodes in which—according to the targets—the consequences occurred.

As can be seen, 76% of the targets said that they came to realize their own faults because of the other person's anger. Furthermore, the target's relationship with the angry person was reportedly strengthened more often than it was weakened (in 48% vs. 35% of the episodes), and the targets more often gained rather than lost respect for the angry person (in 44% vs. 29% of the episodes).[9]

These data suggest that the everyday experience of anger is sufficiently reinforced to maintain a rather high incidence. But we do not have to rely solely on individual reports of outcomes to make this point. Anger has been much condemned on the societal level. As Campbell (1975) has noted, anger is on everyone's list of sins. But there is another column on the list that should not be overlooked. Traditional moral teachings also emphasize the sinfulness of not becoming angry under appropriate circumstances, even when (or especially when) a display of anger might be difficult or unpleasant. The current appeal of assertiveness training suggests that such a notion is not entirely out of date. In any case, there seems to be little need for recourse to biological arguments to explain the prevalence of anger.

How Does Anger Differ from Annoyance?

Straw person. According to most psychological analyses, the major difference between anger and annoyance is one of degree. Anger is more intense than annoyance; beyond that, the question has aroused little interest.

Person in the street. Anger is indeed often more intense than annoyance, but that is not the only, nor even the major, difference between these two emotional states.

To the person in the street, the difference be-

TABLE 21.4. Target's Perception of Longer-Term Changes or Consequences Brought About by the Angry Episode

Type of change	% episodes[a] in which change occurred "somewhat" or "very much"
You realized your own faults	76
You realized your own strengths	50
Your relationship with the angry person was strengthened	48
You gained respect for the angry person	44
You did something that was good for the angry person	39
You did something that was for your own good	38
Your relationship with the angry person became more distant	35
You lost respect for the angry person	29

[a] $n = 80$

tween anger and annoyance is intuitively clear but difficult to describe. One group of 48 subjects kept daily records of all their experiences of anger and annoyance for a one-week period. At the end of each day they wrote a brief sentence describing each experience and labeled it as *anger, annoyance, or uncertain.* At the end of the week, they completed a more detailed questionnaire on the most intense incident of annoyance that did not include anger and on the most intense incident that was representative of anger.

A total of 1,536 incidents were recorded in the diaries: 73% were labeled annoyance, 23% anger, and 4 %uncertain. Subjects apparently were quite able to distinguish between their experiences of anger and annoyance.

Like the straw person of psychology, subjects reported that their experiences of anger were generally more intense than their experiences of annoyance. However, *intensity* can mean different things depending on the context. Psychologists often define emotional intensity in terms of physiological arousal. That is not what the person in the street typically means when he or she says that anger is more intense than annoyance.

According to the descriptions given by subjects

---

[9] People often find positive aspects to negative events. This is true even when the event is so severe as a paralyzing spinal injury (Bulman & Wortman, 1977). Some of the positive outcomes listed in Table 4 also reflect this tendency to find a silver lining in every cloud. For example, subjects who evaluated the overall consequences of an episode as harmful rather than beneficial were significantly more likely than others to say that they came to realize their own strengths because of the incident.

of the two kinds of incidents, *seriousness* would be a better word than *intensity* to describe the difference between anger and annoyance. Subjects often said that the incidents that aroused their anger were more important to them, even when they were not affected directly. Thus, a person might get angry over the killing of baby seals, but only annoyed by someone loudly chewing gum, although the latter could be more immediately upsetting. This brings us back to the issue of blame discussed previously. Anger has a moral connotation that annoyance does not, and morality cannot be reduced to a matter of intensity, in the sense (say) of physiological arousal.

There is also a difference in response tendencies during anger and annoyance. Persons who are annoyed often try to hide their feelings and to leave the situation as rapidly as possible. The angry person, on the other hand, may go out of his or her way to seek confrontation. Anger seems to demand expression. Of course, people do tend to inhibit the expression of anger, either completely (on occasion) or partially (most of the time), but persons who do not want to express their anger at all are probably not truly angry.

The above characterization summarizes some of the major differences in the way people describe their experiences of anger and annoyance. The summary, however, both exaggerates and oversimplifies the differences between these emotional states. It exaggerates the differences in the sense that people can become angry or annoyed at the same object, and they may respond similarly in either case. It oversimplifies the differences in the sense that even when anger and annoyance are indistinguishable in terms of the object or response, people typically have little difficulty identifying the state they are in, although they may have a great deal of difficulty stating the basis for their judgment.

To help clarify what is perhaps the most important difference between anger and annoyance, consider briefly an analogous distinction between knowledge and belief. One person may claim knowledge about a state of affairs, whereas another might only profess belief. As Austin (1961) has pointed out, the difference between knowledge and belief in such instances is not necessarily a matter of certainty (the cognitive analogue of intensity), for people who believe may believe with utmost certainty. Rather, claims of knowledge and belief represent different moves in a social "game."

People who claim knowledge are staking their reputation, offering their guarantee, that what they say is true. People who claim belief, on the other hand, are hedging their bets, refusing to make a commitment.

Like knowledge, anger has a promissory quality. It represents a commitment. As such, anger involves one's self and one's principles in a way that annoyance does not. This helps explain the fact that the person who is easily annoyed may be regarded as moody or touchy; whereas the person who becomes angry too readily or inconsistently, or who does not exhibit an appropriate follow-through, may be regarded as shallow and lacking in character.[10]

In short, the differences between anger and annoyance are qualitative as well as quantitative. Being a little bit angry is not a shade more than being very annoyed. Anger emerges at the interface between the self and society in a different way than annoyance does.

Are Women Less Able Than Men to Experience or Express Anger?

Straw person. There are both straw men and straw women who give affirmative answers to this question, but for very different reasons. The former typically start from a biological perspective, whereas the latter typically begin from a sociological (or, more specifically, a feminist) position. According to the biological argument, males of most primate species are more aggressive than females, and, in humans, a similar pattern has been observed cross-culturally. To the extent that anger is related to aggression, it follows that men are also more prone to anger than are women.

The feminist argument reaches a similar conclusion but starts from a quite different set of assumptions. Feminists argue that women are quite capable of experiencing anger (biologically speaking) but that they are inhibited from doing so by power inequities within our patriarchal society. A

---

[10]It is also instructive in this regard to compare the difference between anger and annoyance to that between loving and liking. Love involves a commitment, and it legitimizes certain kinds of social relationships. It is even possible to love someone without liking him or her (although conflicts an almost inevitable in such cases, as many romantic potboilers attest). In any case, it is not possible to reduce love to a matter of physiological responses, even physiological responses as interpreted in the light of situational cues.

woman's anger, therefore, tends to be experienced and expressed in indirect and often self-defeating ways, including lethargy, depression, and so on.

Person in the street. In the present series of studies, women reported becoming angry as often as men, as intensely, for much the same reasons, and they expressed their anger as openly as did the men. The only major and consistent difference was that women reported crying more often than did men (about four times more often).

It might be thought that the questionnaires used in these studies simply were not sensitive enough to detect subtle differences between the sexes. That is unlikely. For one thing, the differences postulated to exist by both the biological and feminist arguments (and certainly by the two in combination, for they are not completely incompatible) are by no means subtle. For another thing, the questionnaires were sensitive enough to pick up a number of differences between students and community residents. These differences are not particularly noteworthy, because they can be accounted for in terms of the students' living conditions. Nevertheless, there is no reason to believe that students should differ from nonstudents more than women differ from men. Finally, experimental research also lends little support to the notion that women are less prone to anger than men are, or that women are more inhibited in their expression of anger (see Frodi et al., 1977).

I do not wish to imply that there are no differences between men and women in the everyday experience of anger. Obviously, some of the things that a man finds provocative might not affect a woman, and vice versa, and when angry, a man may do and say things that a woman typically would not (e.g., see Frodi et al., 1977). But once we leave the level of specifics, these differences tend to disappear. Women are just as sensitive as men to unfair treatment, to unwarranted threats to their self-esteem, and to negligence or lack of consideration on the part of others; and in response to such provocations, women are just as able as men to make their feelings known clearly and emphatically.

I emphasize this lack of sex differences because it is consistent with a constructivist, as opposed to biological, view of anger. That is, there is little in the social norms pertaining to anger itself to suggest that women should be less sensitive to provocation than men, and since anger typically does not involve a great deal of direct physical aggres-

sion, women should be as able as men to express their anger appropriately and effectively.

But what about the feminist argument? Does the failure to observe marked sex differences in the everyday experience of anger mean that the feminists are simply wrong? In some versions, at least, the feminist argument involves a confounding of sociopolitical and psychological levels of analysis. At the risk of greatly oversimplifying a complex issue, the central premise of the feminist argument may be rephrased somewhat as follows: Women should be more angry than they now are at the unjust conditions they face. The merits of this premise must be evaluated independently of how often, at whom, and for what reasons women actually do become angry during the course of everyday affairs.

The above notwithstanding, the feminist argument does have implications for an understanding of anger as it is ordinarily experienced. For example, if a woman can be convinced that she is really angry, but has been suppressing it, then she may also come to see the object of her anger in a new light (e.g., as involving an injustice) and be motivated to do something about it. This is perhaps as clear an example as any of the potential social uses of anger—a potential that is by no means limited to the feminist movement.

Rebuttals, Rejoinders, and Implications

The view of anger presented by the person in the street can be summarized as follows. Anger is only loosely related to aggression, at least in everyday affairs. That is, aggression is only one of many possible manifestations of anger, even if such highly socialized responses as a verbal retort or the denial of some benefit are included under the general rubric of aggression. Anger occurs most often between friends and loved ones; it is precipitated by some perceived wrong or avoidable misfortune; and although it is an unpleasant experience, it generally leads to positive consequences. Anger differs from closely related states, such as annoyance, primarily in terms of the attribution of blame implicit in anger and in the commitment to action if the instigating conditions do not change. Finally, there appear to be few differences between the anger of men and women under ordinary circumstances.

The above picture is based on only a small

sample of the data collected in a series of studies on the everyday experience of anger, the complete results of which have been published elsewhere (Averill, 1982). The picture is necessarily over-simplified. Nevertheless, were more detail to be added, the basic outline would not change greatly. For present purposes, it is sufficient to note that the picture of anger presented by the person in the street is more consistent with the constructivist view of emotion outlined earlier than it is with the views attributed to the straw men and women of psychology. But before accepting the picture painted by the person in the street, we must consider a number of possible objections. This will also provide an opportunity to explore in more detail some of the implications of these studies on anger and aggression for theories of emotion in general.

Too Much Straw

To begin with, it might be objected that the straw persons I have created should have been made of sterner stuff; they do not convey the diversity and sophistication that characterize current research on anger and aggression. However, before the straw persons are criticized too harshly on these grounds, two things should be kept in mind. First, their task was to present a broad view, a kind of gestalt. We are used to thinking of the whole as greater than the sum of its parts, but sometimes, it is less. Second, my concern here is primarily with anger as an emotion, not with aggression in all its forms. As already described, anger has received relatively little systematic attention from psychologists, although it plays an important role in much contemporary research on aggression.

The reader has undoubtedly also noticed that my straw persons bear close resemblances to implacable experimentalists. The resemblance is not entirely coincidental. Current social psychological theories of anger and aggression rely heavily on laboratory findings. For the most part, however, the issues I am raising are not peculiar to any particular methodology. For example, a common criticism of laboratory research is that studies are often designed to clarify the findings of earlier experiments, with insufficient attention paid to the external validity of the research program as a whole.[11] As Berkowitz and Donnerstein (1982) have pointed out, a similar criticism could be made of many programs of research conducted in clinical, industrial, and other, more naturalistic, settings. But to point out that a criticism must be shared does not invalidate the criticism. Therefore, let us examine the issue a little more closely.

Generalizations from research findings may be of two kinds: situational and theoretical. Situational generalizations involve the extrapolation of findings from one setting (e.g., the laboratory) to another (e.g., "real life"). By contrast, theoretical generalizations involve the significance or emphasis that is placed on findings because of their presumed relevance to underlying mechanisms. In their defense of laboratory research, Berkowitz and Donnerstein (1982) correctly note that experiments are designed to investigate causal hypotheses (e.g., the effects of the presence of a weapon on aggression) and not to provide normative data (e.g., the likelihood that certain kinds of responses will occur in naturalistic settings). In other words, the generalizations that one can draw from laboratory research are theoretical and not situational.

Assuming that an experiment is well-designed and conducted, what factors make theoretical generalizations possible? In physics and certain other areas of science, very small effects, observable only under tightly controlled laboratory conditions, can be highly significant theoretically. This is because the relevant causal hypotheses are quite precise, and they have been rigorously deduced from theories of considerable power and depth. Unfortunately, social psychology is not known for the kind of theories that would lend comparable significance to the rather small effects typically observed in the laboratory. This makes theoretical generalizations from laboratory findings rather tenuous, no matter how well-designed the study may be.

---

[11]Perhaps the best documented case of this is the series of studies on the risky-shift phenomenon (Cartwright, 1973). However, a fair amount of inbreeding is also evident in studies on aggression. For example, Lubek (1979) did a content analysis of research on aggression and related topics published between 1968 and 1977, inclusive. During that 10-year period, 102 articles appeared in the *Journal of Personality and Social Psychology* and the *Journal of Experimental Social Psychology*. Roughly 65% of these used electric shock as the dependent variable, usually in conjunction with some variation of the teacher–learner paradigm. Lubek also noted a marked tendency among researchers to cite their own work and that of a small group of colleagues, and not to cite research more than a decade old. There are, of course, many advantages to such a strategy (e.g., in terms of replicability). However, too much inbreeding can also lead to debility.

Of course, the same thing could be said (perhaps with even greater force) about theoretical generalizations based on other types of psychological research. For the past 40 years, however, our social psychological theories of anger and aggression have rested primarily on the results of laboratory research. As a consequence, our theories have been biased in the direction of variables that have a demonstrable causal effect under laboratory conditions but which nevertheless may be of questionable theoretical importance. To take but one example, unexplained physiological arousal has been demonstrated to facilitate emotional reactivity, including anger and aggression. But what is the relative importance of such arousal in comparison with other determinants of emotional behavior? Probably, it is not great. Yet, one can pick up nearly any book on aggression or on emotion and find elaborate discussions of the role of physiological arousal (and other causal variables frequently investigated in the laboratory). The types of explanatory variables offered by the person in the street for his or her anger pale in significance by contrast (see the earlier discussion of the causes of anger).

To repeat, no particular theorist today would likely endorse the simplified views presented by our straw persons, at least not in every respect. And although our straw persons reflect the tradition of experimental social psychology (with a passing bow to biologically oriented research), the weaknesses they portray are not limited to any particular research paradigm. These qualifications do not mean, however, that our straw persons are made entirely of straw. On the contrary. They present a fairly accurate portrait of anger and aggression as might be found, for example, in an introductory psychology textbook.

If we grant that our straw men and women of psychology are made of sinew and bone as well as straw, then it is only proper that they be allowed a chance for rebuttal. Therefore, let me turn to some potential criticisms of the picture of anger painted by the person in the street.

The Reliance on Self-Reports

Perhaps the most obvious objection to the view of anger offered by the person in the street (or at least that version of it presented earlier) is the reliance on self-reports. What a person says is under conscious, voluntary control, and hence is subject to dissimulation and conformity to social expectations. And even when a person is not dissimulating in an attempt to present a positive self-image, she or he still may not have the ability to report accurately what is taking place internally.

The fact that self-reports are often influenced by social desirability is a shortcoming only if social desirability represents a confounding variable. When social expectations or norms are themselves the focus of interest, then self-reports may be a very useful guide. Validity does not inhere in a particular kind of data as an intrinsic property. Rather, validity is always relative to the inferences being made. In the present case, the inferences I wish to make are not to the internal cognitive processes that help mediate anger and aggression, but rather to the social norms and expectancies that help constitute the syndrome of anger.

I do not deny that there are often good reasons to be skeptical about self-reports. The clinic and many other contexts attest to the powers of persons to deceive not only others but themselves as well. Also, Nisbett and Wilson (1977) have reviewed considerable evidence that people have difficulty identifying the variables that influence their behavior, even when they wish to cooperate and have no reason for dissimulation.[12]

Obviously, this is not the place to begin a detailed examination of the advantages and limitations of self-reports. Nevertheless, a few general observations should be made. Many of the criticisms made of self-reports also apply to other forms of data, especially overt behavior. Even physiological responses, which often are regarded as particularly trustworthy, can be quite misleading and difficult to interpret (Averill, 1974; Averill & Opton, 1968). Why are self-reports treated with such skepticism and searching criticism, however valid, while the limitations of other forms of data are often treated with sufferance?

Hogan and Emler (1978) have suggested that the distrust of self-reports can be traced, in part,

---

[12] Nisbett and Wilson's (1977) analysis is frequently cited as evidence against the validity of self-reports. Without gainsaying some of the important points they make, it should also be noted that their analysis has been extensively criticized on both methodological and conceptual grounds (Adair & Spinner, 1981; Cotton, 1980; Rich, 1979; Smith & Miller, 1978; White, 1980). That the overly negative conclusions reached by Nisbett and Wilson have struck such a responsive cord in spite of these criticisms reinforces some of the observations made in this section (i.e., with regard to the general biases among psychologists against self-reports).

to individualistic and rationalistic biases that characterize much of American society. These biases assume competition in the pursuit of self-interest, in which case it is reasonable to mislead others about one's true intentions, feelings, and wishes. I do not believe we have to cast the net so widely. The distrust of self-reports stems more from the internal dynamics of psychology than from broader cultural biases. After 100 years, psychology is still suffering from an identity crisis. We have been much concerned with convincing ourselves and others that our field is a real science. Consequently, we have tended to downgrade the great stock of knowledge that is embedded in our ordinary language. Science, in the minds of many, deals with the unknown, the esoteric, and the counterintuitive. What people can tell us about their everyday lives usually does not fit this stereotype. Therefore, let us ignore what people have to say; better yet, let us demonstrate that what they say has little relationship to what they do.

I do not mean to dismiss ail the criticisms of self-reports, for there are ample grounds for caution. Nor do I mean to make a virtue out of necessity, even though there is a certain necessity—not just a convenience—about the use of self-reports for investigating a phenomenon like the everyday experience of anger. I am suggesting that psychologists should not impose a form of prior censorship on themselves by excluding from consideration a whole class of data and type of methodology, all in the name of science. [. . .]

Animal Emotions

Let us turn now to a rebuttal that is more theoretical than methodological. If emotions are social constructions, how do we account for emotions in animals? For example, animals do not have the capacity to make the type of judgments (e.g., an attribution of blame) that we have seen are characteristic of human anger. Yet, as a cursory perusal of almost any introductory psychology textbook will attest, our current conceptions of emotion rely heavily on animal research. Am I suggesting that such research is irrelevant to an understanding of human anger?

No. But I am suggesting that its relevance is often misunderstood. It would be fatuous to deny a continuity between humans and animals in emotional as in any other kind of behavior. Moreover, I have little sympathy with the notion that human

beings are basically a pacific species and that all human aggression can be traced to the corrupting influence of society. However, human aggression can take many forms. Not all of these forms can be characterized as manifestations of anger, and conversely, we have seen that not all anger involves aggression.

The relationship of emotion in humans to "emotion" in animals can be compared to that between language in humans and "language" in animals. Human language was made possible by a long series of evolutionary developments. But no species other than humans possesses language, and with the possible exception of chimpanzees and gorillas, none are capable of acquiring the most rudimentary elements of a language, even after careful training. This does not mean, of course, that animals do not communicate; they do, often in subtle and complex ways. An understanding of animal communication may someday help us to better understand the origins and nature of human language. However, no one would imagine that our understanding of specific human languages (e.g., English or Chinese) will be greatly facilitated by studying communication in dogs or rats. Similarly, I would maintain that our understanding of specific human emotions (such as anger) will not be enhanced greatly by studying superficially analogous behavior in lower animals (e.g., aggression in the cat or rat).

The gap between human language and communication in animals is far more evident than the gap between human and animal emotion. However, the obviousness of the gap is due, in part, to the fact that linguists have amassed a great deal of data on the form and nature of various human languages. There is no comparable body of data with respect to human emotions. Hence, it is much easier to draw loose analogies between the human and animal "emotions" than between human and animal "languages."[13]

Authentic Emotions

Let me consider one final objection to the view of anger presented earlier and to a constructivist view of emotion in general. Emotional experiences are often regarded as the epitome of sincerity and authenticity, as "mirrors of the soul" or reflections of one's "true" self. A constructivist position seems to sully this picture by implying that emotions are social conventions or roles that people enact. Social rules, a critic might argue, may regulate, modulate, inhibit or disguise the expression of emotion, but somehow the authentic emotion remains intact throughout the various transformations.

William James once asked us to abstract from the experience of emotion all bodily sensations. What would be left, he queried, other than the cold perception of the arousing event? The question can be turned around. Abstract from the experience of anger (or of any other emotion) all social norms and expectancies regarding the appraisal of the instigating conditions, the organization of the response, the anticipated outcomes, and the attribution of responsibility (e.g., "I couldn't help it; I was overcome by anger"). What would be left of the emotional experience?

In fact, it is very difficult to imagine what an authentic emotion might be like, if we mean by "authentic" a response unsullied by all social norms and expectancies. If that is our conception, then by definition an emotion could be authentic only if innate. A social-constructivist must find a different solution to the problem of authenticity.

In everyday affairs, when we say that an emotion is inauthentic, we typically mean that there is a disjunction between the internal experience and its external manifestation. For example, a person may present a calm and polite exterior while seething inside. Conversely, a parent may scold a child in mock anger while inwardly laughing at the child's antics. When the disjunction is deliberate, as in these examples, we have an intuitively obvious contrast by which to distinguish the authentic from the inauthentic. But what if we ask about the authenticity of an unfeigned emotion, or about the internal experience of emotion? For such a question to be meaningful, we must also have some contrast in mind. What might that contrast be? In addressing this issue, let us begin by considering briefly an experience that is in a sense incorrigible, and hence the authenticity of which is generally beyond question—pain.

Hilgard (1977) has shown that persons who experience reduced pain when given a suggestion of hypnotic analgesia may nevertheless continue to register pain and are able to report the pain through an automatic writing technique. In metaphorical terms, the pain is experienced by a "hidden observer," presumably dissociated from the "hypnotized part" of the self. Which experience is more authentic, that of the "hidden observer" or that of the "hypnotized part"? The temptation is to say

that of the "hidden observer," for its reports conform more closely to the true interests of the individual (avoidance of tissue damage from the applied stimulus). However, Spanos and Hewitt (1980) have demonstrated that the "hidden observer" can be led by appropriate suggestion to experience either more or less pain than the "hypnotized par." That is, the "hidden observer" is also a creation of the hypnotic procedure. To quote Spanos and Hewitt (1980) directly, the experiences of the "hidden observer" result "from subjects' attempts to convincingly enact the role of 'good hypnotic subject' as this role is defined for them by the experimental procedures they undergo" (p. 1201).

In citing this study by Spanos and Hewitt, I do not wish to imply that pain and emotion are equivalent phenomena. They are not.[14] However, the study does illustrate nicely some of the considerations that must be taken into account when deciding the truth or authenticity of an experience.

Authenticity is not an inherent property of experience; it is a judgment about experience. Like any judgment, it is based on a set of presuppositions. For the most part, these presuppositions have to do with the perceived best interests of the individual or, in a more extended sense, with the best interests ("true values") of the group (which sometimes may be contrary to the welfare of the individual). In the case of pain, the best interests of the individual are seldom in doubt, and hence it is only under highly unusual circumstances that the question of authenticity even arises. The emotions are far more complicated in this regard, for they are partly constituted by social norms and expectancies that may vary from one group to another.

---

[13] Analogies between human and animal emotions art facilitated not only by an absence of systematic observation, but also by the way we speak. Anger and many other emotions are regarded as "brutish," "bestial," "primitive," "gut" reactions Elsewhere (Averill, 1974) I have examined the symbolism inherent in this way of speaking and have traced its influence on theories of emotion from classical Greece to the present time.

[14] Pain is more simple, more invariant, and more tied to immediate sensory stimulation than is nearly any emotion. Of even greater importance, pains do not have intentional objects in the same sense that emotions do. For example, I cannot be angry unless I am angry *about* something but my pain need not point beyond itself. Because of these and other differences, I would not extend without major qualification a social-constructivist view of emotion to an analysis of pain. Nevertheless, instructive parallels can sometimes be drawn between these two kinds of phenomena.

Thus, one person's anger, no matter how keenly felt, may be denied legitimacy by another person who approaches the issue from a different ideological stance. In terms of the current argot, the former person (from the standpoint of the other) is suffering from "false consciousness" (cf. the biological and feminist arguments regarding possible sex differences in the everyday experience of anger, as described in an earlier section).

Space does not allow further elaboration of this complex issue. Therefore I will simply state, without the customary qualifications and respect for nuances, what I consider to be the most general case with respect to the sociodynamics of authentic emotional experiences. Emotions are not only social constructions; they also help to sustain and validate the norms and expectancies, the beliefs and values, that provide the blueprint for their construction. Thus, one of the surest ways for a religious or political convert to affirm the validity of a new system of beliefs is by experiencing the emotions considered authentic by the group. This self-validating process is somewhat circular. That is, the emotions are taken as a sign of the validity of the very norms and values of which they are a product. To break the circle (or, more accurately, to obscure its nature, for it is not really broken), a kind of myth is created. According to this myth, emotions-at least authentic emotions—are not social products. Rather, they are uncorrupted and spontaneous events attributable only to the self. (For a more detailed discussion of the relationship between emotions and cultural belief systems or ideologies, see Averill, 1982; Hochschild, 1979; Solomon, 1976.)

Concluding Observations

The above remarks clearly go beyond the data presented earlier. In closing, therefore, let me make a few final observations related more specifically to the study of anger and aggression. *Fear, anger,* and *depression* are what Zuckerman (1980) has called the FAD of emotion theorists. In spite of its centrality in this faddish triad, we know surprisingly little about anger, even in a descriptive sense. Zuckerman has also referred to fear, anger, and depression as the "unholy trinity" Pursuing this felicitous metaphor, we might say that anger is the unholy ghost that presumably begets much aggression, but that seldom has been observed directly.

In another sense, of course, we all know a great deal about anger, because we have experienced it many times in our own lives. And yet our knowledge is largely intuitive and unsystematic. One of the tasks of psychology should be to make such intuitive knowledge explicit, just as one of the tasks of linguistics is to explicate the rules (grammar) of the various human languages. Until that is done—for anger as well as for a variety of other emotions—it is doubtful that theories of emotion can escape the FAD lampooned by Zuckerman or break the cycle of historical fads outlined in the introduction to this essay.

REFERENCES

Adair, J. G., & Spinner, B. (1981). Subject's access to cognitive processes: Demand characteristics and verbal report. *Journal for the Theory of Social Behavior, 11,* 31–52.

Anastasi, A., Cohen, N., & Spatz, D. (1948). A study of fear and anger in college students through the controlled diary method. *Journal of Genetic Psychology, 73,* 243–249.

Arnold, M. B. (1960). *Emotion and personality* (2 vols.). New York: Columbia University Press.

Austin, J. (1961). Other minds. In J. L. Austin, *Philosophical papers*. London: Oxford University Press. (Originally published, 1946)

Averill, J. R. (1974). An analysis of psychophysiological symbolism and its influence on theories of emotion. *Journal for the Theory of Social Behaviour, 4,* 147–190.

Averill, J. R. (1976). Emotion and anxiety: Sociocultural, biological, and psychological determinants. In M. Zuckerman & C. D. Spielberger (Eds.), *Emotion and anxiety: New concepts, methods and applications.* New York: LEA-Wiley.

Averill, J. R. (1979). Anger. In H. Howe & R. Dienstbier (Eds.), *Nebraska Symposium on Motivation* (Vol. 26). Lincoln: University of Nebraska Press.

Averill, J. R. (1980a). A constructivist view of emotion. In R. Plutchik & H. Kellerman (Eds.), *Theories of emotion.* New York: Academic Press.

Averill, J. R. (1980b). On the paucity of positive emotions. In K. R. Blankstein, P. Pliner, & J. Polivy (Eds.), *Assessment and modification of emotional behavior.* New York: Plenum.

Averill, J. R. (1982). *Anger and aggression: An essay on emotion.* New York: Springer-Verlag.

Averill, J. R., & Opton, E. M., Jr. (1968). Pychophysiological assessment: Rationale and problems. In P. McReynolds (Eds.), Advances in *psychological assessment* (Vol. 1). Palo Alto, CA: Science and Behavior Books.

Bach, G. R., & Goldberg, H. (1974). *Creative aggression.* Garden City, NY: Doubleday.

Bandura, A. (1973). *Aggression: A social learning analysis.* Englewood Cliffs, NJ: Prentice-Hall.

Baron, R. A. (1977). *Human aggression.* New York: Plenum.

Berkowitz, L., & Donnerstein, E. (1982). External validity is more than skin deep: Some answers to criticisms of laboratory experiments. *American Psychologist, 37,* 245–257.

Brown, J. S., & Farber, I. E. (1951). Emotions conceptualized as intervening variables—With suggestions toward a theory of frustration. *Psychological Bulletin, 18,* 465–495.

Bry, A. (1977). *How to get angry without feeling guilty*. New York: New American Library.

Bulman, R., & Wortman, C. B. (1977). Attributions of blame and coping in the "real world": Severe accident victims react to their lot. *Journal of Personality and Social Psychology, 35,* 351–363.

Campbell, D. T. (1975). On the conflicts between biological and social evolution and between psychology and moral traditions. *American Psychologist, 30,* 1103–1126.

Cannon, W. B. (1914). The interrelations of emotions as suggested by recent physiological researches. *American Journal of Psychology, 25,* 256–282.

Cartwright, D. (1973). Determinants of scientific progress: The case of research on the risky shift. *American Psychologist, 28,* 222–231.

Cotton, J. L. (1980). Verbal reports on mental processes: Ignoring data for the sake of theory. *Personality and Social Psychology Bulletin, 6,* 278–281.

Dewey, J. L. (1895). The theory of emotion. II. The significance of emotions. *Psychological Review, 2,* 13–32.

Dollard, J., Doob, L., Miller, N., Mowrer, O., & Sears, R. (1939). *Frustration and aggression*. New Haven, CT: Yale University Press.

Donnerstein, E., & Berkowitz, L. (1981). Victim reactions in aggressive erotic films as a factor in violence against women. *Journal of Personality and Social Psychology, 41,* 710–724.

Ellis, A. (1977). *How to live with and without anger*. New York: Reader's Digest Press.

Frodi, A., Macaulay, J., & Thome, P. R. (1977). Are women always less aggressive than men? A review of the experimental literature. *Psychological Bulletin, 84,* 634–660.

Gates G. S. (1926). An observational study of anger. *Journal of Experimental Psychology, 9,* 325–331.

Harré, R., & Secord, P. F. (1972). *The explanation of social behavior*. Totowa, NJ: Rowman & Littlefield.

Hilgard, E. R. (1977). *Divided consciousness: Multiple controls in human thought and action*. New York: Wiley.

Hochschild, A. R. (1979). Emotion work, feeling rules, and social structure. *American Journal of Sociology, 85,* 551–575.

Hogan, R. T., & Emler, N. P (1978). The biases in contemporary social psychology. *Social Research, 45,* 478–534.

Izard, C. E. (1977). *Human emotions*. New York: Plenum.

James, W. (1890). *Principles of psychology* (Vol. 2). New York: Holt.

Lazarus, R. S. (1966). Psychological stress and the coping process. New York: McGraw-Hill.

Lazarus, R. S., Coyne, J. C., & Folkman, S. (1982). Cognition, emotion, and motivation: The doctoring of Humpty-Dumpty. In R. W. J. Neufeld (Ed.), *Psychological stress and psychopathology*. New York: McGraw-Hill.

Lindsley, D. B. (1951). Emotion. In S. S. Stevens (Ed.), *Handbook of experimental psychology*. New York: Wiley.

Locke, D., & Pennington, D. (1982). Reasons and causes: Their role in attribution processes. *Journal of Personality and Social Psychology, 42,* 212–223.

Lubek, I. (1979). A brief social psychological analysis of research on aggression in social psychology. In A. R. Buss (Ed.), *Psychology in social context*. New York: Irvington.

Mandler, G. Emotion. In E. Hearst (Ed.), *The first century of experimental psychology*. Hillsdale, NJ: Erlbaum.

Marshall, G. D., & Zimbardo, P. G. (1979). Affective consequences of inadequately explained physiological arousal. *Journal of Personality and Social Psychology, 37,* 970–988.

Maslach, C. (1979). Negative emotional biasing of unexplained arousal. Journal of *Personality and Social Psychology, 37,* 953–969.

Meltzer, H. (1933). Students' adjustments in anger. *Journal of Social Psychology, 4,* 285–309.

Nisbett, R. E., & Wilson, T. D. (1977). Telling more than we can know: Verbal reports on mental processes. *Psychological Review, 84,* 231–259.

Novaco, R. W. (1975). *Anger control: The development and evaluation of an experimental treatment*. Lexington, Mass.: Lexington Books/ D. C. Heath.

Pepitone, A. (1976). Toward a normative and comparative biocultural social psychology. *Journal of Personality and Social Psychology, 34,* 64–-653.

Plutchik, R. (1980). *Emotion: A psychoevolutionary synthesis*. New York: Harper & Row.

Rich, M. C. (1979). Verbal reports and mental structures. *Journal for the Theory of Social Behavior, 9,* 29–37.

Richardson, F. (1918). *The psychology and pedagogy of anger*. Baltimore, MD: Warwick & York.

Robinson, D. N. (1979). *Systems of modern psychology*. New York: Columbia University Press.

Rubin, T. (1969). *The angry book*. New York: Macmillan.

Rule, B. G., & Nesdale, A. R. (1976). Emotional arousal and aggressive behavior. *Psychological Bulletin, 83,* 851–863.

Schachter, S. (1964). The interaction of cognitive and physiological determinants of emotional state. In L. Berkowitz (Ed.), *Advances in experimental social psychology* (Vol. 1). New York: Academic Press.

Smith, E. R., & Miller, F. D. (1978). Limits on perception of cognitive processes: A reply to Nisbett and Wilson. *Psychological Review, 85,* 355–362.

Solomon, R. C. (1976). *The passions*. Garden City. N.Y.: Doubleday.

Spanos, N. P, & Hewitt, E. C. (1980). The hidden observer in hypnotic analgesia: Discovery or experimental creation? *Journal Personality and Social Psychology, 39,* 1201–1214.

Tavris, C. (1982). *Anger: The misunderstood emotion*. New York: Simon & Schuster.

Tolman, E. C. (1923). A behaviorist account of the emotions. *Psychological Review, 30,* 217–227.

Tomkins, S. S. (1924). Affect as amplification: Some modifications in theory. In R. Plutchik & H. Kellerman (Eds), *Emotion: Theory research, and experience*. New York: Academic Press.

Watson, J. B. (1924). *Psychology from the standpoint of a behaviorist* (2nd ed.). Philadelphia: Lippincott.

White, P. (1980). Limitations on verbal reports of internal events: A refutation of Nisbett and Wilson and of Bem. *Psychological Review, 87,* 105–112.

Zajonc, R. B. (1980). Feeling and thinking: Preferences need no inferences. *American Psychologist, 35,* 151–175.

Zillmann, D. (1979). *Hostility and aggression*. Hillsdale, NJ: Erlbaum.

Zuckerman, M. (1980). To risk or not to risk: Predicting behavior from negative and positive emotional states. In K. R. Blankstein, P. Pliner, & J. Polivy (Eds.), *Assessment and modification of emotional behavior*. New York: Plenum.

Appendix: How to Read a Journal Article in Social Psychology

Christian H. Jordan and Mark P. Zanna • University of Waterloo

How to Read a Journal Article in Social Psychology

When approaching a journal article for the first time, and often on subsequent occasions, most people try to digest it as they would any piece of prose. They start at the beginning and read word for word, until eventually they arrive at the end, perhaps a little bewildered, but with a vague sense of relief. This is not an altogether terrible strategy; journal articles do have a logical structure that lends itself to this sort of reading. There are, however, more efficient approaches–approaches that enable you, a student of social psychology, to cut through peripheral details, avoid sophisticated statistics with which you may not be familiar, and focus on the central ideas in an article. Arming yourself with a little foreknowledge of what is contained in journal articles, as well as some practical advice on how to read them, should help you read journal articles more effectively. If this sounds tempting, read on.

Journal articles offer a window into the inner workings of social psychology. They document how social psychologists formulate hypotheses, design empirical studies, analyze the observations they collect, and interpret their results. Journal articles also serve an invaluable archival function: They contain the full store of common and cumulative knowledge of social psychology. Having documentation of past research allows researchers to build on past findings and advance our understanding of social behavior, without pursuing avenues of investigation that have already been explored. Perhaps most importantly, a research study is never complete until its results have been shared with others, colleagues and students alike. Journal articles are a primary means of communicating research findings. As such, they can be genuinely exciting and interesting to read.

That last claim may have caught you off guard. For beginning readers, journal articles may seem anything but interesting and exciting. They may, on the contrary, appear daunting and esoteric, laden with jargon and obscured by menacing statistics. Recognizing this fact, we hope to arm you, through this paper, with the basic information you will need to read journal articles with a greater sense of comfort and perspective.

Social psychologists study many fascinating topics, ranging from prejudice and discrimination, to culture, persuasion, liking and love, conformity and obedience, aggres-

353

sion, and the self. In our daily lives, these are issues we often struggle to understand. Social psychologists present systematic observations of, as well as a wealth of ideas about, such issues in journal articles. It would be a shame if the fascination and intrigue these topics have were lost in their translation into journal publications. We don't think they are, and by the end of this paper, hopefully you won't either.

Journal articles come in a variety of forms, including research reports, review articles, and theoretical articles. Put briefly, a *research report* is a formal presentation of an original research study, or series of studies. A *review article* is an evaluative survey of previously published work, usually organized by a guiding theory or point of view. The author of a review article summarizes previous investigations of a circumscribed problem, comments on what progress has been made toward its resolution, and suggests areas of the problem that require further study. A *theoretical article* also evaluates past research, but focuses on the development of theories used to explain empirical findings. Here, the author may present a new theory to explain a set of findings, or may compare and contrast a set of competing theories, suggesting why one theory might be the superior one.

This paper focuses primarily on how to read research reports, for several reasons. First, the bulk of published literature in social psychology consists of research reports. Second, the summaries presented in review articles, and the ideas set forth in theoretical articles, are built on findings presented in research reports. To get a deep understanding of how research is done in social psychology, fluency in reading original research reports is essential. Moreover, theoretical articles frequently report new studies that pit one theory against another, or test a novel prediction derived from a new theory. In order to appraise the validity of such theoretical contentions, a grounded understanding of basic findings is invaluable. Finally, most research reports are written in a standard format that is likely unfamiliar to new readers. The format of review and theoretical articles is less standardized, and more like that of textbooks and other scholarly writings, with which most readers are familiar. This is not to suggest that such articles are easier to read and comprehend than research reports; they can be quite challenging indeed. It is simply the case that, because more rules apply to the writing of research reports, more guidelines can be offered on how to read them.

The Anatomy of Research Reports

Most research reports in social psychology, and in psychology in general, are written in a standard format prescribed by the American Psychological Association (1994). This is a great boon to both readers and writers. It allows writers to present their ideas and findings in a clear, systematic manner. Consequently, as a reader, once you understand this format, you will not be on completely foreign ground when you approach a new research report—regardless of its specific content. You will know where in the paper particular information is found, making it easier to locate. No matter what your reasons for reading a research report, a firm understanding of the format in which they are written will ease your task. We discuss the format of research reports next, with some practical suggestions on how to read them. Later, we discuss how this format reflects the process of scientific investigation, illustrating how research reports have a coherent narrative structure.

TITLE AND ABSTRACT

Though you can't judge a book by its cover, you can learn a lot about a research report simply by reading its title. The title presents a concise statement of the theoretical issues investigated, and/or the variables that were studied. For example, the following title was taken almost at random from a prestigious journal in social psychology: "Sad and guilty? Affective influences on the explanation of conflict in close relationships" (Forgas, 1994, p.

56). Just by reading the title, it can be inferred that the study investigated how emotional states change the way people explain conflict in close relationships. It also suggests that when feeling sad, people accept more personal blame for such conflicts (i.e., feel more guilty).

The abstract is also an invaluable source of information. It is a brief synopsis of the study, and packs a lot of information into 150 words or less. The abstract contains information about the problem that was investigated, how it was investigated, the major findings of the study, and hints at the theoretical and practical implications of the findings. Thus, the abstract is a useful summary of the research that provides the gist of the investigation. Reading this outline first can be very helpful, because it tells you where the report is going, and gives you a useful framework for organizing information contained in the article.

The title and abstract of a research report are like a movie preview. A movie preview highlights the important aspects of a movie's plot, and provides just enough information for one to decide whether to watch the whole movie. Just so with titles and abstracts; they highlight the key features of a research report to allow you to decide if you want to read the whole paper. And just as with movie previews, they do not give the whole story. Reading just the title and abstract is never enough to fully understand a research report.

INTRODUCTION

A research report has four main sections: introduction, method, results, and discussion. Though it is not explicitly labeled, the introduction begins the main body of a research report. Here, the researchers set the stage for the study. They present the problem under investigation, and state why it was important to study. By providing a brief review of past research and theory relevant to the central issue of investigation, the researchers place the study in an historical context and suggest how the study advances knowledge of the problem. Beginning with broad theoretical and practical considerations, the researchers delineate the rationale that led them to the specific set of hypotheses tested in the study. They also describe how they decided on their research strategy (e.g., why they chose an experiment or a correlational study).

The introduction generally begins with a broad consideration of the problem investigated. Here, the researchers want to illustrate that the problem they studied is a real problem about which people should care. If the researchers are studying prejudice, they may cite statistics that suggest discrimination is prevalent, or describe specific cases of discrimination. Such information helps illustrate why the research is both practically and theoretically meaningful, and why you should bother reading about it. Such discussions are often quite interesting and useful. They can help you decide for yourself if the research has merit. But they may not be essential for understanding the study at hand. Read the introduction carefully, but choose judiciously what to focus on and remember. To understand a study, what you really need to understand is what the researchers' hypotheses were, and how they were derived from theory, informal observation, or intuition. Other background information may be intriguing, but may not be critical to understand what the researchers did and why they did it.

While reading the introduction, try answering these questions: What problem was studied, and why? How does this study relate to, and go beyond, past investigations of the problem? How did the researchers derive their hypotheses? What questions do the researchers hope to answer with this study?

METHOD

In the method section, the researchers translate their hypotheses into a set of specific, testable questions. Here, the researchers introduce the main characters of the study—the subjects or participants—describing their characteristics (gender, age, etc.) and how many of them were involved. Then, they describe the materials (or apparatus), such as any questionnaires or special equipment, used in the study. Finally, they describe chronologically the procedures of the study; that is, how the study was conducted. Often, an overview of the research design will begin the method section. This overview provides a broad outline of the design, alerting you to what you should attend.

The method is presented in great detail so that other researchers can recreate the study to confirm (or question) its results. This degree of detail is normally not necessary to understand a study, so don't get bogged down trying to memorize the particulars of the procedures. Focus on how the independent variables were manipulated (or measured) and how the dependent variables were measured.

Measuring variables adequately is not always an easy matter. Many of the variables psychologists are interested in cannot be directly observed, so they must be inferred from participants' behavior. Happiness, for example, cannot be directly observed. Thus, researchers interested in how being happy influences people's judgments must infer happiness (or its absence) from their behavior—perhaps by asking people how happy they are, and judging their degree of happiness from their responses; perhaps by studying people's facial expressions for signs of happiness, such as smiling. Think about the measures researchers use while reading the method section. Do they adequately reflect or capture the concepts they are meant to measure? If a measure seems odd, consider carefully how the researchers justify its use.

Oftentimes in social psychology, getting there is half the fun. In other words, how a result is obtained can be just as interesting as the result itself. Social psychologists often strive to have participants behave in a natural, spontaneous manner, while controlling enough of their environment to pinpoint the causes of their behavior. Sometimes, the major contribution of a research report is its presentation of a novel method of investigation. When this is the case, the method will be discussed in some detail in the introduction.

Participants in social psychology studies are intelligent and inquisitive people who are responsive to what happens around them. Because of this, they are not always initially told the true purpose of a study. If they were told, they might not act naturally. Thus, researchers frequently need to be creative, presenting a credible rationale for complying with procedures, without revealing the study's purpose. This rationale is known as a *cover story,* and is often an elaborate scenario. While reading the method section, try putting yourself in the shoes of a participant in the study, and ask yourself if the instructions given to participants seem sensible, realistic, and engaging. Imagining what it was like to be in the study will also help you remember the study's procedure, and aid you in interpreting the study's results.

While reading the method section, try answering these questions: How were the hypotheses translated into testable questions? How were the variables of interest manipulated and/or measured? Did the measures used adequately reflect the variables of interest? For example, is self-reported income an adequate measure of social class? Why or why not?

RESULTS

The results section describes how the observations collected were analyzed to determine whether the original hypotheses were supported. Here, the data (observations of behavior) are described, and statistical tests are presented. Because of this, the results section is often intimidating to readers who have little or no training in statistics. Wading through complex and unfamiliar statistical analyses is understandably confusing and frustrating. As a result, many students are tempted to skip over reading this section. We advise you not to do so. Empirical findings are the foundation of any science and results sections are where such findings are presented.

Take heart. Even the most prestigious researchers were once in your shoes and sympathize with you. Though space in psychology journals is limited, researchers try to strike a balance between the need to be clear and the need to be brief in describing their results. In an influential paper on how to write good research reports, Bem (1987) offered this advice to researchers:

> No matter how technical or abstruse your article is in its particulars, intelligent nonpsychologists with no expertise in statistics or experimental design should be able to comprehend the broad outlines of what you did and why. They should understand in general terms what was learned. (p. 74)

Generally speaking, social psychologists try to practice this advice.

Most statistical analyses presented in research reports test specific hypotheses. Often, each analysis presented is preceded by a reminder of the hypothesis it is meant to test. After an analysis is presented, researchers usually provide a narrative description of the result in plain English. When the hypothesis tested by a statistical analysis is not explicitly stated, you can usually determine the hypothesis that was tested by reading this narrative description of the result, and referring back to the introduction to locate an hypothesis that corresponds to that result. After even the most complex statistical analysis, there will be a written description of what the result means conceptually. Turn your attention to these descriptions. Focus on the conceptual meaning of research findings, not on the mechanics of how they were obtained (unless you're comfortable with statistics).

Aside from statistical tests and narrative descriptions of results, results sections also frequently contain tables and graphs. These are efficient summaries of data. Even if you are not familiar with statistics, look closely at tables and graphs, and pay attention to the means or correlations presented in them. Researchers always include written descriptions of the pertinent aspects of tables and graphs. While reading these descriptions, check the tables and graphs to make sure what the researchers say accurately reflects their data. If they say there was a difference between two groups on a particular dependent measure, look at the means in the table that correspond to those two groups, and see if the means do differ as described. Occasionally, results seem to become stronger in their narrative description than an examination of the data would warrant.

Statistics *can* be misused. When they are, results are difficult to interpret. Having said this, a lack of statistical knowledge should not make you overly cautious while reading results sections. Though not a perfect antidote, journal articles undergo extensive review by professional researchers before publication. Thus, most misapplications of statistics are caught and corrected before an article is published. So, if you are unfamiliar with statistics, you can be reasonably confident that findings are accurately reported.

While reading the results section, try answering these questions: Did the researchers provide evidence that any independent variable manipulations were effective? For example, if testing for behavioral differences between happy and sad participants, did the researchers demonstrate that one group was in fact happier than the other? What were the major findings of the study? Were the researchers' original hypotheses supported by their observations? If not, look in the discussion section for how the researchers explain the findings that were obtained.

DISCUSSION

The discussion section frequently opens with a summary of what the study found, and an evaluation of whether the findings supported the original hypotheses. Here, the researchers evaluate the theoretical and practical implications of their results. This can be particularly interesting when the results did not work out exactly as the researchers anticipated. When such is the case, consider the researchers' explanations carefully, and see if they seem plausible to you. Often, researchers will also report any aspects of their study that limit their interpretation of its results, and suggest further research that could overcome these limitations to provide a better understanding of the problem under investigation.

Some readers find it useful to read the first few paragraphs of the discussion section before reading any other part of a research report. Like the abstract, these few paragraphs usually contain all of the main ideas of a research report: What the hypotheses were, the major findings and whether they supported the original hypotheses, and how the findings relate to past research and theory. Having this information before reading a research report can guide your reading, allowing you to focus on the specific details you need to complete your understanding of a study. The description of the results, for example, will alert you to the major variables that were studied. If they are unfamiliar to you, you can pay special attention to how they are defined in the introduction, and how they are operationalized in the method section.

After you have finished reading an article, it can also be helpful to reread the first few paragraphs of the discussion and the abstract. As noted, these two passages present highly distilled summaries of the major ideas in a research report. Just as they can help guide your reading of a report, they can also help you consolidate your understanding of a report once you have finished reading it. They provide a check on whether you have understood the main points of a report, and offer a succinct digest of the research in the authors' own words.

While reading the discussion section, try answering these questions: What conclusions can be drawn from the study? What new information does the study provide about the problem under investigation? Does the study help resolve the problem? What are the practical and theoretical implications of the study's findings? Did the results contradict past research findings? If so, how do the researchers explain this discrepancy?

Some Notes on Reports of Multiple Studies

Up to this point, we have implicitly assumed that a research report describes just one study. It is also quite common, however, for a research report to describe a series of studies of the same problem in a single article. When such is the case, each study reported will have the same basic structure (introduction, method, results, and discussion sections) that we have outlined, with the notable exception that sometimes the results and discussion section for each study are combined. Combined "results and discussion" sections contain the same information that separate results and discussion sections normally contain. Sometimes, the authors present all their results first, and only then discuss the implications of these results, just as they would in separate results and discussion sections. Other times, however, the authors alternate between describing results and discussing their implications, as each result is presented. In either case, you should be on the lookout for the same information, as outlined above in our consideration of separate results and discussion sections.

Reports including multiple studies also differ from single study reports in that they include more general introduction and discussion sections. The general introduction, which begins the main body of a research report, is similar in essence to the introduction of a single study report. In both cases, the researchers describe the problem investigated and its practical and theoretical significance. They also demonstrate how they derived their hypotheses, and explain how their research relates to past investigations of the problem. In contrast, the separate introductions to each individual study in reports of multiple studies are usually quite brief, and focus more specifically on the logic and rationale of each particular study presented. Such introductions generally describe the methods used in the particular study, outlining how they answer questions that have not been adequately addressed by past research, including studies reported earlier in the same article.

General discussion sections parallel discussions of single studies, except on a somewhat grander scale. They present all of the information contained in discussions of single studies, but consider the implications of all the studies presented together. A general discussion section brings the main ideas of a research program into bold relief. It typically begins with a concise summary of a research program's main findings, their relation to the original hypotheses, and their practical and theoretical implications. Thus, the summaries that begin general discussion sections are counterparts of the summaries that begin discussion sections of single study reports. Each presents a digest of the research presented in an article that can serve as both an organizing framework (when read first), and as a check on how well you have understood the main points of an article (when read last).

Research Reporting as Story Telling

A research report tells the story of how a researcher or group of researchers investigated a specific problem. Thus, a research report has a linear, narrative structure with a beginning, middle, and end. In his paper on writing research reports, Bem noted that a research report:

> . . .is shaped like an hourglass. It begins with broad general statements, progressively narrows down to the specifics of [the] study, and then broadens out again to more general considerations. (1987, p. 175)

This format roughly mirrors the process of scientific investigation, wherein researchers do the following: (1) start with a broad idea from which they formulate a narrower set of hypotheses, informed by past empirical findings (introduction); (2) design a specific set of concrete operations to test these hypotheses (method); (3) analyze the observations collected in this way, and decide if they support the original hypotheses (results); and (4) explore the broader theoretical and practical implications of the findings, and consider how they contribute to an understanding of the problem under investigation (discussion). Though these stages are somewhat arbitrary distinctions—research actually proceeds in a number of different ways—they help elucidate the inner logic of research reports.

While reading a research report, keep this linear structure in mind. Though it is difficult to remember a series of seemingly disjointed facts, when these facts are joined together in a logical, narrative structure, they become easier to comprehend and recall. Thus, always remember that a research report tells a story. It will help you to organize the information you read, and remember it later.

Describing research reports as stories is not just a convenient metaphor. Research reports are stories. Stories can be said to consist of two components: A telling of what happened, and an explanation of why it happened. It is tempting to view science as an endeavor that simply catalogues facts, but nothing is further from the truth. The goal of science, social psychology included, is to *explain* facts, to explain *why* what happened happened. Social psychology is built on the dynamic interplay of discovery and justification, the dialogue between systematic observation of relations and their theoretical explanation. Though research reports do present novel facts based on systematic observation, these facts are presented in the service of ideas. Facts in isolation are trivia. Facts tied together by an explanatory theory are science. Therein lies the story. To really understand what researchers have to say, you need consider how their explanations relate to their findings.

The Rest of the Story

> There is really no such thing as research. There is only search, more search, keep on searching. (Bowering, 1988, p. 95)

Once you have read through a research report, and understand the researchers' findings and their explanations of them, the story does not end there. There is more than one interpretation for any set of findings. Different researchers often explain the same set of facts in different ways.

Let's take a moment to dispel a nasty rumor. The rumor is this: Researchers present their studies in a dispassionate manner, intending only to inform readers of their findings and their interpretation of those findings. In truth, researchers aim not only to inform readers, but also to *persuade* them (Sternberg, 1995). Researchers want to convince you their ideas are right. There is never only one explanation for a set of findings. Certainly, some explanations are better than others; some fit the available data better, are more parsimonious, or require fewer questionable assumptions. The point here is that researchers are very passionate about their ideas, and want you to believe them. It's up to you to decide if you want to buy their ideas or not.

Let's compare social psychologists to salesclerks. Both social psychologists and salesclerks want to sell you something; either their ideas, or their wares. You need to decide if you want to buy what they're selling or not—and there are potentially negative consequences for either decision. If you let a sales clerk dazzle you with a sales pitch, without thinking about it carefully, you might end up buying a substandard product that you don't really need. After having done this a few times, people tend to become cynical, steeling themselves against any and all sales pitches. This too is dangerous. If you are overly critical of sales pitches, you could end up foregoing genuinely useful products. Thus, by analogy, when you are too critical in your reading of research reports, you might dismiss, out of hand, some genuinely useful ideas—ideas that can help shed light on why people behave the way they do.

This discussion raises the important question of how critical one should be while reading a research report. In part, this will depend on why one is reading the report. If you are reading it simply to learn what the researchers have to say about a particular issue, for example, then there is usually no need to be overly critical. If you want to use the research as a basis for planning a new study, then you should be more critical. As you develop an understanding of psychological theory and research methods, you will also develop an ability to criticize research on many different levels. And *any* piece of research can be criticized at some level. As Jacob Cohen put it, "A successful piece of research doesn't conclusively settle an issue, it just makes some theoretical proposition to some degree more likely" (1990, p. 1311). Thus, as a consumer of research reports, you have to strike a delicate balance between being overly critical and overly accepting.

While reading a research report, at least initially, try to suspend your disbelief. Try to understand the researchers' story; that is, try to understand the facts—the findings and how they were obtained—and the suggested explanation of those facts—the researchers' interpretation of the findings and what they mean. Take the research to task only after you feel you understand what the authors are trying to say.

Research reports serve not only an important archival function, documenting research and its findings, but also an invaluable stimulus function. They can excite other researchers to join the investigation of a particular issue, or to apply new methods or theory to a different, perhaps novel, issue. It is this stimulus function that Elliot Aronson, an eminent social psychologist, referred to when he admitted that, in publishing a study, he hopes his colleagues will "look at it, be stimulated by it, be provoked by it, annoyed by it, and then go ahead and do it better.... That's the exciting thing about science; it progresses by people taking off on one another's work" (1995, p. 5). Science is indeed a cumulative enterprise, and each new study builds on what has (or, sometimes, has not) gone before it. In this way, research articles keep social psychology vibrant.

A study can inspire new research in a number of different ways, such as: (1) it can lead one to conduct a better test of the hypotheses, trying to rule out alternative explanations of the findings; (2) it can lead one to explore the limits of the findings, to see how widely applicable they are, perhaps exploring situations to which they do not apply; (3) it can lead one to test the implications of the findings, furthering scientific investigation of the phenomenon; (4) it can inspire one to apply the findings, or a novel methodology, to a different area of investigation; and (5) it can provoke one to test the findings in the context of a specific real world problem, to see if they can shed light on it. All of these are excellent extensions of the original research, and there are, undoubtedly, other ways that research findings can spur new investigations.

The problem with being too critical, too soon, while reading research reports is that the only further research one may be willing to attempt is research of the first type: Redoing a study better. Sometimes this is desirable, particularly in the early stages of investigating a particular issue, when the findings are novel and perhaps unexpected. But redoing a reasonably compelling study, without extending it in any way, does little to advance our understanding of human behavior. Although the new study might be "better," it will not be "perfect," so *it* would have to be run again, and again, likely never reaching a stage where it is beyond criticism. At some point, researchers have to decide that the evidence is compelling enough to warrant investigation of the last four types. It is these types of studies that most advance our knowledge of social behavior. As you read more research reports, you will become more comfortable deciding when a study is "good enough" to move beyond it. This is a somewhat subjective judgment, and should be made carefully.

When social psychologists write up a research report for publication, it is because they believe they have something new and exciting to communicate about social behavior. Most research reports that are submitted for publication are rejected. Thus, the reports that are eventually published are deemed pertinent not only by the researchers who wrote them, but also by the reviewers and editors of the journals in which they are published. These people, at least, believe the research reports they write and publish have something important and interesting to say. Sometimes, you'll disagree; not all journal articles are created equal, after all. But we recommend that you, at least initially, give these well-meaning social psychologists the benefit of the doubt. Look for what they're excited about. Try to understand the authors' story, and see where it leads you.

Author Notes

Preparation of this paper was facilitated by a Natural Sciences and Engineering Research Council of Canada doctoral fellowship to Christian H. Jordan. Thanks to Roy Baumeister, Arie Kruglanski, Ziva Kunda, John Levine, Geoff MacDonald, Richard Moreland, Ian Newby-Clark, Steve Spencer, and Adam Zanna for their insightful comments on, and appraisals of, various drafts of this paper. Thanks also to Arie Kruglanski and four anonymous editors of volumes in the series, *Key Readings in Social Psychology* for their helpful critiques of an initial outline of this paper. Correspondence concerning this article should be addressed to Christian H. Jordan, Department of Psychology, University of Waterloo, Waterloo, Ontario, Canada N2L 3G1. Electronic mail can be sent to chjordan@watarts.uwaterloo.ca

REFERENCES

American Psychological Association (1994). *Publication manual* (4th ed.). Washington, D.C.

Aronson, E. (1995). Research in social psychology as a leap of faith. In E. Aronson (Ed.), *Readings about the social animal* (7th ed., pp. 3–9). New York: W. H. Freeman and Company.

Bem, D. J. (1987). Writing the empirical journal article. In M. P. Zanna & J. M. Darley (Eds.), *The compleat academic: A practical guide for the beginning social scientist* (pp. 171–201). New York: Random House.

Bowering, G. (1988). *Errata*. Red Deer, Alta.: Red Deer College Press.

Cohen, J. (1990). Things I have learned (so far). *American Psychologist, 45,* 1304–1312.

Forgas, J. P. (1994). Sad and guilty? Affective influences on the explanation of conflict in close relationships. *Journal of Personality and Social Psychology, 66,* 56–68.

Sternberg, R. J. (1995). *The psychologist's companion: A guide to scientific writing for students and researchers* (3rd ed.). Cambridge: Cambridge University Press.

Author Index

A

Abelson, R. P. 27, 28, 40, 52, 151, 185
Abraham, K. 328
Abramovitch, R. 187
Abramson, L. M. 59, 285
Abramson, P. R. 285
Abu-Lughod, L. 142, 175–177, 179–181
Ackerman, A. M. 285
Adair, J. G. 348
Adams, H. E. 307, 313
Adelman, P. K. 332
Akiyama, H. 128–129
Akoh, H. 131
Albright, L. 157, 166
Alcock, J. 143, 144
Alexander, R. D. 143
Allen, J. L. 193
Allgeier, E. R. 150
Allport, G. W. 157
Altman, I. 191
American Psychiatric Association 245
Anastasi, A. 338
Ancoli, S. 72, 252–253, 255–264, 266, 268, 269
Andersen, S. M. 49
Anderson, C. A. 28, 40, 325
Anglin, J. M. 53
Antill, J. K. 158
Antonucci, T. C. 133
Apfelbaum, B. 278
Archer, D. 186
Archer, R. L. 240
Arcuri, L. 240
Aristotle 308–310, 312
Armon-Jones, C. 7, 173
Arnold, M. B. 8, 47, 58, 337–338
Aron, A. P. 6
Aronson, E. 360
Asad, T. 134
Asch, S. E. 132, 204, 213
Ashby, F. G. 201
Austin, J. 345
Ausubel, D. P. 285
Averill, J. R. 2, 4, 5, 8, 15, 26–29, 31, 40, 41, 48, 52, 159, 166, 175–177, 291, 299, 322, 323, 326, 327, 337–352
Avertt, C. P. 158
Ax, A. F. 76
Azuma, H. 131

B

Bach, G. R. 340
Bain, A. 67
Bainum, C. K. 266
Baldwin, M. W. 266, 276
Balswick, J. 158
Baltes, P. B. 130
Banaji, M. 140, 158
Bandura, A. 61, 340
Banks, R. 66
Bard, P. 65
Barkow, J. H. 140
Barlow, D. H. 178, 181
Barnes, J. 308, 309
Baron, R. A. 341–342
Baron, R. M. 166
Baron, R. S. 266, 276, 329
Barrett, K. C. 176–178, 187
Bartlett, F. A. 121–123, 127
Bartlett, F. C. 27, 52
Baron, R. M. 157
Bator, C. 189
Batson, C. D. 2, 174
Baumann, D. J. 193
Baumeister, R. F. 12, 15, 174, 179, 282, 295–305, 324
Bavelas, J. B. 266, 276
Beebe-Center, J. G. 62–63
Beeghly, M. 26, 30, 36–37, 49, 53
Bekerian, D. A. 29, 31, 94
Bellah, H. N. 129
Bem, D. J. 49, 357, 359
Bent, D. 259
Berenson, B. G. 233
Berg, J. H. 240
Berkowitz, L. L. 287, 291, 321–323, 325–336, 347
Berntson, G. G. 7
Bers, S. A. 308
Bertram, B. C. R. 143
Bilsky, W. 132
Birdwhistell, R. L. 258, 262, 276
Birnbaum, D. W. 158, 165, 188
Birnbaum, R. 257
Black, A. 266, 276
Blainey, K. 188, 189
Blair, C. 329, 330
Blaney, P. H. 199, 206, 212
Blankstein, K. R. 189
Bless, H. 200–201, 216–226

Silver, M. 2, 181, 282, 307, 308, 310
Simmonds, S. F. 193
Simon, H. A. 57, 175, 240
Simons, R. C. 61
Simpson, C. 28, 52
Singer, J. A. 202
Singer, J. E. 4–5, 13, 71, 76–93, 255
Singer, R. D. 205, 213
Sinha, J. 131
Skinner, B. F. 278
Slade, P. 159
Smith, C. A. 26, 40, 48, 50, 58, 72–73, 94–114, 177, 186, 248, 307
Smith, E. E. 28
Smith, E. R. 348
Smith, G. E. 273
Smith, P. 119, 132
Smith, R. 306, 309, 316, 317, 322, 324
Smith, S. 119, 128, 181
Smith, S. F. 23
Smith, W. J. 266
Smith, W. P. 128
Smuts, B. 266
Snyder, M. 222, 266
Snyder, S. S. 63
Sogon, S. 132
Solomon, R. C. 178, 351
Solomon, R. L. 62–63, 191
Solomon, S. 179
Sommers, S. 221, 225
Sonnemans, J. 4, 177
Sorce, J. 178, 179
Sorenson, E. R. 38, 256
Spackman, M. 200, 202
Spangler, T. J. 59
Spanos, N. P. 350
Spatz, D. 338
Spence, J. T. 158, 161, 167
Spielberger, C. D. 287
Spindel, M. S. 94
Spinner, B. 348
Spinoza, B. 68, 308
Spiro, M. 120, 121
Sroufe, L. A. 62
Srull, T. K. 202, 323–324
Stang, D. 221, 225
Stanislavski, K. S. 277
Stapley, J. C. 158, 165
Stapp, J. 158, 161
Stearns, C. Z. 324
Stearns, P. N. 324
Steffen, V. J. 157, 166
Stein, A. 193
Stein, N. L. 187, 327
Steinberg, J. 193
Steinberg, R. 174, 186
Steinbrenner, K. 259
Steiner, J. 266, 276
Stepick, A. 123
Stepper, S. 5, 13, 228, 230
Sternberg, R. J. 37, 360
Stetsenko, A. 130
Stigler, J. W. 119, 128
Stillwell, A. M. 15, 282, 295–305, 324

Stone, J. I. 49
Storms, M. D. 6, 49
Strack, F. 5, 13, 200–201, 216–226, 228, 230, 240
Stroebe, M. 133
Stroebe, W. 133
Suci, G. J. 26, 39
Sullivan, B. N. 26
Sullivan, H. S. 316
Sullivan, M. W. 186
Sullivan, W. M. 129
Summerfield, A. B. 41, 53, 241
Summers, K. 205, 210
Sunar, 131
Susman, J. R. 187
Svejda, M. 178, 179
Swagerman, J. 58, 64
Swidler, A. 129
Symons, D. 143, 144, 148

T
Tajfel, H. 157
Takata, T. 128
Tangney, J. P. 158, 165, 178, 181, 281–283, 285–295, 297, 301, 304
Tannenbaum, P. H. 26, 39, 326–328
Tarafodi, R. W. 127
Tassinary, L. G. 145, 268, 269
Tavris, C. 340
Taylor, B. 329
Taylor, C. 121, 122, 133
Taylor, D. M. 119, 132, 133
Taylor, G. J. 186, 309, 316
Taylor, S. E. 61, 205, 247
Teasdale, J. D. 11, 59
Teismann, M. W. 144
Tellegen, A. 9
Termine, N. T. 328
ter Schure, E. 94, 95, 107, 108
Tesser, A. 308
Tetlock, P. E. 178
Thayler–Singer, M. 186
Thoits, P. A. 180
Thomas, J. 222
Thome, P. R. 341–342, 346
Thornhill, R. 143, 144
Tice, D. M. 174, 179, 295
Tiller, D. K. 29, 31
Tinbergen, N. 265
Tipton, S. M. 129
Todd, M. J. 37
Olman, E. C. 337
Tomarkin, A. J. 190, 332
Tomkins, S. S. 7, 12, 28, 175, 255, 256, 258, 262, 265, 332, 338
Tooby, J. 140, 176, 177
Tornquist, J. 240, 248
Totterdell, P. 4, 9
Tourangeau, R. 255, 332
Tov–Ruach, L. 313
Trabasso, T. 187
Triandis, H. C. 119, 122, 130, 131, 133
Trivers, R. 143, 144
Troccoli, B. T. 334
Tronick, E. Z. 179, 182

Subject Index

A

Abramovitch, R. 187
accountability 96, 103, 107, 110
action readiness 59–60
activation theory 92
Adams, H. E. 313
adjustment 133–134
affect 4, 10–11
    systems 7
affective contrast, law of 62–63
aggression 2, 281–282, 285–293, 316, 325–335, 337–351
Akiyama, H. 128–129
alexithymics 186
altruism 2
Ambivalence Over Emotional Expression Questionnaire 189
amygdala 5
Ancoli, S. 252–253, 255–264
anger 45–46, 60, 81–83, 87–88, 97, 101, 103–104, 106–110, 187–188, 243, 261, 281–283, 285–293, 321–335, 337–351
annoyance 344–345
Annual Review of Psychology 295
anxiety 97, 101, 103, 105–110, 234, 235, 237, 243
apparent reality, law of 61–62
appraisal 7–8, 10–11, 47–48, 72, 94–114
Archer, R. L. 240
Aristotle 308–310, 312
Arnold, M. 8, 58, 337–338
arousal 261
articles, reading 353–361
ASCAL–4 program 38
Asch, S. E. 132, 204
Austin, J. 345
Averill, J. R. 15, 29, 31, 40, 159, 322, 323, 326, 327, 337–352
Avertt, C. P. 158
Awlad-Ali Bedouins 181
Ax, A. F. 76

B

Balswick, J. 158
Baltes, P. B. 130
Banaji, M. 158
Baron, R. S. 329
Bartlett, F. A. 121–123, 127
Bator, C. 189
Baumeister, R. F. 12, 15, 282, 295–305

Beebe-Center, J. G. 62–63
Beeghly, M. 30, 36–37, 49, 53
behavioral ecolocy view 252
Bekerian, D. A. 29
Berg, J. H. 240
Bers, S. A. 308
Birnbaum, R. 257
Blair, C. 330
Blanckstein, K. R. 189
Bless, H. 200–201, 216–226
Boca, S. 240
Bohner, G. 200–201, 216–226
Bond, M. B. 132
Borgida, E. 165
Bower, G. H. 48, 199–200, 204–215
Boyes-Braem, P. 32, 40, 51
Brekke, N. 165
Bresler, C. 14
Bretherton, I. 30, 36–37, 49, 53
Brewin, C. R. 335
Bridger, W. H. 61
Brief Psychiatric Rating Scale 233
Brown, J. S. 337
Brown, K. 187
Bruner, J. S. 205
Buss, D. M. 8, 139–140, 143–153, 155
Buss-Durkee Guilt Scale 286–288, 291–293

C

Cacioppo, J. T. 145, 216, 227, 228
Campbell, D. T. 344
Cannon, W. B. 4–5, 76, 337
Cantor, N. 42
Carkhuff, R. R. 233
Carver, C. S. 191
Catanzaro, S. J. 189
Chaiken, A. L. 237
change, law of 62–63
Chao, R. K. 131
Church, A. T. 23
Christophe, V. 228, 239–250
Cialdini, R. B. 193
Cicero 316
circumplex 9, 38
Clark, M. S. 214, 214
Clore, G. L. 12–13, 31, 61, 200, 213
close relationships 2

373

Gold, A. 222
Gottschalk, L. 233
Gouaux, C. 236
Grajek, S. 37
Gramzow, R. 281, 285–294
Gray, J. 66
Gray, W. D. 32, 40, 51
greatest gain, law of 66–67
Green, B. L. 244
grief 67
Grossman, M. 167
group pressure 132–133
groupthink 2
guilt 97, 101, 103–110, 187, 243, 281–283, 285–304
Gurwitz, S. 222

H

habituation, law of 62–63
Haidt, J. 171–172, 175–184
hansei 116
happiness 186, 243
Harder, D. W. 286
Harris, P. L. 29, 31
Harter 53, 128
Hartnack, D. 129
hasham 181
Hatfield, E. 227, 228
Hazlitt, W. 307, 310
Heatherton, T. F. 15, 282, 295–305
hedonic asymmetry, law of 63–64
Heidelberg Life Event Inventory 218
Heider, F. 309
Heider, K. 126, 129
Heimer, F. 332
heirarchical cluster analysis 34–35
heirarchical structure 30–40
heirarchy 38–40
helplessness 99, 101, 103, 107, 110, 113, 114
Hepburn, C. 165
Hewitt, E. C. 350
Hilgard, E. R. 350
Hochschild, A. R. 187
Hoffman, M. L. 304
Holland, D. 122
Holmes, T. S. 244
Holocaust 240
Horowitz, L. M. 42, 302
hostility 234, 235, 237, 281–283, 285, 316
Hsee, C. K. 172, 185–197
Hunt, J. McV. 76
Hupka, R. B. 315

I

identity 133
identity formation 127–129
impatience 192
inclusiveness, level of 27
independence 122–123, 129
intensionality 3
interdependence 123–124, 129, 131
interest 243
intergroup behavior 133
interpretive science 177

Isen, A. M. 48, 213, 214
Izard, C. E., 7–8, 12, 30, 36, 48, 328, 332, 338

J

Jackson, D. A. 328
Jacobson, E. 231
Jakobs, E. B. 253
James-Lange theory 76, 312, 333–334
James, W. 4–5, 14, 76, 187, 326, 332, 337, 350
jealousy 139–140, 143–155, 281–283, 306–319
Jensen, S. 23
Johnson, D. M. 32, 40, 51
Johnson, J. T. 140, 157–169
Jourard, S. M. 237
The Journal of Personality and Social Psychology 295
joy 46, 60, 187–188, 243

K

Kagan, J. 29, 52
Kagitcibasi, C. 131
Kahneman, D. 36
Katigbak, M. S. 23
Katz, I. 298
Kelley, H. H. 29
Keltner, D. 171–172, 175–184
Kierkegaard, S. 312
Kim, U. 131
King, L. A. 188–189
Kirson, D. 22, 26–56
Kitayama, S. 8, 15, 115–118, 282, 322
Kleinman, A. 133
Kochanska, G. 295
Kondo,D. 123
Kovecses, Z. 29
Kruglanski, A. 330
Kurokawa, M. 128

L

Lacey, B. C. 60
Lacey, J. I. 60
LaFrance, M. 158
Laird, J. D. 14
Lajya 181
Lakoff, G. 29
Lane, R. D. 188
La Rochefoucauld, F. 307, 315
Larsen, R. J. 139–140, 143–153, 155
Latané, B. 91
Lazarus, R. S. 8, 10–11, 58, 72, 94–114, 240, 255, 322
Leary, M. R. 12
Le Bon, Gustav 227
Lebra, T. S. 123
Levels of Emotion Awareness Scale 188
Levenson, K. W. 126, 129
Leventhal, H. 326
Levine, L. J. 327
Lewinsohn, P. M. 236
Lewis, H. B. 286, 292, 295
Lewis, S. J. 286
Libet, J. M. 236
lightest load, law of 66–67
Lindsley, D. B. 92, 337
Linville, P. W. 192